THE MUSIC OF EDMUND RUBBRA

In memory of Edmund Rubbra

The music of
Edmund Rubbra

Ralph Scott Grover

Scolar Press

Published by
SCOLAR PRESS
Gower House
Croft Road
Aldershot
Hants GU11 3HR
England

Ashgate Publishing Company
Old Post Road
Brookfield
Vermont 05036
USA

British Library cataloguing-in-publication data
A catalogue record is available

ISBN 0 85967 910 1

Typeset by Manton Typesetters, Louth, Lincolnshire and
printed in Great Britain by The University Press, Cambridge

Contents

Preface

At a time when musical experiments of all kinds are pursuing their single-minded course, exploring new instrumental and vocal combinations, sometimes in conjunction with electronic media; when music is thought of in terms of 'densities' and 'textures'; when musical works seldom appear to present a finished and attractive whole, the music of Edmund Rubbra must seem conservative, anachronistic, even dull. Yet critical preoccupation with the avant-garde is a small factor in any attempt to account for the 'scandalous neglect'[1] accorded Rubbra's music over a long span of time. The late Hugh Ottaway, critic, analyst and writer, attributed the neglect to fashion and laziness, explaining the latter more fully in the following passage:

> Superficially, Rubbra's music is 'easier on the ear' than almost anything else being written today. But that is misleading, for there is little contemporary music that so requires our full attention all the time. You cannot happily nod in and out – at every 'in' finding some catchy, surprising, or titillating local event. With Rubbra, the continuity, the stream of thought is everything. Lose that and you are what is called 'disadvantaged'.[2]

Harold Truscott, another writer and thoughtful observer of the contemporary British musical scene, has written more explicitly:

> Edmund Rubbra is one of our most powerfully individual living composers. The neglect accorded his major works is an artistic disgrace fit to rank with the still more complete neglect of Sir Arnold Bax and Havergal Brian,[3] to name only two others. In Rubbra's case, this may be partly the result of a general failure to differentiate intelligently between two entirely dissimilar things, balanced by the absence from his work of anything in the nature of fireworks or gimmicks. Rubbra, at any rate, has pursued a consistent course outwardly more traditional than that of most twentieth-century English composers, and one of a high seriousness. I write 'outwardly' more traditional because continuing experience of the traditional lived at Rubbra's level reveals it as far more disturbing and new in its implications than most of the 'new' trends which splutter and disappear. This is always the effect of true tradition, as distinct from the utterly dissimilar 'conventional', with which it is usually confused. Convention is far removed from any connection with Rubbra's art, which continually startles with the unfamiliarity of the language derived from the traditional; but to perceive and understand this requires application and thought,

and this is another part-reason for the neglect of Rubbra's music, albeit reflecting no honour on the musical elements of our nation.[4]

Put in precise musical terms, the traditional materials of which Rubbra's music consists are those associated with common triads and conventional scalic combinations. In all candour, it must be said that many of the themes that are fashioned from these traditional materials are not particularly distinctive or even memorable. What *is* memorable is the music that results from this often totally unpromising material: it does not sound like music that one has heard before. This is the experience of most first-time listeners to Rubbra's music. Stemming from that experience is an immense satisfaction in the knowledge that new combinations, employing traditional materials, are still possible from the pen of an imaginative and gifted composer.

Still another basic, possibly overriding, reason for the neglect Rubbra's music has suffered is that many of his works are imbued with a serenity and optimism that are hopelessly at odds with modern society, and thus not really understood nor appreciated in our noisy, troubled century. This is certainly not to say that conflict and drama are absent from Rubbra's music, for there are notable instances of each throughout his works. Yet the passages and movements in which they are contained are the products of musical events which often involve diverse contrapuntal lines. In other words, they are not there because the composer thinks that the listener will expect them. Still, no matter how tense the music becomes, there is almost always an underlying optimism, the result not of naïveté but strong spiritual convictions.

It can thus be deduced that Rubbra was an individualist who knew what he wanted to say and how to say it. That he paid dearly for such an independent stance is very evident from the scarcity of performances of his music. Naturally, commissioned works received a first performance, followed usually by one or two further hearings in other places, but after these the shelf appeared to be their eventual destination. Were it not for the occasional BBC Radio 3 broadcasts of Rubbra on record, the silence would be deafening.

Critics and reviewers have also played a part – albeit an unwitting one – in the general neglect of Rubbra's music, as Hugh Ottaway explains:

> So far as critical comment goes, Edmund Rubbra has had a lean time in recent years. Some of the notices of his new compositions – the Third Quartet, for instance – must have irked him considerably, for he is no mean critic himself and knows the folly of *reacting* to what a work is not instead of *responding* to what it is. In the present critical climate the artist who cultivates a well-defined area and whose style is positively related to tradition is likely to be both underrated and misunderstood. Rubbra is an artist of this type, and his single-mindedness – his determination to be himself, regardless of fashions and fetishes – has undoubtedly told against him.[5]

Unfortunately, some of the reviews have so missed the point of Rubbra's music as to advertise in a very public way their writers' insensitivity. In some the ultimate weapon has been ridicule, a favourite device in all areas of human endeavour when something is misunderstood. However, it is good to be able to report that a sizable percentage of reviews is favourable, and that those that are mixed are at least constructive when faults are pointed out.

There is a scattering of general articles on Rubbra and his music together with some in which particular works are discussed in more detail, a number by the composer himself. There is also a thin introductory symposium, each chapter of which has a different author dealing with the music by genre.[6] None of these is an in-depth presentation or longer than ten pages. The symposium also includes an autobiographical sketch of the composer's childhood and adolescence, and an essay by Harold Truscott covering Rubbra's orchestral style. Both Truscott and Ottaway – the other principal contributor along with the musicologist, Elsie Payne – have provided the most food for thought and I gladly acknowledge their contributions. Yet, although this book is a useful introduction it is unlikely to be read, or even seen, by the average person wishing to know more about Rubbra's music, for it was published in a limited edition of 250 copies, and has long been out of print.

It is therefore obvious that a comprehensive study of Rubbra's music is long overdue. I too have structured the book by genre but with variations such as the distribution of the symphonies over three chapters. The reason for dividing the symphonies into three groups is not arbitrary, based on the awkwardness that could result from lumping these large works into one immense chapter. It is, rather, to acknowledge that Rubbra's concept of the symphony changed after the first four, and again after the Seventh.

Except for small portions that contain my own comments, most of which are intended as explanatory links, the first chapter is autobiographical, for, in addition to reproducing *in toto* Rubbra's account of his childhood and adolescence, I have included the transcriptions of three tapes, made with the composer's gracious consent during the summer of 1980. These follow the course of his busy life from where he left off at the age of twenty. Where it has seemed appropriate, relevant background information in the tapes that concerns particular works has been transferred to the chapters where they are discussed; in all such cases the taped source of the information appears in the notes for that chapter.

Unlike many composers who are reluctant to discuss their music and the processes employed in its creation, Rubbra always demonstrated a willingness – even eagerness – to talk about both. The many articles he contributed to leading music journals contain valuable information, much of it analytical, and excerpts from these will be found throughout the book. Some articles, such as those on the Fifth Symphony and certain of the choral pieces also contain music examples in support of the analyses, but because of limitations on length imposed by journals these articles are less detailed than Rubbra might have wished. Therefore, in line with my conviction that the composer should be permitted to 'speak' as often and as fully as is practicable, I have woven his analyses into my more detailed ones.

With regard to the analyses themselves, my opinions and assessments concerning particular parts of works are scattered throughout, rather than incorporated in a general summary at the ends of the discussions. Such a plan better serves the readers because it allows them to gather impressions as they read, thus removing the burden of having to refer to earlier paragraphs and musical examples. No apologies are made for not including thorough analyses of every important work. To have done so would have lengthened the book unnecessarily and exhausted both author and reader.

Reviews – good and bad – of particular works appear at the ends of discussions, exceptions being excerpts relevant to what is under discussion, and included in the text. All reviews including excerpts are presented without comment unless errors or patently unfair statements need correction.

Fifteen of Rubbra's early works remain in manuscript, certainly not a large number in view of his total output. His reasons for withholding them from publication centred on his conviction that in one way or another they fell short of his expectations and his high standards. Believing that a composer has the right to privacy in such matters, I have not attempted to gain access to them in any way. However, this has not prevented a brief mention or even a limited description of some of those for which the composer provided information.

Finally, the book does not pretend to render definitive judgements on Rubbra's music. Naturally, an author's objective and subjective feelings should enter into discussions and analyses to a reasonable degree, but it is the vast body of listeners over a long period of time that hands down the ultimate verdict. With the emphasis on the listener throughout this book, it is hoped that the publicizing of a large body of music containing its share of masterworks will hasten the day when Rubbra is given the attention he deserves. Only then can a fair verdict be reached. In the words of Sir Adrian Boult,

> [Rubbra] is a composer who has never made any effort to popularize anything he has done, but he goes on creating masterpieces, which I am convinced will survive their composer and most of those who are his contemporaries. There is no question that his music has come to stay.[7]

Notes

1 The critic, Ernest Bradbury, used this term in the title of an article in *The Yorkshire Post*, 25 February 1976.
2 Hugh Ottaway, 'Rubbra At 75', *The Listener*, 3 June 1976, p. 710.
3 The situation with regard to each of these composers has now been redressed: Lewis Foreman, *Bax: A Composer and His Time* (London and Berkeley: Scolar Press, 1983); Reginald Nettel, *Havergal Brian: The Man and His Music* (London: Dennis Dobson, 1976).
4 Harold Truscott, 'The Music of Edmund Rubbra', *The Listener*, 9 July 1964, p. 70.
5 Hugh Ottaway, 'Edmund Rubbra and His Recent Works', *MT*, September 1966, p. 765.
6 *Edmund Rubbra: Composer*, Lewis Foreman (ed.) (Rickmansworth: Triad Press, 1977).
7 Printed in the foreword to *Edmund Rubbra: Composer*, p. 7.

Acknowledgements

It is always a great pleasure to acknowledge and thank those who, in large and small ways, have contributed to a book, be they publishers granting permission for the use of copyrighted materials, or particular persons who have given generously of their time by providing materials and encouragement.

Of the music publishers, I am especially indebted to Alfred Lengnick & Co. for their blanket permission to reproduce 265 excerpts from Rubbra's scores, together with their consent to reprint (actually in modified form) their catalogue of Rubbra's music – my Appendix B. I am also most grateful for their kindness in providing, free of charge, the scores of a substantial number of Rubbra's works.

I am also indebted to the publishers who control the copyright of the following works from which I have drawn extracts: Introduction and Fugue for Piano, Op. 19; Five Motets, Op. 37; *The Dark Night of the Soul*, Op. 41, no. 1; *Amoretti*, Op. 43; and Five Madrigals, Op. 51, reproduced by permission of Stainer & Bell Ltd; Sonata No. 2 for Violin and Piano, reproduced by permission of Oxford University Press. The passage from Fugue No. 3 in Paul Hindemith's *Ludus Tonalis*, c.Schott & Co., Ltd., London 1943, is used by permission of European American Music Distributors Corporation.

Two further excerpts are contained in yet to be published works: the Fantasy Fugue for Piano, Op. 161; and the Sinfonietta for Large String Orchestra, Op. 163. Neither extract could have been included without photocopies of the manuscripts, for which I thank, respectively, Michael Hill, pianist and former Rubbra pupil; and Adrian Yardley, Rubbra's youngest son.

For blanket permission to include reviews of Rubbra's music in whole and in part appearing in *Music and Letters* from Vol. 19, no. 2 (April 1938) to Vol. 64, nos. 1–2 (January–April 1983) inclusive, I am indebted to Oxford University Press; and to *The Musical Times* for similar reviews appearing from December 1925 to January 1982 inclusive. The copyrights in this instance are controlled by the authors. However, it has not seemed feasible to try to obtain individual permissions from so numerous a group, many of whom can be presumed to be either no longer living or nearly impossible to trace. In any event, I thank them for their contributions.

For permission to use extracts from three extended reviews by Desmond Shawe-Taylor – 'Symphony No. 5' (15 July, 1950); 'A St. Dominic Mass' (25 October, 1952); and 'Rubbra's Viola Concerto' (25 April, 1953), I am indebted to *The New Statesman and Nation* (latterly *The New Statesman and Society*).

I wish to thank the following periodicals for permission to quote from articles appearing in their pages: *Musical Opinion*, for Hugh Ottaway's 'A Note on Rubbra's Sixth Symphony' (August 1956), and a letter from Rubbra in the February 1957 issue; *The Music Review*, for Rubbra's article, 'Symphony No. 5 in B flat' (February 1949), and Elsie Payne's article, 'Some Aspects of Rubbra's Style' (August 1955); and *Tempo* for 'Edmund Rubbra's Second Symphony: A Note By The Composer' (January 1939).

For permission to reprint materials from the book titles shown below, I thank the following publishers: Eleanor Elder, *Travelling Players*, Frederick Muller, 1939; interview of Rubbra in Murray Schafer, *British Composers in Interview*, Faber and Faber, 1963; and Rubbra's article, 'Missa in Honorem Sancti Dominici' in Robert Stephan Hines, *The Composer's Point of View*, University of Oklahoma Press, 1963.

Extracts from sleeve–notes by Rubbra pertaining to his *Missa Cantuariensis* and *Missa in Honorem Sancti Dominici* on RCA record LRLI 5119; the Farnaby Improvisations, *A Tribute*, and *Sinfonia da Camera* on RCA record RL 25027; and the Improvisation for Violin and Orchestra on RCA record GL 25096, were made possible by kind permission of BMG Records (UK) Limited on behalf of BMG Music International.

Finally, it is my pleasure to recognize and thank the following persons for particular services involving time and effort on my behalf: first, Edmund Rubbra himself for the three tapes which form the bulk of 'An Essay in Autobiography', and Colette Rubbra for making available photographs and copies of letters. But beyond these tangible gifts was the gift of their encouraging and enthusiastic support for the book in all its stages, and the wonderful warmth of their friendship. I deeply regret that they did not live to see the book as a finished product. Their son, Adrian, for cassettes, and in his capacity as successor copyright owner, permission to reprint the first part of 'An Essay in Autobiography' in *Edmund Rubbra: Composer*, Lewis Foreman editor; and the following articles in *The Listener* (courtesy of the BBC): 'Edmund Rubbra, Now 70, Looks At His Eight Symphonies' (27 May, 1971); 'Edmund Rubbra Writes About The Development of His Choral Music' (6 June, 1968); 'Edmund Rubbra Writes About His Eighth Symphony' (31 December, 1970); 'Edmund Rubbra Writes About His *Sinfonia Sacra*' (15 February, 1973). Harold Truscott, for permission to quote from 'Style and Orchestral Technique' and 'Chamber Music' in *Edmund Rubbra: Composer*, Lewis Foreman editor. Jane Ottaway, for photocopies of her late husband Hugh's unpublished articles on Rubbra's symphonies from several of which I have cited passages, and for copies of letters to and from Rubbra. Peter Craddy, for providing me with tapes of Rubbra's music which formed the foundations of a number of my analyses. Lewis Foreman who, in his capacity as proprietor of Triad Press, and editor of *Edmund Rubbra: Composer*, authorized my use of passages from Elsie Payne's chapter, 'Non-Liturgical Choral Music' in the above-named publication. Michael Hill, for his many constructive suggestions while engaged in reading through my entire typescript. As for my wife, Frances, other members of my family, and many friends on both shores of the Atlantic, I can only admire and thank them for their patience during the nine years I was occupied in the writing of this book.

RSG

Abbreviations

The following abbreviations appear in the chapter notes:

The Monthly Musical Record	*MMR*
Music and Letters	*M&L*
The Music Review	*MR*
The Musical Quarterly	*MQ*
The Musical Times	*MT*
The New Grove Dictionary	*NGD*

1 An essay in autobiography[1]

Before Edmund Rubbra is given free rein to talk about his music and his many experiences, space must be devoted to other aspects of his life. Born in Northampton on 23 May 1901, he enjoyed a long and distinguished career not only as a composer, but also as critic, music journalist and teacher. Naturally, his autobiographical account emphasizes his music and some of the events that led to the composition of particular works, but other facets need mention in order to present a balanced account of his full and productive life. Unfortunately, these areas are rarely cited and their importance is thus underestimated.

An examination of back issues of leading British music journals would reveal the frequency with which Rubbra's name appeared as the author of major articles on some phase of music, or on the works of a particular composer. Just as often his reviews of new music appeared, signed 'E.R.' No matter in which capacity he wrote, his careful and dispassionate attention to his subject is readily apparent, and his unobtrusive scholarship is always illuminating. The near half-century occupied by these articles and reviews – 1929 to 1976 – is clear evidence of the importance of this phase in Rubbra's life.

Rubbra also wrote three small books, of which *Counterpoint: A Survey*[2] is the most important. Not a textbook, it is a valuable source of information on the historical development of counterpoint as practised by the greatest contrapuntal composers, and it is packed with discussions of their work, plus musical examples.

In 1947, as his reputation both as composer and writer grew, Rubbra was invited to become a lecturer at Oxford, and thus was associated with Worcester College from then until his retirement in 1968. An overlap in his teaching occurred when he also accepted a position as Professor of Composition at the Guildhall School of Music and Drama in London from 1961 to 1974.

There were, of course, honours. As early as 1938 Rubbra was elected to a Collard Fellowship by the Worshipful Company of Musicians. In 1955 the Company awarded him the Cobbett Medal in recognition of his Services to Chamber Music. Leicester University conferred an Honorary LL.D. in 1959, and in the following year he received the CBE. In 1963 Worcester College made him a Fellow and in 1978 he received an Honorary D.Litt. from Reading

University where, almost sixty years earlier, he had begun his formal studies. He also held an Honorary D.Mus. from Durham University (1949), was a Fellow of the Guildhall School, and a Member of the Royal Academy of Music. In connection with the Durham degree he received a one-line letter from Vaughan Williams, dated 16 March 1949: 'I am delighted to hear of the honour which Durham University is conferring on itself.'

Rubbra was also an excellent pianist, both as a recitalist and as a member of chamber groups, and he appeared in both capacities in England and on the Continent. His first wife, Antoinette Chaplin, was a French violinist with whom he toured Italy, gave recitals in Paris, and made broadcasts. They were married in 1933 and lived for many years at Valley Cottage near Speen in Buckingham-shire, where many of his works were composed. (The cottage is presently occupied by his son Benedict, a well-known painter, and his wife Tessa, who is an excellent potter.) After Antoinette's death Rubbra married Colette Yardley with whom he lived in Gerrards Cross, Buckinghamshire until his death on 14 February 1986.

Now it is time for Rubbra to talk about himself in his own way.

'I was singularly fortunate in having as teachers (Cyril Scott, Holst and R.O. Morris) personalities whose interests, musical and otherwise, were so similar to those that had developed in myself during my most formative years. Because of this harmonisation of interests, my teachers could offer their greatest help at the time it was most needed, and from the store of their own experiences instil in me the knowledge that music does not grow and flourish in a narrowly confined area, but is the product of every force to which one is subjected through the very fact of living an active and expanding life.

'However, it is not my purpose here to say more of the impact made upon me by those whose guidance during my student days was so enriching: but rather to try to equate vividly remembered childhood and adolescent experi-ences with those directions in my musical thinking that have gradually become crucial to my style and general attitude. Some of the correspondences I shall mention may seem to the outsider so subjective as to make them appear ques-tionable as evidence of congruity between particular experiences and important elements in my style. Nevertheless, I shall have no hesitation in mentioning them because, looking back, my intuition strongly upholds the truth of these relationships, however doubtful their validity may appear to others.

'On re-visiting my birthplace, Northampton, some years ago I tried to find the small, box-like, red-brick house where I spent the early years of my child-hood. At that time, No 2 Balfour Road was part of a row of six connected houses surrounded by fields on all sides, and I often wondered why they had been left so isolated, as if forgotten by the builder. A stream issuing from a culvert passed the bottom of the garden, and in wet weather it became a raging torrent, flooding the surrounding fields. The biggest building seen at the far side of a field in front of the houses was Miller's factory, where wooden lasts for boots and shoes were made. My father worked there for a time. Now, however, these houses are included, and almost lost, in an estate that has entirely obliterated the fields that meant so much to me in my childhood.

'One of my earliest memories, and still vividly with me, is of waking one winter morning (I must have been three or four years old at the time) and finding that the usual positions in the room for light and shadow had been completely reversed. The ceiling was bathed in a strong white light instead of being in relative shadow, and the floor, on which the morning sunlight usually lay, was darkened. As I rested wonderingly in bed, with my eyes fixed on that dazzlingly white ceiling, my father came in to see if I was awake, and I asked him why the light of the room was so altered. He told me that there had been a heavy fall of snow in the night, and the light of the morning sun on it was reflected on the ceiling, making the lower part of the room in relative shadow. I suppose I accepted the explanation, but it did not lessen the impact of what I had seen, and its clarity seventy years later is evidence of the deep impression it had made. It is only now, looking back, that I intuitively know that this topsy-turvydom, working subconsciously within me, influenced that way I look at thematic substance and its related counterpoint in my music, these being instinctively so shaped as to be capable of inversion without diminishing their effect. Examples are manifold, but as illustrations of my meaning I give two: the first from the slow introduction to the last movement of Symphony No. 4, and the second from Variation Two in the finale of the cello and piano Sonata.

Ex. A

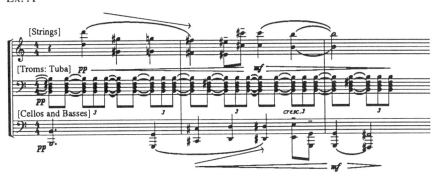

I can now see that these thematic processes, which seemed at the time of writing to evolve naturally through the experience of composing, are linked indissolubly to that unexpected re-distribution of light and shade in the early childhood memory I have described.

'An equally vivid experience, and one that nothing since has been able to eradicate, occurred some years later, when I was perhaps nine or ten years of age (chronology seems beside the point in such matters). It was a hot summer

Ex. B

Sunday, and my father and I went for a longish walk which took us out of the town through a wood known as Harlestone Firs, and which, I remember, contained heaped-up ants' nests that became a seething mass of agitated life when disturbed. Before entering the wood we rested a little, leaning on a gate that gave us a distant view of the town. Suddenly, through the hazy heat, I heard distant bells, the music of which seemed suspended in the still air. I was held motionless, the scenery vanished, and I was aware only of downward-drifting sounds that seemed isolated from everything else around me. I have no doubt now that this experience, held captive for so long in my inner consciousness, gradually became so embedded in my musical thinking as to be the means whereby the disembodied bell-sounds I heard that summer afternoon became transmuted into those downward scales that constantly act as focal points in my textures.

'By this time I was already having piano lessons from a little hunch-backed lady who had a high reputation as a teacher. A longish walk to her house took me beyond the factory I have already mentioned, through some disused quarries and over the race-course. The piano she used for teaching had, I remember, discoloured ivory keys and a silk and fretwork front. This was in marked contrast to the one I used at home, which was a new demonstration upright piano lent to us by an uncle of mine, W.H. Gibson (he married a sister of my father), who owned a remarkably well-stocked piano and music shop at 6, Cowper Street. The point of this loan of a piano was to help us financially at a time when my father was out of work, and it was my duty to demonstrate the quality of the piano to prospective customers. (My demonstration "war-horse" was a Sonata in C by Mozart.) If the customer was pleased with the sound of the piano and a sale was made, we would get a commission. Another piano would then take its place.

'In 1912 we moved from 2, Balfour Road to a more central part of Northampton. The house was in a long, dreary street called Alcombe Road. Here my father took up the work for which he had originally been apprenticed, watch and clock repairing, and this, with a great deal of pressure from my mother, led to the acquisition in 1916 of a modest shop in Overstone Road, where watches, clocks and jewellery could be displayed. A back bedroom was made into a room where I could work, but as the piano would not go up the stairs, it had to be hauled up outside and pulled through the gap left by taking out the window frame. They were tense moments!

'My general musical studies (harmony, counterpoint, piano-playing) had already begun in earnest, but my time for these was restricted because I had to contribute to my parents' meagre income: first, before I left Kettering Road School, by working as an errand boy, and second, when I left school at the age of 14, by working for a short time in the office of Crockett and Jones, the boot and shoe manufacturers. The next step was taken by my father's brother, F.C. Rubbra, who owned a factory that made boots and shoes for the export market (a mine for my hobby of stamp collecting). He suggested that I should start in his office (at 7s. 6d. a week!) and work my way up to eventual ownership of the business, as my uncle had no children to take it over. My mother was very much opposed to the idea, and certainly I could not envisage with any degree of pleasure devoting my life to such a pursuit, however, profitable. So I turned down the proposal, and took a job as correspondence clerk in the Permanent Way Department of the local LNWR Station, made possible by the fact that in my last year at school, having already reached the highest standard, I learnt shorthand. It was a position that held me in good stead when, eventually, Cyril Scott took me as a pupil, for I could travel to London on a quarter fare ticket. By getting up very early in the morning and working in the evening I managed somehow to keep up with my studies in harmony, counterpoint, piano and organ with Charles J. King, a fine local musician and organist of St Matthew's Church (in whose library I excitedly discovered Holst's *Rig Veda Hymns*), and later with Dr A.C. Tysoe, organist of All Saints Church, a strict disciplinarian who gave me a good grounding in Bach.

'It was, however, before I left school that I was first encouraged to begin composing, for I remember being asked to write a school hymn by a Mr Grant, one of my teachers. I have no recollection of what this was like, for the manuscript has been lost, but it would not have been a strange assignment, as I was not only brought up in the hymn-singing milieu of the Congregational Church (Primrose Hill) I attended, but played the piano for the Sunday School hymns. My mother, who had a pure soprano voice, and who would have been a fine singer had she had opportunities for study, was a prominent member of the Church choir, and used to sing the solos in such works as *Messiah* and Stainer's *Crucifixion*. She was also in demand as a soloist in secular concerts, and I learnt a lot of my harmony by writing out transpositions of songs so that they suited her voice. My father had had no musical training, but he played the piano "by ear", and had a fund of popular tunes at his finger tips, although backed-up by sketchy harmonies in the left hand! The most exciting musical event for him was the yearly visit to Northampton of the Carl Rosa Opera Company, and I often went with him to hear his favourite Verdi operas, *Il Trovatore* in particular. He also had a talent for mending musical boxes, and his shop was rarely without one waiting for repairs. The trained musician in my family was Bertram, the blind brother of my father, and I believe he was a fine pianist. As, however, he died when I was about three years old, I hardly knew either him or his devoted sister Elizabeth, who used to dictate to him the piano music he was learning. She did not long survive his death.

'During the crucial years in my early life from 1915 to 1920 Northampton happened to be rich in talented amateur and professional instrumentalists, and I would like to put on record my indebtedness to a fine local violinist, Bertram Ablethorpe. We often met for music-making, and he stimulated me to write a violin and piano Sonata for him. This, my first attempt at a larger form, is not the predecessor of the published second Violin and Piano Sonata. The manuscript is now lost, but the work was performed during my student days at the Royal College of Music by myself and a fellow-student, Kenneth Skeaping. The real No 1 is still extant in manuscript, and is listed as Opus 11. There was also a local string quartet of excellent amateur players. In listening to their rehearsals and eventually writing a piece for them, a new sound-world was revealed to me. Composition was stimulated, too, by fairly frequent meetings with a younger contemporary, William Alwyn, who lived near to me and who was already developing rapidly as a composer [Malcolm Arnold was also born in Northampton].

'A third vivid experience, as deep and lasting in its impact as the other two I have mentioned, had its origin in a Sunday sermon at the church I attended. It was given by a Chinese Christian missionary named Kuanglin Pao, and the stories I heard from him then and during our brief friendship so impressed me that I wrote a set of piano pieces that I called *Chinese Impressions*. The manuscript bears a dedication to him, and I give below the beginning of one of the pieces.

'This new direction given to my thoughts had already been haltingly started by my mother's liking for Amy Woodforde-Finden's *Indian Love Lyrics*, the piano accompaniments of which I used to play for her, and was fostered by my later discovery of the work of Cyril Scott and Holst, both of whom were deeply interested in Eastern philosophy and religion, and by my reading of Mme Blavatsky's extraordinary book *Isis Unveiled* which I found in the Northampton Public Library. These combined stimuli remained as underlying experiences in such works as the one-act opera of 1933, "*Bee-bee-bei*" (which I am re-naming *The Shadow*), the action being located in Kashmir, the first movement of

Ex. C

the Piano Concerto (dedicated to Ali Akbar Khan) and the *Pezzo Ostinato* for solo harp.

'Such interests culminated in my decision, at the age of 17, to give an entire concert of Cyril Scott's music. This took place at the Carnegie Hall (a fine small concert hall in the Northampton Public Library) on 7th November, 1918. As it happened, this concert was central to my development, for the interest shown in it by Scott, after he had seen a programme surreptitiously sent to him by the Rev S.J. Hooper, the Minister of Primrose Hill Congregational Church, led the composer to accept me as his pupil. This, after a year or so, culminated in a Composition Scholarship at University College, Reading, where Holst taught.

'At last, therefore, I stood on the threshold of becoming a professional musician. Exciting as the prospect was, it was painfully tempered by the fact that I had no means to support me during the period of my studies! There were no grants in those days, and it was only through the enthusiastic interest of a fine local amateur pianist, Mr Tebutt (who was a master-printer) that enough money was raised to see me through my years of study at Reading and the Royal College of Music.

'In these autobiographical fragments I have necessarily restricted myself to those events, interior and exterior, that have I believe contributed most to my early development as a composer. But without the love, sacrifice and extraordinary encouragement given by my mother to both myself and my younger brother (who eventually became Chief Designer of aero-engines at Rolls Royce, and was part of a team that designed the Merlin engine used in the Spitfire) the crude realities of very limited means would have seriously and adversely affected the development of our respective careers.'

From this point to the end of the chapter Rubbra's autobiographical account has been transcribed from three tapes, made, respectively, on 28 June, 26 July and 9 August 1980.

'The autobiographical fragment that I wrote for the *Triad Press* book took me to the age of twenty before I seriously studied music: that is, studied music for my whole life. I wanted to leave Northampton and the work I was doing there, and devote myself completely to music. I was then a pupil of Cyril Scott. These lessons came to an end and I wondered where I should go from there.

'Scott had a close friend in Evlyn Howard-Jones, a pianist who was an authority on Brahms. I remember that he played the whole of Brahms's piano music in his later years. He also played Bach Preludes and Fugues, and it was said at the time that he could play them in any key (which *was* a feat), although I never heard him do it. Scott suggested that I go to University College, Reading, where a music faculty of sorts had been established, and study piano with him. Holst was also there as a teacher. They travelled to Reading each week, as they did not live there. They suggested that I try for a composition scholarship, which I won. I thus went to Reading in 1920 or thereabouts. The music facilities were rather ramshackle because there was no new building for such a school. I lodged out in Kings Road, Reading. The room I worked in at the university had an upright piano, it is true, but as it and the room itself were used by other students as well, I didn't get much privacy. However, there was a fairly mature student who didn't belong to the university. She rejoiced in the name of Eurydice Draconi. She was a fine pianist and a pupil of George Woodhouse. She specialized in Scriabin, so I often retreated to where she lodged in Kings Road, and listened to her playing of his Fourth and Fifth Sonatas.

'My other studies were with Holst, but as he had no special room set aside for him we had our lessons in the Great Hall. We studied from the scores of Weelkes and Byrd, whom he considered pre-eminent in early English music, and Victoria, whom he considered greater than Palestrina. For my work, I wrote several songs, and a piano piece – a tone poem for piano and orchestra – which Holst later conducted in a performance at the college with me at the piano. I was ridding myself of the influence of Cyril Scott under Holst but there was a curious mixture of the two composers. It was characteristic of Holst that when he was undecided at a lesson on some point, he would write a postcard from wherever he was and give his solution to the problem. This showed that he carried around with him his pupils' difficulties. [Imogen Holst, in her biography of her father, quotes Rubbra's remark with reference to his training under Holst: 'with what enthusiasm did we pare down our music to the very bone.'[3]]

'I studied piano with Evlyn Howard-Jones [who was early impressed by Edmund Rubbra's gifts, and truly prophesied that the young man would go far[4]]. However, Holst felt that I wasn't really getting the complete musical education that I should have. I went to lectures on other subjects than music, such as English history and Greek philosophy, trying to make up for my lack of education, but they weren't sufficient, of course, to occupy me completely. They certainly contributed nothing to my musical training. So, although I was supposed to remain at Reading for three years, I applied after a year on Holst's advice for the open scholarship in composition at the Royal College of Music, where he himself taught. Thus there need be no break in our association. Although Howard-Jones didn't teach at the college I could have private lessons with him, or with one of his pupils who did teach there. My musical education at the college was very different. I was mixing with students of my own or older age. I remember playing with Gordon Jacob the two-piano arrangement of Stravinsky's *Rite of Spring*, which was then published. We played that constantly because we loved it so much. And Holst was able sometimes to gather together some players from the college who would perform anything that I wrote, and which Holst was interested in. I recall an early song for voice and two violins – a curious combination – but he was very taken with it, and said, "we'll hear that next lesson." So he brought in two violinists and a singer, and we listened to it. Sometimes he would even brush aside all one had done, and concentrate on some work that had just been published. He was, of course, deeply interested in the music of Vaughan Williams – a great friend of his – and when the Mass in G minor was first published when I was a student there, we went through it instead of the lesson.

'Sometimes, when he was away in America (it was the time of *The Planets*) we would have substitute teachers. I remember Eugene Goossens, Balfour Gardiner, even Vaughan Williams (although he wasn't a good teacher), and others of a similar type, and they would take his place. Thus I had plenty of experience. When I had written a large work rather like the sonatas (of course, there were several sonatas before No. 2, which is published), I played them at college concerts with a violinist who was one of the students. I also played in Brahms's F minor Quintet, which I greatly enjoyed.

'Other students were sometimes older. There was Maurice Jacobson, with whom I became great friends, and he became, of course, the publisher who headed Curwen. This was a very useful contact in later years. Constant Lambert was there. I heard his work, *Green Fire*, which is not heard nowadays, and is probably quite forgotten. And so it was a lively and general musical education that I received at the Royal College of Music. It included ear training, and everything else appertaining to a student's musical life. For piano I went to Howard-Jones privately, and even had violin lessons from his wife, Grace Thynne. Although I didn't take to the violin as an instrument (the piano was much more mine), I had a good many years of experience at playing it, and this proved very useful in later life.

'After I had been at the college for three years, I remember one Easter vacation when someone in the Arts League of Service Travelling Theatre asked me if I would take the place of their pianist, who was ill, on their next tour which would take them to Yorkshire. I had no time in answering this telegram to consult Sir Hugh Allen, who was then Head of the Royal College of Music. My acceptance meant that I would miss the last term at College. Now Sir Hugh didn't take kindly to this at all, although I explained to him in an interview that I couldn't have done anything else. I couldn't get hold of him at the time. I was at home when the telegram came, I didn't know where he was, and the theatre was in a hurry to know whether or not I could do it. So I said yes without consulting him, and he said I shouldn't have done that. However, I am very glad that I accepted as the experience would be very valuable, and my being given a year's extra study at the college made no difference.

'In addition to joining the theatre as a pianist I wrote music for various numbers. It was a high-class variety show. We went to villages in Yorkshire, put up the scenery for one night, and travelled around by bus during the day, and then put up the scenery somewhere else. It was all great fun and hospitality was given to us by the local gentry, so there was a variety of experience in that way. My connection with it didn't cease with the six-week tour, but went on for several years until it culminated in my doing the music for an anti-war play called *The Searcher*, written by an American lady librettist, Velona Pilcher, who had settled in England. I wrote this music for a few selected instruments – about five. I think there was a piano, a double bass, a timpani, a flute, and a violin; and it was produced in the Grafton Theatre, an underground theatre in the Tottenham Court Road, London. The theatre doesn't now exist. But in the theatre they had omitted to build a space for any orchestra, so we were lined up single file at the side of the stage. All very awkward! I was at the piano, and then the others followed in a long line. I did what conducting I could from the piano. Well, the first night came and in the middle of the first performance I remember the lights fused, and this added to the confusion. However, we got over that, and the play went on for several more performances.'

Eleanor Elder, co-founder of the Travelling Theatre, has a first-hand account of the important and active role that Rubbra played. It appears in her book, *Travelling Players: The Story of the Arts League of Service*:

> In spite of the fact that we had to rely entirely on a piano, we introduced incidental music in many of our plays. Some of this was traditional and adapted, but a great deal of it was composed for us by Sidney Young and by Edmund Rubbra, who toured with us as pianist for a few weeks in 1924.
> Edmund Rubbra, like Sidney, was delightful to work with. They both had infinite patience with my musical ignorance, and were quick to grasp what effects were required.
> The more difficult the problem the more Edmund seemed to enjoy it: I would go through the play with him marking where I wanted the music and vaguely indicating the crescendos and culminating points. He was always ready to adapt or alter his score when necessary or, if he thought that alteration would spoil it, suggest an alternative. His music, admirably descriptive for ballets and plays, was inclined to be too complex for folk songs with a piano accompaniment. Yet he could reduce it to the starkest simplicity on occasion – as for instance, when we decided to produce Ezra Pound's translation of the Japanese Noh-Play, *Hagoromo*.[5]

After mentioning that 'the music was the problem, as a piano was unthinkable', the account goes on to tell how gramophone records were procured but were found to be 'impossible to dance to; and when we tried them over they were so obviously "records" that we decided not to use them.'

> I sent for Edmund, who immediately suggested an orchestra of members of the company. 'Impossible!' I cried. 'I can only spare four, and only two of them have ever played any instrument in their lives!' 'That will be all right', said he. 'We'll have very simple instruments. What have you got?' A search among our properties brought to light a varied collection. He chose an Indian drum and cymbals, a wooden pipe with four notes, a triangle, and a cowbell. Stephen Jack produced an ocarina, which he played with skill. 'Good', said Edmund. 'All we require now is a xylophone.' And he departed with the gramophone records, to turn up a week later with a score. He had, he said, caused a domestic upheaval by playing the records for a whole week-end, after which, having saturated his mind with Eastern modes and rhythms, he had composed something on the same lines.
> Edmund allotted to the startled actors their various instruments and, true to Arts League traditions, they tackled their parts with a will. The result was pandemonium, but after some rehearsals the final effect was very charming. True, the orchestra was not always perfect, but neither were the conditions under which they had to play, and once or twice hysteria nearly got the better of them. I can still see them, Stephen with his ocarina, dressed for the sea chanties; Hugh Mackay in his black cloak, with

the Indian pipe; Sidney Young in charge of both the xylophone and drum; and Elizabeth Dore, Victorian in checks and pantalettes with the cowbell; all crouched behind the curtains in a wing space two feet wide with only a flickering candle by which to see their instruments.

[Another play that taxed the small company was six scenes from Hardy's *The Dynasts*] there was one scene when, by the light of the warning beacon, the people on the coast gather together in terror of Napoleon's landing. The scene is short but very dramatic. For this Edmund Rubbra arranged the lines as a chorus spoken to drum beats, the voices overlapping each other in a crescendo of terror in a definite series of rhythms. This, added to the movements of the group of speakers, made a striking finish to the first scenes.[6]

Near the end of the generally favourable press comment on the production, there are these lines:

music by Edmund Rubbra that without obtruding hints the passage of troops, the clash of arms; and at the crisis of rumour, a veering eddying crowd on the heath in the baleful glare of the beacon that finely suggests mankind in the play of world circumstances . . . [7]

Rubbra's name appears on the roster of the Touring Companies for 1923–24. Strangely, the two works for which he wrote music, *Hagoromo* and *The Dynasts*, do not appear in the lists for those years, but the former is found for 1929–30 while the latter was a part of the 1933–34 season. Another play for which Rubbra composed incidental music (but which is not mentioned by Eleanor Elder) is *Mahomed and the Spider* (incidental music and chorus; author anon.).

We return now to Rubbra's narrative:

'During this time [the mid-1920s] I was playing for ballet dancers from the Diaghilev Ballet. Holst was very keen on the Diaghilev Ballet, and he took me on several occasions to see their latest productions. Two of the dancers (they were English, not Russian) shared a room – a studio – in Gower Street; and I played for them, and even wrote some music for them. One was called Ilgeranoff, but his real name was Henry Essex – quite English. In that manner I paid my way, although in Northampton enough money had been collected to keep me for two or three years.

'While in London I lodged in Hampstead Garden Suburb in Wildwood Road with a family of spinsters (I was the only male among them), but the woman in charge happened to have been at one time a pupil of Howard-Jones. That's how the connection came about, so it was a musical household in a way, and I was quite happy there. I walked across Hampstead Heath to get my bus to the Royal College of Music.

'Now I must say something about my other principal teacher at the RCM, and this was R.O. Morris. He took me for counterpoint and harmony, and gave me a thorough drilling in those two subjects. He was a great authority on sixteenth century polyphony, and even wrote a very good book on that subject.[8] He was also a composer, although he is not heard nowadays. His music was an extraordinary combination of, say, Purcell and Vaughan Williams. He was related to Vaughan Williams in that his wife was a sister of Vaughan Williams's wife. He was also a keen mathematician and it was even said that he devised the crossword puzzles for *The Times*, although I have no evidence actually, but I can quite believe it. He was also interested in Eastern thought, and when he found that I was too, he lent me Ouspensky's philosophical book, *Tertium Organum*. I don't remember that I took this in at the time, but I was very much fascinated by it. I think R.O. Morris's music ought to be remembered now in some way or another. I recall transcribing for piano a symphony he had composed, and this was a very good exercise for me.

'Now my music had been getting too diatonic under Holst's influence, and R.O. Morris wisely set me on another path. He said, "why don't you write a double fugue for full orchestra based on a chromatic theme?" I followed this up with a triple fugue, also on a chromatic theme. These exercises got me away from Holst's diatonic thought, and they proved to be a very cleansing sort of thing. Holst had steered me away from Cyril Scott, but of course things can go too far, and I had then gone too far. The double fugue was performed at one of the Patron's Fund concerts at the RCM in later years. Holst was present, and I don't think he was very pleased with the result, because he couldn't bear anything in the nature of rich, chromatic music. However, I felt R.O. Morris had done me a good deal of good by suggesting this.

'Sir Hugh Allen, Head of the RCM, was a very gruff man, but he was very kind to me really. I recall one occasion after I had joined the RCM choir (which I had to do) when I suddenly became aware of his baton pointing at me, and his saying, "Rubbra, come and conduct this." It was something by Bach and I hadn't studied it at all. Very nervously, I went to the front of the orchestra and conducted it, in what way I can't remember now. I recall on one occasion he said to the choir, "you are singing like a wheelbarrow being drawn backwards." I don't understand what he meant by that remark, but he had this way of giving vent to his feelings.

'One of my close friends during my college days wasn't actually a student at the college; but one day when I was having a piano lesson (which took place in Eaton Terrace, opposite Caroline Street), Howard-Jones told me of a young musician of about my age who wanted to meet me. He lived there and worked privately. I met him [Gerald Finzi] and we went upstairs and talked about music. Until his death [in 1956] we remained very close friends. He had a great influence on me. We took our music to each other, and criticized it.

'When I left the college, I wrote a piano concerto, which is not published yet, and I don't think it will ever be. It was played by Kathleen Long, a very well known and good pianist, and it had good notices.

'One of the critics who seemed to be very kind to me was Richard Capell. He was not only the critic for *The Daily Telegraph*, but also editor of the house magazine of Augener, the music publishers. He got me to review a lot of new music, which was very good experience. I was interested in writing not only short reviews, but much longer ones when the occasion called for them. I remember trying to review Sorabji's *Opus Clavicembalisticum*, which had just been published by Curwen. It was a three-hour piano work and you can imagine my difficulty in reviewing it. However, I did it, and wrote an article on it which is still available today somewhere. The work is so complicated that sometimes Sorabji wrote his music in five staves instead of the usual two. Thus I had an outlet in reviewing music and writing about it, which served me well in later years. And Richard Capell was quite interested in the music I was writing.

'In the latter part of that decade – 1920 to 1930 – Hubert Foss was making up the catalogue of music for the Oxford University Press. He published three of my early songs, two of which were with harp – an unusual combination – and one with piano. I also wrote a Phantasy for Two Violins and Piano [Op. 16], which was published by him later and reissued by Lengnick. His connection brought me to Constant Lambert, to whom I dedicated my Triple Fugue. I took it to him one day and played it over, and he in turn introduced me to the music of William Walton, whose Viola Concerto I heard for the first time and which I was very excited about. It was during this time that Lambert wrote *Rio Grande*, a tremendous success then. In fact, one paper – I think it was the *Daily Express* – said, "hats off, gentlemen, a genius!"

'I've spoken about Evlyn Howard-Jones and the piano. He was a friend of John Ireland, Bax, Goossens, and that school of music, as well as Cyril Scott. On the other hand, Holst was a friend of Vaughan Williams, and the two schools of thought were much opposed to each other. Howard-Jones said rather nasty things about Vaughan Williams's school, and the other side said equally nasty things (although not quite so much) about the school that Howard-Jones championed. But Holst didn't know much about what was being produced by these other composers, so that, very often, when I had little to show him he would say, "would you play me some piano music" of whoever it might be – Delius, Bax, or Ireland – and he would listen to it very silently and say nothing at the end, so I wasn't aware of whether he liked it or not. But he was interested in hearing it anyway. It was odd that at that time there were these two schools of thought that never came together; they were entirely separate from each other.'

Tape No. 2, which follows, records events and reminiscences from approximately 1930 up to and including Rubbra's service in the army during the Second World War. Some of the army experiences carry over into Tape 3, and it is at that point that it seemed advisable to place them in chronological order in Tape 2.

'It's curious that my first two teachers, Cyril Scott and Holst – we will also include R.O. Morris – were much interested in Eastern thought. Scott had written a piano work called *Egypt*, consisting of five pieces, which he dedicated to Marie Russak, that enlightened seeress who brought back to me information on my past Egyptian lives. (I don't know if you can quite believe that) Holst, of course, had already written the *Rig Veda* hymns and *Savitri*, a small chamber opera, and various other works based on Indian subjects. This accorded with my own instincts very much and I followed them into the same realms. First, I became a vegetarian, which I was until the outbreak of war when I could no longer be one in the army without starving to death, so that was that! Scott introduced me to G.R.S. Mead, whom I suppose one could describe as the intellectual of the Theosophical movement. I even set as my Op. 1 a translation of his from the Greek, *The Secret Hymnody.* My instincts led me to Theosophy and many of its parts. For instance, I went to a camp in Holland which was a yearly event run by Krishnamurti. He used to teach around a campfire each evening. The order was called The Order of the Star of the East. This was an offshoot of Theosophy and it was purported that he would become the modern Messiah; he was brought up by Mrs Besant to be such.

'At the time I was teaching the piano privately in order to earn a living, and I was also teaching harmony and counterpoint to many of Howard-Jones's piano pupils – something he wanted me to do. So I hired a studio in the Wigmore Hall and taught there one day a week. I also moved from my lodgings in Wildwood Road, Hampstead Garden Suburbs, to a place a little farther out.

'The works I was writing at this time were getting larger. They had started by being songs, but they were expanding. They started expanding even at Reading University when I wrote a piano and orchestral piece which Holst conducted. I wrote the Phantasy for Two Violins and Piano, which is a very condensed, contrapuntal work, and very continuous – too condensed, I feel, at the moment. I wrote my first Piano Concerto and also a Sonatina for Piano, which Dorothea Vincent, one of Howard-Jones's pupils, played in the Wigmore Hall. But I later discarded the first two movements as not being satisfactory, and kept the final movement, a prelude and a gigue-like fugue, which Augener published with the opus number 19C.

'But it wasn't until I wrote the Violin Sonata No. 2 that I became recognized largely. This was because when I played it privately at a house – I've forgotten where it was – it came to the attention of no less a person than Albert Sammons – and Geoffrey Tankard – both of whom liked it so much that they included it in their repertory, and played it many times. Also, when Holst was very ill I went to see him and played it to him – this was, I should think, in about 1933 – and he told me it was one of the best modern violin sonatas he had ever heard. So all that gave me great pleasure.

'I moved then to a flat in Camden Town which brought me nearer to London. For a living I played for ballet dancers. I wrote an opera [*Bee-bee-bei*, renamed *The Shadow*, 1933]; and I wrote my first string quartet. But the quartet had a final movement which I later discarded, and I revised the whole first movement – not the second – and added a new finale after the Second World War because Vaughan Williams was so interested in the material of the work. So I dedicated it to him.

'Also, when I was living in Camden Town (it was rather a large flat) I formed a music club to introduce new chamber and piano music. The audience, which numbered about twenty or thirty perhaps, sat about on cushions very informally. They paid so much a quarter to come and listen. I remember Hubert Foss coming to one of them and bringing with him the first printing of Benjamin Britten's *A Boy Was Born*, and we were very excited by it.

'Now about this time, being tired of London and London life, I moved to a remote cottage in Buckinghamshire [near Speen] where I wrote the Sinfonia Concertante for Piano and Orchestra. This was in 1934, and I dedicated the last movement to Holst, who had just then died. For a living I continued to review books and music for *The Monthly Musical Record* which was then edited by Richard Capell. I did recitals for the BBC and I was able to manage. I also taught privately, and I taught in a school in Wimbledon, the main body of which came from Germany at the time of Hitler. They were mostly Jews who had been deported from Germany and had taken refuge in England. They all came to the school – thirty or forty of them – and I taught them music. Among them was Peter Korn; he was later in California for a long time as head of a music department. Now he is head of a music college in Germany.

'Also at this time I was writing song cycles – a new departure – with a string quartet and string orchestra. I went back to Edmund Spenser for the words. The first set was called *Five Spenser Sonnets* and it was for tenor and string orchestra. The second set was *Amoretti*, for string quartet and tenor solo. I went back to Spenser because my general reading then was the metaphysical poets of the early period. I wrote a lot of choral music: five motets, all settings of metaphysical poets; five madrigals to words by Thomas Campion; and even some medieval Latin lyrics. Now these were originally for unaccompanied choir, but I found them so difficult that I decided many years later to revise them. It was after the Second World War, and I made them into Four Medieval Latin Lyrics for Baritone and String Orchestra. This made them more accessible.

'Now I don't remember why I did it, but I suddenly embarked on a long orchestral movement, not realizing that it was a movement for a symphony. I didn't know what it was, but when I finished it I realized it was so final in the way it ended that I couldn't follow it with anything else. It couldn't be the first movement of a symphony, so I decided that it was the last movement. Therefore I had to write two previous movements, and thus my First Symphony came into being. The first movement was very fierce. It was just about the same time as the Walton No. 1 and the Vaughan Williams No. 4, which are both very similar in mood. The first movement was in B minor, and the Symphony ended with this long C major movement that I wrote first. So in effect the whole work really is a cadential movement from B to C, although I didn't realize it at the time. The second movement, Périgourdine, was based on continuous variations on a French traditional theme called "Périgourdine". Sir Adrian Boult, who was then just Adrian Boult, conducted the first performance in the BBC Concert

Hall; and I remember the critics afterwards – one critic [Richard Capell] saying, "this is a symphony, and no mistake." It had a very good press.

'Through the Symphony I got to know the Head of Music at the BBC. This was Owen Mase to whom, with his wife, I dedicated the First Symphony. He introduced me to Alfred Kalmus, who was the London representative of Universal Editions. The score was taken to him, and he deliberated a long time before he decided to publish it because it was a very big work, very expensive to engrave, and so on. But at last I heard to my great joy that he would take it and have it printed and engraved in Vienna. This so encouraged me with symphonies that I quickly wrote the Second, the Third, and the Fourth in the space of five years – from 1935 to 1940. Of course, they were all composed so close together that they were, in a sense, reactions to each other – not separately contained symphonies. No. 2, for instance, wasn't like No. 1. It begins with a single line, and it is more austere and contrapuntal. No. 3 is – I presume one could call it – more lyrical, and then No. 4 is more chordal.

'In between these symphonies and as a sop to the expense of printing them (they weren't all printed, by the way. In fact, No. 2 wasn't, No. 3 was, and No. 4 was still in short score), it was suggested to me that I write smaller works to compensate. Now Universal Editions at the time was an offshoot in England of Boosey and Hawkes and they suggested I should write a suite of pieces for small orchestra, which would be of a popular nature and which would offset the more serious content of the symphonies. So I composed the Farnaby Improvisations. I even wrote a Schoenbergian piece just as an experiment, but it has never been performed. The text for this was written by a painter named Cecil Collins. He lived in a cottage near me, but he was also a poet, and I decided to set this strange poem called "O Unwithered Eagle Void" for small choir and small orchestra in a Schoenbergian idiom. Whether it turns out that way or not I don't know. It would be interesting to see.

'During the war Universal Editions split away from Boosey and Hawkes, so I was without a publisher. These earlier symphonies were assigned to UE even if they weren't printed by them. Then in 1941 I was called up before the Fourth Symphony was finished. I did my basic training at a place called Arborfield near Reading. I was there for six weeks. Then, after one and a half years, I was posted to a remote camp in Towyn on the west coast of Wales. It was a cadet training corps where I had an office appointment because, oddly enough, I had learned shorthand in my youth. They took advantage of this and put me in an office, and I think I proved useful. But it wasn't easy at all to compose, as you can imagine, under army conditions.

'This camp which was, as I said, on the west coast of Wales, was divided into what were then called "batteries". I was in F Battery, but, believe it or not, in E Battery was Alan Rawsthorne! Now he had a dry wit, as you probably have heard, and he was in charge of dealing out equipment to the cadets as they arrived, and when a cadet by the name of Hastings came Rawsthorne found a rifle with the number 1066 on it, which I thought was rather nice! This is a story that has remained with me ever since. Rawsthorne and I didn't work together very much because we were in different batteries, but we remained in contact with each other. I ran a small orchestra there of musical people who were interested in playing, but with terrible results I'm afraid! I was helped enormously by a fine double bass player who had been conscripted from the BBC Orchestra. His name was Bob Morris, and he and his wife lodged in the village and I had many happy hours with them. We even became so efficient – relatively speaking, because some of them were quite bad players – as to give a local broadcast from the camp. It was also here that I heard Rawsthorne's First Piano Concerto, which I liked very much. It was played by a Welsh orchestra that visited the camp. Also, while I was there, I revised the Sinfonia Concertante for Piano and Orchestra, which I had written very much earlier. I rescored and revised it, and it was later published by Boosey and Hawkes.

'After one and a half years I was asked by the War Office – and this came as a great surprise – to be the pianist in the formation of a trio – violin, cello and piano – that would present serious music to the troops. Although I was a pianist, I wasn't used to playing chamber music and I knew nothing very much of the trio repertory. But you can imagine how immensely pleased I was at having been asked to do this. I was made sergeant over the others because of my position, I suppose, but we had to create a repertory, and for many months we rehearsed in London or wherever we could. Sometimes it was in a Salisbury Plain camp. We started our travels which, at first, were all over England, Scotland, even the Orkneys, and finally to Germany, playing chamber music – trios mainly – to the troops. The original idea of three gradually expanded until we had a viola player, a singer and a flutist, so we were quite a crowd. We travelled with our own grand piano which we used (with the legs off) as a seat in the lorry going from place to place. When we arrived at the camps, or camp, where we were supposed to be, we unloaded the piano, put the legs on, and there it was – ready for the concert. I remember on one occasion we arrived at a camp, and the piano that was already there was covered with black leather. It was a terrific piano – about nine feet long, I think, and they said, "you needn't unload your piano because we have one." We all said, "that's very good." It was a pioneer camp at Manchester or thereabouts. We started to rehearse. When we started I counted at least twenty notes that wouldn't play at all. They were stuck. It was absolutely impossible to give the concert, so we called the sergeant in charge and said the notes were constantly sticking. "We can't play a piece of music on this!" His classic reply was, "Well Sir, only six were stuck this morning." As if six were all right, but twenty were a bit beyond the pale! We tuned our piano on the way. I remember having it tuned by the light of a hurricane lamp in the lorry itself. But it was all great fun, and we loved it. We were all very passionately persuaded in our views and the whole time travelling from one camp to another was taken up with one long argument about something or other – either music or politics.

'We were called "The Army Classical Music Group". Now some entertainment officers were so anxious to make a good impression that they wouldn't call us "The Army Classical Music Group" because it would put people off. They wouldn't get an audience. So one entertainment officer advertised us as "Ed Rub and His Seven Piece Band" or something like that. Of course, we had a crowded house, but when I began to explain what we were going to play – we usually began with a Haydn trio – most of the audience stamped out and left only those who were interested. It wasn't a very good thing to do! Once, I remember in Germany – this was in the last year of the war when we went to Germany through Holland (there was terrible destruction) – we went to a camp and did the usual things after the concert. We took the piano to pieces by taking the legs and the pedals off, etc. We thought we had loaded everything, but we had forgotten the pedals, and so when we got to the next camp, we found we had no pedals, and an army runner on a motorbike had to go miles in order to fetch them while the audience was waiting. You can imagine the uproar when they were at last brought, and the pedals were fixed onto the piano in full sight of the audience. It delayed things greatly, of course. We went as far as Berlin, where we played, and I was demobilized from there. [Tape 3 follows.]

'As you can imagine, life in a camp – especially in a remote part of Wales as well as at the camp where I was later in Wiltshire – wasn't conducive to continuous composition. But there were various activities, and I took full advantage of them. I started what I thought might be the Fifth Symphony, but when I received a commission much later on – some years after the war – from the Musicians' Benevolent Fund for their annual concerts in the Albert Hall (I received a commission for a choral work with orchestra), I turned this idea, these sketches that I thought were going to be the Fifth Symphony, into a work called *The Morning Watch* to words by Henry Vaughan, whose work I was very fond of. The first performance was very odd because there were *two* full choirs and *two* full orchestras; and Sir Adrian marshalled them wonderfully.

'Then I had a letter from Joseph Williams, the publishers (they are now connected with Stainer and Bell) asking for a couple of works they could publish as they were building up their new catalogue of music. I took advantage of this offer to revise the five *Amoretti* for Tenor and String quartet that I had written much earlier in the thirties, and also *The Dark Night of the Soul*, also dating from the thirties. The words for the latter were by St John of the Cross and the work was for contralto solo, small chorus and small orchestra. Very much later, again, this was performed at Norwich Cathedral – a very fine and moving performance, and the contralto was Kathleen Ferrier.

'Now during all this time of travel with the trio or sextet, I managed to find time to start and finish the *Soliloquy* for Cello and String quartet, Two Horns and Timpani. I wrote this for William Pleeth, who was our cellist at the time. Later on, before I was demobilized, I received a commission from Canterbury Cathedral for a large, double-choir Mass. But I couldn't find the necessary leisure and peace to carry this through before the end of the war, although I did start it. Funnily enough, I did a little of it at the Choir School in Canterbury where we happened to be stationed at the time. I began the *Kyrie* there, and went on with it in London at some barracks we were at in Chelsea. One evening when I was working on the *Kyrie*, we went to bed as usual. Next morning, we thought, "shall we stay here to have breakfast, or shall we go to Mr Pleeth's house at Finchley in North London?" We decided to go there as it was a change. When we came back we found the place in a shambles. One of these flying bombs had dropped on it so if we had stayed there for breakfast, what would have happened, we didn't know. It was a miraculous escape!

'I was demobilized, as I said, from Germany, towards the end of 1945 and then I found myself in Northampton (because I was born there) to receive a new suit in place of my battle dress. On my way back to the cottage in Buckinghamshire I had an idea that turned into the Cello Sonata, Op. 60. I worked on this when I got back – it went very quickly – and I broadcast it with William Pleeth, and dedicated it to him and his wife, the pianist Margaret Good.

'When I got home I finished the *Missa Cantuariensis*. Oddly enough, I can't remember why, its first performance was a secular one, though later on it was done marvelously at Canterbury.

'My next task, I thought, was to find a publisher. I hadn't a regular publisher, and I felt I needed one now. After much thought, I approached Maurice Jacobson, an old friend who had been a pupil of Holst at the RCM when I was there. Although he was a much older man, I had remained friendly with him ever since. He was quite a good composer, a good pianist and adjudicator, and he was one of the heads at Curwen, the music publisher. They had already published some songs of mine, so I naturally approached him, but he felt that what I was writing was outside their particular catalogue. Thus they couldn't undertake publication, but in the same street – Berners Street – there was Lengnick. I saw the Managing Director, who was then Bernard de Nevers, and talked to him about it. After a time he took me on, and we had a contract. My *Missa Cantuariensis* was the first work of mine that Lengnick published.

'In 1947 or thereabouts, I became a member of the Roman Catholic Church, after my religious wanderings, and to celebrate this I wrote the *Missa in Honorem Sancti Dominici*. I called it this because I happened to be received in the Church on the Feast of St Dominic, not for any other reason, not because I knew anything very special about him. This Mass was performed by the Fleet Street Choir under T.B. Lawrence at the Royal Academy of Music many years later before the Queen Mother, and she remembered it – it must have impressed her – for even as late as 1960 when, at Buckingham Palace I received the CBE investiture, she talked about it, and asked me if I was composing any more Masses.

'About this time I received my Honorary Doctorate in Music from Durham University.

'In 1947 Oxford was forming a new faculty of music. Oddly enough, they hadn't had one before then and Sir Jack Westrup was going to be the professor there; he had known me from the early days of my reviewing for him when he had been Editor of the *Monthly Musical Record*. He knew my music too. When I received a letter inviting me to be a lecturer there, I didn't know what to do, and I delayed a very long time. The regular income would have been most beneficial, of course, but I delayed because I felt unequal to the task of lecturing formally: two lectures a week during term on counterpoint or any works that I liked to talk about; and also teaching generally the students in their degree work. This would occupy two days a week. So he got a little impatient after months of not hearing, and wrote again in the autumn of that year and said, "what about it? Are you accepting?" After that, I decided to accept the offer!

'There was a housing shortage in Oxford at the time, and although professors were supposed then to live in Oxford and be on the spot, it wasn't necessary for me to do so because of the lack of accommodation, and so I was able to travel there from home on two days a week. I was attached to Worcester College, and later became a Fellow there. During this time, oddly enough, I worked on incidental music for a performance of *Macbeth* at Stratford-upon-Avon. Of course, I had done a lot of this before with the Arts League of Service Travelling Theatre, but this had been many years before. The whole thing was a bit of a shambles because I spent a week there rehearsing with the actors. They were notoriously unmusical, and I in my innocence had written music that they were supposed to speak to in rhythm. It was very difficult to get them to do it properly, especially as there was no conductor. The music was recorded, but they couldn't hear it during the performance, so you can imagine that all my special effects were completely lost in the process. However, it was a nice experience.'

Rubbra's brief description of the origins of the Fifth Symphony which followed here appears in Chapter 3, along with his description of the problems associated with the composition of the Sixth Symphony, also moved from its place in this narrative.

'Now the trio which started in the army (Joshua Glazier, violin; William Pleeth, cello; and myself, piano) was loath to disband when the war came to an end because we so enjoyed playing together and we decided to keep it going. We broadcast and played at many music clubs. Later, I wrote a Trio in one movement, and we played this at the then newly-formed Cheltenham Festival. Earlier, I had revised Symphony No. 2 and conducted it at Cheltenham. Then I got a commission from the Griller Quartet to write a second quartet. This was all before 1950, so you can see how busy I was. It was finished for them, and they played a very fine performance on a Decca record.

'I also received (much before 1953 when the coronation of the present Queen took place) a request from the BBC to write something for the coronation. I came up with the Ode to the Queen in three movements to Elizabethan words. It was a work for voice and orchestra. I thought of Kathleen Ferrier's doing it; I imagined her voice. Unfortunately, when it came to having to perform it in the actual coronation year, Kathleen Ferrier was too ill, and her place was taken by Anne Wood.

'Then came the British Council's offer in the early fifties for a Scandanavian tour of the trio. We sailed from a north of England port – I think it was Hull – to Bergen in the most atrocious North Sea weather, and everybody except myself arrived thoroughly sick. We gave our concert in Bergen, and then went to Oslo where we broadcast. Then we went via the Baltic Sea on an icebreaker – which was a new experience – to Helsinki, and gave a concert in the Sibelius Academy there. Then we made our way to Denmark where we played at a place on the northernmost tip, I think it was, called Aarhus, a university town, and we played before the students there informally. It was a most enjoyable experience.

'When we got back, I was faced with other commissions. One was to write a piano concerto for the BBC. This I enjoyed writing because I hadn't done one since those early days at the college. I was very much interested at that time in Indian music and I dedicated the Concerto to an Indian musician named Ali Akbar Khan, whose playing impressed me so much. It had a lot to do with the formal construction of the work, especially the first movement [explained in Chapter 6]. It was first performed by Denis Matthews and conducted by Sir Malcolm Sargent at the Festival Hall, which was then new. Then I had a commission from William Primrose, the violist, for a viola concerto. He played that at the Festival Hall; and later it was performed by Sir Thomas Beecham and Frederick Riddle, also at the Festival Hall.

'During this time I went to Italy to a conference on modern music in Rome. I attended various functions and first heard a work by Elliott Carter – a first performance. It was, I think, his String Quintet, or something of that nature. The conference was enlivened by Stravinsky's being there. He wanted to attend an opera – I think it was by Henze but I've forgotten the name of it. Anyway, it is *de rigueur* on first nights for the audience, especially in certain seats, to wear evening dress, and Stravinsky turned up *not* in evening dress, and he was refused admission! That it should have happened to the great Stravinsky, who was always being followed around by an entourage of admirers, created almost a scandal. I couldn't get near him myself!

'When I returned I started on Symphony No. 6, which wasn't a commission at all.

'Then I had a commission from the Feeney Trust from Birmingham to write a seventh symphony. I finished this in about 1957 I think (these dates are rather hazy in my mind), but it was performed before 1960 in Birmingham Town Hall by the Birmingham Symphony under Panufnik, a Polish composer who had come over to England, and had an appointment for a few years to conduct that orchestra.

'You can imagine that with all these commissions (I was writing articles, too, for *The Listener*) continuing with the trio and expanding its requirements –

we had to go to so many places and travel so much – was impossible. I was loath to give it up, but I just had to disband it.

'I had a commission then for a brass band festival piece, and I wrote a set of variations that was published by Paxtons, the brass band people. Now there is a curious story about this. I was one of the adjudicators in the Albert Hall the day of the competition. Brass bands came mostly from the north of England. All of the adjudicators were in a tent on the floor of the Albert Hall. We were not allowed to go out of it the whole day. Food was brought in and a san-lavatory too. Very necessary! The funny thing I remember about this is that when the competition was over and they dismantled the tent, I was left with the sight of a san-lavatory in the middle of the Albert Hall.

'In 1959 I made my first trip to America. I was invited there to hear performances of my Viola Concerto to be given by Primrose in three towns in New Jersey. It was only a six-day visit so I was able to see only a very little of America: just the towns in New Jersey, and New York City. When I was stepping out of the plane – I arrived about 4am, very tired – I was told (I was brought over by PAN-AM free) that they wanted me to carry a PAN-AM bag. But I hadn't got one, so I hastily borrowed one from one of the passengers. I hadn't noticed that sticking out of this handbag were knitting needles. They photographed me as I came down the steps of the airplane with this bag, and protruding from it were these knitting needles. Then the reporters who were waiting for me asked, "why do you carry a bag with knitting needles?" I don't know why I felt this required a facetious reply at 4am, but I did. I said, "I knit my music." It seemed to satisfy them anyway!

'When I got back to England I rushed to Leicester where I was to receive an Honorary Doctorate of Laws.

'Another new experience in these first years of the 1960s was the fact that I was brought in to play the piano for the ballet, *Les Noces*, of Stravinsky, which demands – has since its first performance – four pianos. I heard this work with Holst when it was first performed by the Diaghilev Ballet, and the four pianos were played by French composer-pianists. The hidden choir was in the pit together with the percussion. But when we did it at Covent Garden, the arrangement was different. All four pianos were placed, two on either side, in the pit. Myself and John Gardiner were together on the right, and on the other side were Richard Rodney Bennett and Malcolm Williamson. The choir was in between us, and the percussion section was behind myself and John Gardiner. We couldn't see the stage or anything that was going on there, and we couldn't hear the pianos on the other side of the pit because of the noise of the percussion behind us as well as various other things, so we had to keep our eyes fixed completely on the conductor. We got through it, but how I just don't know. It was an interesting experience. We did six performances at Covent Garden. [All of the principals in these performances are shown in the photograph on the dust-wrapper.]

'Now when the trio was in existence we had visited various music clubs. One of them was at Evesham in Worcestershire. When it was celebrating its twenty-first birthday the members decided to commission a new trio; and it was thus that I wrote my second trio. For that occasion Erich Gruenberg, William Pleeth, and I played this work. (Gruenberg had replaced Norbert Brainin of the Amadeus Quartet, who, in turn, had replaced Joshua Glazier.) It was as if the intervening years hadn't existed! We came together, and the experience of those war years made us play as though there were only a day or so between! And then we did, not the same programme but another which included my Second Trio, at Birmingham a few months later. We toyed with the idea – at least I did because we so enjoyed it – of continuing the trio, but it was an impossible proposition.

'I was engaged also on my Third Quartet. That had its first performance by the Allegri String Quartet at the Cheltenham Festival one year [1967] and also my Piano Preludes which I played myself.

'There is a biennial festival at Stroud in Gloucestershire and the directors try to get new works for this. One year in the 1960s I was asked to compose a work for choir and orchestra and I wrote the suite called *Inscape* to words by Gerard Manley Hopkins.

'In 1968 I retired from Oxford because I had reached the retirement age in 1967; I was given a marvelous send-off with a concert of my music – an entire evening of it including a symphony – at the Town Hall. I had been teaching a little at the Guildhall School of Music in London. As my teaching at Oxford came to an end, I decided to increase my teaching at the Guildhall, so I did two days a week there instead of going up one day. I liked teaching, and I felt it was a good thing to be in contact with the young musical mind.

'I wrote Symphony No. 8 in 1968. It wasn't to a commission at all, but I dedicated it in homage to Teilhard de Chardin, the French Jesuit, whose writings had influenced me enormously. It was performed a few years later by Sir Charles Groves with the Liverpool Philharmonic Orchestra.

'Symphony No. 9 now was occupying me. It was nothing new, because it began life as an oratorio. My publisher wanted me to write an oratorio, and he compiled the libretto from the Bible. I had started it, I should think, about twelve years before. But I wasn't happy with writing an oratorio. I felt it was an outdated form for me; and although I liked the ideas with which it began, I couldn't get on with it because putting them in an oratorio framework defeated me until I realized that the opening idea could be developed as a symphony. I called it Symphony No. 9, *The Resurrection*. Although it is for soloists, chorus, and orchestra, it is actually symphonically constructed from beginning to end. It had its first performance by Sir Charles Groves and the Royal Liverpool Philharmonic Orchestra in 1973.

'Symphony No. 10 came about by request from the Northern Sinfonia, a small body of very good players. They were asking for a chamber symphony; but I thought that if I was writing for a small body of players, I would write a work in one movement. But this movement compresses all four movements of the usual symphony into what is also the exposition of a sonata: the first part is the exposition, the second part is a scherzo or development, and the third is the slow movement; and then there is a coda. Thus it has all the ingredients of first-movement form, although I call it a symphony.

'Now I was acquainted with a young American critic, named Bennett Tarshish, who lived in California. His father was a rabbi. He was for some reason captivated by English music, and immensely impressed by my music generally. He wrote to me first from California, and then he came over to England where I met him. He was so ill – he was only in his thirties – that soon after he was in England he died. He had an incurable kind of disease. It was a great loss, and his widow asked me if I would write in his memory a string quartet, which I did: No. 4, and I dedicated it to the memory of Bennett Tarshish.

'I then started Symphony No. 11, which occupied me from 1977 to 1979. I had the first idea in 1977, but like most things I compose I like to keep the original idea in abeyance for quite a considerable time in order to digest it. Although I put down the beginnings of Symphony No. 11 in 1977, it was a long time before I got to work on it, and then I completed it in 1979. That's the work that is to be played at this year's Proms [1980]. Since then, I've written the Duo for Cor Anglais and Piano to a commission from a Dutch oboeist, who said that the cor anglais repertory is very limited, and would I write a piece for it and piano. I was intrigued by the idea because the cor anglais is an instrument I love. I completed this work, and it's now in the process of being published.'

We have now reached the end of the three tapes which Rubbra so kindly made in my presence during the summer of 1980. Between then and his death in 1986 nine further works were completed, the last of which was the Sinfonietta for Large String Orchestra, commissioned by the Albany (New York) Symphony Orchestra. This received its first performance on 5 December 1986. Both this commission and the articles and record reviews that have appeared in America in connection with certain earlier works are heartening signs that a composer, who has fared so badly at times in his own country, is receiving the recognition abroad that should have been his all along.

Not mentioned in Rubbra's autobiographical account is his association with the Dartington Dance-Mime Group in 1935–36. This is surely a minor item in his long and varied career, but it is of interest none the less because it demonstrates yet again the depth of his interest in composing for the theatre. The description of the intent behind the founding of the Group and the latter's subsequent flowering is too long and involved to be reproduced here.[9] Suffice it to say that a repertory of dance-dramas emerged, each title of which consisted of separate dances with descriptive headings. That Rubbra was *the* composer for the Group is amply demonstrated by a glance at the four programmes reproduced inside the back cover of *Edmund Rubbra: Composer*. He wrote the music for no less than seven of these dance-dramas, and their titles may be introduced as evidence of their varied content, and consequently, of the different sorts of music required to match their moods: *The Three Marys*; *The Three Sisters*; *Medieval Suite*; *Mothers*; *The Family*; *Epithalamium*; and finally, *Routine*. And the moods within any one of these works change in conformity with the dance titles so the extent of Rubbra's contribution is evident. The piano seems to have been the only instrument involved except for an occasional drum.

One of the intriguing questions repeatedly asked me during the course of writing this book concerns the origin of Rubbra's name, and, indeed, it appears to be a question of interest for almost everyone who is aware of the composer and his music. Michael Dawney poses it at the very start of an interview with Rubbra: 'May I ask you at the outset: is Rubbra really an English name?' The composer's answer follows:

> Until I am able to go thoroughly into the question of the origin of my name, I can't state categorically that it is English. A recent dictionary of surnames gives the spelling of my name with only one *b* – Rubra – and the origin of this form of the name is given as deriving from a village in Devon: Rowborough. How an additional *b* came to be inserted in my name, I do not know; but I have evidence that it goes back at least 150 years, and that the family was centred in the south Midlands. Earlier history is confused, one tradition being that an ancestor of mine named Rubiera was turned out of his home town, Bologna, in north Italy in 1565 for writing some seditious literature, and settled in England. A town named Rubiera still exists near Bologna. In another tradition an ancestor of mine, Carlos Henry Rubbra, came over to England at the time of the French Revolution. It has been further stated that the name is a variant of Rob Roy – Gaelic, red-headed, equals rubra (Italian or Latin for red). Pronunciation: the shortened form would obviously have a long *u* – this is more euphonious, but the two 'bs' could not possibly be pronounced other than with a short 'u'.[10]

Notes

1   The title of this chapter and Rubbra's account of his childhood and early youth were taken from *Edmund Rubbra: Composer*.

2   *Edmund Rubbra, Counterpoint: A Survey* (London: Hutchinson University Library, 1960).

3   Imogen Holst, *Gustav Holst: A Biography*, 2nd edn (London: Oxford University Press, 1969), p. 100.

4   Constance Richardson, letter to the editor with reference to the death of Evlyn Howard-Jones on 4 January 1951 at the age of 73. *M&L* 32, no. 2, April 1951, p. 199.

5   Eleanor Elder, *Travelling Players: The Story of The Arts League of Service* (London: Frederick Muller Ltd, 1939), pp. 162–3.

6   *ibid.*, pp. 164–5; 167.

7   A.S.W., *Manchester Guardian* (n.d.).

8   R.O. Morris, *Contrapuntal Technique In The Sixteenth Century* (Oxford: The Clarendon Press, 1922).

9   The details of the founding of this group, together with sample programmes, are printed inside the back cover of *Edmund Rubbra: Composer*.

10   The interview took place around the time of Rubbra's seventieth birthday; this excerpt appears in *Composer* 39, Spring 1971, p. 7.

2   The first four symphonies

We begin this study of Rubbra's music with his symphonies, mainly because the musical world at large thinks of the composer as primarily a symphonist – an impression that seems destined to remain. However, analytical discussions of these works will take on more meaning if they are prefaced by explanations of the guiding principles which govern not only the symphonies but virtually all of this composer's works.

First among these is Rubbra's very different approach to composition, as revealed in his own words:

> Frankly, I don't give form much thought at all. I never know where a piece is going to go next.... My method of working at a lengthy work is to continue steadily from the opening idea [or, as he has said more picturesquely elsewhere, 'I usually begin at the beginning and go straight through to the end']. The excitement of discovery would be lost if I 'graphed out' where certain climaxes, etc., would be. When I begin, my only concern is with fixing a starting point that I can be sure of. I work each bar as I go along until I have expressed exactly what I want.... My imagination discovers that architecture for me. I never force it to conform to formal rules. I never, for example, consciously search for a second subject; I'm only happy if this comes spontaneously, unexpectedly, and in the right place.[1]

Some of this is made more specific in the following explanation:

> All my works, symphonic or otherwise, stem from a single root idea (usually melodic and vocal in conception). There is no formal division into first and second subjects, etc. If these occur they are the result of the natural proliferation of the material. Each movement, then, is conceived as a single arc of sound, which implies a long growth towards a climax point and then a relaxing of tension.
>
> The texture of my music, whether symphonic, for chorus, or for solo instruments, is largely melodic and contrapuntal in conception. This, coupled with the unmetrical rhythm characteristic of early polyphonic music, makes it necessary that each part of the texture should be given minute attention. The plastic phrasing of each individual part, *however seemingly hidden* [my italics] is of the utmost importance.[2]

In a letter from the composer to Hugh Ottaway, dated 12 November 1949, the meaning of the final sentence above is given emphasis by these words:

> Every part in my symphonies does need to be moulded in an almost vocal way, and

unless that is done (and of course it takes a great deal of rehearsal time) the movement of the music is clogged, and the texture seems turgid.

It should by now be clear that we are dealing with a type of symphony which, in conception at any rate, represents a new, even radical departure from that of Beethoven and his successors: rooted in counterpoint rather than harmony. This point was corroborated by the composer when he told Ottaway that he was not 'greatly concerned with tonality as a basis of construction; the movement of the tonal centre is determined by the development of the contrapuntal thought'.[3] Thus the drama in Rubbra's music (and there is plenty of it) is not brought about by the opposition of tonalities (tonic versus dominant, for instance), but by melodies that in themselves contain tensions, revealed and released by contrapuntal means. Later, as we shall see, Rubbra became more aware of tonality as an integral part of his compositional processes, but it never really supplanted counterpoint as the prime mover. For this reason, most of the analyses throughout this book are not centred on harmonic procedures.

Another of Rubbra's basic premises is his conviction that the diatonic tonal system of the last three centuries or so has by no means exhausted its possibilities despite Schoenberg and his followers. (This is a conviction that seems to be dawning on more and more composers, including some who used to be staunch champions of twelve-tone music.) This conclusion is not at odds with Rubbra's de-emphasis on harmony, for his music does move from tonal centre to tonal centre, but such movement is the result of contrapuntal motion.

There are negative aspects associated with Rubbra's type of symphony, but they involve one's *perception* of the music rather than the music itself. Foremost among these is the *apparent* simplicity of much that the analyst and critic sees and hears: innocent, almost naïve, and quite ordinary figures, many of them scale-wise, and heard hundred of times before in the music of other composers. Can more be done with them? Can they possibly yield new combinations? The answer to both questions is affirmative most of the time, but for many analysts and critics it is 'no'. This is because, first, they are unwilling to admit that large-scale works existing outside the mainstream of 'modernism' have anything important to say; and second, certainly not works that employ traditional materials in what is believed to be a traditional way. I am persuaded that many, if not most, of these people experience real difficulties when they undertake serious investigations of Rubbra's larger works, for what seems simple on the exterior turns out to be exceedingly complex when one delves deeply into the music. Few have either the time or the patience for the task and this constitutes another very negative aspect. I am not averse to confessing that when I begin a detailed analysis of any of Rubbra's larger works my initial reaction is one of perplexity, accompanied by a sense of disorientation when I see no familiar guideposts anywhere along the way. These reactions are eventually replaced – but only very gradually – by the realization that distinct, logical patterns are slowly emerging from previously heard fragments. These patterns often combine, and soon, complex textures result.

With regard to textures in his larger works, Rubbra has been subjected to repeated criticisms which have, from time to time, elicited comments from him. His textures and instrumentations are closely interwoven, for he feels that the function of the latter is to elucidate his linear thought rather than to serve primarily as a colouristic element. That at times it does both is beside the point. In 1955 he told Ottaway that he thought some poor performances originated in insufficient rehearsal time, and not enough study of the scores by conductors.[4] Such performances are, of course, to blame for at least some of the bad reviews. Carrying this to its logical conclusion, performing organizations have contributed – unwittingly, of course – to how Rubbra's music is perceived by the critics (and, through them, the public). All of this is implicit in the passage cited above concerning the need to mould every part in the music, plus the necessary rehearsal time in which to do it.

Nothing anywhere in the composer's writings concerning his compositional methods should be interpreted as indicating that his symphonies and other large works are formless. In the following excerpt Harold Truscott throws a good deal of light on this fascinating subject:

> At first hearing a Rubbra symphonic movement could seem to move harmonically or tonally almost in a casual manner, and simply alight where it happens to rest. Some have written of this music as though this is, in fact, what happens. The composer himself has said that he through-composes, that he thinks about an idea for a long time before he begins to work on it, and that he often does not know where the music is going. I do not think this is the whole of the truth. It may be, on a conscious level. But it is the thinking about an idea for a long time that gives away a deeper truth.... Obviously, much happens at a subconscious level and equally obviously this seems to be what happens with Rubbra. Consciously he may only be aware of the music drifting; subconsciously, he has a very tight hold on what happens and why it happens. There is no other way to explain the purposeful movement of a Rubbra symphony, in which there is no sign of the music drifting where it will.[5]

Proof that his music is not formless is borne out by Rubbra's own statements in various analyses that a particular movement is in sonata or rondo form. When such movements are *first* experienced, the music may *appear* to be drifting because often there is continuous contrapuntal manipulation of the basic material from which the themes are fashioned; and the basic sonata structure lies beneath all of this.

'Improvisatory' is another word that is sometimes used to characterize Rubbra's music, and to many it is a synonym for formlessness, though in experienced hands that is not true. Neither the word nor the ideas behind it can be dismissed, particularly in Rubbra's case in view of the title, 'Improvisation', which is attached to a number of his works. It seems safe to say that all written music is improvisatory in the sense that it is continually expanding and sprouting variants – some obvious, others subtle – in obedience to the melodic, rhythmic and harmonic tendencies of its basic material, and that these variants spawn still others. The only limiting factor is the composer's imagination and in Rubbra's case that imagination is fertile indeed. Rubbra's chosen material leads him instead of allowing itself to be straitjacketed into some pre-existent mould, and it is this that causes much of his music to sound improvisatory. But the word 'leads' does not imply weakness. Rather, there is an imaginative recognition of the possibilities inherent in his material, and the willingness to explore all its ramifications. This causes his music to unfold – many times – with that inevitability that makes one realize its course could not have proceeded differently.

Symphony No. 1

Rubbra's three-movement First Symphony, Op. 44, occupied him from 1935 to 1937 and years later elicited the following comments from him as to its origins:

> When I began writing the First Symphony, there was, as far as I can recollect, no compulsion towards such a work because of the existence of Walton's No. 1 [1932–35] or Vaughan Williams's No. 4 [1931–34].... If there are aggressive factors in all three symphonies, it is probably because they all reflect a prevailing atmosphere, for I certainly did not set out to make an aggressive statement. Indeed, exactly the opposite, for the first movement to be written was the Finale, which is a long essay in the kind of inward lyricism that is common in my later works. Having decided that this *was* the Finale and not the first movement, I was forced into making the kind of dramatic statement in the first movement that would find its resolution in the relatively calm atmosphere of the ending. [It will be recalled from the autobiographical chapter that Rubbra did not realize at the time that this ending was really a symphony movement.] It is a most difficult formal problem to find a first movement for an existing finale (I had the same problem in Symphony No. 6), and I could only solve it by reversing the direction of its diatonic beginning (BC–BA) and inflecting the A to A sharp (A sharp–B–C) thus forming a chromatic fragment. This, dissonantly harmonised, forcibly stated on the brass, and surrounded by active string and woodwind writing that stresses the semitone, starts the symphony off *in medias res*. It is an intense movement, even in its quietest moments.[6]

The word 'tempestoso' following the *Allegro moderato* direction is an accurate indication of the nature of this movement, whose 'quietest moments', restricted to several passages, provide only an uneasy and temporary respite.

As to the movement's basic structure, Rubbra's phrase *in medias res* appears to furnish an important clue. However, the composer's prior knowledge of his procedures has given him a distinct advantage not enjoyed by the first-time listener, who in the normal course of events has reason to believe that the first prominent melodic line in a movement nearly always constitutes a main theme. In the present instance that faith *appears* to be justified, for the rocking chromatic line, shouted out *forte* by horns and trumpets, is just as convincing as the strident and disjunct line with which Vaughan Williams's Fourth Symphony opens, and which is his first theme. But with the conclusion of Rubbra's movement – indeed, well before – there comes the realization that the opening material cannot qualify as the principal theme because it is never repeated anywhere. On the other hand, material introduced in measure 28 and growing directly out of the continuous turmoil impresses itself on the hearer to a greater degree than the material thus far heard. This is because it has a better defined shape that includes an unmistakable starting and finishing point. Also, there is a certain authoritative air that is lacking in the earlier material. Scored mainly for woodwinds with initial help from the trumpets, it totally dominates the texture for eight measures, and not surprisingly it reappears later in the movement.

We return momentarily to the composer's expression, *in medias res*. In one review these words were interpreted as meaning that 'the first movement plunges into the middle, apparently, of the development section'; and this observation is then followed by a reference to the Sibelian method of figures that eventually coalesce to form themes.[7] The trouble with this interpretation is, first, the chromaticism that Rubbra derived from the diatonic line of his finale is *itself* a line. Developments are usually associated with the breaking up of materials, not their presentation and extension, which is the procedure until measure 28. Second, the theme beginning in measure 28 is full-fledged from the start. Furthermore, it is a diatonic theme whereas the foregoing material is fundamentally chromatic. This circumstance enhances the listener's capacity to identify more easily a principal theme. Finally, the movement is not cast in sonata form. Therefore, a term like 'development', which implies an exposition, is meaningless. How then should *in medias res* be interpreted? Probably figuratively in the sense that the music seems to start in the midst of turbulence from which order will eventually emerge – even if only temporarily – when the diatonic theme is heard.

However, there is no doubt that the chromatic material – the raw material of the movement – is the original source of just about everything that follows, including the diatonic theme of measures 28–35. The relationship between the melodic cell of the opening chromaticism and the start of the diatonic theme is indicated in the bracketed portions of Example 1, where each eight-measure passage is shown. A closer examination of the diatonic theme (B) reveals that

Ex. 1

its ensuing segments are derived not from its chromatic origins but from expansions of its own material. There are five further statements of the theme, the first three of which are sounded in succession (measures 216–40). In these statements the scoring is considerably reduced, and the mood is more tranquil, although the steadily repeating quarter-note E flats in the basses preserve the movement's basic intensity. The theme's fourth and fifth appearances occur in measures 244–51 and 256–64.

The most significant segments in the theme are its first four notes, and what for lack of a better term we may call the rounded contour in the fourth measure of Example 1. Sometimes these two segments are joined, as at the start of a long passage (measures 49–74), scored for the entire woodwind section, but they are scarcely audible, embedded as they are in the midst of the eighth- and sixteenth-note texture, and overpowered by the brass. Their function in these measures is purely as a background. Much more prominent during this passage is a string melody in which the rounded contour figure is the terminal point, both melodically and rhythmically, of two four-measure phrases. A particularly effective use of the figure is found in measures 187–204 where it is heard no less than fifteen times in a continuous overlap as it is passed from instrument to instrument. Its rhythm has been altered, and it is preceded each time by two introductory notes as shown in Example 2. The pitches are always the same

Ex. 2

although different octaves are employed. It is actually an accompanimental figure to a restless and highly chromatic but discontinuous line in octaves, given to the violins. This line represents an economical use of previous material, for it is not a new theme at all, but merely a reiteration of the two opening notes of Examples 1A and 2. Its syncopated rhythm emphasizes its restlessness. Another short burst of the Example 2 figure consists of six overlapping entries, which come before and during the first of the three repetitions of the theme shown in Example 1B.

There are other examples of segments stemming from the movement's chromatic beginnings as illustrated in 1A. The first consists of two short, literal reproductions of the intervals contained in the opening four measures. The rhythmic patterns have been changed, though not drastically. Each is scored for brass as was their prototype: horns, measures 68–71; trumpets 72–5. Two further segments with obvious antecedents are also scored for brass, but each is more fragmentary than those just cited. The first is for four horns, and is composed of the rocking semitones extending from the last beat of measure 1 to the end of measure 2. They are arranged in alternate rhythms on different pitches, the first and third horns having the higher line, and the second and fourth the lower. The continuous repetitions have created a rhythmic and melodic ostinato that extends over seven measures (21–7). The second segment involves the trumpets in a dissonant chordal arrangement in which the top line preserves the descending contour in measures 1 and 2. The third trumpet ascends as the others descend, creating a mirror image. This too becomes an ostinato.

The other aspect of the initial chromatic material must now be mentioned: the very agitated semitonal texture given to the strings (Example 3). Far from being merely a temporary atmospheric device designed to underline the 'tempestoso' direction, these semitonal figures pervade the movement to such a

Ex. 3

remarkable degree that of the movement's 275 measures only a very few do not have them. The jerky rhythms and the wide spacing between some of the pairs are potent contributory factors to the general unrest, and this agitation becomes even greater when the interactions between these figures and some of those already described are taken into account.

Without a doubt, one of the dominant characteristics of this movement is the abundant use of ostinatos. The elements of which they are all composed come from both sources: the chromatic material and the diatonic theme. Two examples have already been noted above. The second of these – the chordal passage for trumpets – is preceded by another ostinato, which, in turn, grows directly out of the first statement of the diatonic theme. Two patterns are employed in this ostinato: the more prominent one is closely related to the string figure in Example 3 in that it is made up of pairs of semitones an octave apart in an ascending-descending arrangement. The other pattern is a transposition of the following notes in measures 4–6 of Example 1A: B, D, C sharp, C natural, B, but in a different rhythmic plan. Pattern 1 is scored for flutes, clarinets and first violins, while Pattern 2 is assigned to the second violins, violas and cellos. The two-measure length of each pattern is sounded three and a half times.

All of the ostinatos in the early part of the movement belong to a series, each member of which – whether consisting of two dissimilar patterns arranged one above the other, or a single pattern – contributes to a build-up of tensions that must eventually be released. The release comes just before measure 78, but there is no feeling of even momentary relaxation, for the first violins and piccolo initiate a four-measure phrase that combines the urgency of the first two notes in Example 3 with the falling semitones in measure 3 of Example 1A. A rising and falling ostinato in the lower strings provides a restless accompaniment. The music steadily gathers power again, making economical use of various fragments associated with the original material. The main driving force continues to be the turbulent and irregular groups of sixteenths seen in Example 3, although the jagged contour is not necessarily present. In fact, the profile is often quite low.

With the sixteenths as a background and accompanied by a temporary reduction in the orchestral forces, there is a short series of consecutive, eight-measure passages for solo trumpet, flutes and harp, other woodwinds, and first violins (measures 125–55). If one were unaware of the melodic cells at the very start of the movement plus Rubbra's method of deriving almost everything from them, one might consider these soloistic passages as being the introductions of new themes. Yet, it would be foolish to assume this, for the proliferation of new material is counter to Rubbra's processes, as, indeed, it is to all composers who intuitively sense the possibilities inherent in their basic material. These passages are merely different – even rather obscure – facets of the generative figures, chromatic as well as diatonic. The most arresting of them is the passage for two flutes and harp, seen in Example 4. It stands out by virtue of its syncopated rhythm and tonal colour. So many continuous transformations have preceded

Ex. 4

this passage as to cause one to question the latter's connection with the diatonic theme of Example 1B, but such a connection can be made by comparing the first two measures and the B of measure 3 with the opening rounded figure of 1B.

Shortly after the end of these soloistic passages, the longest of the movement's ostinatos – fourteen measures – helps to bring about the most turbulent of the movement's sections. It consists of a two-measure pattern, set in the high register of the flutes and first violins, and its chromaticism is directly related to that of the movement's opening measures. The remainder of the orchestra has various repeating figures that at first glance appear to be literal repetitions, but upon closer examination these are seen to contain notes that differ from those in earlier groups, although many of the contours are approximately the same.

Following the climax at the end of the turbulent section, the figure shown in Example 2 is introduced and the imitative, overlapping passages already cited lead to the movement's concluding portion. After the three relatively calm statements of the diatonic theme, the full orchestra boils up again in conjunction with the theme's two final appearances. Following their conclusion the scoring is abruptly reduced, and the movement ends quietly. This sort of ending will undoubtedly surprise the listener after he has experienced the raw power and intensity of what has gone before, but in Rubbra's case it is just the first example of what for him becomes normal procedure. The first movements of every symphony up to No. 9 (considered by most commentators to be an oratorio) end quietly. Perhaps one should include Nos 10 and 11 – both one-movement symphonies.

The composer was the first to realize that his tempestuous first movement needed

in the following movement the relief afforded by the ubiquitous French dance tune that I found printed in *Grove's Dictionary* under the heading *Périgourdine*. [There is a more specific reference to the tune's origin in a note at the bottom of the score: the eight-bar theme of this movement is taken from *Essai sur la Musique* (Paris 1780) of De la Borde and Roussier. The original is in G major.] It is a tune which, like the original tune in the Scherzo of the Fifth Symphony, contains within itself all sorts of contrapuntal possibilities, and these I made full use of. Its most prevalent interval is the fourth, which appropriately anticipates the *basso ostinato* that accompanies the main theme of the Finale.[8]

Perhaps the following comment by Edwin Evans was an attempt to answer the perplexity of listeners who may have wondered why such a stern and uncompromising first movement could be succeeded by what probably seemed a naïve second:

Why the following movement should be based on a French folk-song... may be hard to explain, but why should it need explaining? In place of a conventional scherzo a theme was recruited for a movement in free variation form, so why not? The only objection I can see is that it happens to be the name of a Paris restaurant, well known between the wars, and that is insufficient to rule it out.[9]

As we shall soon see, the movement is anything but naïve, and the composer's alertness to its 'contrapuntal possibilities' of which he made 'full use' is enough to dispel any such illusions.

The Périgourdine was a dance from what used to be Périgord, now incorporated into the Départment of Dordogne. The metre was traditionally 6/8 and while the dance was in progress the dancers sang the melody, here pitched a half step higher than in the original. The composer's direction is *Allegro bucolico e giocoso* and the movement is entirely monothematic and essentially through-

Ex. 5

composed. It pursues a course that from its soft and delicate start becomes increasingly boisterous and uninhibited. The basic plan governing its quite headlong progress consists of groups of statements of the full theme that alternate with passages consisting of fragments, recruited from the theme's various segments. Altogether there are twenty-two full statements of the theme.

The movement begins with a group of woodwind entries: solo oboe as seen in the example, solo bassoon and solo flute, all set in F minor despite the look of A flat major. Not shown in the example is the lightly accented supporting bass. This consists of alternating Fs and B flats, the first F being sounded beneath the upbeat in the opening half measure. The more usual (and banal) practice would allow the upbeat to remain unharmonized. The Cs in the melody are supported by B flats, and the ambiguity is strengthened by D flats in the horns at the same places. The first intermediate passage, consisting of delicate fragments distributed around the orchestra, leads to a flute and oboe entry in measure 37, followed by the piccolo and second violins in 45. The second half of the violins' statement is completed by the oboe. The accompanying fragments set up an ostinato in which a 'Three Blind Mice' pattern is used with the concluding note held out. It is this pattern, stated eight times, which is the dominant factor in the passage, not the thematic statements, which form a running background. I think this transfer of interest was intentional and not an accident attributable to poor scoring. After all, the listener has by now thoroughly familiarized himself with the melody, and a slight shift in emphasis is a pleasant change. However, the insistence of this ostinato figure is much more than a diversion, for there is introduced a sense of excitement that constantly mounts as the movement progresses. This is increasingly the result of the fusion of the two elements: the thematic statements, and the fragments derived from them. Adding to the mounting excitement is the more frequent participation of the brass, beginning at measure 83 and continuing with the involvement of the trumpets and trombones in a short canonic passage (measures 112–18).

After a *fortissimo* climax the music softens, and the passage from about measures 140 to 150 sounds rather Ravelian – like the mysterious gathering of forces before the final, great climax in *Daphnis et Chloé*.

It is not long before the music builds again, and at the change from 6/8 to 9/8 at measure 234 the sunny, raucous character of the movement suddenly disappears, replaced by a section that communicates a feeling of uneasiness. The dynamic level is *forte* and *fortissimo*, and all of the material is derived indirectly from the theme. Prior to this change there is a section numbering thirty-two measures that is filled with a typical figure associated with 6/8 – ♪ | ♩ ♪♩ ♪ | ♩. Dominating the orchestra, it is occasionally varied with longer note values, but its content is the same: a kind of summary – repeated many times – of the second and third measures of the theme but with intermediate notes omitted. Most of the theme itself is stated by the solo trumpet in measures 213–20, but it is scarcely heard in the general hubbub. Even the E major entry of the theme in the strings at 226, incomplete as it turns out, has to compete with the dancing figure.

The arrival of the 9/8 section at measure 234 – *fortissimo*, and *poco meno allegro* – indicates a complete change of character, for the dancing figure ceases to dance at the instant its concluding note is taken as the first note in a curiously elongated version of the same figure – ♩ ♩ ♩ ♪ | ♩ ♩ ♩ ♪♩ ♪ | – in the woodwinds and horns. Lumbering melodic fourths and fifths stride across the score in the trombones, while an upward-rushing, two-octave scale figure engages the violins. No substantive changes take place until measure 253, even allowing for the increase in intensity at 249, where the figures merely exchange places as the rushing figures move to the woodwinds and their figure, with slight changes, goes to the strings. The almost grotesque nature of the entire section is emphasized by three-octave harp *glissandi*.

At measure 253 this intense activity ceases, to be replaced by a section which, in terms of its melodic, harmonic and rhythmic content is static. Perhaps it is this general, but temporary, inactivity that serves to communicate an even greater sense of unease than that just experienced during the intense activity associated with the rushing figures and the other ingredients. All of this is short-lived, for at measure 267 the theme returns in a complex, stratified arrangement that consists of a *fortissimo* woodwind and trumpet statement in its original, ebullient form (except for the 9/8 metre which, with its extra beat, gives the theme a new and interesting twist), while beneath, the lower strings and violas share an augmented, canonic version in dotted quarters and halves. The canon breaks off at the point where the lower strings (soon joined by the lower woodwinds) begin to repeat the first half of the theme, thereby creating an ostinato that, with one short interruption, leads to a final, complete (but still augmented) statement. A different dancing figure in quarters and eighths virtually monopolizes the violins, eventually spreading to the woodwinds. It too is an ostinato with occasional breaks and canonic passages, and it extends right to the very end of the movement. But the most extraordinary thing about this final section is the *fortissimo* augmentation in the trombones of the theme. Introduced by a gong stroke, it consists of one note per measure so that, beginning in measure 289 the theme is only completed in measure 333, the last measure of the movement. In the eighteenth measure of this trombone statement the horns and trumpets peal out their version of the theme in dotted quarters and halves.

Thus, here in his First Symphony, Rubbra has demonstrated his contrapuntal skills to a remarkable degree, and the same kind of ingenuity will be seen time and again in future works of a dimension commensurate with such treatment. Yet the effect here and in the works to come is spontaneous and natural. Such layered passages as those just described are no mere sterile exercise; they are an integral part of Rubbra's thinking. Each separate line is indispensable to the totality. The general effect of this particular passage is one of vibrant life – the culmination of a movement whose uncomplicated, almost child-like beginning, gives no hint of the gradually increasing excitement and final, riotous explosion.

The third and final movement, the first to be written, is marked *Lento* and in the article from which the composer's extended remarks on the preceding movements were taken, he reveals that 'this movement is in sonata form'. Rubbra's views on sonata structure were written in connection with his Second Symphony:

> It can no longer be inferred from the word 'Symphony' at the head of an orchestral work that the music is divisible into fairly clearly defined sections, such as, in the first movement [the most usual one for the employment of sonata form], exposition, development and recapitulation. There are, of course, and must be, contrasts in subject-matter, but these contrasts need not be in the places assigned to them by the text-book. Nor need the argument (or development) wait for a double bar, or the recapitulation be anything like a full repetition of the material of the exposition. This does not, by any means, imply a loosening of formal principles: only that the modern composer, in using material – as is mostly the case – that is not strongly anchored to a key-centre, must find other means of making the structure cohere in a logical manner.... Now the nature of the themes of a Symphony determine the nature of the form. If the latter is unsatisfactory, it is usually because the composer has, owing to pre-conceived formal ideas, interfered with the evolution of the melodic thought, instead of allowing it to unfold naturally. It may be thought that if the latter course is taken the music, by continuous suggestion, would move too far afield, and thus lose touch with the initial impulse. This is true, however, only if the composer has no grasp of the formal implications of the idea. Provided he has this grasp, the idea is like a circle which, however much it expands, always has the same centre. When the expansion is at its fullest, then the contrasting idea has every right to appear. This, in turn, will expand and evolve.[10]

While the sonata structure in this movement certainly has the qualities of formal flexibility, it is equally true that in succeeding examples of its use further refinements can (and should) be expected. It is important to remember that the composer's views were written following the completion of the Second Symphony. The part omitted in the quoted passage concerns the application of sonata form in the first movement of that work, and in due course it will be seen that the experience gained from the composition of the present movement – which Rubbra had thought was the first movement until he realized otherwise – was an important factor.

Returning now to the final movement: there is no slow introduction, as there often is at the beginning of a sonata structure, the obvious reason being that the tempo is already slow. Thus Theme 1 in the form of a quiet canon between solo cello and solo viola is heard immediately over an ostinato in the basses. I should like to draw attention to its scoring: the cello is set an octave higher than the viola, whereas normally the reverse would be true. Had the latter course been adopted, the effect would have been quite ordinary. This way, the weightier timbre of the cello even in its high register proved better for the production of the rich tone Rubbra obviously desired than the viola. The violin could not have done it at all, and the viola was needed for its rich, middle-register tone. The opening passage is shown in Example 6. It has been fashionable over the years

Ex. 6

to criticize Rubbra – sometimes severely – for various, alleged scoring faults, one of which is an insensitivity to instrumental colour. This beginning is one instance where the charge is baseless.

Following the entries of the *tutti* strings and most of the remainder of the orchestra in the measure directly after the example, some of the thematic segments are subjected to development and expansion. One of these is the opening figure in measure 1, and another is the falling figure in measure 5. Much is also made of the dotted rhythm that is so important a part of the theme. In fact, it dominates a large part of the movement, sometimes quite dramatically. An early instance of this is found in measures 17–21 where, beginning with the last sixteenth of 17, the three upper string sections have the equivalent of the dotted figure: dotted eighth rests interrupt the flow. The lower strings and woodwinds play the connected dotted figure. The sense of impending drama communicated by this passage is brought about by an alternation in the figure between the upper strings, marked *pizzicato*, and the other instrumental parts. The melodic contour of the figures, portions of which are highly disjunct, increases the interest. Another figure, composed of a falling fifth and a rising fourth, is a direct outgrowth of a short *pizzicato* passage that ends in measure 9. It is easily overlooked here and in measures 30–33, but it comes into its own later when it forms the basis for two modulatory passages, both of which will be discussed in due course.

The slow tempo makes these early developmental passages seem longer than they are, so that when the second statement of the principal theme arrives in measure 22 a feeling of spaciousness has been created. This statement and the much freer version beginning in measure 34 are also in canon, the former between solo bassoon and solo oboe and the latter between ensemble violas and violins. One of Rubbra's most characteristic sounds now comes to the fore: the subdued, poignant timbre of the cor anglais. Here, it is engaged in playing an expressive derivative of Theme 1. The next appearance of the theme starts in measure 50 with a two-note upbeat and the canon which by now is understood to be an integral part of it, is between the first violins and the second violins plus violas. Other instruments have supporting roles. Since each violin part is set in the high register at the unison, this statement is a climactic one, allowing the canon to be heard to best advantage. The sheer sweep of the passage as it reaches for its highest point and then begins its descent is aesthetically satisfying.

The last measure of this statement overlaps the onset of the subordinate theme. It would be difficult to imagine a greater contrast between themes, for whereas the first is introspective and slow to unfold, the second is direct, almost blunt (Example 7). Note the descending figure, borrowed from the fifth

Ex. 7

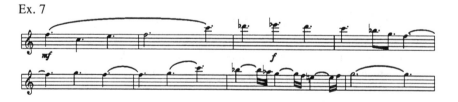

measure of the first theme, and here provided with a different ending. The subordinate theme now occupies centre stage, for there are three prominently scored statements in quick succession. In fact, only two measures intervene between the first and second statements. The latter is an incomplete canon at the octave and at a distance of two measures between second violins, violas and solo trombone. Between the string and trombone entries the first violins begin what would have been a three-way canon, but this is abandoned after one measure in favour of other material.

This 'other material' is not just anything, for since the start of his composing career Rubbra has never indulged in meaningless padding. All of his accompanimental or background passages – whichever one chooses to call them – are composed of organic materials whose sources are either primary materials or derivatives of them. In this instance the important accompanimental passages consist of ascending and descending figures of varying lengths, and their melodic and rhythmic shapes are those of the figures in measure 5 plus the latter's ascending form. A melodically modified version of Theme 1, involving almost the entire orchestra in a *fortissimo* statement, fills measures 95–103. The canon is between the strings and most of the woodwinds on one hand, and the clarinets and brass on the other. It is an extremely intense statement, strongly emphasized by the bass drum and timpani.

A third theme with a distinctive contour and character of its own makes its appearance in measures 102–11. It seems too pedantic and rigid to attach the term 'closing theme' to it, for it has none of the summing-up traits generally associated with that term. It is quiet and meditative, but aside from its intrinsic beauty it is notable for its modal flavour. In its initial appearance its first half is shared by the first trombone and first violins, while its second half is carried by the violins alone. An interesting division in terms of how the melody is harmonized is provided by the two halves. In the first, there are modal harmonies with various instruments participating, but in the second, sustained brass notes and a short countermelody in the cor anglais are substituted. A second statement of the theme follows immediately, its first half scored for solo violin, while its second half is divided between cor anglais and first flute. The theme appears as Example 8.

Ex. 8

Here we must digress for a moment to consider an aspect of Rubbra's art that has received too little attention, most probably because of the much wider recognition accorded his mastery of counterpoint: his harmonic subtlety. It has seldom been written about, much less identified in particular passages. A good general statement, the best I have yet seen, puts it this way:

No composer more than Rubbra can see round a chord in all its aspects and limitations. His powers of modulation are in their way unique, for he is a master of the
shifting semitone and the enharmonic change – which means that his acute ear and
inventive skill so often create sounds pulling in two directions. Thus a C sharp may
in the course of his music become a D flat in his mind and so cause a subtle
modulation as inspired as it is unexpected.[11]

The passage that occasioned this digression is a mere seven measures long, but
in this short span there is contained a transition of surpassing beauty that
clearly demonstrates the composer's mastery of the enharmonic change. The
material employed in this change was mentioned earlier as consisting of a
falling fifth and a rising fourth.

To begin: if we refer to Example 8 we will see an E on the first beat of the
sixth measure, a note that would normally be harmonized by the dominant
triad: A, C sharp, E. (The fact that it is not so harmonized here has no bearing
on the discussion, for it is the reappearance of the E in the solo violin at the
same place in the theme's second statement that concerns us.) With regard to
the second statement, it would seem that the persistent As – the dominant of D
minor – in the first bassoon part, and the rocking figure from F to D and back
again in the second bassoon part, both under the solo violin, were intended
firmly to establish D minor in the listener's mind. This would make it possible
to convince him that the E he is about to hear will also be harmonized by the
dominant chord of D minor. But the E, transferred to the first violin section in
an overlap is left hanging, for not only is it not harmonized as a dominant but
there is no resolution to D minor as in the first statement. The remainder of the
theme (measures 6–10 in Example 8) is shared equally by the cor anglais and
the first flute, but interest has shifted so completely to the first violins as to
thrust them into the background.

Now for the transitional passage itself, shown in Example 9. Taking the
unresolved E as the starting point of the new phrase, the melodic line falls a
semitone to D sharp and then to D natural before dropping a fifth to G. Then
comes a rise to C, a semitone fall to B, a drop to E, and so on through the same
process until B is reached. Melodically, this is quite an ordinary sequence, but
harmonically it is not, for under each member of the melodic series there is a
different chordal structure. Thus the elements of unpredictability and surprise
are strong. Actually, the alert listener will be aware before the E resolves to D
sharp that something is brewing because the harmony is heading away from a
resolution on D. Any sense of inflexibility in the various stages of the transition
is neutralized by the counterpoints in the moving parts, and they, of course,
have as much to do with the changes in harmony as the quarter-notes in the
lower strings. I cannot leave this passage without remarking on its extraordinary
beauty; yet the simplest means are employed.

Once the sequence has ended on B there follows an eight-measure passage
in which an octave C sharp pedal in the violas provides an uneasy stability for a
sinuous line in the lower strings, and a soft chromatic line in the solo oboe. The

Ex. 9

feeling conveyed by this whole passage is one of expectation that something is about to happen. That 'something' is the development section, which begins with vigorous repetitions in the woodwinds and brass of two-note groups at different pitches in the rhythm ♪♪♪♪. These groups, two to the measure, are versions of the rising and falling figures in the first measure of the principal theme. The restless, chromatic line of the solo oboe is repeated at a lower pitch in the first violins and violas. Then, simultaneously with the two-note groups there is a diminution in the horns and second violins of the third theme (measures 140–45), but the sheer weight and gathering momentum of an *accelerando* have obscured the diminution so that it is merely another component in the general turbulence. On the other hand, another statement of the same theme, this time in its original note values and extending from measures 148 to 157, is very prominent. The importance attached to it can be gauged by its instrumentation – trumpets, second violins, augmented in the second half by woodwinds – and the cessation of the two-note groups. Under these conditions the theme rings out over everything. From measures 159 to 180 there is a canonic and *fortissimo* statement of Theme 1 between woodwinds and brass at the distance of a half measure instead of the usual measure. This is only a paper change, however, for the metre is now 2/4. Simultaneously in the trombone parts Theme 2 appears in a half statement.

Upon the completion of these passages at measure 180 a new phase of the development begins. The constant, rushing string figure consisting of dotted sixteenths and thirty-seconds in ascending and descending patterns – a feature of the development since shortly after its beginning – now fades into the background under a particularly beautiful version of Theme 1 in the cor anglais

Ex. 10

(Example 10). Note how a new synthesis has been created. The rushing string figure disappears altogether when an *appassionato* statement of the sequential pattern in Example 9 appears in the first violins to the accompaniment in most of the remainder of the orchestra of yet another synthesis of the principal elements of Theme 1. At first, this new synthesis is essentially background material, but when the sequential pattern ends it dominates everything, for then it moves into the highest reaches of the entire violin section where it functions as a bridge, closing the development and opening the recapitulation.

From the composer's earlier remarks on sonata structure, the difficulties involved in making categorical assertions about any of its broad sections can be appreciated. Dividing lines can be very vague and ill-defined. That is true here with regard to the point at which one can be reasonably sure (but not certain) that the development gives way to the recapitulation. My particular solution is probably not the only one, but I interpret the sequential passage from measures 190 to 199 as constituting the first half of the development's final passage. My choice is influenced by the positioning of the same sequential passage at the same place at the exposition's end. Each of the two sequential passages is then succeeded by a connecting link of approximately equal length – six or seven measures – that leads into the new section.

As for the recapitulation itself, there are convincing reasons for choosing measure 205 as its starting point: 1) the ritard in the preceding few measures, leading the listener to expect something new; 2) the quickening of the tempo in 205 that confirms this expectation; 3) the reappearance of Theme 1 in its original pitches. But the last and most important point concerns the true function of a recapitulation which, first of all, is emphatically not that it is simply a repetition of the main themes of the exposition. True, the latter are often repeated exactly but many composers subtly alter the details of harmonization, rhythm, instrumentation, and so on. Additionally, as Rubbra has said, the recapitulation need not 'be anything like a full repetition of the material of the exposition'. Sometimes the order in which the material was first presented in the exposition is changed, and some themes are even omitted altogether. Finally, there is the concept, admittedly one of feeling rather than reason, that, following the often turbulent and tension-producing procedures to which the movement's basic materials are subjected in the development, a certain 'maturity' envelops these materials when they reappear in the recapitulation – a maturity based on the experiences which they have undergone. The best presentation of this idea that I have yet seen is contained in an introductory book on music intended for the layman:

> The danger in a literal recapitulation lies in its psychological falsification of dramatic untruth. If, in the last chapter of a novel, the major characters appear exactly as they were in the first chapter, one would seriously question the meaning and the value, either to the characters or to the reader, of the cycle of experience to which both have been subjected in the course of the intervening pages. A literal recapitulation implies that nothing really has happened to alter one's perspective with respect to the original presentation.[12]

Returning now to the recapitulation under investigation, three major alterations are very audibly present: changes in the principal theme's instrumentation to horns and cellos, plus the abolition of the usual canon during its first half; the final flowering of the accompaniment derived from segments of Theme 1, and introduced at the end of the development; and the inevitable harmonic changes produced by this accompaniment. By far the most memorable of these alterations is the accompaniment. Although it does not overshadow the principal theme, it is certainly coequal with it, and as a counterpoint it is magnificent. The soaring violins are breathtaking, not only for the heights they reach but also for their long, sustained line and the intrinsic beauty of that line itself. Only the theme's second half is in canon, but before the imitation ends the first trumpet breaks in with a *fortissimo* statement, not of Theme 2 but of Theme 3. The high violin counterpoint continues through the first half of this. At measure 229 the second segment of Theme 1 suddenly appears in the midst of the violin counterpoint and upon its completion the counterpoint will resume as before.

Preceding the final appearance in the recapitulation of Theme 1, there is a good example of how Rubbra reinterprets something he has used before: the sequential passage shown in Example 9. There the passage was slow, expressive, and thinly scored. Here it is part of a denser texture, and it is shorter by one segment. The most interesting difference concerns the harmonic implications. In Example 9 sharps are prominent, but here the passage is constructed around flats. Each passage begins with the same sound, but the spellings are different: D sharp in the first, E flat in the second. B minor is the *apparent* goal of segment 1 in Example 9, a goal that is averted as segment 2 moves more surely towards E minor. In the later passage G minor *is* the goal, which is not only realized but confirmed by segment 2, and it is realized by pitching the segment a minor third rather than a fourth higher. The third and last segment of passage 2 begins on G but F sharp is next – not F sharp as a leading tone to G but as the dominant of B minor. The same *melodic* segment ends passage 1, appearing as though the harmonic goals would be the same for both passages. However, the presence of an E flat pedal in the basses under the G, F sharp, B in the later passage suggests a different outcome, and this becomes clear when Theme 1 returns in measure 258. The B with which the latter opens and the notes that immediately follow it are the same as those that have been heard before, but the introduction of B flat and the persistence of the E flat pedal show that the theme is headed for a different resolution. That is achieved when the theme comes to rest on G flat. During the course of its journey it is, of course, entirely flat-oriented. The theme's halves are instrumentally divided with the first half scored for strings only, and the second for solo oboe with the solo bassoon taking the canonic imitation. There is no canon in the first half. The dynamic level becomes softer as the statement nears its end, and only the oboe and a *pianissimo*, sustained chord above a repeated F in the timpani are left.

The concluding section of the movement is marked *Coda, Fuga*. The reason for the omission of Theme 2 (Example 7) in the recapitulation is now clear: that theme is the fugue subject and its restatement before the coda would have weakened the element of surprise. A further instance of Rubbra's enharmonic thought can be seen when the G flat that ends Theme 1 becomes the F sharp with which the fugue subject begins. The subject is well-suited for stretto treatment, and there are two prominent instances of stretti in two parts. Surprisingly, instead of continuing until the end of the movement as one would expect, the fugue stops not far beyond the halfway point in the coda. This permits space for one final statement of Themes 1 and 3, here combined in a riotous orgy of sound at whose end a stretched-out brass entry of the first nine notes of the fugue subject peals out above a single chord, held for twelve measures, triple *forte*, by all of the other instruments.

At its first performance, under Sir Adrian Boult in London on 30 April 1937, Rubbra's First Symphony attracted a good deal of attention. Richard Capell, music critic for *The Daily Telegraph*, wrote, 'this is a symphony, and no mistake!'[13] Another reviewer felt that

> the Symphony is not only a significant work in itself, but it should place a composer whose talent has hitherto been recognized only in a small way among the hopes for English music which at the moment are more obscure than in the recent past... the symphony itself is not derivative; it may be compared in this respect and in emotional congruity with Walton's. It is a fine work and promises more.[14]

The longest and most comprehensive review was by Eric Blom:

> The immediate impression, agreeable or not, was certainly that of a composer with a mind of his own and technical gifts fully adequate to the rigorous demands he makes on himself as a craftsman. It is good to see such a work published and the composer thus encouraged to continue his labours as a symphonist, for which he is obviously cut out. Even this first Symphony of his shows him to have the root of the matter in him, for it combines strong thematic invention with a natural feeling for genuine polyphony. The masterly fugal coda to the finale exhibits these gifts most clearly; but the whole Symphony is strong, impressive stuff. Harsh, grating, unhappy as much of the music is, one feels all the time that it truthfully reflects real experience. Not once is there a theatrical pose or a mere display of technical ingenuity for its own sake. No doubt Mr. Rubbra will clarify his creative procedures later on and arrive at something more contemplative, more reposeful, more philosophical. But the material for contemplation is there already, for whatever this

Symphony reflects, in abstract and purely musical terms, is life itself, not technical formula or detached aesthetic preoccupation.

The tragic first movement, for all its grimness, is exhilarating because it is uncompromisingly truthful. The second, entitled 'Périgourdine'... is in the nature of things more artificial, though admirably carried out. The long concluding slow movement is the most convincing, if only because music of that kind is the most difficult for a modern composer to write who feels urged to express himself lyrically but will not bring himself to let sentiment ooze too freely. Here is much of that classical quality, so rare in the music of today, of profound feeling perfectly disciplined.[15]

Finally, there are these remarks by Dr Robert Simpson, noted for his own symphonies and string quartets. They were made following a broadcast of the work by the BBC Symphony Orchestra, conducted by Bryden Thomson:

Its dogged power is not meant to endear itself to the listener; and I'm sure it didn't. On the other hand I hope you found its lapidary consistency as impressive as I do. When it first appeared it created a considerable impact. As so often in this country, such events are easily supplanted by other not necessarily more important ones. I don't think it's the public that's the culprit; more likely the professional opinionists and the official bodies who take too much notice of them.... You will probably agree it's a severe, even a stringent piece. It's rather curious that Britain in the 1930s produced three somewhat fierce symphonies: this one, Walton's First, and Vaughan Williams's Fourth. Some mystics think it was the War coming, though I don't see why three British composers needed some clairvoyant excuse for feeling a bit rampant at that time.[16]

Symphony No. 2

The Second Symphony, Op. 45, was composed between February and November 1937, and dedicated to Sir Adrian Boult. The composer revised it in 1950 when he

reduced the scoring from triple woodwind to double, made a cut in the middle of the first movement, and rewrote the end of the finale so that it now closes in D major – D (modal-minor) is the tonic in the first movement – instead of the E flat minor in which it begins.[17]

This is the only symphony that Rubbra saw fit to revise; the task was undertaken following the completion of Symphony No. 5, and Ottaway seems to feel that the timing here is significant. As we shall see in the next chapter, No. 5 does represent new departures in several areas, the most notable of which is an increasing awareness of tonality as a shaping force. The implication of Ottaway's emphasis appears to be that the change to D major at the end of the finale of No. 2, in conformity with the D tonal centre of the first movement, was influenced by the relationship of keys in No. 5. If this implication is correct, then I must question its validity, for, if one aims for consistency, why were the finales of Nos 3 and 4 not similarly revised? The first movement of No. 3 begins and ends in E major, but its last movement ends in C sharp minor. In like

manner, the first movement of No. 4 ends in D major while its final movement
finishes in E major. No, I tend to believe that the Fifth Symphony did not enter
into the matter at all. Further, the latter work could not have been responsible
for the decision to reduce the number of woodwinds, for Symphonies 3 and 4
had already been scored for double woodwinds, perhaps as a consequence of
the triple scoring in the First Symphony.

An excerpt concerning sonata form from Rubbra's article on the Second
Symphony has already been cited. The composer stated that where material 'is
not strongly anchored to a key-centre... other means of making the structure
cohere in a logical manner' must be found: 'if in the present work these other
means are largely contrapuntal, this is because the thought throughout is fundamentally melodic: melodic, not in the square, classical sense, but in that of the
freer patterns of sixteenth century music.[18]

Ex. 11

With respect to the first movement of the Second Symphony, there are two ideas,

> one dramatically tense and the other lyrical... each idea, upon its first appearance, is stated fully, and it is only in the subsequent expansion that attention is focussed upon fragments drawn from the principal themes. Such fragments become the mortar that binds the structure.[19]

The first idea consists of a long, unison string melody, divided into four segments, marked *a*, *b*, *c*, *d* in Example 11. The inherent beauty of this theme is due in no small measure to the natural balance between its ascending and descending members. This presentation is followed at once by a partial breaking up of the melody into its several segments, and then by a vertical synthesis of four of the segments: in measures 8–11 segments *a* and *b* appear as in their initial statement, but in the violins only; overlapping in measure 11 the same segments are in the lower strings. A summary of the vertical synthesis in measures 14–20 shows *c* in the violins (14–16), *a* + *b* in the violas (16–19), and *d* in the lower strings (16–17). A seemingly insignificant figure, which is also a part of this synthesis, furnishes a good example of how early in a movement Rubbra senses new shapes that can be fashioned from a melodic segment. This figure, seen in Example 12, is formed by simply reversing the direction of the

Ex. 12

1st oboe

first two notes of *d*, and substituting a semitone for the original tone, thereby creating the interval of a falling fourth – a characteristic Rubbra sound. When the figure is repeated, naturally there is a rising fourth, an equally characteristic sound. This repeating figure is briefly exploited in the following passage where it is shared by clarinet and horn at the distance of a half-beat before it is completed with flutes and clarinets. The figure is heard just once more in the movement.

The seamless nature of much of Rubbra's writing becomes evident here, for right in the centre of the clarinet and horn presentation of the figure just mentioned Theme 2 (Example 13) makes its appearance. It is a three-part canon at the time interval of a measure and a half and the intervallic distance of a diminished fifth; it is begun by the violas, continued by the lower strings, and

Ex. 13

completed by the violins. Another overlap occurs when the horns begin a statement of Theme 1 – minus segment *d* – simultaneously with the lower string entry of Theme 2. A final and even more abbreviated statement of Theme 1 – lacking both *c* and *d* – appears in the woodwinds to a *pizzicato* accompaniment, and it marks the conclusion of a very short exposition.

Under normal circumstances a development and a recapitulation would follow this short exposition. Indeed, some analysts might call most of the remainder of the movement a development, and insofar as the recapitulation is concerned the composer refers to it when he says that the two themes 'coalesce in the final climax. This is the actual recapitulation, but it lasts only long enough for the climax to die down to a pianissimo'.[20] But a much more recognizable and logical structure asserts itself rather forcefully. It is an unorthodox structure, created by the uniqueness of the materials, and, more importantly, by the treatment accorded them. Viewed in this way the portion of the movement following the exposition can be divided into three large sections (not including the coda's eight measures), each of which has two features: an extended ostinato and a long *stringendo* that steadily increases to a *fortissimo* climax.

With this structure in mind, the first section extends from the last beat of measure 33, where its *stringendo* starts, to 57; its ostinatos begin in 35. Section 2 begins with a flute solo on the last beat of 57, with a short ostinato beneath it, scored for the first horn. Theme 2, scored for violins, enters in measure 65, supported in the lower strings by a rhythmic ostinato. The restless atmosphere is emphasized by the *pianissimo* level. At measure 78 the *stringendo* begins and the dynamic level increases to *forte*. The ostinatos start at 87, and the section concludes with the first beat of measure 129. The final section begins in the same measure with a solo violin passage that extends through 144; its material is a variant of the figure shown in Example 12. Its material consists of nothing more than a falling fourth followed by a falling semitone, and when the drop is sufficient the reverse procedure is adopted. As the values are quarters and halves, the original dotted rhythm is preserved, so that, in effect, the variant is augmented.

Beneath the solo's first half a short, gruff figure is heard in the *pizzicato* lower strings, its four statements separated from one another by a measure and a half. They contribute to what can only be described as a lonely, desolate feeling, for during this first half of the solo passage the only other instruments participating are the first oboe and the harp. During the second half of the solo, however, the remainder of the orchestra begins to gather its forces in preparation for the final climax of the movement. The ostinatos, mostly rhythmic, begin at this point; at the instant the solo finishes the *stringendo* commences. A *fortissimo* statement of Theme 2, its canonic shape now limited to two parts with a perfect instead of a diminished fifth separating them, appears in the horns and strings.

The gruff figure, *forte* and heavily accented, dominates the lower reaches of the orchestra (trombones, tuba, basses). In fact, this figure is responsible for maintaining and increasing the tension during the next passage in which the brass sound increasingly loud, sequential statements of segment *a*. Each succeeding statement is a third higher than its predecessor. At the same time segment *b* and a continuing, non-canonic series of Theme 2 statements supply a running background. Thus another vertical synthesis, compounded of various elements, demonstrates economy of means most effectively. Strings and woodwinds join the brass for the two final sequential statements before the stunning climax that contains a triple *forte* statement of segments a and b (measures 172–5). Upon its conclusion, a wonderfully expressive version of Example 12 in the unison strings leads via a steady *diminuendo* to the *pianissimo* coda. This final, eight-measure section contains the first example in a Rubbra symphony of one of his characteristic touches: a solo oboe or the cor anglais poignantly singing above a series of sustained or slowly moving chords. In this instance the oboe melody is a restatement of *a* and *b*, but each segment is interrupted by short rests. The effect is one more of exhaustion than peace.

No casual reading through or dissection of the score can prepare the listener for the emotional excitement and tensions of this movement. It is music that must be heard and experienced many times.

As though not wishing the tensions of the first movement to be forgotten, the composer hardly allows the first-movement cadence to die away before launching the listener into the equally tense *Vivace assai* of the scherzo: 'attacca subito lo scherzo'. Again, the structure is unorthodox, for here there are no divisions into scherzo and trio sections. This untraditional approach is implicit in Rubbra's explanation that

> the scherzo begins with fragments – alternating violently between forceful statements and quiet lyricism – and ends with fully developed themes. There are five such themes, but as they are all natural developments from the opening fragments they can all, in spite of rhythmic differences, combine. Such a combination takes place in the final climax.[21]

What the composer has just described with respect to commencing with fragments and ending with full-blown themes is analogous to the procedures found in the first movement of Sibelius's Second Symphony.

The fragments to which Rubbra refers are contained within the first eight measures as shown in Example 14 where each fragment is marked. (For those who may wonder what is happening in the score below the example, the answer is reinforcements at strategic points by the strings and brass.) As the fragments are repeated at various pitches some are lengthened until, at measure 41, the first of the five themes to be combined with the others at the climax is introduced. It is spread across sixteen measures in the violins and its lyrical, smoothly flowing material is obviously an extension of segment *c*. I shall label it Theme 1. (As all five themes will appear in combination near the end of the movement, the reader may wish to refer to Example 15 during the course of this discussion.)

Above Theme 1 in the upper woodwinds, and below in the violas, a variant of *b* and *a* + *b* have been organized into groups of running eighth notes, each

Ex. 14

group separated from its neighbour by rests. There are fourteen such groups, and taken together they constitute an ostinato. The importance of this secondary passage is indicated in two ways: each group is composed of octaves allotted to each part (except for the violas), and each group is meticulously marked *mf*<*f*. Further rhythmic accents are provided by the first trumpet's emphatic enunciation of segment *a* throughout the entire passage. What is particularly impressive about this passage as a whole is the balance between the slow-moving theme and the faster moving groups that make up the ostinato. The latter are necessary as a frame, so to speak, for the former. Careful examination of many Rubbra works, mainly orchestral, show this simultaneity to be an important characteristic of his musical thought.

In the closing six measures of the passage just described a quite audible melody, given to the solo trombone, poses a momentary problem. It is so individual and self-contained as to prompt one to expect its reappearance in the climax, or even before, as one of the five themes mentioned by the composer. But it is not heard again. Portions of it have a definite Gregorian flavour, an impression that is strengthened by its easy flow and the modality of some of its progressions. In fact, the thought has even occurred to me that Rubbra might have inserted it in a mischievous moment as if to say, 'identify this, if you can!' More seriously, the melody turns out to be a very decorative variant of some of the elements of Theme 1.

Forceful statements of segment *a* bring the entire passage containing Theme 1 to a close, and serve as a bridge to the antecedent of Theme 2. This is a full-fledged melody in 9/8 metre with a dancelike lilt. Admittedly, this theme, given out twice in the violins and woodwinds (measures 59–70; 72–8), bears little or no resemblance to the much more compact theme in the climax, but similarities in rhythm and contour shapes are demonstrable.

The antecedent of Theme 3 is introduced as a distinct theme in its own right by the solo oboe at measure 107 over empty fifths in the violas and cellos, and a *pianissimo* interchange in the violins of segment *a*. When to this there is added the hollow beat of the bass drum plus a harp chord on the first beat of alternate measures, the effect is one of suspense and mystery. This is dispelled when the horns follow at once with the theme, which is heard twice more in the same form.

Theme 4 appears in the form in which it is found at the climax and its primacy can be judged from the frequency of its restatements. It is first heard in the trombones (measures 116–29), although it is almost eclipsed at times by the horns' statement of the third theme. It is immediately repeated by the trumpets in thirds with unison violins following one measure later in close canon at the interval of a fourth above the trumpets' top line. Another canonic statement at the same time interval involves the horns, first trumpet and trombones (167–78). Two more entries – trombones at 242 and bass trombone and tuba at 253 – lead into the combination of themes at 265. As for Theme 5, it is really an offshoot of No. 3, and appears to have no antecedent of its own.

Ex. 15

Moving to the climax where the five themes interact from measure 264 until the end of the movement at 306, there have, of course, been preparations for some time. These have taken the form of a general tightening up of segments and themes as early as just before measure 200. The volume has been steadily building, and more instrumental parts have become involved. Looking at Example 15 where each of the five themes is numbered, it will be noted that Theme 2 takes the form of a four-measure ostinato, and that the three-note figure in its second measure is segment *a*. As the strings exactly duplicate the woodwinds, they are omitted in the example.

Ex. 15 continued

To conclude: the scherzo is a riot of sound, deliciously confusing at times with all its segments isolated, combined, re-combined, and so on. The fecundity of imagination in this movement is boundless and it illustrates a most important point: the sheer inability of analysis or description adequately to record what is going on in the music. For the latter to be appreciated to its fullest extent the movement must be listened to again and again. All of the components that have been discussed have, of necessity, been isolated, but when the movement is heard as a totality these components become blurred as they weave in and out of the texture. Yet they are all essential if the progress of the musical thought is to reach its logical conclusion. This is the first example in a Rubbra symphony

Ex. 15 continued

of a genuine scherzo if, by that term, what is meant is a driving and, as Truscott says, an 'almost demonical' movement.[22] The most memorable example yet to come of such a piece is the scherzo of the Seventh Symphony.

The slow movement, marked *Adagio tranquillo*, is one of Rubbra's most deeply felt compositions. In this regard it compares very favourably with the Canto of his Sixth Symphony, sometimes referred to as the most beautiful of all the composer's symphonic slow movements. In his article on the Second Symphony Rubbra points out that

> formal freedom is here taken a step further, as there are no contrasting themes. The development of the first simple statement naturally gives rise to variants, but the mood never ceases to be meditative, even when the final climax is reached. When

form develops as freely as this, a magnetic centre must be found: otherwise the effect will be rhapsodical. In this slow movement, such a centre is supplied by a pedal on middle C which persists through much of the second part of the movement.[23]

The entire content of the movement is generated by and flows from the opening idea in the violas, designated x in Example 16. This example deserves close study, for the economy of means displayed in it is truly extraordinary. Look, for instance, at the second violin line (x^1) whose scale-wise descent is taken directly

Ex. 16

Ex. 16 continued

from the violas' first three notes and stated simultaneously. The very expressive x^2 is merely a continuation of the rising fourth in the viola line, while x^3 is a re-working of the violas' two opening measures plus the descending scale line of x^1. All of these elements have important functions as the movement slowly unfolds. One of the most prominent is x^1 following its transformation into a dotted figure. In that form it is responsible for the first big climax of the movement in measure 72, for, beginning in measure 50, it and its variants become a twelve-note ostinato in the second violins. The figure and its subsidi-aries in the violas and cellos – some of the latter creating mirror images as they move in contrary motion – support a soaring expansion of x^2 in the first violins. The figure then takes on added intensity when it is reduced to a four-note ostinato in measure 60, and made the central element over a repeating E flat pedal in the basses. Also in 60 other instruments join either x^1 or its satellites, so that by the time the climax is reached considerable tension has accumulated. It is released most abruptly by means of a *fortissimo*, eighth-note chord whose dissonance is unexpected and, therefore, something of a shock.

At measure 73 the insistent pedal on middle C – the 'magnetic centre' mentioned by the composer – is introduced. Set in continuous eighth notes, it sounds without a break through measure 107. It appears in alternate horn parts until 104 where it is transferred to the trombones so that the horns may sound a climactic figure based on x^2. From measure 97 through 107 the timpani joins in sounding the pedal, but, of course, the pedal is merely a stable reference point for the material surrounding it. Thus at measure 76, and in a slightly slower tempo, x appears in the violins in a version that includes diminution and stretto at the distance of one beat, and at the interval of a fifth, the lower strings following. Upon the conclusion of this short passage of just four measures, another version of x is heard in the lower strings, accompanied by versions of x^3.

At measure 83 the final buildup to the shattering climax of measures 104–10 begins in the *divisi* first violins. For the duration of this entire passage the marvel of musical inventiveness and expansion continues. (During the years I have known and played and replayed the excellent recording of this symphony, I have never failed to respond emotionally to this passage, and to be impressed by the apparent ease with which the tension constantly mounts.) The material employed is, of course, related to x as in measure 83 where the half-step B flat, A – a transposition of G, F sharp in the original – is followed by another half-step, F, E. A new and enlarged figure is thus created, yet it is one that bears only a fleeting relationship to x. Its significance is not a matter of its lineage but of its progeny. Perhaps the first thing that strikes the listener is the realization that the entire passage is harmonically static: A minor in its first inversion, a fact constantly emphasized by the relentlessly repeating C pedal. The problem then is making the A minor bearable over a span of twenty-eight measures. This is where the inventiveness and expansion mentioned are really tested; first, because a slow tempo can cause a long expanse of any key to sound tiresome; second, even though the harmony is static, a way must be found to compensate for this by shaping a melodic line that holds the listener's interest, one which is set in a dynamic rhythm. Both of these requirements are completely satisfied in this passage.

The listener's attention is first engaged by the duality of the melodic line, for although the essence of the thematic material is contained in the upper of the *divisi* violin parts, it is the lower that, by defining the harmony, gives it its characteristic sound, at least initially, for after the tenth measure the melodic line is set in octaves. Space is too limited to give a detailed account of the evolutionary nature of this melodic line. Suffice it to say that although the entire passage of twenty-eight measures impresses one as constituting a unit, it is possible to recognize interior divisions based on similarities of melodic intervals and rhythmic patterns. Within each division, including those where sequential treatment is used, there is melodic variety as new figures evolve. Rhythmically, the excitement mounts as the passage moves from its opening four measures in which the note values are longer, to the next six where they are shorter, to succeeding divisions where they are shorter still. For part of the passage there is a steady *accelerando* and the dynamic level increases dramatically. A *fortissimo* statement of x^3 leads into the quiet and soothing coda during which x returns in the violas, a variant of x^1 is given to the violins, and a gently rocking figure with its origins in x^2 is intoned in the cor anglais. The interaction of this solo with the dotted and chromatic viola line is particularly beautiful. A Rubbra trademark now appears: a surprise change of harmony for the concluding chord. One is led to expect some sort of B minor ending. Instead, the D is raised to D sharp, thus preparing us for the final rondo movement in E flat minor where the D sharp is enharmonically changed to E flat.

With regard to this rondo, the composer remarked that it 'offers a complete formal and thematic contrast to the others. This is deliberate, for I felt that the classical formalism of the Rondo would act as an excellent foil to the unconventional build of the previous movements'.[24] However, even here there is a small bit of unconventionality, for the final *A* of an *ABACABA* plan fails to return, its place having been taken by a long coda.

The attractive 6/8 rondo theme has been given an imaginative setting in which the high and low sonorities of the woodwind section are explored as flutes, then oboes, and again, flutes are joined with bassoons in a two-octave presentation. Underneath, *pizzicato* basses provide a syncopated rhythm. An examination of the theme in Example 17 reveals an interesting division between its members as the distinctive colour of the clarinets interposes itself. At measure 16 the thematic material, becoming ever more varied as it swiftly

Ex. 17

unfolds, is joined by a cheerful 6/8 melody, scored for all the strings with the exception of the violas. It is made up of a rocking motion that involves rising and falling fourths and fifths. But this is not merely a casual melody that is heard once and then forgotten, for it is stated twice more in the course of this first *A* section. It is missing in the abbreviated second *A* but, as the third *A* is an exact duplicate of the initial *A* (scoring changes excepted), it is, of course, present there too. The obvious conclusion to be drawn is that each melody is to be considered as a coequal with the other, both together constituting the movement's principal material.

The theme with which the *B* episodes are concerned is completely different from either of the two parts of the *A* theme. It is in 4/8 metre and there is about it a sturdiness that does not, however, detract from its basically high spirits. Although in each *B* section the key signature has been altered from six flats to two sharps, the shift in tonality has been so gradual as to negate any idea of a sudden transition. Thus when the theme in the first *B* section is perceived not as a D major melody but as a clear example of A major (with Mixolydian associations), there is no sense of a tritone relationship between E flat and A. The same is true of the second *B* where the theme does appear in D major, involving no sudden half-tone shift.

A unifying element linking the *A* and *B* sections is supplied by the clarinet figure in Example 17. In the first *B* section its almost constant presence in the woodwinds and lower strings provides a dancelike backdrop for the *B* theme. The

Ex. 18

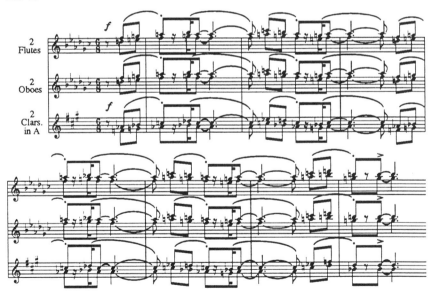

entry of the brass with the first half of the theme in canon is the signal for heavier support for the dancelike figure, and the violins take it up as well.

With regard to two items, the second *B* section is quite different. First, it is much shorter – thirty measures as against fifty-four – and second, it is more heavily scored. Therefore, it is both more concentrated and more massive.

The central episode, or *C* section, of this movement exhibits yet more economical use of material. It has, of course, its own distinctive theme, shown in Example 18. It has Lydian characteristics, is stated twice, and is confined to the woodwinds, but the rocking theme in the *A* sections is also present simultaneously in the lower strings. There are two complete statements of it, one at the start of section *C* in measure 131, and the other in measures 162–9. In addition, several versions of the clarinet figure in the fourth and fifth measures of Example 17 pervade the texture, appearing first as a close stretto in the violins above the rocking theme.

There is a wonderful lightness and sparkle about this central episode that sets it apart even from the *A* sections, where the same qualities are also evident but somewhat more restrained. The contributing factors are the rhythm and the instrumentation. The first of these is responsible for the buoyancy that pervades the section, a quality resulting from an accented third beat tied over to the fourth beat (as in measure 7 of Example 18), and an accent on a tied-over sixth beat (of which there are several instances in the example). Emphasis is provided by syncopations in the lower strings and timpani. The instrumentation is similar to that of the *A* sections: the principal episodic theme is in the woodwinds. One passage that particularly stands out both rhythmically and instrumentally extends from measure 148 through 154. It is scored for oboes, bassoons, harp, soft strings and soft timpani. These all combine to give the passage a rather veiled and indefinite sound. Rhythmically, it is memorable for the patterns indicated above.

The fifty-four measure concluding section, marked 'coda', replaces the final *A*. It is divided into two subsections, the first marked *presto* and the second *maestoso*. Its most notable feature is the majestic reappearance in the *maestoso* portion of x^3 from the slow movement, as it is stated in its fully developed form in that movement's climactic moment. As there, so here in this coda: a *fortissimo* statement by the brass to the accompaniment of a persistent timpani beat. Thus the symphony is brought to a triumphant conclusion.

The first performance of the Symphony took place on 16 December 1938, and elicited the following remarks under the heading, 'Sibelius' Eighth At Last!' This newspaper account then continued,

> Sibelius' long-awaited Eighth Symphony was performed by the BBC Orchestra last night – but the composer was an Englishman, Edmund Rubbra.
> The Finnish Grand Old Man has never been so sincerely flattered.
> If this work had been announced as being by Sibelius the average audience would have believed it, but they might have commented: 'the old man's powers are failing at last.'

The Symphony is organised well and all its orchestral tricks – the woodwind arabesques, the bustling strings, the brass fanfares, the sweeping crescendos are Sibelian, but the sombre brilliance, the thematic fertility, and the big-hearted tunes are missing.

'Three Blind Mice', for example, is hardly adequate material for two movements.

All the same this new Symphony is honest and direct, whatever it lacks in strength and personality.[25]

It seems inappropriate to treat the above 'review' with anything but the contempt it deserves. Silence is the best response surely. As for the 'Three Blind Mice' figure, other composers have employed it – notably Brahms in the third movement of his Fourth Symphony. It appears to be one of those primary musical patterns that from time to time unconsciously rise to the surface; and surely the unconscious element is borne out in Rubbra's comments that

the three movements so far discussed are not only linked in their formal freedom, but have an actual thematic link. This is a three-note descent from the third of the minor scale to the tonic. (I hasten to add that this thematic connection is quite *unconscious* [my italics], for I have only just discovered it myself!)[26]

A responsible approach to the Symphony is contained in this review:

It is not easy to think of a parallel in modern works to the fine unified span of the first movement. Arch-like construction is rare nowadays. His ideas crowd upon each other, lie on each other's backs in an urge of counterpoint. The score is heavily lined, and in the long run tiring to the ear. It is all rather reckless, though not in the way that word usually implies. And it is always interesting. This is not faint praise, for interest is the most lasting quality in music.[27]

The first performance of the revised version took place at the Cheltenham Festival of 1946 and featured the London Philharmonic Orchestra conducted by the composer.

Symphony No. 3

Rubbra composed his Third Symphony, Op. 49, in 1938–39. It was first performed by the Hallé Orchestra under Sir Malcolm Sargent in Manchester on 15 December 1940. The original venue and date for the first performance was to have been London on 23 September, but because of the frequent bombings the capital was undergoing at this time, Manchester was thought to be a safer site. The Symphony, which is in four movements, is altogether more relaxed and lyrical than its predecessors. The score is inscribed 'To Arthur Hutchings' and articles on the Symphony by both him and Wilfrid Mellers have appeared in leading journals.[28]

The first movement, marked *Moderato*, has a very engaging first theme composed of two melodic elements so interdependent as to make it virtually impossible to say for sure which is the actual theme (Example 19). The commonly accepted view is that the theme is set forth by the two oboes in thirds,

Ex. 19

and that the first horn melody, doubled by the violas, is a counterpoint to it.[29] Actually, both elements comprise the theme, for these two melodies, each beautiful in itself, seem to submerge their separate identities so that a more perfect organism might be created by their union. This is true for both the exposition and recapitulation (the movement is in a somewhat modified sonata form). Between these sections the two components undergo separate development, as one might expect. Thus the reunion of the two elements in the recapitulation is all the more effective.

A third element in this primary material consists of an ascending and descending scale figure in the cellos and basses. While this may seem to be merely accompanimental in nature, the transfer of altered segments of it to higher parts shows that it is an important component of the movement. Its initial and subsequent full statements in the lower strings are played *pizzicato*.

The development of these three fundamental constituents begins immediately after the seven-measure statement of the theme has been completed. However, before details of this can be explored, mention must be made of the quite audible echoes of Sibelius, brought about by the combination of the oboe

Ex. 19 continued

thirds and the running *pizzicato* figure in the lower strings. Ottaway mentions this resemblance – the first person to do so – and goes on to say that 'the next three bars strongly confirm it.'[30] It is at this point that the flowing bass figure is transferred to the flutes and oboes where it is expanded in each part to thirds with an octave's separation between the parts. Woodwinds playing prominent figures in thirds produce a characteristic sound in Sibelius's orchestral works and composers who introduce it in their own works are vulnerable, if not to criticism then certainly to comparisons. Yet, disregarding the similarity, it is evident that both here and elsewhere in this Symphony, Rubbra was striving for a more diverse instrumentation than is to be found in his two preceding symphonies.

The passages between the end of the woodwind's thirds and the beginning of the second theme show a keen awareness on the composer's part of the possibilities inherent in his material. During the final measure of the thirds (10) the tonality has shifted from E major to G sharp minor and almost immediately, there is a further shift to D sharp minor (= E flat minor). Within these measures (11–16) parts of the three original elements are still together and by following

Ex. 19 continued

the instrumental lines it can be determined which segments have been selected
to form a new synthesis.

In measures 11 and 12 the first violins have the first five notes of *a* in partially altered values, while the second violins have elongated versions of *b*. In 11
the bassoons, horns and violas have *d*, followed over the barline to 12 by *b*; thence
through 12 and 13 the inverted form of *b* is heard. Starting with the last beat in
13, clarinets, bassoons and violas play an augmented version of *d*. *B* and *c* are
presented in measures 14–15 in the oboe parts, at the conclusion of which the
original form of *d* appears in the second violins and violas. Beneath all of these
passages are the running *pizzicato* eighths in the cellos and basses.

At measure 20 there is a key change to B flat minor (with lowered seventh
and, at one point, lowered second). At the distance of a diminished fifth from E
major the farthest point tonally from the latter key has been reached. From here
to the entry of Theme 2 in measure 27 noticeable changes take place: small
segments of the running eighths – with slight alterations – move to the clarinets
and violas; and the cadence which ended the oboe's contribution to the first
theme in measures 6–7 (see Example 19) has been detached for use as a
separate and repeated figure in the lower strings. The violin melody appears to

be a composite of several segments. When a full cadence has been sounded in measure 27 Theme 2 makes its appearance.

The decision as to which music constitutes the second theme is controversial. Mellers believes that the theme starts in measure 50.[31] Although he is silent on where he thinks it finishes, logic dictates that it ends with the cadence at the beginning of 65. Ottaway remarks that 'such a view of this flute and clarinet line [from measure 50] is a misguided one'. Defending his viewpoint, he continues

> Clearly it is derived from two features of the preceding build-up – the quaver bass (see especially the penultimate bar, p.12) and the reiterated semitonal figure. Better to think of this as the beginning of the development.[32]

Two further arguments against Mellers's claim are, first, the passage recurs in the development in an abbreviated version, and second, it never appears in the recapitulation itself, as Mellers readily acknowledges.[33]

The other choice for the second subject is the passage that starts in measure 27 and ends with the cadence in measure 35. It is antiphonal in character: short, cadential 'answers' appear in the strings following the woodwind statements, similar activity occurs in sections of the brass, and so on. The first part of the theme appears in Example 20.

Ottaway never committed himself to this choice, observing that the 'radical change in texture creates the *illusion* [my italics] of a "second subject!"' Later, in his typed analysis, he says, 'there is, in fact, no conventional second subject', yet in his handwritten copy he referred to the recapitulation of this passage as the 'second subject'.[34]

Ex. 20

Be that as it may, if there is a second theme – and I think there is – I believe it to be here, and for two reasons: first, the section containing it has about it an aura of defined purpose that seems entirely too deliberate to be squandered on what Mellers calls a bridge passage[35] and, second, it is restated in the recapitulation at almost the point at which one would expect to hear it again. (This is, of course, no true criterion, for bridge passages also reappear where they are expected.) The decisive factor in the argument, however, is the force with which the passage returns in the recapitulation: triple *forte* and full orchestra (although the brass do not participate in the playing of the theme).

Having decided which of the two passages better qualifies as Theme 2, it seems reasonable to accept Ottaway's suggestion that the second, rejected, passage at measure 50 marks the commencement of the development and his supporting argument, cited above, is entirely convincing. The running eighth figure at measure 50 in the flutes and clarinets is a transposition of the second half of the cello and bass line in 48 which, in turn, was first introduced in the second half of measure 3. The other running eighths in the passage are similarly derived from the primary material. The semitonal *pizzicato* figure, whose repetitions on different pitches are separated by quarter rests, is an accompaniment and its origin is *b* in Example 19. Following this, the horns sound their version of the semitones, while in the strings there is a short canonic statement of the flute and clarinet line. A small *crescendo* and *accelerando* bring the entire disputed passage to an end on an E flat cadence. Now that its components have been traced to their source, the passage seems without any doubt to belong to the development. The different sound and texture generated by the thin woodwind melody and the *pizzicato* figure make it easy to understand why the passage could have been mistaken for the second subject, although its reappearance at the end of the development rather than in the recapitulation should have been a warning sign.

A quite new phase of the development rushes in almost before the brief E flat cadence has had time to take effect in the mind of the listener, for when it begins in measure 65 with a four-part harmonized flourish on the brass in C sharp minor, a complete change in both texture and atmosphere takes place. The change also extends to content, for the flourish is much more than just a flourish. Its four notes introduce the continuation of the second theme's first phrase, heard now in a four-part brass harmonization but in a broader rhythmic pattern. The flourishes are extended to the woodwinds and strings and their insistent rhythm, varied from time to time, provides the forward impetus for the rest of the development. Even beneath the largely lyrical subject matter that dominates for the next thirty-five measures, the rhythmic pattern ♩ ♫♩ ♩ ♩ ♩ is present in the timpani in the form of an interrupted pedal, which itself creates a pattern – a measure of pattern alternating with a measure of rest. The notes of the pedal are, first, C sharp, and later as the tonality shifts, they become B flats.

The lyrical element referred to presents problems with respect to its ancestry, for immediately following the burst of fanfares a double bar ushers in what

Ex. 21

is virtually a new theme in measure 75 (Example 21). Separating it into its two components is perhaps the best way of tracing its origins. The first measure above, with its half- and quarter-notes on the same pitch, harks back to the first measure of the movement, while the little arch figure in eighths is contained in the running eighths of the lower strings – the third element of the primary material. The second measure of Example 21 is harder to pin down, but the simplest way out of the dilemma is to consider it as a connecting link between the first and third, and the third and fifth measures. Very soon these three half-notes are detached, their direction and intervals undergoing constant changes in the developmental process once they attain their independence. Rhythmically, they cut across the prevailing 6/4 metre in a triple pattern, but over a long trill in the second violins and violas and an ostinato figure in quarters in the lower strings, the triple pattern gives way to a duple one: ♩♩♩♩. Again, the melodic direction and the intervallic content are in continual flux. The tension built up by changing cross-rhythms over a stable metrical pattern is typical of a Rubbra development, as are the constant melodic changes. In time these tensions must be released and in this case in two ways: first, by an orchestra-wide, *fortissimo* explosion of the fanfare figure, and then by another buildup which employs the material erroneously thought by Mellers to constitute the second theme.

The preparation for the recapitulation has been perceptively thought out by Ottaway, and it deserves to be included here:

Notice that while the timpani figure continues on C[♩ ♫♫♩ ♩ ♩, eight measures prior to the recapitulation] a move towards some sort of E tonality is at once apparent in the violins. By the time the drum-note drops to B and Theme 1 returns in a blaze of E major, the emergence of E (a mixture of major, minor and Phrygian) has already become explicit, despite the C pedal. In a way, the repeated Cs are the pivot on which the whole thing turns: as the flatted sixth of E, C has already acquired importance in the semitonal figure [C, D flat, C] in the second violins, measures 125–28, and this figure [B, C, B] is to be the timpani's contribution to the recapitulation. This transitional passage (pp. 29–30) is a fine, broad example of Rubbra's sense of modulation and is well worth studying for a keener insight into his tonal habits.[36]

The shortened recapitulation (thirty measures as opposed to the exposition's forty-nine) contains an almost immediate repetition of Theme 1 in G major after the E major statement. Theme 2 returns as described earlier. Another important difference between the recapitulation and the exposition is the heavier scoring in the former section.

The coda, twenty-one measures in length, is especially beautiful and typical of the way in which Rubbra pulls materials together at the end of a movement. There is the oboe/cor anglais solo that, beginning with the Second Symphony, is to provide an unforgettably poignant touch throughout the symphonies. Here, it is the oboe that thoughtfully recalls fragments of the primary material to a gently pulsating rhythm on the horns and shifting harmonies in the lower strings. With the violin entry there is an upward surge and a brief *crescendo* before all movement dies away as a measure of general pause intervenes. The concluding five measures, *Adagio tranquillo*, bring a return on the oboes of the Symphony's opening thirds, and the movement ends quietly.

To refer to the second movement of this Symphony as a *scherzo* in the commonly accepted sense of that term is as incorrect as it was in reference to the First Symphony, and there are movements in later symphonies where the same is true. There is no word that adequately describes this type of movement which, though playful in nature, lacks the powerful drive of a Beethoven scherzo. Yet it cannot be compared with the type of movement adopted by Brahms in his first three symphonies, for Rubbra's is faster and more energetic. That Rubbra can write a real tense and hard-driven scherzo was amply proved in his Second Symphony and we shall see other examples later.

Returning to the movement in question, there is a family resemblance between the material here and that of the 'Périgourdine' movement in the First Symphony, but it is not at all a matter of note similarity; rather, the likeness is atmospheric. Both themes have about them the qualities of simple innocence that one associates with folk music, although it is only the 'Périgourdine' movement whose theme is derived from that source. Like the latter movement the present one is monothematic, though, of course, this does not mean an endless succession of repetitions, for there are interesting offshoots from the one theme. The theme itself (Example 22) is composed of two overlapping motives, the first of which is identical with the repeated eighths of the first movement's development section. Although for many experienced analysts and musical amateurs such derivations must seem to stem from deliberate choices, more and more proof is being assembled gradually to show that with this composer such is not the case. In this instance Ottaway was told by Rubbra in September 1956 that 'the rhythm of the scherzo was *not* consciously derived from the first movement.'[37] This statement and others like it strongly support the

Ex. 22

concept that a leading composer can create important works which rely more on intuition than on a thought-out plan. Such a procedure may not always produce masterpieces, but certainly in this instance it is responsible for the relaxed atmosphere and the sheer inventiveness with which the music surges ahead.

This inventiveness is apparent at once when the theme is reproduced antiphonally in the first oboe, returned to the clarinet, and given back to the oboe. There is then an inexact canonic passage in which the theme's second member becomes a descending melodic third. A return to the antiphonal texture follows with more instruments participating. This opening section of the movement, twenty-five measures in length, ends with two loud and heavily accented brass statements of the repeated eighths. The key structure throughout the section has shown a drop to F minor from the initial A flat; then to D flat and A minor. This drop by thirds becomes a characteristic of the movement.

An episode now follows during which the two-measure theme is subordinated to the augmentation of its second member. The first such alteration occurs in the cor anglais (measures 27–36), the only use of the instrument in the entire symphony. When Ottaway inquired – also in 1956 – as to the reason for such a limited use, the composer replied that it was purely a matter of colour.[38] A second, third and fourth augmentation appear respectively in the first violins, first oboe and, again, violins. The keys in this section are A minor, F major and D minor.

At the end of this episode a new and much longer section begins in which the tonalities become more fluid and the theme more varied and extended. The instrumentation at the start is thin, but gradually becomes more dense until the whole orchestra is involved in an imitative texture that includes canonic entries. The section, seventy-two measures in length, ends as before with the brass sounding the repeated eighths, this time more loudly.

Ottaway has suggested that the next section of forty measures 'may be regarded, perhaps, as a short trio', one of his arguments being that 'this is the halfway mark and what happens next is a recapitulation.' He also points out a texture change: 'for the first time, the quaver and crotchet rhythm is entirely dispensed with and there is a much augmented derivative of the theme, moving in dotted minims on the violins.'[39] I would be inclined to agree with this view if the 'trio' were a good deal longer and therefore in balance with the other sections. Another objection is the extremely close similarity of the material to that of the first episode, even though the augmentations in this section are longer. (Actually it is only the beginnings and the endings of phrases that are longer, not the entire passage.) Therefore, Mellers is not really accurate when he refers to them as being 'triply augmented'.[40] It is true, of course, that the replacement of the quicker note values by longer ones makes this section different from the previous episode, but nevertheless the reasons given above appear to militate against calling this section a trio. Incidentally, in his notes on a performance of this symphony by the BBC Northern Orchestra on 24 September

1955, Ottaway mentioned this passage: 'extreme augmentations of initial motif (mainly violins) seem forced; the idea becomes insignificant when [it is] so deprived of its rhythmic life'.[41] Another way of looking at the section is that the absence of the rhythmic figures provides welcome relief in a movement that is otherwise dominated by them.

The recapitulation mentioned by Ottaway (whether recapitulation is the correct term for this part of the movement is doubtful) begins in measure 182, four measures before the end of the episode just discussed. Although its length is just one measure shorter than the opening section there are differences in content and instrumentation. The key structure is substantially the same as in the earlier, corresponding section – A flat to F minor but with less emphasis on D flat and A minor. After what Ottaway has referred to as 'the two stamping bars',[42] there is the expected episode, but it is quite different from the first. For one thing, the augmentation is restricted to the violins, and consists of just one passage of sixteen measures rather than three passages totalling thirty.

More significantly, a new melody – derived, of course, from the original material – appears in the lower strings at measure 236 and again the eighth-note rhythm disappears just as it did in the earlier episode, but not until this melody starts to move up through the remaining strings to become an important force. When it first appears it is merely a ground swell, for the primary theme still chatters happily in the other parts. The texture becomes noticeably thinner as the new melody (it cannot be called a theme because it is basically connective tissue) begins its upward climb to the accompaniment of fragments. The G pedal seen in Example 23 continues to sound for three and a half more pages. The object of both the new melody and the pedal is the accumulation of tension, for they both lead eventually to a resumption of the augmentations

Ex. 23

heard earlier in which the first and final notes receive a triple value. This is the cumulative passage of the movement. From measure 348 to the end in 361 the two-measure primary material is heard for the last time, back in its home key of A flat.

The question of structure in this movement is not easily or satisfactorily answered. The rondo principle seems to be at work, but in a very free and uninhibited way. How to fit the final 110 measures into a structural plan is a real problem. Ottaway suggests that they might constitute a coda[43] and this is certainly a possible solution. Yet in round figures such a coda would occupy almost a third of the movement, and this seems rather unlikely. In view of Rubbra's relaxed and unplanned approach to form, preferring to let the structure invent itself as it is moulded by the content, it seems best to give up the attempt to find a suitable name for both the final section and, indeed, the whole movement. One thing is certain, however; we are not dealing with a standard scherzo, trio, scherzo form. Whatever it is, it should be listened to and enjoyed in the spirit in which its creator conceived it: light, playful and relaxing.

The *Molto Adagio ma Liberamente* is not one of Rubbra's most memorable slow movements, despite Meller's claim that it is 'one of the few authentic examples of twentieth-century tragic art'.[44] In commenting on this assessment, Ottaway calls it 'a curious claim [that] seems to be based purely on the D major coda (the beginning of the initial motive is here 'transfigured' in the relative major)'.[45] Like all such claims this is completely subjective and incapable of proof. It is meaningful only to the writer. What *is* 'tragic art' in this century, and how can the authenticity of the example be defined or verified in that context?

The movement is not long – just over one hundred measures – and this is to its credit if one accepts Ottaway's verdict that it is 'a severe, dogged movement whose lyrical structure seems heavy and laboured'.[46] This judgement is fair for parts of the movement, notably the heavily scored passages extending from page 91 to the top of 95. Too much is attempted there, as will be evident when these pages are discussed. I do not, however, feel the verdict is accurate for the first third of the movement.

The movement begins with a dialogue in which three-note figures in the violins are answered by the violas and cellos, accompanied by sustained brass chords (not shown in Example 24), and a *pizzicato* bass. At the eighteenth measure a new figure appears in all of the strings with the exception of the first violins. Its rhythm is essentially that of the dialogue figure, but the quarter between each group of eighths slows the forward progress and imparts a feeling of heaviness: this feeling is relieved somewhat by a new melody given to the solo oboe. Both elements are shown in Example 25. Following sixteen measures of this there is an eight-measure variant of the dialogue with the same kind of brass accompaniment as before, but with a different rhythmic pattern in the basses. Then follows a short bridge passage, supported by a triplet figure in the lower strings. It leads to a new theme in 4/4 metre, enunciated *pianissimo* by woodwinds and strings, and supported at the bottom by the newly-introduced

Ex. 24

triplets. This passage is also short – nine measures – and it is succeeded once
again by the dialogue. This is accompanied by a combination of the triplet
figure and a figure in running eighths that comes from the bridge passage.

Ex. 25

It is this combination of the dialogue with the other elements that most closely fits Ottaway's assessment. How much more effective the dialogue would be had it been more simply set. The triplets and eighths obscure it with what seems like pointless activity, although their probable function is the establishment of a momentum for the purpose of carrying the passage through to the final climax. It is this climax whose texture Ottaway found 'thick and muddy – the trombones on pages 93–94 seemed disastrous. Could this ever be clear?'[47] The problem, stated earlier, is that too much is going on; there is too much doubling, both between instrumental parts and within the parts themselves.

After three full pages of a dynamic level that ranges from *forte* to triple *forte*, an almost impenetrable texture, and a heaviness that becomes increasingly oppressive as the passage moves on, the return of the calm and soft 4/4 theme is very welcome. In the repetition the former supporting triplets are replaced by even quarters. The movement ends very peacefully with the opening figure of the dialogue, followed a measure later by its repetition. One can agree with Mellers that 'this restatement over the major chord, as opposed to the B minor of the beginning, as it were symbolises the resolution of conflict.'[48] What is objectionable is his earlier-cited conclusion, which immediately followed this observation.

The last movement, 'Tema con 7 Variazioni e una Fuga', instructs the conductor that 'there should be the least possible break between the variations'. The eight-measure theme seems at first to be in E major, but by the second measure G sharp is seen not as the mediant of E but the dominant of C sharp minor. The theme and its attendant harmonies are scored for strings only. Its most notable characteristic is the graceful balance between ascending and descending movement. Measures 2–3 and 6–8 (except for the final cadence) are melodically but not harmonically identical. Thus on a very small scale one of

Ex. 26

the fundamental principles of all art is operative here (Example 26): the delicate balance between unity and variety.

Variation 1, nineteen measures long and in 6/8 metre, is scored for clarinets, bassoons, horns, and strings. Its melodic material is based, first, on the falling minor second and the rising major sixth of measures 3–4 of the theme. The pitches are the same: E, D sharp, C = B sharp. The second statement of these intervals is an overlapping one: C, B, G. Almost immediately a second set of intervals is reached, but it is less obvious than that just named. The intervals are contained in measures 5–8 and the notes are (D), C, B, E, A, G, F sharp. Their origin is the second and third measures of the theme: C sharp, B, E, -A, G sharp, —F sharp. The small dashes indicate notes in the theme which are omitted in the variation.

Thereafter, Rubbra's inventiveness takes the material where it seems most naturally to want to go until a repeat of the second set of intervals ends on a cadential E. The accompaniment adheres to the same pattern throughout the variation: an eighth rest, four identical chords, and either a new chord or another repeated chord on the sixth beat. Each chord consists of four notes, but there are doublings so that the *divisi* bass parts are duplicated in the bassoons and the *divisi* cellos and first and second horn parts are identical. This thick texture gives the variation a dark and rather sombre hue, heightened by the inability of the listener to identify some of the chords because of low pitches, and the dissonances between them and the melodic line. Finally, there is an undercurrent of tension caused by the simultaneous pull in two directions of the melody and the harmony: the former is oriented towards E minor, while the latter tends towards A minor. There is a brief excursion in the middle to a form of F minor.

In Variation 2 the restlessness of the first variation gives way to a serene and deeply felt melodic flow which, once begun, continues through all twenty-four measures. The metre is 3/4 and although there is no tempo direction the quarter equals 76. As in Variation 1 the three upper string parts carry the melody, but in the final phrase the oboes replace the first violins. The melodic material consists of the first twelve notes of the theme for its first and last statements. Otherwise, except for a two-measure link whose first measure is an inversion of the theme's first measure, the first six notes are treated sequentially. Starting on E (two entries) each successive phrase is a third higher with the D entry concluding the series. Each final note is overlapped by the next entry's first note, producing some interesting but implied cross-relations: G sharp/natural, B natural/flat.

The accompanimental harmonies are again quite unconventional in places. The lower strings and timpani have a rocking A, D, A figure with later changes to other notes. Dissonances are created between the first of these and the upper string melody, but they are not sufficient to disturb the general serenity. The later shift to other rocking fifths is more in consonance with the melodic material. There are two further accompanimental elements. The first, which goes no farther than the first eight measures, is assigned to the flutes and oboes, and consists of a scalic, Aeolian counterpoint. The more important second element is a brass chordal figure set in an unchanging rhythm: ♫ ♩ ♫. Eight measures from the end trumpets and trombones employing this rhythm alternate between measures containing a major second and a minor third. The final cadence is left unresolved when the major second is tied over into the final chord. A certain uneasiness colours the variation in these last measures.

Variation 3 is marked *Presto leggiero*, the first tempo indication in the set. The piece is over almost before it has had a chance to get started despite the first and second endings indicated for the repetition of its twenty-three measures. The key is an unambiguous G major and the metre is 6/8. Although the whole orchestra is involved the atmosphere is light and graceful. The references to the theme are subtle and largely undetectable because they are fragmentary. The most important fragment thematically, but not audibly owing to the *pianissimo* dynamics, is entrusted to the trumpets and trombones. It is made up of the first four notes of the theme, here transposed to B, G, A, B. These are repeated a third higher, followed by an ascending phrase related to the theme's fifth measure. The same four notes conclude the variation. The initial segment in the staccato woodwind and string parts is derived from the fifth and sixth measures of the theme, and the answering arch form is the natural response. These two alternating shapes – concave and convex – comprise the sole outer melodic content of the variation as distinct from the inner brass melody. The harmonic structure is simple: the variation is basically in G major, but at the end of each woodwind and string segment one of four blocks of sound establishes itself before the start of the next headlong segment. Of these harmonic blocks – G, E, B, G – B occupies twice the space of the others. They are a subtle touch in what could easily have been a rather shapeless and monotonous G major.

Variation 4, *Lento espressivo* (♩ = 76), marks a return to the tempo of the theme as well as that of Variation 2, and like the theme it is scored for strings only. In the short space of eighteen measures the unassuming mastery of contrapuntal techniques is impressive. The first eight measures are occupied in the first violins by an inversion of the entire theme. At the same time the lower strings are in strict canon with the violins at the distance of one beat in the 3/2 metre and at the octave. The second violins engage in free counterpoint until measure 8 where they begin a statement of the complete theme right side up. Two beats later – the metre having shifted to 4/4 – the first violins are in canon with them, but in this instance the intervallic relationships are fluid in conformity with the harmonic direction. The violas, which have had no part in the variation until the eighth measure, enter with occasional references to the theme.

With respect to tonality, the variation is clearly in B flat major until the second half of measure 8, but the prominent D flat on the third beat of that measure ushers in a period of harmonic uncertainty. There is then a mixture of D flat major and B flat minor plus a brief reminder of B flat major. The uncertainty gradually clears in favour of B flat minor despite the *Tierce de Picardie* cadence.

Variation 5, *Allegro scherzando*, 3/4 metre, offers a highly rhythmic version of parts of the theme. The variation opens with the first oboe playing scraps taken from the theme's first measure. Two sequential repetitions of this lead in the fourth measure to the three-note motive that straddles the first barline in the theme. Accompanying the first oboe are the first clarinet and first bassoon with different but related scraps – also given sequential treatment. These four measures are then repeated, after which the three instruments resume their sequential conversation. Seven measures of the latter lead to a canonic passage begun by clarinets and violas with oboes and trumpets following a measure later. The subject of this is the first sixteen notes of the theme.

As for the other instruments, the violins' sole contribution throughout the piece is a figure whose smooth, conjunct quarter-notes provide a balance to the rather nervous-sounding woodwind figures. The horns never do more than provide a continuous foundation in the form of held-over F sharps. Beneath the entire texture the basses and timpani beat out a forty-two measure stream of quarter-note F sharps. This continuous pedal reinforces the already strong tonic nature of the material to the degree that the entire variation really consists of one protracted tonic chord despite the introduction of other notes. The fact that these other notes are not harmonized by the chords to which they normally belong only increases the tonic hold.

Variation 6 in 5/4 metre and marked *L'istesso tempo energico* grows directly out of Variation 5. It is abrupt to the point of sounding almost ill-humoured. Its sole connection with the original material is the four-note, *pizzicato* lower-string figure that is an adaptation of the slow moving four half-notes – also in the lower strings – in the first two measures of the theme. This figure is reproduced sequentially, but it must be admitted that this is purely a score detail, for the listener will find it impossible to distinguish the pitches of this bass figure even though the dynamic level is *forte*. He will be even less able to hear the sequential progress. This is principally because the gruff figure in the brasses completely eclipses it and, of course, the tempo is another inhibiting factor. Thus it must be concluded that the bass is merely an organizing factor in the sense of providing a thematic reference.

The brass figure, like that in the lower strings, is divided into a 3 + 2 pattern. Its gruffness and impatience are products of its rhythmic design: ♩ ♪♫♩. There is no discernable melody. All of the brass instruments are involved, though not always at the same time. There are no woodwind, violin or timpani parts and the violas have only two chords.

After the restlessness of Variations 5 and 6, the balance is restored by the smooth tranquillity of Variation 7. However, in this case balance is not just a matter of externals; it is an interior quality as well. The variation is divided into two contrasting parts, the second of which is a masterly and expressive synthesis of its own material plus that of the first part. The overall tempo, *Adagio* ($\downarrow$ = 44), is the slowest of any of the variations.

In Part 1, which is in c metre, Rubbra has taken two small fragments from the theme – the three-note semitonal figure that crosses the first barline, and the leap of a major sixth – and by means of simple connective tissue has welded them into a new melody of great beauty (Example 27). Its first ten measures are

Ex. 27

scored for strings only. The tonality is fascinatingly ambiguous in this first part. There are four sharps in the signature, but neither E major nor C sharp minor is made explicit until the latter key closes Part 1. There are E sharps in the melody and bass of the first line, which should be interpreted as the leading tone of F sharp minor. An example of the ease with which the composer moves from sharp keys to flat keys occurs in the eleventh measure where a tied-over E sharp in the bass of the preceding measure becomes an F. Above it a new version of the Part 1 theme is heard in F minor. The woodwinds are now heard for the first time. Soon the harmony works itself around to C sharp minor and the cadence noted above.

Part 2 combines the new theme of Part 1 and the original theme. The former retains its duple metre, and is scored for violas and trombones (melody), and the lower strings and bass trombone (accompaniment). The original theme is in a superimposed 6/4 metre, and is entrusted to the flutes and violins. The variation ends in C sharp minor.

Before the vigorous fugue is discussed, it is appropriate to summarize the variations in terms of their interactions with one another and their ultimate effectiveness as a set.

On an elementary level, there is a good contrast and balance with respect to tempi: moderate, moderate, fast, moderate, fast, fast, slow. Key relationships are more complex because some variations begin in one key and end in another. Yet a more symmetrical pattern emerges here than in the area of tempi. In presenting it, the word 'ambiguous' is employed to indicate a possible interpretation other than those given above: 1. ambiguous to E major; 2. A minor to D minor; 3. entirely G major; 4. entirely B flat major; 5. entirely F sharp minor; 6. ambiguous to E minor; 7. F sharp minor to C sharp minor. It will be noted that Variations 3, 4 and 5 occupy a central position with 1 and 2, 6 and 7 falling off on either side. Another pattern that affects only the three central variations is the relationship involving a third: G, B flat, F sharp (= G flat) minor. And the question that surfaces so often in Rubbra's music applies here: was this balanced design consciously planned, or was it accidental? Of course, no one can say for sure, but more and more my own inclination is to regard all such instances as intuitive and, therefore, unplanned.

Another interesting point is whether the variations as a unit are cumulative or non-cumulative, that is, do they build irresistibly to the fugue or not? In my judgement they do not, a view held also by Ottaway who, having remarked that the Seventh Variation fails in 'getting the movement any further', concluded that 'these variations are definitely not cumulative.'[49] This is disputed by Mellers, who tells us that 'the effect of the variations, always tending towards the concluding fugue, is cumulative'.[50] The key to the problem is the slow Seventh Variation which, while hauntingly beautiful, brings the momentum built up by Variations 5 and 6 to a dead stop. The Fourth Variation, though faster than the Seventh, is still slow enough to be another inhibiting factor. In the Seventh Variation, the composer made a conscious decision in favour of the non-cumulative type by placing the slowest variation in the set just before the highly rhythmic and energetic fugue. Aesthetically, was this decision good or bad? Is it better to set the fugue apart from the variations which, in effect, is what has happened even though the cadence of Variation 7 has hardly died away before the explosive force of the fugue is felt? Or would it have been better if the excitement had mounted through successive variations to reach a climactic point in the fugue? There are dangers inherent in the latter course because of the need to create and sustain a steadily mounting level of tension and excitement over a number of variations. It would appear that the non-cumulative type of variation would provide more of a challenge ultimately because sharply contrasting variations offer opportunities for more variety in every area. One need only recall the differing instrumental combinations in this set that a steadily growing excitement would preclude. Finally, in this instance the fugue stands out as a separate unit, compelling the listener's attention.

At first glance the fugue subject, shown here in Example 28, seems not to have any connection with the theme from which the variations have sprung. However, a little detective work reveals that the second group of eighths stems from the theme's fifth and sixth measures. Preceding it with the three initial eighths is a natural reaction. The semitonal figure in measure 5 plus the notes that follow it are a direct transfer of measures 8–9 in Variation 7.

Ex. 28

The answer, which is real, enters at the start of the subject's sixth measure and this overlap continues for the next three entries. One of these entries is irregular with respect to the usual tonic/dominant, subject/answer sequence as shown in the scheme SASSA. There is no formal countersubject in melodic terms, but the illusion of one is created by the consistent presence of various ascending and descending chromatic segments, set in a half-note rhythm. These are distributed throughout the orchestra.

During the course of the last answer in the traditional I–V relationship, what appears to be a stretto entry in the upper woodwinds and first violins turns out to be a false entry. It is the first of a number of such entries that run concurrently with complete entries of the subject. Altogether, including the expository subject and answer entries, the subject is heard fifteen times. Some entries are very close together; two of them, separated by only one measure, are particularly interesting because of their identical pitches but enharmonic spellings (A sharp minor, p. 122, = B flat minor on p. 123). There is probably no particular reason for this except that the end of the A sharp minor statement and the start of the B flat minor statement mark the boundary between pages where sharps predominate and those where flats prevail.

In a fugue where the majority of the statements of the subject are close together there can be few episodes or, at best, very short ones. In this fugue there are just two of any consequence: measures 60–65 and 72–81. In the latter an overlap on the end has been allowed in order to accommodate logical phrasing. The semitonal figure joined to a falling octave that characterized the second episode has its origin in measures 62–4 where the complete figure (featuring a falling fifth rather than an octave) borrowed from Variation 7 is used. Each of the two episodes is orchestrated differently, the second being the most lightly scored passage in the fugue: woodwinds playfully toss the four-note figure from one instrument to another over a doubly augmented version of the semitonal fragment in the strings.

The climax of the entire movement begins in measure 90 and continues to the end at 116. It combines two statements of the fugue subject plus the various episodic fragments derived from it with a full statement in augmentation of the variation theme. The *fortissimo* level and the participation of the whole orchestra ensures a triumphant ending. It is this passage, reserved as it should be until the end, that unifies the movement beyond any doubt. It is a fitting conclusion to a work that solidly established Rubbra's reputation as a symphonist. The recognition of his achievement is contained in all but one of the following reviews:

For five years Rubbra has concentrated with unflagging energy on the problems of symphonic form, undismayed by lack of public recognition and giving never a thought to more immediately popular or remunerative types of composition. The Third Symphony is easier for the average music-lover to apprehend than the other two, and it is quite possible that it may win for Rubbra a popular and lasting success. There is no 'playing down' to the public, but rather a distillation of thought, a clarification of texture, and a more simple handling of form which is the natural outcome of the experience gained by the composer from his two previous symphonies.[51]

A new symphony which will take a high place in modern musical art. Rubbra has evolved his own musical language.... He does not seem to be influenced by any of the aggressively modern idioms fashionable in certain quarters, and if his harmony is sometimes complex, it can be apprehended by listeners who still hold to the usual tonalities. The symphony ... is largely contrapuntal; its ingenuity is proved by the skilful part-weaving and by the constant appearance of fresh counter-themes springing from the main subjects.... The work was most warmly received.[52]

Serene and clear ... touching here and there, especially in the slow movement, depths that the average dashing modern composer leaves unexplored.[53]

There was no mistaking the importance of the work as a contribution to symphonic music.[54]

In a review headed 'Ovation for New Symphony' but unidentified as to author and source, we read that

Edmund Duncan Rubbra, who in his youth was a railway clerk, was given a warm ovation when he mounted the rostrum at the Hallé concert at the Odeon Theatre, Manchester, yesterday [15 December 1940], after the first performance of his Symphony No. 3.

Unlike scores of compositions of the last twenty years it avoids the temptation to be outré or clever for cleverness's sake. One feels that here is a man expressing himself naturally, and who has not let sophistication blind him to feeling.

There is a good deal of generality in the opening movement, and also in the concluding variations and fugue [what this means is anyone's guess]. At first hearing one doubts whether these clinch the symphony tightly, but with one or two exceptions they are wholly welcome for their own sake, and the fugue is very effective.

Here and there one catches backward glances at the idiom of Mr. Rubbra's predecessors and contemporaries, but the themes, which have obvious appeal, are personal and well handled. He writes ably for all sections of the orchestra; the brass will certainly hope for more Rubbra symphonies.

An interesting point is that the symphony did not sound hostile or modish alongside Beethoven's Eighth and Brahms's Second.[55]

The only sour note in these reviews was struck by Edward Lockspeiser:

> This is a fortress of a symphony, grim and unadorned and built on unshakable foundations. The sonata form, the scherzo and trio [sic] and the variations and fugue are the sites chosen, and Mr. Rubbra fills these old forms with themes as hard as rock and with huge boulders for his developments. Here is a consummate technique; but if only some variety were introduced into all this strenuous music! If only the themes were not so constantly hard-driven! Such massive developments end by giving an impression of a mere *tour de force*. Humour is apparently unknown to Mr. Rubbra, though the second movement is not without a suggestion of grace. The orchestra is made to toil unrelentingly, and from one end of the score to the other there is seldom anything that one could call a solo. It has been said that the spirit of Brahms is in this music. It is rather the spirit of Bruckner – a Bruckner who might have lived after Hindemith.[56]

Continuing in a more positive vein, J.A. Westrup says

> Simple and direct in expression, economical in resources the Symphony sets up no barriers between composer and listener. The orchestration is, characteristically, more line-drawing than colouring. The music carries the impress of a confident mind.[57]

Another review contains some thoughtful generalizations before mentioning some of the particular aspects of the work:

> Rubbra owes to the great composers of the past what every sensible composer owes to them, namely, what study and observation will give, and no more. He does not go to them for inspiration. That is entirely his own. He has now evolved a system that serves him well. His music is substantially built on a contrapuntal basis which has only one thing in common with scholastic counterpoint – the fundamental aim, the weaving together of melodic strands in such a way as to secure a satisfactory whole. Nothing is more striking in the Symphony than the neatness of its texture. All four movements bear ample evidence to a workman's fastidious care of his material. Nothing has been borrowed: nothing has been put down thoughtlessly or in apparent haste.... After hearing the admirable interpretation of the Symphony by the Hallé Orchestra conducted by Dr. Malcolm Sargent it was impossible to feel any doubt as to Mr. Rubbra's future. He is one of the men who count, and his goal is well in sight.[58]

Finally, a distinguished fellow-composer, Herbert Howells, wrote the following words to Rubbra soon after he had heard the first performance of the Third Symphony:

> Now and again there comes a work with the power to make one fall in love with music all over again. In such a mood I found myself when listening to your symphony.[59]

One can easily imagine that of all the comments and reviews written in connection with the Third Symphony none pleased its composer more than this one.

Symphony No. 4

The date of March 1942, given for the completion of the Fourth Symphony, Op. 53, is really the date when the full score was finally finished, for originally there was only a short score. Rubbra's call into active army service in 1941 presented a problem for, in his words, the Symphony

> had to be scored in my Army life. I took it everywhere I went in the Army, and in whatever available space I could have I finished it, and conducted it in battle dress, as far as I can remember, at an Albert Hall Prom [14 August 1942].[60]

The work is in three movements. The first movement, *Con Moto*, ♩ = 52, has attracted the most attention, undoubtedly because of its composer's unorthodox use of a very common chord: the dominant seventh, which from the very opening measure appears in its most exposed inversion – the third.[61] In a passage brimming with mischievous, almost perverse, humour Rubbra explained the circumstances:

> Now Holst, when I was studying with him, had particular grievances against certain chords, and he had one against the dominant seventh. I don't remember what he called it, but he said, 'don't use the dominant seventh, ever.' So, I said to myself, 'well, I *will* use it in this Fourth Symphony'; and I used it in its third inversion, and you will find it there very, very frequently. It was a great success.[62]

Ex. 29

This first movement is one of the best examples in all of Rubbra's symphonies of the germinal process at work, for virtually everything can be traced back to the original material, which is composed of two elements, one melodic, the other chordal. It is the second of these that contains the 'forbidden' dominant seventh, made perhaps more 'reprehensible' because it does not resolve to a I_6 chord – either major or minor. In fact, it never does resolve in the orthodox sense, but is perceived as an entity in its own right; as such it imparts a special sound to this movement that is heard in no other symphony by any other composer. It can be seen in Example 29 that it is alternated with triads in root position, but since these are not the natural resolution of the dominant seventh the independence of the latter chord is enhanced. The melodic element is seen to consist initially of a falling fifth and a rising major third, but by the end of the example the fifth has become a fourth and a minor third has replaced the major third.

A new phase of the movement begins in measure 28 when the rising third is filled in, given independence by detaching it from its surroundings, and made rhythmically arresting through a new pattern (see Example 30). At measure 33

Ex. 30

the rising three-note figure is replaced with a second one in which the middle note falls. During this phase the alternating root-position triads and third-inversion dominant-sevenths continue in the accompaniment, but for a part of the passage they are rescored for the lower strings (*pizzicato*). Something like a bridge passage, incorporating the falling fifth and the filled-in rising third (47–50), leads to the start of the movement's first climax.

This climax represents still another phase of the movement, because for the first time there is introduced what seems to be a polyphonic texture in that at its start in measure 51 two of the melodic elements thus far heard are combined: several versions of the opening figure in diminution (flutes, oboes), and the following figure (F sharp, E, F sharp – clarinets and strings). However, the second of these figures is static, and its repetitions over five measures convey the impression of an extended F sharp embellished by the Es. Thus a solidly harmonic support is suggested. As the climax progresses the impression persists that the texture is really homophonic regardless of the elements that have been placed together. The principal reason for such an impression is that one of the new elements – a fusion of the semitonal and the rising, filled-in third – is treated as an ostinato. These combined figures form a pattern one measure in length which is heard twenty times. This ostinato gives harmonic support to a variety of melodic elements, one of which is the original falling fifth and rising

Ex. 31

third in diminution. The slow tempo seems to accentuate the ostinato by making it appear to be longer than it really is.

Upon the conclusion of this first climax in measures 78 and 79, there is a brief respite before new material is introduced in measure 85, or at least what *seems* to be new material. Whether or not this material can be construed as a second theme is a matter of opinion, but a strong 'pro' argument involving the listener's perception can be advanced. In this instance there seems little doubt that he will view it as both new and different (Example 31). Certainly what the listener hears is more important to him than what the analyst sees or tells him he should hear. In this case it matters not to the listener that most of Example 31 can be traced back to elements already heard. The new synthesis is strong enough to appeal to him as constituting a completely new theme, and compelling enough to cause him to forget, momentarily, at least, the material which opened the movement. Thus this new synthesis will be referred to as Theme 2.

The elements comprising Theme 2 are the dominant seventh chords (as well as other chords) in a new rhythm. They are scored for strings and woodwinds, and their top notes form a new melody. The triplet figure in the first violins is more complex in terms of its antecedents because these are less obvious. The falling thirds are the antitheses of the detached rising thirds seen in Example 30 (the rising thirds are, of course, derived from the latter). The G, F sharp, G figure at the start of measure 4 in Example 31 is the minor second transposition of the same figure used melodically from immediately after the end of Example 30 up to the beginning of the buildup leading to the first climax. The figure is, of course, the exact transposition of the semitonal figure that is at the heart of the ostinato passage.

Through having seen and heard many examples in Rubbra's works of similar reworkings and joinings of previous materials, I am entirely convinced that most, if not all, of these new syntheses are products of an unconscious creativity. Edwin Evans reached the same conclusion when he said, 'the composer's thought has developed that way, and it has become second nature to such an extent that probably he is himself often unconscious of it.'[63] Evidence to support these conclusions comes from the composer himself in the form of genuine surprise when the later use of certain materials has been pointed out to him. This is invariably followed by some statement to the effect that he was either unaware of the relationships or had not consciously intended them.

As the new section containing Theme 2 progresses, the two distinctive elements of which the theme is composed maintain their independence: the melody atop the chordal foundation, and the flowing triplet melody. There is eventually an inevitable disintegration of the elements into variants that are closely related both to the theme itself and the original material from which the theme was derived. A tremendous climax gradually unfolds and when it reaches a peak it is, in Ottaway's words,

> one of the biggest things of its kind to be found anywhere in Rubbra's music. Bigness here is certainly not a matter of length – about twenty-five bars, as it

happens [101–25] – or even of linear density, as such; its only measure is the completeness with which all the thematic tendencies of the movement are united and fulfilled. This passage is splendidly climactic, full of tension and cumulative power, but the listener must not expect a dramatic (harmonic) resolution of the tension. That is not Rubbra's way. Having reached this point of fulfillment, he is content to turn aside and reflect on the music's origins: notice how undemonstratively – from a tonal and harmonic point of view, anti-climactically! – the music 'side-slips' into remote flat regions (around fig. 13). Nothing could be more characteristic at such a juncture, and nothing more baffling to those at odds with Rubbra's mode of thought.[64]

This last sentence is obviously directed towards those critics and reviewers who cannot seem to understand that Rubbra's symphonies are not built on a preconceived harmonic foundation.

After the *allargando* and *diminuendo* that mark the end of the climax have run their course, the overall structure of the movement begins to emerge, for the final section that follows is an easily recognizable version of the first thirty-nine measures. This is the section where Rubbra is 'content' to 'reflect on the music's origins'. But as in the dispute concerning the existence of a second theme, there is equal ambiguity here with respect to structure. There are two available options: this concluding section is the recapitulation in a sonata form, or it is the final *A* in a simple ternary structure. Of these, the former is highly improbable, not so much in terms of the section itself but because of the nature of the first third of the movement – the exposition of a sonata form on which the recapitulation is based. In this instance an important factor militates against the acceptance of the first section as a sonata exposition: the appearance of Theme 2 so far into the movement. This would be of little consequence if the movement were proportionally longer, but at just 170 measures the introduction of Theme 2 at exactly the halfway point – measure 85 – is implausible in the context of a sonata exposition. If, however, Theme 2 is regarded as the start of section *B* in a ternary structure, its brief reappearance in the final eight measures of the movement makes sense, for its function there is that of a small coda. Quite apart, however, from these considerations there is the *feel* of the music to be reckoned with, and the first section does not feel like an exposition in a sonata structure because of the continuous development of its fundamental material, in this case the falling fifth and rising third, which are constantly evolving. The process is unhurried and open-ended, unlike the self-contained nature of the usual first theme in a sonata structure.

The middle section, beginning with Theme 2, is closely related to the first section in that its material is derived from that source but, because the transformations throughout the first section have been long and gradual, section 2 impresses by its apparent newness. This relationship of the second theme to the source material of section 1 does not negate Ottaway's conviction that 'each movement is worked out monothematically'.[65] Thus the movement's overall structure is an *ABA*[1], although Westrup says that 'the familiar elements of sonata form – exposition, development and recapitulation' are present, a conclusion with which I must, of course, disagree. One can, however, agree with Westrup's further observation:

> Yet nothing in it follows a formal plan which can be foreseen by the listener; it is rather that the design appears logical when complete. There is a growth of intensity and also of complexity, each new element in the structure suggesting another until the pinnacle is reached. Rubbra's thought is primarily polyphonic; the texture is

Ex. 32

woven of continuous threads. But it also shows a suggestive treatment of harmony. Familiar chords are given new associations.[66]

The second movement, called 'Intermezzo', is aptly named, for it is a pleasant and relaxed piece that bridges the gap between two highly concentrated, serious movements. The listener needs this relaxation after the rigours of the first movement and before the intensity of the finale; and this *Allegretto grazioso* perfectly meets that need. The expressive direction, *sempre delicato*, as well as the waltz rhythm and the light scoring are indicative of the movement's character. These all combine to produce music that is distinctly reminiscent of the ballet. While the movement is monothematic, a fuller explanation of how the material is employed is necessary. The theme is an eight-measure melody, as seen in Example 32, but melodic variants closely related not only to each other but to the parent melody are a characteristic of the movement. In fact, the theme as shown here is sounded only once before being broken up into its constituent parts. After the parts have been isolated, they are often combined polyphonically. There is no growth such as in the first movement, and there is no climactic point.

The final movement, the third, consists of two parts – an Introduction, marked *Grave e molto calmo*, and an *Allegro maestoso*. The first of these is sombre and withdrawn. Its theme, scored for the lower strings, is recitative-like, and this characteristic is accentuated by the held chords against which it is silhouetted (Example 33).

Harmonically, the first twenty-one measures of this movement are interesting because they again demonstrate the ease with which Rubbra moves from key to key by means of abrupt transitions (see also the discussion of this point in connection with the last movement of the First Symphony, p. 44). Up to the last beat of measure 9 the tonality is clearly A minor, made explicit by the held A minor chord. Following the A minor cadence in measure 9 a chord totally unrelated to A minor suddenly appears: E sharp, G sharp, C sharp – the dominant of F sharp major/minor (the chord occupying beats 2 and 3 of measure 10 does not change or affect this two-measure passage). Two further measures of the same harmony in the woodwinds and brass lead not to F sharp major/minor, but to a kind of F minor, and this change is an excellent example of Rubbra's enharmonic methods: E sharp becomes F. While this in itself is not at all noteworthy, the treatment is, for the enharmonic change to F is effected in the lower instruments only (violas, cellos, basses). The more prominent higher instruments are thus freed to take notes that dramatize the sudden semitonal shift that is so arresting. The melody for this portion, again in the lower strings, is decidedly different from its A minor predecessor, yet it is cut from the same cloth, and the phrasing is almost identical. The held F minor triad in the upper parts is harmonically more necessary than was the earlier A minor triad. This is because the melody under it contains notes foreign to F minor – D and B naturals. The triad acts as both a reference point and a control. The F minor segment is just half the length of the opening A minor segment and at its

Ex. 33

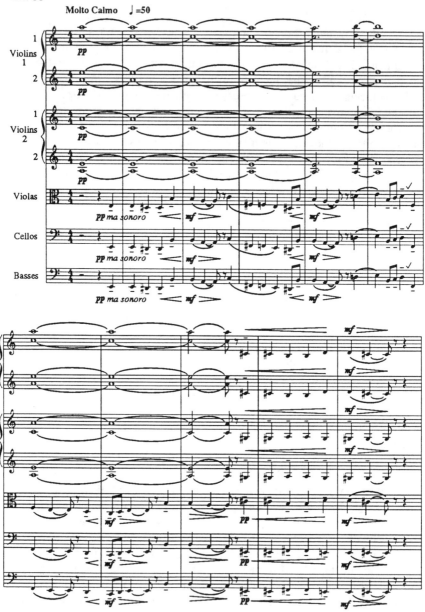

conclusion A minor is restored by the simple expedient of the raising and lowering of tones except for C, which is, of course, common to both keys. Thus a second abrupt transition has occurred; after four measures of still another melodic variant under the familiar sustained chords, a new phase of the movement is set to begin.

This new phase begins with a six-measure canonic passage built at first on the rising sixth and falling second of measures 2–3 in Example 33. Yet short as it is the canonic imitation is a balanced, miniature arch structure, for following the peak the descent employs rising seconds and falling sixths and fifths. Of course, the canon destroys the recitative-like impression that has dominated the movement thus far, but in any case that was weakened four measures before the advent of the canon by a steady timpani beat on A. This serves as a kind of link, for it continues through the canon and the first part of a very expressive section that contains inexact imitations in the strings and woodwinds of short, derivative figures.

The final phase of the slow Introduction, twenty-two measures in length, is dominated by a syncopated figure composed of triplets and eighths. Its first appearance is in the form of a *pianissimo* B minor triad pedal in the trombones and tuba. It serves as a background for two canonic statements (upper and lower strings) of the opening material (see Example 33). The second of these statements is the canon by inversion which was chosen by the composer as one of the musical representations of the ''topsy-turvydom' of his childhood experience as related near the beginning of Chapter 1 (see Example A, p. 3). Further – but non-imitative – development of this material over the syncopations leads to two final, sombre statements of the Introduction's opening phrase. These are given to the woodwinds above a held A minor chord in the strings. The direction, *Attacca*, immediately launches the listener into the *Allegro maestoso*.

In view of the generative nature and consequent growth of so much of Rubbra's material, it is surprising to discover that no thematic relationships exist between the just-concluded Introduction and the *Allegro maestoso*. Indeed, it is sometimes better that such relationships do not exist, for if they are too often present and traceable the results can appear to be inflexible and, eventually, so concentrated as to be tiring for the listener. Yet there is a relationship between the sections, but only in the sense that they complement each other.

The structure of the *Allegro maestoso* is a large ABA^1 and each of its sections is more nearly equal in length than in many other Rubbra movements of similar construction: 62, 61 and 53 measures respectively. The phrase structure is also more regular and predictable than that found in most later Rubbra symphonic movements: $8 + 8 + 8 + 6$; $8 + 8 + 8 + 8$ for the first *A*. The *B* section has no such clear-cut phrase divisions; but the final A^1 returns to $8 + 8 + 8 + 8$ until the concluding twenty-one measures, marked *Trionfale*, defy any phrase divisions owing to the powerful, forward sweep of the music.

The material of the *A* sections consists of three, easily identifiable elements presented simultaneously (Example 34). The most obvious of these is the broad melody scored for violins and horns. Second in importance is the trombone and

Ex. 34

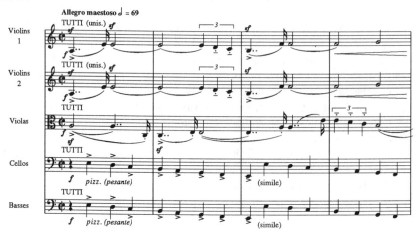

viola countermelody. Under these two elements is the cello and bass ostinato in the form of a descending Phrygian scale. In the twenty-sixth measure of the ostinato, F sharp is introduced, followed in the next measure by C sharp. Finally, in measures 55–6 a clear E major is established when D sharp and G sharp are added.

The start of section *B*, eight measures after the confirmation of E major, affords a further illustration of Rubbra's sudden modulatory changes effected by enharmonic means. D sharp, the leading tone of E, is sounded as a sixteenth note in the violins on the last portion of the fourth beat in measure 117. In 118 it becomes E flat in an E flat minor context. The new key is reinforced by a new ostinato pattern consisting of rising fourths, but this reinforcement proves to be temporary for succeeding fourths move away from the principal scale degrees of E flat. A, D, B flat, E flat, and so on through G, C, F sharp and B are substituted until a descending D major scale is reached. But any sense of D major as an enduring tonality is soon cancelled when it is considerably weakened by G, D and A sharps.

The next twenty-one measures, introduced by another enharmonic change (A sharp = B flat), are lightly scored. A syncopated triplet figure in the lower woodwinds accompanies an E flat minor string melody, whose antecedent is the subdued atmosphere, but not the material of the Introduction. In the second half of the twenty-one measures there is a lovely duet between solo flute and cellos, soon augmented by solo oboe and basses, accompanied now by the triplet figure which has moved to the horns. The tonality is inconclusive – intentionally, one feels – but the reasons for its indefiniteness are not made clear until the next passage, which is, in reality, a new section. It is preceded by a small *crescendo*, a broadening of the tempo, and a double bar.

This new section, marked *fortissimo*, involves most of the orchestra. Its strong, forward drive conveys the unmistakable impression that the tonal uncertainties, so evident throughout the preceding parts of the *B* section, are about to be resolved in a forthright manner. The harmonic structure is centred for eight measures on the third inversion of the dominant seventh of D (it will be recalled that such chords are a very prominent feature in the harmonic landscape of the first movement). Yet the ultimate goal is not D major/minor but A minor by way of very brief touches of B minor, D major and the dominant seventh (third inversion) of C minor. This is all supported by a chromatically falling, double dotted pedal: eight measures of G, three of F sharp, three of F. The material above the pedal is composed of two distinctive elements: an impassioned violin melody whose nucleus is the inversion of the rising fifth heard in the first measure of the *Allegro* (seen in Example 34); and an undulating triplet figure in thirds, given to the woodwinds and violas.

With the arrival of A^1 in the ternary scheme of this *Allegro* the expectations aroused by the passage just described are fully justified. The latter's clearer harmonic focus, the sweep of its violin melody with its hint of the very opening passage of the *Allegro*, and its surging triplet figure are explainable only in the context of the final A^1. In other words, these components have fulfilled a purpose in the larger design. The clearer harmonic foundation gives way to the descending Phrygian pedal, and the violin melody leads naturally into the melody of the first *A*, scored now for horns. The triplet figure assumes a new identity as a full-fledged A minor theme when, in addition to the woodwinds, it is scored for violins. The trombones meanwhile retain the counterpoint of the first *A*. Everything with the exception of the changes just noted proceeds as in the opening *A*, and the phrase structure is essentially the same: 8 + 8 + 8 + 8.

The final twenty-one measures of the movement are occupied by a section marked *Meno mosso, trionfale*. In keeping with its mood the dynamic level is consistently *fortissimo* – even triple *forte*. It marks, of course, the culmination of the entire work, not just of the movement. Being thoroughly rooted in E major (made explicit by the key signature), it represents the final victory of a definite tonality over the tonal ambiguities not just of the movement but also of

Ex. 35

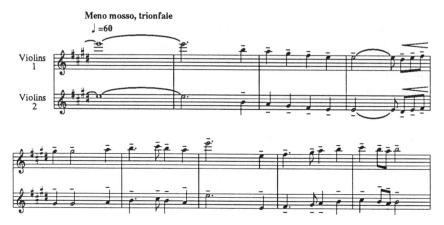

the preceding movements. The melody is chorale-like (Example 35) and there
is exact, though widely spaced, imitation between the trumpets and violins.
Westrup uses the term 'Handelian' to describe the 'finality' and 'massive simplicity' of this concluding section.[67] Richard Tiedman is more picturesque in
the *American Record Guide* for September 1979 when he refers to it as 'the
kind of music one imagines played at the heavenly gates as the believers march
in.'[68] However one describes it, it is certainly impressive enough to bring an
audience to its feet, particularly in time of war (1942) with the composer as
conductor and in battle dress besides! Years later (on 20 March 1950) Egon
Wellesz, authority on Byzantine music and a professorial colleague of Rubbra
at Oxford, wrote about the Fourth Symphony to the composer:

> Thank you so much for having given me the Fourth Symphony... I went through the
> score and admire it very much. The work is so concise and expressive, and it shows
> already the line which is worked out in the Fifth Symphony, though its character is
> quite different from that of the Fifth Symphony.
>   Since I know the First, I think I understand the problems which you are setting
> and solving. It is a great joy to see how your mind works. You do think symphonically
> and the task for the orchestra therefore is an easy one. Every climax develops so
> logically.

Other than the articles by Westrup and Mellers there appear to be no reviews
of the Fourth Symphony – at least none current at the time of the first performance. Insofar as periodical reviews are concerned, the dearth can be explained
by the extremely thin issues (at times no issues at all) during the war years. We
shall, therefore, have to content ourselves with some further observations from
Westrup's article:

> Rubbra's Fourth Symphony shows, even more than his Third, that symphonic in-
> vention need not wrap itself in mystery or extravagance, and that originality con-
> sists, not in the conscious forging of a new idiom, but in the personal handling of a

common tongue. His Symphony is not 'light', since his thought is always serious; but equally it does not strike attitudes nor labour to tell a tale at twice its necessary length.

A composer may show his individuality both in the character of his ideas and in the texture with which he clothes them. With Rubbra the ideas and the texture appear inseparable. To some his orchestration, which rejects almost every device of colour practised at the present day, may seem monotonous. There is no melting of one shade into another, no incidental tinting. There is also no exploiting of virtuosity; the writing may be difficult, but it is never spectacular. Colour is laid on in blocks, and so gives the lines of the composition a direct and simple clarity. The more one studies the score, the more it becomes obvious that this 'monotony' is the natural clothing of the score. Rescored, the work would not only sound different: it would *be* different. One cannot resist the impression that this music has affinities with an earlier period, before colour became an end in itself.

These affinities are apparent also in the development of the ideas. Their growth is spontaneous, as it seems, yet very subtly organised.[69]

With regard to Rubbra's orchestration there have always been (and probably always will be) dissenting voices – those who usually restrict their remarks to generalities that encompass the composer's entire symphonic output. Westrup cites above the most common of these complaints, but then justifies Rubbra's procedures insofar as this particular symphony is concerned. It is therefore with more than passing interest that there are recorded below some objections to specific passages in this work, expressed by one of the composer's staunchest allies, Hugh Ottaway, in a well thought-out passage:

> The homophonic opening of the first movement is free from textural problems, but even here Rubbra thinks in terms of weight of tone (divided strings, pp. 1–5). N.B. the change in texture on p. 9 leads to a revealing thickening of the orchestral sound. The line of thought is fully sustained by the strings: why double with clarinets, bassoons, and horns, and even the heavy brass? This thickens the lines and deadens the sonority. I suspect that a treatment of this passage by strings alone would be more satisfactory. The drop in pitch (omission of violins) also emphasizes the drabness. If weight is the determining factor here, it is the weight of what goes before and comes after that necessitates the doubling, *not* the intrinsic demands of this passage.[70]

These conflicting statements could certainly provoke a discussion, but one that would ultimately prove fruitless. Rubbra has always orchestrated in the manner that to him was most appropriate to the expression of his thought. However, this is not to say that certain passages could not have been scored differently, and the changes made by the composer in the revised Second Symphony are an acknowledgement of that fact. As for me, there are passages in a number of Rubbra's orchestral works that I feel would benefit by being rescored. Many listeners must feel the same with regard to passages – even prominent ones – in the works of numerous composers, but in the last analysis such feelings are personal, and therefore subjective. Hence the futility of taking a stand on the matter of Ottaway's objections.

Two important factors must be taken into account in the consideration of this question, the first of which is so obvious as to make one wonder why it is

seldom, if ever, mentioned: the impossibility of really knowing how a controversial passage would sound in new orchestral dress. Of course, if two versions
of the same work are available for comparison the listener can choose one over
the other, or, more ideally, recognize good and bad points in each. There is no
better illustration of this than Musorgsky's and Rimsky-Korsakov's orchestrations of *Boris Godunov* – both available on record. But this is the exception, not
the rule. To return to the present issue: unless Rubbra had seen fit to revise the
Fourth Symphony, and in the process eliminated the doublings Ottaway felt
were excessive, one could never know how the rescored passage might sound.
The same controversies have surrounded the orchestrations of Schumann, Brahms
and Bruckner; and it is here that the second and more important of the two
factors applies: the realization that major changes in the orchestration would
alter the distinctive sound qualities associated with these and other composers,
and the sound we have become used to would be entirely different.

The solution then is to refrain from making sweeping generalizations which
are all too often parroted indiscriminately. Schumann's orchestration is particularly vulnerable to this sort of injustice. Surely there are numerous movements
or passages in his four symphonies where the orchestration is exactly right. One
has only to recall the scherzo and *Adagio* from the Second Symphony, the 'cathedral' section of the Rhenish Symphony, and so on.

Linking the above to the subject of this study, there appear to be no doubts in
anyone's mind that by temperament and inclination Rubbra was an orchestral
composer. If it were otherwise his symphonies would certainly not have been
made the subject matter of special articles, however short, and they would not
take up three chapters in this book. Yet in certain quarters blanket statements
persist to the effect that Rubbra's orchestration is

> thick, harsh, gray, colorless…. And it is true that Rubbra is more concerned with the
> 'fascinating interplay of inwardly related lines than with the quickly fading experi-
> ences of harmonic color.' An outburst of rhetorical and effulgent color would be
> unthinkable in Rubbra's spiritual world. But to say that his music is colorless is to
> be insensitive to Rubbra's subtle play of harmonic interchange and instrumental
> timbre. Most evident, especially in the symphonies after No. 3, is a pervasive,
> pearly luminosity, like sun-backed early morning clouds. Rubbra has his favorite
> instruments; the oboe is often given prime melodic matter, and always with a tint
> completely individual to the composer. The trombones, both bass and tenor, are
> important parts of the characteristic texture, often with a magnificent bronzen maj-
> esty.[71]

There is, of course, no doubt that Rubbra's orchestration is heavy in portions of
the First, Second and Fourth Symphonies, but if those who generalize so
readily would listen sympathetically, score in hand, they might discover that the
intensity and, in some cases, the recalcitrance of the material require the sort of
orchestration they see and hear. In the symphonies still to be discussed – the
majority of the total number, be it noted – the orchestration becomes lighter
because the materials are less driven.

Finally, at various times Rubbra has expressed the view that his first four symphonies are 'somehow different facets of one thought, and a knowledge of all is necessary to a *complete* understanding of one'. He clarified and enlarged upon this rather enigmatic statement (as recorded in Chapter 1, and repeated here because of its value as a summary) by saying that because the symphonies

> were all composed so close together [1935 to 1940] they were, in a sense, reactions to each other – not separately contained symphonies. No. 2, for instance, wasn't like No. 1. It begins with a single line, and it is more austere and contrapuntal. No. 3 is – I presume one could call it – more lyrical, and then No. 4 is more chordal.

In the following excerpt Rubbra elaborates on the contents of Nos 3 and 4 in terms of how each represents a reaction to its predecessor:

> The texture of No. 3 is open and eschews compact counterpoint, and there is a general relaxation in favour of brightness and clarity of presentation. This reduction of counterpoint is taken a step further in No. 4, the long harmonic paragraphs of which open out like a landscape.[72]

From the composer's remarks it is evident that these four symphonies show a logical progression, based on particular problems which he set for himself. Each has its own distinctive character and aura and it seems only natural that listeners may favour one or two over the others. Few will choose the First Symphony because of its strenuous (some might even say ruthless) exploitation of the possibilities inherent in the materials. Yet the second movement certainly affords relaxation from the rigours of the other movements – something that cannot be said for the Fourth Symphony of Vaughan Williams, composed just prior to Rubbra's First, and often mentioned in the same breath. Each of *its* four movements is filled with tension. Yet I find myself in agreement with Truscott's view that Rubbra's First 'is one of the most remarkable Firsts in my experience'.[73]

As for my personal preference among the four, I favour the Second. The tensions are just as great as those in the First, but because they are more firmly controlled they seem more unrelenting, and thus more exciting for the restraints imposed. This is true not just for the first movement, but also for the second and third. The second movement is also important because it is the first example in Rubbra's symphonies of the hard-driven scherzo, while the third is a wonderful mixture of tranquillity and tension. The concluding rondo is relaxed from start to finish. And so I return again and again to the Second, attracted by its exciting emotional content, its impressive grandeur, and the balanced contrast of its movements. Nothing in these personal reactions is intended as a denigration of the Third and Fourth Symphonies, each of which I feel to be a solid achievement.

Notes

1   Quoted in Murray Schafer, 'Edmund Rubbra', *British Composers in Interview* (London: Faber & Faber, 1963), pp. 67, 71.
2   Quoted in *The World of Music*; further information unavailable.
3   Quoted in Hugh Ottaway's private papers.
4   *ibid.*
5   Harold Truscott, 'Style and Orchestral Technique', *Edmund Rubbra: Composer*, p. 18.
6   'Edmund Rubbra, Now 70, Looks At His Eight Symphonies', *The Listener*, 27 May 1971, p. 690.
7   Printed inside the front cover of *Edmund Rubbra: Composer*.
8   'Edmund Rubbra, Now 70, Looks At His Eight Symphonies', *The Listener*, 27 May 1971, p. 690.
9   Edwin Evans, 'Edmund Rubbra', *MT*, February 1945, p. 44.
10   'Edmund Rubbra's Second Symphony: A Note By The Composer', *Tempo*, January 1939, p. 8.
11   Julius Harrison, *The New Musical Companion*, 22nd edn, A.L. Bacharach (ed.) (London: Victor Gollancz, Ltd, 1964), p. 275.
12   William Fleming and Abraham Veinus, *Understanding Music* (New York: Holt, Rinehart and Winston, 1958), p. 122.
13   Tape of 26 July 1980.
14   Printed inside the front cover of *Edmund Rubbra: Composer*.
15   Eric Blom, *M&L* 19, no. 3, July 1938, pp. 361–2.
16   In addition to his career as a composer, Simpson has edited and contributed to the two-volume Penguin history of the symphony; and is the author of a book on Carl Nielsen.
17   Hugh Ottaway, 'The Symphonies', *Edmund Rubbra: Composer*, p. 33.
18   'Edmund Rubbra's Second Symphony: A Note By The Composer.' The subject of Rubbra's associations with Elizabethan music has generated confusion and misunderstanding. Later in this book it will receive the attention it deserves.
19   *ibid.*
20   *ibid.*
21   *ibid.*
22   Sleeve-note to the recording of the Second Symphony on Lyrita SRCS 96.
23   'Edmund Rubbra's Second Symphony: A Note By The Composer', *Tempo*, January 1939, p. 8.
24   *ibid.*
25   Printed inside the front cover of *Edmund Rubbra: Composer*.
26   'Edmund Rubbra's Second Symphony: A Note By The Composer', *Tempo*, January 1939, p. 8.
27   W. McNaught, *MT*, January 1939, p.63.
28   Arthur Hutchings, 'Rubbra's Third Symphony', *MT*, September 1940, pp. 361–4; and 'Rubbra's Third Symphony: A Study of Its Texture', *MR*, February 1941, pp. 14–28. Wilfrid Mellers, 'Rubbra's No. 3', *Scrutiny* 9, no. 2, September 1940, pp. 120–30.
29   Such a view is held by Mellers in the above-cited article, and by Hugh Ottaway in his unpublished analysis of Symphony No. 3.
30   Ottaway, unpublished analysis of Symphony No. 3.
31   Mellers, *op. cit.*, p. 122.
32   Ottaway, *op. cit.*
33   Mellers, *op. cit.*, p. 123.

34   Ottaway, *op. cit.*
35   Mellers, *op. cit.*, p. 123.
36   Ottaway, *op. cit.*
37   *ibid.*
38   *ibid.*
39   *ibid.*
40   Mellers, *op. cit.*, p. 124.
41   Hugh Ottaway, unpublished notes on a performance of Symphony No. 3.
42   Ottaway, unpublished analysis of Symphony No. 3.
43   *ibid.*
44   Mellers, *op. cit.*, p. 125.
45   Ottaway, *op. cit.*
46   *ibid.*
47   *ibid.*
48   Mellers, *op. cit.*, p. 125.
49   Ottaway, unpublished notes on a performance of Symphony No. 3.
50   Mellers, *op. cit.*, p. 126.
51   Reprinted from Boosey & Hawkes Newsletter in *Tempo*, no. 5, August 1941, p.10.
52   Reprinted from *The Manchester Guardian* in *Tempo*, no. 5, August 1941, p. 15.
53   Reprinted from *The Daily Telegraph* in *Tempo*, no. 5, August 1941, p. 15.
54   Reprinted from *The Times* in *Tempo*, no. 5, August 1941, p. 15.
55   Printed inside the front cover of *Edmund Rubbra: Composer*.
56   Edward Lockspeiser, *M&L* 24, no. 3, July 1943, p. 188.
57   J.A. Westrup, *MMR*, September 1943, p. 161.
58   Arthur Hutchings, *MT*, January 1941, p. 37.
59   Quoted in *British Music of Our Time*, A.L. Bacharach (ed.) (Harmondsworth: Pelican Books, 1946). Chapter on Edmund Rubbra by Arthur Hutchings, p. 202.
60   Tape of 26 July 1980.
61   The chord gave rise to an article by Wilfrid Mellers, 'Rubbra and The Dominant Seventh: Notes On An English Symphony', *MR*, May 1943, pp. 145–56. This was later reprinted in Mellers, *Studies in Contemporary Music* (London: Dennis Dobson, Ltd, 1947), pp. 153–70.
62   Tape of 26 July 1980.
63   Evans, 'Edmund Rubbra', *MT*, February 1945, p. 76.
64   Ottaway, 'The Symphonies', *Edmund Rubbra: Composer*, p. 36.
65   *ibid.*
66   J.A. Westrup, 'Edmund Rubbra's Fourth Symphony', *MT*, July 1942, p. 204.
67   *ibid.*
68   Richard Tiedman, 'Rubbra: Neglected Symphonist', *American Record Guide*, September 1979, p. 38.
69   Westrup, *op. cit.*, p. 204.
70   Hugh Ottaway, unpublished notes on Symphony No. 4.
71   Tiedman, *op. cit.*, p. 38.
72   'Edmund Rubbra, Now 70, Looks At His Eight Symphonies', *The Listener*, 27 May 1971, p. 690.
73   Truscott, 'Style and Orchestral Technique', *Edmund Rubbra: Composer*, p. 27.

3 Symphonies five, six and seven

Rubbra's Fifth Symphony, Op. 63, is different from its predecessors to the degree that it heralds a new chapter in the creative life of its composer. This newness is partially revealed in the introductory paragraphs that Rubbra wrote as a preface to his analysis of the symphony:

> When, at the end of 1941, I was called up for war service, my fourth Symphony was already finished, although not fully scored, and projects had been made for a fifth (choral) symphony. Preliminary sketches for this were actually noted down in 1942, but army life proved not to be the ideal milieu for symphonic thinking. The sketches were therefore put on one side until continuous thought was again possible, and what time I had was devoted to the writing of works in smaller forms (the *Soliloquy* for cello and small orchestra and the *Missa Cantuariensis* being the most important). In 1946 I was free to take up the abandoned threads, but my enthusiasm for a choral symphony had waned, and the sketches for it were turned into an independent setting for chorus and orchestra of Henry Vaughan's *Morning Watch*. In this year, too, I wrote a cello and piano Sonata, fully revised an earlier string Quartet and added a new finale, revised an early *Lyric Movement* for piano and string quartet, and wrote the *Three Psalms* for voice and piano: thus it was not until 1947 that I was able to turn my thoughts to a new, purely orchestral, symphony. This gap of six years between the last two symphonies was equal to the amount of time that covered the writing of all the previous four (from 1935 to 1941), and it had an enormous importance in determining the form and content of No. 5. When symphonies are written in quick succession the characteristics of each are usually the result of a *reaction* away from its predecessor: in other words, although they are independent works they are somehow different facets of one thought, and a knowledge of all is necessary to a *complete* understanding of one. But a gap of six years, a gap moreover spent in surroundings totally inconducive to musical thinking, was sufficient to obliterate the previous symphonic period, and when at last I came to grips with No. 5 I did so with no sense of reference to the other four. In fact, the reference was more to the chamber music that had occupied my thoughts before No. 5 was started in August, 1947.
>
> This was reflected not only in the texture of the new Symphony, but in the greater polarisation of tonality. The cello Sonata and the string Quartet are unambiguously in G minor and F minor, and the tonal centre of No. 5 is clearly B flat. Such a clarity of tonality is *not* a characteristic of the other symphonies: No. 1 starts in B minor, B

seeming to be the leading note of the C major with which the symphony ends: No. 2 does likewise, starting in D minor and ending in E flat major: No. 3 is more clearly in a key, E major, but pushes out at the end to the more (seemingly) majorish C sharp major, and No. 4 gets nearer to a definite key by implication rather than in actual fact. This clear tonality in No. 5 is emphasized (and the same process is more tentatively seen in No. 3) by making the keys of the four movements correspond to the notes of the tonic triad: *viz.* B flat, D, F (as a starting point) and B flat.

Formally the work is in the nature of a triptych, the three 'panels' of which are as follows:

Adagio-Allegro energico : Allegro moderato:
Grave-Allegro vivo.

From this it will be seen that the first movement, with its long *Adagio* introduction, exactly balances the final two movements (for these are played without a real break), the middle movement (a scherzo) affording the necessary bright relief. This formal balance is reflected, too, in the return, at the end of the work, of the motivating phrase played in the first few bars by a solo oboe.[1]

The listener, experiencing this symphony for the first time after having listened to the first four with some degree of concentration, will discover a quality that he will instantly recognize as new but one not directly related to matters of texture or key as discussed in Rubbra's account. This quality, put simply, is a sense of relaxation engendered by a greater flexibility in the handling of materials. Already noted in the analyses of the preceding symphonies is a certain rigidity in some movements that was brought about by an apparent unwillingness on the composer's part to let go of materials that were attractive but the development of which sometimes seemed excessive. However, it should not be assumed that the relaxation in the Fifth Symphony implies any slackening of thematic logic and discipline. Indeed, these are applied just as firmly but in ways that are altogether less obvious.

The composer's short account of the very mundane origin of the first movement's opening idea is a fitting introduction to his analytical comments:

It came to me curiously – the opening idea. The opening bars came to me while I was waiting for a bus on a hot August day in High Wycombe to take me to my cottage. I saw the notes written on manuscript paper – not necessarily heard them although I must intuitively have done so – but I kept them in my mind as a starting point of Symphony No. 5, and they've remained so.[2]

The body of Rubbra's analysis begins with a further reference to the first movement's key structure before going on to talk about the thematic content of that movement and the complex relationships that govern it:

The key of B flat is, at the beginning of the Symphony, arrived at obliquely by dramatic enharmonic harmonies scored for brass and kettle drum. The resolution of these two bars is upon the nearly-related key of E flat minor, but this is seen to be the subdominant of B flat minor when it supports a phrase the contours of which are clearly in the latter key. The mingled augmented and perfect fourths in this oboe phrase form the basic melodic elements in the Symphony. When it is complete, at bar 10, its characteristics have been emphasized by appearing as counterpoint on the bassoon and in augmentation on cellos and basses; moreover the oboe, at bars 9 and

Ex. 36

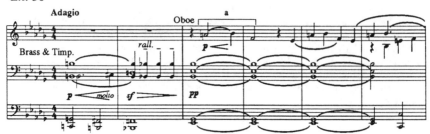

10, modifies its opening phrase by substituting major sixths for the perfect and augmented fourths, and this wider interval is important in later developments. At this point the violins enter for the first time with a phrase beginning (in the key of E flat) with the sixth to tenth notes of the oboe phrase, the accompaniment to it being compounded of the leaping sixth just introduced by the oboe and an inner pedal of B flat that, in spite of the introduction of new keys, keeps the music anchored to a feeling of the tonic. There is an accelerando, and the music moves towards a *forte* statement (in canon on the brass) of the original subject-matter, while the strings soar above it with a quaver pattern first introduced as subsidiary material in the original statement. Five bars of this lead to a long theme developed from all the important elements so far heard:

Ex. 37

This is played by all violins and violas in unison, and when the accompanying counterpoint to it assumes greater importance the theme plays a correspondingly secondary role, developing by compressing into semiquaver patterns some of the quaver outlines just heard. This semiquaver figuration then develops into a forceful diminution of the original oboe theme until, halfway through bar 2 of the above quotation, the music suddenly quietens to admit the statement of the second theme

Ex. 38

(in the related key of D flat major) by solo clarinet. Even here the original subject-matter is not lost sight of, for the rising fourths in the bass refer to it. (Hints, also, of future movements are contained in the semiquaver pattern in bar 3 of the above quotation [*cf*. Ex. 44].)

These elements now develop in combination until the music broadens out into a thematic transformation of the original theme, heralding a real return to the opening mood. The oboe again has the subject-matter, but the pitch is much higher and the key is C minor. Filling the inner spaces is a supertonic pedal, its occasional semiquaver pulsing adding a dramatic element. At the end of this section the rising augmented fourth is used as a modulatory device to arrive at A major.[3]

Ex. 39

Hugh Ottaway's analysis of this A major passage shows exactly how the modulation is effected:

> Once again the oboe's augmented fourths are the root of the matter: when B flat is lighted on, it is a logical step to E natural, the fifth of A; the bassoon arrives at C sharp by a similar route; and the violas and cellos enter (*pp*) on A itself, thus completing the triad. The key is evolved from the movement of the parts; it is not ordained by any element of dramatic structure (the Beethoven method) but is the logical outcome of the linear growth. There are only five bars of this serene A major; the music is then pulled back into the flat keys: the lower strings descend the scale of A to C sharp, only to find that it is now D flat, the first violins having risen from E to F. This enharmonic change is typical of Rubbra at such a moment. For something big is on the move: there is a rapid crescendo, and accelerando, and an urgent use of the augmented fourths; the tension increases, and an emphatic assertion of *a* [see Example 36] impressively detonates the *Allegro* section of the movement.[4]

According to the composer, 'the whole of this *Allegro* section is in reality the development section, but it is a development of rhythmic implications',[5] the chief pattern of which is the figure seen in the middle and bottom staves of Example 40. The triplets in the third measure of Example 40 continue in the woodwinds and strings for a further eleven measures, dominating matters to the extent of forcing the music into a 3/4 metre. It should be noted that in the third measure the triplet figure preserves the outline of the oboe's solo at the start of the movement (the first interval has, of course, been altered to a major second). The remainder of the passage abandons this intervallic structure (with one

Ex. 40

'small exception) in favour of a sequential pattern containing steadily rising pitches. The dynamic level is increased to a *fortissimo* which is intensified during the first eight measures of the triple metre by horns and trumpets sounding empty fifths in the rhythmic pattern seen in Example 40. The excitement thus engendered is shared by the continuing high, unison strings whose legato intensity is in sharp contrast to the heavily accented brass. The latter's participation in the passage ends with held notes and the lower woodwinds and strings continue the rhythmic fifths, extending them to sixths under the still soaring violins. This lighter scoring permits the violins to be heard to greater advantage as they finish their rhapsodic ascent. When the brasses re-enter *fortissimo* the horns sound the opening melodic cell accompanied by the driving rhythmic figure in the first trumpet and trombone.

The composer's analytical comments with respect to the first movement continue with the mention of

> a long 'appassionato' theme based on both the first and second subjects. The key of the second subject (D flat) is now predominant, but it is mainly first subject material that is used, particularly at the climax, where it is in canon [measures 157–61], and later, on a tonic pedal, where it is in diminution and imitated by inversion [measures 162–6]. After an enharmonic change to C sharp minor, duple and triple rhythms are simultaneously used (all three parts using basic first subject material), and this prepares the way for the dual rhythms used when the second subject proper returns.[6]

This restatement of Theme 2 is yet another example of the composer's penchant for altering the note values and the instrumentation of a principal theme when it

Ex. 41

returns. In this instance a comparison of Examples 38 and 41 shows that the second statement is an augmentation of the first. However, when tempo differences and the time lapse since the theme's first statement are taken into account, the listener is really unaware of the change. He will, of course, be aware of the change in instrumentation for in statement 1 the first clarinet and first flute announce the theme. Here, in this restatement the violins have it.

'The tension gradually mounts until, on a supertonic pedal (C), the harmonic ambiguity of the opening finally settles, by way of the augmented fourth, on to B flat major.'[7] Beginning with this interval the subsequent passage is the same as the A major one shown in Example 39, except, of course, that it is in B flat, but whereas the tranquil A major passage led, via a forceful *crescendo*, to the *Allegro energico*, the B flat counterpart is now coda material, 'rounded off by a poignant reference, by the oboe, to its first phrase'.[8]

No greater contrast between Rubbra's two antipodal 'starting points' can be found than those represented by the first and second movements of this symphony. The first movement grows from melodic cells composed of selected intervals; the second movement, marked *Allegro moderato*, is monothematic – built on an eight-measure theme 'announced by unaccompanied solo horn. From that moment the theme, or patterns derived from it, are never absent. It is heard in all twelve keys (including one minor) and becomes truncated, elongated, augmented and turned upside down'.[9] In other words, the theme is an indivisible unit conceived as such in the mind of the composer and not constructed from any melodic cell. However, the theme, shown in Example 42, takes one back in

Ex. 42

spirit to the *Périgourdine* movement of the First Symphony, which, it will be recalled, employed a borrowed French tune. Norman Demuth, although silent on the similarity in character between the two melodies, does suggest a 'French connection' in the following passage:

I do not know if Rubbra has studied the Symphony in B flat by Vincent d'Indy. In any case, the affinity between this second movement and the third in d'Indy's Symphony is spiritual and not thematic.... The opening idea of this movement is redolent of the 'chanson populaire' of France, whose quality is very different from that of this country. No suggestion is made here that Rubbra is not being 'original', and plagiarism of material and spirit is strenuously denied; but the Englishness has gone out of the work for the moment.[10]

I quite agree with Ottaway that the movement is not a scherzo in the generally accepted sense, and as support for this assertion Ottaway cites the various Beethoven scherzos and those from the Fourth and Sixth Symphonies of Vaughan Williams, 'where the note is one of sardonic violence'. He goes on to suggest the term 'bucolic humoresque' as a characterization for its 'engaging gaiety and good humour'.[11] Even within Rubbra's own *oeuvre* this movement cannot compare with the boisterousness and impetuosity of the scherzos in the Second, Sixth and Seventh Symphonies.

Rubbra's imaginative treatment of a theme whose persistent repetitions could easily turn into numbing monotony is demonstrated impressively time after time. Contrapuntal manipulation is at the heart of this treatment, and in the following account some examples of it are cited.

Concurrently with the last note of the unaccompanied solo horn's presentation of the theme, the solo bassoon begins its presentation to be followed in exactly the same way by the solo clarinet. All three entries are in D major, thus firmly establishing the tonic before the start of the almost continuous modulations. The very rudimentary counterpoint accompanying the second and third entries is derived from various segments of the melody. For the bassoon's entry the counterpoint is provided by the first oboe, while for the solo clarinet it is supplied by the violas. A simple bass supports both solos. Even when complexities are introduced this same, simple kind of counterpoint – always traceable to the theme – can be heard dancing and sparkling in the background. As for the theme itself: after the entries just described it may be begun by one instrument or group of instruments and completed by another single instrument or group. Quite often it is shortened to eight measures – sometimes even reduced to a segment or two which may then engage in a sequential modulation from one of the many keys to another.

An augmentation in the violins of (roughly) the theme's first four measures (35–41) represents the initial alteration. The first significant change, however, occurs at measure 132 where,

> after a general pause of two beats, it looks as though new subject-matter has appeared, but closer inspection reveals that the triplet pattern is a rhythmic metamorphosis of the two final bars of the theme, while the slow moving minims of the middle part reveal an augmentation of the theme.[12]

Ex. 43

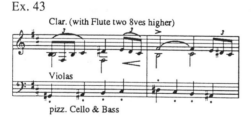

The two measures containing the triplets constitute an ostinato that, altogether, is heard ten times (measures 132–51), the last two of which are in B flat. The very next passage (measures 152–69)

> shows the theme in B flat minor moving against an augmented inversion of itself. At the tenth bar [measure 161] the theme, still augmented, reverts to its uninverted shape, while surrounding it are triplets derived from the tail-piece of the theme. This is the climax of the movement, and it is followed by a quiet recapitulation beginning in D flat major, the theme being played by bassoon with derivative counterpoint on the oboe.[13]

The modulations contained in this movement comprise a topic in themselves. They are always elementary and twice they are so abrupt as to make one smile with the composer, who is obviously thoroughly enjoying himself. All of the modulations enhance in a most delightful way the childlike innocence and naïveté of the movement. There is no intervallic pattern employed in the modulations, a circumstance that contributes to the spontaneity of the movement. However, as observed in Table 1, an interior pattern (marked by brackets) is repeated a half-step lower in the recapitulation.

Table 1.   *Key changes in movement II*

⌐D-A-A flat-C¬G-D flat¬E-E flat¬D-E flat-F-B
(G.P.) B-B flat-B flat minor
⌐D flat-A flat-G-B¬C¬E flat-D⌐

Ottaway correctly sensed the playfulness behind the modulations in the following passage:

> The changes of key do not take us into different rooms [but] the same room with the furniture rearranged. 'There', he seems to say, 'how do you like it that way?' And he shifts into (key?), with the theme on the (instrument?). 'Or shall we put this here?' The theme is passed to the (?) in (key?). But the composer who fidgets with the furniture can be very trying, and it says much for Rubbra's imagination that he sustains the interest throughout the movement.[14]

A careful look at the manner in which the table is arranged shows that a structural design is implicit, however asymmetrical it may appear. The general pause mentioned above by the composer, and indicated in the score, marks the boundary between a lengthy first section and a short second section of just thirty-seven measures. The end of the latter and the beginning of the concluding section are marked *Allargando a tempo*. Rubbra's term for this final section is 'recapitulation', and this lives up to its name by proving to be the counterpart of section 1, measures 10–76. Thus the abrupt modulation in measures 75–6 (E-E flat) is repeated in measures 235–6 (E flat-D). Because of the much lighter instrumentation at the start of Section 2 there is the temptation to think of this portion as a trio (and, in fact, Demuth calls it precisely that in his analytical comments).[15] However, this seems incorrect because at the end of the two-measure triplet pattern the complete theme is stated in B flat minor by the full orchestra. Trio sections are always scored more lightly, and the theme of the minuet or scherzo that precedes and follows such sections is not present in them. Moreover, in this particular instance, the movement is categorically monothematic; thus the whole point of a trio section is missed. Where is the contrast?

To summarize: the movement appears to be a simple example of an asym-metrical ternary form – *A B A*[1] – with plenty of room for argument regarding the exact status of *B*. This is because *B* starts off by exhibiting substantial dif-ferences, but these disappear after just twenty measures.

The *Grave* movement is Rubbra at his most profound and expressive, and as such it ranks with the slow movements of the Second and Sixth Symphonies:

> The most important thematic elements... are those revealed in the first three bars of the cello tune. In fact, there is nothing anywhere that is not germane to the 2nd–5th–4th progression, *although these intervals are not necessarily always in this order* [my italics].[16]

The intervals are thus available in any order for future use, and in and of themselves do not constitute a fixed theme. They do, however, qualify as a melodic cell but not in the same way as the cell which gives rise to the first movement. There, the original intervallic order is more likely to be preserved intact.

Ex. 44

The cello theme, marked *molto espressivo*, extends across thirteen measures. After the intervallic configuration has been established (*x* in Example 44) sub-tle changes begin to appear. When the violins enter at the conclusion of the cello theme 'the basic intervals of fifth and fourth are seen used in the simplest possible way, and embedded in its twelve-bar length is a passing reference to the characteristic augmented fourth of the opening of the Symphony.'[17] The first part of this passage is shown in Example 45 together with the rising augmented fourth (enclosed in a bracket). The second half of this violin passage consists of a duplication two and three octaves higher of the second half of the cellos'

Ex. 45

material. A short bridge passage that utilizes the intervallic cell but with the position of the fifth and fourth reversed, 'gives way to a secondary theme, accompanied by two strands of counterpoint, one a diminished version of the opening, and the other a version retaining the original time-values'.[18]

Ex. 46

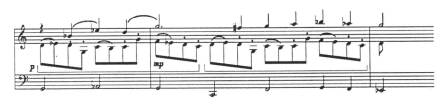

Example 46 shows these strands plus the start of the secondary theme. The diminished version is separable into two distinct figures, the second of which is the inversion of the first. The scalic group of eighths serves as a connecting link between repetitions, and an ostinato is set in motion that consists of six statements. The bracket enclosing the groups of eighths was inserted by the composer, and is intended to emphasize the 'natural grouping of three-two against the four-two of the secondary theme'.[19] Rhythmic tension is thus built up which is released in the first and shorter of the movement's two climaxes.

Before moving on to the next important phase of the movement, mention should be made of two Rubbra characteristics found rather often in all of his major works and present in the preceding example. The first of these is mentioned by the composer in the line just quoted: the simultaneous positioning of two rhythmic versions of the same figure. One of these versions is almost invariably diminished (as here) or augmented. A further example is to be seen in the approaching climax: inversions of the melodic cell, one in quarters and ending on a half-note, the other in eighths and finishing on a quarter-note. The second trait appears in the secondary theme and involves rising fourths in the melodic line. These are especially prominent in the final measure (33) of the secondary theme where sequential movement is heard.

One of Rubbra's most haunting cor anglais passages emerges from the first climax, its sombre, brooding quality enhanced by undulating ostinatos in the

Ex. 47

harp and strings, and by a muffled triplet figure in the timpani. The cor anglais theme (Example 47) is also 'compounded of the characteristic intervals' introduced at the start of the movement by the cellos, and the uppermost of the ostinato figures contains 'a slower version of the same intervals'.[20] A second and far more intense climax follows, built from passages containing sixteenths and thirty-seconds in which are embedded short, right-side up and inverted statements of the original intervals. The triplet figure on the timpani is used 'with tremendous force at the height of the climax. When this has subsided a return is made to earlier material [see Example 45], this time in D flat major, the only difference in texture being the occasional intrusion of the triplet drum rhythm.'[21] The movement ends quietly, trailing off to nothing.

After having heard the *Grave* and absorbed its numerous details, one may perhaps be pardoned for having momentarily forgotten that its relationship to the following *Allegro vivo* is the same as that of the opening *Adagio* to the first *Allegro*. There are good reasons for such an oversight. First, the opening *Adagio* ends with a crescendo and *fortissimo*, alerting the listener to expect something of consequence to follow immediately. The *Grave*, on the other hand, winds down to a satisfying cadence. Second, in each case the harmonic structure prepares one for the expected result: continuation for the *Adagio*, full stop for the *Grave* even though this stop proves to be a very short one. Third, and most important, it becomes apparent as the final *Allegro* gets under way that the relationship between it and the preceding *Grave* is tenuous when compared with the relationship between the first two movements. Possibly this is because the rising augmented fourths and their half-step, upward resolutions – such a prominent characteristic in the first two movements – are more 'ear-catching' than the milder intervals injected into the final *Allegro*: the last four notes of the intervallic cell at the beginning of the *Grave*. (A more immediately recognizable figure for the final *Allegro* is, to my mind, the three notes whose source is the sombre drumbeat in the *Grave*.) However, no matter what one may feel about the relationship between the last two movements, the *Allegro vivo* is certainly one of Rubbra's most rhythmically alive and colourful movements.

Amid the brilliant and bewildering array of themes, deciding in what order of importance to rank them is a difficult if not impossible task. The solution to the problem is not to classify them at all in terms of principal, secondary, and so on, but simply to accept them in the order in which they appear. The first theme, begun by the woodwinds and completed in the strings, makes immediate and obvious use of the transformed drumbeats. Its B flat minor tonality is clear (Example 48). The next theme, containing the characteristic intervals

Ex. 48

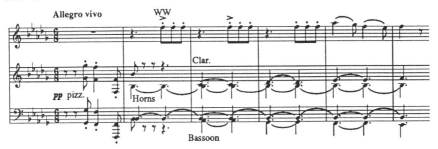

from the *Grave* is scored for violins and is just as tonally unequivocal: D minor, although halfway through its tremendous span (measures 22–68) A minor is introduced. Only its first portion appears in Example 49. In his analysis, the

Ex. 49

composer quotes its first six measures as indicative of 'the close relationship between the two final movements'. He continues by saying that 'the slower melodic element [shown in this theme] and the interjected triplets [seen in Example 47 and also used as an independent rhythmic figure] are foils for each other and develop side by side rondo-wise.'[22] As this theme progresses, its intensity and sweep are magnified in two important ways: first, the melody moves steadily upward, increasing in volume as it goes; second, it is reinforced by other instruments – flutes and oboes scored one octave apart – and by octaves introduced by the *divisi* violins. During this long statement horns, trumpets and trombones proclaim at different times the terse, *forte* first phrase of the first theme (measures 4–6 of Example 48) as well as slight variants of it, and their competition is responsible for obscuring the melodic line as their enthusiasm mounts.

When the end of the long theme is reached in measure 68 another long violin passage begins at once with a two-octave drop from high C to middle C. The material of this new passage has a transitional atmosphere characterized by suspense as the violins start their long climb again. This melodic line moves at a slower pace because of the change in the rhythmic pattern to dotted quarters, some of which are tied. However, the violins are forced to surrender some of their independence when the brass again enter and assume the dominant role. The woodwinds enter with their chattering phrases from the first theme. At measure 85 the first trumpet enters and begins a round of 'joyful phrases with which the word "alleluia" is associated in my mind'.[23] These are shown in Example 50. Against these phrases the lively rhythmic pattern ♪♩ ♪♩, employed

Ex. 50

previously, assumes great prominence in the middle strings as it moves up and down in scalic form. The whole passage reaches its climax with *forte*, stretto statements of the trumpet's phrase – right-side up and inverted – shared by all sections of the orchestra but dominated, of course, by the brass.

From measure 131 to 155 the first half of the long violin theme whose beginning was seen in Example 49 is repeated, and this

> leads to a new tune on trumpets and flutes, accompanied by woodwind two octaves apart, the characteristic features of which are rising augmented fourths and falling sixths, thus recalling the first movement.

Ex. 51

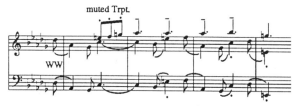

> Snatches of the last bar of the scherzo theme (changed to 6/8) are also heard, and out of this general mêlée of subject-matter emerges a trumpet theme in 3/4 (against a 6/8 background) that in itself draws together and unifies the important thematic elements heard in previous movements.[24]

In example 52 these elements and the movement from which each is derived are shown in brackets. Two measures after the trumpet entrance a four-measure ostinato pattern is initiated by the horns and trombones. This consists of the trumpets' two opening measures pitched one octave lower, followed by a transposition of the same. The complete ostinato pattern is heard four times, but two further statements with altered components are admissible. At the same time

Ex. 52

the strings, in 6/8 metre, are loudly sounding their own ostinato – a descending tetrachord complete in two measures and executed as a tremolo. Its lineage is unambiguous: the 'alleluia' trumpet phrase seen in Example 50. With one exception, this ostinato extends over twelve statements.

The total effect of the conflicting metres and the din created by three simultaneous melodic lines is overwhelming. The Psalmist's exhortation, 'make a joyful noise unto the Lord', aptly describes this entire section, and it can, in fact, be applied to the whole movement.

It is obvious that after such a big climax the movement must soon end. A short bridge passage in which all instruments are in 3/4 metre contains straightforward references to the symphony's initial oboe theme. Its conclusion is marked by a *fortissimo allargando* at the end of which a joyous and exact recapitulation of the movement's first twenty-one measures bursts forth with its chattering woodwind theme. Any hope that the exuberance might be continued beyond the twenty-first measure is dashed when the momentum is 'twice broken by a silent bar before the music changes to the solemnity of the initial mood of the whole Symphony. Full circle is thus made.'[25] In this one-page *Adagio* the cor anglais and cellos sound the first movement's haunting and unforgettable intervals for the last time over a timpani figure only slightly changed from that of the *Grave*. The final gravitation to the B flat major chord produces a most restful and satisfying cadence.

Ottaway's appraisal of this closing *Adagio* section raises interesting points, but I question its validity:

> The intention is clear, but the musical reasoning is scarcely of Rubbra's stamp. It is not that the sense of unity has been pushed too far but in the wrong direction: the *Adagio* is retrospective; it does not grow out of the movement.[26]

My first objection concerns the interpretation put on Rubbra's last sentence, 'full circle is thus made', quoted by Ottaway prior to the above statement. Do Rubbra's words refer to the fulfilment of a structural design or merely the return of the symphony's opening mood? There is no way of knowing for sure. I agree that the *Adagio* 'does not grow out of the movement' and that it 'is retrospective', but I see nothing wrong with that. The ambiguous nature of Rubbra's sentence causes Ottaway's argument to falter when he calls the composer's intention 'clear'; in actuality, it is not. In Ottaway's concluding paragraph there appear to be contradictions:

> Despite this apparent miscalculation, the finale is among the most convincing by modern composers... even here, where the desire to clinch a cyclic argument might have led to exaggerations, the weight and proportions are exactly right.... What could seem more natural than the re-emergence of *a* [the oboe's initial phrase] in the all-pervading rhythmic pattern?[27]

The symphony received its first performance in London on 26 January 1949. One review of the work, written relatively soon after this performance, is very general:

> The whole of the music is of an original cast, and its originality is without strain. Here Rubbra succeeds where many fail, for originality fails in proportion to its effort. His is perhaps the most natural of the originalities now current, for it is the most free from self-consciousness. The symphony is very sincere music. Very often that epithet is used to cover all manner of sins, for some of the world's worst music has been sincere. With Rubbra the quality communicates itself in special terms that come from the inside; and it is a winning quality, or a quality by which we try to be won. How far are we getting? As far as knowing that Rubbra's symphony is neither a winner nor a hit; and liking the composer none the less for that.[28]

How noncommittal and uninvolved can one be? At least the following review takes a stand, even though it is a very disagreeable one:

> The prevailing texture is that of porridge – compounded, no doubt, of the finest and wholesomest wholemeal, but porridge none the less.... Everything, as in an old-fashioned shop, has the air of being tremendously 'good' and 'well-made'; all that is lacking is splendour, effervescence, surprise.[29]

Ottaway's response to this review calls it 'unsympathetic, faintly facetious and far too general', and concludes with the perceptive observation that 'it is still a serious comment, for the writer sees that in challenging the texture he is up against the very substance of the work itself.'[30] This observation strongly reinforces the remarks made by Westrup in his article on Rubbra's Fourth Symphony (see pp. 98–99).

No such perception is demonstrated in the pronouncement by Olin Downes, one of America's most respected critics, after a performance of the symphony by the Juilliard Orchestra, conducted by Jean Morel:

> the Fifth Symphony of Edmund Rubbra, dated 1948, is tiresomely prolix, heavy-handed in its orchestration, and of a length and pretentiousness wholly out of proportion to the worth of its ideas.[31]

One other short review may be included here before two lengthy notices, occasioned by the Melbourne Symphony's recording of the work (Hans-Hubert Schönzeler, conductor) are cited:

> His earlier symphonies were lacking clarity of texture for the reason that he was using for orchestral music an essentially choral polyphony. In his Third and Fourth Symphonies his growing mastery of a true orchestral style was accompanied by

some loss of grandeur [whatever that means], but in the Fifth (1948) the intensity and nobility of the first two reappeared transfigured by luminous orchestration.[32]

One of the record reviews is highly positive in its comments, the other generally negative. We begin with the latter:

I rather doubt whether we shall continue to see no. 5 as the traditional high point in Rubbra's symphonic output. Compared with the mastery and individuality of no. 7, some aspects of its personality now seem to sit uncomfortably upon it, such as the bass lines which, always restlessly striding up and down, are a weakness inherited from Holst rather than a proven legacy from early music; the jaunty feudal tune of the second movement, too, can seem rather anaemic and irritating beside the more pungent peasantries of Mahler [I can only assume that a 'feudal tune' is one that betrays its close resemblance to a folk tune]; and elsewhere some of the gaunt counterpoint shows a puzzlingly oblique relationship to that of Shostakovich. But this very invocation of the 20th-century symphonic tradition as a frame of reference is intended to advocate the acceptance of Rubbra into that tradition, an acceptance which, it may be hoped, will proceed apace with the advent of this compelling recording.[33]

The final review reads as follows:

Prof. Louis Blois has observed, 'Of all non-liturgical works in the literature, the symphonies of Rubbra and Bruckner are the most direct trajectories to a divine presence.' Such a strong statement certainly provokes consideration, though some may dispute it. However, after those of Vaughan Williams, for me Rubbra's are the most imposing symphonies composed by an Englishman, with a lofty grandeur and spiritual integrity that gives credit to the symphonic medium.... Completed in 1948, the Fifth is one of the most highly regarded works in Rubbra's estimable canon of eleven symphonies – in fact, the distinguished composer Herbert Howells found it 'a work with the power to make one fall in love with music all over again.' It is also one of Rubbra's most accessible symphonies, with a lyrical warmth missing from the sterner Second and Seventh. Its long, beautifully shaped, flowing lines evoke a mood of great nobility, dignity, and reverence; the slow, majestic unfolding of the first movement and the elegiac third are especially moving. A gently rollicking scherzo and robust finale provide comfortable contrast.[34]

Evidence that American and Canadian interest in Rubbra's music was growing is provided by the American composer and conductor Bernard Hermann in a letter to Rubbra dated 22 April 1952:

I just returned from New York where I had supper with Stokowski. He had just come back from Toronto where he had conducted your Fifth Symphony, and he was ever so enthusiastic about it. I took this occasion to tell him all about the Third Symphony, and also the Fourth. I certainly think you should send him scores of both. You have, most assuredly, made a friend for your music in him.

Again, in a letter of 17 November 1952, there are these words:

This is just a few words to tell you that the other night they played over the local radio station [Los Angeles or Hollywood] Barbirolli's recorded performance of your Symphony No. 5, and I do want to take this occasion to tell you that I found it a most rewarding and beautiful work. I congratulate you on being able to achieve such moving tranquility and optimism in your music, and also that I think it is different from any of your other works. I thought the contrapuntal weaving and orchestration were of a magnificent oneness, and all I can say is Bravo! again.

Symphony No. 6

Rubbra began work on his Sixth Symphony, Op. 80, in the autumn of 1953 and finished it in the summer of 1954. Commissioned by the Royal Philharmonic Society, it was given its first performance at one of the Society's concerts on 17 November 1954 by the BBC Symphony Orchestra under the direction of Sir Malcolm Sargent.

A month later the composer contributed an article to *London Musical Events* in which he described the genesis of the work. This inadvertently gave rise to a controversy between the musicologist Elsie Payne and Hugh Ottaway, whose writing on Rubbra's music as well as the music of Shostakovich and Vaughan Williams is always thoughtful and stimulating. The argument, conducted in the pages of *Musical Opinion*, was set off by three of Payne's articles, published in other journals. It began in August 1956 and ended in February of the following year. There is nothing like a prolonged and rousing controversy over a large-scale work. It sharpens musical wits while it is alive, and years after it has quieted down it is an important reference point when the work is freshly approached. Lastly, it provides the reader with interesting biographical and/or analytical details. This controversy centred on the four notes, E-F-A-B, which Rubbra in a perhaps unguarded moment placed at the head of his score. How and why this came to be he explains fully in the article mentioned above:

Those unfamiliar with creative processes may assume (and it is quite a logical assumption) that by the time a composer has written six symphonies he has, so to speak, well-oiled the grooves of symphonic thought, thus making each successive symphony run more smoothly and easily. But the exact opposite is the case. The problems get progressively more difficult, unless one is content to repeat oneself, a thing that no self-respecting artist will do. Each symphony, if it is to hold its own in the corpus of one's works, should inhabit a *distinct* world of its own, even though all of them are intimately related at deeper levels. To achieve this *distinctiveness* one doesn't say 'It's about time I wrote another symphony', but wait patiently until inward creative processes throw up an idea that one instinctively knows has symphonic potentialities. I cannot say when this was in my 6th Symphony: the time and the occasion in 1953 have now completely vanished from my conscious memory. All I know is that a movement intended to be the first, grew from a rising series of four notes, E-F-A-B, and was concluded in November of that year. The end of the movement, however, has such an air of finality, that I gradually came to realise that nothing could follow it. Added to which there was a practical difficulty in making this the first movement, for the unaccompanied theme beginning with the notes mentioned above, and which opened the movement, were given to the English horn, an instrument notoriously difficult to play in tune unless well warmed-up before-hand. These considerations led me to make this, the first movement written, into the finale. Such a step created in itself a new problem for me, inasmuch as in my previous symphonies each movement had, so to speak, taken its cue from what preceded it, generally taking the form of a reaction in mood and speed. Having completed the finale first, this creative method could no longer be followed, and I had to find beginnings for an already accomplished end. [Perhaps Rubbra had forgotten that the last movement of the First Symphony had also been written first. See page 16.] Thought couldn't do this, and I had to wait patiently for the origins of the other movements to assert themselves, for I am a fatalist where music is concerned. A sudden light showed where these origins were; viz: in the same four notes (E-F-A-B) with which the finale began. Soon after this discovery, the remaining movements began to take shape, the first from a *chord* containing the first three notes of the basic group, the second (slow) from a fifth consisting of A and E, and the scherzo from a melodic use of E and F. These acted as starting points only, the music of each movement developing *sui generis*, and with its own view of the tonal centre implied by the basic notes. All these movements grew up together, as it were, and I think it is this fact that gives the 6th Symphony its own peculiar kind of unity. The unity of the previous symphonies has been made either by a progressive unfolding of tonality or by a pervasive one. Here, however, in this new symphony the centre is a series of notes the tonality of which is differently conceived in each movement, D minor-F major in the first movement, A minor-major in the second, C major in the third, and Phrygian mode moving to C major in the finale. Instead of giving a key for the symphony, as in No. 5, I place the four basic notes under the title on the first page. (It looks like a capitulation to tone-row methods, but I assure you that this is far from the truth!)[35]

By way of introducing the controversy, I quote the opening paragraphs from Ottaway's major article on the subject:

A composer must be prepared for some curiously specious assessments of his work, yet in publicly acquiescing – 'professional etiquette', I believe – he may surely insist that matters of demonstrable musical fact shall not be falsified. When Edmund Rubbra inscribed the score of his Sixth Symphony with a rising succession of four notes (E-F-A-B), he had a right to expect that critics would use their ears and eyes, and then their ears again, before concocting elaborate theses. But a good deal of nonsense has since been written, and I wonder that the composer has not replied with a personal statement. In a sense, such a statement does exist (see 'London Musical Events', December 1954), though it was written on the eve of the first performance, before the technocrats had had their fling. Rubbra contributed a short article on the origins of the work, with particular reference to E-F-A-B, and left little doubt that the 'motto' (*not* 'motto theme') was of biographical rather than analytical interest.

After a short summary of Rubbra's article, Ottaway continues

Unfortunately, however, E-F-A-B is the sort of bait that many musicians find irresistible; someone was bound to fall for it, only to find himself thoroughly hooked, a major catch! The critic who referred to Rubbra's 'motto' in terms of the two four-note germinal motives in Vaughan Williams's Fourth Symphony shall go unnamed; he was commenting on the first performance and foolishly jumped to an erroneous conclusion which his ear could scarcely have prompted. Since we are all victims of auto-suggestion from time to time, especially at first performances, I shall leave it at that. The comparison, of course, was wholly misleading, for Vaughan Williams's motives are complete entities, important *thematically* throughout the work; they are vitally structural as well as inspirational.

Far more serious is the case of the writer who, several months later and with access to the score, made fictitious claims for E-F-A-B in three major articles, one of which was devoted exclusively to the Sixth Symphony. I refer to the work of

Elsie Payne: 'Some Aspects of Rubbra's Style' (*The Music Review*, August 1955); 'Edmund Rubbra' (*Music and Letters*, October 1955); and 'Rubbra's Sixth Symphony' (*The Monthly Musical Record*, October 1955). These essays have a learned and authoritative air and a passion for categorising every detail of the composer's style. Clearly, Dr. Payne has done a great deal of work on Rubbra's music, some of it really valuable, but in such a context her misrepresentation of the Sixth Symphony is so much the more dangerous. Her predilection for creative subtleties has led to a position which is quite untenable if put to the test of ear and eye.[36]

The thesis set forth by Payne in the three articles named above is summarized below. At the beginning of the excerpt she describes what she believes is the essence of Rubbra's style in a general way (ignoring, however, the equally important tendency to begin a movement with a complete theme that extends over a specified number of measures).

Rubbra's thematic, indeed his whole expression, is the outcome of a thematic unit or idea. Sometimes 'unit', sometimes 'idea' seems to be the more appropriate word to use of the germinal factor, though the difference between the two is not so much a structural one as one of character. The unit or idea is often based on a simple interval or succession of intervals. All the thematic and textural ideas of the Sixth Symphony, for instance, arise out of the notes E F A B and the intervals implied by those notes. The unit itself has only a modicum of individuality; it is, in fact, embryonic. It is sufficiently bare and simple to allow scope for varied extensions and developments, yet sufficiently individualized to ensure some melodic and textural homogeneity between the many aspects of its development. It is very malleable, and furnishes all the melodic and contrapuntal complexity of the work (apart, of course, from definitely contrasted sections, *ostinati*, and so on), and is thus responsible for the synthetic value and power of Rubbra's contrapuntal style.[37]

In her later and more expansive articles Payne develops this thesis and when Ottaway disputed the whole idea, the battle was joined. He was quite correct when he said

Having found that the majority of Rubbra's movements are evolved from some sort of germinal fragment, Dr. Payne has tried to go one better and to discover the existence of a single germinal process pervading an entire work. The Sixth Symphony with its 'motto' inscription appealed irresistibly to this (sub-conscious) desire; so strongly, in fact, that the conscious musician was unable to regain the ascendancy.[38]

Ottaway next pins down his argument in terms of how the four notes are used in each movement:

Take, for instance, the opening movement, where the connection with E-F-A-B is so slight as to be virtually negligible: the first chord of the introduction, which is in D minor, includes the notes E, F and A – and that is the full intent of it! In no real sense can this tiny detail be said to propagate the movement; it does not even dominate the introduction. As Rubbra has said himself, it merely provides a starting-point. The main material of the movement is independent, both of the introduction and of E-F-A-B. Moreover, the frank use of sonata form, with clearly defined (and contrasted) first and second subjects, sets the movement apart from Rubbra's more usual practice. It is a striking exception to the generalisation that his music evolves from a single 'thematic unit or idea'.

As for the remaining movements, in the second

the only connection with E-F-A-B is the open fifth A-E, heard at the outset on muted horns. The motive based on open fifths is fundamentally static, and when it recurs it makes itself felt as an emotional focus not as a germinal 'unit'. The rest of the movement is freely evolved from the melodic material the fifths accompany, and this is quite independent of E-F-A-B....

Only in the scherzo is there any thematic guidance from E-F-A-B, and this is limited to a rhythmic use of the minor second E-F (E is construed as the major third of C, the central key of the movement). This again is a starting-point, and the important opening motive is rounded off with the salient figure from the development section of the first movement. Here is a real cross-reference in the work, and it strikes the ear more acutely than anything to do with E-F-A-B. It is, in fact, this figure that furnishes the movement with most of its 'melodic and contrapuntal complexity' – complexity, not complication.

In the finale, of course, the cor anglais theme beginning with E-F-A-B generates the whole movement. However, other aspects of the theme, notably a falling fifth and an octave leap, become just as important as the first four notes; and when the main *Allegro* is reached a striking new theme is added.[39]

Now that the main argument has been presented, there is nothing to be gained by quoting from the exchange of letters in the pages of *Musical Opinion*, as each letter simply refuted its predecessor. Suffice it to say that at the conclusion of two of his letters Ottaway appealed to Rubbra to settle the issue: 'What a pretty situation! It only remains for the lion to devour *both* his jackals. Forward, please, composer.'[40] And finally: 'On one thing Elsie Payne and I appear to agree in principle – the desirability of a clarifying statement from the composer. I hope Edmund Rubbra will feel disposed to grasp the nettle.'[41] Rubbra did grasp the nettle in a wonderfully tactful letter to *Musical Opinion*, dated 14 January 1957, and published in the February number, thereby putting an end to the E-F-A-B debate:

Sir, – It is a unique task to have to separate, not opponents of a work, but supporters, and I hope I can do so without wounding the susceptibilities of either!

Analysis after the event is something a composer is not vitally interested in, as analysis, for him, is intuitional in the actual processes of creation. So that in order to balance up the claims of these two (or too!) penetrating critics I must as far as possible look at the work from an outside critical angle. When I (perhaps inadvisedly!) placed those four notes (E-F-A-B) at the beginning of the score of my Sixth Symphony, my intention was to indicate, not a key, but the *interval sources* of the music, each movement beginning with a *selection* from these notes (except the last movement, which uses all of them thematically). The crux of the analytical argument with reference to each movement resides in the particular selection *and not the four notes as a whole*. Miss Payne is on safe ground when she stresses the pervasiveness of the four-note motif and its continuation (i.e., the opening cor anglais theme) throughout the finale, and Mr. Ottaway is on safe ground when he disputes the significance of the four notes in the other movements, but both would have got nearer to the truth of each movement if they had confined their analysis to the generating power of the *selected* notes. The E-F-A of the first movement yields a second and a third as motivating intervals, the A-E of the slow movement a fifth, and the E-F of the scherzo a semitone. Analysis will, I think, show that these are the dominating factors in each movement.[42]

As Ottaway has stated in one of the quoted passages, the first movement of the Sixth Symphony is cast in sonata form, preceded by a slow introduction. Rubbra alluded to this when he said that 'the form of the first movement is more "classical" than any of the opening movements of the previous symphonies.'[43] However, in this connection, another comment by Ottaway has particular relevance:

> In a broadcast conversation that he did with me in 1971, I suggested to the composer that this might be a notable exception to the 'rule' – i.e., 'I never know where a piece is going to go next'; but he said that, at the outset, he did not know that he was embarking on a sonata form (Radio 3, December 4, 1971).[44]

Most probably after the completion of the seventeen-measure *Lento* introduction and perhaps well into the *Allegretto* Rubbra sensed from a formal standpoint where his materials were taking him. This may explain the absence of a direct thematic connection between the introduction and the *Allegretto*, for if there were one it seems certain that he would have mentioned it. As it is he writes only that the introduction 'concerns itself, like Haydn's introductions, with indirect preparation for the 6/8 *Allegretto*, the final twist to F major being effected by a change of direction in the final semitone of the opening melodic idea.'[45] Of course, very often there are no thematic connections between a slow introduction and the main body of the movement as investigations of many Haydn and Mozart first movements prove. However, by now having become accustomed to the intricate relationships in every area of Rubbra's *oeuvre*, it is only natural to expect some sort of organic connection here. Lacking any, we may legitimately ask what is the function of this introduction? Are we hearing only an impressive facade? The answer is to be found in the composer's words, 'indirect preparation'. The open fifths and their supporting chords establish the tonalities from which the tonic (F major) will emerge. These preliminary tonalities are D minor, D flat major (the key of the second theme in the sonata framework), a hint of F minor and then the 'final twist to F Major'. In this way the tonic is approached indirectly and made all the stronger thereby.

The tonality of the first theme in the sonata structure is established even more securely by being sounded over a drone-like foundation during the theme's first three statements. These statements constitute a unit by virtue of key, treatment and the fact that they succeed each other without so much as a measure's break between them. No. 3 is an abridged version. As for the instrumentation, the first statement is given to the solo flute and clarinet for the opening three and a half measures, joined in the second half by the oboes and the second flute and clarinet. For the next appearances the strings, woodwinds and horns are united in various combinations.

Now for the theme itself. As can be seen in Example 53 it is jaunty, highly rhythmic, and exhibits a nice balance between disjunct and conjunct members. Certain of the marked segments make important contributions to later developmental transformations, which, in fact, are not long in coming. The main reason

Ex. 53

for their early appearance is Rubbra's intuitive penchant for immediately discovering the growth potentialities of his basic material. It is not necessary for
him to wait until a formal development section arrives; and to do so would be
utterly foreign to his musical nature. The following list summarizes this developmental activity up to the important bridge passage with its new idea (this
begins in measure 59):

1. In measure 27, the cellos have an extended version of the scale figure in
    segment *b*. This occurs during the second statement of Theme 1.
2. In measure 28, the trumpets begin a repeated-note figure derived from *c*,
    heard also during Theme 1's second statement.
3. The upward leap of an octave through the major sixth in measures 34–5
    (woodwinds, first violins) is the inversion of the second limb of *a*.
4. The repeated *pizzicato* notes in measures 35–8 (cellos, basses) come from
    c.
5. In measures 49–50, the three note violin figure comes from the opening of
    segment *d*.
6. In measures 48–50, the rocking sixths in the violas and cellos are suggested
    by the rising and falling sixths of *a*.
7. The woodwind figures in measures 53–59 are similar to those listed in Nos
    2 and 4, and come from *c*.

Ex. 54

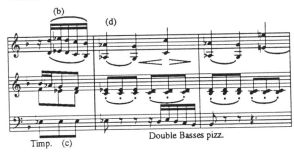

The climactic appearance of the principal theme is in E flat (measures 35–42), and it starts one measure after the end of the third (shortened) version. Again, it is emphasized not by drone-like chords but by the *pizzicato* notes listed above under 4. When they cease, the tympani takes up the same rhythm for the remainder of the statement. In his short analysis accompanying the first performance of the symphony Rubbra observed that the 'details which have been brought forward in the expansion of the first subject are now isolated'.[46] His illustration appears as Example 54. He then remarks on the 'rhythmic tension that culminates in two different forms of the same idea [segment *d* in the opening statement of Theme 1: see Example 55]'.[47]

Ex. 55

Horns

The bridge passage features a new, three-note motive, characterized by the composer as 'a supple and unsymmetrical theme in the tenor register'.[48] In line with Rubbra's usual style, it is not long before inversions and extensions of its three notes are found. The general mood of this whole passage (measures 59–69) is somewhat subdued, both thematically and instrumentally for, with reference to the latter, only the middle and lower registers of the strings, oboes and bassoons are used, together with soft, sustained thirds on the horns. (Later, upper registers are employed, other instruments participate, and a small *accelerando* propels the music toward a D flat statement of Theme 1.) Accompanying the new material of the bridge passage are 'the chord sequences of the introductory *Lento* but a tone lower'.[49] These sequences are very cleverly arranged so that in the *divisi* first violin parts where they appear, each group of three identical chords in the 6/8 metre – containing three notes each, played *pizzicato* – corresponds to one one-measure harp chord of the introduction. The sequence of chords is exactly the same in the introductory and bridge passages, but in the latter the sequence is repeated.

Theme 2, like the last statement of the principal theme, is in D flat. A key relationship of a lower third is thus set up between it and the initial appearance of Theme 1. However, since there is but one measure between the D flat statement of Theme 1 and the commencement of the new theme, it seems an exaggeration to speak of a 'dramatic' use of key in the sonata sense of large structural units being played off against one another. As for Theme 2 itself, it is a tranquil, unhurried melody, introduced and played by the solo oboe for its

Ex. 56

first eight measures. It is reinforced in its second eight measures by the first flute playing one octave higher (Example 56).

The symmetrical length of the theme is another classical association that might have prompted Rubbra's remark (cited earlier) with respect to the more classical cast of this movement. The all-woodwind texture under the melody (except for the first horn's soft D flat pedal) has a chatty sound as the instruments share in contrapuntal combinations involving the falling scale pattern of the theme's third measure. Inversions of this pattern also play a part. At the theme's end the strings enter the conversation, punctuated by brass comments including an unsuccessful attempt by the first trumpet to sound the theme once more. In these final pages of the exposition the mood is one of complete relaxation, and in the final page everyone seems to wind down rather regretfully as if in preparation for the development.

The beginning of the development as it turns out *is* a sobering influence, for the atmosphere is charged with tension as the bridge theme, now extended and altered, is reintroduced. This reappearance seems almost menacing, owing, first, to the absence of the chords first used in the introduction, and whose muffled sound in the first appearance of the bridge passage contributed a degree of softness; and, second, to the presence of the trombones and timpani with their insistent rhythm. The sombre mood is intensified by the instrumentation: violas and cellos, to which is added the first oboe after three measures. With the entry of the first violins, first horn and muted first trumpet the atmosphere takes on excitement, aided by a gradual *accelerando*. This darker phase of the development (from measures 125 to 136) leads to the second and much longer phase in which a bright E flat major replaces the minor tonalities along with a return to the prevailing 6/8 metre. The material most prominently employed in this portion of the development comes from the little three-note fragment in measure 22 – segment *d* in Example 53 – followed by a falling fifth. Scale passages composed of eighths and sixteenths and derived from segment *b* are a secondary feature, along with offshoots suggested by the immediate context with which Rubbra is working at the time.

Following the *allargando* and *fortissimo* return to the F major tonic in measure 168, the abbreviated recapitulation begins in measure 172 with a canonic version of segments *c* and the first three notes of *d* (see Example 53). Lasting just two measures, this has the effect of a fanfare calling attention to the return of the principal theme. The latter, with its characteristic first-measure leap omitted, is divided, its first half assigned to trumpets alone where it becomes an extension of the canonic figure. The trombones, lower strings and timpani are, meanwhile, re-engaged in firmly establishing the tonic by means of the drone figures used in the exposition. The violins and upper woodwinds continue to hammer out the development's main material until they exchange it for the second half of the principal theme. Tension is thus built up briefly over what is, in effect, an overlapping of the development and recapitulation, because, in listening to these few measures, one is not sure which section will ultimately prevail. However, it is not a 'dark' or 'tragic' tension, for everything I have been discussing in this paragraph has a buoyant, even triumphant sound. But the tension serves a vital purpose in the design: it serves notice that a major structural change is taking place. From the last beat of measure 177 to measure 192 the recapitulation and exposition are essentially the same, the only difference being minor alterations in the instrumentation. The diminutive bridge passage of just six measures bears no resemblance at all to its predecessor in the exposition. The brooding theme of the latter, which earlier was so prominent, is not heard again.

Theme 2, now in F, reappears for its one complete statement, begun this time by solo clarinet instead of oboe. The presence of soft, sustained strings and horns plus a softly-rolled timpani part bestows a somewhat gentler quality than was heard in the exposition's all-woodwind presentation. This is emphasized even more when the theme's second half is played in octaves by *divisi* first violins. As in the exposition, much is then made of the rising scale figure and its inversion in contrapuntal combinations, except that here the passage is twice as short.

A very abrupt key change from F to D flat ushers in the striking coda. Its fifteen measures and quiet, reflective mood provide a perfect balance for the introduction and the listener feels he has come full circle, so strong is the sense of unity. The material is derived from Theme 1 and the introduction. Harp and strings are prominent as in the introduction, but the sound is richer. There is a final shift to the tonic – F major – and the movement is over.

Looking back on this first movement as a whole, several features impress the listener. Perhaps foremost is the rhythmic vitality, a great deal of which is the result of tensions set up by 1) syncopations within the basic 6/8 metre; 2) by the simultaneous use for short periods of 6/8 and what amounts to 3/4; and finally, the combination of 1) and 2). Rubbra is careful, however, to establish the macrorhythm first, only gradually introducing syncopations, and waiting until the principal theme has gone through four statements before injecting the more complex microrhythms into the texture. A second point with respect to rhythm that almost any listener will notice is the contrast between these subtleties and the absolutely straightforward 3/4 metre in which the second theme is presented. This difference is welcome simply because rhythmic complications, if allowed to continue for too long a time, tend to lose their appeal and to become tedious.

Still another notable point about the first movement is the control the composer has imposed on his material; it does his bidding. This has not always been the case in the fast movements of some of his earlier symphonies. The happy result here owes much to the directness and uncomplicated nature of the material itself.

The second movement, 'Canto', is widely regarded as one of the most beautiful of all Rubbra's slow movements. At the head of the score, and in Italian, are the first three lines of the poem, 'L'Infinito' by Count Giacomo Leopardi (1798–1837). Rubbra, in his programme notes for the symphony's first performance, provided R.C. Trevelyan's translation of the poem's first six lines:

> Dear to me always was this lonely hill,
> And this hedge that excludes so large a part
> Of the ultimate horizon from my view.
> But as I sit and gaze, my thought conceives
> Interminable vastnesses of space
> Beyond it, and unearthly silences,
> And profoundest calm; [50]

The gentle melancholy of this sonnet, realized to the full in the last line, 'In such a sea shipwreck is sweet', is a continuing characteristic of Leopardi's poetry for, despite the nobility of his background, his family was very poor and his childhood was not a happy one. In addition, he was a lifelong cripple. All of these factors were responsible for a very personal and pessimistic idiom. He also wrote prose works, and was one of the foremost classical scholars of his time.

With reference to the poem, Rubbra tells us that 'although Leopardi speaks of an Italian landscape, it is one that is also intimately mine from the window of my workroom [in the Chilterns]'.[51] In his perceptive remarks on the music of this movement, Ottaway makes an interesting connection between it and the poem. After observing that the music 'has little in common with the English pastoral idiom of the last forty years or so', he concludes that 'it is closer, perhaps, to the poet's Italian landscape: some of the textures have the quality of light that is so familiar from early Italian painting.'[52] While this is, of course, a subjective judgement, there is no doubt that much of the very real intensity of this movement is a matter of instrumental colour. There are passages where the light is brilliant and others where it is darkly glowing. But more tangible is Ottaway's assertion that 'an early music, too, may have played its part – something much more remote than that of our own Elizabethans.'[53]

It must be admitted that attempts to identify this 'early music' in other than the most general terms have proved futile, and the only thing to be said is that vague reminders surface here and there. For example, the traditional cadence figure – eight, sharped seven, eight – in which the first note is suspended above dominant harmony recalls late Renaissance practice when the final resolution is to a tonic, and early Renaissance procedure when the resolution is to an empty fifth that is not a tonic. And in measures 33–6 a hint of organum and discant is heard in the softly rising and falling chords, formed by six string parts (basses, *divisi* cellos, viola, *divisi* second violins) and first and second horns. Above this, the first violins sing an undulating, chromatic melody.

As Rubbra reminds us, the fifth (A–E), stemming from the famous (or infamous) four notes inscribed at the head of the first movement, was intended to serve only as a starting point and the music that follows is 'a gradual enrichment of the bare essentials of the opening'.[54] While the fifths are not germinal, they do serve two important functions: an harmonic background to the melodic segments, and a colouristic element. Both functions are evident in the first fifteen measures, the second of them active at the outset where the bare fifths by themselves establish the sense of loneliness expressed in the poem's first line. By the third measure the fifths form the foundation beneath the unadorned solo clarinet melody. This melody contains in embryo much of the 'gradual enrichment' that follows (Example 57). The solo oboe at measure 17 begins an expansion of this thought

Ex. 57

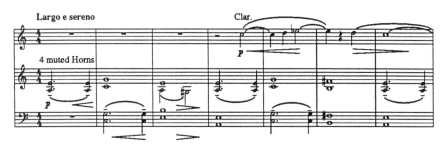

and during its second half a typical Rubbran technique may be observed: a simultaneous augmentation in the harp part of the oboe passage immediately above it (Example 58). Below the harp, violas and cellos, muted and *divisi*, add

Ex. 58

depth to the harp part by doubling it in sixths. Soon the violins enter for the first time, muted, and there is further expansion of the basic material. This includes a one-measure inversion and diminution of measures 9–10 at a higher pitch level. From this point to the double bar after measure 37 the miracle that is the compositional process has taken over to the degree that it is virtually impossible to trace the music back to any particular point, although relationships with respect to individual intervals can be recognized. A completely new line has been forged, the first half of which consists of a close imitation against a background of horn fifths. The second half contains the twisting, chromatic violin line mentioned above with reference to the organum and discant texture.

The double bar at the end of measure 37 introduces a new phase of the movement when, accompanied by another passage of bare fifths, the solo violin enters with the phrase shown in Example 59. (This is one of the passages

Ex. 59

referred to earlier in connection with light – in this instance a momentarily brilliant light, but there is an immediate darkening when the entire string section enters *pianissimo*.) The bracketed portion of the example is the first of a number of ostinato entries distributed throughout all sections of the orchestra. The second, third and fourth statements in the lower strings are skilfully combined with the violins' augmented version of the solo oboe's passage in measures 22–4. Oddly enough, the violins do not participate in the ostinato until the climax of the section (except for one inversion of the figure). The climax is ushered in by trombones and timpani beating out a very tense figure, ♩♩ ♩., spread over eight measures. At the height of the climax the ostinato pattern is heard in diminution for two *fortissimo* statements.

This entire middle section reminds one of the similar section in the slow movement of the Second Symphony, but there are important differences. There, the cumulative force of the much longer ostinato passage is intense and overwhelming, whereas in this movement the section is short-lived and much more restrained. And instrumentation has relevance too: in the Second Symphony it is heavier because more instruments are involved in the ostinatos.

After this peak has subsided some of the opening material of the movement is repeated literally, and scored in the same sparse manner, but fresh variants grow from it and the movement is brought to a tranquil and *pianissimo* close by a typically Rubbran cor anglais phrase. Thus at movement's end an inexact ternary structure has evolved – one whose first and third sections are based more on similarities in mood than on sameness of thematic material. Such a structural interpretation is thoroughly in keeping with Rubbra's improvisatory manner of composition.

The composer refers to his third-movement scherzo as 'unbuttoned in its energy'.[55] Its starting point is, of course, the notes E-F from the basic series E-F-A-B. To these notes are added four others which, by now, are thoroughly familiar for they are the same four from which most of the first-movement development was fashioned. Example 60 shows how quickly these elements are subjected to change and variation (measures 4–8). Most of the subsequent

Ex. 60

attention is concentrated on the four-note figure (*b*) which the composer described as 'ubiquitous, turning up elongated, upside-down, embedded in melody
or accompaniment, and rhythmically transformed'.[56]

With so much going on it is small wonder that the movement is monothematic.
The material is treated so interestingly, and one becomes so involved in its
various manifestations that the introduction of another theme would seem almost an intrusion. Thus there is no trio in the generally accepted sense, but
there is a middle section where different aspects of the same material are
expressed in duple metre rather than in the 3/4 of the two flanking sections. As
for the latter, they are identical except for the non-repetition of the first seven
measures and the final forty-two, the latter having been replaced by a fourteen-
measure, *lento* coda. An unequal ternary structure thus results in which section
B seems to consist of new material, an illusion brought about by the change to
the 3/4 metre, the introduction of triplets, and the development of figures used
earlier. Apropos this structure, the composer says that 'the form is that of a
rondo, but the intermediate sections achieve contrast by virtue of rhythmic
rather than melodic change.'[57]

Owing to the monothematicism of the movement, it is predictably difficult
to separate recurring statements from episodes, but with care it can be done.
The following scheme relating to the first *A* section represents one possible interpretation among several. (Section *B* can be dismissed immediately as not
having its own scheme of statements and episodes because of its short, fifty-
one measure length, most of which is through-composed. The final *A* is naturally dependent on the first *A* and, as we have just seen, the two are unequal in
length.) The scheme is based on the general premise that during the episodes
the four-note figure is restricted to interior or subordinate parts, while more
prominent instruments are assigned some of the new elements that have evolved
from the original material. The most notable example of this is Episode 2 where
harp and celesta – the latter instrument a newcomer to Rubbra's orchestra –
attract attention with ostinato figures of irregular length.

Statement 1	mm.	1–24
Episode 1	mm.	25–51
Statement 2	mm.	51–70
Episode 2	mm.	71–100
Statement 3	mm.	100–145
Episode 3	mm.	146–179

Yet no formal scheme, no matter how varied, seems really important in the face of the music's boundless vigour and seemingly endless capacity for self-renewal. In the first instance, the vigour resides in the inherent nature of the theme itself, but as the movement progresses it is the syncopations and other rhythmic devices which are ultimately responsible for the exciting buildup. The movement is simply propelled to its final climax in a lighthearted manner that quite conceals the complications of its composition. I suppose there must be some listeners who feel let down by the gradual *rallentando* and *diminuendo* that lead from measure 357 to the *lento* coda at measure 365, and then by the coda itself. It takes courage to be different and I know of no other scherzo whose forward motion is deliberately broken so near to the end. Yet interest is by no means lost, for as the texture thins out the solo flute's variant of the theme is the paramount factor, and it ensures one's attention. Also, this soft and slow coda is a unifying element, preparing the listener for the long *andante* introduction with which the fourth movement begins.

This introduction 'commences with an unaccompanied theme for cor anglais, which starts with all four of the basic notes [E-F-A-B]'.[58] (This is reproduced in Example 61.) Its fifty-five measure length raises questions about its structural

Ex. 61

function that are even more pertinent than those associated with the short first-movement introduction. Rubbra's further remarks provide clues when he says, 'for purposes of ultimate development, it is the octave leap between bars 4 and 5 that is important. The antithesis of leaping figure and conjunct thematic material forms the basis for subsequent development'.[59] Thus the introduction would appear to be a repository of motivic material from which the succeeding and main section of the movement will draw. But it is much more than this for, as the composer reminds us, 'it has its development and climax',[60] and the expressiveness with which it moves from the former to the latter is memorable.

The earliest example of this expressiveness is, of course, the cor anglais melody itself, but immediately following it are the two string passages (measures 8–12, 15–18) wherein the developmental process is begun. Other notably expressive passages are those later ones where the timbre of the cor anglais penetrates and enriches the surrounding orchestral fabric with its persistent E-F-A-B pattern (measures 21–2 and especially 36–41). As the material is assimilated and enlarged upon, the rhythmic flow becomes more liquid with the appearance of eighths and sixteenths. A two-measure *accelerando* leads directly into the *Allegro moderato* movement.

When the principal theme of the *Allegro* is sounded in the first violins and first trumpet the relationship between it and the introductory material becomes instantly clear: the latter's octave leaps and conjunct material, couched here in a setting of dotted quarters and eighths, are combined with the theme in close, imitative counterpoint. As for the theme itself, it is a sixteen-measure affair, firmly matter-of-fact in its intervallic construction and rhythmic regularity (Example 62). Altogether, it is heard three times, twice in E flat and the third time

Ex. 62

in A. The material associated with the second statement is quite different from the introductory material surrounding the first statement in that it is not contrapuntal. Its thicker texture is derived from the doubling of instrumental parts, and its dotted rhythm, applied to shorter note values, is more insistent. When the A major appearance of Theme 1 bursts in after a short *adagio*, it is accompanied for its first two measures by a transposition of the material surrounding the first statement, but thereafter more new material produces still greater rhythmic tension. (Despite the references to new and different accompanimental materials in this discussion, it is possible to trace relationships from one to another. Considering Rubbra's compositional procedures, there is nothing startling in this.) This new material consists of a very conventional sequence in sixteenths: I–IV, VII–III, VI–II, V–I.

Between the first and second appearances of Theme 1 there is a subordinate theme, marked *grazioso*, which is similar in its plainness to the first theme (Example 63). Its one repetition, in C (measures 205–11), leads into the final and triumphant thirteen measures of the movement.

Meanwhile, E-F-A-B and its transpositions have by no means been idle, but, significantly, they do not appear while Theme 1 and the *grazioso* theme are

Ex. 63

sounding. I would suggest that the reason for this is to ensure that the listener's attention is directed to the principal material. In the sections between statements of the latter, E-F-A-B is prominent in particular instrumental combinations, but it is never sounded by the full orchestra. Some examples of it are found in measures 74–5, violins; 78–9, first trumpet, first trombone; 107–10, woodwinds (three incisive, *fortissimo* statements, each in the following rhythmic pattern: ♪♩ ♪ ♩ ♪, and starting, respectively, on F, C, and G); 125–31, first horn (two statements, each with a different ending). Following several other entries there is a final one between the end of the A major appearance of Theme 1 and the second entry of the *grazioso* theme (measures 191–7, first violas, cellos and cor anglais). This entry is more complete than those we have just considered, for it contains the octave leap that was such a prominent characteristic of the first statement back in the introduction.

Insofar as structure is concerned, this movement has no formal plan to which a label can be given. Yet certainly no one would ever regard it as formless. The structure is entirely generated by the logical progression and manipulation of all of the material. One is reminded of J.A. Westrup's words in connection with the Fourth Symphony, for they are equally valid here: 'yet nothing in it ... follows a formal plan which can be foreseen by the listener; it is rather that the design appears logical when complete'.[61]

Critical comments regarding the symphony were uniformly favourable. Starting with the most extensive review, we read that

> in his Sixth Symphony Rubbra, long a master in this field, is happily at ease with himself, with his forms and with his colours, and in consequence we can feel the rare and pleasurable thrill of being held in so untrembling and certain a grasp. This effect of clarity and certainty is enhanced by the bright scoring and the happy diatonic tunes. Lest this praise should be counted as damnation in those quarters where 'extravert' is the fashionable term of mild abuse, it should be added that the work is cunningly constructed with many subtle cross-references and the derivation of much material from the falling fifth which is prominent at the beginning [in the introduction to the first movement]. The composer is at pains, however, to make these transformations clearly audible and, musically speaking, dramatic. They are not simply a composer's means of keeping going; there is plenty of straw for the bricks. The work has not unnaturally already had quick success and will doubtless deservedly have more.[62]

Ottaway, without mentioning certain previous Rubbra symphonies, but obviously having some in mind, remarks on this work's

> greater warmth and ease ... the counterpoint is never self-conscious here, for the whole thing has been fully imagined ... a landmark in Rubbra's development.[63]

Three newspaper reviews are also full of praise. In the *News Chronicle*, Scott Goddard refers to the work in the following terms:

> A noble new symphony. There is no gainsaying the intrinsic beauty and power of this music. It is in every way a remarkable work, splendidly proportioned, nobly conceived, a great enrichment of our symphonic music.

Martin Cooper in *The Daily Telegraph*:

> A major success for Rubbra. He has achieved his first unqualified major success as a symphonist. It is a work whose themes are easy to grasp and retain, simple yet skilful in construction. A work which will reveal more and grow in stature with performance. A real triumph for its composer.

Finally, the critic of *The Manchester Guardian* says

> He is first and foremost a symphonist with the gift of distinctive melody and a craftsmanship that, over and over again in this latest work, touches genius.

Each hearing of the Sixth Symphony reinforces one's impression that, except for the hauntingly beautiful slow movement – *Canto* – this is certainly one of Rubbra's most ebullient and extrovert works. Could this be at all responsible for the enthusiasm exhibited in the above reviews? And, conversely, would these reviews have been as enthusiastic had the symphony displayed a larger proportion of inwardness than is contained in the *Canto*? These questions are in no way meant to downgrade the solid achievement which this symphony represents, but simply to report that one often looks in vain for such enthusiasm following the debuts of Rubbra's quiet and more subjective works, not just in the symphonic field but in most other genres as well. As with the Fifth Symphony, there was an encouraging report from America concerning the Sixth, again from Bernard Hermann, who wrote on 9 July 1956,

> I have been asked to come back to London and do some concerts with the LSO next May, and my present plans are to return to England between May 1st and July 1st of next year. I also, of course, will do my utmost to see that we do the Sixth Symphony in public. I shall be most curious to learn if J.B. [John Barbirolli] approved of the changes we made together. I have played the records of it to some of my friends here, and they were all most deeply moved and impressed with your magnificent work. The more I hear it, the more I think about it, and the more I am convinced that not only is it a most glorious piece of music, but to have known it is to have enriched one's life. That, I feel, is the true great mission of music. Again, Bravo, Edmund, and thank you.

Soon after the completion of the Fifth and Sixth Symphonies, Rubbra had sent a score of each to Sibelius. In each case, he had received a note of thanks containing favourable but very general comments – too general, really, to be of value.

Symphony No. 7 in C

'This work was commissioned by and is dedicated to the City of Birmingham Symphony Orchestra. The first performance was given by them under Andrzej Panufnik on October 1st 1957.' So reads the note in the facing page of the score. It occupied the composer during 1956–7 and is Op. 88 in the list of his works.

In a number of Rubbra symphonies there is at least one movement that conforms structurally to one of the standard classical plans. Thus the fourth movement of No. 2 is a rondo, the first movement of No. 3 is a modified sonata form, while the fourth is a set of seven variations and a fugue, and No. 6 opens with a sonata movement. In No. 7 each of the three movements is formally structured: the first is a sonata form, the second a scherzo with two trios (although the usual scherzo after the second trio is replaced by a coda), and the third a passacaglia and fugue (certainly not a classical form, but of the three movements the most rigidly structured).

The overall structure of the first movement is very clear: slow introduction (1–33); exposition (34–131); development (132–227); recapitulation (228–93); and coda (294–305), which features a shortened version of the slow introduction. However, the movement is quite unconventional because of the presence in every section except the coda of a four-note motive consisting of two rising semitones and a falling fifth. It can be seen on virtually every page of the score up to the beginning of the coda. It is introduced in isolation over a C pedal at the commencement of the introduction (Example 64), but it is not itself one of

Ex. 64

the three themes of the movement, although it is incorporated in the second and third themes. Its cardinal importance is clearly demonstrated by the number of its separate appearances (90), and the manner in which it permeates the entire compositional and orchestral fabric. It is always recognizable, even on the few occasions when it is inverted, because its intervallic structure is always preserved, but its most fascinating aspects derive from its extremely varied rhythmic presentations and its distribution throughout the orchestra.

With regard to the first of these aspects there are at least ten different metrical patterns – some of them quite syncopated, especially when the motive is blocked out in quarters against the prevailing 6/8 metre, together with displacements in which the motive begins on the third quarter of the measure and finishes on the third quarter of the following measure. Some patterns are long while others are short. Interesting combinations result when two different rhythmic patterns of unequal lengths are scored simultaneously in pairs, one unequal pair in one orchestral choir and the other in a different section. This can be seen in measure 82 where the longer pattern is in the upper woodwinds and violas while the shorter one is scored for the lower woodwinds and cellos. With the conclusion of the longer pattern on the first beat of 83 the short pattern in the bassoons and cellos is repeated, accompanied by an inversion of the longer pattern in the clarinets and violas. Such interlockings are fairly common, although perhaps not as common as one might expect, given the prototype in Example 64. However, since all these instances are cast in one of the standard 6/8 patterns, they are not as highlighted as the patterns composed of the three quarters. These stride boldly across the whole orchestra and are particularly noticeable when they are scored for brass and/or the high string register.

From this it would be easy to conclude that the four-note motive completely dominates the movement, but this is not so. Although its appearance on any page and in any instrumental part is unpredictable, the motive always functions as an integral member of the total fabric, and as such it flows logically from preceding passages to subsequent ones. Of course, it may, and often does dominate the texture for the moment.

Since this motive is not, in and of itself, one of the main themes, the question may be legitimately raised as to its purpose. Ottaway suggests an answer: 'Rubbra seeks to reconcile the freer, more open experience of No. 6 with the functioning of a basic germinal idea.' But then he denies the motive's germinal nature: 'its presence among the themes of the *Allegro* is that of a common factor rather than an origin.'[64] Since it neither germinates nor is subjected to dissection – the second function of Rubbra's motivic figures – the real reason for its presence in the midst of a sonata structure is unclear.

The *Lento e molto espressivo* introduction serves as the fountainhead for more than just the four-note motive, for material associated with the principal themes in the following *Allegro moderato* has its origin here. Nor is this all, for certain of the scherzo's material can be traced back to this opening.

The principal subject of the *Allegro moderato* is stated by flutes and clarinets in C minor (there is no key signature) and consists of four segments set apart from one another by an eighth rest (Example 65). Except for the rising

Ex. 65

fourth and third near the end the entire theme is conjunct. The rising and falling thirds outlined by the first five notes of segment 2 come from the same figure in measures 19–20 of the introduction (flute and oboe), while the rhythmic figure of two staccato eighths and a dotted quarter with which segment 3 opens is derived from the accompanimental groupings in the woodwinds starting in measure 18. Another rhythmic pattern, starting with the dotted quarter of the fifth measure of Example 65 and ending with the dotted quarter of the sixth measure, has its origin in the introduction in measure 17 where, again, it is an accompanimental figure (strings). Although in this first statement of Theme 1 the two rhythmic figures just mentioned overlap one another they soon operate independently, and the second figure is often shortened through the omission of the last dotted quarter.

Owing to Rubbra's frequent use of 6/8 metre and the diatonic nature of his themes, it is sometimes difficult to distinguish one theme from another, and the difficulty is compounded when his themes are lightly scored. To put it another way, the principal themes are likely to be very similar. A further obstacle to precise identification is the fact that only rarely are there tonic-dominant or tonic-relative major relationships between themes.

Fortunately, in the present instance the very disjunct nature of the second theme is an important identifying factor. The theme consists of two unequal parts in terms of both length and content, and extends from measure 54 through the fourth beat of measure 68. Its first two notes are obviously derived from the staccato notes of Theme 1's segment 3. However, these notes have a new function here, for they introduce a new rhythmic version of the familiar four-note motive, which, as mentioned above, is a part of this theme. Thereafter, the remainder of the theme's first section climbs rapidly in a disjunct contour, as seen in Example 66. The second part of the theme is longer and employs the

Ex. 66

following rhythmic figure: ♪ ♩ ♩ ♩ ♪ . This comes from the third segment of Theme 1. Except for measure 68 it is used almost everywhere and its reproduction at various pitches, as well as small connecting links between some of its appearances, adds up to a melodic line. Upon its conclusion material from Theme 1 takes over, soon joined by various rhythmic versions of the four-note motive.

A third theme appears in measure 86, finishing on the first beat of measure 92. This is composed of a dotted figure and the four-note motive, the latter now in a cross-rhythm of quarters against the 6/8 pattern. Ottaway believes this theme to be the second,[65] but tending to support my view is the fact that the development commences with statements of my Theme 2 – an admission, it seems to me, of its importance. It is quite true that these developmental statements omit the second part of the theme, but this is a completely normal situation given the freedom of the developmental process.

There is a conventional double bar separating the exposition from the ninety-six measures of the development. It goes without saying that the latter contains interesting variants of the principal materials that interact melodically and rhythmically in all sorts of ways. A new variant not heard before is the inverted form of the four-note motive. Altogether, there are only four instances of it, but three of these are prominent in the strings, and are near enough to the original forms to offer interesting contrasts.

In the recapitulation all three themes reappear in keys different from those chosen for their initial statements in the exposition (a common Rubbra trait observed in earlier symphonies and in those still to come), but shortly before the *Lento* coda, there is a strong gravitational pull to C major in which key the movement quietly ends with reminiscences of the slow introduction.

The ground plan of the second movement is asymmetrical: Scherzo 1, 154 measures; Trio 1, 55 measures; Scherzo 2, 76 measures; Trio 2, 37 measures; and coda, 26 measures. This asymmetry causes no discomfort in terms of too much of one section and not enough of another because the great wealth of material and the imagination of the composer in manipulating it have, together, created a strong, virile movement that holds the listener's interest from first to last. The almost bewildering abundance of material is under strict control, yet at the same time the impression of unrestrained improvisatory freedom is preserved.

If the wealth of melodic material is examined more closely, what appear to be new melodies prove to be quite subtle variants of some of the segments into which the primary scherzo theme can be divided. Thus what might have seemed an overly long Scherzo 1 is divisible into nine unequal sections of which six are variations on some aspect of the basic theme. The melodic substance in some of these sections is so transformed as to require great effort in tracking it to its origin. Yet the basic elements of the scherzo theme are not overlooked, for loud brass passages employing the characteristic figure in measure 2 abruptly terminate sections 2 through 5. As section 6 with its concluding fermatas leads directly into a shortened version of the scherzo theme, no brass passage is needed. At the end of section 8 *fortissimo* woodwinds, followed by brass, prepare the way for the final section of the first scherzo – a free statement of the theme.

This theme, shown in Example 67 where its important segments are within brackets, is a very terse affair of eight measures. As the example indicates, the theme is divided between strings and woodwinds. Within the first segment two small fragments are important: the opening three-note dotted figure, which seemingly originates in measure 105 of the first movement, and the downward-leaping diminished fifth that frequently becomes an augmented fourth. (Whichever way this interval is spelled, its typical sound is one of the hallmarks of Rubbra's style – it dominates the Tenth Symphony, as we shall see.) Halfway

Ex. 67

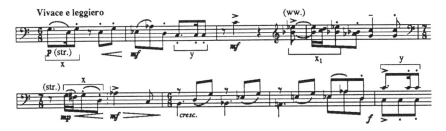

through the second, but altered, statement of the theme, a woodwind figure not previously heard (measure 15) assumes importance as the movement progresses. It is merely a filled-in, descending fourth (set in thirds for pairs of instruments). It also appears to originate in the first movement (measures 34–5, the head of that movement's first theme).

Measure 24 marks the opening of the very short second section in which there is a violin melody consisting of the augmented fourth referred to above and the five-note figure of measures 1 and 2. The accompanimental pattern in the bassoons and lower strings is a combination of the dotted quarters and two eighths of measure 6. This is one of the simpler examples of Rubbra's compositional methods regarding the evolution of materials. The forthcoming variants are, for the most part, far more complex and subtle because they involve the transformation of fragments into new and almost unrecognizable entities through the addition of notes before, in the middle of, and following the fragments. Significant changes in pitch contours also occur. To trace the exact derivation of every note in each variant is thus obviously impractical. With this in mind, a few further examples from the remaining scherzo sections will suffice.

The third and fourth sections, separated by the brass passage, are both violin-dominated. In section 4 use is made for the first time of an ascending figure in thirds, first heard in the woodwinds in measures 13–15. Here the violins have it and descending motion is added. Between sections 4 and 5 a particularly striking *fortissimo* statement of the brass figure in canon and augmentation is heard. The fifth section is more easily traced back to its source, for the descending four-note first violin and viola figure comes from measure 15. Its exact counterpart with slight metrical differences appears in the violin parts of measures 114–18, first movement. Between sections 5 and 6 an augmented brass statement intervenes. Section 6 features a syncopated figure in the strings, dominated in the first violins by a falling diminished fifth and major second (source: measure 2). Above, in the woodwinds, is heard a rather dry little melody made up of previously heard figures. A shortened version of the main scherzo theme (section 7) is followed in the next section by alternating metrical patterns: 7/8 and 5/8, and later on, 9/8 and various other metres. The woodwinds and violins play an ingenious melody composed of fragments of the principal theme, linked together by logical threads. This section moves smoothly into the last of the nine sections, a free rendition of the original material.

A possible second internal structure involving the first scherzo section can be argued, based solely on metrical divisions. Thus the first thirty-four measures are taken up with materials set in 6/8, 5/8 and so on, the next sixty-five are in 3/4 with the exception of one measure of 5/4, while the concluding fifty-five measures return to the metres of the first metrical division. I doubt very much that this second internal structure was the result of conscious planning, and it may even well be that the nine sections pointed out above are entirely fortuitous.

The two trios are very different from one another. Trio 1, in duple metre except for occasional changes, is composed of two distinct parts. The first of these, marked *giocoso*, is very lively and high-spirited, while the second consists of a rather poignant and dry melody in the woodwinds over an ostinato in the low strings. This section broadens considerably at its end into a blazing *crescendo* containing elements of the scherzo theme, and it leads naturally into the second appearance of the scherzo.

The first half of Trio 1 immediately shows that its source is segment x^1 of the scherzo theme (see Example 67) but the segment x^1 figure appears in the second violins two beats after its inverted form has been sounded in the first violins. Thereafter both forms of the figure merrily pursue their way through all sorts of combinations and extensions including scale-wise passages derived from the descending fourth of measure 15. When Part 2 is reached, the little melody in the first bassoon turns out to have also originated in segment x^1, most probably via the second violins at the start of the trio. The second bassoon's opening counterpoint comes from this same second violin part and the ostinato figure in the low strings is a direct transposition of the opening of the first violin's *giocoso* melody. As Part 2 proceeds, the thirds in the woodwinds are also seen to be related melodically and rhythmically to segment x^1.

After an abridged return of the scherzo (seventy-six measures), the stately melody of Trio 2, introduced by a soft gong stroke, comes as a surprise. Even more surprising is the discovery that the majestic ostinato figure, which strides in syncopated half notes through the brass, and rhythmically right across the string melody, is intervalically identical to the second violin's figure in measure 1 of the first trio. The string melody begins with a quarter-note version of the same intervals and the same pitch as those of Trio 1, measure 1, before dissolving into extensions of various kinds. Another big buildup similar to the one that ends Trio 1 leads to the free treatment of the shortened scherzo in the coda.

In looking back on this movement it is, perhaps, instructive to quote the composer's words: 'here, everything grows out of a rhythmic scheme, ♩♪♪ rather than a melodic one, with intervening tunes that are thrown out, as it were, haphazardly in the general bustle.'[66] As one listens to the interaction of these rhythmic elements with the astonishingly inventive expansion of thematic material, the thought keeps coming back that many a composer would be delighted if he could only be this 'haphazard'.

The third and final movement of the Seventh Symphony is a passacaglia and fugue. The passacaglia is very unusual in that it is cast not in the traditional triple metre but in 8/8. Other unusual features are that the concluding two measures of the theme's eight-measure length are identical to the first two, and the fifth and sixth measures are inversions at different pitch levels of the two opening and closing measures. The theme, shown in Example 68, is quiet and meditative but some of its later sections reach great peaks of intensity.

Ex. 68

I digress here for a moment to deal with a statement by Ottaway with which I am in complete disagreement, and which perplexes me. His statement reads: 'the very closely-knit finale, a passacaglia (*Lento*), *looks* as if it must be one of Rubbra's most satisfying achievements; but in performance this tends to move heavily, impaired by the burden of its own insistence.'[67] Taking the last clause first, is it not the nature of all passacaglias, chaconnes and ground basses to repeat to the extent that the word 'insistence' can be applied to all of them? The major characteristic of all these processes (*forms* would be the wrong word) *is* their insistence. Whether or not this insistence becomes a 'burden' seems to be a matter of personal taste. As for the heaviness, it almost goes without saying that this quality is a natural characteristic of most movements and pieces built on the ground bass principle. This is because of the slow tempi and solemn, often stately nature of their themes. When the other quality of insistence, caused by many repetitions is present, naturally the whole movement or piece will tend to move heavily. Thus it appears that Rubbra is being criticized for something that no composer of passacaglias, chaconnes and ground basses can avoid. Of course, from time to time in all works of these types changes in texture and/or scoring will considerably lighten the sound. This is very notice-able in Bach's organ passacaglia when the theme moves from the pedals to the manuals, particularly at those points where it is contained in delicate *arpeggios*. The last movement of Brahms's Fourth Symphony is another example where there are many changes in volume and texture as the full orchestra gives way to lighter instrumental combinations.

Rubbra's varied orchestration likewise provides many opportunities for con-trast between heavier and lighter textures. An important process in the achievement of this variety is the sharing of the theme by various instruments during the course of any one complete passacaglia statement. For example, in the first entry, cellos and basses set out the whole theme, joined by horns 1 and 2 from the end of the second measure through most of the fourth, at which time they rest; the violas enter with the triplet figure in measure 4 and remain through measure 8. This is one of the simpler distributions. Much more complex instrumentations may be observed during the eighth statement (beginning at measure 46). Here, oboes, first trombone and cellos are assigned the first two measures; the theme is then taken for the next two measures by clarinet 1, horns 1 and 3, and the top line of the *divisi* violas. The triplet is shared by oboes, first clarinet, bass clarinet, horns 1, 3, 4, first violins and violas 1 and 3, but only the oboes and first violins complete measures 5 and 6, and only the first violins go on to complete measures 7 and 8.

The score reveals, of course, the overlapping of sections caused by the sameness of the first and final two measures. Where there are no overlaps, it should not be assumed that sections are entirely independent at such points. To illustrate, section 7 finishes in measure 46 as expected, but this measure contains also the usual notes for a new entry of the subject. Measures 45 and 46 are therefore identical in this one respect. Which to choose as the correct start of a new statement? The principal criterion is the fact that the theme pursues its normal course after measure 46 and concludes in measure 53. The score tells us this, but a less sure answer is provided when the score is translated into sound. Then the notes of measure 1 (in measure 45) are heard more prominently than they are in 46 owing to the strength of the first trumpet, which is reinforcing the violins. However, if the listener follows closely the progress of the violins *after* the apparent new entry in 45, he will hear a soaring line that commands his attention, not with the familiar notes but with a sequential treatment of them. In measure 49 the violins sound the triplet figure in the expected pitches, and the theme concludes four measures later as it should. Counting back from that point the true start is heard to be in measure 46 where the first trombone cooperates with the oboe and low strings in announcing the start of the theme, but not so as to detract from the violin's individuality.

Unlike the Bach organ passacaglia and the chaconne from Brahms's Fourth Symphony, Rubbra's passacaglia is not divided into sections where a particular texture, melodic figure, or rhythmic pattern is singled out for special attention. Rather, it is unpredictable, a quality made immediately apparent by the non-variational approach and the manner in which the theme is not preserved as a unit in any one choir or group of instruments, but is divided up and shared by diverse groupings. This unpredictability is one of Rubbra's characteristics, and is the reason this movement seems more flowing and less rigid than the Bach and Brahms pieces. However, it is certainly no less a passacaglia for these reasons. In fact, its flexibility is the quality that contributes so much to its expressiveness because no restrictive formal considerations inhibit it.

When the theme is first stated little promise is given of the flexibility to follow but shortly after the beginning of the second statement, the free treatment and the emotional intensity to come are apparent as the first violins in measure 9 embark on a counterpoint that steadily rises in pitch and expressiveness to its peak in measure 14. In approaching and reaching this climax, the passage ignores the start of the third statement, and in straddling the line between statements – a normal procedure throughout the movement – the theory is confirmed that the movement was not conceived as a set of variations but as a continuously flowing entity. Each of the passages leading to subsequent peaks is longer, and the climaxes themselves are more intense as the movement progresses.

An intriguing aspect of this passacaglia is the manner in which short portions of the theme, acting as counterpoints to the same or different parts of the theme, weave in and out of the fabric. Since some segment of the theme is always present, it is obviously necessary for the counterpoints to appear on pitches quite different from any of those sounded in the recurring statements, for to do otherwise would obscure the basic plan of the repetitions. Rubbra is careful to preserve the integrity of the basic plan not only in this respect but also by sometimes staggering the contrapuntal segments rhythmically. Thus when they enter a beat or two later than their 'legitimate' counterparts, the latter's importance is assured, but by the same token Rubbra also preserves the independence of the counterpoints. Sometimes the counterpoints are inversions of their thematic counterparts and this thrusts them into prominence.

The whole idea of introducing segments of a recurring theme as counterpoints to that theme is fraught with danger, but Rubbra successfully overcomes the difficulties by making the momentary ambiguities intelligible. The best illustrations of this can be found beginning with measure 18. There, in the flutes, first bassoon, second violins and violas, the equivalent of measures 1 and 7 is heard, but anchored on F sharp. This figure is completed in measure 19 (corresponding to measures 2 and 8). Simultaneously with the B flat on the second beat of 19 – the conclusion of the counterpoint – another appearance of the same figure on B flat is heard in the horns, while on the second half of the third beat an inversion of the same figure commences in the first trumpet and violins, concluding on beat 4 of measure 20. All this time the bassoons, cellos and basses are occupied with the sixth through eighth measures of statement 3 of the theme and, of course, because of the normal overlap, the first two measures of statement 4. Other examples of this same procedure are found later in the score.

One of the challenges implicit in pieces or movements build on a recurring bass is that of providing harmonic interest and variety in conjunction with the repeating and unyielding theme, but without jeopardizing the fundamental unity that is so important in pieces of this sort. Rubbra's passacaglia is rather ingeniously constructed in this regard, for the harmonic indefiniteness of its subject implies E flat major and C minor. This leaves him free to suggest first one, then the other, and he does so by harmonizing the frequent Gs as the mediant of E flat, the dominant of C minor/major and also I in G minor. Variety is provided through dissonances of a mild sort, brought about by the contrapuntal movement of melodic lines.

One further passage just prior to the fugue deserves mention. What seems like the start of the fourteenth and final statement of the passacaglia theme is heard in measure 90, but by the middle of 92 it is obvious that the theme has given way to free treatment. However, threads of the original remain, for the first oboe in its *molto espressivo* sixteenth notes of measures 92–3 condenses the first four measures in the form of a diminution, and the first violins continue with the triplet figure and the leap of the minor sixth before abandoning the theme. The first trumpet in measure 95 repeats the triplet and goes on to complete all of measure 6 except the fourth beat. The answering downward leap of a major sixth in the first violins is from A to C, not C to E flat, and the stage is set for the fugue. The *fortissimo* and *allargando* climax of measures 95–6 is a fitting conclusion (although there is no cadence) to this deeply moving passacaglia, which, despite his reservations, Ottaway pronounced, 'one of the finest things that Rubbra has given us.'[68]

The brief fugue flows directly from the passacaglia's final measure, as the solo clarinet softly intones the gentle subject. In a letter to Ottaway, the composer observed that this subject is 'free of definite suggestion of the passacaglia theme except for the reference to the middle of the theme with its leap of a sixth'.[69] In Example 69 this relationship is bracketed. The answer is real; the

Ex. 69

remainder of the exposition proceeds normally, the answer coming in the first bassoon, the subject's second statement in the first oboe, and the second answer in the cellos and basses. There is no countersubject. After a short episode the subject appears, *forte*, in the second violins and violas, accompanied by its diminution in the flutes and oboes. Two further *forte* entries (horns followed by trombones and *pizzicato* strings) give way to the fugue's longest episode. 'Towards the climax, the theme is used simultaneously with its inversions.'[70] When these entries are concluded the brief *fortissimo* climax contains the subject right-side up. Following one more simultaneous but abbreviated entry of the subject and its inversion, the fugue breaks off, its remnants continuing over into a quiet half statement of the passacaglia theme.

I myself am grateful for this brief reminder of the passacaglia, for I must confess to ambivalent feelings with respect to the fugue. Sometimes I am happy with it while at other times I feel it is too academic, and an anticlimax after the inspired passacaglia. Undoubtedly these are personal and subjective reactions, but they find an echo in Harold Rutland's review of the symphony's premiere in Birmingham Town Hall, 1 October 1957: 'I was a little puzzled by the final fugue, which seemed to have small relevance to the rest of the work.'[71]

Further excerpts from Rutland's review appear below:

> The new symphony is not only an impressive piece of musical architecture; it gives evidence of a strength and a warmth of feeling that have not always been present in Rubbra's previous works.... At a first hearing, I felt that the Scherzo might have provided a more striking contrast with the two outer movements [I disagree entirely with this last observation] ... and I felt that, even in this work (though to a lesser degree than formerly), the composer too often had recourse to contrapuntal devices to keep the music moving. Subsequent performances of the Symphony may, however, cause me to change my mind.[72]

Following the symphony's next performance, Ernest Bradbury had this to say:

> On 8 October, the night after the première of his *Festival Gloria*, Edmund Rubbra returned to the Festival Hall for the first London performance of his Seventh Symphony. It was given by the City of Birmingham Symphony Orchestra under Panufnik, a week after its world première in Birmingham. And if there is light and air in the new *Gloria*, these qualities are certainly to be found in the new Symphony – especially light, which is indeed suggested by the key of the work, C major. It is possible to imagine a performance of greater intensity than the one on this occasion, also a performance in which the undoubted beauty of the music would flow with greater ease. Much has been made recently of Rubbra's 'emancipation' from his allegedly gloomy, or stodgy, musical past, and perhaps our orchestral players must also learn to appreciate his music in this 'new light'. Still, Mr. Panufnik had obviously taken pains with the Symphony's preparation, and he left his audience on the whole grateful for his work.[73]

The most probing review was penned by Alan Blyth:

> Out of joint with the times he may be, but sound workmanship as exemplified in the interesting construction and logical development of this symphony is not so easily come by; it may well outlive today's violent and exotic fashions.... In this symphony, unlike some of the earlier ones, the orchestration is finely calculated; the music's inner logic can be heard as well as seen. Perhaps the ideas themselves are not always very memorable; their treatment nearly always is.[74]

Just over a week after the Symphony's first performance on 1 October 1957, Rubbra received a letter from Bernard Stevens, composer, and Professor of Composition at the Royal College of Music. Dated 9 October, the letter reads:

> Many congratulations on No. 7. A great achievement, and the Passacaglia is one of the most moving things I know in music.

Notes

1   Edmund Rubbra, 'Symphony No. 5 in B flat, Op. 63', *MR* 10, no. 1, February 1949, pp.27–8.
2   Tape of 9 August 1980.

3   Rubbra, *op. cit.*, pp.28–9.
4   Hugh Ottaway, unpublished analysis of Symphony No. 5.
5   Rubbra, *op. cit.*, p.30.
6   *ibid.*, pp.30–31.
7   *ibid.*, p.31.
8   *ibid.*
9   *ibid.*, p.32.
10 Norman Demuth, 'Symphony No. 5.' In the booklet accompanying the 78 rpm recording of the work by the Hallé Orchestra, conducted by Sir John Barbirolli.
11 Ottaway, *op. cit.* It is interesting to recall that for the 'Périgourdine' movement of Symphony No. 1, Rubbra supplied 'bucolico' in connection with the tempo.
12 Rubbra, *op. cit.*, p.32.
13 *ibid.*
14 Ottaway, *op. cit.*
15 Demuth, *op. cit.*
16 Rubbra, *op. cit.*, p.32.
17 *ibid.*, p.33.
18 *ibid.*
19 *ibid.*
20 *ibid.*
21 *ibid.*, p.34.
22 *ibid.*
23 *ibid.*
24 *ibid.*, pp.34–5.
25 *ibid.*, p.35.
26 Ottaway, *op. cit.*
27 *ibid.*
28 W. McNaught, *MT*, March 1949, p.90.
29 Desmond Shawe-Taylor, *The New Statesman and Nation*, 15 July 1950. Printed in Hugh Ottaway, 'Rubbra's Sixth Symphony', *MT*, October 1955, p.528.
30 Ottaway, 'Rubbra's Sixth Symphony', *MT*, October 1955, p.528.
31 Olin Downes, *New York Times*, 3 December 1953.
32 Dyneley Hussey, 'Music in Great Britain After 1945', in Rollo H. Myers, (ed.), *Twentieth Century Music*, London: John Calder, 1960, p.191.
33 Stephen Banfield, *MT*, January 1982, p.36.
34 Walter Simmons, *Fanfare* 4, no. 6, July–August 1981, p.158.
35 Edmund Rubbra, 'Symphony No. 6', *London Musical Events*, December 1954.
36 Hugh Ottaway, 'A Note On Rubbra's Sixth Symphony', *Musical Opinion*, August 1956.
37 Elsie Payne, 'Some Aspects of Rubbra's Style', *MR*, August 1955, p.200.
38 Ottaway, *op. cit.*
39 *ibid.*
40 Hugh Ottaway, letter dated 4 October 1956, and published in the November issue of *Musical Opinion*.
41 Hugh Ottaway, letter dated 5 December 1956, and sent to *Musical Opinion*.
42 Edmund Rubbra, letter dated 14 January 1957, and published in the February issue of *Musical Opinion*.
43 Edmund Rubbra, programme notes for the first performance of the Sixth Symphony.
44 Hugh Ottaway, *Edmund Rubbra: Composer*, n.6, p.96.
45 Rubbra, programme notes for the first performance of the Sixth Symphony.
46 *ibid.*
47 *ibid.*

48   *ibid.*
49   *ibid.*
50   *ibid.*
51   Rubbra, 'Symphony No. 6', *London Musical Events*, December 1954.
52   Hugh Ottaway, 'Symphony No. 6, Op. 80', *Hallé*, March 1955, p.3.
53   *ibid.*
54   Rubbra, programme notes for the first performance of the Sixth Symphony.
55   This characterization was used by Rubbra a number of times to describe his joyously unrestrained movements.
56   Rubbra, 'Symphony No. 6', *London Musical Events*, December 1954.
57   Rubbra, programme notes for the first performance of the Sixth Symphony.
58   *ibid.*
59   *ibid.*
60   *ibid.*
61   See Chapter 2, pp.92–93.
62   Ivor Keys, *M&L* 36, no. 3, July 1955, p.305.
63   Ottaway, 'Rubbra's Sixth Symphony', *MT*, October 1955, p.528.
64   Hugh Ottaway, 'The Symphonies', *Edmund Rubbra: Composer*, p.38.
65   From Hugh Ottaway's private papers.
66   Letter of 27 July 1957 to Ottaway.
67   Ottaway, *op. cit.*, p.38.
68   Hugh Ottaway, *M&L* 40, no. 1, January 1959, p.97.
69   Letter of 27 July 1957 to Ottaway.
70   *ibid.*
71   Harold Rutland, *MT*, November 1957, p.629.
72   *ibid.*
73   Ernest Bradbury, *MT*, December 1957, p.680.
74   Alan Blyth, *MT*, November 1968, p.1033.

4   The last four symphonies: a new approach

The Eighth, Ninth, Tenth and Eleventh Symphonies represent a new departure for Rubbra in terms of the basic organization of their materials, although not necessarily in their treatment. (The Ninth Symphony, a choral work throughout – except for a relatively short orchestral section – and with soloists, is a special case, although it fits the general pattern of the new approach.) The composer provided the basis for his new departure when he said, 'in much of my later music a particular interval rather than a key underlies the building of the structure.'[1] Of the three purely instrumental symphonies the Eighth has the most complex structure, as each of its movements evolves from the intervals set forth in the first. The structures of the Tenth and Eleventh are simpler because, as one-movement works, the selected intervals are not subjected to as much transformation. But the results of this new approach in all four works are a greater sense of unity, and music that becomes increasingly more intense.

Symphony No. 8

Rubbra's Eighth Symphony, Op. 132, dates from 1966–68. Its overall structure corresponds to that of the First, Fourth and Seventh Symphonies: three move-ments. It is, however, much closer to the Seventh because of the lively scherzo centred between two generally slow movements. At the head of the score an inscription reads, 'Homage à Teilhard de Chardin'. The scientific and philo-sophical world-view of this French geologist, paleontologist, philosopher and Catholic priest (1881–1955) is much too complex, and his accomplishments too numerous for inclusion here, but their relevance to this work is set forth in the final paragraph of Rubbra's long article on the symphony:

> A word should be said about the subtitle to the symphony: *Homage à Teilhard de Chardin*. The works of this controversial priest-scientist have, from the beginning of their publication in England, exercised an enormous influence on me. His cosmic

view of evolution gives, if one responds to it, a picture of a purpose, a oneness, that makes nonsense of any fundamental antagonism or real separation between the world-view of science and of Christianity. The energy that is responsible for life as a whole and for later self-consciousness has not ceased with the evolution to man but becomes concentrated in him, so that with the spiritual insights given by religion he can act as a spearhead for further evolutionary development. It was no part of my intention, even if possible, to translate these ideas into music: but they meet, I hope, in a like optimism.[2]

All of the commentators who reviewed the first performance of the Eighth Symphony on 5 January 1971 were at pains to point out the great gap separating it from the Seventh (ten to twelve years). None of them suggested reasons for this symphonic silence, although Desmond Shawe-Taylor came closest when he declared that 'Rubbra was writing, not an old sort of symphony in a new way, but a new sort of symphony.'[3] The implication that can be deduced from this remark is that time is needed for new ideas to season before being put into practice. Hugh Ottaway, acknowledging that 'one might speculate at length on the reason for this gap', believes it 'unlikely that it was mainly chance, aided and abetted by commissions for other types of work'.[4] However, there is no evidence to support his statement that 'the way in which [Rubbra] has written about the background to No. 8 ... suggests that he may have felt some dissatisfaction with the consolidation which No. 7 represents'.[5] Shawe-Taylor's remark seems closer to the truth: No. 8 simply represents a new compositional concept rather than dissatisfaction with its predecessor.

In the following excerpts from his article, Rubbra spells out this new approach:

There comes a time, usually late, in a composer's life when perspectives and direction reveal themselves with a clarity such as was never known when, earlier, deep involvement with one work after another seemed merely to lead to an addition to a growing list of opus numbers. After fifty years of almost continuous writing, I am now aware of the map of my development, and although this knowledge makes for a certain amount of self-consciousness, in the sense that there is present a known reference-point, ample compensation is given in the freedom which it releases. This freedom expresses itself in detachment from concern about style or idiom, whether it is up-to-date (whatever that means!) or not, and whether it is influenced by any contemporary figure or figures. For good or ill, the continuous struggle over the years to bend the material of one's art to a shape that satisfies the demands of the 'inner voice' – demands that can never be stilled – results in inescapable conclusions. The problem *then* is not to make the conclusions conclusive, for this leads to easy acceptances and thence to mannerisms, or to a style that solidifies into formulae. If this is to be avoided, one must be careful to resist the temptation to be entirely at home in the area of thought so painfully formulated, and to sit back cosily while one's thoughts move in well-oiled grooves.

It was at such a critical point in my development that my Eighth Symphony (1966–1968) was written. My thoughts had gradually crystallised into a knowledge of the dramatic value of intervals as such, i.e., that their juxtapositions and interpenetrations could cause tension or illumination equally with harmonic or tonal changes. But I was afraid that, if I allowed a new work to grow from a knowledge of this, it would lose the instinctiveness that I had always treasured as part of the creative process: that intervals would, as it were, detach themselves from other aspects of the music and become entities that, in my new awareness of their possibilities, would be liable to cerebral manoeuvring. This at all costs I wished to avoid (for the prime excitement of composition is when things click into position without the will being consciously involved), and to counter it I resorted to a method of composition that I had never used in previous symphonies. I had always sketched out the music for these on three or four staves, indicating only the salient instrumental colours, and orchestrating fully only when all the music was finished. This inevitably puts the accent on line, and is rather like making a black and white drawing to precede a painting, with pencil indications of the main areas of colour. But as the ideas for the Eighth Symphony slowly formulated themselves, I decided to fix them straight away in orchestral terms. There was thus no preliminary short score to be filled out later, but a *full* score in which the balance of sounds was an integral part of the formal growth of the music. This not only made the composition of the work far more exciting, but the score itself was made all the richer by reason of the instant clothing of each idea with its appropriate colour.

The tonal centres of all three movements (Moderato, Allegretto con brio, Poco Lento) have their origin in the widely-spaced held chord of C-G-C with which the symphony open: but although the first movement ends on this chord, and the second and third come to rest on G, the two notes of C and G are not to be thought of as having any real relationship to the inferred keys. Indeed, the ends of both the first and last movements introduce – the one on flutes and the other on celesta – falsifying overtones that disperse any settled key feeling. Out of this initial chord (C-G-C) evolve also the interval characteristics of each movement. The interval of the perfect fourth, so highly prominent in it (G-C), sets in motion the complicated interplay of fourths that shapes the first idea, and when it contracts, as it does very soon, to a third (E flat-A flat contracting to E natural-G) the basic interval argument has been formulated.[6]

The first movement opens quietly with the above-mentioned perfect fourths moving disjunctly in a rocking motion against the held background chord, C-G-C. It should be noted in Example 70 that each of the two melodic lines comprising the fourths outlines an augmented triad, but the ambiguous nature of such

Ex. 70

harmony is partially neutralized and checked by the background chord. As the movement progresses the triadic outlines in the streams of fourths (and there are other outlines besides the augmented form) are far less important than the sharply disjunct contour of the figure itself and its variants. One of the movement's chief characteristics is a figure consisting of three accented notes on the same pitch.[7] These notes are often joined to the rocking figure, and they are

Ex. 71

also attached to such variants as that seen in Example 71. They also assume an independent existence.

As the rocking figure is heard so often, one might assume it is the principal theme of the movement, but its lack of direction and focus renders it unsuitable for such a role. The earliest statement of what might appear to be the principal theme is in measures 7–9, but a comparison of this with the actual first theme in measures 15–18 proves that the former is an embryonic version of the latter. As shown in Example 72 the careful balance between conjunct and disjunct elements and the attention given to the melodic curve have produced a principal

Ex. 72

subject that contrasts well with the surrounding disjunct material. Including its first appearance, there are twelve statements, the first three of which precede the introduction of Theme 2. Nos 1 through 5, 11 and 12 are alike with respect to their presentation in fourths, effected by *divisi* writing and interaction among parts. Another characteristic, common to entries 1 through 4, 11 and 12, is a simultaneous mirror image in one or more parts.[8] This is clearly visible in Example 72. A third classification can be made on the basis of treatment: the mood of entries 6 through 10 is much lighter than the earlier entries, owing to rhythmic patterns containing shorter note values, plus the absence of the fourths. Conversely, in all of the entries containing the fourths there is a weighty sound not unlike that of strict organum. One further detail should be noted: the F sharp in Example 72 is just the first of the theme's twelve different endings. In fact, nine of the twelve statements adopt their individual resolutions two to three notes earlier than is the case in this example. The flexibility associated with these individual endings enables the theme to move on to new harmonic contexts.

Continuing with pertinent excerpts from Rubbra's analysis, 'after the first climax [measures 31–34, the third statement of Theme 1] there is a long passage in which clarinets in thirds and horns in fourths maintain a close but rhythmically varied partnership.'[9] This passage and its immediate repetition on flutes and bassoons (measures 40–44) are extended instances of the 'basic interval argument' mentioned above. The fourths in the horns and bassoons are of the highly disjunct, rocking variety first heard in the opening measures (see Example 70). Sounding them with the entirely conjunct thirds, set in eighths and sixteenths, demonstrates the 'rhythmically varied partnership'. The first two measures of the passage are shown in Example 73, where a contrasted but complementary texture

Ex. 73

of great transparency can be seen. Both passages are part of a long transition leading to the 'second and longer climax, a forceful and urgent statement of the initial interplay of fourths [measures 61–8]'.[10] The start of the gradual buildup to this climax overlaps the end of the flute and bassoon passage and involves, first, the complete figure shown in Example 74 and, second, the separation of this

Ex. 74

figure into its two components: the three-note motive containing the octave leap (x), and the three accented notes on the same pitch (y). The first of these components presently serves as a rhythmic ostinato in the lower strings, sometimes alternating with the accented notes, now stretched out to fill the 6/8 measures. Above the ostinatos variants are heard, then the three accented notes, and finally, the rocking fourths, each statement of which ends with the repeated notes. As the dynamic level increases, so does the tension, which subsides only when a diminuendo announces the arrival of the second theme. This transition between themes is dramatic and masterfully handled.

> [The] long second subject which is in 6/8 as against the 6/4 of the opening, is quiet and relaxed, scored for strings and harp (without basses), and yet in the counterpoint given to the violas, which moves between the poles of a fourth, has internal relationships with the opening.[11]

Another relationship with previously used material can be demonstrated by a reference to Example 75 where segment x, first introduced in Example 74, is an integral part of this second theme.

Ex. 75

Although in itself the second theme is 'quiet and relaxed', this is not neces-sarily true of the entire section of which the melody is a part. Indeed, as the section unfolds, it becomes increasingly apparent that, while the tension-pro-ducing fourths have disappeared (only temporarily), a new version of Example 74 continues to generate a certain restlessness. This version takes two forms: one, an arch, the other, an inverted arch. Each of these forms appears in succession in the solo oboe at measures 78–81, just before the first statement of Theme 2 has been completed. (There are only two other statements of Theme 2 in the entire movement, and these are joined together: recapitulation, measures 148–62.) Although the oboe entries are subdued, it is clear from the markings – *espress. e intenso* – that Rubbra meant them to stand out. Between these oboe statements and one shared by cellos and basses in measures 89–92, woodwinds and strings have the arch figure simultaneously but in different rhythmic patterns. Rubbra is obviously alluding to these latter passages when, in his analytical comments, he says

> in the course of the development of this second subject, a technical feature that has increasing significance begins to assert itself. I refer to what is known as heterophony, in which the same material is presented simultaneously in two different rhythmic forms.[12]

The detached, three-note, same-pitch motive is prominent, and it becomes more so in all parts, both as a member of the figure from which it came, and as a separate entity. At measure 90 the fourths return (clarinets followed by horns), and from measure 101, delicate arpeggiated garlands of fourths in the woodwinds and harp provide a soft background to derivative material in the brass and violas. The last seven measures before the recapitulation begins at measure 118 are filled with heavily accented statements of Example 75 in the trumpets and first violins, and the tension which accrues from their repetitions is emphasized by falling fifths (not fourths) in the woodwinds, second violins and violas, and by raucous and accented major seconds in the horns.

The word 'recapitulation' having just been used following a discussion of Theme 2 implies that there is no development *per se*, a fact acknowledged by Rubbra's failure to mention one, for continuing from his previous quote,

> The characteristics of the recapitulation, which follows the enlivening of second-subject material are: 1. the overspill into it of the triplets established by the second subject; 2. a speeding-up of a slow dotted rhythm found in Subject 1 so that it becomes a dancing figuration; and 3. the emergence on strings, and later on trumpets, of a theme that is a remoulding and elongation of first-subject material. This latter comes back in its original form at the *tutti* climax of the movement.[13]

From Rubbra's comments, and very certainly from the experience of the music itself, there is little doubt that the recapitulation contains modifications sweeping enough to reinforce the argument that much of the section is virtually new. If we recall that of twelve statements of the principal subject, the exposition contains but three, the difference in this one area alone sets exposition and recapitulation far apart. Further significant differences are clearly indicated in Rubbra's analysis, which we shall now consider point by point.

'The triplets established by the second subject' sweep in in descending chains over the *fortissimo* re-entry of Theme 1, now in its original key of C major. Scored in octaves for flutes, oboes and first violins, they are a powerful rhythmic element having the ostinato characteristics so typical of Rubbra's style. During the next entry of Theme 1 – No. 5 which follows almost immediately – the triplets are scored for unison bassoons and lower strings. The ensuing passage (measures 126–30) contains the fourths shown in Example 70, but with the accompanying thirds missing. Substituting for the latter are the triplets, now reduced to a rhythmic figure containing the three-note, single-pitch motive that is so important throughout the movement. The fourths are assigned to second violins, violas and the middle register of the harp. The upper harp part has its own triplets, and all of the triplets together urge the rhythm along to the next passage – a more fully scored version of measures 40–44: flutes and clarinets in thirds, first violins and harp in fourths, sustained tones and derivatives in other parts. The brass instruments are silent. Rhythmic urgency is ensured by steady triplets in the timpani. Such rescoring is only one of numerous instances in Rubbra's symphonies of subtle changes in colour, and these changes are detailed here in order to refute the charges that little attention is paid to subtleties in instrumentation. Still another difference between this passage and its counterpart in the exposition concerns pitch modifications: here, the thirds and fourths are a minor third higher. The conclusion of the passage, marked *poco accel.*, gives way to a *Quasi Allegretto*.

In terms of its extent and predominantly jovial atmosphere, this new tempo constitutes an entire section within the recapitulation. In fact, it is a miniature scherzo. Besides corresponding to Rubbra's second point – the appearance of a 'dancing figuration' derived from Theme 1 – it contains entries 6 through 10 of the principal theme (referred to earlier as being light in character), and one extended statement of Theme 2 (measures 148–62). The dotted figure (actually double-dotted), borrowed from the 'slow dotted rhythm found in Subject 1', is easily seen and heard, especially because of its *staccato* markings, but it quickly turns into a figure composed of undotted sixteenths and eighths. This figure is shared imitatively by almost all parts including the celesta, the first time in this symphony that the latter instrument has appeared. The sixth statement of Theme 1 is the first of the light – perhaps even playful – versions of what has heretofore been an impressively serious subject, and it corresponds to Rubbra's third point: the 'remoulding and elongation of first-subject material'.

Concluding this entry, there is a rhythmic transition to the second theme, accomplished by introducing the opening notes of this 6/8 melody into the middle of the 3/4 measure just prior to the reintroduction of the 6/8 metre. Two purposes are served by this transition: first, the attractive second theme is permitted another hearing, this time in an extended version; second, opportunities are provided for the presentation of the scherzo-like entries of Theme 1 (7 through 10). Thus when entries 11 and 12 are heard in their 'original form at the *tutti* climax of the movement' (Rubbra's final point), they are all the more impressive.

Rubbra's concluding comments on this movement mention

> the quiet five-bar coda [which] consists of three bars of overlapping fourths (horns) and two bars of thirds (flute), each surrounded by the held C-G-C of the opening of the symphony. The two salient intervals of the movement are thus heard in isolation.[14]

Looked at now from a structural viewpoint, the first movement seems to suggest two possible ground plans. The simpler of these is built on the premise that there are three sections (not including the coda) of which the first and third are approximately equal in length – seventy and seventy-six measures respectively – and a much shorter middle section of forty-seven measures. Thus an *ABA*/coda form results in which *A* is concerned with Theme 1 while *B* contains Theme 2. The trouble with this plan is that although the *A* sections are almost equal numerically, their content is unbalanced: the second *A* contains nine statements of Theme 1 compared with three for the first *A* and, as we have seen, five of these differ from the original form because of the introduction of a scherzo-like subsection. Also, the reintroduction of Theme 2 in the second *A* section is hard to justify in this structural plan.

Given all of the circumstances, the second ground plan is by far the more plausible. It assumes that there are but two sections: a normal exposition containing the usual principal and secondary themes, and a shortened recapitulation in which a development of sorts (the *Allegretto*) is inserted. If one *must* apply a label, 'enlarged sonatina' seems the most likely candidate. But, in view of Rubbra's whole compositional approach, 'the improvisatory feeling for form',[15] to use Ottaway's expression, is the dominant force here.

One item not yet mentioned is the role played by the rocking fourths (Example 70). Even though they constitute neither the primary nor the secondary theme, their appearance at important points cannot be dismissed, for they are highly audible. My suggestion is that they are a connecting thread – perhaps a motto employed as a unifying device. Whatever their purpose, they make an indelible impression on the listener, and persuade him that they are only slightly less important than the main themes.

The second movement, *Allegretto con brio*, is a colourful and scintillating scherzo, that builds steadily in intensity and excitement. Not only is it a joy to hear, but it is a marvellous example of Rubbra's consummate skill in contra-

puntal manipulation. There are four main themes. A fifth enters at the beginning of the extended, sixty-five measure coda. According to Rubbra, the first of
these themes has for its source the short flute passage in thirds that concludes
the first movement. This passage 'sets the pattern, not only for the thematic
substance of the following Allegretto con brio, but for its harmonic support
consisting of contrary motion thirds'.[16] Thus the fourth, which governed the
first movement, has given ground to the third to the extent that fourths of any
kind are very rare in the second movement.

The first theme (Example 76) is more notable for the future use and shapes
of its constituent parts than for its existence as an independent entity. Of the

Ex. 76

three marked segments, *x* and *y* are of paramount importance, for *z* ceases to
exist as a recognizable unit.

Transformations of *x* and *y* occur as early as measures 6–8 where in the
lower strings both segments are inverted. In measures 10–12 another inversion
is shared by upper and lower strings.

A second theme, 'which soon follows on low strings, is again designed
round the third'.[17] Extending from measures 13 to 17, it is shown in Example
77. Accompanying it in the woodwinds are the sixteenths of segment *y*, changed

Ex. 77

now into running connected groups, whose source is obvious. This second
theme, unlike the first, retains its original identity to a far greater degree, the
only slight deviation being a simultaneous mirror image in measures 51–5
(original in the first violins, inversion in the cellos), and a shortened, heterophonic
stretto entry in flutes and violas (measures 52–5). Fragmentations of the theme
into segments capable of inversions, and combinations with elements drawn
from other sources are frequently seen.

'Subject III turns the opening material upside down, changes the rhythm
from 2/4 to 3/8, and treats it as an inverted canon (two oboes).'[18] Example 78

Ex. 78

shows that although segment *x* clearly dominates the theme, the bracketed tail-piece is derived from segment *y*. This derivation, perhaps unimportant in itself, has a direct bearing on Theme 4, which, following soon after No. 3, stems from the last five notes of the tailpiece, and thus indirectly from *y* (Example 79).

Ex. 79

After mentioning that the fourth subject 'is again a variant', Rubbra's description reads 'spaced at three octaves distant on high flutes and low bassoons, it is accompanied heterophonically by strings spaced one octave apart'.[19] After the presentation of all four subjects, there is a quite lengthy stretch that consists of all manner of combinations involving the themes and their individual segments, 'until the long 6/8 coda, where a new theme on violas is accompanied by woodwinds and horns in thirds. This process gathers to a climax, notable for its augmentation of the opening idea of the movement'.[20]

Despite Rubbra's brief summaries of the thematic bases of the movement, the alert listener soon becomes aware that the themes are, *in themselves*, relatively unimportant: they are primarily reference points. Certainly, they provide the fundamental materials without which the movement would be shapeless, but their significance lies in the myriad developmental possibilities suggested by the segments of which they are built. A good illustration of how secondary the themes really are is supplied by the second subject (see Example 77). It has a distinctive shape, preserved throughout five complete statements. All of this the *score* readily reveals. Yet, when the movement is heard, a very different impression emerges, for the theme, although not losing its identity, is so scored as to blend into its surroundings even during its one appearance in the first violins (measures 51–5). At that point, it is cast in thirds, a circumstance that reduces the incisiveness which attended its first appearance in the lower strings. The centre of attention in this violin statement is really on the violas and flutes.

These parts, also in thirds, form a canon with the violins at a distance of one beat later. The violas are at the same pitch level as the violins, and this situation, plus a different time interval, obscures the primary line and weakens the violins' authority. The flutes, pitched an octave higher, challenge the violins' primacy even more. And violas and flutes both engage in a short augmentation of the theme against the original time values – another heterophonic variant.

It might be assumed that with the three other themes even less individualized than Theme 2, a sense of unity in the movement as a whole would be missing. This is not so. Paradoxically, the unity results from the many small segments derived from the themes as they combine with one another and metamorphose into new shapes. It is these shapes, however changeable, that are the constants. One shape, the six-note figure marked y in Example 76, is present a great deal of the time, either in its original form or with the first and sixth notes lopped off. In the latter event, the four sixteenths are joined with others to create a strong, continuous line which provides much of the movement's rhythmic vitality. Naturally, each group of four sixteenths is subtly altered to fit the needs of the moment in terms of direction, new patterns, and so on.

Large structural divisions are readily apparent, each one marked off by a theme. Thus the inverted canon of which Theme 3 is composed starts the second section in measure 75. Rubbra's intent to designate this section as a structural unit is made clear by the double bar that separates it from the preceding section, the metre change from 2/4 to 3/8, and the conspicuous absence of the running sixteenths. Without these and with the instrumentation scaled down, the texture is buoyant; the effect is that of a trio interrupting the scherzo. But it is an interruption destined to be brief, for the section ends with the first beat of measure 99. A three-measure transition gives way to a new section featuring at its beginning Theme 4. This is heard twice as is Theme 2, and Theme 1 also returns. A slightly longer reappearance of the trio, together with changes in the instrumentation, is indicative of another important structural division. A transition leads to the coda, which, with its own theme (No. 5), is quite unlike either of the two other main sections. However, the coda contains derivatives from the previous sections which are combined in new ways. Yet, no formal plan ever tells the whole story, for the structure described here is not a 'closed' form in the usual sense, but a 'becoming'. It is the *becoming* that creates the form, and this is what Ottaway understood when he wrote, 'that Rubbra is primarily concerned with Being – a Bach-man rather than a Beethoven-man – should not need stressing; it is implicit in almost everything he has written, at least since the Second Symphony (1937).'[21]

The following is pure speculation and should be understood as such: I suggest that there is a demonstrable point of contact between Rubbra's music in this movement and one of the ideas espoused by Teilhard de Chardin. It is reasonable to suppose this in view of Rubbra's acknowledgement of the 'enormous influence' Teilhard exercised on him. But this point of contact is in terms of the most basic philosophical belief in the lives of both men: the Unity perceived by each as the fundamental principle underlying the universe and all things in it. Teilhard used the term 'cone of space-time' to describe the 'whole evolutionary process ... at whose base lay multiplicity and chaos and whose apex is the point of ultimate convergence in complex unity that he called "Omega".'[22] Rubbra's concept of unity is, of course, ingrained in his music: 'each new work, whatever its emotional content is a reaffirmation of "unity of being": new ways of giving this embodiment, not new musical styles, are what he gets excited about.'[23] Another writer put it this way: 'in an age of fragmentation, Rubbra stands (with a few others) as a composer of a music of oneness.'[24] What all this means with reference to this particular movement is that the various themes, the large number of fragments derived from them, and, in turn, their interactions with one another, present a balanced, unified whole that corresponds to Teilhard's concept of unity as having emerged from multiplicity. I do not for a moment believe that Rubbra consciously thought of this correspondence when he composed this movement. It was, quite simply, the result of a conviction independently arrived at, but perhaps reinforced by Teilhard's writings.

The last movement, *Poco Lento*, characterized by the composer as being 'in many ways the emotional core of the symphony',[25] is by far the shortest of the three. Rubbra describes its intervallic structure as follows:

> It was stated earlier that the fourth contracting to a minor third was the basis of the argument in Movement I. A further contraction takes place from Movement II to Movement III, when the interval of a third (G-B) found in the final chord of the former is contracted to a second (A flat-B flat). With the addition of a sixth (which was prominent in Movement II as an inversion of the third) one arrives at the basic chord that shapes both melody and harmony in Movement III (A flat-B flat-G). Indeed, the movement is a long meditation on this chord (with the third adding its accompanimental quota), and even the more relaxed and lyrical second subject (violins) contains these intervals and is accompanied by seconds on the woodwinds.[26]

Ex. 80

Example 80 shows these intervals arranged harmonically as the accompaniment (horns) and melodically as the principal theme (violins). The descending segment in the second measure (cellos, basses) demonstrates the ease with which the melodic head motive (G-A-F sharp) can be inverted, and the third measure shows the inversion of the entire theme, plus the introduction of a new rhythmic pattern. Following this and continuing until the introduction of a second, yet clearly related, theme, there are complete statements of the principal subject in its original and inverted forms, as well as fragments derived from both. The material is well suited to canonic treatment, of which there are two short examples: the first in the violins (measures 23–4, a distance of two beats and an interval of a sixth), the second a canon by inversion between woodwinds and lower strings (measures 27–9, also a distance of two beats but at the interval of an octave). Running concurrently with the first of these canons is an augmented statement of the theme (solo trombone, measures 23–5).

Perhaps the most memorable passage in the first section of this movement is that growing out of the statement of Theme 1 given to flutes and oboes. This passage, assigned to solo oboe and consisting of spun-out fragments, is supported by an accompaniment whose unusual nature centres around the harp and violas. Both of these parts have alternating As and Cs in quarters against the oboe's liquid flow of eighths, but it is the combined sound of all elements that is so arresting with the harp's harmonics and the detached *sul ponticello* on each viola note commanding, perhaps, the most attention. Yet the scoring is so transparent as never to divert one's attention away from the oboe's pensive melody. The passage ends at the point where the first canon and the trombone augmentation begin.

Soon a second example of this same kind of scoring makes an appearance, but the steady timpani beat and restless eighths in the octaves of the first violins convey a suppressed excitement to the accented thirds shared by the harp and lower strings (tremolo, *sul ponticello*). Near the end of the passage, brass and lower strings (*naturale*) engage in simultaneous presentations of the original material: right-side up and inverted.

A second theme follows immediately (Example 81) and Rubbra's remark concerning its intervallic structure should be recalled. Certainly the sixth plus

Ex. 81

the second – two of the three basic intervals in this movement – are obvious (C-A-B), as are the accompanying seconds on the woodwind, the third organizing interval. And the three stressed Ds in the third measure of the example are a clear reference to the first movement's same-pitch figure. It is this second theme to which Ottaway is referring in the following passage: 'when a more extended theme emerges on the violins, it has the magic of a new discovery, yet this, too, is drawn from the basic material.'[27] The theme is repeated in the harp and violas, the scale figure with which it concludes leading to still another passage scored in the same vein as the two already described. The harp is joined this time by first and second violins playing an octave apart (tremolo, *sul ponticello*), and the oscillating thirds are restored to the prominence they enjoyed in the first such passage. A new version of Theme 2 soon follows (solo clarinet, joined two measures later by solo flute). The *crescendo* and *poco allargando* directions that conclude this passage generate an utterance typical of a number of Rubbra slow movements (the Second Symphony particularly comes to mind): single-pitch, accented eighths in strings and timpani over which other parts enunciate either the current thematic material or fragments of it. In this instance, most of the other instruments participate in one way or another. At the end of this there is one more full statement of Theme 2 (violas and cellos, measures 66–9).

A cancrizans version of the second subject in the first violins serves as a preparation for the final climax, where 'the shape of the prevailing melodic fragment is made more forcible by being expressed *in* sixths'.[28] More fragments are heard and 'the movement ends calmly with [another] cancrizans statement of Subject II on flute, and then a colouring of the final G major chord with overlapping fourths made into a mysterious chord on celesta',[29] the only appearance of this instrument in the movement.

Where the two retrograde versions of Theme 2 are heard, the attentive listener is sure to notice the small but significant link with the first movement: the one-pitch, three-note pattern with which the retrograde melodies end. Considering Rubbra's improvisatory approach to composition, the question of whether this reappearance of the three-note pattern was planned or not seems unanswerable and, indeed, unimportant. Certainly the recognition of the motive close to and at the very end of the movement furnishes tangible proof that the symphony has come full circle. It is but another example of the unity that pervades Rubbra's music. In the final analysis, a listener is more likely to respond to a simple instance of unity such as this than he is to explanations of intervallic structures, which he may or may not be able to translate into sound. But the composer's final statement with respect to these structures is interesting and informative because it shows the path his mind took – the ultimate philosophical 'leap', as it were: 'there is an odd parallel, in the intensity generated by the progressive contraction of intervals [from one movement to another], to the energy engendered by the astronomical phenomenon of star contraction.'[30] Such concepts link him to Teilhard de Chardin's unified cosmology in ways that no atmospheric or outright programme music could.

Martin Cooper, in his review of the symphony's first performance, made a rather feeble attempt to make a connection between Rubbra's music and Teilhard's work:

The relevance of Teilhard de Chardin's cosmology only becomes apparent in the symphony's finale, where the themes have a note of awe; the rarified orchestral palette suggests, perhaps, "the air of distant planets" and the diatonic insistencies of the earlier movements are less pressing.[31]

Still another reference to Teilhard tells us that

Perhaps the symphony's dedication ... helps explain its faint air of sententiousness. When composers start thinking about 'cosmic unity' and the discovery of 'peace in a Divine purpose', one fears the worst – not cynically, but because these things are themselves the aim, not the subject matter of good art. To my ears, Rubbra's Eighth is about security and nostalgia, and its 'serenity' (one would rather call it tranquillity) is portrayed rather than deeply achieved.[32]

At least three questions are posed by this second review: why are not 'these things ... the subject matter of good art'? Are 'security' and 'nostalgia' merely the reviewer's words for the composer's tonally-oriented style at a time when most critics consider this to be hopelessly outdated? Finally (and perhaps this is quibbling), what *exactly* is the difference between 'serenity' and 'tranquillity'?

It seems entirely possible that Rubbra's explanatory article from which I have so liberally quoted, and which was published a week or so before the symphony's first performance, inadvertently helped to fuel the generally unfavourable notices. This idea is not as far-fetched as it might seem, considering the rather negative remarks concerning the symphony's intervallic structure that appeared in three of the four London reviews. Had Rubbra not emphasized this aspect so strongly, the reviews might have concentrated on details of melody, instrumentation and the like, although to be fair some of these are mentioned in a lukewarm fashion.

It remained for Ottaway to see the work as a whole, and to take the measure of it from all angles:

the musical result is excitingly fresh and creative. All that one has come to value most in Rubbra's music is renewed and transformed: the lyricism, the linear textures, the improvisatory feeling for form, the capacity for growth from small beginnings – these are immediately recognizable, and yet different. There is great freedom of invention, but at the same time a high degree of discipline.

The third (last) movement provides the readiest illustration. [A two-sentence explanation of the generating intervals follows.] Although variants of the initial chord and melodic phrase are almost constantly present, the impression one receives is of something gently floating, borne along by an unobtrusive current.... And at every step there is a warm poetry, a sensuous expressiveness, an inner radiance and composure. Indeed, the whole work is a splendid vindication of Rubbra's independence, consistency and refusal to be side-tracked by passing fashions; at the same time it establishes a new perspective and makes us look again, with fresh insights, at the achievements that preceded it. Strangely, there have been few performances, and for most of our concert-giving organisations this symphony seems not to exist.[33]

Symphony No. 9 (*Sinfonia Sacra*)

The *Sinfonia Sacra*, as it is more commonly known, also carries the further subtitle, 'The Resurrection'. Rubbra felt strongly that the work was his finest achievement, but unfortunately he never explained why he thought so. However, I suspected at the time he told me this that his conviction had much to do with the work's subject matter. One must allow, of course, that composers (and all creative artists) are often very subjective about their works, and are thus unable to make impartial judgements. In my opinion this is the case here, for I think that Rubbra allowed his enthusiasm (perhaps 'fervour' is not too strong a word) for his subject to obscure the objectivity that was almost unfailingly present throughout his life. We begin with his detailed article on the work.

I began work on my *Sinfonia Sacra* at the beginning of the Sixties. The original title was 'The Resurrection', and it was planned as a full-scale oratorio on a text, compiled from the New Testament, that began with the Crucifixion and ended with the Ascension. To formalise the structure, each section was to end with a chorale, using 17th-century tunes in a reharmonised form. With this structure in mind, I wrote the Crucifixion section ending with the first chorale, and continued into the contralto narration beginning with the words 'Now in the place where He was crucified'. While working on this narration I began to feel doubts as to the validity, in our time, of a large-scale oratorio based on the familiar pattern of recitatives, arias and choruses. Would a preordained scheme of this kind go against the present-day listener's expectation of a developmental arc leading him forward uninterruptedly from the stark impact of the Crucifixion to the joy and light of the Resurrection and the Ascension? These doubts so radically affected my original conception of the work that I felt compelled to put aside the music that I had already written, although I knew intuitively that it would remain valid as the germ of all that would follow.

Only after the completion of my Eighth Symphony in 1968 did I see the formal problem of the new work as a symphonic one: the desired unity could be achieved only by shaping the material and textures to symphonic ends, however strongly they would have to conform to the diverse moods of the text. Having decided this, the next thing was to overhaul the original text, which, being designed for an oratorio, was too long and diffuse, as well as offering far too much recitative material. The drastic word-cutting which I undertook made symphonic cohesion more possible, but the text still lacked strong focal points, and my work on it was not complete until I had the idea of breaking up the narrative by the introduction of four traditional Latin hymns to be set for chorus: they would act as periodic summings-up. Lastly, instead of setting the words spoken on the road to Emmaus, I decided to substitute a purely orchestral movement, 'Conversation Piece', which would be preceded by the narrator speaking the following words in order to make more specific the intention behind the orchestral section: 'And behold, two of them went that same day to a village called Emmaus... and they talked together of all those things that had happened. And it came to pass that while they communed together and reasoned, Jesus himself drew near, and went with them. But their eyes were holden that they should not know him.' This interlude would offer the necessary instrumental variety.

Having thus considerably pared down the text, and decided where the Latin choruses should be placed, I felt that at last I was in the right frame of mind to continue where I had left off so many years before. The work, for which the title *Sinfonia Sacra* seemed appropriate (although I view it as being, in essence, my

Ninth Symphony) was quickly finished: the scoring was completed on Good Friday 1972.

The following description of the major areas of the *Sinfonia Sacra* contains explanations of some of the further technical means whereby the composer sought to invest his work with deeper meanings:

> The opening, Crucifixion, section is headed by the words 'There was darkness over all the earth until the ninth hour', and both the harmony and instrumental colouring are suffused in darkness. The quiet, almost stifled dissonances, are scored for full muted brass, with muted violas doubling the first trumpet; and the three varied statements of this four-bar motif are interrupted either by the timpani or by *pizzicato* cellos and basses that spell out in linear form some of the main notes of the opening chord. Indeed, from this chord spring not only the basic tonal centres of the work, but the intervals that shape so much of the vocal writing. It is basically a chord in which the outer notes, clearly delineating an A minor tonality, are clouded by an internal diminished fifth (B-F), and it is the latter interval – heard early in the baritone solo setting of *Eli, eli, lama sabachthani* – that is used to invoke the deepest meanings in the vocal line. Also of great importance is the interval of a perfect fourth between the two bottom notes of the opening sequence of chords, which often brings stability to the upper harmonies. A simple example is heard early on when the baritone's chromatic line, a setting of 'It is finished: Father, into Thy hands I commend my spirit', is accompanied by the stabilising use of an ostinato moving from F sharp to B on harp and low strings. Following this is the climax of the opening section, a powerful and somewhat chaotic re-statement of the opening music in a condensed form, with a dramatic timpani part. An abrupt transition to music that develops from the chromatic intensity of the baritone setting leads to a statement of the opening chords on muted strings: these underpin the first full choral section, a setting of the *Crux Fidelis* in which the diminished fifth plays a specially important part. The first chorale (a tune by Johann Crüger) which ends the Crucifixion section is instrumentally stated at first, but its chromatic undertones disappear when it is followed by a four-part harmonisation for unaccompanied choir.
>
> At this point the narrator's recitative begins, describing how Joseph of Arimathea, having asked Pilate for the body of Jesus, laid Him in a new sepulchre, sealing it with a stone: and how the two Marys, wishing to anoint the body, found the tomb empty except for two angels 'in shining garments'. The first recitative ends here, and the words of the angels are set for divided tenors, with each phrase of the first tenors echoed by the second. Throughout the recitative and the tenor chorus the binding force of the diminished fifth is very much in evidence.
>
> The Disciples' disbelief in these events, related by the narrator in a short recitative, seemed to call for the insertion of an affirmatory chorus. Musically, too, it was apt, for the slow pace of the music up to this point needed the more vital movement afforded by the *allegro vivo* choral setting of the second of the four Latin hymns I had chosen, the Easter Sunday introit *Resurrexi, et adhunc tecum sum, Alleluia.* The vigorous postlude to this ceases abruptly with the resumption of recitative music in an indeterminate D minor accompanied by woodwind and harp. This narrative, linked to much of the earlier music, ends with Mary Magdalene's recognition of Jesus when He appears to her, and with Jesus's words (baritone) announcing His Ascension. The section ends with a choral setting of the *Regina caeli* (characterised by a continuous crescendo), followed by an arrangement of a chorale tune by Teschner.
>
> It is here that the orchestral 'Conversation Piece' intervenes. Melodically this is dominated by the diminished fifth: indeed, all the following Ascension music is developed from harmonic or melodic hints found in the opening section of the work.

The ending, using all the available choral and orchestral resources, including bells, juxtaposes a setting of the Latin hymn *Viri Galilaei* with a final chorale tune by Hassler, ending in a triumphant A major.[34]

Appearing as Example 82 is the impressive chordal opening of the *Sinfonia Sacra*, and as the reader/listener examines it, he should refer to the composer's detailed description of this passage, noting the composition of the first chord, and absorbing the menacing atmosphere of the timpani and the *pizzicato* lower strings.

Ex. 82

Another impressive passage from the work is the divided tenor chorus in the second section, also mentioned in Rubbra's article. The words of the two angels telling the Marys that the tomb is empty are very imaginatively set 'with each phrase of the first tenors echoed by the second'. This is obviously intended to suggest the extent and probably the mysterious atmosphere of the empty tomb, to say nothing of the awe inspired by the dazzling appearance of the angels. In Example 83 the last line of the contralto narrator's lengthy recitative is also included. Note the frequent use of the diminished fifth in the tenor chorus – pointed out by the composer – as well as the dramatic contour of their line.

The *Sinfonia Sacra* received its first performance by the Royal Liverpool Philharmonic Orchestra and the Liverpool Philharmonic Choir, conducted by Sir Charles Groves, on 20 February 1973 in Liverpool. The three major reviews exhibit quite diverse opinions, the first one calling the work

Ex. 83

Ex. 83 continued

the product of an independent rather than an obviously original mind, and while best described as a 'Passion', its place in Rubbra's output is that of a Ninth Symphony inviting comparison with Beethoven's 'Choral', a far more innovatory work in every respect. The parallel harmonic movement at times recalls Vaughan Williams, as the interval of the diminished fifth which dominates the 'Conversation Piece' and is readily noticeable elsewhere recalls Rubbra's former teacher, Holst. The mysticism of Holst's *Hymn of Jesus* is however nowhere evident in the more Catholic *Sinfonia*. Placing *The Planets* in the same programme was perhaps a mistake: its strongly directional content made the *Sinfonia Sacra* seem more slow-moving that it might otherwise have done.[35]

The author of the second review begins by saying that the *Sinfonia Sacra* 'shows both fastidious craftsmanship and an imaginative handling of texts concerning the Resurrection'. He continues:

There are vivid contrasts, which range from the lugubrious harmony and scoring (as far as one can tell from the cues of the vocal score), depicting darkness at the opening, to a radiant final chorus. The contralto narrator has the lion's share of the

solo work, the baritone sings Christ and the soprano the small part of Mary
Magdalene. The choruses are in basically four parts with some division, and the
writing is not at all difficult. The central chorus, 'Ressurrexi', has a particularly
vigorous momentum, and the composer has incorporated into the work three of the
most familiar German chorales.[36]

The most thorough and thought-provoking of the three reviews tells us that the
Sinfonia Sacra

> has one moment of sheer magic, in the mezzo-soprano's brief narrative of Jesus
> being taken up into heaven in the act of blessing the disciples; and the final sturdy
> harmonisation of a chorale tune by Hassler, as joyfully devout and untouched by
> irony as if the whole of our calamitous century had never been, is difficult to listen
> to dry-eyed. Otherwise it is a work of noble euphony (its harmonic dependence on
> the diminished fifth notwithstanding) and almost painful sincerity. For all its mixture
> of Catholic and Lutheran musical traditions, the quiescence – even passivity – of
> spirit is strangely Oriental in effect.
>   The music is almost ego-less, in the sense that, for a mystic, egolessness is a state
> aimed at so that something else – the divine, perhaps – may speak through the void
> where the ego used to be. In Vaughan Williams, for instance, and Holst – mystics
> both, though of very different temper – one sometimes feels that something of the
> sort has actually happened. But not (to my ears) in Rubbra: the temple is raised by
> faith and prepared with all due ceremony, but the spirit declines to take up its
> lodging. The *Sinfonia Sacra* deserves great respect for its decency and gentleness,
> its utter unconcern with effect and abiding singleness of purpose as a personal
> testament; but it remains too slow too much of the time, too earthbound, too
> unwilling to move out of the middle registers; and its civilised decorum of expression
> somehow keeps the terrific events that are being evoked too effectively at arms
> length.[37]

One further, very succinct notice points out that the *Sinfonia Sacra*

> is more noteworthy for its devotional fitness and sincerity than for any specifically
> symphonic quality. The true Rubbra symphony of recent years is the very fine no.
> 8.[38]

In her lengthy summary of the *Sinfonia Sacra*, Elsie Payne begins by saying that
the work

> is not only a statement of [Rubbra's] own religious beliefs and attitudes ..., but also
> a statement of his accumulated musical styles and idioms, above all of his symphonic
> techniques and his methods of setting words to music.... It re-states much that had
> gradually evolved in both his instrumental and his vocal work. It is a culmination
> and, although it is Rubbra's first choral symphony, it does not lay claim to be an
> essentially new departure.[39]

Having examined the *Sinfonia* in some detail and listened at length to the tape
of it, I feel certain that Rubbra's main reason for regarding it as his finest work
was his conviction that in it he had fused the basic elements of the symphony
with the special requirements needed in the composition of choral music. In
other words, he would have agreed with Payne's thesis. It would have been
entirely natural for Rubbra to have aimed for such a fusion, because these two
genres – the symphony and choral music – are the most important areas of his

music. Finally, after a description of the four sections of the work (although in this summary they are called 'movements', a term I find inappropriate and misleading) Payne offers and then defends her view that the work is a symphony:

> In a free, twentieth century sense, the work may rightly be called a symphony. For it possesses the essential elements of the symphonic genre – at one extreme event and drama, at the other contemplation and un-event, plus the necessary moments of relaxation. And certainly it possesses symphonic profundity. It is, as symphonies generally are, a summary to date of all the facets of the composer's musical thought. In it are to be found characteristic germinal ideas and their expansions (especially profuse here in so far as this is a choral as well as an instrumental work) – melodically, an intervallic preponderance of minor thirds, semitones and diminished fifths; rhythmically, an adherence to the natural sounds of both English and Latin words; in addition, more subtle symbolisms and rhapsodic, melismatic stretches of melody.... There are also frequent fluctuations of momentum within each of the separate movements [as the sections are joined together, the use of the word 'separate' is misleading] which are very characteristic of Rubbra's music whatever the overall tempo may be. And, above all, there is in the work the heterogeneous amalgam of material and/or styles which has typified Rubbra's most recent mosaic-like large-scale structures – English words are set against Latin ones, seventeenth century tunes introduced in twentieth century settings, and – although only in one place – the spoken word instead of recitative.[40]

In the last analysis, most listeners will not care whether the *Sinfonia Sacra* is a symphony or an oratorio, and it is probably useless to favour one category over the other. Proponents of the symphonic thesis will cite Stravinsky's *Symphony of Psalms*, Vaughan Williams's *A Sea Symphony*, and two works by the American composer, Roy Harris: *Symphony for Voices* and the *Folk Song Symphony*. That there is confusion about the status of the Rubbra work is undeniable. The composer refers to it at the end of the first long quotation from his article as being 'in essence', his Ninth Symphony, yet Payne, who argues in favour of the symphonic status does so in a chapter entitled 'Non-Liturgical Choral Music'. I do not for a moment doubt that the work is much more tightly knit because of the parings and alterations Rubbra undertook, and which he describes above, and I agree with Payne that 'characteristic germinal ideas' are to be found in it, but I find it difficult to think of it as a symphony when it is mainly composed of choruses, recitatives and solos, and the lengthy, orchestral 'Conversation Piece' does not sway me.

As for the careful thought and planning that went into the revisions and alterations, I cannot share Rubbra's apparent confidence that the listener will be able to distinguish between the structure of a standard oratorio and one that has been symphonically conceived. I will concede that the listener will be conscious of the series of forbidding and sombre chords with which the work opens – certainly one of the germinal elements. He will hear these chords again almost immediately, and he will recognize them near the end, but from his point of view such reminders, as well as repetitions of other germinal elements, will be less important than the text being sung above them. All through this work the text is the dominant element, influencing, as it should, the shape and content of the orchestral accompaniment. Thus, try as one may not to use it, 'oratorio' seems to be the only appropriate word to describe what is being heard, and it is not in the least disparaging to apply it here. Another term, suggested by our first reviewer, is 'Passion', but this is incorrect as only a tiny portion at the beginning of the work is devoted to the sufferings and death of Jesus. This portion is, of course, necessary to an understanding of the Resurrection and the events that follow. The very fact that Rubbra chose these portions of Scripture rather than the much more commonly set events of Passion week is important: it is a clear indication not just of his religious convictions but also of his inherent optimism.

Despite the arguments concerning the status of the *Sinfonia Sacra* (symphony *versus* oratorio and Passion), there is no disputing the emotional appeal of the subject or the sensitive, thoroughly appropriate music with which the text is clothed. The work should enter the standard repertoire of every major choral society and orchestra, and be performed during the Easter season as a complement to the frequently heard Bach Passions in Holy Week.

As for Rubbra's belief that the *Sinfonia* is his finest achievement, I cannot agree, for in my opinion the mere application of symphonic methods to a choral work cannot justify such a stand. I must confess that if there is another reason for his view, I have been unable to discover it.

Symphony No. 10 (*Sinfonia da Camera*)

Before Rubbra's Tenth and Eleventh Symphonies were composed, the most well-known, one-movement symphonies comprised these works: Samuel Barber, Symphony No. 1; Roy Harris, Symphony No. 3; Schoenberg, Chamber Symphony No. 1; and Sibelius, Symphony No. 7. Of these, the Sibelius work is probably the best known and most often played. It goes without saying that all of these symphonies are notable examples of extreme compression and were, in each case, the result of some inner compulsion on the part of the composer. To illustrate: for Sibelius the seeds of this compression were sown as far back as his Fourth Symphony. However, an entire set of new problems greets every composer who undertakes such compression.

Chief among these problems is the need for structural coherence, a problem that must be solved by the establishment of contrasting divisions of one kind or another without causing significant interruptions in the music's flow. The most conventional way of accomplishing this involves the presentation of the elements of sonata form – exposition, development, recapitulation – in some sort of compressed synthesis. Obvious tempo changes are also important factors in marking off structural divisions. These usually correspond to the tempi assigned to the contrasted movements in a conventional four-movement symphony. Of the works listed above, the Rubbra Eleventh and the Harris Third do not adhere to a sonata framework and even Rubbra's Tenth, while conforming to its outlines, demonstrates the melodic, contrapuntal and rhythmic independence, which in some of his previous symphonies has been at odds with a sonata structure.

The *Sinfonia da Camera*, Op. 145, was finished on 5 August 1974. It owes its existence to a commission from the Northern Sinfonia, which gave the work its first performance on 8 January 1975 with Rudolf Schwarz conducting. Rubbra accepted the commission

> with great enthusiasm, for after writing Symphony No. 9, which involved choir and soloists as well as a full orchestra, my thoughts had already turned towards using far smaller forces for my next symphony, perhaps dispensing with the heavy brass, but retaining percussion. This imagined scheme, however, had to be still further modified when I started work on a symphony that would have to be geared to the instrumental forces of a particular orchestra, namely, one flute, two oboes (with occasional change to English horn), two clarinets, two bassoons, two horns and strings. Such a drastic pruning of the number of instruments also gave me the opportunity to put into practice some formal pruning that had long been in my mind: to compress the usual three movements of a symphony [more usual for Rubbra, as most well-known symphonies have four] into a continuous movement that would, at the same time, mirror the three sections of a normal *first* movement, i.e. exposition, development, recapitulation. In the Tenth Symphony this works out as follows:
>
> Section 1, Lento = Sonata form exposition
> Section 2, Scherzando = Sonata form development
> Section 3, Lento (slow movement) = Sonata form recapitulation
> Section 4, Adagio (five bars only) = Sonata form coda
>
> The ending of each of these sections is clearly defined, not by the presence of a normal cadential ending (for this would bring the music to a full stop), but by brief interruptions of sound that, far from breaking the thread of the thought, are so placed as to lead the listener to expect a change of mood and pace.[41]

As we have seen, this slow-fast-slow structure occurs in previous Rubbra symphonies, the difference, of course, being that here one movement is involved rather than three. Yet the middle section of this symphony is not really fast, for the directions at the beginning of the score tell us that 'the basic tempi of the work fluctuate between 42 and 52, whether these refer to a quaver, a crotchet or a dotted crotchet. Between these extremes the music should move very freely.' Restricting a work even of this relatively short duration (playing time is approximately eighteen minutes) to such a narrow tempo range invites a number of problems, not the least of which is a tendency toward monotony, but in this instance the limitations are appropriate, for monotony is never a factor. This sense of rightness is attributable to the serene and contemplative character of the symphony's basic material, which, although unfolding throughout in a leisurely manner has intense and even passionate moments.

The pre-eminent interval with which this work is concerned is the diminished fifth. In the first instance this interval is the product of alternating major and minor seconds, which, beginning with B, end on F in the solo cello's ascending segment (Example 84). (An augmented fourth results from the inter-

Ex. 84

action of the G in the cellos and basses with the C sharp in the solo cello, but the sound is, of course, the same.) This interval 'moulds both the melodic shapes of the first section and its supporting textures'.[42] But the cello statement is not just a casual introduction, for besides being isolated by rests on either end to emphasize its importance, 'it contains within it all the main structural elements of the work.'[43] Nor should 'the first note of the symphony, a quiet A on double basses [and cellos]' be dismissed, for it is 'followed immediately by the first note of the solo cello entry (B)'; and these two notes outline the 'predominating tonal centres of the symphony'.[44] Immediately after the cello's statement 'the music settles to the hushed reiteration of F sharp octaves, and this note repetition is used much later to usher in what can be called a second subject'.[45] At this point the F sharps constitute a stabilizing pedal, above and below which the solo cello, now joined by all the cellos, plays a descending segment. This descent is balanced by simultaneously ascending segments in other string parts during the course of which a diminished fifth (A-E flat) is outlined. In the fifth and final measure of this concentrated opening section, the melodic line continues to rise – *poco accelerando, crescendo* – to a dramatic climax consisting of three detached, heavily accented sixteenths, played by the principal strings and woodwinds. These notes, plus rests at the start of measure 6, call attention to the initial statement of the principal theme.

This theme, in which two diminished fifths are rather subtly outlined, unfolds in a very satisfying way on the cellos over a repeated *pizzicato* A in the basses. It will be noted in Example 85 that the basic tonal idea (A-B) is again

Ex. 85

emphasized. The theme is terminated rather abruptly by a rest at the beginning of measure 9 and by four descending notes quietly enunciated by the bassoons. Thus the principal subject, like the opening cello segment, is set apart, but far more conspicuously. We shall meet the same demarcating rests and notes later, but under somewhat altered circumstances.

Only one measure, the ninth, occupied solely by the bassoon's descending notes, separates the conclusion of Theme 1 from the beginning – also in the

Ex. 86

cellos – of what appears to be a new theme (Example 86). However, a careful comparison with Example 85 shows that the apparently new material is drawn from the first theme. Its most notable characteristic is the real beginning of the exploitation of the diminished fifth. This theme or melody (for purposes of identification it will be referred to as Theme 1A) leads an independent life, for literal and prominent repetitions of enough of it to be easily recognized turn up later. For now, altered forms of it move up through the strings to the first violins, where rhythmic variants of its first four notes are sounded in octaves in a short ostinato passage. But the diminished fifths are far from absent, for violas and horns sounding with the violins outline them melodically, and they are beginning to show up in the chord structure, which is the product of the melodic lines. The climax of the passage (and the first in the symphony) begins when, in measures 20–21, a canon is set up between violins and violas in which eighths and quarters from the first measure of Theme 1A are used. Thus vertical as well as horizontal diminished fifths are heard. The canon is short-lived, but the music is urged on by means of strong accents and *sforzandi* applied to the basses (*pizzicati* acting as substitutes for the absent timpani), horn passages containing diminished fifths, and string tremolos. One of Rubbra's most hauntingly beautiful melodies connects the end of this climax with the second theme. It is illustrated in Example 87. Assigned to flutes and oboes one octave apart,

Ex. 87

poco ƒespress.

its two segments of four falling sixteenths come from Theme 1. That Rubbra thought of this melody in more than casual terms is demonstrated by its later repetitions.

Theme 2 (Example 88), ushered in by the note repetitions mentioned earlier, is one of those broad, singing melodies so characteristic of Rubbra. Scored for

Ex. 88

violins and violas, it exhibits a fine balance, first, between conjunct and disjunct motion, and second, between the directions of melodic flow so that just the right number of notes in one direction is offset by a turn in the opposite direction. Its four-note descending figures are also traceable to Theme 1. Several ornamental extensions of its four concluding notes plus a one-measure connection introduce three measures of string tremolos, which, reinforced by heavily accented notes in all of the other parts, lead to the second statement of Theme 1 in measures 47–53. It is a *fortissimo* statement in the violins, and it represents the first part of a climactic summary of the symphony's basic material (excluding Theme 2).

The next stage in this process begins in measure 54, when a variant of 1A emerges from the final, held note of Theme 1. The main characteristic of 1A is, of course, the diminished fifth, and this interval is concentrated in all those parts which have the thematic material. Its outline is heard again and again. Particularly outstanding is the *forte* horn passage in measures 60–63. Its diminished fifths are sounded just when the force which has sustained the high and sweeping first violin part is spent. But there is no let up in the tensions that have pervaded the climax up to this point, for detached sixteenths in the 6/16 metre restlessly and *poco a poco crescendo* outline the diminished fifth (F-B) in the lower strings. Above this relentless, eleven-measure beat the violins and violas join in sounding the first two measures (roughly) of Example 87. The use of this very beautiful fragment in the midst of the exposition's final passage is not in itself remarkable. Rubbra's compositional procedures often join melodic segments from earlier sources in long lines that always surprise one by their apparent newness. What makes this segment memorable is the horns' simultaneous and overpowering augmentation of this fragment, thus extending the two-plus measures to five and a half. The exposition closes in the same way as Theme 1 was introduced in measure 6: melodic lines ascending to heavily accented sixteenths, followed by 'brief interruptions of sound'. Here, because of the sectional division, a more dramatic effect is called for and this is obtained by heavily accented melodic lines, *fortissimos*, higher pitch levels, and more massive scoring.

> The quiet and relaxed opening of the scherzando section [the development] offers an immediate contrast to the preceding climax, but the hold of the initial material is still there, for the oboe solo moves *downward* from F sharp to B, thus reversing the direction of the symphony's opening statement.[46]

This new direction is seen in Example 89. Although Rubbra may have been entirely unaware of the origin of this phrase, it is possible to trace the source. By taking the solo cello's F sharp in measure 2 as a starting point and proceeding in retrograde motion to the initial B, and ignoring F natural, the exact source of the falling fifth is revealed. The metrical configuration is different, for the prevailing metre of the *scherzando* section is 6/8, and this is sufficient to convert the falling fifth into a dancelike figure, especially when, from time to

Ex. 89

time, a phrase extension is added. The basic figure is distributed about equally in the woodwinds and strings, but only two instances of it are found in the horns (three if a more elaborate version is counted). The choice of a descending perfect rather than diminished fifth for the development (a notable exception is measures 144–51) lends a tranquillity to the section that contrasts well with the restlessness of much of the adjoining sections.

Another figure that commands a great deal of attention first appears simultaneously with the oboe's falling fifth, and in subsequent passages it is second only to it in importance. Actually, it is not so much an established melodic shape as it is a rhythmic pattern whose melodic content changes in response to developmental processes. It is composed of chains of sixteenths, which completely fill all but two or three of the section's ninety-nine measures. While the direction of the flow varies, there is an approximately even division between ascending and descending forms. In many instances the direction is opposite to that of the prevailing material, such as when the downward-moving fifth is accompanied by rising sixteenths, but at other times, as developmental changes dictate, the direction may vary considerably. Nearer the end of the section the sixteenths lose their identity and become merely chains of repeated notes and arpeggiated figures. Whatever their direction or shape, the figure is distributed throughout the orchestra (although its appearance in the horns is almost nil). Sometimes it grows out of the basic material, but more often it appears in parts that are subordinate. The origins of these rising and falling sixteenth figures are, not surprisingly, to be found in the symphony's opening measures.

Any listener who has been exposed to the usual 'recipe'[47] for sonata form will find himself asking how or why a full-blown statement of a main theme can be 'legal' in a development section. Are not developments supposed to consist of thematic segments with, perhaps, one 'permissable' new theme, but certainly no full statement of a theme previously set forth in the exposition? Yet, in this development; Theme 2 makes not just one but three complete appearances. The answer to our question can be expressed in a reaffirmation of the principle that each example of sonata form, while complying with the outer structure (exposition, development, recapitulation), and including principal themes in its design, is autonomous with respect to how the inner details are worked out.

In this instance a sonata structure is unfolding at a leisurely pace. Its themes are not dramatic in themselves, although the tensions to which they are subjected are, at times, dramatic. There is a noticeable difference between the two principal themes in that the second contains no diminished fifths, and is predominantly conjunct – factors that make it suitable for inclusion in the relaxed atmosphere of the development, a section that in the vast majority of cases is tense and restless. Here, the only really tense moment comes with the reintroduction of diminished fifths in measures 144–51. The second theme's first two appearances in the development section (violins, violas: measures 115–20; cellos, basses: measures 120–25) take up space almost midway through the section. They immediately engage the listener's attention by acting as a focal point and a shift from the fragmentary nature of the proceedings up to that point. But whereas in usual developments thematic fragmentations often produce tension, especially where modulations are involved, here the fragments seem leisurely, so that the sudden appearances of Theme 2 are not out of character. Following the theme's second statement, there is a return to the melodic fragments until diminished fifths from Themes 1 and 1A (cellos and basses) and repeated sixteenths (violas) darken the mood and generate tension. As this gradually subsides, Theme 2, with slight pitch alterations, makes its third appearance (measures 161–5). Rubbra carefully marked it *caldo e molto sonore*, an indication of its importance and of the part it plays in the approach to the development's final pages. The section's last few measures are filled with segments drawn from the middle portion of the first theme. These rise to a climax made more striking because of the quasi-canon between strings and horns.

The recapitulation, which begins in measure 175, is introduced in the preceding measure by the three-note descending figure first heard in measure 9. Here, as there, the figure is sounded by one part only (cellos) and is prefaced by a rest, the whole serving to mark off the recapitulation from the development in the same way as it separated the first appearances of Themes 1 and 1A. Referring to the recapitulation, Rubbra observes that 'the inwardness of the slow movement starts with a rescored version (English horn in contrast to cellos) of music heard in the first section, but develops it at greater length.'[48] This rescored music is none other than Theme 1A, but the rescoring is not confined to the cor anglais, for its accompanying figures are also rearranged instrumentally. The result is, for all intents and purposes, new: the dominant role of the cor anglais has created an entirely different atmosphere.

That atmosphere, is, of course, the 'inwardness' mentioned by the composer. It is responsible to a great extent for forging such differences between the exposition and the recapitulation as the order in which the basic materials appear in the latter, and their further development, to say nothing of a multitude of new details. In fact, the recapitulation is an almost wholly new synthesis of the original subject matter as the following discussion shows.

The three measures growing out of the conclusion of the cor anglais solo contain the elements of Theme 1A, and although they are substantially the same as in measures 20–22, they lead to a new development that is really a subsection. This begins introspectively with hushed string chords over which the first oboe and muted first horn tenderly intone melodic fragments. Interest shifts to the strings (more fragments) and then to oboe and flute soli. Their material and that

of the succeeding *poco accelerando* is drawn largely (and probably unconsciously) from the rising and falling fourths embedded in the solo cello's
passage in measures 1 and 3. (The little three-note motive, consisting of two
sixteenths and an eighth in measure 4 also plays a part.) Further development of
the fourths includes, first, a restatement of the A-B motive that symbolizes the
symphony's tonal centres, and second, a final, poignant statement by the cor
anglais in measures 217–21 of Theme 1A. A steady increase in tension characterizes all of this subsection from just prior to the *poco accelerando* to the cor
anglais solo. Theme 2 tries hard to be heard before a complete, but rhythmically
free version of it is given to the solo violin, followed by another for solo viola.
After a short climax, a brief summary of the important elements of the *scherzando*
development is heard. This leads into the symphony's final climax – an impassioned statement of Theme 1 at the pitch level first heard in measures 6–8. This
is the only reappearance of Theme 1 in the recapitulation.

> A calm and very brief coda stresses, in its melodic shape, not only the prevailing
> diminished fifth interval, but, in moving from the tonal centre of B to that of A,
> underlines the importance of this shift throughout the symphony.[49]

The coda is introduced by the three-note descending figure (cellos and basses)
which has served twice before as a divider. It is not easy to describe the essence
of these five concluding measures, which are among the most beautiful in all of
Rubbra's music. We have met passages like this before, and it is the haunting
sound of the oboe or cor anglais that makes them so memorable. Harold
Truscott tells us why:

> What becomes more and more evident is that Rubbra's tempi have a tremendous
> effect on the sound of the instruments he uses, to such an extent that they can sound
> as though one has never heard them before. Particularly is this true of the oboe (and
> the cor anglais on occasion). Rubbra has a way of giving his last utterance in a slow
> movement or at the end of a work to the oboe, and this instrument gains from the
> extreme slow tempo an unforgettable feeling it never has in the work of any other
> composer.[50]

Of course, the melodic content of such passages also contributes in no small
degree to the total expressiveness. 'Often... the melodic line involves an augmented fourth with the upper note rising further by a semitone, and this intensifies the sound, so that it pinpoints Rubbra immediately.'[51] The solo oboe in this
coda has exactly this type of melodic line, but in the final two measures of the
symphony the emphasis shifts to the flute and first clarinet as the haunting
melody, first heard in measures 30–31, returns, and with a subtle note change
the tonal centre shifts to A.

Surely this symphony's most remarkable attribute, and one that even the
most casual listener can hardly fail to note, is its melodic spontaneity. The lines
possess an extraordinary diversity and flexibility, as the unceasing developmental process unfolds in a lyricism that Rubbra found was 'burgeoning more
freely than in anything else I have written'.[52] Yet, throughout the work the

directions of the flow can be traced to the two opening measures – the 'first cause' of everything. A careful balance between these directions is always maintained, but life-giving tensions in which the pull of opposite directions is very evident are allowed to develop.

The music's effortless flow is promoted by a varied assortment of metres. These call to mind Rubbra's choral music where the metrical patterns stem directly from the textual rhythms and accents, and in this sense there is a resemblance to the fluidity of the choral works. Table 2 summarizes this rich variety by showing the metres employed in each of the symphony's main sections. Some metres run on for long periods while others may occupy only one or two measures. In order to simplify the table, no attempt is made to record the changes from one metre signature to another in a successive fashion, as some of these changes are very frequent.

Table 2

Section	Metre signatures
Exposition (75mm)	3 4 5 2 5 3 4 6 9
	2 4 4 4 8 8 8 16 16
Development (99mm)	9 6 2 3 4 3 12 9 18
	8 8 4 4 8 8 16 16 16
Recapitulation (85mm)	4 3 4 3 5 3 5 4 6 7
	4 2 8 4 8 8 16 16 8 8
Coda (5mm)	8
	8

In view of this rhythmic flow which goes hand in hand with the melodic flow, I find Arnold Whittall's admittedly mild but none the less damaging inference very puzzling. It was the result of Ottaway's statement that Rubbra's musical thinking is based on 'the germinal idea and the "logic of intervals"'. Whittall deduced from this that the composer's 'declared preference for continuing "steadily from the opening idea"' may be responsible for 'the occasional loss of impetus, which it is possible to sense even in as recent and admired a work as the Tenth Symphony'.[53] Possible to sense where in this symphony? Certainly not at those planned points where 'brief interruptions of sound' (Rubbra) define the underlying architecture and relieve the accumulated tension. And how has the tension accumulated? By the very technique that

Whittall questions, and that has produced the melodic flood whose impetus needs to be momentarily halted. I agree that this criticism is valid for some of the earlier symphonies where Rubbra's technique had not fully matured, but it is not valid here.

No account of this symphony would be complete without reaffirming and emphasizing the work's real title: *Sinfonia da Camera*. On the score 'Symphony No. 10' appears beneath the title in parentheses and in smaller letters. Examples too numerous to be dealt with in detailed fashion attest to the chamber-music qualities of the work. Such examples are, of course, most obvious in the instrumentation right from the start where the solo cello gives out the fundamental material from which everything grows. The thematic material itself, none of which is of large dimensions requiring massive instrumentation, is also in accord with the concept of chamber music. The result of both elements working together – thematic material and instrumentation – is music of the utmost sensitivity. Certain movements in the earlier symphonies approach the Tenth with respect to these characteristics, most notably the last movement of the Eighth, yet during the impassioned climaxes as well as the passages leading up to them, one senses that the boundaries between chamber and non-chamber music are being crossed again and again. Thus the Tenth Symphony seems a blend of both.

Passages from two short letters, written by the dedicatee, Sir Arthur Bliss, express his delight with this work. The first, written on 14 August 1974, just over a week after the completion of the Symphony, mentions the dedication:

> You do me much honour. It is with the greatest pleasure that I learn that your Chamber Symphony will bear my name as dedicatee, and I look forward eagerly to hearing it on January 10th next.

The second, dated 18 February 1975, contains his reactions after receiving

> a tape of your/my Symphony, and I have twice played it through.... Without a score detailed comment is impossible, but I can say straight off that it fulfills two of my cherished convictions about music. 1) The Symphony moves steadily and sometimes majestically forward to a nodal point. No stop go – stop go. 2) The sound is always beautiful – indeed, the long contrapuntal interweaving of the strings is quite ravishing. I hope it has many performances, and I am proud to have my name associated with it.

Symphony No. 11

Two remarks made by Rubbra in connection with his two last symphonies seem contradictory. With reference to No. 10 we are told that 'this symphony says all I want to say.'[54] The second remark preceded the first performance of No. 11: 'My new symphony, the Eleventh, is a culmination of all my symphonies compressed into one movement.'[55] The first statement seems to imply that the composer planned to write no further symphonies after his Tenth, while the second shows that he must have felt the need for some sort of summation of his accumulated symphonic thought. Certainly the Eleventh Symphony calls for interpretation on this retrospective level as well as an assessment of its intrinsic worth as an independent entity.

The Eleventh Symphony, Op. 153, which occupied Rubbra intermittently from July 1977 to February 1979, is dedicated to his wife, Colette. It was commissioned by the BBC for the 1980 Promenade Concert season, and was first performed on 20 August of that year by the BBC Northern Symphony Orchestra under the direction of Nicholas Cleobury. As usual, Rubbra provided an explanation of the symphony's structural details, this time in the form of an interview on Radio 3, broadcast on 17 August. (Excerpts from this interview appear as they become relevant to the discussion.)

This symphony and its immediate predecessor are alike in two entirely exterior respects: both are one-movement works, and both take somewhere between fifteen and eighteen minutes to perform. With respect to the latter point, Peter Stadlen's comments in his review of No. 11 appear below:

> The difference between clock time and time experienced is driven home by Edmund Rubbra's Eleventh Symphony. It seemed hard to believe that barely fifteen minutes had elapsed when the BBC Northern Symphony Orchestra under Nicholas Cleobury concluded the world premiere of this BBC commission at an Albert Hall Prom. A compliment to the 79-year old composer is implied and indeed, intended: for the frequency of compositional action and the density of compositional thought is unusually high. In fact, I found the bar-to-bar progress more readily perceptible than the overall design.[56]

Stadlen's concluding sentence points up one of the more important differences between the two symphonies: the one-movement sonata design of the Tenth and the seemingly amorphous character of the Eleventh. (I shall have more to say on this difference as the discussion unfolds.) Still another dissimilarity lies in the instrumentation: the Eleventh Symphony marks a return to the standard orchestra (give or take an instrument or two) of the Sixth, Seventh and Eighth Symphonies.

The most striking similarity between the Tenth and Eleventh Symphonies is, of course, the selection and employment of a pervasive interval. Concerning the interval chosen for the Eleventh and its place in the work, Rubbra's radio interview is instructive:

> All my life I've been involved with the interval of the fifth – not consciously – but it's cropped up everywhere; and this opening idea started entirely with the fifth. It's a long theme, based on horns; and when I realized that the fifth was so prominent in it, I decided to make the whole movement revolve round the fifth. I say 'revolve' because I didn't realize at the time how it would resolve at all. But as it went on, I found it was so important that I don't think you will find a single bar in the whole symphony which is without it. The listener views it as a huge improvisation, but a controlled one in which the fifth has an all-important role to play.[57]

The opening theme (or material, as I prefer to call it for reasons to be advanced shortly) is shared by the first and third horns. It divides naturally into segments, the first two of which play an important part in the proceedings as the symphony progresses. Its predominantly disjunct contour is accompanied for much of its sixteen-measure course by a balancing conjunct, descending figure in the lower strings: B-A-G sharp. These notes, correctly described by Colin Seamarks in his programme notes for the first performance as constituting 'the basis of the stepwise movement in the symphony',[58] are heard later in passages where greater significance is attached to them. Roughly the first half of this opening passage is reproduced in Example 90.

Ex. 90

Hns.

Cellos, Basses

It is not long before secondary material is heard (measure 25ff). According to the composer, it 'consists of intervals which are much narrower than the fifth', although 'the fifth becomes an accompanimental figure, and is heard as such quite clearly'.[59]

Since themes are very important form-building elements, and repeated hearings of this symphony solidly confirm Rubbra's assertion that 'the listener views [the work] as a huge improvisation', there is clearly a need to investigate the place of these melodic materials in the total scheme. Certainly the work contains no analogy to sonata form, and the very words 'theme' and 'subject' seem to confuse the issue, even though the composer himself used them in his interview. If one accepts the usual definition of a theme or subject as a structured melody, which is heard and recognized several times in the course of a movement or piece, and which, by its presence helps to shape the overall form, then these two melodies are not *bona fide* themes, for there is no literal or even free repetition of either. Thus no conclusive structure is established and the listener waits vainly for a familiar landmark to reappear. Under such circumstances it would seem more fitting to call the work 'Improvisation for Orchestra' rather than symphony. The latter term creates expectations in the listener's mind that are not fulfilled. A case in point is the opening horn melody (Example 90), which sounds more like the material for a slow and majestic introduction than a main theme. 'Brucknerian spaciousness' is the way one reviewer describes it,[60] and I think the listener, hearing the work for the first time (perhaps every time) is justified in viewing this beginning material in this way. But when what is thought to be a slow introduction gives way to passages containing no identifiable theme, the listener is somewhat disconcerted, and even the appearance of the second melody at measure 25 does little to relieve his perplexity. This is partly because, if one adheres to symphonic principles, there is no simple explanation for the material between the conclusion of the horn passage and the beginning of the second melody. Much of this confusion could be avoided by renaming the work as I suggest above.

There is no doubt that the fifths contained in the horn melody are responsible for most of what occurs later. As Seamarks puts it, 'the whole symphony is, in fact, one huge development of the first page.'[61] In the tracing of this development, the interval's size plays a large part because it makes everything so easily recognizable. Other than the fifths in the horn melody's second half (which stem directly from those in the first half), the first fruits of the very opening measures appear underneath the oboe solo, which begins in measure 17. Here, the violas introduce an accompanimental figure in eighths that, excluding the first note, follows the contour of the fifths in measures 5 and 6 (see Example 90). This figure is immediately expanded to include another fifth higher than the second one, so that the ascent and descent produce a wavelike motion. The figure is distributed throughout the orchestra, and is present about one sixth of the time. Beginning in measure 25 and with few exceptions thereafter it is expressed in sixteenths rather than in eighths. It is the same figure mentioned above by the composer as constituting an accompaniment to the secondary idea. He refers to it again in connection with the climax of the symphony, but prior to that reference he provides a quite novel explanation concerning the interactions of his basic materials:

> This process of change – kaleidoscopically if you like – of the fifth throughout the work is very important. It's almost, as I said, like an improvisation, because I like to think it is as naturally developed as possible – not intellectually but as naturally; and one should listen for the fifth coming in at a natural point rather than being forced in because it's the structure of the movement.[62]

The application of this interesting metaphor assumes greater clarity later on when

> the accompanimental notes of the opening horn tune (B-A-G sharp)... become at the climax [measures 150ff] the principal theme. In the middle are four horns, and the fifth is a dancing structure round it [the reference is to the sixteenth-note figure previously mentioned]. So the roles are reversed; but they are all there in a different way. In a sense, I'm transferring all the time the elements like a kaleidoscope: in other words, shaking them up.[63]

The slow section which starts in measure 176 just after the above-mentioned climax has run its course, contains a 'newish tune – I suppose it's a newish tune – but it's accompanied by the fifth'.[64] This melody, heard as an oboe solo, *does* attain the status of a full-blown theme in the sense in which the latter was defined earlier, for it is heard later in its entirety in the strings (measures 202–9), reinforced by woodwinds at one point. However, the first two measures of

Ex. 91

this second statement of the theme are obscured by the brass, so that recognition of the melody as a theme is somewhat diminished. A glance at Example 91 shows the melody to be largely conjunct until near the end when downward leaps of a fifth restore it to its middle range. The accompanimental figure is in the basses (*pizzicato*) and the bottom of the harp, and consists of two rising and two falling fifths adjusted to the triple metre and *adagio* tempo. Separating the two complete statements of the theme are a clarinet solo, a short flute passage, and a violin passage in octaves that leads directly into the second statement. All of these passages are highly lyrical and are marked *espressivo*. Melodically they have nothing in common beyond a tendency toward chromaticism and downward leaping fifths. A little past the halfway point between the two theme statements – immediately following the oboe and flute passages – the prevailingly calm mood is slightly ruffled by the same one-pitch rhythmic figure ($\sqrt{}$) that was so prominent in the first movement of the Eighth Symphony and the passacaglia theme of the Seventh.

Any further accounts of the intervallic structure of this work would be both space-consuming and tedious. This is because the symphony is different from the other works treated in this chapter. Both the Eighth and Tenth Symphonies are also constructed on an intervallic premise, but in each case the chosen interval (the fourth in No. 8, the diminished fifth in No. 10) is incorporated into recognizable themes that can *themselves* be analysed and fitted into structures, albeit of individual kinds. In the Eleventh Symphony the motives and figures are too fragmentary for a thoroughgoing analysis to have any real significance. This statement is certainly not intended to imply that relationships between short motives or figures are non-existent. Such relationships not only exist but are demonstrable even when the motives and figures are widely separated by numbers of pages in the score. The ear, however, does not discover the relationships as easily as does the eye, because the materials composing the relationships are not members of themes that implant themselves in the memory through repetitions. To put it another way: part of the difficulty (if difficulty is the right word) is that the fifth is too omnipresent for the ear to properly sort out the various ways in which it is used. Stephen Banfield expressed his reservations in another way when he said that the fifth

> stands out from the score on every page, yet one is not conscious of this being a symphony of fifths, probably because they are not used vertically but are skilfully co-ordinated as melodic elements with traditional counterpoint whose consonances are thirds and sixths. That being the case, the symphony is disappointing, for there is not much else to latch on to.[65]

Heyworth sees a structural problem when he remarks, after first pointing to Rubbra as 'a composer who is often held up as a model of symphonic coherence', that 'the thinking remains surprisingly episodic.'[66] I prefer the term 'mosaic-like' to 'episodic' as I think it comes closer to Rubbra's kaleidoscopic analogy. To draw a natural conclusion here: the result of the improvisatory element in this work is a large proportion of through-composed writing, possibly more than in any other Rubbra symphony.

Both cause and effect – improvisatory viewpoint leading to degrees of through-composition – are traceable to Rubbra's fundamental approach to composing, an approach to which I have alluded several times in these chapters. During Rubbra's BBC interview of 17 August this approach was reaffirmed, for when the composer was questioned about the accidental element in his music (an element that is the outcome of the improvisational approach), he replied

> I do arrive by accident; and a critic who was very familiar with my music couldn't understand why these things happened accidentally. But it isn't so, really. It *seems* like accident, but it has to be a *controlled* accident if that can be so envisaged.
>
> Q.   I think I remember reading somewhere that you never sketch works beforehand; you allow them to grow.
>
> A.   No, I don't like to be tied by sketches. I have known composers to write in that way, and then string them together afterwards – put them together. But I don't work in that way. They wouldn't go together for me.
>
> Q.   You have no idea at all what's going to happen?
>
> A.   Not a bit. That's the excitement of it, you see. If it turns out right, *that's* the excitement of it.[67]

It follows that if the music collectively is the result of a 'controlled accident', then the harmonic structure must also be subject to chance – an assumption that is correct. The 'accidental' harmonies emanate, however, not just from the varied combinations of the innumerable fifths but also from the interactions of the latter with conjunct and often chromatic lines. Some of the harmonies are mildly astringent, particularly at those points where outpourings from the brass create dissonances with other parts.

Some of the most interesting passages harmonically and instrumentally are those that in a more conventional symphony would be termed transitional or developmental. Here, owing to this work's improvisatory nature no satisfactory term can be found for such passages, but as parts of the improvisatory process they all have a definite role to play. Each of the three I have chosen for special comment has a strangely visionary quality, which one recalls even after some of the symphony's climactic moments have receded from the memory.

The first passage (measures 69–79) contains a rather impersonal melody in the violas. It is surrounded by empty fourths and fifths in the *divisi* violins, rising and falling fifths in the lower strings, and an undulating scale figure in octave triplets on the celesta. Near the end of the passage the solo horn intones, in triplets, the pitches heard in the symphony's three opening measures. The entire passage sounds reserved – even remote – and this feeling continues as the woodwinds enter above *pizzicato* triplets.

The second passage, coming soon after the beginning of the final slow section (measures 191ff), is interesting because of its bare harmonies and thin instrumentation: empty consecutive fifths, syncopated and set in the rhythmic figure quoted above (♪♪♩) and separated by an octave and a half in oboes and bassoons. Beneath this, cellos and basses have an ostinato, triadic figure – tremolo, *sul ponticello* – while timpani and harp mark out a syncopated rhythm.

In the third passage (measures 223–31) a gently flowing cor anglais melody is supported by two sets of rocking fifths, one set in the harp and violins, the other in the lower strings. A somewhat exotic atmosphere is created which is heightened when the first bassoon doubles a small portion of the melody one octave lower. In measure 228 the cellos enter to double the remainder of the cor anglais melody, the violins' fifths are transferred to the flutes, and the harp is given arpeggiated fifths. The whole passage has an aura of delicate, shimmering magic, and one wishes it could last a little longer. All three of these passages help to refute the charge that Rubbra's instrumentation is dull and unimaginative.

To summarize: writing about the Eleventh Symphony has not been an easy task. In fact, of all Rubbra's symphonies the Eleventh has been the most problematic from the points of view of form, thematic content and harmony. Trying to determine why Rubbra considers the symphony to be 'a culmination of all my symphonies' brings *me* anyway to the inescapable conclusion that the Tenth represents the culmination for the very reasons that the Eleventh Symphony *is* a problem. The Tenth has a well defined structure that is not, however, in any way rigid or inflexible, and in this respect it is a worthy successor to – indeed, a culmination of – all of those earlier movements in which the same freer tendencies were manifested. And I feel more than ever that Rubbra was right when he referred to the lyricism of the Tenth Symphony as 'burgeoning more freely than in anything else I have written'. The wonderfully flowing melodic line has produced a combined rhythmic and harmonic texture in the Tenth Symphony that is not quite matched in the Eleventh.

My remarks must not be construed in any way other than in the context of a comparison with the Tenth Symphony, for in the last analysis the Eleventh Symphony in its own right is an impressive achievement. A number of hearings – not just one or two – are necessary if the listener is to absorb the symphony's main points, to say nothing of its subtleties. Unfortunately, if the past is any criterion such opportunities will not materialize. One, perhaps two performances, and the work will be shelved for years. Hasty and sometimes preposterous judgements will be made, based on the initial performance only. In fact, this has already occurred, for Heyworth handed down his verdict of the Eleventh Symphony in stinging terms: 'a stuffed carcass'.[68] Happily, another review exhibits understanding and sensitivity and I am pleased to quote it in full:

> The symphony is well-made; it is constructed with that quiet, unobtrusive logic which distinguishes the best of Rubbra's scores. It manages to draw a richly varied collection of material from its unprepossessing generative idea of the interval of a fifth. The mood, set by the horns and solo oboe of the opening, is wistful; this slightly detached, reserved approach persists even through the music's more agitated moments. Passion seems restrained by a noble eloquence; we hear an intelligible language, well used, but we do not sense the feelings which give impulse and meaning to that language.[69]

With respect to the final qualifying sentence in this review, I would like to suggest that the music's reserve and one's inability to 'sense the feelings' behind the language may be simply the fruits of that philosophical and tranquil frame of mind that one finds in the late music of composers who live to a ripe age. Those same mental and spiritual attitudes, gleaned from a lifetime of musical creativeness, are responsible for much of the detachment that marks the late works of Bach, Beethoven and Brahms, to name only three. Such attitudes are sadly out of fashion in today's world. In Rubbra's case, these mental and spiritual attitudes toward life have not been confined to advanced age, but have always been the norm to a degree. Their transference to his symphonies is a natural process which may be seen in most of his music. Here and there, a few perceptive writers and reviews have recognized this. In a short article, 'Rubbra: Neglected Symphonist', Richard Tiedman writes

> Foremost, is that the spiritual content of his music is profoundly at odds with contemporary values. Rubbra is a man of powerful religious conviction. This conditions his work in no obvious ecclesiastical way; rather his music is imbued with a pervasive serenity and strength. The ten symphonies [the Eleventh was composed following the appearance of this article] are probably the most beneficent and positive works in the form that this century has produced.[70]

Two further excerpts underscore the same thought. In Wilfrid Mellers's words,

> It is significant that Rubbra has referred to his symphonic movements as, in the philosophic sense, 'essences' – as manifestations of creative life through the medium of sound. It should be clear that ... such a conception necessarily involves a religious attitude to one's experience; and I am inclined to think that Rubbra's achievement has depended on his being endowed with what is, for a man of the contemporary world, rather a peculiar spiritual make-up.[71]

Harold Truscott put it this way:

> Ultimately, and as perhaps the most potent facet of his style, all his music is about God – this is its motive force. Bruckner is far enough in the past, now, that we can listen to his Masses and symphonies as set pieces of musical structure and expressive sound without being too disturbed by what they are saying, or what set them off; although a good deal of Bruckner's musical point is missed this way, of course, which may account for some of the mistaken and bumbling assessments of his music with which we are still pestered from time to time. But Rubbra is too immediate, and, in fact, thrusts what he says before us so that we cannot ignore it unless we ignore him altogether, as we have come close to doing. His concern with his subject makes him at present an unfashionable composer; but it also makes him a permanent one.[72]

That Rubbra felt he still had something to say symphonically was made apparent during the summer of 1985 when he told me that he had embarked on his Twelfth Symphony: the title page bears the date '25.3.85'. Unfortunately, it is impossible to ascertain what the symphony would have been like, as nothing exists beyond the page reproduced in Plate 1.

Plate 1

Notes

1   Quoted by Lewis Foreman in his remarks on Rubbra's Fourth String Quartet: *Tempo*, no. 124, March 1978, p.29.
2   'Edmund Rubbra Writes About His Eighth Symphony', *The Listener*, 31 December 1970, p.925.
3   Desmond Shawe-Taylor, 'Rubbra's Return', *The Times*, 10 January 1971.
4   Hugh Ottaway, 'The Symphonies', *Edmund Rubbra: Composer*, p.39.
5   *ibid.*
6   'Edmund Rubbra Writes About His Eighth Symphony', *The Listener*, 31 December 1970, p.925.
7   Although, as noted earlier, a gap of at least a decade separates the Eighth from the Seventh Symphony, the resemblance between this accented, single-pitch figure and that of the passacaglia theme in the Seventh Symphony is too strong to be ignored. The tempo of both movements is approximately the same, and this fact emphasizes the similarity. It seems very likely that its appearance in the Eighth Symphony is entirely fortuitous but, as we shall see, it recurs in the Eleventh Symphony.
8   This is a further example of the 'topsy-turvydom working subconsciously' in Rubbra and experienced in his childhood, as related in Chapter 1.
9   'Edmund Rubbra Writes About His Eighth Symphony', *The Listener*, 31 December 1970, p.925.
10 *ibid.*
11 *ibid.*
12 *ibid.*
13 *ibid.*
14 *ibid.*
15 Ottaway, *op. cit.*, p.40.
16 'Edmund Rubbra Writes About His Eighth Symphony', *The Listener*, 31 December 1970, p.925.
17 *ibid.*
18 *ibid.*
19 *ibid.*
20 *ibid.*
21 Hugh Ottaway, 'Edmund Rubbra and His Recent Works', *MT*, September 1966, p.766.
22 Michael H. Murray, Article on Teilhard de Chardin in *Collier's Encyclopedia* 22, London: P.F. Collier, Inc., 1978, p.113.
23 Ottaway, *op. cit.*, p.767.
24 Ronald Stevenson, 'Concerted Works', *Edmund Rubbra: Composer*, p.43.
25 'Edmund Rubbra Writes About His Eighth Symphony', *The Listener*, 31 December 1970, p.925.
26 *ibid.*
27 Ottaway, 'The Symphonies', *Edmund Rubbra: Composer*, p.40.
28 'Edmund Rubbra Writes About His Eighth Symphony', *The Listener*, 31 December 1970, p.925.
29 *ibid.*
30 *ibid.*
31 Martin Cooper, *The Daily Telegraph*, 6 January 1971.
32 Stephen Walsh, *The Times*, 7 January 1971.
33 Ottaway, *op. cit.*, pp.40–41.

34 'Edmund Rubbra Writes About His "Sinfonia Sacra"', *The Listener*, 15 February 1973, p.220.
35 Robert Orledge, *MT*, April 1973, p.409.
36 Peter Dennison, *M&L* 54, no. 3, July 1973, p.373.
37 Calum MacDonald, *The Listener*, 10 December 1981, p.731.
38 Hugh Ottaway, *MT*, December 1973, p.1249.
39 Elsie Payne, 'Non-Liturgical Choral Music', *Edmund Rubbra: Composer*, p.83.
40 *ibid.*, pp.84–5.
41 Sleeve-note to the recording of the Tenth Symphony on RCA RL25027.
42 *ibid.*
43 *ibid.*
44 *ibid.* With reference to these notes (A and B), Rubbra remarks: 'Before, however, analytical sleuths get to work on this fact, I hasten to point out that it has nothing to do with the initials of Sir Arthur Bliss, to whom the work was dedicated!'
45 *ibid.*
46 *ibid.*
47 Charles Rosen's choice word for the textbook definition of sonata form in *The Classical Style: Haydn, Mozart, Beethoven*, New York: W.W. Norton and Co., Inc., 1972, p.31.
48 Sleeve-note to the recording of the Tenth Symphony on RCA RL25027.
49 *ibid.*
50 Harold Truscott, 'Style and Orchestral Technique', *Edmund Rubbra: Composer*, p.28. Other Rubbra symphonies and the movements in which the oboe or cor anglais have the final say are No. 2, third movement; No. 3, third movement; No. 5, first and fourth movements; No. 6, second movement.
51 *ibid.*
52 Quoted in *Edmund Rubbra: Composer*, p.41.
53 Arnold Whittall, Review of *Edmund Rubbra: Composer*, *M&L* 59, no. 4, October 1978, p.471.
54 Quoted in *Edmund Rubbra: Composer*, p.41.
55 Printed in the *Radio Times*, 20 August 1980.
56 Peter Stadlen, *The Daily Telegraph*, 21 August 1980.
57 BBC Radio 3 interview, 17 August 1980.
58 Colin Seamarks, BBC Proms Programme Notes, 20 August 1980.
59 BBC Radio 3 interview, 17 August 1980.
60 Peter Heyworth, *The Observer*, 24 August 1980.
61 Seamarks, *op. cit.*
62 BBC Radio 3 interview, 17 August 1980.
63 *ibid.*
64 *ibid.*
65 Stephen Banfield, *M&L* 64, nos 1–2, January–April 1983, p.144.
66 Heyworth, *op. cit.*
67 BBC Radio 3 interview, 17 August 1980.
68 Heyworth, *op. cit.*, p.
69 Nicholas Kenyon, *The Listener*, 28 August 1980, p.284.
70 Richard Tiedman, 'Rubbra: Neglected Symphonist', *American Record Guide*, September 1979, p.37.
71 Wilfrid Mellers, *Music and Society*, London: Dennis Dobson, Ltd, 1950, p.174.
72 Truscott, *op. cit.*, p.29.

5 Other orchestral music

Rubbra's non-symphonic orchestral music is not extensive, but it does include four works that deserve to be more widely known and performed. However, before these are considered in some detail five earlier essays should be mentioned. The first two, the Double Fugue, Op. 9 and the Triple Fugue, Op. 25, remain in manuscript. Both are student works despite the widely separated opus numbers, for Rubbra was at this time (the 1920s) a student at the Royal College of Music. His counterpoint teacher was R.O. Morris and he was also studying composition with Holst.[1] As related in Chapter 1, Morris set Rubbra on a new course designed to get him away from the overly diatonic influence of Holst. The result was the two fugues, both of which were, fundamentally, exercises in chromaticism. Some years later, the Double Fugue received a performance which elicited the following remarks:

> Of the five works played at the Royal College of Music Patron's Fund Concert on Friday [no date] under Mr. Boult, two at least 'promised' well. Edmund Rubbra's so-called 'Double Fugue', angular in subject matter, austere and powerful in orchestration, showed 'character'.[2]

Holst, who was in the audience, was not enthusiastic, a not surprising reaction in view of his antipathy to chromatic music.

The ballet music for *Prism*, Op. 48, is another unpublished work. Rubbra referred to it obliquely in Chapter 1 by telling of his associations with two English members of the Diaghilev Ballet, for whom he wrote music.

The last of the early works are orchestrations of piano music by other composers: Op. 40, the well-known Prelude in G minor of Rachmaninov, and Op. 47, Brahms's Variations and Fugue On A Theme by Handel. With regard to the second of these Edwin Evans makes some interesting points:

> Between his Second and Third Symphonies Rubbra orchestrated Brahms's Variations and Fugue On A Theme by Handel. Why? Was anyone pining to hear that overworked composition played by an orchestra? I venture to say that it was a false move. Rubbra is less a colourist than a line-draughtsman. He is no disciple of Rimsky-Korsakov or Ravel – not that their methods would have helped him in this instance, for the work does not invite colour. But the absence or paucity of colour accentuates the pianistic quality of the music, which the piano itself is quite competent to do. I

can understand Ravel orchestrating Moussorgsky's 'Pictures', which obviously pleaded for colour, but not Rubbra orchestrating a completely self-contained and self-satisfied set of pianistic variations – though, to be sure, Weingartner *did* orchestrate the Hammerklavier Sonata.[3]

Rubbra inadvertently answered Evan's question as to why he orchestrated the piece when he said, 'I always felt that as a piano work it wasn't successful – I always felt it needed something more.' This statement is followed by accounts of several performances:

> It was first performed by the Philharmonic Society. But not much notice was taken of it for some reason until it was performed in New York by Toscanini. I tried to listen to the performance because it was broadcast, but it was four o'clock in the morning and the reception was terrible. It was later taken up by Ormandy and the Philadelphia Orchestra, and even recorded by them on a Columbia record. This was a brilliant performance.[4]

Improvisations on Virginal Pieces by Giles Farnaby

This piece, Op. 50, the first of the four main works to be discussed, is surely one of Rubbra's most engaging compositions. Written about 1939, its first performance took place at the Bradford Subscription Concerts in January 1940. The following passage explains its origin and describes it in general:

> Until they were taken over by my present publisher (Lengnick), my first four symphonies were assigned to Universal Editions, and, in order to offset the cost of engraving and printing the full score of my First Symphony in Vienna (1937), it was suggested to me that I might like to write a lightweight work that would be less costly to produce and, at the same time, have a more popular appeal. This was the origin of the Farnaby Improvisations. As a pendant to my interest in sixteenth-century polyphonic music I had long been fascinated by Farnaby's perfectly fashioned keyboard miniatures, and I decided to use five of them as the basis for a small orchestral suite, being careful in enlarging them to retain as far as possible the crystalline freshness and idiom of the music. The titles of the first three, 'Farnaby's Conceit', 'His Dreame', 'His Humour', suggest that the composer was trying to encapsulate some personal characteristics, but the fourth and fifth, 'Loth to Depart' and 'Tell me, Daphne', seem more impersonal. They are probably based on well-known tunes of the period, and Farnaby's arrangement of the latter takes the form of a set of variations. I have not, however, simply orchestrated these to form the finale of the Suite, but have written my own set, taking care to retain the concision of the original music.[5]

The work is scored for a modest ensemble which, in addition to strings, includes two each of the following: flute, oboe, clarinet, bassoon, horn, trumpet and timpani. However, according to the composer's note in the score, the second flute, oboe, bassoon and trumpet are not obligatory. The five movements are balanced as to tempo and mood – rather like the pyramidal contour of which Bartók was fond. Thus the first, third and fifth movements are fast and extroverted while the second and fourth are slower, quieter, and more reserved.

Doubtless Rubbra's choice of these particular Farnaby pieces as well as their placement in the suite was at least partly dictated by this question of balance and contrast. All five come from the *Fitzwilliam Virginal Book* (hereinafter referred to as *FVB*), which contains the known bulk of Farnaby's work in this medium – some fifty pieces. Each of Rubbra's movements preserves intact Farnaby's melody and rhythm. Most of the harmonic structures are also the same, certainly at the beginning of movements where Farnaby's melody is first presented, and often later. However, superficial as well as major deviations – the latter involving Rubbra's own materials – justify the word 'improvisations' in the title.

The word 'conceit' in the title of the first movement is said by Gustave Reese to be related to the word 'toy (toye)', which was 'a short, light genre piece'.[6] Farnaby's original (*FVB*, No. 273) is a tiny miniature consisting of only seven of our modern measures (Example 92).

Ex. 92

Rubbra's treatment begins with a straightforward presentation of Farnaby's entire piece, but with each half repeated. Including the initial statement there are seven distinct sections, each closing with the rhythmic grouping of Farnaby's final measure. (Actually, each of Farnaby's originals concludes with a held chord occupying a whole measure following the final measure in each of our examples, but since Rubbra does not include these in his suite, they have been omitted here.) Except for small changes in the instrumentation, several of the sections are exact duplicates of one another, each a repetition of Farnaby's theme. Thus the first, fourth and sixth are alike. The second corresponds to the seventh, but some variety is achieved in the treatment of the first half of the melody. Sections 3 and 5 are dissimilar, the former being in the minor key entirely while the latter employs both major and minor modes. There are also other differences. Each deals with subordinate figures derived from Farnaby. While there is not much variety in terms of alterations to the original piece, the movement as a whole has charm and vitality. There is also a fulfilment of expectations as the rhythmic grouping of Farnaby's final measure comes around each time to close the section, but the attractiveness of the material prevents the repetitions from becoming in any way monotonous.

The second movement, 'His Dreame' (*FVB*, No. 194), is hauntingly beautiful, an effect created by Rubbra's original material in conjunction with Farnaby's melody, the first four measures of which are shown in Example 93. The melody

Ex. 93

is stated twice, first by the first oboe and then by the violins. Rubbra's original material, presented *con sordino* throughout the movement, consists, first, of chords in the lower strings and a rising two-note figure in the first violins. This underlies most of the oboe's statement, and the gentle undulation of the carefully phrased figure above the steady quarter-note chordal movement is most effective. During the violins' presentation of the melody, this material is replaced by suitable, short figures assigned to various instruments. The chords return, there is a one-measure reappearance of the two-note figure, and the movement quietly dies away to nothing.

The third movement, 'His Humour' (*FVB*, No. 196), is a driving allegro with an abundance of good spirits. In his setting of the melody in Example 94

Ex. 94

Rubbra always places each statement of the first and third phrases in the piccolo and flute (except for one statement for piccolo only, measures 77–9, 81–3), accompanied by a syncopated and *pizzicato* figure in the strings. The second and fourth phrases are always stated in the first trumpet part (plus second trumpet, measures 79–81, and first oboe, measures 83–5). There is thus an antiphonal effect, and it is this alternation of phrase settings, the piccolo's shrill sound and the syncopations, that heighten the genial and delicately playful atmosphere. Between these full statements of the first four phrases, there are presentations of some of Farnaby's later phrases as well as Rubbra's free treatment of various motives drawn from the original accompanimental material.

Farnaby's setting for 'Loth to Depart', No. 230 in *FVB*, takes the form of six variations on a rather subdued, even melancholy theme (Example 95). Rubbra, however, does not follow the variation scheme in his setting. The melody in its entirety is heard but twice, first by the solo viola and then by the horns and first

Ex. 95

violins, the final portion being shared by woodwinds when the horns diverge. These appearances are followed by a statement that omits the first four measures. However, the most striking feature in this movement, unlike any of the preceding movements, is the composer's harmonic treatment. Following the G major cadence concluding the first statement, there is an echoing cadence in E major; this is followed at once by the second statement in C major. Halfway through this statement there is a sudden shift back to Farnaby's original G minor. The abruptness of these changes reminds one of the similar changes in Vaughan Williams's Fantasia on a Theme by Thomas Tallis. A particularly lovely passage – not, however, related to these changes – occurs from measure 37 when the first clarinet (joined presently by the second), the second violins, and the violas play the abbreviated melody accompanied by a steady stream of generally rising quarters derived from Farnaby's opening measure. The entire passage increases in volume and culminates in the third appearance of the G major cadence. An echoing E major cadence then ushers in transitional passages, some of which are chromatic, based on the original tune. The movement ends with a truncated statement of the main melody, scored for first oboe and first violins above a repeated and muffled D in the timpani. It is a movement that lives up to its title, for its quiet beauties make one 'loth to depart'.

'Tell me, Daphne', No. 280 in *FVB*, consists of a theme and two variations in Farnaby's setting. Rubbra, in this, his final movement, also employs the variation format but expands the number to six. However, as already cited, Rubbra took pains to 'retain the concision of the original music'. Concern for brevity is underscored by the fact that each of the variations except the last is eight measures in length, thus conforming to the eight measures of Farnaby's melody.

After an entirely straightforward exposition of the theme in the first violins, accompanied by the woodwinds lightly reproducing Farnaby's scale passages, Variation 1, still in 4/4 metre, changes the accents when the theme appears in the first flute. Variation 2, *Vivace*, isolates the rising thirds contained in the eighths of Example 96 (A-C, C-E, E-G), and alters them to *staccato* triplets and an eighth.

Ex. 96

These four measures are repeated. Variation 3, *Lento*, subdued, features but three instruments: the two clarinets in a variant of the theme, accompanied by scale-wise triplets on the solo cello. The fourth variation is a heavily accented, dancelike, *fortissimo allegro* in which a variant of the melody is contained in the rhythmic figure ♩ ♪ ♩. The fifth variation begins in A major and ends in F sharp minor. Here, the characteristic rising, five-note figure in Farnaby's first measure is shown in quarters and retrograde inversion with the D omitted.

Except for the scale in the clarinets that connects this variation with the final one, the instrumentation is for strings only. The concluding variation is also in A major for most of its length, its last ten measures reverting to the original A minor. Marked *Allegro bucolico*, the variation in its major key section features short figures that are recognizable as having been derived from the thematic material, yet are different enough to contrast with the full statement when the latter returns in minor for the final ten measures.

In his short review of the work, Edward Lockspeiser observes that 'the mood of these characteristic virginal pieces is never violated in the improvisations on them, free though they are in harmony that is nevertheless kept strictly diatonic.'[7] (We have seen that certain passages, notably in 'Loth to Depart', are not 'strictly diatonic'.)

A Tribute

For some strange and inexplicable reason, *A Tribute*, Op. 56, is not available in full score from Lengnick, the orchestral parts only having been published. Therefore, the recording of the work (now unfortunately deleted from all catalogues) must suffice. The composer has provided us with a brief account of the circumstances surrounding the work's origin:

> I was already in the Army and stationed in a remote part of Wales when, in 1942, I was one of six composers [actually seven, the others being Alan Bush, Patrick Hadley, Gordon Jacob, Constant Lambert, Elizabeth Maconchy and Robin Milford] asked by the BBC to contribute a short piece to a programme to be broadcast in honour of Vaughan Williams's 70th birthday [12 October]. After much manoeuvring behind the scenes I was granted a week's leave to fulfil the commission, and during this time I wrote and scored for small orchestra what I originally called 'Introduzione e danza alla fuga'. While exactly describing the form of the music, it was a ponderous title for such a small piece, and when I revised the score for its inclusion in a broadcast programme of my work on the occasion of my 70th birthday I re-named it 'A Tribute'. There are no specific references in it to Vaughan Williams's music.[8]

The core of the slow section is a gently rising and falling scale figure: C, D, E flat, F, E flat, D. This is set in what appears to be a 6/4 metre. First heard in the lower strings, it soon becomes apparent that the six notes are to be treated as an ostinato figure. Melodic fragments begin to sprout against it in various instrumental parts, and it is not long before the ostinato figure itself moves into the woodwinds and other parts. As it does so, the pitch contours are changed so as to accommodate evolving harmonies. The melodic fragments begin to coalesce and a full-throated theme finally emerges. The main impression gained from this quiet first section is that of a pastoral meditation based on the ostinato figure.

The *Allegretto* (presumably) grows directly from the introduction, and is in a triple metre. The rhythmic lilt of this section is most attractive and there are some interesting cross-rhythms. The Mahler of the *Wunderhorn* songs as represented in 'St. Anthony of Padua's Sermon to the Fishes' makes an appearance in the descending triadic constructions emphasized by the triple metre. The gentle Mahlerian irony is also present in the woodwinds and other instruments. During the course of the section another ostinato figure becomes prominent.

It must be assumed that the 'danza alla fuga' part of the title was applied to the piece before the revision spoken of by the composer, for no fugue or even fugal writing is apparent. After a *forte* climax, a much modified and curtailed version of the slow introduction concludes the work.

Festival Overture

Whether the use of the four-note rhythmic figure, ♫♩, throughout much of the Festival Overture, Op. 62, was unconscious or a deliberate evocation of the first movement of Beethoven's Fifth Symphony is, perhaps, beside the point. It is rather difficult to believe that the composer could have been unaware of it and it is equally difficult to understand why Harold Truscott made no mention of it in his record-sleeve analysis of the work. Reference to Beethoven *is* made: 'the overture is... mainly an extrovert composition – unbuttoned, to use the term Beethoven employed at times to describe some of *his* extrovert pieces.'[9] The work was written for and received its premiere performance at the Elgar Festival in Malvern on 18 July 1947, under the direction of Julius Harrison. Chronologically, its composition immediately preceded the beginning of work on the Fifth Symphony.

The overture is cast in a modified sonata form. The first subject is stated immediately in the woodwinds and violins, although in the preceding half measure which actually begins the overture and concluding on the first beat of the first full measure, there is an inversion of the four-note figure. However, to

Ex. 97

assert that this inversion and the principal theme are Themes *b* and *a* respectively is analytically inaccurate. So is the labelling of the marching quarters in the lower strings and brass (measure 3ff) as Theme *c*.[10] The only one of these 'themes' to be preserved intact in future statements, thereby qualifying it as a principal subject, is *a*. C is out of the running altogether as its only function is to provide a strong harmonic support for the activity going on above; *b* has no identity of its own beyond its initial statement. Yet Truscott correctly identified the second theme (calling it 'a sort of second subject').[11]

Between the first and second themes Truscott has found another (Theme *d*) which he says is 'imitated between treble and bass in Rubbra's characteristic bi-tonal writing'.[12] Only five measures in length (*fortissimo*, measures 27–31), the composer apparently considered it important enough to reintroduce at the start of the coda (measure 169), where an augmented version of its first measure and a half is given to the horns and all the bass instruments. Despite this shortened climactic reappearance, I tend to think of its initial statement not as a theme in its own right but rather as a momentary concentration of material from previous passages that is undergoing a metamorphosis. Truscott is, of course, correct about the imitation (actually, the passage is a strict canon at the distance of one measure and the lower interval of a fourth), but I cannot accept his statement with respect to bitonality. Nevertheless, specific points bearing on the present passage must be raised here. First among these is the question of key: C sharp minor for the treble parts and its relative major – E – for the bass. With six tones always common in such a relationship (seven if the natural minor is involved), the concept of bitonality is not even debatable. All that occurs in the present instance are very mild dissonances. If Donald Grout, in citing Milhaud's bitonality in the first movement of the latter's Fourth Symphony can say, 'of course no listener hears the two tonalities of B major and G major.... What he hears is G major with a few dissonant notes which he probably interprets as *passing tones* or *non-resolving appoggiaturas* [my italics]',[13] how much more is this reasoning true in Rubbra's passage, where the keys are *closely* related.

Returning to a brief consideration of the two themes contained in the overture's exposition, Theme 1 (shown in Example 97) appears twice: measures 1–5

Ex. 98

and 34–8; and Theme 2 has three statements of which the first two are in strict canon at the minor seventh, as shown in Example 98. Between these two statements, each scored for first clarinet and first bassoon, there is a short variant for solo flute and oboe, also in canon. Again, bitonality is postulated because of the B flat major theme set against the 'marching alternation of E flat and B flat' in the lower strings and timpani;[14] once again it is an untenable notion. A far more reasonable explanation is that the combination resulting from treble and bass parts is an example of what, for lack of a better term, has been called 'wrong-note harmonization' or 'wrong-note style'. And even if the E flat

and B flats are consistently reversed throughout the passage, there are still harmonic clashes. What we are hearing and seeing, I think, is an example of light-hearted humour.

However, what the listener will probably remember most about this overture is the very frequent reiteration of the original and inverted four-note figures, which are such distinctive features of Theme 1. Both figures are especially effective when they are reproduced in long chains of rising or falling sequences – a fact Beethoven was quick to recognize in his Fifth Symphony. But whereas tension dominates this symphony's first movement, the mood in Rubbra's overture is festive and jovial. Some of this geniality is traceable to the sparkling, scalic counterpoint that often provides contrast; whereas in Beethoven's movement even the second theme furnishes but scant relief from the overriding tension. There are other differences too, for with Rubbra the motive does not expand beyond its original leap of a fourth (the very rare downward leap of a fifth is not an expansion when the note of resolution is the lower octave of the final note reached by the upward-moving fourth). Nor is there ever a contraction to a third – something that would be a very obvious reference to Beethoven. Thus the figure remains static when compared with Beethoven's ever-changing motive. Still other examples of the static nature of Rubbra's figure are those occasions, mainly in the development section, where the repeated notes resolve to a half-note rather than being links in a sequential chain, but even here the surrounding counterpoint provides the necessary motion.

The development section is lengthy and all of the elements that make up the two themes are presented in various guises and combinations. But even here, despite the static qualities, there is the feeling that the four-note motive is undergoing development – an illusion probably linked to the constantly changing tonal centres. A new theme in the first violins is introduced in measure 105, and it occupies the remainder of the development. However, when this theme is examined carefully, a substantial part of it is seen to consist of an eighth-note figure first introduced in measure 11 as sixteenths where it, in turn, is discovered to be the inversion of the sixteenth figure first heard in measure 1. The eighths in the theme introduced here in the development serve as connectors to half-notes that are distinctive elements in this new melody. In the sixteen measures before the recapitulation the melody consists entirely of halves and quarters, the eighths having migrated to the woodwinds, which so far have been resting. The broadening effect of the longer note values in the melody and the re-entry of the brass, together with an increasing dynamic level, signal the approach of the short recapitulation. This begins in the brass with a *fortissimo*, augmented version of the first two measures of Theme 1. The remainder of this passage leads to a very different arrangement of melodic patterns heard in the exposition. There follows a literal repetition of the two statements of Theme 2 and the intervening related material. A triumphant coda, scored for full orchestra, brings the work to a brilliant conclusion.

In retrospect, the Festival Overture presents no problems for the listener; he need do nothing but listen and enjoy. Even the four-note motive, so reminiscent of Beethoven, is embedded in surroundings very different from those earlier ones with which the listener is so familiar, and he quickly adjusts to Rubbra's festive interpretation. The motive, although organically a part of Theme 1, leads an independent existence most of the time and it is this feature that the listener recalls. Rhythmically, there are no complications in the guise of cross-rhythms or syncopations.

Resurgam

The second of Rubbra's two overtures, *Resurgam*, Op. 149, was completed on 9 May 1975. With respect to other major works of the same period, it followed the Tenth Symphony and immediately preceded the Fourth String Quartet. According to the composer's note at the beginning of the score,

> this work was commissioned by the Plymouth Symphony Orchestra to celebrate its Centenary in 1975.
> In March 1941, the Church of St. Andrew lay in smoking ruins after a bombing of the town. Only the tower stood intact, epitomizing the City motto 'Turris fortissima est nomen Jehovah'. A board was fixed over the North Door, upon it the single word 'Resurgam'. Hence the title of the Overture.

The work received its first performance in November 1975 not in Plymouth but in London.

Structurally, *Resurgam* is a conventional sonata form with a *Lento* introduction and a concluding *Adagio*. The *Lento* is organically connected with the main-movement *Allegretto*. This is achieved through the introduction of embryonic material that reaches its full potential in the exposition. The first third of the introduction has a dreamlike aura that seems to suggest the sense of unreality so often associated with wholesale destruction. The entire string section is engaged in playing accented block harmonies – *pianissimo*, tremolo – and all the parts except the basses are additionally directed to play *divisi, con sordino*. Although the notes of the individual parts change, the harmonies remain essentially the same as the chords move in a ghostly procession of half and whole notes (the metre is 5/2 until there is a change to 4/4 just prior to the end of the passage). The harp is also a member of the procession, duplicating in its eight-note chords the notes of all the other strings. Above, the first oboe and first horn, the latter muted and in a short mirror canon with the oboe's first phrase, hauntingly feel their way toward more substantial material. The three notes at the head of the oboe and horn soli are to become important later on. Presently, the first clarinet replaces the oboe and is, in turn, superseded by the first flute. All of their materials are scalic in character and comparisons between them and those of Themes 1 and 2 will show direct relationships. As other instruments join in (the tolling effect of the strings and harp having now ceased), a feeling of confidence takes hold, turning into momentary defiance when the solo trumpet hurls a challenge above *fortissimo* strings in the form of the three notes heard in the opening oboe and horn soli. A very brief quiet spell intervenes before the first climax begins to build. The mood is one of sheer defiance on the part of all instruments, and this is accentuated by timpani, the tolling of bells and tremolo strings.

The *fortissimo* material, moving in eighth notes and sounding in sixths in both trumpets and flutes, is very intense. It contains two figures of prime importance – *x* and *y* in Example 99. *X* is common to Themes 1 and 2, and *y* is a

Ex. 99

Fls, Tpts.

prominent component of Theme 1. The first time that *y* is heard in the above example, it is also heard in the bells and violins, but there are accented quarters in place of eighths – another example of Rubbra's skill in combining two rhythmic expressions of the same motive. In the violins the quarter-notes are spaced a seventh apart. When these dissonances are combined with the sixths in the trumpets and flutes the resulting intensity is greater.

The change of mood from the *Lento* introduction to the *Allegretto* exposition is both sudden and unexpected. The principal theme, carried by flutes and oboes, is lighthearted and exuberant, characteristics greatly magnified by the infectious rhythms. These are not confined to the theme itself, but are very much an integral part of the *pizzicato* string accompaniment's block harmonies. These consist of carefully marked *sforzandi* on syncopated parts of each measure. The rhythmic vitality of the entire thematic presentation derives from the interaction of two different sets of accents: one for the theme and the other for the string accompaniment. The former, incidentally, contains one full and one slightly altered instance of segment *x*, while in the strings segment *y* makes two appearances. It must be conceded, however, that because of the dominance of the theme in the flutes and oboes plus the *pizzicati* and opposing accents in the strings, *y* is not easily heard. Nor, perhaps, is it meant to be, for such references

Ex. 100

in the works of any composer are the interior scaffolding on which parts of the structure depend. The theme is shown in Example 100.

Following a very short transitional passage which includes two prominent instances of x – the first, an inversion in the woodwinds – Theme 2 makes its first appearance in the strings (Example 101). It is as calm and soaring as Theme 1 is energetic and buoyant. Note segment x in the middle.

Ex. 101

The development section, which follows immediately upon the completion of Theme 2, marks a return to the cross-rhythms and a heartiness of expression, but with a higher degree of dissonance. This increase is brought about by the greater horizontality of the writing, for all parts, especially the brass, have scraps of melody to contribute, and in their enthusiasm to be heard they generate an almost joyous raucousness. This comes to a head when segment x is expanded and rhythmically vitalized to become the subject of an energetic fughetta comprising five entries (violins; violas and cellos; trombones; horns; violins). There are moments in the development when not just the metre and tempo (6/8, ♩. = 54) but also the scalic materials recall the development in the Tenth Symphony.

Important changes in the scoring and key (E rather than C), and a somewhat different transition to Theme 2 that involves two measures, mark the recapitulation of the first theme. Otherwise the music is the same. Theme 2, slightly slower than in its first statement, is also reproduced exactly, but on the cor anglais instead of the strings, and there are other scoring changes too. Alterations of this kind in all of Rubbra's recapitulations are common as we have seen in the symphonies, and they always have the same effect: the repetitions *seem* like new music.

An upsurge in volume at the end of Theme 2 leads directly into a nine-measure, two-part coda. Part 1 involves the whole orchestra in what appears to be an uplifting and heartfelt celebration of victory. Just as suddenly this gives way in the second part to a sense of total spiritual serenity and fulfilment, and, as is so often the case in Rubbra's orchestral music, it is the oboes that have the final say. Doubled by the first bassoon, they intone the appoggiatura figure, F sharp-E. This was an integral part of Theme 2, and it was first heard in the slow introduction at a different pitch. Readers familiar with Mahler's *Das Lied von der Erde* will, I think, recall how unforgettable this figure is in 'Der Abschied', set to the word 'ewig'. The same atmosphere of unearthly peace prevails here.

It might appear from the foreword to the score that *Resurgam* is concerned only with the destruction of St Andrew's Church and the determination to rebuild it. However, the bluff and jaunty confidence that permeates so much of the music is a persuasive argument for the belief that the overture depicts Plymouth as a dynamic seaport – a sailors' town, which has seen famous ships and figures come and go through the centuries. But the defiance of the city in time of war is also clearly evident in the music. The undestroyed tower of St Andrew's, the largest church in Devon, was as much a symbol of hope for Plymouth in those dark days as the dome of St Paul's was to Londoners. Hence, it seems appropriate to end the work with music that radiates an inner confidence and an unshakeable faith in the future. This the appoggiatura figure does, especially if one mentally supplies the word, 'ewig'.

Notes

1   Rubbra's assessments of these composers and teachers are contained, respectively, in 'R.O. Morris: An Appreciation', *M&L* 30, no. 2, April 1949, pp.107–8; and *Gustav Holst: Collected Essays*, Stephen Lloyd and Edmund Rubbra (eds) London: Triad Press, 1974.
2   Printed inside the front cover of *Edmund Rubbra: Composer*.
3   Edwin Evans, 'Edmund Rubbra', *MT*, February 1945, pp.44–5.
4   Tape of 26 July 1980.
5   Sleeve-note to the recording of the Farnaby Improvisations on RCA RL25027.
6   Gustave Reese, *Music in The Renaissance*, rev. edn (New York: W.W. Norton & Co., Inc., 1959), pp.835; 847, n.125.
7   Edward Lockspeiser, *M&L* 27, no. 4, October 1946, p.272.
8   Sleeve-note to the recording of *A Tribute* on RCA RL25027.
9   Sleeve-note to the recording of the Festival Overture on Lyrita SRCS 96.
10   *ibid.*
11   *ibid.*
12   *ibid.*
13   Donald Jay Grout, *A History of Western Music*, 3rd edn (New York: W.W. Norton & Co., Inc., 1980), p.702. Milhaud is the composer most often cited when bitonality is under discussion.
14   Sleeve-note to the recording of the Festival Overture on Lyrita SRCS 96.

6 Concertos and concerto-related works[1]

The shameful neglect accorded Rubbra's output in this area is even more thorough than that encountered in the symphonic field. There are no introductory articles such as those cited in connection with the symphonies and the works in the concerto category are less frequently heard than are the symphonies. What makes this state of affairs so regrettable is that the public, which traditionally has always had an appetite for the added excitement that a soloist can furnish, is being denied the opportunity to hear and know several works of superior quality. Although none of these works is a display piece on a par with most of the popular concertos for various solo instruments, there is nevertheless much to delight and impress the thoughtful listener. There are moments of genuine excitement and virtuosity but, as in the best concertos, such moments unfailingly arise from purely musical considerations, and are never an end in themselves. Works with an immediate appeal are the relatively early Sinfonia Concertante, which elicited enthusiastic reviews, and the later Improvisation for Violin and Orchestra; certain other works require a longer time for the listener to fully realize their value.

Piano concerto, Op. 30

The earlier of the two piano concertos, Op. 30, was composed in 1931–32, and consists of three movements in the usual fast-slow-fast sequence. The concerto was written for Kathleen Long (1896–1968), a pianist with wide-ranging tastes. She was noted for her Mozart and Bach performances with the Boyd Neel Orchestra, and for her interpretations of Debussy, Ravel and especially Fauré. Her reputation in France was very high, but she was also a champion of contemporary English music. Her performance of Rubbra's concerto attracted the following notice:

The orchestral rehearsal held in connection with the Royal College of Music Patron's Fund yesterday was conducted by Mr. Geoffrey Toye, who obtained from the New Symphony Orchestra supple accompaniment to the three solo pieces.

The first of these was Mr. Edmund Rubbra's concerto for pianoforte and orchestra, which had never before been played in public. The overgenerous acoustics of the hall did not seem well adapted to a concerto so richly scored, and not a few of the passages admirably played by the soloist, Miss Kathleen Long, were barely audible. The last movement, in particular, showed the balance between soloist and orchestra tilting heavily.

There is, however, abundant evidence in the first and second movements of courage and originality. Mr. Rubbra is not afraid of a dramatic phrase because dramatic phrases are not fashionable just now. He has, moreover, an ear for orchestral colour, which he uses in a characteristic way, and often with telling effect.[2]

A passing reference to the concerto in a review of the First Symphony points out that it 'should have had more than the one hearing it got at a Patron's Fund Rehearsal a few years ago'.[3]

Rubbra's evident dissatisfaction with the concerto, a conviction he continued to hold, has prevented its publication. One of the outstanding memories in connection with this performance is 'laboriously having to write all of the orchestral parts out myself. That taught me a lesson!'[4]

Sinfonia Concertante

In spite of its low opus number (38), the Sinfonia Concertante for Piano and Orchestra is not Rubbra's first large-scale work to be published, for, although it dates from 1934–36, it was revised and rescored in 1942–43 while the composer was stationed with the army in Wales. It will be recalled that the original version was written at the cottage near Speen in Buckinghamshire to which Rubbra had moved in 1934. There are three movements: *Fantasia*, in which an individualized structure is created by alternating sections of *Lento* and *Allegro*; *Salterella*, a driving and exciting *Allegro vivace*; and a Prelude and Fugue marked 'In Memoriam Gustav Holst, 1874–1934'. The first performance took place in August 1943 at a Proms concert conducted by Sir Adrian Boult, with the composer at the piano.

Ex. 102

The *Fantasia* opens with two contrasted yet subtly related ideas: related in that seconds – major and minor – have an important role in each. These two ideas are 1) a rising piano figure, and 2) a gently rising and falling curve in the strings (marked respectively *x* and *y* in Example 102). The entire movement is an outgrowth of these ideas and the developmental process begins at once. This statement thus acknowledges that two of Rubbra's most important and recognizable characteristics are fully operative in this, his first published work for a soloist and orchestra.

The first instance of organic development is found in measures 4–5 where the piano's C-E-F sharp-A pattern, embedded in the figure shown in Example 102, has been detached, set in sixteenths, and alternated between the hands. At the same time and beneath this new pattern, the F sharp-G-F sharp figure (*y* in Example 102) turns into a simultaneous alternation of B-C-B in the right hand and C-B-C in the left. Both lines are in quarter-note values. Before the end of this short section (really an introduction such as those that precede the main *allegro* movements in some of the later works) there is a return in the piano part to the basic melodic and rhythmic shapes seen in Example 102, although with variations. This allows an elaboration of the original string figure (*y*) to be heard to better advantage.

With the start of the *Allegro* in measure 20, the second section gets under way, and the expansion of both the piano and orchestral material proceeds swiftly. Regarding this expansion, some of the small details are worth noting, as they give us a clear picture of the composer's thought processes at this early stage in his career. The first point to be noted is the bass of the piano part as seen in Example 103. Its C-E-F pattern, used here as a left-hand accompani-

Ex. 103

ment, is a modification of the C-E-F sharp of the opening. The first E-F in the right hand emphasizes the semitone introduced in the strings (Example 102) while its second appearance is part of the altered main figure. This one measure is repeated three times, followed by another two measures of the same material but at different pitches. The interesting point is that these six measures, plus another quite different one, are background for what appears to be a main

Ex. 104

theme in the strings (Example 104). However, this turns out to be an intermediate stage between the germinal phrases of the beginning and the theme that comes to dominate the movement (Example 105) with its seventeen statements.

Ex. 105

By comparing Examples 102, 104 and 105, the evolutionary transformations can be traced, foremost of which is the change from the upward moving sixteenths of Example 104 to the falling thirty-seconds in Example 105.

The theme finally chosen, with its urgent rhythm at the beginning and end, is striking enough in itself to command attention, but it is thrown into high relief by the heavily accented, *forte*, *pizzicato* chords in the divided second violins, cellos and basses. These magnify and sharpen the theme's inherent tension. The piano, meanwhile, occupies itself with its opening material, here arranged in double octaves. It then has one solo statement of the theme in rolled chords. This is followed by a 5/4 statement of Example 105 in the violins, accompanied by *pizzicato* chords in the cello and a decorative extension of the theme in the first clarinet.

The development of both the piano's and orchestra's materials, together with unaltered statements of each, occupy the ensuing *Allegro*. Although this section accounts for only twenty-eight measures it contains a tremendous gathering of tension, which is attributable more to the dramatic nature of the themes and their treatment than to the increasing dynamic level, impressive though that is. If this were not true, the section would consist merely of noise without substance. This first climax ends with the piano's electrifying and dramatic flourish, made up of *fortissimo* octaves in both hands, and featuring the head of the principal theme, accompanied by a rolled B flat in the timpani.

The tension is broken in the following section with a return to the *Lento* and the material of the movement's first six measures, the only changes being the lowering of the pitch by a whole tone and minor differences in orchestration. The next fifteen measures, while retaining the same tempo, do not correspond in any way to the twelve measures that follow the opening six, for at this point the principal theme is given out in an overlapping fashion by solo instruments: cor anglais, oboe and flute. Scale figures in the rest of the orchestra and delicate figuration in the piano make up the accompaniment. An abrupt change comes in the second half of these measures when the descending third in its characteristic rhythm (Example 105, first measure) is detached from the rest of the theme and assigned, first, to the piano and then to the strings and first horn. The piano urges the whole passage forward with cascades of notes in various groupings, and with a final *glissando* and *accelerando* the passage gives way to a new section – *Doppio movimento*.

This new section, which begins in measure 95, resumes the development begun in the first *Allegro* but at a more subtle and less recognizable level. The characteristic rhythm of the main theme is altered from ♫♩. ♪ to ♫. ♩. Another evolutionary development occurs simultaneously in the piano with a series of ascending three-note patterns, separated by rests and obviously derived from the triplet figure in the first measure of the piano's part (see Example 102). As this second *Allegro* proceeds the shredding of themes continues, and new contrapuntal combinations result from the fusion of the fragments. In addition, there are three statements of the entire theme.

If anything, this second *Allegro* is more vigorous and tension-filled than the first. The piano passages are certainly more difficult and fiery, and in listening to them as well as to the whole of the second-movement *Salterella* one realizes just how able a pianist was Rubbra in his prime to have performed this work in public. Like the first *Allegro* the dynamic level of this section is *forte* and *fortissimo*, and the constantly mounting tension is brought about by the inherent tensions of the material and its treatment. Upon the conclusion of the *Allegro* there is a seven-measure repetition of the opening *Lento*, this time at the original pitch (measures 155–61). Its continuation, which is shorter than at the corresponding place following the opening *Lento*, reverts to more basic patterns with respect to the material. A five-measure upward surge brings the movement to a *fortissimo* close.

From this it can be deduced that the movement is structurally well organized and balanced despite connotations sometimes associated with the word 'fantasia'. The *Lento* introduction and its two repetitions serve as reference points between which the two dissimilar *Allegros* run their course. A link between this outer structure and the movement's title is implied in the following general observation: 'the fantasy of the first movement lies mainly in the presentation of the material, which in itself is anything but loose-limbed.'[5]

To one who has become used to only the quieter and more contemplative side of Rubbra's music, the following passage, taken from the same review, may seem exaggerated, even bizarre:

> If this highly individual work has any affinity it is towards the best of Bloch's work, of which one is reminded by the emotional intensity of the melodic phrases, the heavily-treading ostinato basses and the *barbaric splendour* [my italics] of some of the climaxes.[6]

Another reviewer speaks in the same vein of the 'exotic wildness, reminding me of Bloch and Holst'.[7] Both apply to the *Allegro* sections of the first movement and to the *Salterella*, for the final movement contains little if anything that corresponds to such descriptions. The emotional intensity *does* remind one of Bloch, not in terms of any particular thematic resemblances but because certain turns of phrase produce the charged atmosphere and rhapsodic freedom that are associated with Bloch. As for Holst reminders, I would have to say that the ostinatos are the most obvious references.

The *Salterella*, marked *Allegro vivace*, can be considered an early example of the headlong and sometimes boisterous scherzos with which we have become familiar in Symphonies 2, 6 and 7. Of course, it is not entirely accurate to think of this movement as a scherzo because of the specific dance connotations of the title, but the general atmosphere is the same as that of a scherzo. The movement is monothematic if allowance is made for a countersubject that is derived from the *Fantasia*.

Ex. 106

The basic theme as shown in Example 106 is four measures in length, and it is transposed Phrygian. Except for several occasions when the upward leaps of a fourth and fifth are replaced, respectively, by leaps of a third and fourth, plus five places where the Phrygian cadence is altered to a conventional one, the contour of the theme is unchanged. It is undoubtedly this Phrygian sound, coupled with the number of times the theme is heard (twenty-seven) thus helping to perpetuate the sound, that is responsible for much of the 'exotic' flavour, but the 'wildness' (if the reviewer's words apply to this movement) can be attributed to the relentless rhythm and the dissonances resulting from the piled-up texture.

After the theme's initial statement by the solo bassoon, it is sounded in turn by the first clarinet, first oboe, first violins, piano, solo flute and solo oboe. A feature of all these statements, as well as others later on, is the overlap of a measure between the end of one and the start of the next. This same, seamless continuity obtains between incomplete statements of the theme by various instruments or groups. Each incomplete statement usually consists of exactly two measures: half the normal length. Soon after the opening statements, the theme is given to pairs of instruments – some the same, some diverse like oboe and piano. Eventually, either entire sections or at least the most important members of them sound the theme (complete and incomplete). These statements not only add weight to the texture but also help to keep the momentum going. A little over two-thirds of the way through the movement there is a break from the prevailing *Allegro vivace* to *Lento*. Although it is only eight measures in length, the slower tempo provides a respite from the breathless pace and a preparation for its resumption.

The countersubject in embryonic form makes its unobtrusive first appearance in the oboe at measure 11, immediately following that instrument's solo presentation of the principal theme. A comparison of Examples 107 and 104

Ex. 107

shows the derivation of the countersubject from the material in measures 20–23 of the *Fantasia*. However, the countersubject's appearance in measure 11 is not followed by a series of entries as might be expected. Indeed, the next entry does not come until measures 70–77 in the piano, where it is heard in combination with the main theme in the woodwinds. The violin's statement in measures 85–8 is more prominent because the material in the woodwinds and violas is subordinate, consisting only of repetitions of the main theme's first four notes, some of which are varied intervalically. Measures 95–106 contain partial augmentation in the horns and trumpet of the full countersubject as presented by the piano. A later and different version of the countersubject is the chordal one given out by the piano in measures 122–9.

Augmentations are an important feature of the principal theme. The first instance comes in the form of octaves in the oboes at measures 53–60, although only the second half of the theme is sounded. The full theme in normal note values is simultaneously running its course in the cor anglais and clarinet parts, the obvious aim being for both statements to finish together. Measures 110 to 121 contain, first, a four-measure augmentation in the woodwinds of the theme's first half, accompanied in the violas by a conventional half statement. At the end of the four measures an augmentation of the entire theme begins, joined after two measures by a normal statement of the theme in the woodwinds and piano.

A very ingenious passage brings the movement to an exuberant and boisterous conclusion. From a technical standpoint it is a *tour de force* and one might think from a description of it that it is merely that and nothing more. However, everything that Rubbra commits to paper serves the larger musical purpose, and is never technique for its own sake. In this instance the contrapuntal complexities have created a tight web of sound, the sheer excitement and joyous din of which are breathtaking. The whole orchestra and, of course, the piano are involved. The passage starts in measure 168 with a 4/4 presentation of the first half of the principal theme in continuous eighths. This leads without a break of any kind into a similarly altered full statement, as shown in Example 108. The instruments involved in both statements are cor anglais, clarinets, bassoons and lower strings. Above the full statement is a part of the augmented form of the

Ex. 108

countersubject in the violins, while above that there is the first half of the theme in its original 12/8 version. When the piano enters in the measure following our example, it reinforces the 4/4 statement with alternating octaves in each hand. The riot of sound continues *fortissimo* in all parts until the end of the movement is reached, but before that all of the instruments are brought into the 4/4 fold.

The concluding movement, dedicated to the memory of Rubbra's teacher, Gustav Holst, and called Prelude and Fugue, does not in my estimation present a problem simply because 'we have enjoyed ourselves so much in the *salterella* that it's asking much for us suddenly to stop smiling and be serious and, indeed, be invited to remember the dead.'[8] After the unbridled high spirits of the *Salterella* something more subdued is certainly in order. And unless one knew of the dedication to Holst, either by means of the score or a programme note, the music would not seem different in atmosphere from, say, the theme and slower variations in the last movement of the Third Symphony.

The melodic material of the Prelude is stated in the left hand of the piano's entry, and also in the parallel line of the right-hand's bottom notes (Example 109). One of the most important intervals in the passage is the falling fifth at

Ex. 109

the end. Up until the twelfth measure this line is repeated in various contexts, one of which is a muted and *pianissimo* string passage containing ethereal, shifting harmonies that result from unashamedly chromatic movement (Example 110). At the fourteenth measure a theme emerges, the first four notes of which are based on the minor seconds of the opening material (Example 111). An interesting combination of Examples 109 and 111 appears in measures 21–4, where the strings have the former and the piano the latter. Thereafter, the

Ex. 110

Ex. 111

theme dominates the remainder of the Prelude, but with subtle differences. Much of the piano's contribution in this half of the movement consists of decorative passage work, but in the two-measure *Adagio* preceding the Fugue, the piano has a solo, chordal passage of extraordinary beauty that is a variant as well as a reworking of the string passage seen in Example 110.

The Fugue is the emotional summit of the entire work, rising to several peaks of intensity. It is a piece which is far more complex than performances of it would indicate, evidence yet again of how art conceals art. There is more freedom and flexibility than one normally associates with a fugue, a statement amply borne out by the frequent variants and the ease with which these flow into and out of statements of the subject. Yet the integrity of the fugal process is never compromised.

The subject is first announced by the cor anglais, a most appropriate instrument in view of the subject's mournful character (Example 112). The answer

Ex. 112

comes in the solo clarinet, and the third statement in the solo flute. (It may be recalled that the fugue at the end of the Seventh Symphony also employs woodwinds for the giving out of the subject's first three statements.) A rising scale figure that is a continuation of the subject's initial entry (seen at the end of Example 112) accompanies the answer, giving promise of being part of a genuine countersubject when it also finishes the third statement.[9] However, the absence of any one particular sequence of notes following the rising figure and, indeed, the absence of the figure itself on many occasions suggest strongly that there is no countersubject in the usual sense. Yet roughly a third of the way through the Fugue, most of the piano's first utterance is given over to a passage (Example 113), which incorporates the falling fifth employed in the Prelude as well as the rising scale figure. This melody is characterized by Stevenson as a

Ex. 113

second subject,[10] but it fails to qualify as such because of its frequently short-ened version and its spotty distribution throughout the rest of the fugue. However, its more placid nature contrasts sharply with the angular intensity of the subject. To put a label to it, the disputed material is better described as an independent strand of melody that weaves in and out of the fugal fabric in various instrumental parts and at various pitches. By frequently preceding and at times overlapping the beginnings of subject entries, it serves as a cohesive and unifying force. Admittedly, the piano's first statement of any sort in the fugue isolates this material, thereby creating the impression that a second subject has made an appearance. However, this impression is soon dispelled by the inconsistencies in the melodic figure. In the three measures following the piano's exposition of this new figure, attention shifts to the woodwinds where a series of close stretti involving the figure leads to another round of subject entries.

Stretti are also an important element with reference to the subject, the first instance starting as early as the fourteenth measure at the fifth above with a time distance of two beats. Among other examples, the most interesting in-volves the subject in the oboes and first violins, plus its inversion in the trombones at the lower seventh, again separated by two beats (measures 52–3). This passage convincingly demonstrates the composer's concern for a balanced instrumentation: the *forte* of the trombones does not overwhelm the oboes and violins, both of which have been carefully marked *fortissimo* in compensation.

The most comprehensive of the reviews, from which two excerpts have been already cited, calls the work

> a forthright example of the breadth and power of the conceptions we have come to expect of its composer. Counterpoint is indeed the life-blood of the style, and in these masterful hands it is a splendid means of achieving diversity in unity which is the essence of symphonic writing...
>
> The piano part is truly 'concertante'. There are hardly a dozen unaccompanied bars in the work; indeed in this contrapuntal style it is difficult to point with certainty to passages in which the pianist should unequivocally take the lead; never-theless there seems to be no bar which could be omitted or transferred to other instruments without essential loss.[11]

The reviewer for *The Times* sums up the work by saying

> it is more symphony than concerto in that the thought is organic from beginning to end, and the piano is used less for purposes of virtuosity than for the quiet enuncia-tion of what is cardinal in it.[12]

As for the deafening silence which the Sinfonia Concertante has had to endure over the years, Stevenson has the perfect answer:

> Such a humbly proud, individual and profoundly-felt work somehow won't permit me to bemoan it with the customary epithet 'neglected': it is the *audiences* who are being neglected when such a work isn't performed.[13]

Piano Concerto in G

The second of Rubbra's two piano concertos, Op. 85, was commissioned by the BBC and received its first performance on 21 March 1956 at the Royal Festival Hall by the BBC Symphony Orchestra under Sir Malcolm Sargent; Denis Matthews was the soloist. The same forces are featured on the current recording of the work.

The Concerto is in the usual three movements, but this is the only context in which the word 'usual' can be employed, for, with the possible exception of the third-movement rondo, the structural approach is highly individual, and the harmonic scheme of the entire work is completely unorthodox. As is true in so many of Rubbra's large-scale works, the individuality causes genuine problems in analysis; were it not for the composer's helpful explanations in this instance of some of the more puzzling aspects, the analytical process would be much more painful than it is. Even so, there are problems, the answers to some of which may prove indecisive.

Rubbra has described his first movement in the following terms:

> [The work] is dedicated to the Pakistani musician, Ali Akbar Khan, whose phenomenal performances on the 'sarod', a complex Indian stringed instrument, so impressed themselves upon me during the composition of the Concerto as to influence my attitude to the ideas in it.
>
> A prominent feature of the improvisations of Eastern musicians is the slow, almost tentative approach to the main body of the music, as though the musician is at first just 'feeling his way'. Such an approach is reflected in the opening of the first movement of the Concerto, where the pianist 'feels his way', as it were, into the music by means of a simple discourse round a slow G minor arpeggio.[14]

The initial section of the first movement is the first of five sections arranged in a pyramidal configuration: *Adagio, Allegretto, Allegro, Allegretto, Adagio*. The piano's slow, two-handed, ascending *arpeggio* is ingeniously arranged so that each *arpeggio* moves according to its own metrical pattern, the left-hand one cutting into the regular 3/8 pattern of the right (Example 114). Answering *arpeggios* in both piano and orchestra, some of them descending, lead to the next stage in this process of 'feeling one's way' into the music. This consists of a gradual tightening up of the piano part via a series of ascending, unrelated and unresolved dominant seventh chords until the *arpeggios* are vertically expanded

Ex. 114

into triads. At the same time, the orchestral parts gradually lose their tentativeness as they congeal into definite melodic units. The result, of course, is that both piano and orchestra gain in depth, body and purpose.

The thematic material in this movement is very difficult to identify, certainly from the viewpoint of clearly differentiated, readily perceived subjects. This difficulty is caused by the inherent nature of the materials themselves, and not the seemingly irreconcilable structural concepts that lie at the base of the movement. In the following passage Rubbra mentions both the thematic and the structural elements:

> This movement has the title *Corymbus*, a botanical term signifying an 'inflorescence of stalked flowers springing from different levels but making a flat head'. The stalks are thus of increasing length. Musically expressed, this means that each idea, whether important or unimportant is always added to on its reappearance. The overall shape is, however, very close to Sonata form, for after the slow opening there is an *Allegretto* that soon leads to the second subject in 7/16 time and is characterised by a highly decorative piano part. This is recapitulated in G major, and the movement ends with a gradual return to the slow and reflective opening.[15]

Strangely, there is no mention of a first subject in the composer's explanation, yet, if there is a reference to a second subject, there must be a first.

Since the opening *Adagio* is entirely occupied with the gradual, 'almost tentative approach to the main body of the music', it can be assumed that Theme 1 will not put in its appearance until the beginning of the first *Allegretto*. This assumption proves to be correct, and it is indeed confirmed by the reappearance of the same material at the corresponding place in the second *Allegretto*. The theme is not the sort one associates with the opening movement of a piano concerto, for the usual orchestral assertiveness, followed by brilliant virtuosity on the soloist's part as the first theme is announced by each partner are entirely missing. In fact, the theme is introduced by two clarinets, accompanied in the lower strings by a triplet figure containing repeated Bs (Example 115). Tension

Ex. 115

Quasi allegretto

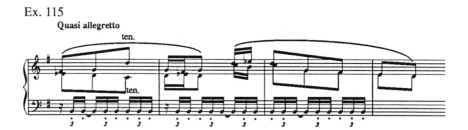

is built up as this figure continues, and it increases when the first violins enter with an ostinato-type figure derived from the third and fourth measures of the theme (Example 116).

This figure is important because of its great rhythmic and dynamic prominence later in the movement. The piano's entry in the ninth measure of the

Ex. 116

Allegretto contains two *fortissimo* statements of the figure, and these lead directly into the first statement of the second theme in the first oboe and first horn parts (Example 117). The theme, together with the instruments chosen for its

Ex. 117

presentation, again differs from orthodox notions concerning 'normal' concerto material. (This whole business of 'normality' obviously confused the reviewers of the Concerto, as we shall see later in this discussion.)

An interesting link with Theme 1 can be seen in the unobtrusive continuation (flute 1, harp, celesta) of the violin's ostinato figure seen in Example 116. This is merely a further instance of the unity inherent in almost all of Rubbra's music. Whether or not the listener is always conscious of the musical means whereby unity is achieved makes little difference, and is really beside the point. However, it seems certain that if such unifying elements were absent, the music would be much less satisfying, although the listener would probably not know why.

Thus far the structure of the *Allegretto* has complied with the basic requirements of sonata form, even to the extent of placing the second theme in the dominant key (D) – something not often found in Rubbra's sonata structures. This same faithfulness to the sonata principle continues with a development section, which is contained within the central *Allegro*, and in the second *Allegretto* there is a recapitulation of both principal themes in the tonic key. An eight-measure *Adagio* brings back the mood of the opening.

Structurally speaking, the novel and unusual corymbus analogy is of much greater interest than the sonata form, which, in this instance is conventional. It was said earlier that the two structural concepts are 'seemingly irreconcilable', but a little reflection will show that this is not so. The lengthening of 'each idea, whether important or unimportant ... on its reappearance' – the corymbus concept – is accomplished within the limits of the encompassing sonata form. In fact, if one rereads the composer's lines one will see that the 'overall shape is, however, very close to Sonata form'. Thus to say in a review of the work that 'in the first movement Rubbra has invented a new musical form' is misleading and inaccurate.[16] I would be the first to give credit where it is due, but here there is surely no 'new' form. What we have is, rather, a *process* that is part and parcel of the sonata structure. Unfortunately, the composer's booklet remarks on the subject came much later than any of the reviews. Had things been the other way around, some of the remarks contained in certain reviews might have been more moderate than they are and here we are not talking just about the first movement but the Concerto as a whole. Several instances of the corymbus principle at work may now be examined.

First, there are the lengthenings of the principal sectional divisions: the second *Allegretto* is just over three times as long as the first *Allegretto* (ninety-three measures as compared with thirty). The natural conclusion to be drawn from this is that both of the principal themes undergo a lengthening process. In Theme 1 the ten-measure statement grows to twenty-five with the significant changes coming in the second *Allegretto* as early as its ninth measure. There, the *arpeggios* from the very start of the movement reappear in G major rather than G minor (solo trumpet) and a short connecting figure leads to a *forte* passage in which the ostinato figure in Example 116 loses its first note. Through all of this the piano is silent until one measure before the start of the recapitulation of Theme 2.

The part of the second *Allegretto* containing Theme 2 has been expanded from the original twenty measures to sixty-eight. The first seven, allowing for differences in instrumentation and key (tonic rather than dominant), are a reproduction of the theme as it appears in the first *Allegretto*. Thereafter the theme is repeated but there is no lengthening of it. In fact, the two principal themes of the movement are unchanging, and the material which is 'always added to on its reappearance' comes from the opening *Adagio*. Thus the 'natural conclusion' referred to in the last paragraph turns out to be wrong!

The piano has the lion's share in the enlargement of the *Adagio* material, for the descending triadic *arpeggios* first heard in measures 7–8 are now preceded by supplementary material that becomes longer with each succeeding phrase. The piano dominates these pages (40–49) and as ideas whose origins are in the *Adagio* continue to develop and expand, the conviction grows that nothing illustrative of the corymbus analogy is in any way inconsistent with many of Rubbra's usual developmental procedures.

Speaking personally, I find other aspects of this first movement to be of greater interest than the lengthening of certain materials upon repetition. Chief among these is the threefold organization of all of the elements which is not restricted just to the first movement, but is evident throughout the Concerto. Two important manifestations of it in the first movement are the triadic arrangement of the melodic lines as seen in the *arpeggios* of the first *Adagio* as well as of later sections, and the triple metres, 3/8 and 3/16, which dominate most of the rhythmic flow. Still another expression of this threefold organization concerns the frequent major/minor third relationships between keys. Some of these involve changes in which a modulation from C to E flat, for example, is accomplished by treating G, the fifth degree of C, as the third degree of E flat.

While this is an extremely usual modulation, it is an effective one here. Similar changes are scattered throughout the movement, but there are also other modulations involving a third relationship in which varying degrees of preparation are evident. But no matter how this type of key change is effected, the time span allotted to each key is very short – not more than five or six measures in most cases, and often not even that much. Thus the harmonic structure in sections other than the two *Allegrettos* – where the principal themes maintain their traditional sonata form relationships – is very fluid.

The second movement is entitled 'Dialogue', 'the idea behind it being a philosophical and at times impassioned discourse between soloist and orchestra'.[17] The very fact that the word 'dialogue' was chosen as the title of this movement invites comparisons with the second movement of Beethoven's Fourth Concerto even though the latter has no title. The overall lengths are different, Rubbra's being slightly longer, and the tempi are different, Rubbra's *Lento* being slower than Beethoven's *Andante*. Each movement begins with a statement for strings alone (the unison harp passage and two unison notes in the muted horns do not fundamentally alter Rubbra's string sound), answered immediately by the piano, but whereas in the remainder of his movement Beethoven's orchestra consists of strings only, Rubbra soon employs the full orchestral palette. Another important difference can be seen in the relationship between the orchestra and the piano: Beethoven separates these elements entirely while Rubbra mixes them in long passages during which the piano part is sometimes purely decorative against the orchestra's presentations of thematic material, while at other times these roles are reversed. Still another important difference centres on the distribution of material assigned to the participants. In Beethoven's movement the theme allotted to each element is never shared by the other, and it is precisely this separation that induces the drama of which the listener is so keenly aware. The gruff string statements, softened by degrees in response to the soothing piano passages suggested to Liszt the image of Orpheus taming the wild beasts with his lyre. There is nothing like this in the Rubbra movement where the thematic material is shared by both entities (although not at first), and the emotional level of both elements is the same. However, the concept of persuasion operates here as in the Beethoven movement, but in an imperceptible way, for one is not really conscious that the orchestra 'gradually gets won over to the new point of view',[18] accomplished through its sharing of the piano's material. The idea here is one suggestive of a rational interchange of thought, once the orchestra perceives the sense of the piano's argument, and as the composer said, the discourse during this process is 'at times impassioned'. With Beethoven, on the other hand, the underlying concept involves the drama of a sensitive entity – the piano – in opposition to a blind, obdurate orchestra.

'The opening A minor statement is made by low strings and harp, and there is a decided query when it ends with an unexpected twist to D flat major.'[19] The 'decided query' at the conclusion of many of the orchestral statements results when the harmony shifts upward a major or minor third, another manifestation

Ex. 118

of the threefold organization in this work. All such passages are made more poignantly expressive through the hesitancies created when the eighth rest intervenes between the statements and the two-note questions. But the key structure itself is of great interest right at the beginning of the movement because of the ambiguities immediately apparent in the very first orchestral and piano statements (Example 118). The composer's remarks indicate that for the orchestra he had A minor and, for the piano, D flat major in mind. However, repeated hearings have not succeeded in eradicating the strong impression that what one *really* hears are D minor and F minor respectively. Pursuing this further, the greater stress accorded the D in the first measure (a half beat longer than the E) seems to establish it as a tonic, attended on either side by the supertonic. In measure 2 the A acts as a dominant, modified by the leading tone G sharp. The decisive factor seems to be the return to D as a tonic in measure 3. The soloist's entry in the fourth measure can more easily be interpreted in the composer's D flat, but here again the F pedal in the strings suggests an F minor

Ex. 118 continued

tonic, and the piano's three Fs in measures 4 and 5 strengthen this impression. Also, the penultimate beat in measure 4 has D flats which are interpreted as appoggiaturas to the Cs which are, in turn, the dominant of F. At the corresponding point in the fifth measure the Gs may be interpreted as appoggiaturas to the A flat and F, while the strong Cs in the same measure may be thought of as the dominant of F minor. The next two measures (6 and 7) gravitate to B flat minor (piano) followed by a confirmation of that key in the strings. The upward twist to D flat major at the end of the string passage is unequivocal this time, for the soft D flat pedal under the piano's entry is heard unmistakably as a tonic.

The key structure for the remainder of the movement duplicates the type seen in the first movement, but minus the stabilizing influence of a first and second theme set in a tonic-dominant relationship. Tonalities are established by the methods with which we have become familiar in the first movement: modulations by major and minor thirds. Other, sometimes abrupt, modulations are also found. The various tonalities appear to last longer than those in the first

Ex. 118 continued

movement because of the slow tempo (*Lento*) but the time allotted to each is approximately the same for each movement.

Looking at Example 118 from a thematic viewpoint, it will be noted how easily the material given to the orchestra and the piano is capable of segmentation. It might seem that the Es and Ds at the start of the orchestral entrance should be placed within a separate bracket like the D flats and Fs at the end. However, the former notes are not so distinctive as the latter, and they do not enjoy an independent existence anywhere in the movement because they are always important members of the four-note motive in segment *a*, which is always treated as a unit. One of Rubbra's important melodic characteristics is prominently displayed in segment *a*: a rising augmented fourth which resolves a semitone higher.[20]

The highly expressive piano material restates this melodic characteristic in the second of its two opening measures. Other segments not related to those announced in the orchestra are *d*, *e* and *f*. The last two are likely to be overlooked as each is merely a counterpoint to the higher melodic line, yet these often unperceived and apparently insignificant melodic figures turn out to have important later roles. This is especially true in the case of segment *f*, which, in conjunction with its longer extension, dominates one particular passage in a very intense and expressive manner (Example 119). This passage leads to a short

Ex. 119

con intensità

section of twelve measures scored for piano only in which there are three further statements of *f*. The first two of these include the extension and a small derivative of *f*. All of these statements ride the crest of the melodic line in the right hand, separated by short connecting links that are directly related to some portion of *f*.

The expressive heart of this movement is contained in a section that encompasses rehearsal numbers 19 and 20 (measures 68–87). The entire passage is soft, delicate and hauntingly beautiful. It is introduced on the cor anglais by a statement of *a*, and all of *b* and *c*. Following this are close imitative entries, fuguelike in character, that are shared by the soloist's right-hand part and the muted first violins. The material is based on the accented notes with which segment *d* begins. The imitative texture breaks off when the muted violins and violas sound segments *b* and *c* two octaves apart. Just as *c* is dying away the muffled timpani begins a steady beat on F in groups of three – an obvious reference to the repeated notes of segment *d*. Meanwhile, the piano is engaged in an introspective monologue consisting of a delicate right-hand embroidery of basic material against a measure-long ostinato pattern of chords. Actually, what we are hearing at this juncture is a feeble attempt on the orchestra's part to resume the dialogue which has, temporarily anyway, received a setback. However, before the dialogue is fully revived, a sudden and very beautiful change is effected with the entry of the cor anglais over the timpani's Fs and the start of the piano's most decorative figure. This steers the music to a soft and indeterminate tonality, regularly punctuated again by the timpani and the bass drum. The effect of the change is magical, particularly when the piano softly answers with the haunting five-note cor anglais figure seen in Example 120. Thereafter the full dialogue resumes with segments *a* and *b* on the strings followed by the soloist with *d* and *a*[1], above which is heard segment *f* in the woodwinds. Following these four measures a one-measure climax leads to the peaceful conclusion of the movement in a radiant A major.

Ex. 120

pp – *espress.*

Looking back over the movement, one might wish to take issue with the composer's remark that the orchestra 'gradually gets won over to the new point of view'. Piano and orchestra seem to share about equally in the unfolding of the material. However, this is a very small point, and certainly not one over which to agonize.

The third movement, entitled 'Danza alla Rondo' and marked *Allegretto gioioso* is, as the adjective indicates, joyful. The unrestrained high spirits are interrupted only once, and then close to the end by a sizable section which is divided into two very dissimilar parts: first, a subsection in triple metre whose very majestic content sounds oddly Russian; and second, the piano's *cadenza retrospettiva* which, as its name indicates, summarizes some of the materials used in the preceding movements. It also contains a subdued version of themes from the rondo. This leads to a very soft and mysterious sounding coda in which the *Allegretto* is restored. There is a sense of suppressed excitement that is released in a final, loud, staccato chord, but the joyousness so evident throughout the first two thirds of the movement does not fully return.

The rondo structure of the movement is inevitably affected, for what has just been described takes the place of the final *A* in an otherwise normal *ABACABA* design. Consecutive and unrelated thirds, instantly recognizable both audibly and visually, are the most important ingredients of the *A* sections, thus carrying out in this movement the threefold idea of the previous movements. For their first appearance the thirds are introduced quite dramatically by the timpani, which themselves have alternating notes a third apart. Example 121 shows the

Ex. 121

start of the movement. In the twelfth measure a countermelody begins, evenly distributed throughout the strings and woodwinds. It is kept in the background, very much overshadowed by the piano and timpani, but when the second *A* section comes around – shortened to eleven measures (72–83) from the original twenty-nine – the countermelody is stronger because of more instrumental doublings and louder dynamic levels. In this case the subtle change provides an interesting difference between the two *A* sections, but a greater difference is the omission of the introductory timpani flourish and the piano thirds as seen in Example 121.

Between the two *A* sections the *B* episode has an interesting and unusual theme, shown in Example 122. A comparison of its oscillating thirds with those

Ex. 122

Solo tpt.
mf

contained in the timpani's opening flourish (Example 121) not only reveals the origin of the new theme but again confirms the basic unity that is always at work in Rubbra's music. The piano is only indirectly involved with the thirds, which are contained within a graceful, leaping figure over a series of repeated chords. With the conclusion of the theme's first statement, the woodwinds have it, followed by a piano statement. There is then a short transition to the abbreviated return of *A*.

Section *C*, which begins at rehearsal no. 29, is divided into two almost exactly equal subsections, the first being sixteen measures in length and the second fifteen. In both the emphasis is on the orchestra with the piano assuming a largely decorative role. A sweeping eight and a half measure violin melody in octaves dominates the first subsection. Rhythmically, it contains another example of the braking action noted in the *Allegro* movements of some of the symphonies: a four-beat pattern cutting across the prevailing 6/8 metre.

The second subsection in 2/4 metre features a syncopated melody introduced by the solo oboe. The strings soon take it up, and the piano joins in with decorative triplets. There follows a forceful restatement of *A*, now restored to its original length, but in keeping with Rubbra's compositional habits rescored with respect to its details. An abbreviated *B* section follows.

Mention has already been made of the majestic 3/4 section and the *cadenza retrospettiva* which follows it. Although one cannot deny the effectiveness, indeed, the impressiveness, of the first of these sections, the reason for it remains both obscure and puzzling. The tempo is within the *larghetto* range, while *trionfale* denotes the expressive content. The dynamic level is at a consistent *forte*. The thematic content of the section is highly serious, and this is accentuated by the timpani's steady beat on every quarter-note. In addition, an organ pedal on F sharp is called for, although the 'ad lib' instruction provides for the absence of an organ. The modal turn of the melody and the frequent drop to the temporary tonic (F sharp) are characteristics of Russian music. Their sudden appearance here is hard to explain or justify, particularly when the movement up to this point has been so joyous and carefree. The soloist is not a participant during the first fifteen measures of this section, but when he does enter – *giubilante, fortissimo* – with triplet octaves in each hand, some of the Russian character is dissipated.

The piano's *cadenza retrospettiva* grows out of the passage just described. The temporary silence of the orchestra allows its material to grow steadily more calm and meditative. The metre has reverted to 6/8 and the various themes previously heard begin to pass in review in the right hand, accompanied in the left by a constant rhythmic pulse. The first theme to be reviewed is a chordal version of the downward-moving *arpeggios* in measures 7–8 of the first movement. Next is a *molto espressivo*, extended account of the upward-moving thirds that open the last movement. The second movement is soon represented by segments *a*, *b* and *c*. From this point on nothing but small thematic fragments are heard until the cadenza concludes with a full statement of the rising G minor *arpeggios* of the first movement together with the answer given originally by the oboe. The *allegretto* and delicately scored coda conclude the Concerto.

As I have become increasingly familiar with this Concerto, I have been unpleasantly surprised at the insensitivity and lack of understanding demonstrated by some of the reviewers whose problem seems to be their inability to think of a concerto in other than traditional terms. This concerto is decidedly untraditional, both in its basic approach and in its choice of materials. One reviewer, who appears to sense some of these differences, addresses the problem as follows:

> Whoever sets out to perform the solo part in this particular work will have to think out the problem of concertante presentation afresh. Rubbra's work stands midway between the romantic display concerto and a work like Falla's 'Noches' which relegates with the most exquisite effectiveness, the piano to the level of one orchestral instrument among many ... Rubbra moves easily through his chosen perspectives. He never fumbles, nor is he at a loss for the next move. There was a time when he seemed in danger of evading issues that would lead beyond a narrowing set of conventions. That time has passed, as the two latest symphonies [Nos 5 and 6] and works of the same period show.[21]

But if the piano's role was seen as something different in the above citation, it is completely misunderstood in this excerpt:

> the composer at no stage seemed to solve the central, crucial relation between piano and orchestra, never to have decided, in fact, what sort of a concerto it was going to be, whether the piano was to dominate, to play power politics, or to merge. Mr. Rubbra's concerto certainly did not allot the solo instrument a brilliant solo role – the keyboard writing, incidentally, was oddly lame for a composer who is himself so accomplished a pianist – nor was that close-knit integration secured, as so frequently

happens in Mozart's concertos.... As the work progressed the piano ceased to function as a point of focus and slipped rather disconsolately into the background. At such moments we still did not have a concertante concerto in the old style, but simply a piano concerto without a piano.[22]

A similar misconception concerning the piano's province in this particular concerto is contained in these lines:

Although Rubbra is an able pianist himself his writing for the instrument is nearly always rather austere and reticent. It is treated here as a *concertante* rather than a solo instrument. Even the 'Cadenza retrospettiva' in the last movement, in which the themes of the previous movements are recalled in *reverse* order [my italics: not entirely true. See the foregoing discussion] provides no opportunity for solo display of any real brilliance. Elsewhere the writing, although often extremely florid, is not showy, and in the performances that I have heard has been almost too modest in effect.[23]

In these last two excerpts we are told what the Concerto is *not*, at least with respect to the piano's role. The point that is consistently missed in these negative opinions is that the composer deliberately chose not to write the usual brilliant and extroverted concerto. That decision is in keeping with the independence and individuality one has come to expect from him. More than that, this Concerto is the expression of a composer who eschews any sort of brilliance and display unless these qualities are inherent in his basic conception, or are a natural and logical outgrowth of evolving ideas. That neither is the case in this work is a fact that dictated the kind of concerto that emerged. If reviewers could recognize that a composer of Rubbra's stature and experience is sensitively aware of his options, they just might cease to fault him for not conforming to their notions of what a concerto ought to be. All of this is not to say that I consider this work to be entirely without flaws, as my remarks concerning the *trionfale* section of the rondo prove.

Another review approaches the Concerto with mixed feelings, but an almost flippant attitude detracts from it:

For better or worse the modern piano concerto with few exceptions, has become very much a public utterance. Rubbra has never been a Marble Arch composer, and the platform manners of his pianist are almost comically exposed when he sits down and unaccompanied begins pianissimo a slow arpeggio, *calmo e quasi improvisatore*. The impatient may say 'Do your improvising beforehand and begin your concerto when you have found something to say', but Rubbra declares in the title of this movement, 'Corymbus', that we are to assist with sympathy this involuted self-communion and watch the making of the main bloom from a multitude of flowerets. As a construction the movement appears flawless, and the piano part, as throughout the concerto, is rich in idiomatic detail. It is the melodic material which seems uncompelling, paying perhaps too high a price for its flexibility.[24]

The characterization of the melodic material as 'uncompelling' is not particularly alarming or even unjustified. Similar words have been used to describe Rubbra's thematic materials in the symphonies, and they will be encountered from time to time throughout the remainder of this book. It *is* one of the prices

Rubbra has had to pay, not so much perhaps because of the 'flexibility' of his material as the fact that critics, who progress no further than the material itself, fail to appreciate Rubbra's novel ways of using it.

I end on a different note by citing two short statements. The first pronounces the Concerto 'masterly in its contrapuntal structure'.[25] The second opinion is prefaced by the wise observation that there are choices involved in approaching the task of writing a piano concerto. The comments are contained in the booklet that accompanies the record album of British concertos, and from which Rubbra's explanatory remarks were extracted:

> Few of the composers involved here have followed the course set by Tchaikowsky, Grieg and Rachmaninov, each preferring to tackle the concerto form with an individuality much to be admired. The Bliss and Tippett concertos are, perhaps, the closest to the older tradition; Bliss because of his declared intention of writing a romantic concerto in the grand tradition and Tippett because he uses the traditional framework which he clothes with his unique blend of romantic polyphony ... Rubbra's concerto is perhaps the most overtly serious and searching concerto in this anthology.[26]

I am not sure in exactly what sense 'searching' is used here, but it seems appropriate to take it in its literal sense as looking for (and finding) a different solution to the concerto problem.

Soliloquy

We turn now to those works written for solo stringed instruments and orchestra, the first of which in the order of opus number is *Soliloquy*, for cello, string orchestra, two horns and timpani, Op. 57. It will be recalled that during his army service Rubbra was directed to form a group for the performance of classical music – The Army Classical Music Group', as it was called. William Pleeth was the cellist in that ensemble, and *Soliloquy* was especially composed for and dedicated to him. Owing to the seemingly constant movements of the Group in connection with its frequent performances at army camps, Rubbra worked on the piece in about twenty different places. It was published in 1947. The work is in one continuous movement, but there are four tempo divisions – *Lento, Adagio, Allegretto grazioso* and *Adagio*. The prevailingly contemplative mood of the work is not substantially altered by the faster tempo.

A few words should be said concerning the scoring which, though not unusual, is carefully planned for maximum effectiveness. All of the strings except the basses are provided in the score with two staves so as to accommodate the *divisi* writing, although there are numerous unison passages. In the *Allegretto* where a lighter texture is desirable, there is a reduction to one staff per section. The horns are used sparingly and are mostly occupied with doubling various string parts, but they do enjoy a few independent moments. The timpani is effective as a tension builder and at climactic points. It too is employed sparingly.

There is no introduction, and the solo cello and orchestra begin together. Two well contrasted ideas, one for the cello, the other for the orchestra, appear simultaneously. The more important of the two is, of course, given to the soloist. It is shown in Example 123. It would be difficult to say which of its

Ex. 123

segments is of greater consequence in terms of future use and development, for everything finds a place later on, not surprisingly in altered form. Thus the theme consists of several germ cells, placing it in the same category as other Rubbra themes discussed in earlier chapters. There is much sharing of this material with the orchestra, and indeed, the orchestra proposes variants which the cello accepts and alters further.

The same is not true regarding the second of the two basic ideas, for this is the exclusive property of the orchestra. It is scarcely a theme, being instead a rising and falling chromatic progression set in half- and quarter-notes. It is also essentially background material against which the cello's leisurely ruminations are projected.

From these remarks, it might seem that *Soliloquy* has nothing to offer except serenity, as desirable as that might be. Yet there is real drama in this piece, not the high drama in some of the symphony movements to be sure, but drama none the less. The first example occurs in measures 56–73. In this section of the opening *Lento* two strands of melody, one in the solo part and the other in the higher part of the divided first violins, unite to produce very expressive harmonies (Example 124). The thematic material has evolved from the beginning of the piece to this

Ex. 124

point, so that what is seen in the example appears to be unrelated,, but this is not so. These harmonies are supported in the lower first violins, the divided seconds and violas, as well as the timpani, by the following rhythmic pattern whose pitches are altered in accordance with the harmonic changes: ♩♪♪♪ ♩♪. The passage is divided into two sections, the first of which is not permitted to grow very much in either volume or intensity. A hushed *pianissimo* introduces the second section where an acceleration and a *crescendo*, plus the added weight of the cellos bring the passage to only a *forte* level. All of this does not, of course, seem very dramatic, but its understatement leads me to believe that this is the passage Ronald Stevenson may have had in mind when he characterized *Soliloquy* as 'a meditation with flashes of interior drama'.[27]

The two principal climaxes in the work are identical with respect to their material, but the second (measures 236–50) is set a half step higher than the first (measures 116–30). The material of, roughly, each second half is that of the soloist in measures 56–62, but in each case it has been assigned to the violins. However, its transference from the soloist to the violins, and the addition of the horns plus a dynamic level of *fortissimo*, have not resulted in as great a sense of drama as that exhibited in the passage described above. The orchestra's chromatic line, which in that instance coalesced so expressively with the cello's melody (Example 124) is completely absent as are, of course, the resulting subjective harmonies. Gone too is the rhythmic figure cited above, which built up suspense and an underlying tension. In its place is a syncopated figure in the timpani and lower strings. In sum, these later passages seem more usual, whereas the earlier one has about it an air of mystery and, ultimately, greater intensity.

The *Allegretto grazioso*, after the opening *Lento* the longest of the four sections, contains a further example of one of Rubbra's rhythmic trademarks: a basic 6/8 metre overlaid with 3/4. Here, the orchestra establishes the basic metre before the cello's entry in the twenty-fifth measure of the section and, unlike many previous occasions, the triple metre is specifically indicated. Later, the metres are exchanged, and there are also alternations of metre within each element – solo part and orchestra. However, the combination of these metres does not, as in other Rubbra movements, produce a real slowing or 'braking' effect. Perhaps this is because the tempo of the 6/8 is not so fast as in some of the *allegro* or scherzo movements, and the portion of this section where the two metres interact is short in comparison with full-length movements.

The thematic material of the *Allegretto* is related to the principal material with which the work opens, but it is so transformed as to be virtually unrecognizable. As in other sections, cello and orchestra share the material.

There are two general characterizations of portions of *Soliloquy* with which I have reservations. First, the orchestra's opening passage is not in my opinion 'a saraband, symphonically developed in flexible tempo'.[28] The passage may look and even sound superficially like a saraband because of the heavily accented second beat in a slow triple metre, but the effect is cancelled by the soloist's fluid line which cuts across the metre. Second, I can more readily subscribe to the view that the 6/8 *Allegretto grazioso* is 'a pastoral *siciliano*',[29] at least until the soloist's 3/4 entry, at which time the cross-rhythm negates any *siciliano* feeling.

Soliloquy is a work that can be easily underestimated at a first or even second hearing. Its thematic material may, at times, appear to be aimlessly drifting, whereas in reality it is subtly related to and evolving from that which has preceded. Therefore, the piece is more unified than it might at first seem. In sum, while it is not one of the composer's major works, it is certainly an attractive piece – well written for both soloist and orchestra. It should be in the repertoire of every capable cellist.

Viola Concerto

Rubbra's Viola Concerto, Op. 75, was commissioned by and dedicated to William Primrose, who, with the BBC Symphony, conducted by Sir Malcolm Sargent, gave it its first performance on 15 April 1953 at the Festival Hall. The Concerto is in the usual three movements, but the customary tempi have been altered to slow-fast-slow, the first of the composer's three-movement works to be so ordered. Such a reversal demonstrates not only Rubbra's independence and individuality but also a certain courage, for to begin a concerto with a slow movement is to risk listener apathy, especially when the solo instrument is not noted for its brilliance.

Ex. 125

Ex. 125 continued

The first movement begins with a twenty-three measure introduction, marked *quasi una fantasia*, the primary purpose of which seems to be to introduce material that will reappear either literally as in parts of the first movement, or in scarcely recognizable form in the second and third movements. Insofar as the listener is concerned, the introduction establishes a mood of utter tranquility, and for him this certainly takes precedence over considerations involving structure.

Soloist and orchestra begin together, the soloist's material consisting of a long, lyrical line whose uninterrupted flow ceases only when the introduction is brought to a conclusion. This line is, however, capable of division into several segments without doing violence to the whole. Of these the most important in terms of future use and/or development are x and y as seen in Example 125. Indeed, the developmental possibilities of x begin to assert themselves in the soloist's initial presentation, where rhythmic compression is employed (x^1). Later, and beyond the example, there is a mirror image of x, a characteristic Rubbran touch noted elsewhere. However, as memorable as segment x may be it does not play an active part in the movement, at least not in the form in which it first appears. The cadenza at the end of the movement is the only place after the introduction where the soloist refers to it, and the orchestra's references are confined to one appearance in the introduction (lower strings) and two statements in the main movement (violins). As for the other main segment in the

Ex. 126

Ex. 126 continued

viola's opening material, the dotted figure in measures 8–9 of Example 125 has
a more significant future role, but as a rhythmic rather than as a melodic entity.
Oddly, the rising fifth in the sixth measure is not so prominent as might be
expected, although as a harmonic interval it has a place in the cadenza.

Perhaps a more clearly defined purpose behind the viola's material is expressed in the word 'interval' for it soon becomes obvious that the melodic
thirds in the initial measures are changed to harmonic thirds in the orchestral
parts – most noticeably in the woodwind parts of both the first and second
movements. But melodic thirds are also prominent, for immediately after the
soloist has completed the principal portion of his expository material, he launches
into a lengthy passage consisting of chains of descending thirds arranged in
triplet groups. It is these mosaic-like figures that lead to the next large section:
the 12/8 *moderato*.

On the basis of two *moderato* sections separated by two *meno mosso* divisions, a rather unusual A-B-B^1-A^1 structure has been formed (the superscripts indicate substantial changes from the parent section). Of course, sections A and B have their own themes. A balance in terms of listener interest is provided by the fact that the A theme is assigned to the orchestra, while the B theme is the viola's province. Harmonic thirds are an important feature, but again there is a sense of balance, for those associated with A *are* the theme as opposed to those in B which *accompany* the theme. Both sets are derived from segment x in Example 125. The viola's only participation in the A theme is restricted to one statement of the thirds assigned to the woodwinds in measures 3–4 of Example 126. In A^1 this participation is much abbreviated. For purposes of comparison the B theme follows immediately in Example 127.

Ex. 127

Thematically, this is one of those Rubbra movements whose melodic stream moves effortlessly, seeming always to renew itself. Yet the gentle, leisurely flow that characterizes the entire movement need not (in fact, does not) imply a lack of direction. This would appear to be the implication in one reviewer's observation that, 'as usual with Rubbra, formal fantasy is held on a fairly tight rein'.[30] (In this statement the reviewer is referring to the entire movement, not just to the *fantasia* of the Introduction.) Another commentator is not so kind:

'there are passages of serene beauty, and others during which we begin to wonder whether the composer has fully distinguished between the serene and the sleepy.'[31] His comment also appears to be critical of the composer's choice of tempo, for he says 'it is not allegro but moderato.' Of course, had it been *allegro* the thematic content would have been quite different, and the comment would have been unnecessary. Within the tempo as it is there is a well considered metrical scheme that enhances the melodic flow and prevents it from becoming 'sleepy'. It consists of frequent metrical changes – the macrorhythmic framework – and assorted cross-rhythms involving both the orchestra and the soloist – the microrhythmic details.

Rhythmic vitality also pervades the middle movement where the tempo is *molto vivace*. The powerful, forward thrust of the music and the need for regular accents to keep the momentum going dictate that successive metre changes are not nearly so frequent as in the first movement. However, this drive, which in the scherzos of the Second, Sixth, Seventh and Eighth Symphonies is relentless and tension-filled, is here moderated and checked. The technical means employed to accomplish this involve the simultaneous use of two metres: the prevailing 12/8 of the orchestra and the viola's 3/2. Similar interaction on a far smaller scale is also found between sections of the orchestra, for example, 6/4 in the violins and 12/8 in the other parts. The result is the application of the braking action so often seen in Rubbra's music. The slower layer is in the foreground – the viola.

The more leisurely pace generated by the rhythmic combinations has instilled a relaxed atmosphere that is significantly reinforced by the diatonic material and the presence of large numbers of parallel thirds, the latter a legacy from the first movement. The structure in which this is cast is that of a rondo with a ground plan of *ABACAB*/coda.

Several interesting features of this movement merit attention. First, the rhythmic pattern ♩♩♩ ♩ᵧ♩♩♩ ♩ᵧ♩ is so pervasive throughout the entire movement as to make the few places where it is slightly altered or not present stand out in relief. The frequency with which the pattern is passed from one orchestral section to another, as well as the instrumental combinations to which it is given are responsible for shifting colours. These range from the delicate hues of the woodwind passages to the darker tones of the combined brass and string sections. One example of the former has various solo woodwinds always in pairs, and these alternate in the playing of an ascending and descending figure that is set in the rhythmic pattern (measures 87–95). Continuous modulations are another trait of this passage.

Second, the thematic material of the entire movement operates within the rhythmic framework. An important eight-measure phrase in parallel thirds, individual enough to qualify as a theme, is cast in this rhythm. Example 128 shows its beginning. However, this theme is a central element in each of the *A* and *B* sections where it is a potent unifying force. (Perhaps it is confusing to call it a theme, for in order for a rondo structure to establish and preserve its

Ex. 128

identity each of its sections must have its *own* theme.) In the present instance the *A* and *B* themes are unmistakable, but the material in section *C* is ambiguous to the extent that no clear melody emerges. The fact that this material contains vestiges of *A*'s theme, accompanied during its first nine measures by the woodwind modulatory passage mentioned above, suggests that *C* might be a small development section. In that case we would be justified in thinking of the movement's overall structure in terms of a sonata-rondo. Other evidence for such a conclusion lies in 1) a brief flurry of imitative entries between solo trumpet and strings of a highly rhythmic figure derived from the movement's basic pattern. These entries are accompanied by 2) vigorous triplets in the solo part and a repeated flourish on the side drum. This whole passage is dancelike and it leads to a concluding six measures that contain 3) a *fortissimo* 6/4 'braking action' composed of an ostinato figure. One other rhythmic figure is present: a duplet grouping in the lower brass and strings. A certain tension is thus built up from all of these elements, which is at variance with the movement's other sections to the degree that the idea of considering it to be developmental is entirely plausible. The final two measures of *C*, marked *fortissimo* and *appassionato ed allargando*, lead into an abbreviated return of *A* where the tension is released.

Rubbra's choice of key for this middle movement – E flat – is in a tritone relationship with the flanking A minor movements. This relationship is also present in the first movement between the two principal themes. Insofar as the keys defining the rondo elements within the second movement are concerned, they are also distant from one another: E flat for the three *A* divisions and the coda, and E for the two *B* sections, although most of the first *B* is in F. However, the two changes from E flat to E are not abrupt. In the first of these modulations a measure containing the second inversion of a C major chord intervenes between the IV of E flat (A flat, C, E flat) and the I of E. The modulation is thus not really sudden, for E is a common tone to C and E. In the second modulation the C major measure is omitted and the A flat is tied over to a G sharp. (There are innumerable instances in Rubbra's music of such enharmonic tied-over notes. They enable him to move easily from flat to sharp keys and vice versa.) The change from E to F in the *B* section, like the change from the C major chord to E, is accomplished through a common tone: A, the fourth degree of E major is the third degree in F. As the second *B* section, like the second *A*, is shortened, the entire F major portion is dispensed with.

The final movement bears the intriguing title, 'Collana musicale', or 'musical necklace'. It consists, according to the composer, of 'nine interrelated meditations... without central theme, but linked together in spirit'. Appropriate metronomic indications introduce each meditation, but with one or two exceptions these are not appreciably different from one another. Each of the nine sections is assigned a Roman numeral in the score, and separated from its neighbour by a double bar. Yet the music is continuous with no full cadence occurring until the end of the movement.

Pursuing the imagery implied in the title, it might be assumed that, in the absence of a central theme, some common melodic element forms the string or chain on which the 'beads' of the necklace are strung. However, this is not true, or, at least not in the way we normally envision such a procedure. Instead of a common element, the material of each section consists of a very small segment drawn from the material set forth in the first thirteen measures of the soloist's part. Each selected segment is usually, but not always, restricted to one particular meditation, and these segments may or may not be literal copies of the original. When they are not they may merely conform to the general contour of the original without preserving the exact intervallic structure. The viola's material is shown in Example 129.

Ex. 129

Other meditations such as III summarize one or two of the original segments by incorporating them in various ways. In this instance the meditation starts with the drop of a minor seventh in the violins and the almost simultaneous sounding of E, D sharp, E in the solo part. These intervals summarize, respectively, those in measures 9–10 and 6–7 of the illustration. An example of a literal use of a segment is seen in the clarinet part at the beginning of IV: the reproduction of the entire segment in measures 3–4. The pitches are identical; only the rhythm is changed. The repeated Es of measures 1–3 are softly intoned in the first horn as a background in this brief (nine measures) but very beautiful portion of the meditation. The soloist incorporates the segment in measures 3–4 (omitting the E) at the ends of two passages in triplets. Later, the G sharp, A, C, A of measures 4–6 also appear as part of a longer triplet passage. The rest of the meditations treat their borrowed segments in the same general manner as those just discussed. In each of them, once the derivative material has been stated, the Rubbran process of melodic expansion runs its course.

For some, this movement may appear to be a set of variations; certainly the numerals at the head of each meditation suggest such a structure as does the employment in each of them of the soloist's principal material. Yet Rubbra's assertion that the movement lacks a 'central theme' precludes this idea. The melodic segments are simply too small and, in many cases, too obscure to be recognizable. Often they are buried in the surrounding texture. But they serve the composer's organizational needs well and they give the movement unity. Unity is also provided by the generally meditative character of the sections; not even the *Allegretto* of No. V upsets that mood, for the metronome marking is not appreciably different from those of the other sections. A conspicuous exception is the ninth meditation, for the movement (and, of course, the Concerto) ends vigorously and *forte* with what one reviewer calls a 'commonplace bustle'.[32] I cannot but agree, for to break the mood that has been built up during the movement seems almost ruthless. A dissenter from this view is Donald Mitchell, who says, 'the brisk A minor conclusion I, unlike the majority of my colleagues, did not find inappropriate. It lent the movement a coda in true finale style, a rounding-off touch which the concerto would otherwise have lacked.'[33]

In addition to the first performance the Concerto was broadcast the following night, 16 April, on the Third Programme. The performing forces were the same. In comparing the two readings Desmond Shawe-Taylor touches on a problem with which many composers are unfortunately familiar, especially those who may have to wait a long time before another live performance: the quality of the playing. In the following report he does not mince words:

> The effect of the live and the transmitted performances was curiously different. From my seat in the hall, the solo part was inclined to vanish: one often saw Mr. Primrose imperturbably fiddling while one's ear reported little more than the buzz of an imprisoned bluebottle. On the air, he had no difficulty in making his presence felt; here it was rather the orchestral part which tended to lose outline. After making all allowances for the acoustics of the Festival Hall and for a possibly poor BBC transmission, doubts remain both about the performance and about the work itself. *How well did conductor and players know the score? Had they had enough rehearsal?* [my italics] More than once in recent months, this orchestra and this conductor have disappointed us in modern works of the kind which demand continuous care for the niceties of balance. Concerto accompaniment is perhaps their weakest point.... It seems likely, therefore, that there may be more beauty and clarity of sound in Rubbra's new work than has yet emerged... and no doubt familiarity and better performances will reveal beauties that now escape us.[34]

That 'better performance' was not long in coming. The venue was the same, but the violinist was Frederick Riddle, and the conductor was Sir Thomas Beecham. As Rubbra put it,

> it was a marvelous performance. I expected the worst from the rehearsals, which seemed to me not very exacting, but the performance – it was sheer perfection! Something that only Sir Thomas could bring about.[35]

Unfortunately, Primrose makes no mention of the Concerto in his memoirs other than that he commissioned it. However, the fact that he played it at least five times (probably more) would certainly appear to indicate approval. Yet, to be fair, it seems not out of place here to observe that in his memoirs Primrose referred a number of times to the Walton concerto, and pronounced that of Peter Racine Fricker 'as perhaps the finest viola concerto in the repertoire'.[36]

One of the very few references to American performances of any Rubbra work comes in a letter the composer wrote to Ottaway on 20 October 1959: 'I am off to America on the 31st. Primrose is giving four performances of the Viola Concerto with the New Jersey Symphony Orchestra; and they've invited me over – paying all expenses.'

The most pressing problem with which every concerto composer must deal involves the balance between the solo instrument and the orchestra. The problem is perhaps most acute in a viola concerto and it was obliquely referred to in Shawe-Taylor's review of the two performances of Rubbra's Concerto where, in each instance, the physical surroundings may have influenced the balance to the detriment of the performance. In view of these unsatisfactory occasions, it seems unfair to suggest that the composer was at fault unless this can be proved. Yet, in the earlier part of his review Shawe-Taylor seems to imply that the balance problem was the composer's fault:

> The most fascinating part of the viola's compass – its first two octaves, the two on either side of middle C – lie just where there is bound to be a good deal of harmonic filling-in and background. The cellist's A string can cut a broad golden path through such impediments but the charming husky voice of the viola is more easily lost; in order to dominate it must soar aloft – where it encounters a fresh problem, that of seeming to emulate the brilliant upper register of the violin. Of course, these difficulties can be surmounted; and like all problems of technique they are capable of stimulating a composer's imagination.
>
> Rubbra, for all his gifts, is not the sort of composer who is particularly excited by technical problems of a textural kind. Each of his three movements contains passages in which the grave eloquence of his thought is perfectly matched by the sensuous beauty of the tonal fabric. Each also has a tendency, once lyrical statement merges into development and climax, to lose quality – and not only textural quality, but quality of composition too.[37]

One could wish that Shawe-Taylor had provided an example or two of where he felt that Rubbra had gone wrong in terms of balance.

A different viewpoint with respect to balance is voiced by Mitchell in the review from which I have already quoted. After speaking of the *Collana musicale* movement as, in his opinion, the 'most inspired', Mitchell continues:

> Although in the first movement and scherzo one had already noticed the deft handling of the textural relation of his solo instrument to the orchestra, it was in this most beautiful finale that the nature of the music really seemed to derive all its eloquence and very genuine passion from the basic capabilities of the viola – an achievement which can only have been brought about by brilliant cognizance of the viola's limitations. Thus, in a sense, this originally conceived and impeccably executed movement stands as a study of the viola's potentialities, besides providing a substantial glimpse of Rubbra's gift for a deep lyricism which never deteriorates into sentimental rhapsodizing.[38]

Another review that addresses the balance problem speaks of how 'the inimitable character of the viola dominates, to the exclusion of any orchestral tutti, the first movement'. And again, 'the whole movement [the third] is suffused with the colours of the solo instrument for which the composer has an obvious affection.'[39]

Finally,

> Once again an English composer has made a major contribution to the viola repertory. This beautiful work is designed with the finest skill for the combination of viola and orchestra, and the wealth of musical thought it contains will not be exhausted in many hearings. The intellectual interest is admirably combined with lyrical quality, and the series of variation-like movements in the finale (called by the composer a 'necklace') will surely win a grateful welcome from every ambitious viola player in the world.[40]

Improvisation for Violin and Orchestra

The Improvisation for Violin and Orchestra, Op. 89, was composed in 1956 in response to a commission from the Louisville Symphony Orchestra, whose governing board and conductor, Robert Whitney, were engaged in an enlightened and far-seeing programme of inviting major composers to write works for their organization. In this way over one hundred works by eighty-seven composers were commissioned and recorded. Other composers besides Rubbra who responded with major works were Copland, Milhaud, Krenek, Piston, Sessions, Schuman, Hovhaness, Martinu and Bliss. In the following account Rubbra supplies us with the details of the Improvisation's origins, and some of its particulars.

> I was particularly glad of such a commission, for it gave me the opportunity to drastically revise and reshape a *Fantasia* for violin and orchestra that I had written in the mid-thirties, but which I had put on one side as being unsatisfactory in shape and scoring. I had, however, always been happy with the material of the long cadenza (unaccompanied except for a quiet timpani roll) with which the early *Fantasia* opened, and when the commission was received twenty years later I felt able to build upon it with greater assurance, give a firmer direction to its improvisational material, and score the music with a finer precision and clarity. The latter was made easier by the fact that in the re-thinking of the original material I reduced the orchestra to woodwind, horns, trumpets and strings using percussion, celesta and harp as colouristic elements.
> The original *Fantasia* was one of several works contemporaneous with it in which I admitted chromatic elements into my thematic and harmonic thinking in such a way as to loosen the hold of key centres and diatonic progressions without, at the same time, weakening the structural hold exercised by these devices. (The most radical of these works is the still unperformed *O unwithered eagle void* for choir and small orchestra, a work that is almost atonal in its freedom.) Such a loosening is evident in the long lyrical lines of the cadenza that sets the scene for the *Improvisation*.[41]

The Improvisation is in one continuous movement, although four loosely defined sections plus a coda are distinguishable. However, these sections are not based on thematic differentiation, key relationships, or even recapitulations of material. They are determined by changes in emotional moods brought about by tempo changes regardless of what thematic material is under treatment at the time. But, as the new tempi are gradually introduced by *accelerandos* and *ritardandos*, the actual points at which new sections commence is sometimes ambiguous and open to personal interpretation. Perhaps the most logical plan is that shown below:

Section 1	mm	1	through	73	slow, reflective
Section 2	mm	74	through	109	fast, vigorous
Section 3	mm	110	through	188	slow, reflective
Section 4	mm	189	through	274	fast, vigorous
Coda	mm	275	through	300	slow, reflective

More important than the structural plan of the Improvisation is the underlying conception of the work: the concept of two contradictory forces – the rhapsodic, impulsive and fantasia-like freedom of the solo violin versus the more restrained and rigid orchestra. (This conception presents an interesting contrast with the short, one-movement *Soliloquy*, which is gentle and reflective, while the Improvisation is rhapsodic and dramatic in addition to being reflective.) This is generally true even considering parts of section 4 where the orchestra shares the unfettered freedom of the violin. It is this contradictory concept that produces tensions, which are communicated to the listener and which keep him wondering what will happen next. Yet, the forces are in balance often enough to provide moments when the tensions are relaxed.

The piece begins with a twenty-one and a half measure cadenza for the solo violin against a continuous E flat timpani roll, twice reinforced by a low E flat octave on the harp. Thus the tonality is centrally controlled by means of a constant reference point, yet the rhapsodic freedom of the violin can express itself in a very wide range of pitches and brief excursions to distant tonalities. The entire cadenza is to be performed *sempre liberamente* and the directions concerning *stringendo, ritardando,* and *a tempo* indicate more precisely how this freedom is to be achieved. However, within this general framework the soloist is at liberty to interpret individual measures and phrases with their peaks and valleys.

And peaks and valleys there are, for the melodic line of the cadenza is generally angular and disjunct, although there are smoother and more conjunct passages near the end. In fact, at first sight, the jagged melodic contour of the material suggests a tone row (Example 130), an impression strengthened by the seven separate pitches with which the principal theme opens. However, as the four measures which comprise the theme proper unfold, the repetition of tones already sounded and the insistent recurrence of B flat in a dominant relationship

Ex. 130

to the all-pervasive E flat timpani roll quickly dispel the idea. It is also note-worthy that, except in measure 5, the ascending major seventh in the first measure is consistently altered to its inversion – the minor second – in all subsequent statements and transpositions both of the theme and the two-measure segment derived from it. This reduction in angularity further dispels any impression of serial construction. Judging from Rubbra's reluctance to publish 'O Unwithered Eagle Void', which he called his 'Schoenbergian piece', one realizes that the serial approach never appealed to him or suited his particular talents. Yet the Improvisation is tonally more free than many of the other works, a fact readily admitted by the composer when he mentioned the 'loosening evident in the long lyrical lines of the cadenza'.

The moment the orchestra enters at measure 22 a restraining hand is sensed, although as if in anticipation the violin has gradually become more subdued in the preceding measures. A limited and quiet dialogue between violin and horns over two incomplete statements of the principal subject by cellos and basses then follows. The solo violin is not to be kept down, however, for at measure 29 when the strings attempt unsuccessfully for the third time to present the theme in a carefully measured manner, the violin, an octave and a half higher, impatiently demonstrates how it can be done in half the time. Its tiny version consists of different intervals and in the succeeding measure breaks off, to be followed by an irritated, double-stopped, thirty-second note version of measure 4. This leads at once in measure 31 to a double-stopped variant of measure 7 and, in the next measure after a thirty-second rest, to a heavily accented suggestion, also double-stopped, of the future second theme. At measure 33 the violin, now quite subdued, resumes its more leisurely and reflective course, accompanied by flute and clarinet. What has just been described is a perfect example of the two forces at work: the volatile violin and the sober orchestra whose differences of opinion provide tension and interest.

At measure 74 the vigorous second section begins, prepared previously by an *accelerando*. Measures 75–82 feature a solo diminution of Theme 1 – the only other statement of the theme by the solo instrument after its initial appearance in measures 1–5. The odd fact that the theme occupies twice as many measures as in its original presentation is accounted for by the change from 4/4 to 4/8, plus four non-consecutive measures of trills. However, the tempo having steadily increased, the effect of the diminution is total. The woodwinds, meanwhile, have been introducing the first segment of Theme 2, a dancelike sixteenth note figure. It remains for the violin to state the theme completely after its diminution of Theme 1 is finished. Example 131 shows this extroverted and

Ex. 131

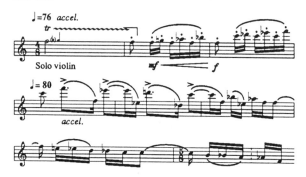

jubilant theme. Soon, the orchestra finds it necessary to apply brakes with a statement of Theme 1 under the solo instrument's mounting excitement, and this theme's concluding notes are stated by the violin alone in an *allargando* tempo. The striding dotted figure in the fourth and fifth measures of Example 131 becomes the dominant characteristic for the next dozen measures in the woodwinds and strings.

Section 3 is ushered in by a full statement of the first subject in the clarinets and violas to the accompaniment of a new and eloquently expressive melody in the solo violin (Example 132). This melody's predominantly scale-wise contour functions as a perfect counterpoint to the main subject's angularity. Its first half is immediately repeated by the violins while the second half appears at a higher pitch level in the flutes and bassoons. The remainder of this highly expressive section features variants of Theme 1 and the counterpoint, shared equally by soloist and orchestra.

Section 4 (measures 189–274) begins with a coupling of Themes 1 and 2. Theme 1 is scored for horns and solo trumpet and Theme 2 for strings – a new and incomplete version. With the soloist's entry things become more and more uninhibited, and even the orchestra participates unashamedly. One of the striking effects of this section is the way in which each of the three statements of Theme 1 is framed in 3/4 metre rather than in the quadruple metre used for all of the preceding statements. This metrical alteration does not affect the rapid flow of the material associated with the second theme, but it does throw the first theme into sharp relief when the pattern changes from even quarters and eighths to ♩ ♩ | ♫♩ in the first half. The silhouette is even more obvious when, as in measures 189–96, the theme is assigned to the horns and solo trumpet, and in 251–8 to trumpets alone. The theme's second statement is heard in the flutes and harp, and there it is, of course, less conspicuous.

The effect of all three appearances of Theme 1 in this fourth section is to slow down the combined unrestraint of the solo violin and those instruments allied with it. This slowing down does not take full effect until measure 258 when the violins play an impassioned statement of the counterpoint seen in Example 132. This soaring melody, begun *fortissimo* but then steadily dimin-

Ex. 132

Ex. 132 continued

ishing in volume, brings us to the quiet and moving coda where fragments of Theme 1 appear in the solo instrument and orchestra. A magical touch comes at the end of the coda when, over quiet tremolo strings, the violin divides the first theme with the harp, the latter playing in harmonics an augmented version of the first half, followed by the soloist's finishing of the theme in its original note values. The entire theme is now restored to its quadruple form, and with all the angularity gone, the effect is deeply peaceful. The work concludes with a four-measure solo horn passage made up of derivative material.

It is typical of Rubbra's compositional technique that the cadenza with which the Improvisation opens is divisible into small melodic segments that are destined for further use as occasion may require. Some of these segments may now be mentioned in the order in which they first appear following the exposition in the cadenza: the descending quarter-notes of measure 3, obtained when the eighths on the second half of beats 2 and 3 are eliminated; the two descending thirds in measure 4 followed by the rising second in 5; the rising thirds of measure 7 where the first double-stopping occurs; and a descending chromatic figure in measure 18 (the lower line of the double-stopping).

The rising thirds of measure 7 appear to be the most useful and important of these segments from the viewpoint of future exploitation. After a brief suggestion of them in the double-stopping of measure 31, a version in fast, dotted rhythms appears in the first oboe (measure 90) and later in it and other parts in conjunction with the dancelike second subject. In that same vigorous section they appear to advantage in triple metre in the bassoon, oboe and horn parts. They are also capable of great expressiveness as in measures 144–7 (solo violin), 165–6 (woodwinds, lower strings), and particularly in measures 275–86 where they are employed in a slow, soft ostinato (oboe 1, cor anglais, harp, violin 1) – one note per measure – accompanied by the solo violin's four-measure poignant utterance, in which triplets outline the thirds, and quarter rests emphasize the expressiveness.

The other segments mentioned above also find future uses and some of the most interesting appearances occur in combinations where one segment is accompanied by another (measures 22–32). Here, fragments are joined to large segments of the principal subject.

A detailed study of the Improvisation with emphasis on its material and the uses to which it is later put reveals the appropriateness of the title. It would certainly seem that *Rhapsody* or *Fantasia* could just as well have served as the work's title. *Fantasia* was, as we have seen, the name for the earlier piece from which the opening cadenza was taken. Why, then, the later change to Improvisation? The answer seems to lie with the solo violin, whose material, except for the initial presentation of the principal theme in the cadenza, its later diminution and its completion of the theme near the end, is largely fragmentary. The basic material of the cadenza with its cellular construction proliferates variants whose nature is improvisatory, and these seem particularly suited to the liquid flow and pliant freedom with which the violin is so richly endowed. In this connection, it is significant that the only complete statement of the principal theme by the solo violin after the cadenza is the impulsive and impatient diminution of measures 75–82. There it is rhythmically free, while in each of the orchestral statements it is strictly metrical, even sternly so. The tensions produced by the contrast of these opposing forces appears to spark still more improvisatory freedom from the violin. Finally, at the work's conclusion, a peaceful balance of the two forces has been achieved.

In an extended review of the Improvisation as performed at the Royal Festival Hall by Frederick Grinke and the BBC Symphony under Sir Malcolm Sargent, Donald Mitchell had this to say:

> This new piece (performed first, I believe in America) is intendedly slighter than much of Mr. Rubbra's music, but it bears all the marks of his recent development and thus has more weight than its title would suggest. Certainly we notice that growing feeling for a subdued yet quite personal orchestral colour which has been evident in all Mr. Rubbra's later works; the cyclically conceived exit and entrance of this Improvisation [?] place the whole in a most delicate and poetic frame. The form of the piece, fittingly, was very free; it built itself, spontaneously – compositional 'sweat', in this context, would be fatal – out of the solo violin's opening rhapsody, whose yearning first phrases, in melodic character and rhythmic articulation, were distinctly – and unexpectedly – 'gipsy'. This, I thought, sounds a new note in Mr. Rubbra's music. I can hardly imagine that he has shifted his national allegiances. Has he, perhaps, been eavesdropping on Bartók's violin concerto? The solo invocation over, the work extended itself through a series of loose improvisations (or variations) [no!] on and about the basic material; slow episodes were frequently haunting, especially from the harmonic point of view, the quick ones less so, where the lyric substance of the piece seemed disinclined to assume a climactic shape. The coda was beautiful; as were, for the most part, the finely laid-out textures, which sensitively accommodated the soloist. Mr. Rubbra's ear, if I may humbly remark upon it, hears more and more.[42]

In another review, the independent nature of Rubbra's musical thought appears to have been misunderstood by the writer. Indeed, a certain confusion and even frustration are evident:

> Rubbra still presents a problem. Basically, he seems to be a diatonic conservative with modal leanings, but he is apt to do some queer incidental things, witness the opening of his 'Improvisation'. What key is it in? E flat supplies the final chord; but the rhapsodic opening melodic passage is as full of augmented and diminished intervals as a note-row; indeed, it looks very much like one, at first glance, but it is not even as simple as that. An evanescent tonality is felt in it, and the E flat pedal survives flat contradiction in a context of sharps. This complex opening section has a contrasted section, *lento*, of stark simplicity [section 3] which returns at the end; a somewhat spiky and forbidding piece, interesting rather than soothing.[43]

What further proof is needed to demonstrate the simple fact that Rubbra is not a composer who can be categorized and pigeonholed?

Violin Concerto

Rubbra started his Violin Concerto, Op. 103, in 1958 and completed it in the summer of 1959. In terms of large, multi-movement works involving the orchestra, it follows the Seventh Symphony. It is in the usual three movements but without a slow introduction such as those found in the preceding concertos: Viola, 1953; Piano, 1956. In a letter to Ottaway, dated 20 October 1959, the composer tells us that this omission was 'deliberate, as I wanted to write a first movement that plunged straight into the material and speed'. The three movements are marked as follows: *Allegro*; *Lento, ma non troppo* (subtitled 'Poema'); and *Allegro giocoso*. What was true of the earlier concertos is equally true here: the performer or listener who is looking for a typical display concerto will be disappointed. The work is primarily lyrical, although this is not to suggest that the prevailing mood is 'English pastoral' or that there are not dramatic moments.

Indeed, the first phrase of the first movement is quite dramatic, and as might be expected, this opening phrase with its octave leap, minor and major thirds, minor seconds, and minor sixth provides most of the material for the movement in one way or another. The very next phrase, scored for violins and woodwinds and coming between the first phrase and its inversion, employs the same rhythm but slightly varies the intervals. Seemingly new material dominates the sixth through the tenth measures but the ascending seconds and the dotted rhythm in which they are set are traceable to the first measure. The material in measures 8 and 9 comes from the violin and woodwind figures in 3 and 4. The entire first theme is reproduced in Example 133.

Ex. 133

An eight-measure bridge passage, roughly the first half of which is scored for flutes and oboes and the second for violins, leads to the first entry of the solo violin. It is supported throughout in the lower strings by eight ostinato statements of the four-note figure containing the octave leap at the end of the first phrase (and the theme as a whole). A glance at the bridge material in

Ex. 134

Example 134 shows how segment *a* is fitted in. This sort of economy is standard procedure throughout the movement.

   It is interesting that the soloist's material, except for a literal repetition of the
first phrase of the principal theme, is both a summary and an expansion of that
theme. Its high placement is coupled with a change in character from the
dramatic nature of the opening phrase to a more gentle and reflective mood. In
due course the soloist has the bridge passage, its accompaniment having changed
from the ostinatos to chords, and this leads directly into the second theme,
which is also assigned to the soloist. A comparison of this theme in Example
135 with the bridge passage shown in Example 134 reveals a further economical use of material, for the rising and falling thirds of Theme 2 come from the
former.

Ex. 135

   From this point until Theme 2 is repeated in its entirety in the orchestra, a
rather nebulous, even, at times, visionary, development of all of the material
thus far heard takes place. Some of this consists of a long double-stopped
passage for the solo violin which, after a two and a half measure trill, leads to a
particularly beautiful section for both soloist and orchestra. In spirit and even in
certain details this seven-measure passage reminds me of a similar but longer
passage in the first movement of the Prokofiev First Violin Concerto. It has the
same high and delicate tremolo flutterings for the soloist, accompanied in the
orchestra by soft, triadic harmonies. The spell is completely shattered by the
repetition of Theme 2 in a sturdy D flat major (first violins and oboes), above
which the soloist plays decorative sixteenth figures and trills. When a short
extension of this is over, the formal development section is near, for what we
have in this first movement is a freely conceived sonata form.

   Considering that Rubbra's large-scale structures always involve some development of his materials throughout the exposition, how does one determine with
any degree of accuracy where a *formal* development section begins? With Rubbra

the latter are not ever predicated on the sudden appearance of foreign keys any more than his expositions are restricted to tonics and dominants. Thus other criteria must be proposed. The two most often seen are the fragmentation of the expository materials and the combining of these fragments into new phrases. This is exactly what happens here when, in measures 93–8, the falling octaves from the opening phrase of Theme 1 and the rising and falling thirds at the start of Theme 2 are combined – not vertically but in alternate succession. It would certainly appear that the development section was well launched, especially in view of the fact that the thirds have not only been changed to minor but the connecting note in the first third is a half step above the starting note. However, in measure 99 the solo violin initiates a complete statement of the bridge theme, accompanied in the lower strings by one-measure statements on various pitches of the falling octave motive plus a delicate tremolo involving thirds in the violins. Whether this should be included in the development or the exposition is not a matter of earth-shaking importance. It merely confirms Rubbra's relaxed approach to composition. And so, without attempting to settle the issue, we can move on to the measures and pages following the bridge passage where there are no doubts at all that formal development is occurring. The selection of particular passages for closer analysis is not the simple task it might appear to be, for many are outstanding in this predominantly lyrical development.

We begin with the passage that flows from and is a continuation of the bridge theme (measure 106). The solo violin, after a half-beat rest, has dropped almost two octaves from D to F and seems about to repeat the bridge theme, but instead combines its thirds with the falling octaves. The orchestra is engaged in a continuation of its activity during the bridge theme. What makes the passage memorable are the harmonic progressions brought about by the interaction of the two elements – solo violin and orchestra. Although these progressions are not at all unusual, they are enhanced by the balance in terms of the melodic direction in each line and especially by the contrary motion when the lines are combined. The effect produced by all of these ingredients is one of quiet intimacy and contemplation. This mood changes to one of growing intensity in the very next passage when the orchestra engages in a closely-knit interplay involving the falling and rising octaves.

One of the most sensitively beautiful passages in the entire movement is that in measures 138–48. Its starting point is really in measure 137, but because there is at the end of this measure a complete change in tonal direction, metre and content, the observer is correct in thinking of the passage as starting in 138. Also, 137 is omitted in the passage's repetition. But far more important is the sense that a new theme is being offered here (Example 136). It is, of course, very true that certain elements in it are traceable to material in earlier themes: the first three notes are an inversion of the E, F, D of the opening of Theme 1; the downward-moving scale figure is first heard at the end of the solo violin's first entry (measures 29–30 from where it is transferred to Theme 2); the octave leap comes from the first phrase; and the rest evolves from Rubbra's magical

Ex. 136

spinning-out technique and using the most common intervallic combinations. The B flat at the theme's end serves as a springboard for the repetition – an exact transposition a half tone lower. The orchestral accompaniment for the first eight of the eleven measures involved in the two passages consists of gently rising and falling scale figures in which a higher peak is reached at the top of each rise; when the repetition of the theme is at the bottom of its range the accompaniment is at the apex. The violins are muted at that point so as not to eclipse the soloist.

In due course, the recapitulation is reached, but the first phrase of the returning first theme is overlapped by the final phrase of the *fortissimo* climax that brings the development to its conclusion. (This climax is made up of a slightly truncated statement of Theme 2, together with suitable counterpoint above its second half.) Thus the fabric at the point of the overlap is continuous. An unusual feature not often found in the first part of Rubbra's recapitulations is the disposition of the material in the same key as in the exposition. This does not last long, however, for the remainder of the recapitulation is transposed a fifth higher, or a fourth lower depending upon instrumentation and the placement of materials. In such cases, a mixed transposition in the same passage may result.

The cadenza is in scale with the length and lyrical content of the movement. That is to say, it is not a lengthy exhibition designed to show off the technical abilities of the performer, and the listener who expects such a cadenza will inevitably be disappointed. Near its conclusion, there is again an overlap, this time with the eight-measure coda at the beginning of which the first phrase of the first theme is sounded for the final time.

A lasting impression of this first movement, gained from repeated hearings, is that while lyricism is predominant, it is a very intense and passionate lyricism. In this respect it is no different from other similar Rubbra movements, and to drive home the point, the words 'appassionato' and 'intenso' are affixed. Another of the composer's characteristic means of increasing tension is present here: a steady drumbeat. Indeed, this appears at the very opening of the movement, and is a portent of things to come. Thus even though the role of the soloist is never spectacular in the sense that it is in other concertos, it would be a serious error to misinterpret 'lyrical' as being synonomous with 'tame' or 'dull'. It is exactly here that many critics and reviewers of Rubbra's music miss the point.

The second movement, 'Poema', lives up to its title. Three clearly differenti-ated themes are involved, each set forth in a distinctive manner. The first, announced by the second violins and violas, is the most introspective and poetic of the three (Example 137). It is entirely surrounded by the remaining

Ex. 137

strings which together form a chordal texture consisting of octaves slowly moving in contrary motion, thus creating a mirror image. The significant inter-val in each octave is the major second, and its presence contributes much to the introspective atmosphere. There is a slightly modified repetition of the theme, but the surrounding string texture is altered so that its octave chords move in the opposite direction. This change creates subtle harmonic differences.

The soloist makes his first appearance in the movement with the playing of the second theme, which is immediately repeated by violas and cellos to the accompaniment of slow, expressive octaves in the woodwinds and violins. The composer obviously considered these octaves to be important adjuncts, for in succeeding repetitions they are heard in the same manner: as a counterpoint to the second appearance of the theme in each pair, and each time the counterpoint is sounded the solo violin is silent. Both elements, theme and counterpoint, are seen in Example 138.

Ex. 138

The third theme is given out by the solo oboe. The shape of its sixteenth-note figure appears to have its origin in the inverted form of the three accented

Ex. 139

eighths of Theme 1. It too has an accompanying counterpoint and each element is seen in Example 139.

Once all three themes have been stated it is reasonable to expect that developmental processes will yield new music. This is exactly what happens, but before several instances are cited, attention should be called to a short passage (measures 42–7) that vividly recalls the 'Canto' of the Sixth Symphony. The ascending and descending open fifths in the orchestra create the same bleak atmosphere, which is only slightly relieved by the presence of the solo violin.

The first of our developmental examples begins in measure 49 with the orchestra's restatement of the chords which open the movement. Above these in measure 50, the solo violin has a climbing figure that is an inversion of the two descending sixteenths and an eighth (measure 25) at the start of Theme 2. In measures 51 and 52, still over the orchestra's chords, the violin continues with repetitions at succeeding higher octaves of a three-note sixteenth figure. This is a more animated version of the fourth measure of Theme 1. There follows a page of very expressive music whose exact lineage is hard to trace because the violin's part is filled with rising and falling scalic figures that occur everywhere in Rubbra's music. Their most likely origin is Theme 2. The underlying orchestral chords are vaguely related to the immediately preceding chords in 49–52.

Theme 2 and its counterpoint retain their original form for their second and third statements with very minor exceptions. Different tonalities are introduced. Such literal repetitions preclude development, and even the solo violin with its triplet scale figure during the first repetition, and thirds and sixths during the second does not suggest genuine development. Since the only one of the three themes preserved intact throughout the movement is the second, the intent seems clear: it is the centrepiece, both melodically and expressively.

The third theme is subjected to moderate development following its repetition and this process begins in measures 77–80. The positions of theme and counterpoint are reversed from those in the original statement. Soon the movement enters its final phase – introduced by alternate rising and falling *arpeggios* from Theme 2. A further expansion of Theme 1, begun *fortissimo* but then becoming quieter, brings this sensitive movement to a close.

The only observation to be made from the viewpoint of structure is that the thematic restatements and developmental passages occur in the same order in which the themes were originally presented. Thus the movement assumes the following shape: Theme 1, Theme 2, Theme 3; development of Theme 1; restatement of Theme 2; expansion of Theme 3; further expansion of Theme 1; restatement of Theme 2; and a free return to the music of Theme 1 for the close.

The final movement, marked *Allegro giocoso*, is a light-hearted, highly rhythmic *scherzando* type of piece. The rhythmic structure is entirely shaped by the principal and subordinate materials, and since both are very asymmetrical in length, metrical changes are a constant feature throughout the movement. 3/4, 7/8, 3/8, 6/8 as well as other metres are employed in rapid succession, often occupying only one measure before giving way to the next metre. The resulting rhythmic patterns combine to create a rich and varied flow that is interrupted just once by a rather strange two-measure ritard three measures before the conclusion of the movement.

Structurally, the movement appears to conform to some recognizable rondo design, but careful investigation proves this to be false. Sectional repetitions come and go with no apparent adherence to a prior plan, but there is no sense at all of a haphazard structure. The impression that is left is one of an entirely spontaneous structure that is evolving from the thematic materials. In fact, there is a very subtle approach to structural form, and the spontaneity of everything sometimes leads the listener to believe that he is hearing new material when actually he is hearing an unexpected repetition of a phrase in new scoring. Episode flows uninterruptedly into episode in an often boisterous display of high spirits. The element of surprise is always strong.

The basic thematic material of the movement is divided into two parts, and is contained within the first five measures (Example 140). The first part consists

Ex. 140

of open, parallel fifths plus the melody that runs along the top (and bottom) of the fifths. The second part includes the material in the 7/8 and 3/4 measures. Most of the musical events throughout the rest of the movement have their origins in one or the other of these parts.

The first instance of such derivations occurs in the solo violin – measures 6–11. In this passage the double-stopped fifths that begin the theme are broken up into a single line of rising fifths. In measures 10–11 the sixteenths of which these rising fifths are composed continue by following the contour of the melody made by the top line of the original fifths. Other examples of these particular derivations are liberally scattered throughout the movement.

In measures 86–105 what may seem to be a new idea is heard, but closer scrutiny shows that this is composed primarily of the first six notes (transposed) that run along the top of the original fifths. The main reason for thinking that a new theme is present is that a different rhythmic pattern has emerged: two dotted eighths in a 3/8 metre in which the supporting parts conform to the normal patterns for that metre. Such cross-rhythms are not at all unusual in Rubbra's music, but there is always an element of surprise about them to the extent that the associated thematic materials often seem completely new.

In sharp contrast to the alterations made in later appearances of the Part 1 material is the absence of any real change in later appearances of the 7/8 measure of Part 2 (the following 3/4 measure need not concern us as future appearances of it are adapted to local circumstances). The impression grows that this lack of change is deliberate, and is intended to counteract the ever-evolving material in the remainder of the theme, thus giving stability to the movement.

There is something to be said, I suppose, for Ronald Stevenson's observation that 'the finale is a peasant's dance'. He defends this view by saying that 'its harmonic aesthetic is based on the open fifth, bridging the medieval age and our own.'[44] It is certainly true that there is no scarcity of fifths, for in addition to being a part of the basic material, fifths are often found in the supporting texture, sometimes in chains. The medieval metaphor is carried a bit further when, just before the end, the 'sudden swirl of notes in E flat minor' is likened to 'a momentary glimpse of the Angel of Death. For a moment the dance of life has become a dance of death – but only for an instant.'[45] Whether or not one agrees with this subjective view, there is no doubt that the change of mood and tempo, followed by a silence at the end of the passage, is dramatic. The 'sudden swirl of notes in E flat minor' is a reference to the soloist's ascending and descending natural minor figures in thirty-second notes. The harmony under these figures – a held E flat minor chord – supports a melodic fragment – B flat, C flat, F, E flat – whose relationship to the descending figure in the second measure of Theme 1 in the first movement (Example 133) seems too close to be coincidental. The reference is more subtle than it is at similar points in some other works – the end of the Fifth Symphony, for example – but its purpose is the same: to unify the opposite ends of a work. Here, however, there is a difference: a reversion to the movement's prevailing mood of light-hearted gaiety. There is another medieval allusion with respect to the sudden intervention of the E flat minor passage, and that is the tritone relationship between E flat minor and the A minor and A major passages that, respectively, precede and follow it; 'Diabolus in musica' as it was known in the Middle Ages. Perhaps the medieval allusions are not so far off the mark as they might seem.

This finale is certainly the most difficult of the movements for the soloist and it goes far towards satisfying those listeners who look for virtuosity in a concerto. It is hard to predict, however, what will satisfy the critics. The following review reported the Concerto's first performance at the Festival Hall, on 17 February 1960. Endre Wolf was the soloist, and the BBC Symphony Orchestra was conducted by Rudolf Schwarz.

Heard immediately after Hindemith's colourful and spirited Symphonic Metamorphosis of Themes by Carl Maria von Weber, Rubbra's tonal palette seemed more than usually dull in tone, and indeed the greater part of his Concerto sounded as though it might just as well have been written for strings alone.... He also appeared to be worrying lest he should overstay his welcome. At least two of the movements were concluded rather arbitrarily instead of being given more expansive treatment [which two is not specified]. To offset this carping is the composer's obvious sincerity, and the slow movement, called *Poema*, reminded us that Rubbra has often something of paramount importance to say.[46]

On 21 March 1960, just over a month after the first performance of the Concerto, the composer wrote to Ottaway:

> I was so expecting to hear from you after the Concerto. I hope everything is all right; or perhaps you couldn't bear the work and didn't like to write! I have never had such a set of uncomprehending notices. On the other hand I've had some wonderful letters from musicians whose judgment I respect.

Perhaps Rubbra added the following, later, 'uncomprehending' notice to his collection: 'One thing in the Violin Concerto is worthy of note; in the middle of some gritty grey texture a simple, innocent, diatonic tune appears, like an astonished child lost in lowering city streets. There is something significant there.'[47]

In addition to the 'carping' cited above, parts of an article by Ottaway include anonymous remarks directed against the Concerto. After mentioning that the Concerto 'is predominantly lyrical and gives the soloist little scope for self-indulgent technical display', Ottaway continues:

> The thought of Rubbra making concessions to virtuosity is hardly less bizarre than the suggestion that he might have spiced with 'wrong notes' a passage like Ex. 3 (from the slow movement, *Poema*) [my example 137]... incidentally, the soloist who interprets *molto espressivo* with any trace of insincerity will have given himself away many times already in the previous movement. To the listener who describes such diatonic lyricism as 'nobility run tame' one can only reply that Rubbra writes this sort of passage without any sense of self-consciousness. [This is a reference to Theme 2 in 'Poema', seen in Example 138.][48]

Passages from several of the 'wonderful letters from musicians whose judgment' Rubbra respected now follow. Two of these letters were from Cyril Scott, who, it will be recalled, took Rubbra as a private pupil before the Reading University days. The first was written on 18 February 1960, the day following the Concerto's first performance:

> We listened with great interest to your highly impressive Violin Concerto last night. It really *is* an impressive work with its wealth of colour, variety and all those elements which go to make a satisfying work of art. But of course one needs to hear it more than once to take it all in. Congratulations!

The second – really just a postcard – was dated 21 February:

> Was delighted to hear your V.C. again last night. Took it in more on 2nd hearing. What a knowledge of the violin you have! Altogether was greatly impressed. What a fine contribution to violin literature.

A number of other musicians had also heard a second performance, among them Herbert Howells, whose undated letter begins

> Just a brief line to tell you that I much enjoyed the broadcasts of the Violin Concerto. Specially the Saturday night performance, and it seems to me that this was not only because I had heard the work before but also the performance seemed

in every way superior. Much that was not at all clear on the air on Wednesday was far better balanced (and I thought played) on Saturday. For one thing, Wolf's intonation and double stopping were far surer. It is a pity those very odd people the critics couldn't have waited before showing off in print!! For me, the slow movement is much the clearest and most beautiful anyhow up to now.

From Maurice Jacobson, Rubbra's friend from their RCM days, a letter dated 21 February said

There's no doubt about it. The Violin Concerto is a fine work. Sue and I went to Maida Vale to hear it tonight – both deeply impressed. Your run-through here at Christmas helped much, and much was familiar to me as a result.

The announcer used the word 'lyrical'. It's too powerful for that (though I see what he means). I should have said rather 'drammatico-lyrical' – not quite right either, for the first two movements have an impassioned quality as well.

A letter from the soloist, Endre Wolf, dated 21 February, thanked Rubbra for his 'very kind words' about the first performance, and went on to say that he

felt that last night's performance was at least as good as the one on Wednesday. I was certainly more relaxed. I am looking forward to listening to tapes.

I am finding the contrasting reviews rather amusing: as far as my performance is concerned the extremes are Colin Mason on the generous end and the Sunday Times who put my name in brackets.

Finally, a very welcome letter, dated 20 February 1960, came from a very respected critic, Neville Cardus:

Owing to severe flu I was kept away from the Festival Hall and the performance of your Violin Concerto. But I listened to the broadcast last night and feel I must write to you to tell you that I heard in it many deeply expressive and beautifully written passages. To be honest among composers nowadays is to be a man marked out of a thousand. In your Concerto I felt a deeply experiencing nature at work, with an artist-musician, and a craftsman, shaping conceptions into recognisably fine music.

You mustn't expect to get from my colleagues notices of positive approval until you have played fast and loose with atonalism, etc. Besides, most of my colleagues seem to think that a critic reduces his stature whenever he praises. Quite the contrary.

Notes

1   In this chapter the concerted works for piano, followed by those for strings, will be treated chronologically rather than in opus number order. The same procedure will be followed in Chapter 7, 'Music for solo instruments'.
2   F. Bonavia, critic of *The Daily Telegraph* (n.d.). Printed inside the front cover of *Edmund Rubbra: Composer.*
3   Printed inside the front cover of *Edmund Rubbra: Composer.*
4   Tape of 26 July 1980.
5   Ivor Keys, *M&L* 28, no. 2, April 1947, p.199.
6   *ibid.*
7   W.R. Anderson, *MT*, November 1951, p.501.
8   Ronald Stevenson, 'Concerted Works', *Edmund Rubbra: Composer*, p.45.
9   Interestingly, this rising figure is exactly the same – melodically and rhythmically

– as the figure Mendelssohn employed for 'Shouldst thou walking in grief', from the chorus 'He Watching Over Israel' in *Elijah*. The coincidence (for I am persuaded that it is such) serves to reinforce the point that much of the material used by very many composers is substantially the same. What matters is that composers adapt it to their own needs in different and individual ways.

10 Stevenson, *op. cit.*, p.45.
11 Keys, *op. cit.*, p.199.
12 *The London Times* (n.d.).
13 Stevenson, *op. cit.*, p.45.
14 Printed in the booklet accompanying EMI Record Set No. SLS 5080, entitled *Twentieth Century British Piano Concertos.*
15 *ibid.*
16 Colin Mason, *M&L* 41, no. 4, October 1960, p.403.
17 Rubbra's analysis in the booklet accompanying EMI Record Set No. SLS 5080.
18 *ibid.*
19 *ibid.*
20 Two other prominent instances of this intervallic combination were cited earlier in connection with the Fifth and Tenth Symphonies.
21 Scott Goddard, *MT,* May 1956, p.258.
22 Donald Mitchell, *MT,* May 1956, p.264.
23 Mason, *op. cit.*, p.404.
24 Ivor Keys, *M&L* 39, no. 4, October 1958, pp.415–16.
25 Brian Kelly, *MT,* September 1960, p.564.
26 Bryan Crimp, booklet accompanying EMI Record Set No. SLS 5080.
27 Stevenson, *op. cit.*, p.46.
28 *ibid.*, pp.45–6.
29 *ibid.*, p.46.
30 Ivor Keys, *M&L* 35, no. 3, July 1954, p.204.
31 Desmond Shawe-Taylor, *The New Statesman and Nation*, 25 April 1953.
32 *ibid.*
33 Donald Mitchell, *MT,* June 1953, p.276.
34 Shawe-Taylor, *op. cit.*
35 Tape of 9 August 1980.
36 William Primrose, *Walk On The North Side: Memoirs of A Violist* (Provo: Brigham Young University Press, 1978), p.188.
37 Shawe-Taylor, *op. cit.*
38 Mitchell, *op. cit.*
39 Keys, *op. cit.*, p.204.
40 Richard Capell, *MMR,* June 1953, p.129.
41 Sleeve-note to the recording of Improvisation for Violin and Orchestra on RCA GL 25096.
42 Donald Mitchell, *MT,* March 1956, p.149.
43 Peter Pirie, *M&L* 38, no. 1, January 1957, p.105.
44 Stevenson, *op. cit.*, p.48.
45 *ibid.*
46 Stanley Bayliss, *MT,* April 1960, p.245.
47 Peter Pirie, *MT,* March 1963, p.199.
48 Hugh Ottaway, 'Edmund Rubbra and His Recent Works', *MT,* September 1966, p.767.

7   Music for solo instruments

In view of Rubbra's earlier career as a very fine pianist, it is both surprising and strange that so little solo music for the piano has come from his pen. It would be easier to understand – even accept – this paradox if all the piano works had been composed at about the same time, but a considerable span of years separates the earliest from the latest: probably the late 1930s to the autumn of 1982, when the Fantasy Fugue, Op. 161, was completed. All of the solo piano music except the Fantasy Fugue and the immediately preceding Invention On The Name Of Haydn is contained on one LP (Phoenix DGS 1009), recorded 29 April 1981 in St James's Church, Clerkenwell Green, London, by Edward Moore. This record was a complete surprise to Rubbra when it was presented to him on his eightieth birthday. Unfortunately, it has already disappeared from the record catalogues. All of the pieces are sensitively performed: Op. 19, Introduction and Fugue; Op. 69, Prelude and Fugue On A Theme by Cyril Scott; Op. 74, Nine Little Pieces; Op. 104, Introduction, Aria and Fugue; Op. 131, Eight Preludes; and Op. 139, Four Studies.

Before these works are discussed in detail, I would like to point out that I take issue with many of the statements contained in Michael Dawney's article, 'Edmund Rubbra and the Piano'.[1] Although the article's intent is so obviously commendatory, this is not what comes through in statement after statement as one reads how a particular work or set 'suggests' or 'reminds one' of some other composer. The list is impressive considering the eight-page length of the article and the superficiality of its content. Bach, Purcell, Stravinsky, Schumann, Brahms, Chopin, Liszt, Vaughan Williams, Britten! Singling out two of these statements, we are told that the 'frequency of Preludes and Fugues... immediately suggests Bach as a model', and that because Rubbra linked each of his Eight Preludes thematically, there is thus a reminder of Schumann's *Carnaval*.[2] As occasion demands, further 'reminders' will be cited.

Introduction and Fugue

Rubbra's first published piece for solo piano is his Introduction and Fugue, Op. 19. The two independent members that make up this work are very different. The Introduction is reserved, even inward-looking, while the Fugue has the typical gigue-like sound that a fugue in 6/8 usually enjoys. But despite the metre the Fugue lacks the high spirits of its extrovert sisters such as the Bach Fugue in G major – the 'Gigue' Fugue.

The Introduction has neither a key nor a metre signature. Dotted lines are substituted for barlines and the rhythmic pulse is flowing and free. The tempo is *Lento ma non troppo: rubato*. There are two contrasting ideas in this short piece of only two pages: a rounded figure with skips, and an ascending scale line whose first two statements end with a falling fifth. These figures are marked *A* and *B* respectively in Example 141. *B* is much the freer of the two,

Ex. 141

for in its third phrase the rising fifth leads directly into a statement of *A*, while in others the line continues to ascend, and in two instances there is a long descent.

Figure *A* lends itself perfectly to the close imitation with which the piece begins. Six entries are involved before the imitative pattern is broken, each pair being separated by a fifth. Before long the two-voiced texture is expanded to three, and then chords appear. Further statements of *A* are embedded in the middle of this thicker texture until, on the second page, they are isolated in the right hand in the form of thirty-seconds and sixteenths. The rhythmic displacement of the figure, caused by its organization into groups of seven and five notes, then into triplets comprised of sixteenths, imparts a fantasia-like flavour which is emphasized by the special *rubato* direction above the passage. The piece ends quietly in an *adagio* tempo with a return to the chordal texture. *B* reverts to its original shape, and there is one further statement of *A*.

The Fugue sounds deceptively simple. The subject itself, seen in Example 142, may have something to do with this, for its straightforward, almost childlike

Ex. 142

innocence seems to contradict the possibility of any complications. But the appearance of a whole tone instead of a semitone in the cadence at the end of the subject, and its consistent use at the same points throughout the Fugue imparts a modal flavour. This in itself would not cause any ambiguities with regard to the tonality. What does is the appearance of a significant number of D and A naturals plus pedal points on E and B. The result of these when they are coupled with the modal flavour is a slightly blurred, out-of-focus sound, and the combination tends to weaken the G sharp minor tonality. It also makes one almost forget that this is, indeed, a fugue. However, analysis soon shows that fugal processes are very much at work.

The real answer enters in the measure following our example, but the third voice enters with related material two measures before its expected and normal statement of the subject – a rather unorthodox procedure. Unorthodox too is the pattern, established at the very start of the Fugue and carried straight through to the end, of paired entries, sometimes in the same voice but most often with each member of the pair placed in a different voice. The members are usually separated by no more than a note or two, and there are also several pairs in which there is an overlap of almost a measure. The entire ground plan of the Fugue is most easily set forth in tabular form (Table 3).

Table 3

Pair 1	mm	1–8	Episode 2	mm	58–68
Pair 2	mm	11–18	Pair 6 (Inversions)	mm	69–77
Pair 3	mm	18–25	Pair 7	mm	77–84
Episode 1	mm	26–30	Pair 8	mm	87–94
Pair 4	mm	31–38	Pair 9	mm	94–100
Pair 5	mm	41–48	Episode 3	mm	101–108
Single entry	mm	48–51	Pair 10	mm	109–116
Single entry	mm	54–57	Pair 11	mm	117–124

A little arithmetic shows that there are twenty-four statements of the subject in all. There is also one false entry in Episode 1. It is a bit surprising not to find more than two inversions, for the subject lends itself so readily to such treatment. And there are no stretti, although the slight overlaps mentioned above suggest this device. Taken as a whole, this early opus number represents a thoroughly workmanlike essay, which should certainly find its way into the repertoire of discriminating pianists.

Prelude and Fugue on a Theme by Cyril Scott

The theme from the slow movement of Cyril Scott's Piano Sonata No. 1, on which Rubbra's Op. 69 is based, appears at the head of the latter score not just in its melodic form but in Scott's fully harmonized version. We are thus able to observe Rubbra's procedures in this piece, which was composed in honour of Scott's seventieth birthday (27 September 1949). The keys (D flat) are the same although Scott uses no signature. His theme, complete in three measures whose respective metres are 5/8, 7/8 and 8/8, rides tranquilly along the tops of chords which are supported at the very bottom by a tonic pedal. In Rubbra's version of these measures the first four notes are highlighted in octaves, but the remainder of the theme pursues its course in interior voices, and a dominant pedal is substituted. Scott's theme is shown in Example 143.

Ex. 143

The first four notes of the theme and their inversion (five notes if the resolution is counted) form the backbone of the Prelude. Although these and other figures derived from them suggest frequent repetitions of the theme, the latter is heard only twice more in its entirety before the commencement of the Fugue – about a third of the way through (measures 12–14) and again just before the Prelude finishes (measures 30–32). This final presentation and the material following are exact duplicates of the Prelude's initial eight measures.

One of the very interesting aspects of the Prelude is the gradual sounding of the components which will make up the fugue subject (illustrated in Example 144). These are not, however, presented in the order in which they will appear

Ex. 144

in the subject. The first to be heard is the descending pattern which makes up the third member of the subject (measures 3–4, marked in Example 144 by bracket *c*). It is the inversion of Scott's initial ascending figure and as an inversion, it is an important ingredient in Rubbra's Prelude, appearing many times. The four Fs which open the subject appear to originate in the accented A flats on the first and fifth beats (in 8/8 metre) of measures 8–12 where they are separated by the ascending and descending patterns (the original and the inversion of Scott's opening figure). An embryonic form of the subject's second member (*b*) appears in the bass of measure 9. In measures 15–16 the accented C flats and an inverted form of *b* are sounded in octaves in the right hand above a quite ordinary accompanimental pattern. This is followed a measure later by an irregular diminution of the exact notes of the subject's third member, placed in an interior voice. Two measures later these same notes are heard in the top voice in a rhythm almost identical with their appearance in the subject. From this point to the final full statement of Scott's theme there is connective material leading to another preview of the fugue subject, this time minus the opening repeated notes, and placed in E minor.

Considering the Prelude as a whole, an asymmetrical *ABA* structure is seen in which the initial *A* extends through measure 14, the point where Scott's theme completes its second statement. Section *B* is concerned mainly with the presentation of the elements employed later in the forthcoming fugue subject, while the shortened final *A* closes the Prelude in the manner already described.

There is some difference between the Prelude as perceived on the printed page and as it comes across in performance. Most noticeable is the fact that, despite its identification at the head of Rubbra's score and at the start of the piece, Scott's theme loses its individuality when it is heard because it is so completely absorbed in Rubbra's counterpoint. Tempo appears to be a factor in this difference, for the movement from which Scott's theme was taken is slow. Rubbra's tempo is undoubtedly faster – *Allegretto tranquillo*, ♩ = 126–132 – and his treatment of the theme at this speed makes it quite difficult to identify. All of this is probably as it should be, for, looked at in this way the theme serves only as a point of departure for a piece shaped to Rubbra's distinctive style.

The four-voiced Fugue is severely plain, as a glance at the subject shows. However, this subject is admirably suited to the introduction of such fugal devices as diminutions and stretti, and these sustain interest as they grow out of the contrapuntal fabric. But it must be said that unless the tempo is exactly right the diminutions sound hurried. Whether this is the fault of the composer or the performer is uncertain. At any rate, in the recorded performance the first diminution (in the top voice at measure 17) is slowed rather perceptibly as though the performer became suddenly aware that the eighth notes were moving too fast. Yet in the score no tempo change is indicated at this point. This slowing would be less obvious if there was not at the same time a statement in the bass of the subject in its original note values. When the second diminution is reached two measures later in the tenor, the tempo has become stabilized, possibly because there is no normal statement of the subject appearing simultaneously, although in the next two measures the tempo is again unsteady. Clearly there is a small problem here requiring adjustments of some sort.

The first stretto comes in measures 21–4 between soprano and bass at the interval of a lower fourth. A rather complex passage occupies most of the remainder of the Fugue. It starts in measure 28 with a second stretto between the soprano and alto at the distance of an octave. The alto part lacks segment *c*, its place being taken by chromatically rising quarters. The soprano line is a diminution with an altered segment *c*. A third stretto follows between tenor and soprano, again at the distance of an octave. The *b* segment is in diminution in each voice, but in the soprano the segment is repeated once a minor third higher in sequential fashion. A final stretto is announced *fortissimo* between the bass and alto. Added interest is provided by augmenting the three accented notes of *a* in the bass. Segments *a* and *b* in the alto are in diminution while *c* is dispensed with. The bass line's segment *b* is in diminution with a repeated sequential leg. The Fugue ends quietly with an altered restatement of measures 17–18 of the Prelude, a procedure I myself do not find wholly convincing although I appreciate the sense of unity thus conveyed.

The differences in mood between the Prelude and the Fugue are as great as those between the Introduction and the Fugue of Op. 19. The liquid flow and almost bell-like sounds of the Prelude are nicely contrasted with the reserved and austere Fugue. The entire work has been arranged by Bernard Rose for organ, and the choice of version – piano or organ – is a matter of personal preference. Certainly the sustained tones and perhaps the counterpoint are heard to better advantage on the organ.

Nine Little Pieces

The Nine Little Pieces, Op. 74, provides high-standard teaching and examination materials for children. Each piece bears a descriptive title, contains a minimal amount of fingering directions, and is designed in such a way as to supply an equal number of technical problems for each hand through the distribution of the same or related material. Thus the hands can develop technically at the same rate. In the published edition each piece is graded in terms of the order of difficulty. No piece is longer than two pages, and of the nine only three reach this length. (It is interesting to note that both William Alwyn and Malcolm Arnold, Rubbra's fellow composers from Northampton, have contributed children's pieces to the same Lengnick series.)

The first three pieces, 'Question and Answer', 'Pipe Tune', and 'Hurdy Gurdy' are in the 'very easy to easy' group. Each restricts the novice to the basic five-finger position and each is marked 'Quickly'. In the first of these there is an alternation between hands of the single-line questions and answers. An example of the gentle humour that crops up from time to time throughout the set is heard near the end when a question breaks in before the previous answer has been completed. This two-beat overlap and the concluding chord are the only times in the piece that the hands play together. In the first half of 'Pipe Tune' the hands have the same melody an octave apart, and the second half is taken up with an equal division for the hands of material derived from the first half. In the third piece the characteristic drone of the hurdy gurdy is suggested in the left hand through the first half, while above it a little figure is heard at various pitches.

'Slow Dance' and 'Catch Me If You Can', nos 4 and 5, are graded 'easy to moderately easy'. The fingering is now extended to include 'thumbs-under' patterns. The first piece consists essentially of two-part counterpoint with some excursions into three-part chords, created by held-over notes. The rhythm produces suspensions for the first time in the set, and these, together with the relatively slow tempo, encourage expressiveness in the young pianist. In measure 20 parallel fifths are created by the perfectly natural contours of two melodies. One cannot but smile at the dismay of pedants visualizing young minds being harmonically corrupted by the parallels! 'Catch Me If You Can' is the perfect title for the strict two-part canon at the octave and at the distance of a half measure, which pervades the fabric of this charming little piece.

'Peasant Dance', no. 6, is a two-page piece. It and its successor, 'Cradle Song', are in the 'moderately easy to moderate' class. Both introduce the young pianist to the problems associated with a homophonic texture in which dissonant harmonies play a large part. In 'Peasant Dance' rhythmic problems are also met when the vigorous melody, composed of smoothly flowing eighths, is punctuated by accented notes (preceded by graces), most of which fall on second and third beats of the triple metre. The accompaniment consists entirely of open fifths, the majority of which move in a stream of quarter-notes that continually oscillate in parallel fashion between F-C and G-D. This pattern produces very frequent clashes with the melody, an effect that suggests the uninhibited nature of most peasant dances, but which also introduces the pupil to interesting and less conventional harmonies.

'Cradle Song' is, in my opinion, the jewel of the set. It is a study in slow, duple metre of sonorities and *pianissimo* control, directed to be played 'with two pedals throughout'. The chords making up the sonorities are the unrelated triads frequently heard in Rubbra's music. Here, they are arranged in two separate streams, one for each hand. Not only are the two streams unrelated harmonically but even the triads in the same hand bear no relationship to each other. In the accompanimental bottom flow each triad occupies a full measure and there are three pairs of triads, arranged so that the chords in each pair alternate. Thus a slow, rocking motion is set up. When the second pair takes over after ten measures the fundamental harmonies change from an F sharp-E axis to one centring on E-G. There are eight measures of this followed by the third pair of triads: B-C sharp. All triads except those on G are minor. Above, in the right hand, a poignant little melody runs along the tops of the shifting triads. The entire piece has a Satie-like wistfulness about it.

The last two pieces in the set, 'The Donkey' and 'The Shining River', are each two pages long and both challenge the pupil with more advanced problems. In 'The Donkey' these are centred on sixteenth-note patterns, some of which engage both hands simultaneously, and tone clusters composed of two and three notes. The two-note clusters have an accompanimental function, while the three-note clusters, placed on alternate beats and separated by an octave, represent the braying of the donkey in a charming and humorous way. In 'The Shining River' the pupil is confronted by the familiar Brahmsian pattern of twos in the right hand against threes in the left, all to be played in a singing manner. Since the right-hand part consists of three-note chords along the tops of which flows a melody, the *cantabile* requirement is a demanding one.

Both of these pieces introduce the pupil to small ternary form. In 'The Donkey' each *A* section is sixteen measures in length, and these are separated by a miniature *B* of just four measures. Its material is derived from *A* and there is no interruption in the rhythmic flow. The ternary structure in 'The Shining River' is more obvious because the *B* section, now eight measures long, is in the tonic minor. Its material is also derivative. Indeed, the original bass line of *A* is simply transposed to the minor key under the same types of chords.

Unless one has heard the Nine Little Pieces, it would be easy to dismiss them as adequate for their purpose, well-written to be sure, and containing difficulties appropriate to the various stages of a young pianist's growth, but essentially no different from thousands of other pieces with the same goals. However, in performance they are refreshingly different from the run-of-the-mill teaching materials, for, besides displaying the vitality and naturalness suggested by the titles, it also reveals unexpected subtleties. Harold Truscott has expressed their essence perfectly: 'Any student set to master these pieces [the later Four Studies are also included in his judgement] is going to gain in the only musical technique that really matters, for it contains all the others – the technique of musical understanding.'[3]

Introduction, Aria and Fugue for Harpsichord (or Piano)

As the title of Rubbra's next keyboard work, Op. 104, indicates, the primary instrument is the harpsichord, but in its absence the composer has authorized the piano as an acceptable substitute. Opinions may and do vary as to which instrument is more effective for the transmission of Rubbra's thought. Truscott believes that 'a piano will convey the composer's thought well enough'.[4] Frank Dawes, the principal reviewer of the work, looks at the problem from the performer's standpoint:

> The introduction sounds better on harpsichord than piano; the aria, with its very close part-writing, is more comfortable to play on two keyboards than one; the fugue is a piece of pure polyphonic reasoning that would suit almost any medium. But the whole is eminently playable on either instrument.[5]

Having myself played the work on both instruments, I find myself in agreement with Dawes in principle regarding his conclusion, but I feel the rich harmonies of the Introduction deserve the fuller sound of the piano.

At the present time the reader has no opportunity to judge for himself which instrument is the better medium, for the Phoenix record cited above is no longer available, nor is the harpsichord version, played by Michael Thomas to whom the work was dedicated.

The very short Introduction (a fraction over nine measures) is marked *Grave ma appassionato*. Its material centres on a falling third and second in each of its first two phrases, the second of which is an exact sequence of the first. This figure, marked with a bracket in Example 145, dominates the Introduction. Its

Ex. 145

rather dramatic nature and the distribution of its notes over a wide area give it a rhapsodic and improvisatory character. There is, however, another figure composed of four sixteenths that outlines a falling second and rising third. It follows the sequential statement of the original figure and overlaps a very shortened version of that figure. The remainder of the Introduction is concerned in one way or another with these two figures.

The gently flowing Aria, marked *L'istesso tempo*, is more than twice as long as the Introduction from which it issues without a break and whence its material is derived. Its first two measures feature the second of the two figures. Near the end of the piece there are some interesting combinations of the figures in which both hands participate. Except for its first and last two measures the flow of triplet sixteenths is constant and there are many instances of two sixteenths cutting across this basic pulse. In two places near the end the first figure runs along the top of the triplets for two measures. Despite the leisurely flow the Aria has its moments of tension, especially during its final third where the dynamic level is *fortissimo* and both hands are busy with separate versions of the figures.

The three-voiced Fugue, besides being the longest of the three components, is certainly the culmination of the work. There is no hint here, except perhaps in the concluding line, of the freedom that characterizes its companion pieces. Its four-measure subject is divided into complementary halves, the first of which is diatonic and the second moderately chromatic (Example 146). The first half is introduced over the two concluding measures of the Aria. Thus the

Ex. 146

entire work is continuous. Dawes in his review describes the second half of the subject as being 'constantly inflected flatwards, a feature that reflects itself in depth right through the harmonic tissue'. He then observes that

> the third fugue of *Ludus Tonalis* has a very similar melodic series in the second half of its subject, and there is perhaps some Hindemith influence to be observed in Rubbra's fugue – fully absorbed be it said, but salutary, as a comparison with the earlier, and more expansive and rather folksy fugue of Op. 19... will show. That, for all its skilful contrapuntal writing, sounded slightly parochial. This emphatically does not.[6]

There is certainly a parallel between the two subjects at these points (Example 147 shows Hindemith's subject) but the deciding factor in the question of

Ex. 147

influence, absorbed or not, is what occurs texturally when all the voices have entered and interacted with one another. Considered in this light there are sufficient differences between the two fugues to ask whether, in fact, there is any Hindemith influence at all. For one thing, the chromatic second half of Hindemith's subject is almost twice the length of Rubbra's, and there is therefore almost twice as much chromatic interaction in his fugue. The areas of tonal instability are thus greater in extent. The two textures are markedly diverse as well, Hindemith's being spare and Rubbra's flowing, even luxuriant. (Tovey's reference to Hindemith's 'lean, athletic style' comes at once to mind.)[7]

Throughout Rubbra's Fugue the flow is entirely natural. The three principal entries of the subject are precisely joined, leaving no space for short interim episodes. The first episode, therefore, is rather long – nine and a half measures – but the literal transpositions of the subject's second half are so prominent as to almost convince one that complete statements of the full subject are being heard. The same is true of the next, shorter episode. Altogether, there are six subject entries. The last three are in left-hand parts, leaving the right hand free for interesting contrapuntal derivatives, which grow in intensity until, above the final *fortissimo* entry – shared by the bass and middle voices – an equally *fortissimo* top voice turns into an elaborate melisma. This concluding line of the Fugue is dominated by groups of thirty-second notes, and a short flourish of sixty-fourths brings the Fugue to an end.

Important expressive features of the entire work are the Baroque-style ornaments scattered throughout all three components. At the bottoms of the pages the composer has identified some of them by name, and in some cases has supplied performance directions. This entire work, like many of Rubbra's others, reveals its secrets and details rather slowly, but repeated hearings bring their rewards, and convince one of the accuracy of Truscott's assessment: it 'contains some of his finest music on a small scale'.[8]

Eight Preludes

Written in 1966, the Eight Preludes, Op. 131, were first performed by the composer a year later at the Cheltenham Festival 'in a curious programme which included some jazz music as far as I remember; anyway, they were mixed up with jazz music of some kind. They wanted to liven things up, I suppose.'[9] The Preludes also appeared on the programme in Oxford Town Hall, 28 May 1968, on the occasion of Rubbra's retirement. About the work itself, Rubbra had this to say (as quoted by Truscott):

> These preludes form my first large-scale solo piano work. I use the word 'work' advisedly, for although each of the preludes is self-contained there is an overall unity of material, and the order of the pieces is fixed by logical transitions from one to another. All the preludes spring from the melodic idea with which no. 1 begins.[10]

Truscott has further emphasized and clarified these essential points:

> I think it is fair to say that the melodic connection is not obvious but it can be perceived. However, what matters is the sense of unity that comes across from this varied collection of pieces, or movements. They do form one work, and although the moods and styles vary it can be heard that there is a controlling force binding them together, essentially in the order in which they appear, and that force stems from the first piece. A work to study and absorb into one's system.[11]

In sharp contrast with Truscott's views are two rather hostile comments which, unfortunately, typify the thoughtlessness and misunderstanding that are responsible for a great deal of the neglect Rubbra's music has suffered. Susan Bradshaw's categorical dismissal assures us that the Preludes 'show [Rubbra] still, in 1967, devoted to an exhausted harmonic language'.[12] The other comment, by Dawes, states tersely 'there are no innovations or fresh revelations here.'[13] It is easier to accept Bradshaw's assessment because she seems so obviously convinced that within the bounds of triadic harmony there is nothing further to be said. She is entitled to her opinion, which, apparently nothing can shake. Rubbra's music, of course, continually proves her wrong. Dawes's comment is more disturbing because it appears as though he had listened to the Preludes with an open mind, but then failed to grasp what this composer's music demonstrates again and again: 'fresh revelations' in terms of new and interesting treatments of conventional materials such as triads, scale figures and common intervals. Returning to the word ' innovations', that quality is also present in this work, not in the sense of the novel use of novel materials, but again in terms of the wealth of possibilities disclosed by imagination and intellect.

Each prelude is a distinct entity with its own special character and emotional flavour, and *only* in this sense can the set be compared with Chopin's and

Debussy's Preludes. There is no overall related key scheme, and, indeed, within some of the pieces the tonality is extremely vague despite the use of key signatures. But nowhere in the set is there the slightest hint of the atonality Michael Dawney speaks of in connection with the four-note series which gives rise to the work as a whole.[14] As we have seen a number of times in this book, such a concept is wholly foreign to Rubbra's thinking.

Prelude I, like VI and VIII, is but one page in length. The four-note pattern that opens it (Example 148A) is, not surprisingly, subjected to transformations

Ex. 148

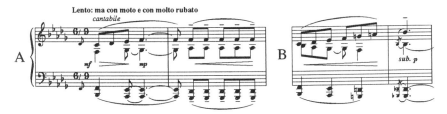

almost at once. Measures 6–7 show three types of transformation simultaneously: the original ascending movement, and two descending movements (Example 148B). A similar extension of the four-note pattern appears in measure 9 in an interior voice. Later measures where the same kinds of alteration are to be seen are 14–17. Other materials growing naturally from the four-note nucleus serve not only as connective tissue in Prelude I but also as important thematic elements in the later preludes, where they are considerably altered. They include the repeated notes/ chords in measure 2, the rising triadic and melodic figure in 9, and the rocking figure in 12–13.

Rhythmically, this first piece captures one's interest not just through the occasional interjection of a nine-beat measure, but more importantly in terms of the three-beat patterns, one example of which is the descending bass line of Example 148B. These become much more frequent and insistent as the Prelude continues, and the cross-rhythms they create against the eighth-note flow do much to enliven what could have been merely an ordinary piece. These interactions result in tensions that are heightened by the accents placed above and beneath the intruding quarters, and by the gradually increasing dynamic level from the middle of the piece onwards. All of this culminates in a massive climax six measures before the *pianissimo* ending.

The fragile, fantasy-like quality of Prelude II is brought about in its first and third sections by the combination of two very disparate elements. The first of these, composed of quarters and eighths in the top line, is derived from the seminal four-note figure, although the relationship is not obvious until the third measure where an accented quarter and triplet outline the ascending tetrachord. Several other like combinations and, near the end, a heavily accented group of octaves also confirm the kinship. Leading up to and linking these derivatives are fragments of the four-note pattern. They include the opening minor second and its inversion. However, it is the second of the two elements that contributes most to the underlying fragility of the Prelude: the falling and rising groups of sixty-fourths and thirty-seconds (some groups are varied by having a sixteenth as the concluding note). These must be fitted between the quarters and eighths of the top line, and also reconciled with the triplets – not an easy task, particularly when a sub-group appears at the bottom as in Example 149.

Ex. 149

Throughout the contrasting second section the right hand executes a tremolo (interrupted once by a short *roulade*), while the left hand is entrusted with two tasks: sounding a two-note pedal (F sharp/B) which the damper must sustain, and playing passages above the right hand consisting of fourths whose rocking motion comes from measure 12 of Prelude I. Perhaps this section with its persistent tremolos was in Dawes's mind when he questioned the suitability of the Preludes for the piano, claiming that few of them appear to have been idiomatically conceived.[15] Considering Rubbra's wide experience as a pianist and his undoubted ability to write well for his instrument, the question seems impertinent, but whichever side one chooses in the issue, the effect of this middle section is magical.

The sixteen measures comprising Prelude III make this piece the shortest of the set. Certainly it is the most restrained. It is a strict two-part canon whose bottom voice is a major third below the top and at a distance of one measure later. Opinions may vary as to Dawney's assertion that the piece 'would make an excellent definition of bitonality for an encyclopaedia'.[16] From the visual standpoint this is true, but repeated hearings fail to confirm two keys. This is because the thematic material is tonally vague, not conforming to key restrictions. Thus the interaction of the two voices produces an even more indefinite situation bordering on a sort of 'benign' atonality, which makes for a very appealing sound. Its basic material is easily traceable from its source in Prelude I (the ascending and descending tetrachords).

Prelude IV consists of two equally interesting yet very different components, one in each hand. The upper one, composed of oscillating triads in the form of sixteenth triplets, is derived from the same rhythmic figure with a similar contour in Prelude I, measures 12–13. The flow is anything but monotonous, for relief is provided by offbeat accents created through changing pitches and occasional irregular phrasing. In other words, agogic accents have a part to play in what is really, at times, a complex rhythmic pattern. In several places the oscillations outline both the ascending and descending tetrachords.

Concurrently with this right-hand activity, the left hand is engaged with octave rearrangements in eighths of the basic fourth: 1, 3, 2, 4 and its inversion (or retrograde), 4, 2, 3, 1. These tend to alternate and some are also in single notes. Harmonically, there is almost continuous modulation from one tonal centre to another, initiated by the right-hand triplets and confirmed by the left-hand groups. As in a number of other Rubbra works the centres are a third apart. Here, the quality of all of them is somewhat clouded by the Phrygian properties of the 1, 3, 2, 4 segments of the bass line and the flatted sixth degrees in the 4, 2, 3, 1 sequels.

All these qualities combine to make this Prelude one of the most beautiful of the set. The rather sombre dignity of the low-set, left-hand octaves combined with the calm, liquid flow of the triplets has produced a very satisfying sonority. This, in turn, underscores the deeply tranquil mood, one undisturbed by the mild dissonances and subtly shifting rhythms.

It is immediately obvious that Prelude V, marked *Allegretto quasi scherzando e capriccioso*, strikes a totally different mood. There is good-humoured bite in the major seconds which make up much of the texture, but all is not sweetness and light, for the interaction of all elements produces tension from time to time. This is because two quite different types of passage are, if not in conflict with one another, at least in the position of being rivals. One is composed of variants of the original four-note pattern in the shape of five- and six-note extensions in the top line, and further, more distantly related variants. The other type is made up of note repetitions – chiefly As and Cs – in sixteenths, the prevailing rhythmic unit of the piece. Their appearances in the beginning, middle and end demonstrate their importance in the total fabric, for repeated hearings lead one to the realization that they are a restraining influence on the rather rough exuberance of the first category.

The passages in the latter group rise ever higher, sometimes in a straight scale pattern, sometimes more indirectly. One is composed of a three-note scale pattern with each succeeding segment pitched a whole step higher. The entire passage takes four measures to reach its goal two octaves higher. Other passages rise more precipitously. In the end, the repeated notes have their way, and their chattering effect remains in the memory as perhaps the dominant characteristic. However, it would never have occurred to me to say that this trait 'reminds one of Chopin's famous *Raindrop Prelude*'.[17] The contexts in which the repeated notes are heard in each prelude, to say nothing of tempo and harmonic factors, are too vastly dissimilar for any comparison, implied or otherwise, to be valid. In the Rubbra piece there is a certain waywardness and rough humour most assuredly not found in Chopin's Prelude – characteristics implied by the *capriccioso* direction.

Prelude VI, marked *Grave e profondo*, is the most serious and introverted of the set. Assuming that all of the Preludes are performed on a recital programme it fits perfectly between the two extroverted flanking Preludes. Its texture is almost exclusively chordal and often dissonant, the majority of the chords in each hand containing four notes. Most of the time both hands play in the bass clef, thereby creating full-bodied, dark sonorities. These sonorities are particularly effective when, simultaneously in each hand, there are four-note, repeated chords, separated from each other by up to an octave. With the exception of one passage these chords are the product of an arpeggiation in each hand, and the left hand arpeggiation is the inverted form of the right. With regard to the origin of the rising *arpeggio* in measure 1 of Example 150, it seems to emanate from

Ex. 150

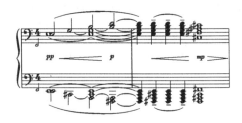

the rising triad in measure 9 of Prelude I; all that is needed is the extra third for the outlining of the seventh. The repetitions in measure 2 stem from those in the same measure of Prelude I. Yet the extended repetitions in measures 4 and 20 (five chords in triplet rhythm, preceded by a tied-over chord) are even more faithful to the original model where exactly the same pattern occurs in 6/8 metre. As the Prelude progresses the distance between chords becomes greater, creating an impression of unfathomable depths, made more mysterious by the very slow tempo and the soft dynamic level.

Prelude VII, like V, is capricious but in a more delicate way. Its *Allegretto grazioso* tempo is approximately similar to that of the earlier piece, but the latter's rhythmic drive is missing here, replaced by a more casual pace. The entire Prelude is dominated by a basic rhythmic figure and although the rests on either side of it are very short, their presence seems to check the forward movement for just an instant. Of course this kind of figure can generate a continuous rhythmic texture through omission of the rests, and indeed two passages are so constructed.

The thematic material is organized into phrases that match the length of the rhythmic segment then prevailing. Many of these phrases contain ascending and descending variants of the original four-note motive and in the inner parts there are also some exact intervallic reproductions, but leaping, disjunct intervals, particularly fourths, fifths and sixths, dominate much of the Prelude. A group of phrases amounts to a complete melody, and each melody is cast in a different tonal centre. (The word 'key' would be inappropriate, for the fabric is too dissonant.) Separating the centres are terse, dissonant cadences, all easily recognizable owing to their similar construction and the fact that their pitch is noticeably lower than that of the preceding and following phrases. The composer has marked each cadence *sub.mp*, and either *rit.* or *cédez*. The first complete melody and its cadence are illustrated in Example 151.

Ex. 151

The last Prelude of the set has an appropriate air of finality about it. It is a one-page fantasy in bravura style, *forte* and *fortissimo* throughout, based on a five-note figure and its inversion. The piece builds up cumulative power through a left-hand ostinato in the G clef. This consists of a transposition of the opening five-note figure. For its first five measures it is scored in eighths, followed by three measures of sixteenths, and ending with two of thirty-seconds. Its five-note length insures that the pattern begins on a different portion of each measure and as the note values increase so does the frequency of repetition. Above these ostinato repetitions the right hand plays mostly octaves, which contribute even more forcefulness owing to their exposed position. Tension piles up because of the restless, accented, non-resolving harmonies, for nowhere is there any tonic until the three cadential chords re-establish the D flat major of Prelude I (these chords are actually written in C sharp major).

It is virtually impossible to establish a relationship between the material of Prelude VIII and that of the first piece. Probably the best that can be said is that the original thought has become absorbed in the manner so often seen in sets of character variations.

Thus ends a most satisfying collection of preludes. Each piece has that indefinable quality, possessed by so much of Rubbra's best music, of having been seemingly improvised. Of course one is well aware that this did not happen; the Preludes were all carefully composed. However, one of the attributes of well-made music in any genre is that one is unaware of the efforts, even struggles, that attended its creation.

Four Studies

It is a measure of Rubbra's musicianship that his Four Studies, Op. 139, written to fulfil the Series Nine, Grade Three examination requirements at the Guildhall School, are included in the recording of his piano music. (The same is true, of course, of his Op. 74 pieces.) These studies, each just one page in length, call for greater skills than the most advanced of the Op. 74 pieces. Their titles, no longer fanciful, indicate at once the problem to be mastered. All are written in a mildly dissonant style that is appropriate for a candidate's understanding of some of the idioms of this century.

'Study in Sixths', in G major, moves gracefully in its 6/8 metre. It is a rather poignant little piece whose two halves are alike except for some left-hand harmonic alterations. A wistful 9/8 measure with a hint of minor, *sub.p* and *poco rit.*, separates the halves. The lilting melody is confined to the right hand where it rides on top of the chord structure, but the inner parts of the four-voice texture are also melodic in character, particularly when sixths are formed with the topmost voice.

'Study in Tonality' is the most interesting and unconventional of the four pieces. Although the key is C major, there is a novel signature of F sharp and B flat. The sharped fourth imparts a distinctive Lydian flavour while the flatted seventh belongs to a number of modes. Both sounds are combined in the descending pattern C, B flat, A, G, F sharp, E, C, which is heard a number of times. As in the first piece the metre is 6/8 but, unlike the latter, rhythmic irregularities are common, owing to syncopations: quarter-notes on the last two beats as well as on second and third beats. Since the texture is two-voiced and some of the piece is canonic or otherwise imitative, these irregularities are very prominent.

'Free waltz time' is the designated tempo for 'Study in Thirds', but late in the piece the standard 3/4 metre is interrupted by two measures of 2/4. All of the dissonances are generated directly from the interactions of the two streams of thirds – one in each hand. Many of the dissonances are non-dominant sevenths in root positions or inversions while others are appoggiaturas. The effect of all of these plus the waltz rhythm is that of a spritely dance and this is intensified by the one-measure phrases in antecedent-consequent arrangements. A brief change of key in the middle from the prevailing C to A flat provides contrast. With the return of the home key new patterns of thirds are introduced together with the duple measures.

The slow procession of half-note chords in 3/2 metre as seen on the printed page conveys the unbroken serenity of 'Study in Cantabile Chord-Playing' nearly as much as the sound itself. In the first half mild dissonances are almost continuous as the unrelated, mostly second-inversion triads create a gently undulating melody against open fifths in the bass. The fifths occupy a whole measure and are unrelated either to each other or to the chords above them. However, at no time is there any vagueness regarding the key (E flat), for at the start of every fourth measure the melodic line and the bass gently come to rest on an E flat chord. Between these points there are brief references to the key. The only accidentals in the piece occur in the first half when two measures of cross-relations (G flat against G natural) slightly ripple the surface. In the second half both hands are occupied with second inversions, moving at times in contrary motion, but still the tonality is carefully preserved. Despite its innocuous appearance and almost bell-like sound, this is not an easy piece and one is reminded here, as in the previous studies, of the original intent behind their composition.

Invention on the Name of Haydn

This piece, Op. 160, was written to commemorate in 1982 the two hundred and fiftieth birthday of the great Austrian. For those who might wonder how musical notes are obtained from the letters H, Y and N (A and D being obvious), there is an explanation. H is the German nomenclature for B and this originated because in the early history of notation the natural sign as it was then formed resembled an H. Explaining how notes are derived from Y and N is more difficult; the process involved in the derivation is certainly an artificial one. An alphabet is used over which is placed the musical portion of the alphabet (A through G) in such a way that A appears over H. The final G in the musical series then appears over N. Another series finishes over U, and part of a third yields D over Y. Thus Haydn's name expressed in notes is B-A-D-D-G, in which the second D is written an octave lower than the first (or 'legitimate') D. In Rubbra's piece these notes appear on a staff under HAYDN at the head of the first page. Other composers also wrote their own similarly derived pieces for the world celebration of Haydn's birth.

Rubbra's setting, dedicated to the English pianist-composer, John McCabe, is simple and straightforward. The four notes are sounded in various rhythmic patterns and pitches throughout the two pages. The first statement is set in half notes as are several others, but the four-square severity of the musical signature is offset by a running counterpoint in eighth notes that eventually turn into triplets. Some statements of the signature are incomplete, and near the end the triplet figure assumes an ostinato-like status for three measures. Despite the strong sense of G major in the four-note signature, there is no predominant tonality, as the piece is in a constant state of restless movement, indicated by the large number of accidentals. However, the final destination is D major, made unequivocally clear as the end of the piece approaches.

The overall impression left by this piece is that of a composer having fun with five rather intractable notes, which, however, prove to be flexible as the exercise progresses. It is not the sort of piece one would like to hear for too long, and the composer was wise to sense its limitations.

Fantasy Fugue

Rubbra's last piano work, the Fantasy Fugue, Op. 161, was completed in the autumn of 1982 'for a one-time Oxford pupil of mine for first performance in Wigmore Hall, London, on June 3rd next'.[18] In his programme notes for this performance Rubbra tells us that the work's title

> probably recalls for him [Michael Hill, the dedicatee and pianist for this occasion] all those detailed lectures I gave on the whole of Bach's '48', lectures that gave me in preparing them hitherto unrealised insights into the structure and musical possi- bilities of each subject. The present Fantasy Fugue, although free and seemingly improvisational, likewise utilises all the minutiae of the subject-matter, even in those contrasting sections where the music becomes less contrapuntal and more harmonic.[19]

The piece is short – just five minutes in length – quite chromatic, slow and very expressive. The feeling one gets from it is that a Baroque concept is being realized in contemporary terms, the latter emphasized by dissonances and unex- pected harmonic twists. The subdued and contemplative fugue subject could, with respect to its melodic contour, pass for a late Bach subject (Example 152).

Ex. 152

With the entry of the answer in a higher voice (seen in the example), the freedom implicit in the first word of the title is felt at once in the form of diminutions that take effect before the answer has even been completed, and this freedom is manifested throughout the remainder of the piece notwithstand- ing the fact that there are three further complete entries of the subject, for in all of these most of the original note values have been altered, allowing further diminutions. The most interesting of these entries is the second, because for half of its length its notes are heard at the top of a right-hand chord series. In the last of the three – a *fortissimo* bass entry in octaves – a change in pitch to A and D flats in the subject's third measure creates new harmonies.

Immediately following the completion of this bass entry (approximately two-thirds of the way through the piece) a short and very expressive section, marked *calmo*, acts as a structural division. Its material, consisting of three- note parallel chords high in the right hand against a single left-hand line in the middle register, bears only a tenuous relationship to the fugue subject. Beneath this material an octave pedal on B in the bass resounds softly for three and a half measures before shifting to B flat, and thence to G. The impression left by this section is one of suspended activity, made more palpable by the static pedal. After a return to the types of treatment previously employed, the piece ends with an *adagio* and *pianissimo* restatement in modified terms of the *calmo* section.

In my estimation, a perfect balance has been achieved in the Fantasy Fugue between the control exercised over 'all the minutiae of the subject-matter' and the wonderful freedom and sensitivity that are everywhere present. Again, in my opinion, it is Rubbra's finest piano piece and one that I hope many pianists will soon discover.

Meditation for Organ

This short piece, Op. 79, written in 1953, is Rubbra's only work for organ if the arrangement of Op. 69 by Bernard Rose is disregarded. It is dedicated to James Dalton, who, as an organ scholar at Worcester College, Oxford, was one of the composer's students.

Meditation is but nineteen measures long, yet within this limit there is much substance, unlike many another organ piece bearing the same title. Everything grows from the descending four-note figure of the opening, as seen in Example 153. By the third and fourth measures the motive has reversed direction. Soon a

Ex. 153

freely evolving countermelody containing elements of both the ascending and descending forms appears in the right hand in quarters. In the left, the descending form in its original time values is retained. Thus far the texture has consisted of two single lines above a C pedal, which is held throughout the entire piece. At just about the halfway point sixths are introduced in the left hand, and in the measure where they are introduced in the right-hand part, the left-hand sixths are reduced to thirds. By this time – even a little before – the material has progressed to where parts of it assume the role of connective tissue, binding together the evolving statements of the four-note motive and those with which the second half of the piece is concerned: a flowing form of the motive incorporated in a flowing eighth-note pattern. Although the piece is through-composed, the almost continuous presence of the motive (except for the connecting links) ensures unity.

The most obvious component of the motive is the mordent, but its very generous use throughout the piece is misunderstood by one reviewer. He begins his notice by saying that the piece's 'closely-woven, slow-moving texture is developed from a motive of four notes, and the effect is incantatory and delightful'. But,

It is not a very expert production so far as writing for the instrument is concerned. There are no fewer than forty-nine mordents in its twenty bars [actually nineteen, as the penultimate measure is divided by a dotted line in accordance with its 5/2 metre]. If they are a feature of the style they are a very tiresome mannerism.... If they are intended as accents they are unnecessary, for a skilful organist knows several ways of giving a melodic accent to a note. In my opinion the piece sounds better without most of them.[20]

What is misunderstood is that the mordents are, from the very start, integral parts of the basic material and to dispense with them would be equivalent to stripping away the organic ornamentation from many a Baroque keyboard theme. The mordents are not a 'mannerism' here nor are they to be thought of or interpreted as 'accents' that somehow got out of control. Admitting that *Meditation* is certainly not a Baroque piece should not preclude the introduction of mordents into a theme (or motive, for that is a more accurate term for this basic material) whose character would be totally different if they were absent.

I find Farmer's other complaint that the registration is 'too specific'[21] somewhat misleading. It would be only very rarely that an organ would lack such basic stops as a solo oboe or 8 and 4 ft flutes, to say nothing of a standard 8 ft stopped diapason. What he should have mentioned is that there are no provisions in the score (such as rests, which in any case would have altered the character of the piece) for the frequent registration changes to be negotiated by hand, for many smaller organs are not equipped with a liberal supply of manual pistons and toe studs by means of which the changes can be made smoothly. As the piece is written, the hands are simply too busy for the registration changes to be made without the aid of these conveniences. All of this may limit the places where the piece can be adequately performed, but there is no question that on well-equipped instruments it is effective. Registration is mentioned briefly in the following review:

> Rubbra offers a new 'Fantasia on one note', this one on a pedal C. A scrap of theme, characterized by a mordent, is woven in expressive convolutions above it with a typical blend of angularity and smoothness. This distinguished and beautiful piece is of no technical difficulty, but it requires a smoothly-judged registration in its brief rise and fall.[22]

Variations on a Phrygian Theme for Solo Violin

We turn now to the first of three works for unaccompanied strings: the Variations on a Phrygian Theme for Solo Violin, Op. 105, composed for the fiftieth birthday of one of England's leading violinists, Frederick Grinke (8 August 1961). Grinke has performed widely, acted in the capacity of a judge in international violin competitions, and served on the faculty of the RAM, of which he is a Fellow. He was the leader for ten years of the Boyd Neel Orchestra. Lennox Berkeley, Gordon Jacob, Kenneth Leighton and Vaughan Williams have also

Ex. 154

composed pieces for him. The Phrygian theme is Rubbra's own, and the piece
consists of twelve numbered variations and a coda.

The theme (Example 154) is seen to consist of four segments of which the
first and last are melodically identical, the accompanying counterpoint in each
case being different. The Variations as a whole are, in their freedom, similar to
those in the fourth movement of the Third Symphony. Variations 1 through 4, 6,
9 and 12 employ segments from the theme in different ways, while Variations
5, 7, 8, 10 and 11 maintain very tenuous connections with the theme. The coda
is a forceful reworking of the materials of Variation 2. Variations from each of
these groups will serve to show the wide divergencies in the set, and not to be
discounted by any means is the lower-voiced counterpoint that accompanies the
theme, for in some of those variations wherein the theme is either not present or
extremely difficult to trace, elements of the counterpoint are present.

From the first group, Variation 4 makes the greatest use of the thematic
segments, and it is also rhythmically interesting. Most of it is double-stopped
and the various segments, including two instances of one long one from the
counterpoint, are very prominent in the upper part. Various metre changes and a
tempo indication of *Vigoroso* provide rhythmic excitement.

Also from Group I, Variation 12 is more obvious in its faithfulness to the
thematic segments. It consists entirely of sixteenths in another *Vigoroso* setting
and the notes of the segments are heavily accented and placed at the beginning
of each group of sixteenths in the 4/4 metre. In the first measure segments *a* and
b overlap. The counterpoint has a big part to play in the proceedings, for the
descending and ascending groups of sixteenths reproduce its tetrachords.

Variation 5, marked *Lento espressivo e molto sostenuto*, is an appropriate
choice to represent the second group. Its only connection with the theme seems
to be the Phrygian half-steps and possibly the three opening notes, which could
be a transposition of the B, C, B of segment *b*. A more likely source for these
notes is the opening of Variation 3, whose first five notes match the contour of
those in 5. There is also an interesting internal structure in this Variation, for its
fifth and sixth measures are the same melodically as the first two, but the
rhythmic organization is quite different. Chromaticism is another area which
sets this Variation off from the theme.

Viewed as a whole, the shape of this set describes an arch with the middle
variations – 5 through 8 – as the apex because of their tenuous connections with
the theme. The chromaticism of these middle variations is also a factor in the
arch structure, although, as usual with Rubbra, hard and fast lines cannot be
drawn: chromaticism spills over into Variations 10 and 11 where it is primarily

figural, as the tonality in each variation is that of the set – A minor. Speaking of tonality, it does not seem presumptuous to question the use of the word 'Phrygian' in the title, for with A as the tonic towards which the theme and most of the variations gravitate, the E-F Phrygian characteristic loses its identity. For A minor to be considered as transposed Phrygian, B flat would have to be prominent. Therefore, the set appears to be in the Aeolian or natural minor mode.

It might appear from the number of variations that the set is long. Quite the contrary is true: it is complete in four pages. Naturally, some variations are longer than others, but none is longer than sixteen measures and only one reaches that length. One further observation may be made: Variations 7 and 8 are joined together as are nos 9, 10 and 11. Thus the set is a fusion of the continuous and discontinuous types.

Meditations on a Byzantine Hymn for Unaccompanied Viola

This second piece in the series of works for solo strings is based on 'O Quando in Cruce'. A note at the front of the score tells us that 'this work was first performed by Maurice Loban in the B.B.C. Home Service programme on December 20th 1962'. In the complete list of the composer's works, it is Op. 117. An arrangement of it for two violas was made by the composer himself: Op. 117A.

The entire hymn is printed in two versions together with an explanatory text on pages 12–14 of the booklet accompanying vol. 2 of *The History of Music in Sound*. Before the music of the hymn and Rubbra's treatment of it are examined, the valuable informational text is included here as historical background:

> In early days many Greek chants were introduced into the Latin churches and sung in Greek. At a later date they were first sung in Greek and then repeated in Latin to the same melody. In the third stage the Greek was dropped and the melodies were sung in Latin only. But in those parts of Italy which were under Byzantine domination the custom of singing in both Greek and Latin was maintained for a long time. Bilingual versions of the Good Friday hymn 'Ote to stavro – O quando in cruce' have been preserved in eleventh- and twelfth-century Graduals from Beneventum and Ravenna. A comparison between the versions from Beneventum and Ravenna on the one hand... and the contemporary Byzantine version on the other... shows that the Beneventan version must be regarded as the incrustation of a very old version of the Greek hymn, whereas the Byzantine version shows a richly ornamented later development of the melody.[23]

Rubbra's Meditations are built on the Byzantine version, which is ten lines long in modern notation, but he has chosen roughly the first two lines. These, stated like a theme at the start of his piece, are reproduced in Example 155.

The absence of a time signature which, of course, conforms to the rhythmic flow of the original chant is a characteristic of the piece, the sole exception being Meditation 12, where a 6/8 metre is introduced. Yet there are other meditations where a metrical feeling is certainly present but without the stipu-

Ex. 155

lation of a time signature. There are sixteen numbered meditations and a coda. Although 'variations' or 'improvisations' might appear to be equally appropriate words for the title, 'meditation' more accurately describes the majority of the components in this work even though no. 9 is marked *Allegretto giocoso* and no. 12 *Allegretto amabile*. Certainly the source and nature of the theme suggest subdued treatment, and the viola is the ideal stringed instrument for its transmission.

The meditations are grouped in such a way as to yield an overall ternary structure. However, the second *A* section is not to be thought of as constituting even a free return to the actual contents of the first *A*. Rather, the divisions are more general, but there are common threads. First, Meditations 1 through 7 are to be played without a break; nos 8 through 11 all have cadential endings; and nos 12 through 16 are again continuous (the coda can be counted into this final group also). Second, there are similarities between certain meditations belonging to those groups where the music is continuous. Thus Meditations 3 through 7 and the second half of 13 through 16 are set in sixteenths. The middle group, nos 8 through 12 and the first half of 13 are set in larger values, no. 10 being made up of quarters and halves and the others of eighths. And since the theme and coda are each twelve measures in length, with the latter a double-stopped restatement of most of the theme, the formal structure becomes more obvious.

The techniques employed throughout the work are virtually the same as those already met in the unaccompanied violin variations: the selection of particular motives from the hymn and their elaboration. The first such motives are the B-C-B and the falling melodic third bracketed in Example 155. These dominate the first Meditation. In the second, the falling as well as the rising thirds which soon appear in the theme are the important characteristic. Against these and on strong beats there are octaves. Some meditations, such as nos 4, 7, 8, 14 and 15, are based on lengthy segments of the hymn, and in all of them except no. 8 the segments are clearly stressed in the upper of the two voices, the lower being filled with running sixteenths. In addition, no. 15 outlines an inversion of its particular segment. The materials of other meditations are so close to parts of the hymn as to prompt intensive searches of the latter in an effort to establish sources, but these merely confirm the composer's inventiveness, which has communicated the spirit rather than reproduced the letter of the hymn.

Improvisation for Unaccompanied Cello

The last of the three variation-type works for a solo stringed instrument is Improvisation for Unaccompanied Cello, Op. 124. Written for and dedicated to William Pleeth, it differs from its two predecessors in two ways: the music is continuous so that there is no cadence until the end, and there are no numbers to indicate separate improvisations or sections. The generating notes (in no sense can they be called a theme) are A-F-E-D in descending order. In his review of the work Robert Anderson points out an obvious similarity:

> Rubbra's careful workmanship and thoughtful style are fully in evidence.... The first four notes of the piece provide the basic intervals, and these happen to be the same as Tchaikowsky's at the start of the first piano concerto. Rubbra is less prodigal than Tchaikowsky and never allows us to forget his intervals for a moment, the result is a cogent piece of musical logic that attractively exploits the cello's capabilities.[24]

Not to put too fine a point on it, Anderson's statement about the omnipresence of Rubbra's intervals is not entirely accurate, for there are passages in the middle and toward the end of the piece where they are missing. Such places provide relief from what could have been too much sameness – something of which the composer must have been aware. Another factor furnishing variety is Rubbra's usual rhythmic flexibility, achieved through metre changes and cross-rhythms, although the metrical changes are nowhere made explicit, for in the three pages that comprise the work there is not a single metre signature. The work has its very expressive moments both dynamically and in terms of tempo, and each of these areas is carefully marked.

Pezzo Ostinato for solo harp

Considering Rubbra's fondness for the harp as evidenced in so much of his orchestral music, it is entirely natural that he should have written for it as a solo instrument. Although there are but two works that fit into this category, each is uncommonly interesting.

The first such work is *Pezzo Ostinato*, Op. 102. Composed in the late 1950s, it bears a dedication to Peter Crossley-Holland, an ethnomusicologist of some distinction who wrote numerous articles on Celtic, Tibetan and native American music. In 1965, after the publication of this work, he became editor of the *Journal of the International Folk Music Council*, and in 1976 Chairman of the Council on Ethnomusicology. He is also a composer, having written music for choral groups, solo voices and various recorder combinations.[25]

Rubbra's dedication takes on meaning when one discovers that the piece has Eastern and therefore ethnomusicological associations, for it may be recalled that *Pezzo Ostinato* was mentioned by the composer in Chapter 1 as having been influenced by contacts with Eastern thought and philosophy. Alan Blyth in his review of the piece following its performance at a retrospective concert at the Purcell Room, on 24 April 1969, was somewhat more specific when he referred to it as 'raga-inspired'. Continuing, he praised it as being 'another original-sounding piece: calm, untroubled music, worlds away from the present mainstream, unfashionable, too, in caressing rather than assaulting the ear'.[26]

The ostinato on which the piece is constructed is a four-measure pattern which incorporates the melodic fourths (in this case ascending) so often found in Rubbra's music. A glance at the pattern in Example 156 shows that the

Ex. 156

fourths are used in three of the four segments, and that the second segment is varied rhythmically. The B naturals in the third segment are a wonderful touch – a consequence, of course, of the absence of B flat in what to some may appear to be a strange-looking key signature.

There are twenty-two complete statements of the pattern and a three-measure coda. The first statement is, of course, unadorned. The pattern is by no means restricted to either the top or bottom parts, but is assigned with certain exceptions to one or the other in a group structure. Thus statements 2 through 4, 10 through 12, 18 and 21 are given to the lower part. Nos 5, 13 and 22 are unevenly divided between top and bottom, and all of the remaining statements are in the upper part. Of course it is the interactions of the ostinato pattern and the figurations that surround them that individualize and give life to the piece, and it is with these that we shall be concerned in the following examinations of some selected statements.

In nos 2–5 the right-hand figurations are made up of continuous sixteenths that form a different pattern in each ostinato statement. That in no. 2 is itself an ostinato. In no. 6 where the original pattern is transferred wholly to the right hand following the division in no. 5, the bottom part traces another ostinato. This consists of a sixteenth-note repetition of the ascending fourth as it appears rhythmically in the first measure of each statement. Beginning with statement 7 and continuing through 13 the metre is altered to 10/16 so that in all of these statements except no. 8 the principal ostinato pattern is reduced to two measures from the original four. This means, of course, that it is moving twice as rapidly. Intriguing cross-rhythms are created in nos 7 and 9.

It would be incorrect to assume that the statements are cumulative in the sense of a gradual increase in tensions, and, in fact, the latter word is really inappropriate at any point in this piece. The cross-rhythms just noted do not become more complex, but some of the figurations take on more animation when their values are increased to thirty-seconds. Still, one cannot speak of tension. The texture thickens in no. 18 and the alternating chords in each hand, marked *fortissimo*, are forceful but never agitated. Even the clusters of major and minor seconds, used from the very beginning as an integral part of the ostinato figure and continuing in all subsequent statements except nos 20 and 21, are never astringent enough to produce a sense of gathering tension. Perhaps the most suitable words that can be used to describe the effect of these clusters are 'veiled' and 'indefinite'. Certainly they help to delineate the overall ethereal atmosphere of the work, an atmosphere made more explicit by the cascades of *pianissimo* thirty-seconds in statement 16. But one's lasting impression of *Pezzo Ostinato* is the almost hypnotic spell cast by the constant repetition of the short pattern throughout seven pages, and to make sure that it is nowhere broken there is the composer's direction to that effect at the bottom of page 1. As for the faintly exotic flavour of the piece, the augmented seconds – B natural to A flat and back again – are largely responsible.

Transformations for Solo Harp

Of all Rubbra's solo instrumental works *Transformations*, Op. 141, is the most considerable in terms of length – thirteen pages – and perhaps even in difficulty. We are speaking now of one continuous work, and whereas the Eight Preludes are exactly the same length, they cannot be compared for obvious reasons. The dedication is to the harpist, Ann Griffiths, who also edited and fingered the piece. The title is a clear reference to the changes effected in two chord streams, one ascending in the left hand, the other descending in the right. What happens to these streams is analogous to the design on the cover of the score: beginning in the upper right corner and moving in a diagonal plane are four drawings of Rubbra's face. The second is considerably less distinct than the first, and so on until in the lower left corner the features are indistinguishable.

The initial chord streams, each composed of four chords and moving at a different rate of speed are shown in Example 157. They may remind some

Ex. 157

readers of certain Debussy piano works by reason of their 'sideslipping' appearance, as well as the intervallic structure of the chords, all of which are of the same size (allowing for differences between major and minor thirds). These chord streams very soon change in one way or another, and the remainder of the piece is concerned with these transformations. But the changes are not effected in the sense of variations – either separate or continuous. The music itself is continuous, but there is no perceptible formal structure, and the best that can be said is that the work is through-composed and improvisatory.

As one leafs through the score an ordered progression from simple to complex is quite graphically revealed, first, in terms of harmony: the first page contains no accidentals of any sort, and the same is almost true of the second and third pages. Thereafter there is a modest increase until pages 8 and 9 are reached. Second, important alterations can be seen in the composition of the basic chords that form the nucleus of the piece, and some of these changes are brought about by the increasing harmonic complexities implicit in the appearance, just noted, of more accidentals. More important that those changes is the breaking up of the patterns set forth at the outset (Example 157), and this process takes various forms, some of which may now be mentioned. First, the rigid chordal flow as seen in Example 157 disappears after the first page to be replaced by a flexible line that allows changes of direction within longer phrases. Thus on page 2 the top line moves resolutely upwards in a long scale-wise passage, balanced soon after by other conjunct phrases flowing in gentle melodic curves. Beneath this series of phrases, set in major and minor thirds, the downward-moving chords originally assigned to the top part maintain their identity, but even here there are directional changes. Later in the work, octave chords, bare octaves and series of parallel triads, as well as more complex chords are busily engaged in creating a full texture. But a great deal of the time it is possible, no matter what the complexities, to pick out patterns of descending melodic fourths and their ascending counterparts from the midst of phrases in which they are embedded. And at various points in the work there are long stretches filled with chains of chords exactly like those heard at the beginning. Thus there are constant factors that hold the piece together, the most important of which appears to be the descending fourth in whatever guise it appears melodically: at the tops of chords or independently. With that in mind, the cover design showing four descending and progressively indistinct countenances makes sense in terms of a graphic representation of the transformations found in this work.

The music's flow is, to a considerable extent, a product of the frequent metre changes, cross-rhythms and syncopated accents so characteristic of the composer. From an expressive viewpoint, dynamic markings are frequent and meticulously indicated. Unfortunately, the work is not presently available on record, but it looks like a valuable addition to the harp repertoire.

Notes

1   Michael Dawney, 'Edmund Rubbra and The Piano', *MR*, August 1970, pp.241–8.
2   *ibid.*, p.242.

3   Sleeve-note to the recording of Nine Little Pieces, and Four Studies on Phoenix DGS 1009.
4   *ibid.*
5   Frank Dawes, *MT*, February 1964, pp.129–30.
6   *ibid.*
7   Donald Francis Tovey, *Essays and Lectures On Music* (London: Oxford University Press, 1949). Reprinted in *The Main Stream of Music and Other Essays* (New York: Meridian Books, Inc., 1959), pp.311–14.
8   Sleeve-note to the recording of Introduction, Aria and Fugue on Phoenix DGS 1009.
9   Tape of 9 August 1980.
10 Sleeve-note to the recording of Eight Preludes on Phoenix DGS 1009.
11 *ibid.*
12 Susan Bradshaw, 'The Twentieth Century', in *Keyboard Music*, Denis Matthews (ed.) (Harmondsworth: Penguin Books Ltd, 1972), p.366.
13 Frank Dawes, *MT*, January 1969, p.68.
14 Dawney, *op. cit.*, p.248.
15 Dawes, *op. cit.*, p.68.
16 Dawney, *op. cit.*, p.247.
17 *ibid.*
18 Letter of 14 November 1982 to the author.
19 Edmund Rubbra, programme notes for the first performance of the Fantasy Fugue on 3 June 1983.
20 Archibald Farmer, *MT*, November 1953, p.515.
21 *ibid.*
22 Ivor Keys, *M&L* 35, no. 1, January 1954, p.,77.
23 Gerald Abraham (ed.), *The History of Music In Sound* (Oxford University Press, RCA Victor) 2, p.13.
24 Robert Anderson, *MT*, January 1969, p.67.
25 Paula Morgan, *NGD* 5, pp.63–4.
26 Alan Blyth, *MT*, June 1969, p.652.

8　The chamber music

Rubbra's long and successful association with chamber music began with the First Sonata for Violin and Piano, Op. 11, which remains unpublished, and ended with the Duo for Cor Anglais and Piano, Op. 156. In between is a wide range of works whose diversity compensates for what is a modest list in terms of numbers.

Phantasy for Two Violins and Piano

Rubbra's first published chamber work is the one-movement Phantasy for Two Violins and Piano, Op. 16, composed in 1927 and dedicated to Gerald Finzi. The title was probably not chosen by the composer, for it seems likely that he was one of those who benefited from the terms described in the following passage. Certainly the time-frame as well as the other conditions apply to the work:

> In the first years of the twentieth century, Walter Willson Cobbett, a keen amateur devotee of chamber music, offered prizes and commissions to British composers for single-movement pieces, without conditions as to the form to be employed. To these (on the advice of the Musicians' Company) he applied the name 'Phantasy', taking the suggestion from the sixteenth-century English Fancy. Over forty of these compositions were heard between 1905 and 1930.[1]

With the exception of the unpublished violin sonata, the Phantasy is Rubbra's first large-scale work in any genre. It is significant not so much for itself – although it is an important achievement for a composer of twenty-six – as for the way in which some of its technical traits point to the future. The first of these is in the area of formal structure. Certainly in previous chapters where large structures have been dealt with, we have grown used to seeing unconventional forms, some of which have fused sonata structure with other designs of the composer's own devising. It would be a mistake to claim that such a fusion can be discovered in the Phantasy, but the germ is clearly there. Proof of the misunderstandings that can be generated even in such an early work as this is provided by Cobbett's statement that the Phantasy is in 'loose sonata form'.[2]

This is just not true, for the usual ingredients of the form are not present to any convincing degree. Certainly a recapitulation of the first fourteen measures from measure 181 through 194 is not enough to qualify for sonata form, especially when these measures are followed by fifty-seven measures that contain no trace of a coda. Of course from the beginning of his composing career it has been known that Rubbra as a predominantly contrapuntal composer paid but scant attention to the tonic/dominant or the tonic minor/relative major relationship pertaining to first and second themes. This has been amply demonstrated in this book wherever sonata form has been employed. In the present instance these tonal relationships do not exist. More to the point, the first theme has none of the qualities that normally characterize sonata form: drive, tension and capabilities for dynamic development. It, like the second and third themes, is very lyrical. Also, the very title, 'Phantasy', belies the idea of any formal rigidity, and leads the listener to expect some kind of free form, which is exactly what occurs here. It was probably the brief but exact recapitulation – even though it comes too soon – that persuaded Cobbett to call the Phantasy a sonata form.

Ex. 158

In possibly the earliest mention of Rubbra in a journal, he is described as being 'particularly fond of taking a simple phrase and exploiting it throughout the whole of a composition, viewing it from different angles and taking scraps of it for development and transformation. An example of this is the Phantasy for Two Violins and Piano',[3] a description that is entirely accurate, except that here there are three phrases. In the discussion that follows I shall refer to these as themes.

Example 158 includes the first two themes, and shows the similarities between them, enabling them to exchange material in one way or another. At first, Theme 2 appears to be a counterpoint to Theme 1 until further investigation reveals that its many literal repetitions prove it to be a theme in its own right. The principal points to be noted are the close canon between piano and second violin, and the three-way canon, marked by brackets and connecting lines, in measures 6–8. Note also in these measures the ease with which Violin II appropriates the first violin's material. All of these canons are merely the start of a long series in which both themes receive canonic treatment in two and three parts.

There are far fewer statements of Theme 3, seen here in its initial appearance in measure 57 (Example 159). Indeed, it seems as though the composer had

Ex. 159

forgotten it for it does not reappear until measure 115, and then only in a subordinate position in the second violin. However, very shortly after the conclusion of this statement it is heard in a three-way close canon.

Of the three themes it is the third that offers the great opportunity for development, largely because of the two groups of sixteenths. It is true that in this very early stage Rubbra's developmental techniques were somewhat limited: in this case to rising sequences of the bracketed figure in Example 159. These are restricted to the passage leading up to the climax where the gathering tension, particularly in the piano, is clear evidence that the work has entered a new phase. But another figure has been detached from Theme 3 and transferred to the piano as a series of full chords: the typically 6/8 rhythmic figure of measures 1, 3, 5 and 6 in Example 159. These two instances of thematic fragmentation are reassuring in view of the earlier parts of the piece where one begins to feel that the constant repetitions of the entire themes, whether singly or in canon, are becoming excessive. And the canons themselves are perhaps carried to an extreme. However, all of this can be excused in a young composer who was eagerly testing his wings and finding, no doubt to his delight, that he had a special aptitude for contrapuntal complexities.

Ivor Keys in his review of the work twenty-four years later rightly uses the expression *tour de force* to describe it, and goes on to say that if it is

> to be called a Phantasy it can only be in a sense even stricter than the normal Elizabethan one, for it is a large-scale tissue of continuous counterpoint, almost monothematic, often canonic and as closely knit as one is likely to see. Some fine climaxes and striking modulations relieve what would otherwise be a tiring piece of essentially undramatic music. With two *cantabile* instruments the piano is content to play a mainly subordinate part which is, however, rich and deep in its sound. In a sense the music is not technically difficult, but it requires considerable musicianship to grasp the underlying shape.[4]

Lyric Movement

In 1929 Rubbra composed a work called Lyric Movement (Op. 24). It had been planned earlier as a string quartet, but the composer was not happy with it for, following four revisions and rescorings, it assumed its present form: a movement for string quartet and piano. In the Lengnick catalogue it is listed as a piano quintet, although Rubbra preferred the title which he gave it. I am inclined to the view that his title is closer to the true nature of the piece, for the quartet and piano in Harold Truscott's words 'seem to move in a sort of co-operative independence'.[5] This view is reinforced from the start with music that is substantially different in terms of the quartet, which functions as a unit, and the piano. The latter's material consists of triplet figures, mostly in the right hand; full chords of various kinds, some of which are heavily stressed, while others are syncopated; and passages containing material previously heard in the quartet. Some of the latter double what is occupying the quartet at the moment, particularly at climaxes, but others are more independent although obviously derived.

The quartet's material measures up admirably to the work's title, for the principal theme in this ternary form is a leisurely, smooth-flowing, singing *legato*. However, even though the music is tightly organized and contrapuntal, both characteristics are much more relaxed than in the Phantasy and this in itself is a notable advance. The imitative writing has none of the relentlessness of the earlier work. There, the excessive employment of canon gives the impression that the composer was almost hypnotized once he discovered how easily his materials yielded to canonic treatment. In the Lyric Movement the canonic passages, although fairly numerous, seem more moderate because of the greater relaxation of the material. In the Phantasy the majority of the canonic entries are only a half measure apart, and this increases the tension. Here, except for the approach to the climax and the climax itself, there is a measure's distance between entries, sometimes more.

The principal theme, first announced by the viola, appears in Example 160. The first violin enters at the corresponding point in the next measure, followed by the second violin one measure farther on. The cello is a non-participant in

Ex. 160

the theme until later, being content before then to play a simple *pizzicato*, arpeggiated figure which is detached from its neighbour figures. Were it not for the absence of a consistent tonic/dominant relationship between parts at this beginning stage, the listener would think that the quartet was embarking on a fugue above a free piano accompaniment. I use the word 'consistent' here because the crucial I-V relationship between a subject and its answer has been altered to a minor sixth, but between entries 2 and 3 the I-V relationship is present: B minor/F sharp minor. Thereafter the fugal characteristics disappear, and what emerges in their place is a network of imitative entries in which melodic extensions, sequences and fragmentations play a significant role. Such procedures are, of course, developmental, and they emphasize once again the technical advances that set this work apart from the Phantasy.

As early as the tenth measure the first of these procedures has been put into operation, and in the next measure there is an inexact sequence of the extended material. Immediately after, the first opportunity in a published work to observe one of the means by which Rubbra composes his long lines may be seen. At first sight, the material of measure 12 and the first half of 13 appears to be new, but having observed in earlier chapters the economy which Rubbra has always practised, and which for him has remained a fundamental principle, what we see here should not be surprising. However, the soaring line seen in Example 161 may well surprise because of its appearance so soon after the almost

Ex. 161

constant repetitions in the Phantasy; there, not much happened except the repetitions. We begin with the inexact sequence in measure 11 of the material in the preceding measure; three of its four notes are marked x. In measures 12 and 13 these same notes are similarly marked. What is left unmarked is simply connecting material that extends the line in an elegant way. The new figure in the second half of 12 is repeated in 14, and after the high sustained E, the triplet and quarter figure in the second measure of Example 160 is used. In fact, these triplets and quarters have been a very prominent feature in all of the quartet parts up to measure 9.

The long line in Example 161 is duplicated at the same pitch in the second violin and cello parts at appropriate time intervals, but soon there is a reversion to the shape of the opening theme accompanied by some rescoring. Following this the expansions return, but with less of a time lapse between entries. The *pianissimo e sereno* soon becomes *poco a poco crescendo*, and this coupled with the shorter space between entries generates a tension which grows greater when the piano abandons its triplets and occasional statements of the main theme in favour of a strongly supportive role. This takes the form of a chordal doubling of the first violin part, and an octave doubling of the cello line – both heavily stressed. Fragmentation – one of the developmental procedures mentioned above – occurs when overlapping, eighth-note entries of the second, third and fourth notes of the original figure appear throughout the quartet and, to a lesser extent, the piano. The climax is shared equally by both quartet and piano in a series of *fortissimo* statements, some of which are strict, and others free. A two-measure unison and octave passage – played tremolo – accompanied by contrary-motion chords in the piano brings the climax to an end, and several measures later section *B* begins.

This new section is divided into two unequal subsections: the first is marked *Grazioso* and contains twenty measures; the second and much longer one has sixty-one measures, and is marked *Allegro (Doppio movimento)*. The eighty-one measure length of the entire section is exactly equal to that of section *A*. The 6/8 *grazioso* subsection contains an eight-measure theme whose two complete statements are presented by the second violin. In the fourth measure of statement 2 the viola overlaps with what turns out to be an incomplete statement, and in the final measure of the violin's second statement the first violin also begins an incomplete presentation. The piano is silent up to the concluding six measures, its material consisting of derivatives. The entire quartet is active throughout the subsection and those members not involved with the theme play material related to it. Thus there is continuous counterpoint surrounding the theme.

The *allegro* subsection, separated from the preceding subsection by a double bar, 'gives us, on a small scale, a preview of the methods of symphonic writing which were to appear roughly seven years later and grow into an astonishing series of major orchestral works'.[6] First among these methods is a four-measure ostinato for the piano, stated three times. Its material in the form of chords consists of the first four notes in the second measure of the *grazioso* theme plus a further descending note which, in the fourth measure of each ostinato pattern, is eliminated. However, the most intriguing feature about not just the ostinato passage but the entire subsection is the rhythm, and this, it will be recalled, is another dynamic characteristic of Rubbra's symphonic developments. The first three measures of the ostinato pattern are in 3/8 metre while the fourth is in 2/8. In itself this is not remarkable but the rests, introduced on the second beat of the second 3/8 measure and the first beat of the third – plus the unexpected shift to 2/8 and the return to 3/8 for the start of the repeated patterns – have combined to produce an early example of Rubbra's rhythmic ingenuity. However, the score reader should not be fooled by the different metres simultaneously allotted to the quartet and piano for, contrary to similar passages in later works, these do not signify complex cross-rhythms even though the barlines do not coincide. The quartet's 2/8 and the piano's 3/8 measures are nothing more than accommodations for different accents. The same situation is found on the following page when six quartet measures of 2/8 equal one 6/4 measure in the piano.

The quartet's material in this second subsection is yet another early instance of Rubbra's growing developmental skills. At first it seems entirely new and, in fact, its construction and ebullience strongly suggest that 'the tunes ... have something of the folk-element in them'.[7] Presumably his plural means also the theme of the first subsection, for there is nothing folk-like about the movement's principal theme. Returning to the quartet melody, the series of rising thirds (measures 106–9) is traceable to the three opening notes of the theme in subsection 1 (measure 82). After the sixteenths of measure 5 the next significant derivations are the C, B flat, G of measures 6–7, found in B, A, F sharp and E, D, B in measures 2–3 of the first subsection's theme. Having once derived the essentials, any composer with imagination can supply connecting links and extensions. Not only does Rubbra do that, he gives us an exciting passage in which all four parts are involved in exact imitation. But, in turn, this passage is combined with a complete statement in the piano of the first subsection's theme – that from which the quartet has derived the figures just described. In consideration of the different rates of speed at which the quartet and piano are moving, several statements of the former's material, plus repetitions and other derivatives, are required before the piano has completed its theme. It is a daring concept, brilliantly conceived and executed. The subsection ends with another exciting statement of the quartet's material, this time without the piano. A shortened final *A*, containing rescorings and significant changes, brings the work to a quiet close. An important achievement, this, which deserves a solid place in the repertoire.

Four Pieces for Violin and Piano

Rubbra's next chamber work in order of opus number (29) is Four Pieces for Violin and Piano, but since it bears a copyright date of 1927, its composition antedates the Lyric Movement by some two years. The music is simple, and the titles, 'Cradle Song', 'The Spinning Wheel', 'Slow Dance', and 'Rondel' show that the work is intended for teaching and recreation.

Violin Sonata No. 2

The Second Violin and Piano Sonata, Op. 31, composed in 1932, was preceded not only by the unpublished First Sonata but by one before that which dates from Rubbra's student days. This was performed by Kenneth Skeaping and the composer at the Royal College of Music; unfortunately, the music has been lost. What we know as the Second Sonata attracted a good deal of attention, both at the time of its first performance and years later: six reviews of which I am aware and possibly more. I begin with the two accounts of its first performance, both undated and unsigned, but presumably from Reading newspapers:

> On Wednesday evening a recital was held, by permission, in the Hall of Reading University, in honour of one of the artists, Edmund Rubbra, pianist and composer, whose early musical education was gained at the University. Mr. Rubbra has obtained much recognition recently, and his compositions have been performed at many important concerts, and it was right and fitting that Reading should have the opportunity of hearing one of our gifted younger composers.
>
> The major work performed on Wednesday was his Second Sonata for Piano and Violin, with the composer himself playing the piano part and his wife, Antoinette Rubbra, the violin. It is interesting, and to some no doubt, refreshing, to find that it is still possible for a young man of today to write in the style of forty years ago, to be able to be original without using the modern idiom. The first movement is romantic in feeling and opens with a broad lyrical melody which flows on smoothly and easily, the one big emotional climax occurring in the development section. The slow movement is quietly reflective, and the finale a surging rhythmical rush, sweeping along without cessation from the first bar until the last. The two artists gave a vivid interpretation of the work, with perfect ensemble and unity of feeling, and it was most warmly received.[8]

The second review has information about other aspects of the programme, and these have been retained as matters of interest, for they identify other areas of Rubbra's musical life.

> Mr. Rubbra's Second Sonata for Violin and Pianoforte was played for the first time at Grotrian Hall on March 21 by Miss Antoinette Chaplin [her professional name] and the composer. Some of his songs were sung at the same concert by Miss Beryl Thurstan with the composer accompanying. Mr. Rubbra also played a group of Debussy for pianoforte solo – he therefore appeared in the threefold capacity of composer, pianist, and accompanist. His pianoforte playing is perhaps unduly modest for its competence, but as a composer his equally sure touch is bolder. His Sonata is modern in idiom (Mr. Rubbra was once a pupil of Holst, though he has long since found his own phraseology), but it is purely lyrical and romantic in feeling. He is not of the dessicated school of composition; and even in the brilliant finale of his Sonata a kind of pathos more prominent in the earlier movements obtruded itself among the energetic passages of a *perpetuum mobile*. Of the songs 'In Dark Weather' was immediately attractive, though the others also had a reflective charm in their fidelity to the moods of the poems. Mr. Rubbra speaks in his music with a quiet but distinctive voice.[9]

The first movement, marked *Allegretto liberamente e scorrevole*, ♩. = 60 in the 6/8 metre, begins with the violin's exposition of a sixteen and a half measure

Ex. 162

theme that is lyrical and graceful. Seen here in Example 162, parts of it resemble in a general sense the first theme of the Phantasy and the *grazioso* theme of the Lyric Movement. This is normal for a composer who is still feeling his way, particularly in view of the 6/8 metre where certain patterns seem to come more automatically to mind than they do in other metres. The theme is cunningly constructed so that measures 9–12 are actually a link between the C major/A minor half of the theme and the curtailed C sharp minor repetition. Although these intermediate measures do have a role to play in succeeding parts of the movement, they cannot be thought of as constituting a theme in their own right, as it appears illogical for a new theme of only four measures to separate two statements of the principal theme. Therefore, I consider these four measures to be an integral part of Theme 1. But these measures serve a purpose other than just acting as connective tissue, for they are seen to be the primary source of Theme 2 (Example 163) whose first statement is also given to the violin.

Ex. 163

From the basic material provided by these two themes Rubbra has reared a structure peculiarly his own. It has strong rondo characteristics, but these do not conform to the usual rondo structures: *ABACA, ABACABA*. Instead, the themes alternate so that Theme 1 is stated five times, and Theme 2 is heard four times. Of course, it is not that simple, for during the violin's second statement of Theme 1 in measures 37–44, Theme 2 is sounded simultaneously in the piano, and for its third appearance in measures 60–69 Theme 1 is in canon between the two instruments. In measures 98–115 the same theme, in the violin, has undergone a metrical transformation from 6/8 to 3/4 while simultaneous developmental processes are occupying the piano. In measure 116 the original 6/8 returns and there is a curtailed statement in the piano of Theme 2, accompanied by free imitation in the violin. The first theme's final appearance in the violin in measures 130–46 is an identical recapitulation, one octave higher, of the opening statement. Except for different accompanying harmonies in the first four measures, the piano's part is also identical. An *Allegro vivo* coda follows almost immediately, but although it contains reminders of the foregoing music, it gives the impression that the composer simply provided an expected, brilliant conclusion. Both instruments have rushing sixteenths whose breathlessness fails ultimately to satisfy because they are so commonplace. Their patterns have been heard before many times in works by other composers. Perhaps this is one of the passages that caused one reviewer to say that 'somehow it keeps me asking where this or that bit has happened before'.[10] (I shall have occasion later to refer to other parts of this review.)

Harmonically, this movement falls somewhere between the non-modernity and the modernity mentioned in the reviews at the beginning of this discussion. The harmony is constantly changing, but in such a way as to suggest that even at this early stage the composer is making deliberate choices. This is the gist of Eric Blom's remark that Rubbra

> is one of those composers – rare, but fortunately rather strongly represented in the British school of today – who can vary their style according to the nature of each work they write and, while not forswearing idiosyncracies of their own, save themselves from becoming a prey to mannerisms.'[11]

Truscott's observation (p.402) is also relevant here: Rubbra uses whatever devices or styles that seem appropriate for his purposes at the moment.

The second movement, marked *Lento e dolente*, ♪ = 72, is entitled 'Lament'. Structurally, it is a ternary form whose *B* section of forty-eight measures is flanked by *A* sections of twenty-five measures. A fifteen-measure coda concludes the movement.

One of the criteria for determining the length of the first section is not so much the actual thematic material – divided into three long phrases – as it is the cessation of the unmistakable sound caused by the rocking augmented second.

Ex. 164

Although this interval is not wholly absent from section *B*, its use there is negligible in comparison with its pervasiveness in the *A* sections. It establishes itself in the opening measures of the violin's theme, where it is marked in Example 164, but it then gives way to more usual intervals. In the piano part it dominates the fabric throughout the section, mostly in the interior voices where it is, nevertheless, easily heard and recognized; it too is indicated in the example. The effect of the augmented second and its constant repetitions is rather hypnotic, and reminiscent of some non-European music.

There is a notable difference in accompanimental treatment between the second and third phrases of the soloist's thematic material (for reasons of convenience labelled *b* and *c*). Whereas *b* is accompanied by the same rhythms and chord structure that support *a*, *c* has virtually the same chords beneath it, but an eighth-note pattern accompanied by arpeggiated sixteenths provides a much more varied texture. This change lightens the atmosphere, and prepares the listener for the generally tranquil mood of the forthcoming *B* section.

It is not really possible to discover a particular theme in this middle section as opposed to the clearly defined one in the flanking *A*s. Yet it is no less an independent section, even though its material is readily perceived as having emanated from *A*. Its most memorable feature is the delicacy and rhythmic subtlety of the piano writing, where sixteenths in both hands as well as for one hand only, characterize the whole section. In the solo part wisps of melody in longer note values stand out in relief. Some of its fragments are adaptations of the material of the *A* sections, while others have been adapted from first-movement material.

Two instances of rhythmic subtleties in the accompaniment should be cited. In the first, the right hand's rising and falling pattern – E, F, G sharp-F, E, D sharp, C, B, an obvious statement of the augmented seconds of section *A* – is but a mere sixteenth ahead of the same notes in the left hand; there is, of course, an octave's difference between the two. This same rhythmic overlap is found in the two preceding measures which began the new section, for the E, F, F, E pattern is handled in the same way. Note also the melodic relationship of this pattern to Theme 2 in the first movement. The second instance of rhythmic subtlety is another early example of the cross-rhythms that pervade so much of Rubbra's music: the violin conforms to the usual 6/8 patterns (later, there are some patterns that stress the second and third, fifth and sixth beats), while the piano's patterns are essentially those that fit a compound quadruple metre; the three sixteenths and dotted eighth in each group can be considered either as triplets or as basic units in 12/16 time.

A soft and delicate *calmato* section with oscillating sixteenths in the piano, and supported by various intervals on the first and fourth beats, plus melodic fragments in the solo line, leads to the concluding *A*. This section, of course, repeats the principal elements of the first *A*, but the treatment of them is quite different: the *pianissimo* resignation at the start of the movement is replaced by a *forte* for both instruments, and an *appassionato* for the violin. The figure containing the augmented second is retained by the piano, but the violin's re-entry for two and a half measures constitutes a restatement of a figure it had played several measures previously. Thereafter, the soloist repeats his earlier *A* material exactly but one octave higher. When the second phrase of the principal theme is repeated, its first half is double-stopped in sixths, and its second half, which is made up of graceful arabesques, is given to the piano. While these are being played, the violin insistently repeats the augmented second figure: C, D sharp, C. All of these changes have been cited to show that, at this early stage, Rubbra has begun to introduce on a fairly large scale his practice of signifi-cantly altering previous materials in such a manner as to take the listener by surprise, particularly when the material steals in almost unnoticed. The coda makes use of material associated with both the *A* and *B* sections and the move-ment ends *pianissimo*.

The final movement, marked *Allegro vivo e feroce* ($\quad$ = 138) with the added instructions, 'Strident and very rhythmic', is a *tour de force* in the *perpetuum mobile* tradition. Structurally, it is an unconventional rondo that follows a design of *ABAB, A+C, AB, A+C, AB*/Coda. The material of the *A* section inevi-tably reminds one of Bartók in one of his wilder moods. It is strange that no review – at least none that I have read – has mentioned this point, for in the fourth measure of Example 165, a typical Bartókian figure appears: D, C sharp,

Ex. 165

B flat in triplets with the expected resolution to A coming at the start of measure 5. The wild rhythms in both instruments are also typical of the Hun-garian master. The mood grows ever more frenetic as the movement goes on and there are formidable passages for the violin, among which is the syncopated and *pizzicato*, quadruple stopping in the second of the *A + C* sections. That may have been one of the passages that caused one reviewer to single out the 'feroce' direction in the tempo for special comment.

The *B* sections, while allowing no slackening of the rhythm in the piano, do provide relief for the violinist and, it must be said, for the listener. The melody given to the violin in these sections is broad and singing and only in the *B* section just before the coda are there any note values smaller than a quarter. The second half of the melody is slightly different in each succeeding statement, but not enough to cause a recognition problem. The designation of *C* or *D* in the two compound sections is recognition of the fact that the material flowing from the *A* statements is, in each case, sufficiently different to warrant a separate identity.

Within the basic ground plan given above there are some variants in addition to the melodic ones just set forth. These include transpositions of entire sections to other keys and subtle rhythmic refinements that reveal themselves only when listening itself becomes refined enough to take in details that go beyond the hearing of obvious, pounding rhythms.

In addition to the favourable comments relating to the entire Sonata that were reproduced at the beginning of this discussion, there are others, including some by McNaught (mentioned earlier, p.298):

> The Sonata is a work of earnest and accomplished art with quite a big A, abounding in the right expressions and tactics.... The whole sonata is written in the very best vein, but a good deal of it seems to have little to do with Rubbra as we know him [the final sentence is probably accurate, considering that the review dates from 1947].[12]

The Sonata must also have been performed in mid- or late 1937, for the following three reviews appeared respectively in January, February and April of 1938:

> Violinists in search of an interesting sonata would find themselves repaid by turning their attention here, for the three movements... go from good to better. In especial the Lament and Finale are full of feeling and fire. Mr. Rubbra's imagination is strong on the wing: it carries him through the sonata without those forced descents which mar so much music.[13]

The next review addresses the ever present problem of balance, a problem that is of the greatest importance in every work that involves two dissimilar instruments:

> The Sonata for Piano and Violin (No. 2), which has now been published, has the characteristic I have always admired in his work – clear, logical thinking and a fine, forceful impulse. The medium chosen is, perhaps, the most difficult of all; the obstacles in the way of a satisfactory balance of power between piano and violin are many. Rubbra has overcome most of them – not all. In the first Allegretto 'liberamente e scorrevole' the equilibrium is impeccable; in the slow Lament which follows the problem is, mostly quiescent, as happens when a leisurely tempo gives each instrument time and opportunity to exhibit its special tone-effects. The problem becomes acute in the third movement, 'Allegro vivo e feroce', which is not a bit too 'feroce' for the piano but much too 'feroce' for the violinist.[14]

Finally, the Blom review, from which a remark was quoted earlier, continues:

> This Sonata is beautifully written for an always difficult instrumental combination; it has form without formality and style without constraint; and while it is far from easy to play, its effect is always greater than the players' effort, for it aims above all at being music.[15]

String Quartet No. 1

The composition of Rubbra's four string quartets was distributed over a period of forty-four years, Quartet No. 1 having been written in 1933 when the composer was thirty-two, and No. 4 in 1977 when he was seventy-six.

Quartet No. 1 in F minor, Op. 35, bears the inscription, 'To R.V.W. whose persistent interest in the original material of this work has led to the present revisions and additions'. It is obvious from this that, for one reason or another, the composer was dissatisfied with the original version. He did, in fact, withdraw it following its inaugural performances by the Stratton Quartet at the London Musical Club, 29 November 1934 and in a Liverpool reading on 31 January 1935 at Rushworth Hall. According to the review of this second performance, 'it is, perhaps a tribute to the composer that, at a first hearing [in Liverpool] it was clearly understandable, revealing some intelligent writing and not a small measure of culture.'[16] What this first version was like is not altogether known, for Rubbra destroyed the original finale. The new finale as well as the other revisions – the rescoring of much of the first movement, and changes at the end of the slow movement – were not undertaken until 1946, a delay brought about by the composer's war service.

The first movement of this three-movement work, marked *Allegretto moderato* ($\downarrow$ = 108 circa), is a fine example of a quite symmetrical sonata form in which the exposition and recapitulation are almost exactly equal in length – eighty-six and eighty measures respectively. There are the usual contrasted themes and a transition to a third, or closing, theme. All of the elements are repeated in the recapitulation. Theme 1 is exactly reproduced in all of the instrumental parts, as is Theme 2 where some very minor rescorings are found. The closing theme has some changes at the end, which are preparations for the end of the movement. The significant difference between the exposition and recapitulation is that all of the second theme's material is transposed a minor third higher.

The first theme begins in the cello and continues in the second violin, a fact made clear by the dotted line drawn between the two instruments. The theme is divided into two parts, which are complementary in the sense that the first is a question and the second an answer. It is the latter that receives the most attention, for it is passed from instrument to instrument in an imitative fabric that is closely woven. There is no transition to Theme 2 and there will doubtless be some who will argue against the very existence of a second theme. There is no question as to its origin; it is an outgrowth of the figure in measures 4–5 which itself is a derivative of the question-answer segments of Theme 1. Yet it is a completely independent entity – a statement capable of proof in several ways: first, the *ritardando* at the end of Theme 1, followed by a resumption of the original tempo, suggests that a new phase of the movement is about to be heard; second, three instances of the semitone D flat-C engage the listener's attention; third, although the figure that follows the final semitone is none other than the first violin figure in measures 4–5, the material leading away from it is different enough to persuade the listener that it is new; finally, the flowing triplet accompaniment in the middle instruments is an important new feature, that is even more persuasive than the melody. (At several points the mirror image of parts of the accompanimental figure appears simultaneously with original, an early example of the technique Rubbra associated with the 'topsy-turvy' experience of his childhood as told in Chapter 1.) To facilitate comparison, both themes appear in Example 166. The section enclosing the second

Ex. 166

theme and its attendant material is the same length as that which contains the first theme – fifteen measures. Yet, unlike the latter it is repeated, with the repetition also numbering fifteen measures. There are variants in the repetition both with respect to the theme itself and many of its details.

Harmonically, Theme 1 is unequivocally in F minor, but Theme 2 is indefinite tonally. Thus the fourteen/sixteen measure transition between Theme 2 and the closing theme – also tonally vague – is not a link in the usual sense of bridging the gap between two keys. It is difficult to define its exact function here, for its individuality gives it almost the status of a separate theme. Yet it would be incorrect to call it that, for the main idea of the whole transition is rhythmic, not melodic. This is apparent from the simultaneous sounding of two and three rhythmic patterns which, in turn, result from the interactions of 5/4, 6/4, and 3/4 metres with the basic 4/4. These metres appears in the score, as do the non-coinciding barlines. The transition's enigmatic fourteen/sixteen-measure length is thus explained: it depends upon which of the four lines is being counted. There are two fairly strong influences at work in this transition: the second movement – *Assez vif* – of Ravel's String Quartet, and Bartók. The first of these is evident in the *pizzicato* cello part and the accompanying syncopations and other irregularities. The grace and delicacy of Ravel are also present. The Bartók sound follows immediately when pounding, syncopated, *forte* rhythms succeed the Ravelian passage. Neither passage lasts long, and no specific Ravel or Bartók melody comes to mind, yet the stylistic auras are unmistakably present.

The return to metrical and overall rhythmic regularity in the closing theme is a nice touch, which effectively separates the rhythmic irregularities of the transition on one side, and those of the development on the other. The theme itself consists of two figures, the second of which is the cello figure that opened the movement, but minus its first and last notes. The first figure is by far the more important of the two; during the course of the twenty-five measures comprising the section it generates a substantial amount of imitation.

The development, which starts in measure 87, is made up of several distinctly different phases, each one a miniature and self-contained unit. It is an early demonstration of the economy that characterizes Rubbra's larger works, for right at the start of the section three prominent figures from previous sections are joined vertically. Reading down, the first violin has the second figure in the closing theme; the second violin has the rhythmic sixteenth/eighth/triplet figure in the transition but in double stops; an octave lower, the viola plays the first violin's figure, but extends its first note from one beat to four prior to maintaining the violin's rhythm. As the development moves on some of these elements change places for a brief period until, at measure 100, the second phase begins. This is dominated by highly rhythmic, imitative entries which at first suggest that a miniature fugue might be in progress, but this proves to be unfounded. Summarizing the entries: the sixteenths are a variant of the group of five at the end of the Bartókian passage; the sudden, isolated bursts of two sixteenths and an eighth in double stops are terse reminders of the accompanimental figure in the transition; and the ascending, chromatic eighths can be traced to measure 3. As this unit progresses, development of some of the elements in the unit itself occurs, making the ending of the unit quite different from the beginning. Two transitional measures lead into the next unit: a transposition a semitone higher of the complete Ravelian passage. The development concludes with a rapidly intensifying passage that is full of ascending and descending scale segments, plus the familiar double-stopped sixteenths/eighths/triplets on the viola. The recapitulation unfolds in the manner already described.

It is obvious from the systematic organization of this first movement that the composer has perhaps not yet come to terms with the adaptations of sonata form that will become such a distinctive feature of his symphonies and concertos. The proportions seem too regular, and the repetitions too literal, even allowing for the transpositions of materials. However, one of the prime requisites of sonata structure is missing: key relationships between themes, and these have, for the most part, been ignored throughout Rubbra's movements in sonata form.

Quite aside from its conventional structure and unassimilated influences, this movement has much to recommend it. Its thematic material, while not remarkable in itself, is well presented, and the contrast between themes is striking. There is a good balance between materials of a tranquil kind and those that are more active. Finally, the movement as sound is both interesting and exciting.

The middle movement, marked *Lento*, ♪= 84, is a ternary structure whose third section is shortened and much altered. There are two distinct parts to the *A* section, yet a common factor unites them: the singular texture that is a result of the combination of from two to three elements. Most of the section's first part is relatively simple, consisting of a viola melody which is surrounded by three-note *pizzicato* chords in all of the other parts. The effect of these nine-note chords and their changing harmonies is extraordinarily rich. The viola solo moves in a languid fashion, and its tone is rather elegiac. However, there are *staccato* thirty-seconds in the solo passage that take on an increasing urgency when, accompanied by a slight tempo increase they are allotted to the other three instruments. But for this gathering sense of tension to be fully effective, the *staccato* notes must be carefully separated.

Nothing thus far has been said about the viola solo *per se*, and this is not an oversight. The melody seems vague – almost as though it were groping toward something more definite. Its search (if that is the right word) is concluded at the beginning of the second part of the section, when the first violin assumes command and shapes the melody that the viola then amplifies from measure 16

Ex. 167

on; and it is this version that appears in Example 167. Also shown are the *staccato* thirty-seconds that unite the two parts of the *A* section, and a very disjunct figure that is nothing more than the logical expansion of the semitones that are basic to the entire quartet. Again, poor articulation of the *staccato* notes and an imprecise rendering of the wide leaps could mar Rubbra's conception of the music.

Section *B* contains the initial statement of a theme followed by six tiny variations on it. Its second appears to be an unconscious reference to the four-note figure in the second theme of the first movement. Connecting the theme with the first variation, and between some of the succeeding variations, there is a measure of free material. The shape of the theme in the variations is never altered, but harmonic changes are introduced. A gradual *crescendo* from variation 4 reaches its peak just before variation 6 (dynamically and otherwise it is the climax of the movement), and the music melts into the movement's final section.

The third part of this ternary form consists of seventeen measures as opposed to the first *A*'s twenty-six. In them, free versions of the material are heard, surrounded by the same rhythmic and much of the same harmonic textures that were so important in the first section. It opens with a set of four overlapping and accompanied entries, whose I-V relationships suggest a fugue. The material comes from the viola's 'unorganized' melody at the beginning of the movement. The cello never participates, being occupied with an oscillating figure at the bottom of the ensemble. This figure also appears as an accompaniment beneath the restatement of the *pizzicato* chords and a slightly different version of the viola's melody. The movement concludes with a final statement of the complete theme, shared in succession by the second violin, first violin and cello.

The last movement, Vivace ($\downarrow$. = 69), grows out of the last cello phrase of the slow movement, and its single theme is introduced by the viola. It is a hard-driving movement with simultaneous metre signatures of 6/8 and 3/4, affording opportunities for an abundance of cross-rhythms. The complete theme, the first phrase of which is derived from the second-movement theme as shown in the preceding example, appears only three times: at the start of the movement (Example 168); four measures after its completion (second violin and viola);

Ex. 168

and in the first violin shortly before the end of the movement. There are also two partially complete statements, but these are widely separated, the first coming about a quarter of the way through, and the second just prior to the final complete statement. Between these statements, complete or incomplete, there is much treatment of material stemming from the theme's various segments. A cursory glance at the bracketed portions will reveal the possibilities. First and most apparent are the quarter-note segments, for their metrical status enables them to cut across the prevailing 6/8, and in this capacity they are very prominent. Their melodic characteristics are preserved throughout the movement, providing easy identification as they unite to produce new melodic lines. There are three inversions of the whole of segment *a*, the second and third of which come just before an incomplete thematic statement (measures 48–9; and 180–81). As for the uses to which the remaining segments are put, space limitations preclude mention, for they are far too numerous. The music constantly changes directions, generating melodic renewal and imitations. One of these imitative passages is quite extensive (measures 125–54) and it is also one of the finest examples in Rubbra's music of the strict type. It is divided exactly in half with the same material common to both halves. The time and pitch intervals are the same throughout the passage: one measure and a lower fourth. In the first half the first violin initiates the imitation, and the opening note for each part moves straight down to the cello – F, C, G, D. In the second half the violins are reversed as to the order of entries, but the downward movement is the same: F sharp, C sharp, G sharp, D sharp. The entire passage is notable not only for the strictness of the imitations, but also for the total lack of running eighths in the 6/8 metre – in evidence almost everywhere else in the movement. Rhythmic variety is achieved by means of the groups of two eighths – duplets – which are a standard feature of the material throughout the passage. At the conclusion of the imitations the eighths reappear, their usual *staccato* markings often reinforced by accents, and it is thus that, together with the reintroduction of the opposing quarters, the movement is brought to a rousing finish.

This final movement is important in the totality of Rubbra's larger works because it is the first manifestation in the chamber music of a type of movement we have already met in the symphonies. Truscott's remarks in the following passage summarize not just the technicalities of this particular movement, but also those of the type as a whole:

> Here we have all the elements that mark many of Rubbra's finales: the rapid movement, the marching bass, at half-bars, up and down the scale and oscillating, the eventual cross-rhythm... which grows mightily as the movement progresses, applying a brake to the rapidity which in this case, for once, seems to make the speed more rapid still. The wonder is that, his mind thinking as naturally as it does in these terms, he has managed to produce so many finale movements which, although having shared family features, are individuals and vastly different from each other. In spite of these resemblances no one could foresee the course of one of them from a knowledge of the others. The thought behind the music is what counts most, and the technique will adapt itself to that. I will not say that, for me, this is his finest finale; I could not choose from such a body of work. But I will say that I do not think he has surpassed it.[17]

As usual, critical comments on the Quartet were mixed:

The first movement, in sonata form, moves with assurance in a slightly pastoral atmosphere, but the writing occasionally suggests that the composer has not fully succeeded in containing his ideas within the medium employed, and that they might have been more completely realized by a larger string body. In the two remaining movements, thought and medium go hand in hand, and the final rondo [*sic*] is notable for its ingenious interplay of rhythms and its sustained vitality.[18]

The specific passages in the first movement where Chapman felt the ideas to be too large for the medium are not indicated. Anyway, surely this is a subjective question to which there is no definitive answer. There are movements in Bartók's and Shostakovich's quartets when the material seems hardly able to remain within the bounds of the medium, yet somehow it does, and in a convincing fashion. Naturally, some material seems intrinsically more suitable for a larger ensemble, but even here this appears to be a matter of personal taste. Who is to say whether Schoenberg's *Verklärte Nacht* is more effective as a string sextet or in its full string orchestra version?

Another review, singularly unenthusiastic, tells us that

the thematic matter is dull, as it is in nearly all British music today. The slow movement has the expected modal music, which he performs well. There seems a slight French tinge in the composer; that should be good for any Briton.[19]

The word 'expected' is, of course, a sarcasm, but the 'French tinge' is most probably a reference to the first movement's Ravelian passages.

The most complete and carefully considered review brings our discussion of the Quartet to a close:

This Quartet is dedicated to Vaughan Williams, and sharing with his Fourth Symphony the key of F minor it partakes also of its power and severity. Indeed the Quartet is couched in terms almost morose, from which there is little relief. A carefully designed first movement contains within its symmetry a very wide harmonic range; for all the enharmonic freedom of the harmony there appear to be no loose threads nor indeed any superfluous notes. The principal subjects are both *cantabile*, the first in 4/4 and the second in 3/4; by way of contrast there are ostinato accompanying rhythms which have an exciting cumulative effect. Rubbra's polyphonic skill enables him to write with remarkable economy of material. It might be felt that this economy is carried too far in the slow movement, which is long in spite of the fact that it leads into the last movement instead of recapitulation. It is a threnody largely coloured by the viola, which has an important solo part. The last movement is a highly polyphonic *Vivace* in mingled measures of 6/8 and 3/4. It is an athletic piece, skilful as ever in canonic device and inversion. The themes are bleak rather than striking, but it is obvious that their importance is susidiary to the overall impression of events crowding in upon each other with ever-increasing speed.[20]

The Cello Sonata

One of Rubbra's most expressive chamber works dates from 1946, the same year as the revised First Quartet: the Sonata in G minor for Cello and Piano, Op. 60. It bears a dedication to William Pleeth and his wife, the pianist Margaret

Good, and it was an outgrowth of the composer's close association with Pleeth during the war years when both were members of the Army Classical Music Group. The Sonata was written immediately after Rubbra's demobilization, and was first performed by the dedicatees in a 1946 BBC broadcast. The cellist, Jacqueline du Pré, also performed the work, and went several times to 'Lindens', the Rubbras' comfortable home in Gerrards Cross, for interpretative sessions with the composer. There are three movements: *Andante moderato* ($\flat$= 72 circa); *Vivace flessibile* ($\downarrow$. = 184 circa), and seven variations on an original theme, rounded off by a fugue.

The first movement is a very free rondo structure – $ABA^{1}B^{1}A^{11}$ – in which the A sections are rather intense *Andantes* in 4/4 metre, while the two intervening episodes are in a faster and less weighty 3/8. True to many of Rubbra's formal structures, none of the repeated sections is exactly like that section's first statement. Sometimes the differences involve key changes and the presence or absence of the cello; at other times the differences in details are considerable. Yet taken as a whole, the dissimilarities are never great enough to prevent recognition of the returning material. For example, in the A sections, measures 62–6 are equivalent to measures 6–10, while in the B sections, measures 106–21 are like measures 33–48. In each case the piano part is preserved, although with differences in key: measures 62–6 are a whole step higher than the original, and measures 106–21 are a whole tone lower than their equivalents. The cello's participation is also very different in each instance. With regard to the B sections, and again using measures 33–48 and 106–21 as areas of general correspondence, there are twelve measures in B before the start of the cello trills in 33, and twenty-seven in B^{1} before the trills in 106. Yet the two sections are almost equal in length: forty-two measures for B, forty-five for B^{1}. Following the conclusion of the trills in each section there is a further discrepancy in length: twenty-seven measures in B, fifteen for B^{1}. However, in listening to this movement, the structure is clear and the sections, despite the considerable differences, are nicely balanced.

An interesting point worthy of mention concerns the cello's nobly expressive opening theme (Example 169): it is never given to the piano, and it is not heard again in its entirety. At the start of the transition from B to A^{1}, signified by a gradual decrease in tempo, its first phrase is in C sharp minor at the very bottom of the cello's register, and slightly more than the first phrase appears

Ex. 169

fortissimo in the home key of G minor just prior to the five-measure *Adagio* that closes the movement. Other notable features of this striking movement are the rich and beautiful piano sonorities in the two *Andante* sections, and the cello's exploration of the extremes of its high and low registers. Another of Rubbra's favourite practices is introduced: the gradual increases in tempo that connect the slow and fast sections. Such *stringendo* passages are heard to best advantage in the Second Symphony. (By this time, the first four symphonies had been composed and the experience thus gained was an important factor in the Cello Sonata.)

The second movement is a vigorous *scherzo* in 9/8 metre, which demands technical facility from both players. Except for two places where short-lived *rallentandos* slow the pace, the rhythm is unflagging, and with the exception of the opening measure and four connected later ones – all for cello – there are no measures of rest for either instrument.

Structurally, the movement does not conform at all to the usual scherzo-trio-scherzo ground plan, which, of course, is not intended to imply that the movement is aimless or wandering. Quite the contrary for, as in many of Rubbra's larger works, the basic material creates the structure as it proceeds. Here, there are two ideas: one, an energetic and leaping piano figure, the second, a generally conjunct cello figure in longer note values. We have met this contrast before in other works, where the smoother, more spacious material has appeared to control its more fiery opposite, constituting a braking action. One of the clearest examples of this concept is to be found in the Improvisation for Violin and Orchestra, Op. 89. It does not apply here in the Sonata, where the cello is just as enthusiastic as the piano, often adopting the latter's characteristic rhythm: ♩♪♩ ♪♩ ♪ Conversely, the piano borrows the cello's longer note values and this interchange of materials between the instruments provides unity as well as variety. The fairly frequent cross-rhythms, expressed in three groups of two eighths each per measure, are shared by the players, although but once simultaneously, and then for an extremely short period. Nowhere do these groups have any effect on the headlong pace of the movement.

The texture of the movement ranges from as little as three lines – two in the piano, one in the cello – to large supporting chords whose content is often an accumulation of held-over notes, but none of these larger chordal textures seems at all heavy. The tempo is too fast for the listener to distinguish anything but the individual lines, which are either one octave apart or divergent, and the more moderately sized chords.

The *Adagio* theme which introduces the third-movement variations is both broad and serene (Example 170) and the piano accompaniment is an important and integral part of it, setting it off to advantage. It is interesting to note that the piano's descending eighths in both hands – G, F sharp, F sharp, E, E, D, D, and so on – are the transpositions of those which Brahms used in the first setting of *O Welt, ich muss dich lassen*, No. 3 in his eleven chorale-preludes for organ: F, F, E, E, D, D, C, C, and so on. In the seven continuous variations that follow,

Ex. 170

only particular segments of the theme have been selected for treatment. Variation I, also marked *Adagio*, throws into relief in the piano the ascending, melodic fifth at the start of the theme. The upward movement in quarters is continuous, so that as each fifth is reached on the first beat of each measure, there is an overlap as the fifth becomes the starting note of a new series. This process occupies six measures (there are only seven measures in the variation), but at the bottom of the piano only three and a half measures are involved in the same manner because of half- instead of quarter-notes. The cello line, decorative and rhythmic, can be traced to the rising and falling fifths of measures 1 and 10 respectively, as well as to the rising fourth in measure 9. The second variation is linked to the first in three ways: first, by the continuing *Adagio*; second, by the rising fourths in the cello which, in the piano, have become falling fourths. This phase of the variation is a strict canonic inversion, and is both mentioned and illustrated by the composer in the chapter on canon in his book, *Counterpoint: A Survey*.[21] Third, the descending octaves and single notes in the piano at the end of the variation are simply the reverse of the rising pattern in Variation I and, before that, the theme. The repeated notes in both parts stem from those of the piano accompaniment to the theme, and the cello sequences of measures 29–31 are, with the exception of two falling sixths, transpositions of the figure in measures 9–10 of the theme.

While Variations III and IV are not linked in terms of tempo – *Con moto* and *Allegro* – they are more closely coupled with respect to material than are their predecessors. Movement in the piano is by sixteenths and the patterns chosen for each variation consist of four notes in a continuous chain. The pattern in the third variation derives from a cello figure in measure 6 of Variation II, and its inversion is inevitable as are the resolutions to a fourth above and a fifth below. The first pattern in Variation IV comes from the fifth measure of the theme. The cello's material through the third and the first half of the fourth variations is composed of freely adapted thematic segments.

At just under the halfway point in the variations the theme, minus measures 11–13, is heard in its original key and note values. Beginning just before the middle of Variation IV, its first four measures are stated in heavily stressed octaves by the piano, and the groups of sixteenths surrounding the octaves are filled with derivatives of the figures that have been heard in the variation up to this point. Interest shifts to the cello when the theme's next six measures are given to it. However, the last two of these (measures 9–10) have been extended to four, and placed in Variation V where, in both instruments, they form the core of the material. Marked *con moto* and with no note values smaller than an eighth, Variation V maintains the brisk tempo of its immediate predecessors, but it is quieter. The thematic material of measure 9 dominates, and is shared in alternate fashion by the players. Except for the piano's octaves at the end of the variation, the texture has been reduced to three strands of melody. The marching quarters at the bottom of the piano come from the ascending and descending fifths of the first measure.

Variations VI and VII continue the trend established in V toward a relaxation in the areas of texture and tempo. Following the conspicuous statement of the theme in Variation IV and the isolation of its final segment in V, it seems reasonable to suppose that in terms of the theme or any portions thereof Variation VI should be the most obscure of the set. The reason for this is that in the final variation (of this or any set) the listener expects some sort of reminder of the theme, and to include too much (or even any) summarizing in the penultimate variation would spoil the climax. The composer has observed this psychological truth by omitting any reference to the theme in VI, but at the end a two-measure F sharp trill engages our attention and leads directly into an augmentation of the theme's first eight measures. This is accompanied by a continuation of the piano's theme-derived figures which supported the cello throughout Variation VI. After a *forte* and *appassionato* climax, the music winds down to a *pianissimo* ending in which a key transition leads to a C minor tonic in preparation for the concluding fugue.

The dignified, four-voiced fugue is real (in the sense of 'real' and 'tonal' answers), and the first statement of the subject is given to the cello (Example 171). Thereafter, the three remaining voices in the exposition appear in the

Ex. 171

piano. Immediately preceding the fourth entry there are two false statements of the subject, one in the cello, the other in the piano. Each intones just the first four notes of the subject. Three further complete statements of the subject – piano, cello and an inverted entry for piano – bring the fugue to a close. One more false entry consisting of an inversion of the first four notes is heard just before the final, inverted statement. There is no consistent countersubject although one is led to believe there will be one because of the consistency of the passages following the completion of the first two entries. There is, however, no continuation of these in later statements. Because of the brevity of the fugue and the length of the subject, there are no episodes.

There is, however, one item of greater interest in the fugue: the displaced rhythm. This can be seen in Example 171, but the ear does not pick it up until the entry of the answer. From that point until the end of the fugue the rhythm is perceived as having been displaced by the value of one eighth note. This creates many syncopated passages which continually surprise, and hold the listener's attention.

Two reviews of the Cello Sonata are reproduced below. The first contains serious misapprehensions that cannot be overlooked – at least not at this stage of our study of Rubbra's music:

> One has the greatest admiration for Mr. Rubbra's fluent technique. He is a builder, and what he builds is solid and well founded.... In form, in the logical sequence of ideas, the work is faultless. But it is a work that has the defects of its qualities: this very pre-occupation with formal perfection for its own sake can easily lead to an indifference to the beauty of detail. The themes are somewhat hard-driven and so, too, are the instrumentalists, at any rate the cellist who, throughout the three movements, can count on no more than nine silent bars.[22]

The 'misapprehensions' concern the phrase, 'this very pre-occupation with formal perfection for its own sake'. I see two false assumptions here. The first and more immediate is the notion that this particular work is formally perfect. In rebuttal, I offer the opening *Andante* and the second-movement scherzo as evidence: the former has an asymmetrical rondo structure that is by no means easily grasped; in fact, like many Rubbra movements, the structure has yielded its secrets only after patient study. With regard to the scherzo, it is so entirely moulded by its material as to suggest that it is formless. Thus, except for the variations and fugue of the third movement, the Sonata exhibits the indifference to formal perfection that is a dominant trait in many works by this composer. This unconventional approach to structure *per se* has been an important theme throughout this book and it stems, of course, from Rubbra's unconventional approach to composition itself. If we accept his oft-repeated statement that he had no idea where a piece was going next, formal perfection was irrelevant because the structure was being decided as the music unfolded. The second false assumption involves the reviewer's use of the word 'preoccupation', and the phrase, 'for its own sake'. Both reveal not only his misunderstanding of the Sonata's formal aspects, but also his misconception concerning the status of form in Rubbra's works as a whole.

The second review tells us that the Sonata

> is an addition of the first importance to the 'cello repertory, in which the difficult combination is superbly handled, and the texture... is refreshingly clear. Its mood (but not its idiom) recalls the last works of Brahms, particularly in the gently wayward first movement.[23]

Suite: The Buddha

It would appear that Rubbra's incidental music for *The Buddha* – a play by Clifford Bax, the brother of the composer Arnold Bax – should be saved for Chapter 11, 'Miscellaneous works', alongside the incidental music for *Macbeth*. However, its scoring for flute, oboe, violin, viola and cello assures its place in the chamber music category. Actually, what we see and hear is not Rubbra's original scoring nor even the complete music, but a suite drawn from the latter – the work of a friend and colleague as the composer explains on the title page:

> I wish to acknowledge my indebtedness to Mr. Adrian Cruft, who, at a time when I was too busy to do so myself, admirably fulfilled my intentions in this arrangement of music written for Clifford Bax's play "The Buddha".

The Suite, Op. 64 and dedicated to the play's author, dates from 1947 and consists of five pieces, whose titles suggest that the play is based on stages in the life of Buddha: 1) 'Prince Gautama', the latter being the name of the wealthy and royal family into which he was born; 2) 'The Peasant Girl', for flute alone (words are appended which, according to a note at the bottom of the page, 'in the original were sung, [and] are printed here merely to indicate the mood of the movement'. The poem speaks in a simple and unaffected way about the close relationship between the peasant girl and Brahm Creator of all things; and is probably intended to symbolize Prince Gautama's dissatisfaction with the sheltered life his father provided for him); 3) 'The Ascetics' represents the midpoint in the young prince's journey towards enlightenment, a stage he soon abandoned in favour of more constructive approaches to life; 4) 'The Chariot Ride', may refer to a vision or something symbolic in Prince Gautama's quest; and 5) 'The Buddha', represents the end of that quest when, sitting and meditating under the Bo tree, Gautama achieved his goal and became The Buddha, or The Enlightened One.

The music in these sections seems appropriate and a common theme unites the first and fifth pieces. However, the extreme brevity of the Suite makes it highly unlikely that it will ever appear on any programme of chamber music, and, of course, without the play for which the music was written there seems little point in a performance.

Meditazioni sopra 'Coeurs Désolés'

This first piece in Rubbra's impressive list of works for the recorder was completed on Easter Monday, 1949. It is based on a theme from Josquin des Prez's four-part chanson of the same name, and scored for tenor recorder and harpsichord. Alternatively, it can be performed by flute or oboe, and piano. It bears a dedication to Carl Dolmetsch and Joseph Saxby, whose research and performances have done so much to restore the recorder family and the harpsichord to the respectability they once enjoyed. As a measure of the excitement that was generated by Rubbra's piece (Op. 67 in his *oeuvre*), I cite Arthur Hutchings's account:

> As soon as 'Coeurs Désolés' arrived, I played it to two of my colleagues here, singing the recorder part to 'ah'. My singing, like my piano-playing is bad. One of the listeners said: 'How extraordinary that something using only triads can be so charged with emotion.' The other said: 'My God! It's no miniature. It's Rubbra himself in the best grand manner. Once he begins "in form" he screws me up and I can't relax tension until the last note has stopped sounding.' Later on I found an undergraduate who plays the recorder well, and we played to a circle of young men, one of whom – a person who never shows off – said that he found himself 'pent up' when Rubbra persisted in moving slowly to climax in one tonality; 'an enharmonic swerve' came just when he felt 'fit to burst'. I have mentioned these remarks instead of defending the piece on technical grounds, because the first two speakers were technicians and analysts of music by profession, and the third a young man at that stage when young musicians are greedy for new music and new techniques, faced with the work of a dogged conservative. Yet each 'first reaction' expressed the *emotional* effect of the new work.[24]

This piece marks the first use in Rubbra's music of the term *meditazioni*. Its English equivalent we have already met in the much later Meditations On A Byzantine Hymn, Op. 117. However, in whichever language the word appears the intent is the same: to place before the listener a number of sections, some but not all of which are reflective and musing in character. In the present work there are *meditazioni* marked *Con moto*, *grazioso*, and *Allegretto*. Thus the word should not always be interpreted as indicating sections that are slow, soft or pensive – certainly the popular understanding of its meaning. Rubbra's concept centres on a stated theme which, in this case at least *is* pensive in consonance with the text of Josquin's chanson. The theme's cadential form, shown here in Example 172, was chosen for practical reasons, although it does not occur in

Ex. 172

the chanson until the start of the third system in a modern edition. Instead of selecting large and easily recognizable segments of the theme for treatment, the composer has limited himself to small, even readily forgotten segments of it, plus – and this is important – fragments from later portions of the chanson, none of which is a part of the theme. All of these fragments, from whatever source, give rise to imitations, and these are presented in a very concentrated manner. Each meditation is numbered, and separated from its successor by double bars, although the music in all cases is continuous.

Hutchings called this piece 'an epitome of his art'.[25] It seems appropriate here to mention some of the ways in which this statement is true. First and most obvious are the ostinatos in the harpsichord parts of Meditations 1, 2, 3 and 6. These differ widely in terms of the lengths of the patterns and the treatment of the repetitions. For example, the ostinato in No. 1 has a pattern of four measures, stated three times note for note (plus the first measure of a fourth statement that gives way to the second meditation). On the other hand, the ostinato in No. 2 has a one-measure pattern whose seven melodic repetitions have received different figurations in the two accompanying lines. The ostinato in No. 3 is interesting because the first four notes in the one-measure pattern are inverted in the fourth, fifth and sixth statements; the two rolled chords per measure in the bass remain the same throughout the meditation. But the greatest variety is found in the ostinato of No. 6, the *grazioso* section alluded to above. The four-measure pattern consists of three measures of 3/2 and a concluding measure of 2/2, and it is stated four times, but between the second and third statements two measures are inserted, only the first of which has a direct relationship to the ostinato pattern. The pattern itself is asymmetrical both rhythmically and melodically, and there is an exact sequential reproduction a fourth higher of each first measure. But this is not all, for each repeated *total* four-measure pattern is a sequence of the preceding total pattern. The distance is a major third higher. Thus four statements of the pattern bring us back to the original tonality: A minor; C sharp minor; F minor; A minor.

A second frequently encountered Rubbran practice can be found in the almost continuous canons of the eighth meditation. A third trait, heard in the same section, is the simultaneous mirror image of figures. It must be said, however, that these passages as well as the ostinatos, while not losing their identity when the recorder line is heard, are far less noticeable than when they are isolated for examination or played alone. Their purpose, however, seems clear: they balance the often rhapsodic freedom of the recorder's music and this contrast between freedom and restraint is yet another Rubbra characteristic.

Harmonically, the meditations tend to remain within the limits of the particular tonality assigned to them. Thus much of the harmony is static and it is this that helps to build the tension described by Hutchings in his account. I am inclined to think that the passage that caused the young man to feel 'pent up' was the persistent D major tonic of Meditation 8, which is defined and strengthened by the fleeting presence of the dominant and other harmonies associated with the tonality. When the change is made to the *fortissimo* restatement of the Josquin theme, the first note of which is harmonized by the first inversion of a B flat major chord, the effect is electrifying, and the sense of release is almost physical. Yet the simple harmonies of the rolled chords and the theme which they define permit no real emotional release until the last of the three A major chords dies away.

The more one studies and hears this work the more remarkable it seems. The various technical devices recorded above never get in the way of the expressiveness of the music; they only add to it. The piece certainly impressed Edgar

Hunt, who said, 'in my opinion [it is] the finest recorder piece of the present century.'[26] But no tribute could have pleased the composer more than this one:

> Edmund Rubbra understands not only the poetry of harmony but also – which is much rarer – the poetry of sound. It is his use of pure sound... that gives his 'Meditazioni sopra Coeurs Désolés' a very special charm. This does not mean that other elements are neglected: it means that the Meditations give the impression, not of a more or less able adaptation... but of a work conceived for the instruments for which it is written – recorder and harpsichord. Of course the music can also be played on the flute (or oboe) and piano. But I do hope the first performance will be given not by substitutes, but by artists skilled in harpsichord and recorder, like Carl Dolmetsch and Joseph Saxby to whom the work is dedicated.[27]

Piano Trio in One Movement

1950 saw the composition and first performance of the Piano Trio in One Movement, Op. 68, the first of two works in this genre. It has three uninterrupted sections, clearly indicated by tempo markings with respect to the first and second, and *Tema* at the start of the third. These divisions correspond in mood and tempo to the three movements of the Cello Sonata; an opening *Andante moderato*, a middle *scherzando*, and a concluding theme with three *meditazioni* instead of the six variations in the earlier work. A short coda rather than a fugue brings the work to a triumphant close.

The theme of the *Andante*, stated in octaves by the two strings, is decidedly autumnal and elegiac in character (Example 173). As it has no theme of its own

Ex. 173

in this opening section, the piano is almost exclusively an accompanimental instrument, providing in its mid- and low ranges a rich, dark timbre that matches the elegiac tone of the strings. Most of its figures are those conventionally associated with long stretches of triplet movement, and the frequent 6/8 patterns that grow out of that movement. In this instance other figures interpose themselves between those just mentioned, but the longest lasting is equally conventional in its way: four groups of four moderately slow sixteenths per measure in each hand.

The extent of the octave and two-octave doublings between the violin and cello is yet another surprising feature of this section: approximately 38 measures, slightly over one-third of the section's 108 measures. Of course, these are not consecutive. While doublings are an effective means for directing the listener's attention to particular themes and passages the composer wishes to emphasize (the opening of Beethoven's Quartet, Op. 95, is just one of many examples that could be cited), their over-use can defeat that purpose by dulling the listener's perception. Second, doubled passages in any chamber music combination temporarily reduce the number of real parts, but in a trio the reduction by one part is more noticeable than in a larger ensemble. Hence, the criticism and concluding suggestion in Colin Mason's review are to my mind constructive and justifiable:

> the 'scoring'... exploits none of the effects of colour that can be achieved with these three instruments. Rubbra may not want to write colourful music, but a few hours with, say, Dvorak's 'Dumky' Trio would perhaps have led him to a more effective use of the medium. As it is, there is much uneconomical doubling, and one has the impression that the work would benefit by transformation into a sonata for violin or cello.[28]

More about this review and Rubbra's reaction to it at the end of our discussion.

The *Episodio Scherzando*, marked *Allegro vivo e leggiero* ($\downarrow$. = 88), grows directly from the concluding *fortissimo* measures of the *Andante moderato*. It has its own theme – light and delicately playful, as seen in Example 174. While not

Ex. 174

a member of the theme, the four-note figure in measures 7–10 of the example has a more important claim on our attention than the theme itself. We have heard these four notes before: they were seen in Example 173 at the very start of the *Andante*'s theme. Yet the rest of that theme has never reappeared, although in contrast there have been numerous restatements of the four notes. Thus this motive appears to have other purposes and functions, one of which is easily determined: it is a unifying agent. But when it appears in all three sections of the Trio in the midst of passages with which it has no demonstrable relationship, it is more than that: it is a motto in the cyclical sense.

The *Scherzando* is very different from the preceding section in that the piano is an active participant in the thematic materials. In fact, in this regard the contrast between the two sections is so great as to suggest that it was the result of a deliberate choice. If this is so, why would the composer have virtually encouraged the kind of criticism embodied in Mason's review, for although no mention is made of the piano *per se*, 'scoring' and 'colour' certainly apply to what the piano is or is not doing? Before an attempt is made to answer that question, I quote a significant sentence that concludes another critical – but softer – review which appeared the month after Mason's. Here, the writing for the piano is being called into question. This 'tends to be thick, and the upper registers are almost completely neglected. *But the composer is a fine enough pianist to know his intentions* [my italics].'[29] Assuming the correctness of this, it stands to reason that Rubbra also knew his intentions regarding the sectional differences in the matter of the piano's participation. However, the Trio's third and concluding section may well be a factor in providing the solution to the whole problem. Remarks in two further reviews supply helpful hints, but before these can be explored the concluding section must be examined.

As the *Scherzando* nears its end following a boisterous climax, the tempo becomes slower in metronomically indicated stages, and the music grows gradually tranquil until a small *accelerando* and a *crescendo* lead directly into the concluding theme and three meditations. The theme is one of the composer's longest and most traditional from every standpoint – melodic, harmonic, rhythmic and in terms of phrase length (Example 175). Yet for all its anachro-

Ex. 175

nisms it seems right here, for it achieves the expressive goal set by the composer – a blend of great dignity coupled with an increasingly joyous exultation as the dynamic level gradually increases.

It remains for only two of the meditations quietly to reflect on particular aspects of this material, for the third, which is also the shortest, reverts entirely to the motto announced at the beginning of the Trio. There is a very conventional but none the less effective enharmonic modulation from the A flat theme to the E major in which the solo piano begins the First Meditation. The most obvious fragment selected for its musings comes at the very end of the theme, and it is nothing more than the upward leap of a fourth followed by a conjunct descent within the key (see measures 11–12 in Example 175). In the piano it becomes B, E, D sharp, C sharp, G sharp. This is immediately inverted, and statements of both versions are then heard. A secondary fragment from the theme's midpoint (measures 6–7) becomes G sharp, A sharp, B, E, and is woven into the fabric of the piano's presentation. These six measures for piano alone mark only the second (and final) place in the Trio where the strings are silent together. When the latter resume it is to mull over very quietly the fragments first proposed by the piano, which then turns to a background of soft, repeating chords. These change at the beginning of each measure and occasionally some of them are mildly dissonant against the dotted half-notes in the bass. The entire meditation is highly expressive.

The Second Meditation is, as expected, more distantly removed both from the source of its material and from the transformations of that material in the First Meditation. Although it is still recognizable, the material has been fragmented, and it is confined to the piano where its *pianissimo* and *molto legato* thirty-seconds outline the falling and rising thirds established in the First Meditation. Set against the serenely chromatic, mostly quarter-note movement in the violin's high register, the thirty-seconds are basically ornamental. The contrast between them and the strings (the cello eventually doubles the violin's line three octaves lower) is one of the high points in Rubbra's chamber music.

The Third Meditation leads into a coda whose triumphant character becomes increasingly evident. Besides the steady *crescendo* for all three instruments, the descending scale – common property of all English bellringers – is prominent in both string parts, and it is strengthened by the syncopated D, tolling at the bottom of the piano. Above this pedal D major is exultantly asserted and amid a combination of octaves, chords and variants on the bell scale – all in the piano – several statements of the motto in the violin, both right-side up and inverted, bring the Trio to an *allargando* and *fortissimo* close.

The passages in the two reviews mentioned above may now be cited. Each of the writers speaks of the Trio's third section in much the same way:

> But there is no trace of everyday 'domestic' emotion; indeed, the remarkable visionary power of the *Tema con tre meditazioni*, culminating in an exultant Coda breve… suggests some kind of rare spiritual adventure far removed from the province of the ordinary man.[30]

The comparisons between the Trio and the Cello Sonata in the next review stem from the latter's performance on the same programme as the premiere of the Trio: 13 July 1950 at the Cheltenham Festival. The Rubbra-Gruenberg-Pleeth Trio were the executants in the new work as they were to be at its first London performance on 5 November of the same year.

> The, to my mind, genuine mysticism of this music makes me overlook many of its stylistic anachronisms (which in a mystical composer we should always forgive), its austere string writing, its ascetic invention, and the formal defects of its first section where a slow theme is treated rather aimlessly in the manner of a chorale prelude [I see no resemblance whatever to a chorale prelude, because the melodic sources of such pieces are far from aimless]. The Cello Sonata (1946) which was also performed at this concert – 'mystical' music too, but more inventive than the trio – succeeds in its very similar first movement through having a theme that is capable of acceleration and retardation, thus producing two climaxes within the movement. The *scherzi* of both works… are remarkably telling. But it is not until the last section that the Trio reaches the spiritual heights of the Cello Sonata. In the 'Tema' and the two [*sic*] 'Meditazioni' a deeply serious and God-fearing musicianship is revealed.[31]

It is now my firm conviction that Rubbra intended his Trio – the entire work, not just the Third section – to represent a spiritual quest, and that each of the three sections is meant to portray a stage along that route. This is not to say that I am prepared to proclaim the work an unqualified success. The first section is, in my opinion, unfocused or 'treated rather aimlessly'. But having said that, is it not true that all inquiries of whatever nature tend to begin in an aimless, unstructured fashion? It does not seem amiss to suggest that Rubbra *wished* to convey that impression in the *Andante moderato* section.

Any serious attempt to solve this and other problems relevant to the Trio must take into account two opposing viewpoints, which can be held simultaneously. The first considers purely musical matters such as structure, distribution of materials, instrumental colour, the appropriateness of the materials themselves, balance and equality of parts, and so on. Mason's review judges the work from these standards. The second viewpoint considers the Trio as a piece of programme music in the most non-specific sense: the musical representation of a search for things spiritual, with that goal either achieved or very nearly met at the end of the work. The concluding remarks in the two reviews support this stance without, however, employing or even suggesting the word 'programmatic'. There is a conflict between the two viewpoints, the gist of which is that regardless of the extramusical connotations of a work, that work ultimately stands or falls on its merits as a piece of music *per se*. If the *Andante moderato* section of the Trio is judged from the first viewpoint alone, it is not a success, but if it is considered from the programmatic perspective, allowances can be made for its deficiencies. This does not alter my expressed agreement with Mason's comments, but it does provide me with a plausible reason for the movement's shortcomings. Assuming that the programmatic thesis is correct, at least some misunderstandings could have been avoided if the composer had indicated his overall meaning in an article or programme note. However, there is a very slight hint from his pen that the Trio is not to be taken altogether at face value – that it does, indeed, operate at a deeper level. This hint is contained in a letter to Hugh Ottaway, dated 1 September 1951:

> Yes, I saw *The Musical Times*, but really it was so naive and un-understanding about my Trio that I didn't give it another second's thought. Who was responsible for it? Do you know?

Following Ottaway's reply, he answered on 17 January 1952:

> Now I know that the notice in *MT* was by Colin Mason, I see light a little more clearly. A complicated personal issue is involved – not so much with me as with my publisher; and I feel he is letting these personal things influence his criticism. He used to be a good friend to my music.

We leave our consideration of the Trio on a more positive note, for a letter to Ottaway of 17 July 1950, just four days after the Cheltenham premiere, offered these thoughts:

> How very nice of you to write about my Trio. It seems to have made a tremendous impression all around, and I certainly think it is one of my best works, if not *the* best. It is difficult for me to judge.

Air and Variations

In Op. 70, also composed in 1950, Rubbra returned to the writing of music for the recorder – in this instance a recorder quartet: descant, treble, tenor and bass. There are alternative provisions for a quartet of pipes and the work is dedicated to the Pipers' Guild. The piece, entitled Air and Variations, consists of just three pages, and the four variations of quite different lengths are enclosed at either end by the five-measure Air. Each variation has a title, and is inscribed with a child's name. Thus, 'Cradle Song – For Adrian'; 'Carillon – For Julian'; 'Carol – For Judith'; and 'Dance – For Jannie'. The first two names are those of the composer's sons, while the two girls are the daughters of friends. A short cadence followed by double barlines concludes the Air and each variation, but there is little or no cessation of sound as the work proceeds.

The brevity and seeming naïveté of this little work belie the thought and sophistication that went into its composition. The Air, for instance, has a stately, dignified quality that is, in miniature, reminiscent of the court music at Versailles during the reign of Louis XIV. The Baroque ornaments evoke these

Ex. 176

qualities still more (Example 176). But there is also a strong flavour of medieval organum as evinced by the parallel fifths and fourths, and the absence of cadential thirds except for the first two beats in measure 3. (In considering the fifths, the reader must be aware of the composer's instruction regarding the treble recorder.) Yet the Air is no mere evocation of past eras; the 7/4 metre and the harmonic clashes are of this century, and the mixture of diatonicism and modality – represented by D major and A major plus a sprinkling of C naturals in the bass recorder – is a Rubbra trait. This mixture, created by the different key signatures, continues throughout the variations.

Each variation is built on some small segment of the Air. Thus in 'Cradle Song', which at twenty-eight measures is the longest of the four, the continuous 6/8 motion of the descant recorder is a replica of the bracketed descending and ascending fourths in measures 1 and 2, plus later modifications of these. The three lower parts are in 3/4 metre, their quarter-note patterns creating uninterrupted cross-rhythms with the descant recorder. Their material consists of leaping or filled-in fourths, which are also derived from the first and second measures. Later, there are separate upper and lower neighbour figures, derived from those shown in measure 1. The constant repetitions of all these figures achieve the desired soporific effect of a cradle song.

'Carillon', in 2/4 metre, contains the obligatory, fast-moving scales used by bellringers. In the first half of the variation they are arranged in alternate descending fashion: D major for the descant; A major (an octave higher than written) for the treble. In the second half the scales – both descending and ascending – are confined to the treble recorder. The lower parts represent the larger bells by means of their *sforzando* and accented quarters. Sounded on each second beat in fourths, and tied over the barlines, they are very clearly heard.

Of all the variations 'Carol' is the only one not obviously related to the Air melodically. Harmonic derivations are more easily seen: parallel fifths, for example. 'Dance', on the other hand is heavily indebted to the Air, for all of its movement in a 7/8 *Allegretto* rhythm is either reproduced or adapted from the first figures in measures 1 and 2. Its *delicato*, soft texture is just right for a young girl.

As mentioned above, this charming little work ends with an exact repetition of the Air, but the dynamic level is now *pianissimo*.

String Quartet No. 2

Rubbra's Second Quartet in E Flat, Op. 73, was composed in 1951. The Griller Quartet, who commissioned it and to whom it was dedicated, gave it its first performance at the South Kensington Museum, on 11 May 1952. Of the composer's four quartets, it is the only one with four movements.

Contrary to the First Quartet's first movement, which is a clear example of sonata form, the evolving structure of the first movement of the Second Quartet

Ex. 177

is based on two melodic cells, marked *a* and *b* in Example 177. The first is announced at the start by the second violin and repeated in the first complete
measure by the viola, where it is inverted. The question-and-answer idea thus
suggested continues until measure 6, where the cell's rising semitone is expressed
in quarters rather than eighths. In measure 7 the first violin enters with cell *b* – a
falling fourth – but the semitones and repetitions of cell *a* extending from it are
of greater significance, for, as the movement proceeds, cell *b* is very secondary
in the scheme of things.

What we see from the example and hear in performance is not a theme,
inasmuch as these notes never return in this order, but it is possible to call this
progression of notes a melody because, in the first line of the example, alternating rests enable the listener to hear the melodic segments as they unfold. In the
second line there is, of course, no problem as everything is stated by the first
violin over inactive parts. The melody, then, extends from the first note to the
A-B flat semitone in measure 13. Continuing, a melodic contour in the first
violin, extending from measures 14–17, is of particular interest because of the
striking resemblance it bears to that of the solo oboe at the start of the Fifth

Symphony (see Example 36 p.106). True, Rubbra's distinctive, rising augmented fourth is missing, but the rising minor second is followed by the falling
interval. Also the note values (but not the metres) are the same. The similarities
seem entirely coincidental, for here the figure is a natural development of cell
a, while in the Symphony it *is* the cell. Another first violin passage soon after is
also of interest: the inversion in measures 25–30 of measures 8–13. From this
point to a new phase that begins in measure 66 there is little change in the basic
material, cell *a* for the most part retaining its original and inverted shapes in its
original rhythmic pattern. It appears in all four instruments, but cell *b* is present
in only the cello part, where it provides a shifting harmonic bass.

Following the movement's first *fortissimo* climax, crafted from sustained
chords and a combination of both cells, the music gradually grows softer, and
the new phase is entered. This is characterized by an irregularly timed interchange of duple and triple metres plus a concluding seven measures of 6/8. Cell
a has dropped its first note in both its original and inverted forms, and its
rhythm has been altered to a triplet. A further transformation occurs in measure
79 when the rising semitone in the original figure, and the falling semitone of
the inversion are combined to form a new, compressed figure.

A sudden modulation from three flats (the 'official' signature of the Quartet)
to two sharps replaces uncertain, shifting harmonies and a solidly established B
minor introduces the next section with the movement's first memorable melody.
Scored for first violin, the melody forms a symmetrical, arched span consisting
of eight measures. Beginning and ending with the inverted form of cell *a*, it soars
via a filled-in diminished seventh to a B, jumps to its highest point on D, and
descends in two stages to its concluding B. However, these eight measures are
merely the start of what will become a short, but graceful interplay in which all
but the cello take part. The viola initiates it by inverting the first segment and
continuing with the ascending diminished seventh. During the trill on the seventh's final note, the first violin reverses the direction of the seventh, and
during *its* trill, the viola follows suit. The violins then take up – in canon at the
octave – the inverted first segment; the viola answers with the ascending
seventh; and the violins follow with separate falling sevenths. What appears to
be the start of a new round, based on this material and scored for the second
violin, is abruptly halted, and an entirely new phase is initiated. The whole
section occupies only twenty-seven measures, but it is one of the most attractive in the movement. Rhythmically too, it is not without interest, for all of the
melodic segments are duplets within the 6/8 metre, which is confined almost
entirely to the cello.

Measure 113 marks the beginning of a transition to the movement's longest
section, a transition that features a twelve-measure melody forged from cell *a*
and scored for second violin. During its first four measures it is enclosed above
and below by the original and inverted forms of *a*. When the first violin rests, it
becomes a high solo that concentrates on the figure in measures 14–16, cited
earlier for its similarity to the Fifth Symphony's oboe figure. A lovely touch is

added when the solo's concluding measures are transferred to the first violin. An unexpected drop of an augmented second – B to A flat – brings the solo to an end, and introduces in all parts a quite gruff series of figures containing cell *a*. Understandably, tension mounts and is increased as the passage grows steadily louder and faster. It is released with the start of the movement's lengthiest and most serene melody, scored for the high register of the first violin. It is also the melody that most commands the listener's undivided attention because of its accompanimental background: groups of repeated, *staccato* sixteenths in the three lower parts. The cellular derivatives in the melody are not as easily recognized as those in earlier passages – not surprising in view of some of the evolutionary changes that have occurred throughout the movement.

Following the conclusion of this melody of seventeen measures, another short transition leads to a repetition of the duplet melody featuring the ascending diminished seventh, and another imitative interplay among the instruments ensues. Unlike its first presentation, the accompaniment here is made up of the sixteenth groups which, indeed, continue as background until almost the end of the movement. One further violin melody is heard in which (if one really concentrates) more derivatives of cells *a* and *b* are distinguishable. The remaining quartet members share, at different times, a new sixteenth-note ostinato figure drawn from *a*. A peaceful *Adagio* coda containing more cell *a* references brings the movement to a close.

Although no rigid formal structure can be either proposed or demonstrated, the movement is in no way haphazard. There is an overall design – very simple – consisting of nothing more than an irregular (in the sense of length) alternation of non-lyrical and lyrical sections. The former are more literally and, therefore, obviously related to the generative cells, while the latter are more subtly – even obscurely in some cases – derived from them. Yet it should be recalled that even while the singing melodies are running their courses, more obvious cellular variants can be heard in the accompanimental background, but each of the melodies is more complete and satisfying as the movement proceeds. A remarkable sense of unity has been created through the interplay of these diverse elements and this is not disturbed even when the melodies are cut short by the intervening transitions.

The second movement, marked *Vivace assai*, ♩. = 144, is entitled *Scherzo Polimetrico*, which Rubbra has defined in the following passage:

> [It is] an essay in the unification of metrically diverse parts. Even where barlines do coincide, as infrequently happens, the beat-units within the bar are obliterated by a variety of neutralizing elements. This is to develop a procedure that is strongly in evidence in the Elizabethan madrigal and the instrumental 'Fancy'.[32]

The basic metre is 21/8, the seven units of which are always in patterns of 4 + 3 with a dotted line to indicate the divisions. The metre changes to 12/8 or 9/8 and back again as circumstances dictate. The score should be looked at vertically in order to see the relationships between the parts at any given moment. There are places – a surprising number, actually – where all four parts simultaneously have the same metre, but one or more parts eventually adopts one of the other metres. This results, for example, in two parts moving in 21/8 while the other two are in 12/8, or three parts in one metre versus one in another. There are numerous possibilities. Although this may seem complex when viewed in the score, it is less so when the music is heard. There are, of course, internal rhythms that cut across the prevailing groups of three eighths, the most forceful of which consists of six quarter-notes. But these cross-rhythms are no different from many we have already met in Rubbra's larger works. So, despite the interesting title bestowed on the movement, I find myself in general agreement with Lester Trimble's assessment: 'all this notwithstanding, the movement sounds like a plain 2/4 or 6/8'.[33] My conclusion is not meant as a detraction in any sense, for regardless of how the metres interact this is one of Rubbra's most vigorous and exciting scherzo movements – completely on a par with the better known ones from the First and Fifth Symphonies.

Yet the vigour and excitement of this music are not the only qualities that recall the symphony movements, for the thematic material has much the same *chanson populaire* flavour of the earlier scherzos. However, there are funda-

Ex. 178

mental differences in treatment for, although the symphony movements and the quartet scherzo are conspicuously monothematic, the theme in each of the former is simply repeated, while the latter is more intent on discovering interesting derivatives. Looking at Example 178, it almost goes without saying that the most frequently heard offshoots will be based on the three eighths with which the theme opens, and this is, indeed, the case. The theme is heard twice in its entirety, and twice more in slightly shortened form, and each of these statements is accompanied by a torrent of eighths, arranged like those in the example in groups of three. In terms of intervals and directions these groups diverge from the illustrated source, some gradually expanding as they fall and rise, while others move up or down by step. These are the predominant patterns of the groups throughout the movement and the second group – those that move up or down by step – is organized into two sub-patterns: six ascending eighths, three descending eighths, and an upward leap of a fourth. The second of the sub-patterns is the inversion of the first plus the downward leap of a fifth. In nearly all instances the first sub-pattern is answered in another instrument by the second sub-pattern. Both sub-patterns comprise one ostinato unit, and two fairly prolonged passages, one near the beginning and the other near the end of the movement, are filled with such ostinatos.

All of the groups of three eighths, regardless of pattern, are the rhythmic workhorses of the movement, and as such have little in the way of melodic interest. This is concentrated in the generally high, slower moving first violin part, and later, in the second. These slower melodic segments are related to the rising and falling scale figures comprising the second half of the theme (see Example 178). Their most striking characteristic is, however, the tight braking control exercised over a very fast basic tempo (also found in the last movement of the First Quartet).

To summarize: this scherzo, like those others in which two or more interior rhythms are simultaneously present, is more outstanding for the cumulative effect of the resulting macrorhythm than for its thematic material. There is here a sparkling, constantly shifting surge of sound – another example of music simply 'becoming' rather than having been foreordained. The movement's sole theme is purely a point of reference, for its repetitions are rather obscured by the derivative material. Had the theme been too prominent and its repetitions too pronounced, the flashing spontaneity of the movement would have been weakened.

The third movement, an *Adagio tranquillo* (♪ = 63), is entitled *Cavatina* and is a very beautiful and utterly serene instrument song. Structurally, it is a freely unfolding improvisation on the various intervals of the movement's only theme, and neither the complete restatement of that theme nor the imitations of its first half have any effect on this process. Preceding the theme (reproduced in Example 179) are two introductory measures for viola and cello, and a first hearing will undoubtedly deceive the listener, for the lovely viola part certainly sounds like the start of a main theme. Indeed, one wishes it were so. Still, the

Ex. 179

three accented Bs in the first measure of both parts should not be discounted, for they play a role later on.

Unlike the Scherzo where the derivatives from the one theme are obvious, some of those in the *Cavatina* are positively obscure, but prior to tracing two of them to their source, an important point needs our attention: even a casual hearing will disclose melodies that seem to qualify as independent themes. This will confuse the listener, who has just been told that the movement has but one theme. However, what appear to be new themes are derivatives whose content is equally lyrical; for just as the Scherzo theme dictated its type of melodic progeny, so here lyricism begets lyricism. The result has produced some of the obscurity mentioned above, two instances of which we now examine.

The first example is contained in measures 8–12 of the second violin part. The melody there could, in other circumstances, function perfectly as an independent theme. Its intervals are as follows: a falling fourth; a rising and falling sixth; a rising second; another falling fourth; and two filled-in rising thirds, separated by a falling fifth. A comparison of this passage with the theme shows that all of these intervals except the rising and falling sixths are present in the parent melody. The falling fifth is, of course, the inversion of the theme's rising fifth, and the last figure in the new melody is an inversion of the figure on the second and third beats in the fourth measure of Example 179. That Rubbra intended this melody to stand out from the other instruments is indicated by his *molto espressivo* direction as well as his dynamic markings. The second derivative melody is much more obscure. The first violin in measures 12–16 employs the falling fourth, rising fifth and falling octave of the theme, but in a completely reorganized and inverted order. This melody's equally dominant status is indicated by *con intensita* and appropriate dynamics.

A further metamorphosis in the first violin, shorter but not too dissimilar, connects this melody with a new one characterized by gracefully flowing triplets. Scored for the most part in the high register, copious use is made of all of the theme's intervals in an entirely new and eloquent synthesis. Its last note (D flat) is also the first of still another triplet melody, which is based on chains of meticulously accented (<>) rising and falling fifths. Directed to be performed *molto legato*, each chain is begun in a new part as the preceding part finishes; the cello does not participate in these, as it provides harmonic support. Thus a slow, undulating motion is created. The longest chain is in the second violin, and the series ends with an ascent by the first violin. The melodies generated by the chains furnish an object lesson in how a simple interval like the fifth – extracted from the theme – can be isolated and used to form a most attractive section.

The next phase of the movement opens with stretto quotations of the theme's first two measures, again scored for all but the cello. The first violin then sounds the complete theme in its original G major, but one octave higher. The stretto entries plus the full theme, coming as they do in almost the centre of the movement, appear to have two functions: first, to remind the listener of the basic material after the various digressions, and second, to act as a structural division, for the balance of the movement is quite different from everything heard so far. It is heavier, a feeling induced by the detached and repeated quarters, the notes with which the movement began.

Taking its cue from a five-note fragment in the second and then the first violin, the viola embarks on a beautiful, twelve-measure melody in which the fifth is again a favoured interval. The viola's entire range is included from the beginning of the melody in its highest reaches through the gradual descent to the lowest notes. The accompaniment in the other three parts is composed of the repeated quarters, but in an entirely new disposition that includes shifting pitches and harmonies.

The penultimate section of the movement issues from the end of the viola's melody. The repeated chords surrounding that melody are now concentrated in the viola and cello, leaving the violins free to exchange a melodic fragment introduced during the course of the viola solo. This fragment undergoes intervalic alterations as it proceeds, plus two instances of inversion. During the seven measures of this passage the composer calls for a gradual increase in volume and tempo, both to be concluded on the final notes of the seventh measure. An *a tempo* and *subito pianissimo* are indicated at the very beginning of the next measure.

The first half of the final section begins in an extraordinarily expressive way, and very suddenly as has been indicated. The melodic fifths, which have up to now played so important a part in the proceedings, have become repeating harmonic fifths, double-stopped, and placed first in the cello and then the viola. Each group of three fifths is lightly stressed and there is one harmony per measure. The violins, a third apart, return to the beginning of the first movement for their material: a new version of the original and inverted forms of cell *a* (see Example 177). The original form, preceded by dotted quarters, occupies the first measure, followed in the second by the inversion. The third and fourth measures continue this succession at higher pitches, but in the next four measures gradual changes come about, although in the first three the harmonic fifths continue, this time in the viola. It is not merely the combination of materials that makes the passage so expressive. It is also the sound produced from a span of about three and a half octaves between the top and bottom with nothing in between. The span remains constant, for as the violins rise higher so do the fifths at the bottom.

The second half of the concluding section is very different. A B minor chord, high in the violins, and a gently dissonant E in the viola – sustained for five measures – form the soft background for a high and generally conjunct cello melody. This is traceable to portions of this movement's theme: the three-note rising figure in measure 5 of Example 179, and the rising fifth of measure 4, which in the cello's melody is inverted. The passage ends on a quiet D major chord with the third conspicuously absent. Here the movement could have ended, but Rubbra carefully steers the harmony to a clear E major via its dominant, reached in the violins by two four-note figures moving in contrary motion, and a four-note cello figure involving a leap. E major is established via three simultaneously sounded stepwise figures, two of which are again in contrary motion. A short viola passage closes the movement to a sustained chord in the other parts. It is an exact repetition of its opening phrase, but in different note values.

It might be thought that a movement containing so much lyricism in the form of solo passages against a harmonic background would be devoid of harmonic interest, but this is not true. On the evidence of the first page, it would be easy to dismiss the whole movement as essentially homophonic, undergirded by a conventionally harmonic foundation, but this is a superficial view, based on one or two hearings. More than a few hearings are required before this view can be discarded. Anyone who has taken the trouble to listen carefully to Rubbra's music knows that 'things are seldom what they seem'. In a very short while, even by the end of the first page, concentrated listening will disclose the contrapuntal nature of the movement, and harmonic interest will be seen to have been generated in two ways: first, by the horizontal movement of individual parts, resulting in mild dissonances, and second, by the sudden modulations and transitions for which Rubbra is well known. And, like most of Rubbra's movements, the key in which this movement ends – E major – is different from that in which it began – G major.

The fourth movement, an *Allegro* ($\downarrow$ = 108), is like the first in that later developments result from the initial material, but with this difference: in the first movement the evolution is easier to trace, because in each of the sections there are new and distinctive references to the initial material. In the fourth movement the sectional structure is much less obvious because the evolution is not nearly so clear, although there are distinctions based on figural alterations. As in the first movement, there are goals towards which everything is pointing. There, it was the seventeen-measure violin melody, the gradual return to melodic fragmentation, and the climax. In this movement the goals are the swiftly paced section marked 'Chorale', and the lovely, high cello phrase with which the movement ends.

The source of much of the movement is a four-note viola and cello motive spaced one octave apart and set in triplets. Immediately following the introduction of this figure, the second violin answers in the first complete measure with a non-triplet and freely inverted rendering which takes up two measures. The angularity of the segments that follow in measures 3 and 4 contrasts well with the smoother contours of the preceding figures, and the whole line is attractive enough to be considered the principal theme of the movement. But this particular sequence of notes never reappears in the order seen in Example 180, and the idea must be rejected.

Ex. 180

The viola and second violin figures, identifiable as to their origins in terms of their upper or lower neighbour classifications, are prominent during the course of the first twenty-two measures; most of them remain in the triplet configuration. The majority are in the three lower parts where, in alternating fashion, they support a first violin melody composed of those same figures plus others of a scalic nature. Thus the basic situation with respect to the making of a melody from motivic fragments is similar to that in the first movement. With the arrival of the 6/8 metre in measure 23 which, along with 9/8 and 12/8, entirely replaces the beginning 3/4, the three eighths making up the first half of the second violin's figure are altered so that all three have the same pitch level. These figures, like those just mentioned, are confined to the three lower parts. They are arranged vertically into triads, but there is a horizontal progression that harmonically sets off each group of three from its neighbours on either side. Above these in the first violin is a melody composed of mostly scalic figures and several instances of the original patterns.

This section takes up twenty-three measures and it is superseded by the section that leads to the chorale. Whereas the former is not easily defined as to its antecedents, the latter is much clearer in that regard. The initial viola figure, altered from its triplet form to three eighths, receives greater melodic definition when its semitone becomes a third. The upward leap of a fifth is retained, but a falling fifth is appended, followed in the succeeding measure by a loosely constructed inversion. The addition of two further measures results in a four-measure melody. The tempo has become somewhat faster, urged on by octave leaps in the cello which are themselves variants of the original viola figure.

Accented, dotted quarters in the violins, played *tremolo, sul ponticello*, contribute to the gathering excitement. The four-measure melody, repeated in the second violin, leads via further transformations to the first large-scale use of the angular segment in measures 3 and 4 at the start of the movement. It is simplified and reduced to three quarter-notes per measure, appearing first in the second violin and then in the first; in the 6/8 metre it generates another powerful example of Rubbra's braking action. When it has run its course, more such action is supplied by four dotted eighths per measure. The dynamic level has now reached *fortissimo*, and the cello's leaping octaves are reinforced by the same figure in the viola, although at different pitches. A slight ritard and then an *accelerando* lead directly into the concluding chorale section.

The chorale itself presents something of a problem if one clings to the notion that all later developments in a movement are explainable in terms of initial or, at least, previous materials of some kind. This is one of the dangers facing anyone engaged in analyses of Rubbra's music. The temptation to try to relate *all* later developments to what has gone before must be resisted, for Rubbra's music never was the type that can be forced into rigid moulds. It should be recalled that the fugue which ends the Seventh Symphony is unrelated to the passacaglia which precedes it. The situation here is analogous, although a case can be made for relating the very broad and flat arch of the chorale's first phrase to the narrow arch of the viola's cellular beginning. But this seems very far-fetched. In my opinion the entire chorale, whose long phrases are divided successively among the four instruments, is an independent entity, unrelated to anything that has preceded it. (For those who may be curious about the provenance of the chorale tune, I have it from the composer that the melody is entirely original.)

In spite of the length of each of the two principal reviews, I reprint them here in full because of the obvious thought that went into their writing, a quality unfortunately absent from many others.

This quartet makes an immediate impression by its warmth of feeling, often expressed in a most euphonious style. The composer has now reached that mature mastery which can dispense with clear-cut key schemes and clear-cut formal treatment of thematic material by way of recapitulation and the like. Close examination reveals a highly organized texture, gradually evolving, in the first movement, from the first four notes, with the addition from time to time of new melodic material which seems to spring naturally from incidental occurrences in previous developments. There is a certain amount of recapitulation of recognizable complete themes, especially in the Scherzo Polimetrico (second movement), but it is on the whole exceptional. Yet how very fitting is the new theme (marked 'Chorale') which appears at the end of the finale! The key schemes within the first, third and last movements would, if considered by themselves, appear haphazard in the extreme. Yet how very satisfying is the sudden return to the E major chord at the end of the Cavatina (third movement)! The scherzo is rather less subtle in these matters. Instead we have considerable rhythmic complexity. The title 'polimetrico' refers to the simultaneous use of different time-signatures in different parts (such as 12/8 with 21/8). But since this is arranged in such a way that the dotted crotchet beat is

constant (the bar-lines not necessarily coinciding) and not in the much more complex way in which all bars would be equal in duration, the general effect is that of a
continuous stream of three-quaver groups in which the listener can only be guided
by thematic repetitions, ostinato figures and the melodic shape of the slower-moving principal themes. He may never even suspect a half of the complexities which
engage the score-reader and worry the players. But this movement stands apart from
the others, which are very homogeneous – there are certain definite similarities of
melodic intervals and harmony, notably a series of alternating chords appearing in
the first and third movements. This is one of the most satisfying quartets to appear
for many years.[34]

The Griller Quartet introduced Edmund Rubbra's E flat Quartet, No. 2, at the South
Kensington Museum on May 11. It is a work of a fine musician's high maturity, full
of beauty and thought. This is music with a long ancestry, going back to the
seventeenth-century English viol school, though it is not a moment archaic in style.
The spirit of the composition is aloof from contemporary disputations and assertiveness; it moves on a plane of singular security. At a first hearing much was, no
doubt, unapprehended of the detail of the intricate texture, but the supreme distinction
of the writing was unmistakable. Merriment was achieved in the scherzo by very
complex means, and a rare serenity in the slow movement by relatively simple ones.
The work has a convincing unity. It will, perhaps, never be music for the many, but
there may be expected for it devotees like the guests at Landor's dinner-party, 'few
and select'.[35]

The critic, Desmond Shawe-Taylor, also thought highly of the work, for in a
letter to the composer of 27 November 1952, he wrote:

Thank you so much for the score of your Second Quartet, which seems to me – after
three hearings of the record – a most impressive and beautiful work: original by
nature, and without the slightest striving after originality.

Fantasia on a Theme of Machaut

Rubbra's next chamber work, composed in 1954 – four years after the completion of the Second Quartet – is one of his finest works for recorder: the Fantasia
on a Theme of Machaut, Op. 86, scored for treble recorder, string quartet and
harpsichord. At its first performance at the Wigmore Hall on 11 February 1955,
the players were Carl Dolmetsch, to whom the piece was dedicated, the Martin
String Quartet and Joseph Saxby.

Guillaume de Machaut (*c*.1300–77) was the principal composer of the French
Ars nova. He was also a poet; secretary to King John of Bohemia, with whom
he travelled all over Europe, until the latter's death at the Battle of Crécy in
1346; and finally, in fulfilment of the holy orders which he had taken in his
youth, Canon of Rheims. Besides his famous *Messe de Notre Dame*, Machaut
wrote isorhythmic motets, ballades, rondeaux and virelais. The text of one of
the two-part virelais, *Plus dure*, deals with a favourite subject of the time –
unrequited love: 'Harder than a diamond or a lodestone / Is your harshness /
Lady, who feel no pity', and so on. It is the melody of this virelai that has

provided the material for Rubbra's piece, and the entire melody has been used rather than a portion. In setting it out, Rubbra has distributed it among all the instruments, being careful to append the word 'tema' to the new instrument each time a new portion of the theme migrates.

The tempo at the beginning is *Quasi grave*, ♪= 66 circa. A note at the bottom of the page advises the performers that 'the metronome markings are approximation only, and there should be a good deal of freedom within each tempo. The transitions from one tempo to another should always be gradual and never abrupt.' The first line of the theme, divided into a short and a long phrase, appears in Example 181. The cadence at the end of the first phrase (measures 3–4) is a perfect illustration of what is sometimes called a 'Landini cadence' – named for

Ex. 181

Francesco Landini (1325–97), the most prominent Italian composer of the fourteenth century, in whose works it appears. Its presence here in the Machaut piece and, indeed, in many of the French composer's works, plus its frequent use in the works of the later Burgundian composers, raises questions as to why Landini's name became attached to it. A better name for it is 'underthird' cadence, which describes its melodic contour: leading tone (7), down to 6, then up a third to 8. At the same time the lower part moves downwards in a stepwise fashion so that, in Machaut's piece, the first four measures (in a modern transcription) are harmonized respectively by the notes G, F, E, D. The sixth below the C sharp, and the octave in Machaut's fourth measure are characteristic sounds in all such cadences. Rubbra observes this convention, except that other notes besides G and F are used in the first and second measures. As for the migrations of the theme, the composer has moved measures 7 and 8 from the first violin to the viola, then back to the violin for the cadence at the end of the first line. The next phrase of the theme (beyond the example) is in the top voice of the harpsichord's rolled chords, doubled two measures later by the second violin. The first half of the succeeding phrase is scored similarly, but its second half is in a lower harpsichord voice with the violin continuing as before. The final line is taken by the recorder with the viola doubling its first, and shorter, phrase. During the second phrase the quartet rests, except for a short, non-thematic viola passage. The entire final line is supported by a chordal harpsichord accompaniment. Owing to the disposition of the five stanzas in Machaut's virelai, there are two endings: *ouvert* and *clos*. Rubbra uses the second of these, but instead of allowing the C sharp to ascend to D at the cadence, he has enharmonically altered the C sharp to a tied D flat; it is here that the Fantasia begins.

Except for three measures near the end of the piece that are exact reproductions of the three measures with which the Fantasia proper begins, the work is through-composed and its continuous flow is seamless. In his very favourable review, Donald Mitchell claims that the work consists of 'five (or six?) interlinked variations',[36] but I do not agree. Rubbra has always shown great care in choosing a title which, in his view, most nearly describes the processes involved in his treatment of an original or a borrowed theme, and, of course, this also applies to such movements in his larger works. One needs only to review the list to see variations, improvisations, meditations, passacaglias and fantasias with subtle, and sometimes not so subtle, distinctions among them. In the present work, 'variations' is not the right word to describe what is occurring, and for these reasons. First, the expansions of the thematic segment selected for treatment occupy a disproportionately large space for a first variation, if one considers the twelve-page length of the piece. Second, if these expanded segments were to constitute a variation, there would be no space for more than two further variations, and certainly not the number specified by Mitchell. Third, and most important from the listener's viewpoint, the music lacks the character and, therefore, the sound of variations. It is not possible here to recognize sections in which different aspects of the theme are explored, yet even in an interlinked set of variations, the latter are usually distinguishable. No, this is a piece in which ideas derived from the theme evolve and expand to the point where the theme itself seems incidental, even irrelevant. Perhaps this is why the composer restates the most characteristic portion of the theme – its first four measures – a little over a third of the way through in measures 28–31. There then follows another excursion away from anything closely related to the theme, and a restatement of measures 1–13 ensues. Five more measures containing references to the underthird cadence lead to the repeated measures referred to earlier, and the work ends quietly. The unpredictable nature of the music in terms of where the piece is going, plus the frequent tempo changes, are so close to improvisatory techniques that another suitable title might well be 'Improvisations'.

The remainder of Mitchell's review mentions Rubbra's 'very striking sonorities' and the full exploration of 'his range of instrumental colours'. He concludes: 'Altogether a masterful little work, dashing, yet tender; alive to the past, yet by no means neglectful of the present; and worth many a hearing in the future.'[37]

Colin Mason calls the Fantasia 'a characteristically meditative piece, of quiet beauty, that builds up to a finely timed climax of considerable subdued excitement and tension.'[38]

Sonata for Oboe and Piano

Rubbra's three-movement Oboe Sonata, Op. 100, dates from 1958. It bears a dedication to the leading oboist of the time, Evelyn Rothwell who, with the composer at the piano, gave it its first performance at the Arts Council Drawing Room on 17 October of the same year.

Born in 1911, Rothwell studied the oboe with Leon Goossens at the RCM. From 1931 to 1939 she played in various orchestras, but following her marriage to the conductor John Barbirolli in 1939, she embarked on a solo career. In addition to the Rubbra Sonata, Gordon Jacob, Arnold Cooke and Elizabeth Maconchy all wrote oboe works dedicated to her. She has written four books, each devoted to various aspects of her instrument. She became Lady Barbirolli in June 1948 when her husband was knighted.

The first movement, *Con moto* (♪ = 63–66 circa), is a quite short (142 measures) and perfectly balanced ternary form, whose two *A* sections of virtually equal length (fifty-three and fifty-five measures) enclose a *B* section of thirty-four measures. Besides differences in their materials, the *A* and *B* sections are set apart by a change in key signatures: three flats for the *A* sections – C minor for the most part – and two sharps for section *B*, which in this case means D major and a rather fluid and, at times, indefinite tonality. However, as in many of his repeated sections, Rubbra's extraordinary harmonic sense is exercised in effecting a key change. More often than not the change steers the music to a tonality different from that announced at the start of the movement. Here, the change eventually causes the movement to end in C major rather than the D major with which the first *A* concludes. Measure 127 is the place where the necessary adjustment is made, and from there to the end the entire passage has

Ex. 182

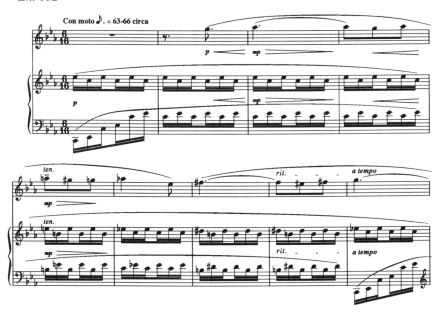

been transposed down a whole step. Another change takes place at the very start of the second *A* with the transfer of the oboe's initial eight measures to the piano above the original rocking accompaniment. However, neither change is enough to cause recognition problems for the listener, and it is therefore not necessary to label the section *A*[1].

The overwhelming impression made by this movement is one of a soaring lyricism in both instrumental parts. Yet it is a lyricism under tight control and directed every step of the way without any discernible loss of spontaneity. Looking at the graceful flow of the music in Example 182, it is easy to understand why the Sonata as a whole has attracted the listener, and established it as one of the most esteemed of all Rubbra's works. But a more detailed inspection of the example will reveal the highly integrated semitonal organization of the oboe's music and, to a lesser extent, that of the piano's (note measures 5–6 where the E and B naturals are a semitone away from the E flats and Cs). Many other instances of semitonal, writing for both instruments will be found in the *A* sections, but in the *B* section the situation is different. There the emphasis has shifted from the obvious use of semitones, as seen in the oboe melody of Example 182, to a more subtle application in the new material. In Example 183

Ex. 183

seconds are abundantly present in both hands of the piano's presentation of the new material, but the listener will identify the dominant figure in the first measure by its melodic thirds rather than by the seconds of which it is composed. This figure appears numerous times in each instrument and at various pitches, but the material that follows it is not at all consistent in either instrument, making it impossible, therefore, to speak of an explicit theme. Of course, there is no question as to whether the *A* sections have a real theme, because the melody in Example 182 is heard not only at the start of the sections but also in the piano 8 measures before *B*, and at the corresponding place at the close of the movement. Perhaps it is the presence of a balanced formal structure that leads one to expect formal, easily remembered themes, but in my opinion it is their absence in this movement that is responsible for the noticeably relaxed atmosphere. Everything stems from the basic materials presented in the *A* and *B* sections; there is not the slightest doubt of the movement's cohesiveness. In the final analysis, then, it matters not what the basic materials are called or how long they are.

In terms of its harmonic progressions as well as its expressive qualities, this movement is one of the most Romantic in all of Rubbra's music. The most outstanding of the former involve brief enharmonic transitions and the movement has barely begun when the first instances occur: measures 6–7 in Example 182, when the E flat of C minor becomes the D sharp of B major, and measures 8–9 where there is a reverse transition. One or two further instances can be found in Section *A*, but it is in the *B* section that, coupled with the rising sense of exhilaration, these transitions are more marked. Rubbra carefully established D major at the beginning of the new section (see Example 183) before settling on a measure of F sharp minor. This in turn initiates the section's first enharmonic transition, effected by a measure of that tonality's dominant – C sharp major – which then moves to F major (E sharp = F). However, once the new tonic is sounded it is immediately left in the same measure. Another enharmonic transition follows soon after when the third inversion of the dominant seventh of A major (but with a C natural in the, by now, familiar figure) gives way to D flat major (G sharp = A flat).

Other kinds of transition are scattered throughout the section, but these, like the enharmonic ones, are abrupt. Perhaps the most exciting feature of this section and, indeed, the movement is the variety and expressiveness of the supporting harmonies beneath the omnipresent figure. The variety is brought about by two factors: the different pitches assigned the figure, and the free movement of the supporting parts.

Finally, in spite of the important differences between the materials of the *A* and *B* sections, a subtle but not readily apparent unity binds them together. It stems from an oboe figure near the end of the first section: C, E flat, D, C, E flat, D, C. The *B* section figure (Example 183) is really just an inversion of this, but near the end of the section (and once in the middle) the unity becomes clearer when there is a reversion to the shape of the prototype: G flat, F, E flat, G flat, F, E flat. It is the rhythmic differences between the figure as it is sounded in each section that make it harder to immediately recognize the unity.

The short slow movement is entitled 'Elegy'. Its plaintive theme (Example 184), first sounded by the oboe and then imitated in part by the piano, is notable chiefly for the drop of a diminished fourth and a rising minor third. An element of surprise is introduced by the C naturals because they are foreign to the G sharp minor tonality. Another surprise comes with the immediate restoration of the tonic note G sharp, but where another composer might have been content to sound just the G sharp, or perhaps even drop the C to a B, Rubbra outlines the minor third: G sharp, A sharp, B. His intent that the listener be made completely aware of the restoration is indicated by the *ritardando* over just those notes. It is, of course, the diminished fourths and the re-establishment of the tonic that are responsible for some of the elegiac mood, but nowhere is there a

Ex. 184

sense that these contours have been overworked. Indeed, by the tenth measure they have disappeared, not to return until measures 53–4, shortly before the movement ends.

The discussion of the movement's main theme implies a ternary structure, but while this is true, it is a loose one, as there is no similarity between it and the unusually symmetrical structure of the ternary first movement. In fact, the only relationship existing between the *A* sections of this movement is the initial material, for all else is different: thematic disposition; piano figures, a number of which are arpeggiated in the concluding *A*; and the typical Rubbran change of key from the opening G sharp minor to the C sharp major that brings the movement to a close.

The *B* section cannot claim a theme of its own; in its stead are several fragments assigned to each instrument. Two of them in the piano's right hand have been joined to form a three-measure ostinato unit. The first of these measures is filled with an ascending, conjunct figure – C, D, E, D, E, F sharp – while the third is a sequential replica of the second. Moreover, both halves of the second and third measures form internal sequences. Thus: G, G, C; F sharp, F sharp, B; E, E, A; and D, D, G. There are occasional note changes in the figures, but they are not drastic enough to alter the basic ostinato pattern, even when the fourth and final statement of the pattern is pitched higher. Were it not for the unorganized left-hand octaves as well as the oboe's music, the twelve measures of ostinato would seem perfunctory. Even so, considering the thirty-four measure compass of section *B*, twelve measures of the same piano material does seem rather excessive.

Harmonically, the two *A* sections of the slow movement are rich in the kinds of mild dissonance that emphasize their serenely elegiac quality. Basically, the chords are major sevenths in root position and their grave beauty is enhanced by the contrary chromatic motion with which they are approached and quitted. The *B* section harmonies are simpler, moderating the elegiac mood, but my reservations regarding the long ostinato passage remain, for the harmonies produced by the entire piano part and the oboe are not up to the standards of the rest of the section.

In the headlong and agitated third movement, a broad, singing oboe melody is set against a piano passage consisting of a series of rapid, ascending thirds laid out in triplets. As the brackets in Example 185 show, the first note in each

Ex. 185

of the first four groups is a member of an outlined, descending seventh. With the exception of several places where this pattern is incomplete, the overall design is consistent wherever the passage is heard, and the design is also present in other keys. The pattern is present only once in the oboe part.

The oboe theme, also shown in Example 185, is heard only twice more, both times in the piano beneath the latter's distinctive figures, although in the first of these repetitions the oboe completes the piano's statement. In view of the significant fragments of the theme that adorn the oboe part, it would be incorrect to assume that total ownership has been transferred to the piano. Yet some of the fragments are not easily recognized owing to different rhythmic patterns, extensions, inversions and intervening fragments that function as connectives. Aside from the initial thematic statement the entire oboe part gives the impression of having been improvised. The fact that this is not so is unimportant, for its relaxed playfulness is a perfect foil for the more structured piano part, which is now seen as unobtrusively exercising control over the seemingly capricious oboe. In this movement, the interaction of these quite different components has not produced the tension that was so noticeable in the Improvisation for Violin and Orchestra, and in some other movements.

Any attempt to categorize this movement with reference to a standard or even an unorthodox formal design leads to frustration because of the differences in the instrumental parts: the essentially through-composed oboe part versus the piano's repeating figures. Owing to the two repetitions in the piano of the main theme, plus other materials that interpose themselves between the restatements, some variety of rondo structure is suggested. But the through-composed oboe part resists this notion. The alternative, then, is to say that the movement appears to have been composed in one sustained, creative burst – reason enough for the inability to discover a particular structure.

Following his observation that the first English performance of the Sonata 'had the immense advantage of an impeccable interpretation by Evelyn Rothwell', the work's principal reviewer goes on to say that

> in this individual and often very beautiful music, Rubbra's fresh, cogent invention is expressed with unfailing grace, though his essentially lyrical treatment provides less variety of pace and mood than the three-movement design seems to require.[39]

Notturno for Recorder Quartet

An interval of four years separates the Oboe Sonata and *Notturno* for Recorder Quartet (Descant, Treble, Tenor and Bass, with an alternative scoring for Piccolo, Flute, Oboe and B flat Clarinet), Op. 106. The only important works composed during that interim were Variations on *The Shining River* for Brass Band, and the Violin Concerto. Dating from 1962, *Notturno* bears a dedication to the four children of Carl Dolmetsch – François, Jeanne, Marguerite and Richard – each of whom played the recorder.

Having experienced writing for recorder quartet in the slender Air and Variations of 1950, Rubbra was prepared to attempt something more substantial and serious for this ensemble, and *Notturno* is in every respect a worthy successor. Its material consists of just one theme and several accompanying figures, and the figures are well contrasted with respect to each other and the theme. The latter dominates to the extent that it or its variants are present in almost all of the work's fifty measures. The almost continuous repetitions – most of them in the original key of C minor – the 3/2 metre, the *Andante* tempo, and the rigid character of the theme are all attributes of the ground bass principle, although in this work the melody is never placed in the bottom voice.

Looking now at the theme, reproduced in Example 186, it will be observed that it is eight measures long (less one beat); that it is made up of three unequal

Ex. 186

segments; and that it is completed in the treble and not the tenor recorder. Such migration to another part is standard procedure throughout the piece, although the completing recorder is not necessarily the treble. The second entry of the theme furnishes the most intricate example of migratory movement. Begun as before in the tenor recorder, the theme's second segment moves to the descant, while the third segment moves first to the tenor and then to the treble. The composer has indicated the third segment's migrations by dotted lines.

Of the theme's eight statements, Nos 3, 5, 6, 7 and 8 are incomplete owing to the absence in all but No. 7 of the second and third segments; No. 7 lacks only the third. In addition, there are two brief false entries which do not figure into the total.

Three statements are of particular interest for other reasons. No. 5 in the tenor recorder has directly beneath it in the bass its mirror image beginning on G rather than C. (Another mirror image between the same two parts involves not a statement but the counterpoint under the last part of 6 and the transition into 7.) Statements 3 and 6 are interesting harmonically because the final note of the upper neighbour figure – D, E flat, D – which concludes their first (and only) segments, has been altered to E natural, creating in each case an abrupt transition. In statement 3 a G sharp under the E leads to the dominant of D minor which, through contrapuntal movement, is carefully established over two measures. The D minor for which this has been the preparation lasts for two measures only, and constitutes one of the false entries. When statement 4 begins, C minor has been abruptly re-established. The situation with regard to the end of statement 6 is the same as that of 3 except for the mirror image referred to above. The ensuing D minor passage, however, lasts through statement 7, at the end of which the transition back to C minor for statement 8 is just as sudden as it was when statement 4 was introduced.

Speaking now from a purely personal standpoint, I find *Notturno* is more satisfying than any of Rubbra's other recorder works. This is probably due to my preference for the homogeneous sound of a whole consort of recorders rather than the broken consort represented by a work such as the Fantasia on a Theme of Machaut for Treble Recorder, String Quartet and Harpsichord. The placid, almost aloof sound of the recorder consort in *Notturno* is Renaissance, and it is in complete accord with the work's detached and impersonal ground bass.

String Quartet No. 3

According to the note on the first page of the Third String Quartet, Op. 112, 'this quartet was written for the Allegri String Quartet and first performed by them at the 1964 Cheltenham Festival.' As with other important works, Rubbra has written a short but fairly detailed article on the Quartet from which passages will be drawn as they become relevant.

> This work was completed in 1963. Although each of its three movements is distinct in mood and form, there is no actual break in the music, the two links consisting of a note held over from the final chord of movements one and two. In the first instance it is a low C sharp held by the cello after a C sharp major chord has ceased, and in the second, a G held by the viola.[40]

Even the casual listener who is familiar with the Second Quartet will sense a wide difference between it and the Third Quartet. The writing in the latter is more self-assured and the composer's complete mastery of the medium is very apparent, a mastery recognized by Hugh Ottaway when he referred to the Quartet as 'the deepest and richest work from this period' (he cites the Missa à 3, *Lauda Sion*, *Inscape*, and *Veni Creator Spiritus* as the other principal representative works from this period). Ottaway's assessment continues:

> Vocal in feeling, instrumental in range and capability of expression, the substance of this Quartet embraces nearly everything that really matters in Rubbra's imagination, and it is realized with a naturalness and an intensity that are immediately perceptible.[41]

'Vocal in feeling' is quite different from saying that

> the mixture (Tudor polyphony and the English folksong tradition) is as before, and it is hard to see just what place it really has in a string quartet, for the constant eventfulness of the music, with its elaborately interwoven textures and rich sonorities, seemed at odds with the real nature of the medium.[42]

Exactly where in the score this 'mixture' can be identified or separated into its components is left unsaid, to say nothing of what its proportions might be. Likewise, there is no indication of what Rubbra works the reviewer might have had in mind when he used the phrase 'is as before'. Also, and for a long time now, there has been general agreement that Rubbra's music is *not* in the 'English folksong tradition', and no evidence has been forthcoming to prove that it is.

In the light of such reviews, another of Ottaway's observations is pertinent here:

> So far as critical comment goes, Edmund Rubbra has had a lean time in recent years. Some of the notices of his new compositions – the Third Quartet, for instance – must have irked him considerably; for he is no mean critic himself and knows the folly of *reacting* to what a work is not instead of *responding* to what it is.[43]

What the three movements of this work are is a complex organism that grows from intervallic beginnings. In Ottaway's opinion, the opening of the first movement is 'probably the most closely-packed and the most far-reaching of all Rubbra's germinal beginnings; even the two major triads (D flat and C) which mark the ends of phrases have a long-term influence'.[44] Rubbra's analysis provides the details:

> The introspective largo (3/2) with which the work begins is in the nature of a weighty introduction, that contains in the first eight bars three melodic intervals and two keys that vitalise the whole work. The former are the semitone, the fourth and the fifth, and the latter the keys of D flat major and C major. (The last movement ends D-flatwards, but by a contrary motion of outer parts, G flat to G natural and D flat to C, resolves onto C major.) The growth of this introduction stems from two elements found in the opening, its melodic aspect from the interval of the fourth, and its harmonic from a shifting semitonal movement. This reaches its climax with a return to the beginning idea, with, however, a greater movement surrounding it in order to prepare for the following Allegretto (2/4).[45]

Example 187 shows the organizing intervals (indicated by brackets), and the two chords (indicated by arrows) that pertain, respectively, to D flat major and

Ex. 187

C major. Two and a half measures beyond the example, a passage in the violins composed of lowered semitones and rising fourths is reminiscent of the opening melody of the Piano Concerto's finale (see Example 121, p.224). Everything about the two passages is different: the metres, harmonies, the subdued atmosphere of this introduction as opposed to the rollicking character of the concerto movement. Yet the comparison is relevant because it illustrates a truth inherent in Rubbra's music that becomes evident only after much concentrated listening:

> As will have become abundantly apparent by now, there are characteristic intervals producing characteristic themes, and often the intervals help greatly to produce the tension in the music; as also should have become clear, the potential in these things is limitless, and is constantly responsible for very different music, saying very different things.[46]

Neither the composer nor Truscott in his short account of the Quartet mentions the extent and quality of the dissonance contained within this introduction, although Rubbra suggests dissonance when he speaks of 'a shifting semitonal movement'. Mild instances of this movement can be seen in the lower parts of the above example, but they give way later to an increasingly biting series of dissonances, made more forceful by repeated and accented block chords in the mid-to-low ranges of the three lower parts. The normally dark colours of these chords are made darker by double stopping, and further emphasis is provided by varied rhythmic patterns, which include stressed eighths tied over, and heavier accents on second and fourth beats in 4/4 measures and third beats in 3/4 measures. Above this activity, the first violin, incorporating the above-mentioned melodic intervals in its line, seems almost detached, owing to the distance between its generally high *tessitura* and the low pitches of the other instruments. At one point the first violin is marked *appassionato*, and this contrasts rather noticeably with the sombre, almost morose, sound of the accompanying chords.

Following very short *fermatas* in the thirty-fourth measure of the introduction, the mood shifts with the arrival of the 2/4 Allegretto.

> In this, the main body of the movement, an extrovert lyricism dispels the introspection of the opening, without, however, dispensing with its predominant intervals: in this case, the second and fifth.[47]

The theme containing these intervals (Example 188) is immediately imitated in the cello and though there is no tonic-dominant relationship, it appears as if a

Ex. 188

fugato passage might have started. However, in the third entry (first violin) everything after the rising fourth is omitted, and soon there is heard in the viola an inverted entry, whose second half is a free imitation of the first half. From this point until the introduction of a 6/8 section fifty-four measures later, the material develops along intervallic lines. It is enlivened by unbroken sixteenths which, begun just prior to the *Allegretto*, cease only with the change to 6/8. This 6/8 section contains, according to the composer, a second theme, 'but even this new subject adheres to the basic intervals of the first'.[48] Not only does it adhere to the first theme's basic intervals, its first half *is* the first theme expressed in inverted form, although as is so often true of Rubbra's music its subsequent statements are far from literal.

The continuous intervallic evolution inherent in music derived from germinal beginnings makes it virtually impossible to determine exactly where a formal development section starts. That there is such a section in this movement is clear from the composer's next statement:

> they [the basic intervals] define, too, the nature of the subsequent development, which is fairly strenuous, until a serener 'molto meno mosso' section intervenes (the fourth again prominent) and moves into a much truncated version of the introduction.[49]

If measures 154–9 are compared with measures 13–18 (this is how abridged the version is), it will be seen that except for small details and having been transposed a semitone lower the two passages are identical. Rubbra's final remark about this movement is confirmation that a very freely conceived sonata form has been heard: 'for the recapitulation, subjects I and II are only briefly referred to before the final build-up to a rhythmic coda'.[50] Yet even though the listener may recognize for an instant all of these brief thematic returns, the nature of the material and its continuous intervallic evolution strongly militate against the aural acceptance of any closed form.

> The Adagio (4/4) that follows without any break in sound stems from the opening viola theme, a theme that again brings into prominence the interval of the fourth. Its distinguishing feature is, however, the accented appoggiatura effect, which in subsequent development gives to the whole movement its emotional urgency. The textures are rich, and there is much canonic writing.[51]

The listener may be pardoned for thinking that he is about to hear a fugue, and there is little doubt that had Rubbra chosen to treat the theme in Example 189

Ex. 189

as a consistent fugue subject, the result would have been very striking. Yet a fugue would probably have inhibited the free development of the various thematic segments. So far as the listener's perception of the theme as a fugue subject is concerned, this segmental development quickly proves his assumption wrong as early as the end of the apparent answer in the second violin. There, segment *y* is extended by one note and repeated sequentially a semitone lower. Also, segment *z*, certainly the most conspicuous of the segments, is missing in the 'answer'. This is the 'appoggiatura effect' mentioned in the above quotation. (It is commonly known as the 'Scotch snap,' and on the continent, 'Lombardic' rhythm.) As the movement progresses all three marked segments achieve independent status as detached elements. Again the Scotch snap figure is the most prominent. In only three passages is its shape altered from the original fourth, and in each of them the alteration is to a rising third, but in conjunction with inverted fourths. In fact, the inversions have an important place in the movement. Although I agree with the composer that the appoggiaturas impart an 'emotional urgency', I feel that segment *x* provides a longer-lasting urgency because of its inherent restlessness, and number of appearances – seventeen in a movement of just sixty-nine measures. The tension is also increased by virtue of the canonic interaction among its statements.

> After a climax, built-up by a pattern of notes derived from the opening intervals of the viola tune (E, F, G) and speeded up, a new element of repeated notes plus a mordent [an inverted mordent] is heard as a background to a harmonic version of the main tune.[52]

This note pattern is none other than segment *x*, and the speeding up refers to a pattern of continuous sixteenths – first rising, then falling – derived from *y*. They are a major part of a short but powerful climax, set in motion by four appearances of *z*, ascending through an entire octave. The harmonic version of the theme is in contrast with its opening statement, whose only accompaniment at that time was the cello C sharp, held over from the first movement. Melodically, this final version bears little resemblance to the original: *x* is missing, and *y* precedes the inverted form of *z*. In measures 66–7 the inverted forms, followed by the rising thirds mentioned above, have been altered to even eighths.

In terms of emotional depth this *Adagio* must rank among Rubbra's finest slow movements. The tension is cumulative from the start, and is even more impressive because of the economy of the material. Choosing the right word or phrase to characterize its mood is not an easy task. 'Pensive', 'melancholy', 'brooding' and 'introverted' are all appropriate.

The repeated notes and the inverted mordent introduced at the end of the *Adagio* tie in with 'the final Allegro (6/8), as the basic idea of this consists of repeated notes followed by what is in effect an upward or downward mordent'.[53]

Ex. 190

The figure (Example 190) which includes these two elements bears a resemblance to that which opens the scherzo in Sibelius's First Symphony (Example 190). However, whether this represents a deliberate or unconscious borrowing on Rubbra's part seems immaterial even in view of his detailed knowledge of Sibelius's music. In fact, this knowledge makes it more likely that the similarity came about unconsciously. Whichever stance one adopts, there is no doubt that the figure's rhythmic explosiveness serves both composers equally well, for in both instances it is responsible for generating the rhythms that vitalize each movement. Yet in each case the repetitions of the figure and the materials that flow from them are vastly different. Those in the Quartet occur at irregular intervals, and rarely in the same way. The scoring will vary and the tonality will change, often precipitating a fundamental harmonic change. Connecting the repetitions is a constant flow of eighth notes, whose patterns are directly or indirectly derived from the generating figure's repeated notes. 'The dancing quavers of this movement never cease until the final bars, and are constantly bringing in their wake new tunes'.[54] These new melodies occupy the space between statements of the generating figure. They stand out from the omnipresent eighths by means of slower and syncopated rhythmic values, and through pitch contours that are widely different from those of the surrounding texture.

This alternation of the basic rhythmic figure with new melodies suggests some kind of rondo, but at best such a structure would be extremely irregular and difficult to follow. No system of lettering could be devised that would prove to be satisfactory; and even an *ABACADA...G* plan is inadequate for mapping the course of the music. It is true that the most individual and important of the interim melodies, a trifle over sixteen measures, occurs twice – measures 22–39 and 148–63 – but between these statements no formal design can be found.

Rubbra concludes his analysis of the Quartet in the following passage:

> But the rhythmic framework is not always 6/8: there is an important and elusive 7/8 section with an ostinato accompaniment, and one section combines 3/4, 6/8 and 2/4. The climax is forcefully rhythmic, but it dies out to place the accented appoggiatura motif of the slow movement into relief. The dying-out is, however, deceptive, for the final two bars briefly and quietly return to the dancing rhythm of the movement.[55]

The effect of the passage containing the combined metres, as well as some having conflicting and syncopated accents, is Stravinskyian.

Harmonically, this final movement is interesting, even fascinating, because of the way in which it wavers between long periods of relative stability, and sections where strong dissonances have been created by the complex movements of individual parts. These latter sections are tension-producing, but in a rough and jocular fashion. In the end, the balance between these extremes is aesthetically very satisfying.

As one grows familiar with this work, experiencing its varied emotional states, and becoming more and more aware of the consummate skill that went into its composition, the more preposterous becomes the condescending review printed at the start of this discussion. That there were other negative reviews is evident from Rubbra's letter to Ottaway, dated 5 August 1964. The composer had enjoyed a short holiday abroad following the Cheltenham premiere of the Quartet, and wrote:

> The Quartet is one of my best works, I feel, and I am glad you think so. Your response to it greatly heartened me after some of the notices. Martin Cooper seemed very disgruntled. The three notices were splendid, so one must be thankful that one's message was understood in some quarters.

Writing soon after a retrospective concert of Rubbra works at the Purcell Room, 24 April 1969, Alan Blyth said of the Quartet,

> [It] is a fine example of Rubbra's well-known contrapuntal skill and each movement is tersely, urgently argued with a slow movement subtly worked out and at the same time introspective, eloquent. This is a piece that should be heard more often.[56]

Passacaglia *sopra 'Plusieurs Regrets'*

The Passacaglia *sopra 'Plusieurs Regrets'*, Op. 113, dates from 1964 and is the second of Rubbra's works for treble recorder and harpsichord. Like its predecessor, *Meditazioni sopra 'Coeurs Désolés'*, the piece is based on a chanson by Josquin des Prez – in this instance a five-part one – and like it, flute and piano can be substituted. The work was dedicated to Carl Dolmetsch.

The treatment of Josquin's theme in the Passacaglia differs from the treatment in both of the previous recorder pieces where a borrowed theme has provided the point of departure. In the *Meditazioni* Rubbra selected fragments, while in the Machaut Fantasia the entire theme was employed. In *'Plusieurs Regrets'* Josquin's theme runs to twelve measures in a modern barred edition, but Rubbra's borrowing amounts to eight measures including the cadence in measures 11–12 of Example 191. This is explained by the fact that Rubbra has not used Josquin's repeated segment in measures 5–7 except in his first statement. There, it appears in close stretto in the recorder part above the original segment in the harpsichord. As for the remaining discrepancy, Rubbra employs smaller note values for the three whole notes in measures 8–9.

Looking more closely at Josquin's theme, measures 2–3 and 11–12 contain the same cadential formula as that seen in Example 181 (p.335) – the underthird

Ex. 191

Table 4

Statement 1	Begun in the harpsichord; completed by the recorder.
Statement 2	Entirely in the harpsichord; recorder has decorative figures.
Statement 3	Entirely in the harpsichord; second half in close canon between the instruments.
Statement 4	Begun in the recorder; short canon between the instruments; statement completed in the harpsichord (LH) with free imitation in the recorder.
Statement 5	Entire statement in the harpsichord, composed of accented eighths formed into intervals in both theme and accompaniment. Accented quarter-note octaves in the theme's second half. Recorder rests.
Statement 6	Entirely in the recorder; free chordal imitations in the harpsichord; final cadence in canon between the instruments.
Statement 7	Key shift from a freely interpreted D minor to an equally free C minor. Theme begun in the recorder; finished in the harpsichord. Four-measure extension which includes imitative segments.
Statement 8	Entirely in the recorder; figural imitations in the harpsichord. Final note of cadence changed so as to effect a return to D minor. Extension of one and a half measures.
Statement 9	Entirely in the harpsichord (RH); five-note ostinato pattern composed of eighths in the recorder, each group separated by an eighth rest.
Statement 10	Entire statement in the harpsichord; second half has dissonant, rolled chords. Few eighths in either part. Recorder has related figures. Between the end of 10 and the start of 11, a three-measure *Adagio* intervenes, containing in the recorder an ascending chromatic figure.
Statement 11	Entire statement in the harpsichord; recorder rests until just before the end.
Statement 12	Entire statement in the harpsichord; recorder has ascending chromatic line, followed by a broken descent and a repeated three-note figure.
Statement 13	Very broad 3/2 presentation, half of which is shared by the instruments in simultaneous, long notes to a running eighth-note accompaniment. In the second half, recorder has its own running eighths.
Statement 14	After an imitative, extended beginning (harpsichord), the statement is an exact duplicate of No. 1.
Statement 15	First four measures (harpsichord) are an exact replica of No. 2; last four are close approximations. Recorder part in first three and a half measures duplicates its passage in No. 2; then a series of high triplets. Final cadence is extended.

cadence used by Machaut in the virelai which inspired Rubbra to compose his Fantasia. During Josquin's lifetime the underthird cadence was almost obsolete.

Altogether, there are fifteen statements of Josquin's theme in the Passacaglia, and the best and simplest way to gain an appreciation and understanding of their rich variety is to summarize the statements in tabular form. Because tables necessarily preclude details, one characteristic common to the majority of the statements in the harpsichord, and to a lesser extent in the recorder, must first be pointed out: the flowing eighths that accompany the statements, enlivening them and imparting a relaxed atmosphere. Where they are absent the table will show their replacements (see Table 4).

With regard to tempi, there is a carefully indicated plan in which the fifteen statements are grouped as follows: 1 through 5, *Allegretto moderato*; 6 through 10, *piu mosso*; 11 and 12, tempo I; 13 through the first part of 14, tempo II; second part of 14 to the end, *Molto meno mosso*. In addition, there are the usual directions between some statements for slowing and accelerating.

Dynamically, the piece moves primarily in a *mezzo forte* to *fortissimo* range. Harmonically, the work is mostly the result of the contrapuntal movement of parts, thereby creating interesting dissonances.

Although there was no attempt on the composer's part to create a triptych or even suggest one based on the three recorder works derived from Josquin and Machaut, an appropriate concert performance could be planned that would place the Machaut Fantasia at the centre (it has the largest instrumental resources), and at either end, one of the Josquin pieces, each of which is identically scored. Such a performance would be balanced and unified with regard to the sources of Rubbra's material, and it would show an audience that here is a composer who has done much to restore the recorder to its rightful place.

First Study Pieces for Treble Recorder and Pianoforte

In the same year, 1964, Rubbra wrote a charming little work called simply First Study Pieces for Treble Recorder and Pianoforte (Op. 118). Its six titles are descriptive: 'Air', 'Musette', 'Gossamer', 'Valse', 'Bells' and 'Dance'. Each except the last tells the recorder player what the total range is and this increases from piece to piece: a third in 'Air', a fourth in 'Musette', and so on. The pieces grow more demanding in other areas as well, for the essentially stepwise motion in No. 1, and the one skip in No. 2 give way in Nos 3–6 to frequent leaps of a third, fourth and fifth. Rhythmically, the beginner is challenged when the easygoing *Andante* eighths of 'Air' are replaced in the next two pieces by sixteenth-note passages in brisk tempi. 'Valse' contains extended passages featuring the common syncopation ♩ ♩, but the most rhythmically demanding piece is 'Dance'. Marked 'Gay (one in a bar)', there are three instances of notes tied over the barline, plus a line composed primarily of sixteenths. All of the pieces have carefully thought-out breath marks.

Study pieces that are interesting melodically and rhythmically should also possess harmonic appeal and this quality is abundantly present in the piano parts of Rubbra's little set. The inflexible C major of the first four pieces is eased by the introduction within the key of non-dominant sevenths, and some of the recorder's notes are harmonized by chords outside the key. There are no accidentals of any kind in the recorder's music anywhere in the set, and this leads to an interesting situation in the final piece, 'Dance'. There, the piano part maintains a signature of one flat and, to avoid any misunderstanding, the composer has placed a signature of B natural in the recorder line. Since the piano part in the 3/8 metre consists of one chord per measure, there are places where B flats clash with the B naturals in the recorder line. But these are of short duration due to the swiftly moving recorder part. Considered separately, the piano part is indisputably in F major, and the recorder is in C major until its melody line moves to a long-held F, after previously establishing that F was the goal towards which it was tending. When the two parts are put together, the expected bitonal effect is less than one would have thought.

Altogether, these six pieces are a delightful introduction to the art of recorder playing. As in Rubbra's other studies – the nine piano pieces of Op. 74; the Four Easy Pieces for Violin and Piano, Op. 29; and the still-to-come Graded Pieces for Violin and Piano, Op. 144 – technical problems are interwoven with interesting music of genuine worth.

Discourse for Harp and Cello

Rubbra's lifelong fascination with the harp expressed itself in the scoring of a majority of his symphonies and concerted works, and in the two works for solo harp. *Discourse* for Harp and Cello, Op. 127, written in 1969, is the one remaining work not yet discussed. Several years prior to 1969 the composer had planned a concerto for harp and orchestra and some of the material in *Discourse* was to have been used in its slow movement. It is regrettable that this work never materialized.

Discourse, which like *Transformations* was dedicated to the harpist, Ann Griffiths, is an aptly descriptive title for a piece that is a musical conversation between equals, and like human conversation, the topics expand and become more involved.

The harp opens the piece with the germ of an idea: three widely spaced, accented chords extending over two measures in 3/2 metre, the top notes of which define a major second – A flat, B flat, A flat. The cello responds in the low treble register with a minor second – F, G flat, F – but goes on to create a full-length theme from it (See Example 192). There are three exact repetitions of the chord sequence above the cello's evolving theme before the harp takes any notice of the cello's melody. When it does respond the bracketed first segment of the melody is selected in a quarter-note version below a chordal

Ex. 192

rendition in the original note values. The beautiful dialogue that ensues is harp-dominated, and accentuated by the cello's two *pizzicato* statements of the marked segment beneath the harp's presentation of the full theme plus the segment in an inner voice.

While the cello continues with two further statements of the bracketed segment in eighths, the harp simultaneously introduces into the conversation a rising three-note figure in accented quarters – C, D flat, A flat – the origin of which is found four measures earlier, also in the harp. There, the three notes were A flat, B flat, F. The second note came at the end of a phrase, hence its longer value – a dotted half – and the third note initiated a new phrase. Under the circumstances it is impossible for the listener to associate the original three notes with the new, modified pattern, whose pitch has also been altered. Two further connected statements, each at a higher pitch, result in a rapid ascent to G where an inversion of the three notes ends on B. In the faster moving and concurrent cello line these notes are also present, but they become absorbed into the rhythm of the two bracketed segments. As expected, and in a very short time, changes are made in accordance with the evolutionary nature of such figures: the fifth becomes a third; and now with the harp following suit, it is the cello that is responsible for the change.

A new and more important topic of conversation soon follows, based on a five-note pattern, which occurs in the middle of a five-measure cello passage (Example 193). The bracketed portion is immediately detached and discussed

Ex. 193

at length at various pitch levels, and the interchange is enlivened by the frequent alteration of the pattern to sixteenths, together with occasional extensions of the falling third. The repeated Gs preceding and following the five-note figure have also been detached and augmented, but their harmonic function attracts more attention than the melodic, and for two reasons: first, the three notes lie atop four- and six-note chords that support the harp's share of the bracketed pattern; second, the even and accented rhythm of the three chords interacts strongly with the syncopated, asymmetrical five-note pattern. Variants of the three chords provide interesting alternatives. One of these has a different chord in the centre, while a second variant consists of three different chords. This second alternative has seven notes in it, and it supplies the accompaniment for the cello figures below. This section of *Discourse* culminates in a forceful climax that opposes two simultaneous statements of the material in Example 193: the stressed repeated notes, and the marked segment. Of the two statements the harp's is the more important, for both melodic patterns are augmented, and in the original key. The cello's statement is in the original rhythm, but the key is C minor. Following the completion of both statements there are further interchanges of the five-note pattern, two of which are simultaneously sounded.

Roughly the last third of *Discourse* reverts to topics previously discussed, but because the dynamic level at the start and midpoint of this concluding section is *fortissimo*, emphasized by frequent *sforzandi*, the discussion is intense. The harp's rigid insistence on a chordal, four-statement ostinato pattern underlines the intensity. The pattern is composed of the semitonal intervals which began the piece and at the same pitch level (A flat, B flat, A flat), but the introduction of other notes yields a longer pattern. The chord series directly underneath provides the mirror image. The cello's restatement of its entire theme (see Example 192) during the harp ostinatos relieves somewhat the inflexibility of the latter. Three overlapping and climactic statements of the bracketed segment in Example 193 – one in the harp, two (double-stopped) in the cello – lead via a passage filled with various fragments to shared restatements of the three-note figure, C sharp, D, F. The cello's version in two eighths and a quarter contrasts with the harp's modified augmentation. The gradual *diminuendo* and ritard of the last line lead to a peaceful ending of great beauty based on the harp's beginning chords and its final, soft reminder of the cello's poignant opening segment.

Discourse is particularly interesting harmonically because of the dissonant writing that occurs at climaxes and at other points where tension between the instruments is indicated. The result is a beautifully balanced whole in which the principle of tension/dissonance, release/consonance is fully operable. The carefully planned instrumental balance ensures that neither instrument ever overpowers the other, yet it enables one or the other to dominate as needed. All of this contributes to a thoroughly satisfying and beautiful sound. Hopefully, *Discourse* will be rediscovered and will take its place in a slender repertoire where there is always room for pieces of this high quality.

Sonatina for Treble Recorder and Harpsichord

This three-movement work, Op. 128, is the most extended and difficult of Rubbra's recorder pieces. In his dedication the composer again acknowledges

Carl Dolmetsch and Joseph Saxby, who first performed it at the Wigmore Hall
on 3 February 1965. The composer's programme notes for this performance are
both interesting and valuable, and the section dealing with the first movement
is reproduced below. The movement is in 3/4 metre with a tempo indication of
Allegretto comodo.

> The first movement takes its origin from an idea I noted down some time before, but
> which had not then been given any particular instrumental colouring. Taking it up
> again, I was suddenly aware of its relevance for recorder and harpsichord. The idea
> in question is built round a succession of fourths. This is heard first as an
> accompanimental figuration, and only afterwards are the fourths incorporated in the
> solo line. The second subject is also built round this interval, but is given freshness
> by a key change which leans more to the major. The form is classical, even including
> a repeat of the exposition. In the more dancelike development the metre changes
> from 3/4 to 3/2 (with an occasional 7/4), but the fourth still persists as a dynamic
> part of the texture.[57]

Although the structure of this movement could easily qualify as an example of
'textbook' form, the simple material that produced it contains subtleties that are
not so straightforward. To begin, the idea containing fourths to which Rubbra
referred, and which first appears in the harpsichord accompaniment, consists of
two parts: a four-note figure and its inversion, marked x^1 and x^2 in Example 194.

Ex. 194

The alternation of these halves continues over the next four measures. Note
also the fourths in the harpsichord bass: A–E. With respect to the recorder's
music, a flowing, mostly conjunct line is heard from the first measure up to
where the fourths are 'incorporated in the solo line'. (It seems odd that these
attractive measures, which appear to be an important part of the principal
theme, are not repeated at the start of the recapitulation.) The fourths introduced in the recorder part are those of x^1: and all of the following fourths are
derived from either that figure of its inversion, x^2. In fact, the very next figures
in the recorder line are replicas in quarter-notes, and at a different pitch, of the
three bracketed notes before the double bar in the example. An example of
Rubbra's subtleties occurs a few measures later when the first three notes of x^2
are contained in groups of eighths. Some of the notes are repeated, thus altering
the rhythm and, in effect, hiding the figure. Meanwhile, the harpsichord has had
its share of fourths: immediately after x^1 has been introduced in the recorder
line, it is sounded in the right hand over a period of three measures, and in the

left for two measures. The distance between the hands is one octave and the repetitions are so arranged as to form a close stretto. Next comes the alternation of the two original figures, but x^2 now leads off. A new element is introduced when, under the eighth-note passage in the recorder, fourths are employed vertically in chords.

The advent of Theme 2 does nothing to lessen the frequency of the fourths; if anything, they are even more numerous, but they are employed in a new and more animated way. The theme itself in the solo line is in D major, which represents an unprepared and, therefore, abrupt change from the A minor of the preceding three measures. The new theme's most prominent figure throughout its eight-measure length and beyond is the first three notes of x^2. The same is true to an even greater degree in the harpsichord, where the figure has assumed ostinato status. Yet the frequency of the figure in either part does not seem excessive because of the rhythmic variety accorded it. This is manifested principally in terms of rhythmic displacements of the three notes, plus combinations of weak and strong accents that make the figure less obvious. Tied notes and phrase markings also contribute to the varied rhythms.

As Rubbra observed in his programme notes, the exposition is repeated and two very different endings have been provided for this purpose. The first permits the music to return to the C major/A minor of the opening, and the second takes the listener into the quasi-B flat minor that occupies the first third of the short development section.

The composer's statement that the fourth 'still persists as a dynamic part of the texture' in this development is, of course, true, but the sudden emergence of fifths cannot be ignored. They are melodically prominent in both parts, but their harmonic incidence is far greater. However, these vertical fifths are less obvious aurally than visually because, although they are 'shamelessly' parallel over a span of ten measures, their sharp rise and fall in the accompaniment's left hand is obscured by the right-hand part, as well as by the high solo line.

The recapitulation is somewhat shorter than the exposition due to the absence of the latter's first six measures. Also, Theme 2 and its accompaniment have been lowered a whole step so as to conform to the C major/A minor tonic of the principal theme. Thus the Classical practice of placing both themes in the recapitulation in the home key has been observed.

Before proceeding to the slow movement, mention should be made of the extraordinary effect produced by the dissonant chords in the harpsichord's left hand at the start of the development section. In the 3/2 metre, which has replaced the exposition's 3/4, there are six chords per measure. By themselves, they are only mildly dissonant, and even when the eighths in the right hand are added the dissonance is not excessive. But that judgement results from playing the passage on the piano. When it is heard on the harpsichord, the effect is entirely different – almost unpleasant – for the *staccato* chords are sharp and biting, and the melodic line above them in the right hand does nothing to relieve the impression. This is because the right-hand part is itself rather biting, as it is composed of groups of four eighths, each of which is divided into two slurred and two *staccato* notes. The angularity of much of the line is still another factor. The entire accompaniment, that is, both hands, is also very exposed because, above its first two measures, the solo line has long notes, while during the last three measures of the passage the recorder rests. It must be assumed that Rubbra was aware of and wanted the brittle, incisive sounds of this passage, for he was certainly conversant with the harpsichord's capabilities and limitations.

With the exception of a cadenza near the end, the recorder part in the short *Adagio mesto* second movement consists of an elegiac, songlike theme. Below this in each 4/8 measure is a rolled chord divided evenly between the hands, each hand playing the same notes an octave apart, and there is but one chord per measure. However, riding on top of each chord are two quarter-notes arranged as appoggiaturas, the second quarter of which is the resolution, always a semitone higher. These upper notes in each hand define a mostly chromatic melody that climbs slowly but steadily, and, of course, there is a dissonance on every first beat. The whole accompaniment provides a poignant background for the beautiful solo line. The *molto liberamente* cadenza furnishes a short interval before a much abbreviated return to the opening material brings the movement to a close.

The Sonatina's last movement, marked *Moderato scherzando*, consists of five continuous variations plus a coda on 'En la fuente del Rosel', by the sixteenth-century Spanish composer, Juan Vasquez. It is contained in a collection called *Romances and Villancicos Españoles*, discovered in Mexico. Not many details pertaining to Vasquez's life and career are available, but the principal known facts are given below:

> Vasquez, born in Badajoz, entered the service of Don Antonio de Zúñiga, in the Andalusian area, probably before 1551. If the composer is the same Juan Vasquez whose name appears at the end of the license in Fuenllana's *vihuela* book of 1554, he was in the service of a certain Juan Bravo, perhaps identical with Count Juan of Urueña (in the province of Salamanca), called 'el Santo'. Vasquez was living in Seville in 1560 .... Vasquez's secular music is of excellent quality.[58]

On the first page of the movement Rubbra has reproduced intact Vasquez's villancico, without, of course, including the words. The texture is in four parts except at the beginning, where the voices engage in imitative entries. There is not a note nor a harmony that is foreign to sixteenth-century practice. The villancico's popular vein is very apparent, but in this instance as in many such works of the period there is enough polyphonic writing to appeal to more sophisticated performers and listeners. Rubbra has the recorder double the tenor voice in two places on this first page. The first half of the theme appears in Example 195 and following it, I have reproduced the final cadence because it is the motivating force in Variation I.

The final note of the cadence marks the beginning of Variation I, which is in C minor; the metre is 2/4, and the tempo remains that of the theme. The

Ex. 195

material is derived from the three-note cadential pattern A, C, B, except that
here is it C, E flat, D. In the right-hand part of the harpsichord accompaniment,
these notes are repeated many times in the original rhythmic values, and at two
pitch levels. The left-hand part is in the form of an ostinato, composed – with
one exception – of four eighths per measure. The basic pattern is one measure
long, and it contains the three cadence notes plus one other that leads to the
repetition of the pattern a minor third higher. Thus a larger, two-measure
pattern has been created, but because the first measure is sometimes repeated at
the original pitch, there is also a three-measure pattern. Rubbra makes the
divisions clear by meticulous phrase slurs, and as the right-hand repetitions of
the three notes do not often coincide with the ostinato patterns, an almost
seamless texture results. The solo line also makes use of the three-note cadence
figure, but always in longer values. The addition of new material to these notes
is responsible for the creation of an independent melody.

In Variation II there is a metre change to 3/8, but the tempo again remains
the same. A slightly modified version in the harpsichord of the harmonized
second portion of the theme is complemented in the solo line by the beginning
of a new melody, which has almost nothing in common with the theme. Following a short ostinato, the accompaniment embarks on an even shorter passage
whose biting sound stems from accented, *staccato* non-dominant sevenths, as well
as other dissonant chords. The variation concludes *fortissimo* with a descending
trill in the recorder, under which the accompaniment shares the solo line's
earlier music.

Variations III through V have one common characteristic: the sources of
their materials are obscure enough to require the composer's aid in the form of
programme notes. Thus the material of III springs 'from a pattern (F-E-D)
found in the body of the tune'.[59] The pattern is, in fact, buried in the tenor part
where it is not likely to be noticed, for it is only a passing contrapuntal
fragment. In the Variation, which is in 3/4 metre and marked *espansivo*, the descending third is completely absorbed into the melodic fabric; the original pitch
is nowhere reproduced. The Variation is divided into two parts, each composed
of ten measures, each half containing exactly the same music but with the
second half transposed down a major third. Of all the variations it is the most
unusual in the treatment of its material and in my opinion this is the result of
deliberate planning. Consider first the means whereby the Variation has been
set off from its fellows on either side: the A minor of Variation II is cancelled in

one stroke when A flats announce a kind of F minor as the recorder introduces the descending third – A flat, G, F; on the other side, a modulation to C major and a change to 2/4 return the listener to a harpsichord statement of the theme's first half. This statement effectively separates Variations III and IV, but it also serves two other purposes: it recalls the theme in case the listener has forgotten it – a real possibility in view of the obscure fragments with which the preceding variations have been concerned – and it sharply defines the movement's overall structure at approximately its midpoint.

Two particular features mark Variation III as the most outstanding of the set: the harmonies and the harpsichord trills. These harmonies are not in themselves unusual, but they seem unusual because of the more conservative harmonies of the other variations. The accompanimental harmonies in the first six measures, and in the first six of the Variation's second half, are virtually static (the following description of the first passage is valid for the transposed second passage): A flat octaves held through each measure but not tied over, and having continuous trills on the lower note, are supported by a chord – A flat, B flat D flat, E flat – alternating with the third inversion of a half-diminished seventh – A flat, B flat, D flat, F flat. Another abrupt semitone drop, occupying four measures, takes the music to the transposed passage and, at the conclusion of the latter, the same process is repeated.

Following the harpsichord's solo statement of the theme's first half comes Variation IV, at thirteen measures the shortest of the set. Again, Rubbra's explanatory remark is helpful: ' … this variation (2/4 C minor) takes over and exploits ornamentally [the theme's] two final notes'.[60] These notes, C-B (a final C in the harpsichord completes the cadence), are changed to a trilled E flat-D (measure 1), a trilled G-F (measure 2), and an inverted mordent on the first note of E flat-D in the third measure – all in the solo line. The accompaniment consists entirely of ascending and descending chords firmly anchored in C minor, but containing mild dissonances. The Variation ends on a half cadence in which a rolled G in the accompaniment is topped by a written out mordent in the solo line.

Variation V, marked *Largo*, is 'a free canon [so designated in the score] that takes its cue from the mordent that ends the previous variation'.[61] The canon is so freely constructed as to be largely unrecognizable in the score, and totally so in the hearing. Four factors are responsible for this: first, the recorder melody is an inversion of the harpsichord's melody contained in octaves; second, the two canonic voices move at different speeds because of different note values; third, some intervals contained in one voice are omitted entirely in the other; and fourth, parts of the Variation are not in canon at all. The mordent that initiated the Variation is only incidentally present and in some cases it is, of course, inverted.

The brief coda marks a return to the original tempo and it is an exact restatement by the solo harpsichord of half of the theme. A lively, sixteenth-note passage in the recorder, amply supported by the accompaniment and ending in a prolonged trill, brings the Sonatina to an exciting conclusion.

A brief notice tells us that 'if Rubbra seems to overrate the power of the recorder on the bottom notes, the writing in general is wonderfully apt'.[62]

Violin Sonata No. 3

It is hard to believe that Rubbra's Third Violin Sonata, Op. 133, privately commissioned, and composed in 1968, had to wait until 1985 for its first London performance, which took place on 13 June at the Wigmore Hall. The occasion was a concert celebrating the fortieth anniversary of The Composers' Guild of Great Britain and in addition to Rubbra's Sonata there were solo and chamber works by fellow members Sir Lennox Berkeley, Alan Bush, Arnold Cooke and William Alwyn – all, like Rubbra, founder members and octogenarians. Two deceased founder members were also represented: Vaughan Williams and Sir Arthur Bliss. I was privileged to be there as a guest of the Guild and I heard the Rubbra work superlatively performed by the Israeli violinist, Yossi Zivoni and the English pianist, Rosemarie Wright. Unfortunately, the concert attracted but scant attention in the press insofar as reviews are concerned.

That Rubbra's Sonata is held in high esteem is best illustrated by the remarks that open Harold Truscott's brief but discerning summary:

> The thirty-six years which separate the composition of the second and third Violin and Piano sonatas are a sufficient explanation of the complete difference of outlook from the one to the other. There is a unity, as well as a textural clarity, about the third sonata which speaks of deep experience coupled with a strong sense of exploration rather than the exploration of youth which seeks experience.[63]

The first of the three movements of which the Third Sonata is comprised is marked *Allegro*, a tempo that except for several minor ritards is maintained until the closing *allargando*. The metrical design, however, is not so simple, for despite the opening ¢ metre the majority of the movement is in 3/2, and other metres intervene, usually for only a short time. No matter what metres are in force, cross-rhythms and syncopations abound, and with respect to these, I cite the following statement, with which I concur:

> This rhythmic complexity, rather than creating tension and vitality, tends to break down the pulse so that the accompanying figuration becomes a harmonic colourwash. Against this the diatonic lyricism of the violin stands out impressively.[64]

This is an intervallically conceived movement, and the chosen interval – in this case the fourth – is a building block whose importance cannot be minimized. Let us look in some detail at the nine measures in Example 196, which constitute the movement's principal theme: all of the important events stem from the actions of fourths, as the connecting lines show; and everything else helps to define and highlight the fourths. These additional notes are not only necessary connecting links, but their conjunct movements balance the leaping fourths. The next stage involves recognition of the units that make up the theme, and

Ex. 196

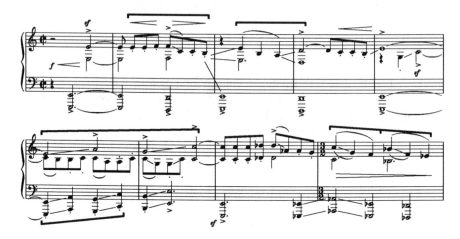

these have been isolated under brackets in the example. The soloist enters in the tenth measure, and his material there begins with the figure in measure 3 plus the upward resolution to a fourth, and so on. The pitches are considerably higher and different, as they should be for the solo instrument's first entry.

Having thus established the primacy of the fourth in the various units of his theme (which in themselves represent a taut developmental process), the composer is free to let his material expand and go where it will, but most of the time with reference to the fourth. An extraordinary concentration of this interval occurs in the piano part in measures 16–19. In the right-hand part of measures 16–17 descending octaves outline fourths – A to E, D to A respectively – in association with an eighth-note figure in the same hand that contains ascending fourths in a descending pattern. The same idea is present in 18–19, but the directions in 18 are reversed. In three of the four measures under discussion, the left hand has chords containing fourths, while in the second measure accented octaves – E, F, G – resolve on octave As in the next measure, thus outlining a fourth melodically. (See measures 16–18 in Example 197.)

Of the many more passages involving fourths in developmental stages, one in particular deserves mention: a moderately long passage composed of double-

Ex. 197

stopped fourths at approximately the midpoint of the movement.

One of the problems confronting a composer who elects to build a movement of some length that is based on an interval is form. Fascination with a chosen interval *per se* is a temptation that can easily cause a composer to forget that that interval is merely a building block, intended to serve a larger purpose. Rubbra always manages to evade this trap in whatever movement is intervallically conceived, and here in the first movement of the Third Sonata he strikes a careful balance between allowing the fourth to dominate completely, and not allowing it enough exposure. In other words, it always does serve the larger purpose of creating expressive music, and participating in the formation of a workable structure.

Rubbra begins by reminding the listener not, in this case, of the entire theme that results from his intervallic building block, but enough of it to provide easy identification. To make this clear, his thematic material has been essentially separated into two levels of importance. The lesser one consists of the figure in measure 4, together with its resolution to a fourth in the following measure. In a variant of this, the resolution is omitted, and several of the figures are linked sequentially. But neither the original figure nor its variant can match the dominant sound of the violin's initial figure, sounded one measure after Example 196 (see above). It goes without saying that the principal reason for its dominance is its dramatic sound profile, but Rubbra has confirmed its importance by assigning it a dynamic level of *forte* or *fortissimo* each time it is heard. It also has an important function as a definer of form – in this instance, a very free ternary structure. Accordingly, the conclusion of the first *A* section is fixed in measures 35–41 by an exact repetition of all of the material for violin and piano in measures 10–16. Similarly, the reintroduction of the second *A* section is announced *fortissimo* in the violin, but with an interesting difference: the two connected figures have been reversed so that their shape is now that seen in measures 2 (second half), 3 and the resolution to the fourth in 4. But this is not all, for the violin continues with the piano's material, including the inner leap of a fourth in measure 5, and the eighth-note figures in measures 6–7. Attention is drawn to the approaching reintroduction of *A* by a two-measure trill on Ds, separated by an octave, plus a one-octave scale in thirty-seconds at the very end of the measure prior to *A*'s reentry. Other restatements of this basic material are heard during this final section.

The material of the middle or *B* section of the movement is proof that the composer is flexible in his interval-dominated movements. This section, therefore, should reassure those who might think that materials are forced to conform to the shape of a foreordained interval. That is not true here nor in any other interval-oriented movement. Rubbra has never permitted his consummate technique to overrule his innate musicianship – not even in those early works in which he sometimes became too relentless with regard to ostinatos and canons. There are fourths in this section, but they are less conspicuous.

Nevertheless, the materials in *B* are shaped differently from those in the flanking *A*s, enabling a balance to be struck between the latter's angular, disjunct fourths and the smoother, melodic fourths of the middle section. The movement as a whole is so tightly knit as to make the texture virtually seamless, and were it not for the landmark fourths pointed out above as sectional dividers, the movement's structure would be far less clear than it is, which is not saying much. Compounding the difficulty is the fact that *B*'s initial material is, strictly speaking, not new. It is, rather, a restatement of the descending scale figure in the violin above the piano's concentration of fourths in the first measure of Example 197, and as such it belongs to section *A*. It is immediately enlarged upon in successive measures, and eventually given to the piano. In its expanded form its most noteworthy trait is the total absence of fourths. The natural divisions of the figure as it descends are fifths, a feature made plain either by rests that separate the various segments, or by a longer note on the concluding fifth. Soon, the descent by fifths is eased in one way or another and, as always with Rubbra, movement in the opposite direction is introduced. This comes at the point where the above-mentioned double-stopped fourths are heard, but since the emphasis is on melodic progression – in two instances by ascending fifths, and between these by mixed directions – the fourths seem less important. Where fourths do assume great importance in this middle section is a bit later on in the piano when accented quarter notes outline bell-like descending fourths: E flat to B flat. Altogether they are stated six times, and each time they are embedded in a surrounding chordal texture consisting of three chords per measure in the 3/2 metre. Near the end of the section the fourths very gradually become more numerous until the *fortissimo* fourths, mentioned above, reintroduce a *very* different and at times almost unrecognizable *A* section.

To sum up: the more this movement is studied and heard, the more structurally complex it appears. While the outline of a ternary form is undeniably present, it is an outline that is not only vague, but one that begins to recede in importance. Replacing it is the conviction that here Rubbra's natural instincts led him along improvisatory paths that only incidentally resulted in a loose ternary structure. The whole feel of the movement is improvisatory, but that does not, of course, rule out structural considerations. In fact, some sort of structure is vital in improvisatory-type movements, otherwise a shapeless, musical mishmash will result. A delicate balance must be achieved between these seemingly irreconcilable approaches to composition. The goal of all truly improvisatory writing is to create music that utilizes the intuitively inventive facet of the composer's mind without imposing a rigid, formal structure on the flow of ideas. It is my belief that in this movement of his Sonata Rubbra found that balance.

The slow movement, marked *Andante poco lento e mesto*, is a gently moving instrumental song whose most arresting feature is the treatment of fifths, as seen in Example 198. However, the specific contour in the first measure is not repeated in the violin until the *fortissimo* climax six and a half measures prior

Ex. 198

to the quiet and peaceful conclusion. Between the end of the example and that point the solo line is continuously unfolding in Rubbra's unhurried way, and, of course, rising and falling fifths play an important part in that process.

The harmonic richness of the accompaniment is due in no small part to the unrelated, second-inversion chords in each hand that underlie the first third of the movement (see Example 198). The dark and sombre colour of these chords is very striking for, as the example shows, both hands are playing in the lower register of the piano. An examination of the chords reveals a melody in their topmost notes, which becomes more active beyond the limit of the example. With one very small exception one looks in vain for later references to this melody, either in the piano part or the solo line. This is surprising, but Rubbra undoubtedly had his reasons for abandoning the melody. Nevertheless, every pianist involved in a performance of this work should be aware that these chords are much more than merely inducers of a particular mood. Although unrelated to each other harmonically, their linear importance is evidenced by the carefully indicated phrase slurs, and these must be observed together with the dynamics.

A subdued passage containing various dissonant chords, including a large number with major or minor seconds, links the second-inversion passage with the rest of the piano's contribution, which is a fully developed, rich partnership with the violin in the sense that the piano now shares and develops the latter's material. The fifths, so prominent at the beginning of the movement in the solo line, are now the principal elements in the musical landscape of both parts. The piano's chords in the second half of the movement have increased in size and complexity, and a number of them are quite dissonant. Again, sonorities are stressed but to a lesser degree and in a different way, for the hands are very widely separated at times, whereas in the second-inversion passage they were together in the bass clef. The chords are all heavily accented, the upper ones outlining the falling fifths of the violin's opening measure. The soloist's fifths are mixed with ascending and descending scalic passages as in the opening measures, and their rhythmic flow offsets the weighty piano chords. A *fortissimo* climax is reached with the violin's repetition of the first four measures of its theme, this time in 4/8 rather than 4/4 metre. Supporting the melody is an augmented version, not of the theme, but of the fifths alone. They are contained in the large chords, which now are no longer widely separated. The movement trails off to nothing – 'niente' – as the violin fifths rock back and forth. At the very end, the second-inversion chords reappear under the last of the fifths.

The slow movement has been very inward looking and for the final movement a complete change in mood is imperative. This is effected in the form of a theme and eight continuous variations. There is a concluding coda which, except for a moderately changed piano part and an extension at the end, is a restatement of the theme. The caustic humour of the highly rhythmic theme, marked *A Tempo di Marcia*, is uncharacteristic of Rubbra, but delightfully vigorous and refreshing. Violin and piano have combined to form a perfect partnership, the elements of which are beautifully contrasted and balanced: the violin line balanced within itself as to conjunct/disjunct movement and directional change; the firmly anchored, dissonant piano chords, whose syncopations and accents help to define the violin melody (Example 199).

Ex. 199

Of all Rubbra's variation movements, this one is possibly the easiest to follow in terms of the relationships between the theme and its variations. It is, of course, the nature of this particular theme that makes this possible: its distinctive rhythms and arresting intervals. Thus the connection between the end of the theme and the start of Variation I is largely imperceptible – or it would be if it were not for two things: the sudden shift from G to A flat major, and the compositional change in the piano's chords. With regard to the change in key, it could be argued that this same (but less sudden) shift has already occurred in the theme without initiating Variation I. Countering that point is the care with which Rubbra returned to G major before the end of the theme so that he could *again* shift to A flat for the Variation. As for the piano's chords, the changes there are away from the rhythmic punctuations associated with marches. What replaces them are chords whose right-hand segments are highly disjunct: leaps of a fourth, fifth and octave. The rhythm of the chords is that of the violin, which, in turn, is the rhythm of the theme. The violin's melodic material is both a restatement and a restructuring of two of the theme's segments.

The jerky rhythm of both the theme and the First Variation continue in Variation II, but short scraps of dialogue based on various thematic segments, and alternating between the instruments, constitute the new feature, and are the main points of interest. Some attention is also given to the repeated note pattern in measure 5 of the theme. An *allargando* leads into the *meno mosso* of Variation III, where the key signature of one sharp has been restored. But this key change is meaningless in terms of G major until the last two measures, for the tonality is clearly B minor without a C sharp. This perfectly fits the main focus of the Variation: F sharp, C, B, and so on down to D. This is a rhythmically smoothed out version of the same notes in measures 3–4 of the theme. Here, only the first three notes are in the violin, but the entire note sequence plus some variants of the descending scale figure are embedded in a richly beautiful and graceful piano part. Although only seven measures in length, this Variation is a wonderfully expressive link between Nos II and IV. A violin trill on D that lasts a measure and a half, and a final *allargando* measure concluding with *fermatas*, lead into Variation IV.

Marked *subito doppio movimento*, this Variation has the characteristics of a scherzo, albeit a miniature one. Accented *staccato* sixteenths in groups of three dominate the entire Variation, being used at the start to outline in the piano's right hand the theme through the D on the first beat of measure 4. The chattering continues throughout the piece, much of the time on a single note or on double-stopped thirds. Following the thematic segment in the piano, only fragments of the theme are heard in both instruments. The most interesting feature of the Variation is the harmonic dichotomy between the instruments. Tonally, the instruments are rarely together, for when one is temporarily stable, the other is either assuming a new key or modulating to one. This has produced situations where, for example, a short G major passage in the violin is opposed by B major in the piano, or a violin transition to B major is accompanied by a temporarily stable F major. Bitonality is obviously a factor here, but the bitonal effect is the product of melodic movement, not of a deliberate vertical plan. This is true of all Rubbra's alleged bitonal passages, and in the final chapter of this book, where his musical style and processes are summarized, his pronouncements on the subject will be found conclusive.

Variation V is a continuation of IV in two respects: the tempo is the same, and the chattering sixteenths are present, but in greatly reduced numbers. References to the theme are nebulous, and for the most part consist of tiny fragments joined together in the violin part to form a new melody. The piano's role is more accompanimental than it was in Variation IV, although near the end its series of rising octave fourths are distinct references to the theme's. Harmonically, the key of the Variation is primarily D flat, causing the signature of one sharp to seem rather odd.

Variation VI has a metre signature of 3/4, basically a continuation of the 9/16 of V. The highly expressive violin part is double-stopped for slightly over fourteen of the Variation's twenty-two measures. The melodic material is even more obscure than that of the preceding variation, and what there is is found in the lower voice of the violin's double-stopped line. However, the main interest is concentrated in the exchange of instrumental parts: invertible counterpoint. In measures 9–15 the violin has a flowing line composed of even eighths, and the upper line in the piano (bass clef) is sounding intervals of various sizes above C sharps in the lower parts. From measures 16–20 the lines are exchanged, the violin playing the intervals and the piano the flowing line. The usual octave transposition is observed, that is, the violin's eighths are transposed down an octave, and the piano's intervals are placed an octave higher. The inverted passage is shorter than the original by two measures, due to a relaxation of the material in both parts before the Variation ends.

In the *Allegretto* of Variation VII, at five measures the shortest of the set, approximately the first half of the theme reappears in the violin in sixteenth notes. At the same time, the piano has as much of the theme in eighth notes as can be accommodated in the same time span.

The march tempo returns in Variation VIII along with the jerkiness, as sections of the theme in both instruments prepare us for the full recapitulation of the theme and its accompaniment in the concluding coda.

Piano Trio No. 2

Rubbra's Second Piano Trio, Op. 138, was composed in 1970 to celebrate the twenty-first anniversary of the founding of the Evesham and District Music Club. The Rubbra-Gruenberg-Pleeth Trio, formed during the Second World War as a service for the soldiers and reluctantly disbanded upon its conclusion, was reactivated especially for the first performance of the work, which took place in Evesham. As Rubbra remarked (Chapter 1, p.24), the three musicians played 'as if the intervening years hadn't existed'. A second performance of the Trio with the same players took place in Birmingham a few months later. The

Trio has only two movements – a *Tempo moderato e deliberato*, and an *Allegretto scherzando*.

The first of these movements is generally intense both melodically and harmonically, a quality evident from the start in the nine-measure theme in octaves between the strings, which is supported by impressively sonorous piano chords. In Example 200, where the duplicate upper notes in the violin have

Ex. 200

been omitted, the important segments have been marked, and it will be seen that their repetitions in altered form have shaped those remaining parts of the theme shown in the example. However, these nine measures are never wholly repeated, and it is therefore the task of the segments to shape the movement. Thus it would be accurate to say that, in the largest sense, the movement is through-composed, for even though certain segments – even large portions of the theme – return, the surrounding contexts are very different in each instance. Always, though, the harmonic context is rich and full, but this statement does not mean that the intensity mentioned above is never relaxed. It is, but in an alternating manner: tension, release, tension, release. These alternating passages do not, of course, have definite boundaries, but such words as *espressivo* and *teneramente* are indicative of the relaxed sections, while buildups in volume and dissonance are signs of tension that is released right after climactic points.

The basic theme has barely finished when melodic and rhythmic changes begin to unfold. Not surprisingly, the first of these occurs in a softly expressive section, thus providing the necessary relaxation after the rather tense opening presentation. It takes the form, at least in the beginning, of close, flowing imitative entries involving all three instruments. These entries are based on segment *a*, but they incorporate two alterations: the first note – B – has been extended to three quarter-notes, and in the first entry high in the violin, the falling third and its resolution have been inverted. A 'spinning out' of the notes of the inverted figure follows.[65] When the cello and piano enter, each reverts to the original form of the figure at the end of *a* before pursuing independent paths that, again, involve *Fortspinnung*. Upon the completion of its improvised melody (for so it seems) the violin embarks on one further entry over two octaves lower, which again contains the previously heard inversion. Immediately following its completion, there is an upward leap, and the violin sounds the four notes seen in the lower bracket of Example 200, altered now to three eighths and a quarter. In their three later, widely separated appearances the same equal note values prevail. These figures are cited not only for their expressive importance, but also because they illustrate the Rubbran technique of making a figural pattern seem new by employing something as elementary as a rhythmic change. By this I mean not just a change in note values, but a basic change of accents and, in this case, the alteration of a figure whose notes are shared by two thematic segments (*a* and *b*).

Tension begins to build slightly in the piano through sequential repetitions that rise by semitones, but they occur only in the right hand. The left hand supplies the harmonic foundation in a non-sequential passage. When the sequences have reached their highest point (which is only an E flat), the melodic line engages in repetitions of *a* in both its original and inverted forms. The violin and cello meanwhile are pursuing an independent course with respect to the piano and each other. Their flowing, generally short phrases are improvisatory in nature, and most of them involve *a*, which is ingeniously woven into the eighths and sixteenths that make up the phrases. Towards the end of this passage, however, both instruments abandon *a* and the way is cleared for a formal statement in the cello of *a* + *b* at the original pitch level and rhythm, but in notes of half their original value.

These musical events are representative in the most general way of those in the remainder of the movement. By this, I mean that the primarily improvisatory style, based on ever new combinations of the various thematic elements, is punctuated by formal statements of the theme's first half or enough of it to reorient the listener. Attention is drawn to these statements by a higher pitch or dynamic level, or both.

This movement should not be left without calling attention to its most expressive passage, which begins not quite two-thirds of the way through. The first three notes of *b* are sounded – *teneramente* and *molto espressivo* – in the cello over a series of chords of which the first three are a version of *a*. The rests separating the short components in the cello's passage are potent factors in the expressiveness. As in other Rubbra movements, the relative isolation of this melody together with its construction strongly suggests a fugato section, but this is not supported by the second and third entries – both assigned to the violin, and both sounding the cello's initial notes as well as some of its later ones.

The concluding movement of the Trio, *Allegretto scherzando*, with its playful, high-spirited rhythms and melodies, provides an excellent foil for the serious and sometimes rhapsodic first movement. Structurally, there appear to be rondo elements in it, but most of the boundaries between contrasted sections are very blurred and ill-defined. In fact, the more this movement is studied, heard and absorbed, the more untenable the rondo theory becomes. There are developmental processes involving the principal theme, and they are fairly continuous. Sonata form is no alternative because the basic structural requirements are not present in sufficient proportions; the development section would far exceed the other sections in size and importance. Continuous variations are out of the question, as there would be no way of distinguishing one from another. The only reasonable alternative, therefore, is an evolving form, which really means a free form. All of this will now be considered in greater detail.

There is no mistaking the principal theme (Example 201), which is readily identifiable by its characteristically jerky rhythm, as well as by its melodic

Ex. 201

content. After the opening thirteen measures during which the rhythm and content are consistently present in every measure – thus constituting a section – there are nine measures where both are absent. It is these that first prompt one to feel that a *B* section is present, a feeling considerably strengthened by the almost literal restatement of the principal theme in approximately the next seven measures. Two things conspire to upset this idea that a rondo structure is unfolding. First, evolutionary processes are at work in the alleged *B* section and these can be traced, both rhythmically and melodically, to the original theme. Thus the independence of a *B* theme, or first episode, would be compromised. Second, and more important, the measures following the restated theme lead past a double bar and into a somewhat faster section in which the principal theme's basic rhythm is present in nearly all of its measures. Complicating things further, this section is forty-eight measures long for the piano and forty-three for the strings, the result of conflicting 3/4 and 2/4 metres. In this lengthy section the participation of the piano in the jerky rhythms and the thematic material equals that of the strings for the first time. There are new combinations of the basic material as the section moves on, but the main impression is one of unrestrained merriment. (This is the section that would qualify as the development if a sonata form were in progress.) All this ends, however, in an accented *fortissimo* passage marked *allargando molto*.

The interesting thing about this change is the sudden reversal in mood as the strings loudly remind us of the opening material of the first movement in the form of a new synthesis of its segment *a*. This is followed by a measure of *fermatas* ending with a double bar. The sudden change has a very sobering effect on the next section, a thirty-four measure expanse marked *lento ma non troppo*. It seems as though the music were suddenly tiptoeing after a stern warning, for the dynamic level is soft, but there is no change in the material. It is still lighthearted, if subdued, and the jerky rhythms persist. When the initial tempo returns following another ritard and increase in loudness, the material reverts to a literal repetition of the opening section of the movement, a few notes in smaller values having been added. If the structure of the movement were a rondo this section would be called *A'* or *A"*.

The last page of the movement is really a coda. The rhythms have been smoothed out, and the music is slowly being steered towards what proves to be a quotation of the material from the end of measure 8 to the end of 12 in the first, not the second movement. This is the passage singled out in our discussion of the first movement for its soft expressiveness, coming as it does right after the drama of the opening presentation. But where in that earlier passage all three instruments had engaged in close imitative entries, here at the end of the Trio the piano furnishes its own version. This takes the form of a simple left-hand octave statement of the inverted *a*, followed in the right hand by a single-note statement of the original form of *a*. Over these entries the violin engages in a lovely, continuous spinning-out of *a* that grows ever softer and slower. The final cadence settles on a G major chord. Thus in a sense the Trio has come full circle.

This work was written in the full tide of Rubbra's maturity and as such there is a surer and firmer hand than is evident in the earlier Trio in One Movement, for despite the sometimes rhapsodic nature of its first-movement material, this second trio displays an economy and a tight rein not found in the preceding work. This is to be expected, for twenty-two years separate the two. All the more deplorable then is the absence in the major musical journals of any significant assessment following either the Evesham or the Birmingham performances.

Graded Pieces for Violin and Piano

In his Op. 144, Graded Pieces for Violin and Piano, Rubbra provided material for the Guildhall School's examinations that is similar in purpose to the Graded Pieces for Piano, Op. 139, written for the same institution. Here, there are five titles: 'Swinging', 'Strolling', 'Riding', 'Gliding' and 'Striding'. In each case the titles are, to some degree, descriptive of the principal musical figures. The grades represented by the pieces are, respectively, Introductory; Preliminary; Grades 1, 3 and 4.

The materials in these pieces are both interesting and challenging, something we have found to be true in all of the composer's pieces designed for students. The amount and quality of dissonance introduced in some of them is rather surprising, but this is all to the good as students are thereby exposed to contemporary idioms while they are yet young.

Harmonically, the most interesting titles are 'Strolling' and 'Striding'. In the first of these, the violin part is unmistakably in D minor, although the single B is natural (the piece has no key signature). The piano part, however, while certainly not bitonal, is ambiguous. The right hand consists almost entirely of ascending and descending chains of thirds which, except for a central C major portion, are clearly in D minor. The ambiguity arises from the open fifths, G-D, that are present in the left hand under the thirds. The uncertainty disappears when the fifths gravitate to the dominant of D minor, and then to C-G in support of the C major section. The piece returns to a more sharply defined D minor and, except for a very momentary shift to F major, this is solidly confirmed at the end.

'Striding', the last of the five pieces and therefore the most difficult, immediately tests the violin student's intonation with three successive, upward leaps of a major seventh in the first three measures: A-G sharp; G natural-F sharp; F natural-E. In the event that the student was not entirely successful with these, there is another opportunity to prove oneself with the same intervals at the end of the piece. Between these passages there are several similar leaps, but they are isolated. Following all the instances in which leaps are involved, the student is seemingly given the chance to regain composure, and to correct any faulty intonations in simple, scale-wise passages, but even here one is not on completely solid ground. The reason is that the piano accompaniment is just as uncompromising under the scale-wise passages as it is beneath the leaps, perhaps more so. It really offers almost nothing in the way of encouragement, and a perusal of the score will show the clashes between the instrumental parts. It is these that severely test the student's intonational capabilities. Yet these difficulties serve a far larger purpose than merely testing one facet of the student's technique. They end by encouraging and developing one's overall musicianship, which is, of course, their prime purpose. The student must recognize that in this particular piece the melodic line as a whole is the important thing, not the individual interval. Next, the student must grasp the relationship between the melodic line and the accompaniment, and then by placing both in proper perspective, will have understood the piece and what it is trying to teach. Would that all teaching pieces everywhere, for whatever instruments and for whatever grade were written with the specific goal in mind of producing really musical performers.

String Quartet No. 4

Rubbra's last string quartet, Op. 150, was composed in 1977, and first performed on 27 November of that year at the Sheldonian Theatre, Oxford, by the Amici Quartet. Although the composer, Robert Simpson, was the dedicatee, the score bears the following inscription: 'In Memoriam Bennett Tarshish 1940–1972'. Tarshish was a 'young American whose passionate advocacy of Rubbra's music brought a decidedly English flavour to his Californian radio series'.[66] (For further remarks see Chapter 1, p.25).

The Quartet, like the Second Trio, is in two movements of which the first is divided into two distinct parts: *Andante moderato, ma liberamente* and *Allegretto scherzando*. In the score these sections are designated I(a) and I(b), labels we shall retain throughout the forthcoming discussion. There is no break between them. The second movement, an *Adagio*, is that part of the Quartet obviously intended as the elegy for Tarshish. The *scherzando*'s position between an essentially slow section and a slower movement preserves Rubbra's familiar three-movement plan.

As in many of the composer's works, there is an organizing interval – in this instance the seventh, both major and minor – yet the organization is not nearly so obvious as it is in earlier works, for the melodic seventh is employed only sparingly. Block harmonies made up of superimposed sevenths whose initial notes are B-C between the violins, and D-E between the viola and cello, open the Quartet (Example 202). Perhaps the large number of sevenths and the resulting dissonances is the reason the passage extends no farther than the seventh measure, but a more probable explanation is that the first violin's melody in those measures provides all of the basic material for section I(a).

That the composer regarded the first twenty-nine measures as introductory seems to be borne out, first, by the manner in which his basic material is soon

Ex. 202

I (a)

broken up and disseminated among the instruments. While this dismantling process is going on, the listener is aware only of a mass of sound from which nothing very definite is emerging. Second, this largely undifferentiated sound eventually coalesces into something more definite. Third, an *allargando* and *subito piano*, as well as a hardly perceptible cessation of sound, introduce a *Poco meno mosso* section with a recognizable theme. This theme is an amalgam of figures and intervals heard during the introduction, and, in turn, these

Ex. 203

can be traced to the dissonant measures shown above. The theme (Example 203) is stated in its entirety only once more (measures 98–100), but two partial statements are heard – the first in the second violin and viola (measures 49–50), the second in the form of an inversion in the cello (measures 51–2).

A second theme, easily identifiable by its falling fifths, and given out by the first violin, occupies measures 63–6, where a series of double-stopped sevenths in both lower parts forms a rather forbidding accompaniment. Its material is also derived from the introduction. This entry is soon followed by a partial repetition, also in the first violin, and then by a complete second-violin state-ment, and one further partial entry in the first violin. This close round has produced an essentially imitative texture. An expressive feature is introduced by the second violin prior to its second-theme statement: a tremolo passage just over seven measures in length. It consists largely of ascending and descending fourths. A second tremolo passage in the same part adds a sense of drama just before the introduction of I(b), the *Allegretto scherzando*.

This second part of the first movement has a flowing principal theme, whose several members are so akin to Gregorian chant that I confidently expected the composer to supply me with information as to their source. Furthermore, in view of the Quartet's origins, it seemed reasonable to suppose that some parts of I(a) might be related to Jewish chant. A nice theory, to which Rubbra responded in a letter of 12 August 1983, 'Sorry to disillusion you about those chants. Not guilty!'

The chant-like theme appears as Example 204, where its members are indi-cated by brackets. While all of these segments are ideally suitable for some sort

Ex. 204

of development, the composer has reserved this treatment for a short middle section only, electing in the outer sections to preserve their contours, or to alter them only very slightly.

Providing an exciting background to the segments are rather long *pizzicato* passages in the second violin and the two lower strings. Since the dynamic level much of the time is *mezzo forte* and *forte*, and in one passage the two lower strings are double stopped, the *pizzicato* portions are energetic and forceful. The materials comprising the *pizzicato* passages have been borrowed from the chant-like theme, and reduced to smaller figures that are repeated many times. In an especially ingenious touch Rubbra has the *pizzicato* cello part playing the mirror image of the viola's line, although not during the entire passage. There are two short *pizzicato* passages also involving mirror images, the first scored for the violins, the other for the second violin and viola. This latter passage helps to bring the first section of I(b) to a *fortissimo* and abrupt conclusion.

The short middle section that follows this sudden stop is marked *Cantabile e grazioso*, and its material is *derived* from the theme instead of *being* either the full theme or one or more of its unaltered segments. Thus this middle section functions as an informal trio in the context of scherzo-trio-scherzo, a role I believe the composer intended.

The concluding section is very different from its counterpart at the beginning of I(b) in terms of scoring and distribution of the returning melody and its parts, but it is not so different as to cause any disorientation. When the whole of I(b) has been heard and assimilated, the impression of having heard a central trio remains. The sense of uninhibited joviality and high spirits is very strong in I(b), but it is completely cancelled by the elegiac *Adagio e con molto espressione* of the second and final movement (see Example 205).

Ex. 205

There are two figures in this movement, the one heard first being of greater frequency and importance than the second. Neither is the source of a true theme, although the first statement of the first figure does give rise to a promising pattern of notes that sounds as though it might expand into a full-fledged theme. Not only is there no theme, but the note pattern itself does not return and most future patterns also disappear after one hearing. It is the first figure – *x* – that remains in the memory rather than the varied material that follows it. I believe the composer intended this, for the figure is widely distributed throughout much of the movement, being heard sixteen times altogether. In sharp contrast, the second figure (*y* in Example 205) has a more rounded and thus more restful contour which balances the angularity of *x*. It has seven statements, and is heavily concentrated in all four parts over an eight-measure span in the first third of the movement.

The final impression one receives from this elegy is a kind of frustration with the fact that no theme emerges. This, I feel, is what Rubbra was attempting to convey here: some idea in music of the brevity of Bennett Tarshish's life. What better way than to inhibit the formation of a full-length theme? Figures *x* and *y*, particularly the former, suggest the incompleteness in a very tangible way. Yet the movement never seems anything but natural; the materials that grow out of the figures are improvisatory in essence, but always in the background there is the haunting sound and memory of figure *x* to suggest brevity and mortality.

Fantasia on a Chord

Fantasia on a Chord, Op. 154, is Rubbra's last recorder work. Scored for treble recorder and harpsichord with an *ad lib* part for viola da gamba, it was written in 1977 to celebrate the tenth wedding anniversary of a couple known to the composer. The husband expressed fascination with this particular chord, and asked Rubbra to compose a piece based on it. The chord appears at the head of the score, and is reproduced above. The work was first performed at the Wigmore Hall, London, in March 1978 by Carl Dolmetsch, his daughter, Marguerite, and Joseph Saxby.

It almost goes without saying that a piece which concentrates on one particular entity such as a chord must, of necessity, be short so as to avoid monotony. Hence, Rubbra has restricted his Fantasia to just forty-six measures. In them, however, he is exceedingly generous with the appearances of his chord, as well as the uses to which it is put. It is first exposed, quite naturally, in the opening measure where all of its notes except the F natural are rolled out consecutively. On the last half beat in the 3/2 metre, the entire chord is rolled under the recorder's first note, F. Variants of this rolling out continue until, in measure 9, the chord is sounded vertically three times, but with an added A sharp in the right-hand part. More rolled-out variants are heard, and then in measures 16–22 only the three bottom notes are employed in an accompanimental capacity. The chord disappears entirely during the next ten measures, reappearing in time for the first ending, which takes us back to the fourth measure. From the second ending at measure 36 through 44 the chord is rolled out and vertically structured. For the latter statements, Rubbra has placed the D at the bottom as an anchor tone, but in the final measures F sharp major is firmly established as the piece comes to a quiet ending.

The fluid and improvisatory recorder part contains no melodic reference of any kind to the chord, and it is as though the latter never existed. Aside from the repetitions of one or two short phrases the part is through-composed. The *ad lib* viola da gamba part borrows from the recorder line, and from both the right- and left-hand harpsichord parts.

In sum, the chord merely provides the framework – albeit a significant and impressive one – for the recorder's often searching but always interesting line, and the dissonances inherent in the chord provide an ever-changing harmonic background.

Duo for Cor Anglais and Piano

Rubbra's last chamber work, Duo for Cor Anglais and Piano, Op. 156, was commissioned by the Dutch oboeist, Peter Bree, concerning whom the following intriguing account appeared in the press the day of the first performance (January 1982). Entitled 'Con brio', it tells us that

> on his last visit to England in 1979 [Bree] commissioned composer Edmund Rubbra to write a piece for him but found when it was delivered that he couldn't afford to pay for it. So he asked the Arts Council if they would like to find the £600 for him, even though he wasn't English. After some demur, the Arts Council paid up.
>
> Next, Bree invited the Queen Mother to come and hear him play the piece at the Wigmore Hall. She was otherwise engaged. Nothing daunted, Bree asked if she would like a copy of the record in view of the fact that she liked Rubbra's music. Yesterday saw Bree and his pianist Paul Komen present the record in question over a glass of sherry at Windsor.[67]

Over a series of large, mildly dissonant chords the cor anglais unfolds a very free and unstructured melody, none of whose members ever merge into a theme. The same is true of the piano part. In the final analysis, the piece appears to be about a cor anglais part whose goal is to show the instrument's capabilities by exploiting range, phrasing and dynamics, and piano sonorities, many of which are impressive. But, of course, it is the combining of these two elements that is the important thing, and this is done with Rubbra's usual skill and attention to details. The carefully placed expression marks in both parts ensure a balance that is never compromised by the dominance of one instrument over the other.

This well-written piece deserves the attention of cor anglais performers everywhere who may (and should) be on the lookout for worthwhile additions to the instrument's virtually non-existent repertoire outside the usual celebrated orchestral passages. Audiences too would benefit from the opportunity to become more familiar with the beautiful sounds of this instrument.

Notes

1   Percy A. Scholes, *The Oxford Companion To Music*, 9th edn (London: Oxford University Press, 1955), p.792.

2   Cobbett's *Cyclopedic Survey of Chamber Music*, 2nd edn (London: Oxford University Press, 1963), vol. 2, p.308.

3   Unsigned article, 'The Younger English Composers', *MMR*, February 1929, p.39.

4   Ivor Keys, *M&L* 31, no. 4, October 1951, p.395.

5   Harold Truscott, 'The Chamber Music', *Edmund Rubbra: Composer*, p.56.

6   *ibid.*

7   Kenneth Avery, *M&L* 28, no. 3, July 1947, p.292.

8   Printed on the inside of the front cover of *Edmund Rubbra: Composer*.

9   *ibid.* An interesting point concerns the discrepancy between these two reviews, this one telling us that the Sonata 'is modern in idiom', while the first one speaks of the composer's non-use of the modern idiom. Rubbra must have been puzzled by these diametrically opposed statements, perhaps even amused by them.

10   W. McNaught, *MT*, June 1947, p.196.

11   Eric Blom, *M&L* 19, no. 2, April 1938, p.233.

12   McNaught, *MT*, June 1947, p.196. It would seem that the reason why much of the Sonata fails to represent 'Rubbra as we known him' is because McNaught's review appeared in 1947, and the Sonata dates from 1932. It seems hardly fair to criticize an early work for failing to measure up to the music for which the composer was known fifteen years later.

13   Marion M. Scott, *MT*, January 1938, pp.58–9.

14   F.B., *MT*, February 1938, p.119.

15   Blom, *op. cit.*, p.233.

16   Unsigned review, quoted in *Edmund Rubbra: Composer*, p.62.

17   Truscott, *op. cit.*, pp.63–4.

18   Ernest Chapman, *Tempo*, no. 2, New Series, December 1946, p.23.

19   W.R. Anderson, *MT*, February 1947, p.64.

20   Ivor Keys, *M&L* 29, no. 1, January 1948, pp.111–12.

21   Edmund Rubbra, *Counterpoint: A Survey*, pp.50–51. Rubbra incorporated the example from Variation II in his 'Essay in Autobiography', (Chapter 1, p.4) to illustrate the 'topsy-turvydom' experienced in his childhood.

22   Edward Lockspeiser, *M&L* 29, no. 1, January 1948, p.112.

23   Ernest Chapman, *Tempo*, no. 18, New Series, March 1947, p.25.

24   Arthur Hutchings, *Musical Opinion*, n.d.

25   Arthur Hutchings, 'Music in Britain 1916–1960', *New Oxford History of Music* (London: Oxford University Press, 1974), p.535.

26   Edgar Hunt, *The Recorder and Its Music* (New York: W.W. Norton & Co., Inc., 1963), p.146.

27   F.B., *MT*, March 1950, p.100.

28   Colin Mason, *MT*, December 1950, pp.482–3. This review followed the first London performance of the work, given by the Rubbra-Gruenberg-Pleeth Trio on 5 November 1950.

29   Ivor Keys, *M&L* 32, no. 1, January 1951, p.92.

30   J.O.C., *MT*, August 1950, p.317.

31   Paul Hamburger, 'Cheltenham Festival (Second Week: July 10th–15th)', *Music Survey* 3, no. 2, December 1950, p.121.

32   Rubbra's programme notes for the first performance on 11 May 1952.

33   Lester Trimble, Review of Record London LL 1550, Griller Quartet, *MQ* 44, no. 4, October 1958, p.555.

34   H.J., *M&L* 34, no. 2, April 1953, pp.177–8.

35   Richard Capell, *MMR*, June 1952, p.130.

36   Donald Mitchell, *MT*, April 1955, p.210.

37   *ibid.*

38   Colin Mason, *MT*, August 1957, p.431.

39   R.H., *MT*, December 1958, p.672.
40   Edmund Rubbra, 'String Quartet No. 3 (Op.112)', *Musical Events*, July 1964, p.8.
41   Hugh Ottaway, 'Edmund Rubbra and His Recent Works', *MT*, September 1966, p.766.
42   Stanley Sadie, *MT*, September 1964, p.673.
43   Ottaway, *op. cit.*, p.765.
44   *ibid.*, p.766.
45   Rubbra, *op. cit.*, p.8.
46   Truscott, *op. cit.*, p.67.
47   Rubbra, *op. cit.*, p.9.
48   *ibid.*
49   *ibid.*
50   *ibid.*
51   *ibid.*
52   *ibid.*
53   *ibid.*
54   *ibid.*
55   *ibid.*
56   Alan Blyth, *MT*, June 1969, p.652.
57   Edmund Rubbra, programme notes for the first performance of the Sonatina for Treble Recorder and Harpsichord.
58   Gustave Reese, *Music In The Renaissance*, rev. edn, p.612.
59   Rubbra, programme notes for the first performance of the Sonatina for Treble Recorder and Harpsichord.
60   *ibid.*
61   *ibid.*
62   Edgar Gordon, *MT*, November 1967, p.1033.
63   Truscott, *op. cit.*, p.69.
64   Michael Waite, *M&L* 52, no. 1, January 1971, p.103.
65   'Spinning-out' is a legitimate expression for this kind of writing. First introduced in German musicology, where the word for it is *Fortspinnung*, it denotes a continuous unfolding and expansion of melodic elements in a spontaneous flow.
66   Lewis Foreman, *Tempo*, no. 124, March 1978, p.28.
67   Unnamed and undated (except for January 1982) newspaper item.

9 The choral music

Rubbra's primary reputation as a composer of symphonies has tended to obscure the fact that he has written fifty-nine published choral works, which, beginning with Op. 3 in 1924 and ending with Op. 164 in 1984, extend throughout his creative life. The list grows more impressive with the realization that some of these works consist of from two to five separate pieces (for example, Five Motets, Op. 37). Of the fifty-nine works, thirty-eight are unaccompanied while the remaining twenty-one are scored for accompaniments of various kinds: piano, organ, small chamber groups, and orchestras of differing sizes. It should by no means be inferred that the unaccompanied works are necessarily shorter, simpler in style, or less difficult to perform than the accompanied ones. Quite the contrary, for some of the former are long, and present tremendous intonational problems, especially those in which the tonality is ambiguous and the style dissonant. The *Te Deum* for eight-part choir, Op. 115, is a good example.

Rubbra's choice of texts demonstrates a wide and discriminating knowledge of literature – a fact confirmed by even a cursory look at the shelves of his study. His special interest in religious and philosophical texts is apparent in forty-two of the fifty-nine works. Most obvious are the Mass settings, various other Catholic liturgical texts and hymns, and passages from the Old and New Testaments, but there are also texts that range from Alcuin of York through such metaphysical poets as St John of the Cross, Donne and Vaughan, to Gerard Manley Hopkins. Various others of the same persuasion supplied other texts.

Several small choral works and three larger, unpublished ones precede the important Five Motets of Op. 37. The first of the small pieces is *Dormi Jesu*, Op. 3, no. 1, also known as *The Virgin's Cradle Hymn*. It is an unaccompanied 'setting of Latin words copied by S.T. Coleridge from a print found in a German village, dating from 1924 when I was finishing my studies under Holst... it was the first piece of mine to be published.'[1] Next come three pieces on Scottish texts: *Afton Water*, Op. 6, an *a cappella* setting of three of the six verses of Robert Burn's poem of the same name; *Dear Liza*, Op. 7, for two voices and piano; and *My Tocher's the Jewel*, Op. 10, a five-part *a cappella* arrangement of a Scottish folksong, set to a dialect poem of Burns. For the second of these pieces, the text and music were collected from Scottish sources by Hugh Mackay, and the third piece is dedicated to him. (Mackay will be remembered as one of the principals in the Arts League of Service Travelling Theatre.) The last of the small pieces is a unison carol on an anonymous text for children's voices and piano, called *To Him We Sing*, Op. 34. While all of these works are charming and well-written, they contain no particularly outstanding characteristics.

The three larger works, all in manuscript because the composer considers them unworthy of publication, are significant mainly for their texts, all of which are highly imaginative, and point towards the religious and mystical texts of the later works. The first of these is *The Secret Hymnody*, Op. 1, scored for SAATBB and an orchestra of strings, harp, celesta, timpani, percussion and organ. Its text, translated from the *Hymn to Hermes* by the theosophist, G.R.S. Mead, is of Gnostic origin. It was performed at Reading University. The second work, *La Belle Dame Sans Merci*, Op. 12, is a setting of Keats's poem, and is scored for SATB and small orchestra. Its first performance took place at Morley College, but it was also sung at St Martin-in-the-Fields, and Newcastle-upon-Tyne under the direction of Dr W.G. Whittaker. *The Mystic Trumpeter*, on the poem by Walt Whitman, is for SSAATTBB and orchestra. Of these unpublished works, it is the most substantial and Elsie Payne's description of it merits inclusion here:

> The melodies do not by any means follow the words closely: neither is their meaning made particularly clear, for the counterpoint often confuses the words. The work indeed is virtually an independent one – one which might probably more successfully have been scored for instruments alone. The main theme, above all (a kind of 'trumpeter motif') is instrumentally conceived, and has no connection, even rhyth-mically, with any of the words. It is a rhapsodic stretch of melody which has an important role: it permeates a great deal of the first part, it is reiterated in the accompanying texture of the second part, and is recapitulated at the end of the third part, thus serving as a unifying agent in what is otherwise a disjointed, sectional form. The work is in this respect an early example of what has come to be one of Rubbra's characteristic methods of forging shape out of free, quais-improvisatory musical material.[2]

Five Motets

Rubbra's first important choral work, the Five Motets for Unaccompanied Choir, Op. 37, was composed in 1934. In an article on his choral music the composer writes that in these motets

> the use of choral forces became assured and at the same time outward-searching in harmony. This is particularly so in the third motet, *Hymne to God the Father* (Donne), where the choral dissonances foreshadow those in *The Dark Night of the Soul*.[3]

From the textual viewpoint, the Five Motets present a unified front with respect to the poets, all of whom were contemporaneous with one another. Besides Donne, the other poets represented are Robert Herrick (no. 1), Henry Vaughan (nos 2 and 4), and Richard Crashaw (no. 5). All are noted for their religious and mystical texts, and Rubbra's interest in them is apparent from his remark that 'my general reading then was going back to the metaphysical poets'.[4] There is a notable kinship in spirit among the texts, even though there is diversity in their subject matter. However, this unity does not always extend to the musical treatment. None of the motets has a key signature, and in each of them the unit of metrical value is the half-note.

The text of the first motet, *Eternitie*, is by Herrick (1591–1674), a poet perhaps more widely known for his light love lyrics, but also, as here, the author of many poems expressing religious intensity. There are three stanzas, the first of which reads: 'O yeares! and Age! Farewell:/Behold I go, /Where I do know/ Infinitie to dwell.' Rubbra's 3/2 setting is for SSAATTBB, and represents a balance between chromatic polyphony and block chordal style. The polyphonic passages are restricted to lines 2–4 of the first stanza and line 1 of the second stanza. The different motive assigned to each of these lines is reminiscent of the points of imitation technique of the Renaissance motet composers with whom Rubbra had far more than merely a nodding acquaintance. But whereas these composers often extended the practice to the entire motet, Rubbra here limits it not just to the lines cited, but fails to carry the imitative entries throughout all parts in his setting of line 1, stanza 2. Still another resemblance to Renaissance practice comes to light in the balance, noted above, between polyphony and chordal style, for lines 2–4 of the second stanza are chordal. However, the motet is thoroughly of the twentieth century by virtue of the dissonances created through the interaction of the polyphonic lines.

Interwoven through the polyphonic passages and the texts to which they are set the word 'farewell' appears and reappears, but in no particular order with regard to parts. This textual liberty is rather striking, particularly at those points where the word is set to a rising fifth, fourth, or even third, for the mostly *pianissimo* level in combination with the intervallic structure suggests a distant bell. The word is also set to a descending, chromatic scale segment. After the last line of the poem – 'Drown'd in one endlesse Day' – the repeated 'farewells' finish the motet. The final one, sung by the sopranos and first altos above sustained notes in the remaining parts, is marked *ppp*, and enclosed in a bracket, the purpose of which is made clear in the note at the bottom of the score: 'if possible a semi-chorus, while other sopranos and altos sustain G.'

The second motet, *Vain Wits and Eyes* to a poem by Vaughan (1622–95) and scored for two SATB choirs, is a contrapuntal *tour de force*. Choir 1 begins the proceedings by establishing in the first measure two canons at the octave, the first between soprano and tenor, the second between alto and bass. Each pair is two beats apart, but only one beat separates each of the four entries. Starting with the second measure Choir 2 does exactly the same. Thus the corresponding parts of each choir are also in canon a measure apart. That the composer was not really satisfied with this procedure is clearly evident from the following passage:

melodic overloading clogs the texture when, in a canon of more than three parts, the leading voice is always purely melodic. This I found to my cost when in 1934, after having set some words by Henry Vaughan for four-part choir with two strict canons, tenor echoing soprano and bass echoing alto, I discovered by accident that a second choir singing the same music as the first choir, but a bar later, fitted perfectly, i.e. there were now two different four-voice canons (called canon 8 in 2):

Ex. 206

The excitement of this discovery overruled the purely musical aspect and resulted in a choral sound, the individual parts of which were indistinguishable.[5]

With the exception of some very minor adjustments, both choirs continue in the fashion described above until just past the halfway point. From there to the end two new canons, also at the octave, appear in Choir 2, the first between altos and basses, the second between sopranos and tenors. Choir 1, meanwhile, continues its two canons for the third time, but the centre of interest has shifted to Choir 2, whose second canon completely dominates by virtue of its high *tessitura*. At the concluding *allargando* all of the canons are resolved in preparation for the final cadence where the Choir 2 sopranos sing a high B flat and C before joining the Choir 1 sopranos on an A.

Three notable attributes in this motet are its rhythmic drive, created by a combination of its relentless quarter-note movement and its tempo ($\downarrow$ = 84 circa); the feeling of massiveness produced by eight parts in strict canonic combinations; and its extraordinarily simple tonal scheme: the entire motet is an expression of the D minor natural scale, although an occasional B natural is heard. The interaction of these three elements has produced an emotional intensity that well matches that of the words.

From the viewpoint of the poetic content Motet 3 could qualify as the central panel of a balanced, five-part design. Its text, *A Hymn to God the Father* by Donne (1573–1631), is the most deeply personal of all the poems. It is flanked on either side by visionary and essentially impersonal poems by Vaughan, while the poems to which the first and fifth motets are set fall somewhere between these types, although Crashaw's text for the fifth motet is the most sensuous of all. This interesting theory regarding a five-part design breaks down, however, when the musical treatment is considered. In the first place, the choral forces are diminished in size after the eight parts of Motets 1 and 2, becoming SSAATB for no. 3, SATB for no. 4, and SAB for no. 5. Also, while a parallel can be drawn between nos 2 and 4 in that both are canonic, the technical manipulation in no. 4 is simple compared with the phenomenal no. 2.

Returning now to the third motet: its first two stanzas are set to the same music, differing textual details accounting for minor rhythmic alterations. The third and final stanza is set to completely new music, although the rhythm is similar. The texture throughout the motet is block-chordal, but the dissonances which are so important a part of the fabric all result from the horizontal movement of the individual voice parts, each of which is a distinct melodic entity. Thus the whole is the sum of its parts. The harmony of the third stanza is centred on A flat minor, a startling and very effective change from the D minor of the preceding stanzas (a more modal D minor because of the total absence of C sharps). The texture in the third stanza is more chromatic – most probably a reflection of the 'sinne of feare, that when I have spunne/My last thred, I shall perish on the shore.' Following another abrupt harmonic shift to a general feeling of D minor, the motet ends with four *fermata*-marked chords, undoubtedly meant to emphasize 'I feare no more.' This technique, first noted in the motets of the fifteenth century (Arnold de Lantins, Dufay, Josquin and others) is employed here for the same reason as it was in the motets of these composers: to highlight particularly important words, names, or ideas. The line which opens the third stanza (see above) is reproduced in Example 207. The dissonances will surprise those who think of Rubbra as being not quite twentieth century.

Ex. 207

Note particularly the dissonance on 'feare' – a fine example of contemporary word-painting. (In order to conserve space, the summary of the voice parts as provided in the 'for rehearsal only' or actual accompaniments will be used throughout this chapter whenever it is practicable.)

Motet no. 4 to Vaughan's *The Search* marks a return to polyphony, but with none of the technical display that tended to divert one's attention from the substance of *Vain Wits and Eyes*. The polyphony is chromatic and of a greater intensity than that found in *Eternitie*. In fact, assuming that the motets were composed in chronological order, *The Search* demonstrates a greater skill in text-setting than do any of the preceding motets, even though, as noted above, its text is impersonal, perhaps even obscure. The vocal lines are longer, and with their rise and fall, altogether more plastic. The canonic imitation with which the motet begins soon ceases, giving way to free imitation. Later, there is a short chordal section. Throughout the motet there is a swelling and thinning of parts as the basic four parts increase to five and six, and then revert to four. Perhaps the most expressive section is found on the last page, where the text reads, 'Search well another world; who studies this,/Travels in clouds, seeks manna where none is.' The effect of the long conjunct lines remains in the memory as the sopranos begin a slow climb and divide, the upper part finishing on a high B flat.

The final motet, *A Song*, to words by Crashaw (1613?–49), carries forward the same liberating process of long-breathed lines and carefully moulded rhythms. There is a fine balance between chordal and polyphonic styles. The latter includes two passages in canon between soprano and alto, while the bass pursues its independent course. The second of these passages is a note-for-note transposition of the first a half-step higher. The final line, 'Dead to my selfe, I live in Thee', has a lifeless quality, enhanced by the empty fifths and the *pianissimo*.

The Five Motets were first performed at a BBC Contemporary Music Concert on 3 April 1936. One reviewer's estimate reads as follows:

> A sameness of atmosphere was due not only to the uniformly mystical character of the texts but also to the composer's attitude towards them. Sincere, dignified, even sombre at times, these skilful settings revealed a deep appreciation of the words and paid them logical tribute.... What one missed was rather a movement, a line of thought, a development dictated less by the detailed inflection of the words than by the inexorable logic of the music itself.[6]

A much lengthier and more detailed review was penned by Eric Blom:

> A choral technique influenced partly by the Tudor madrigalists and partly by Holst makes of these compositions in four [actually three] to eight parts a remarkable new flowering of unaccompanied English vocal music, for a distinct and striking new personality expresses itself in them with force, conviction and originality. Whether the composer writes vertically in chords, as in Herrick's 'Eternitie' and Donne's 'Hymn to God the Father', or horizontally in elaborate polyphony, as in 'Vain Wits and Eyes' and 'The Search', or both combined, as in Crashaw's song, 'Lord, when the sense of Thy sweet grace', he achieves a burning, mystical beauty while he

impresses one by a sometimes almost alarming contrapuntal skill. He can use ways and means that are beyond most contemporary composers, who have more contrivance than craft and can do more with colour than with line. 'Vain Wits and Eyes' is, until about halfway through, not only a double canon for four voices, but the whole fabric is repeated by a second choir at a bar's distance. It must be confessed that to the eye and at the keyboard the effort gives itself away in a certain crabbedness; but this is no doubt much attenuated when the tone-colour of different voices gives perspective to the intricate texture, and it must be said that Mr. Rubbra can write quite simply when it suits him, as in the exquisite Crashaw setting, though never without distinction.[7]

Finally, there are these words:

The composer brings to these settings... something of the austerity and integrity of his master, Holst. Such devices as contrapuntal imitation and enharmonic changes are introduced only to give emphasis to the texts, and often elaboration is swept aside in favour of simple recitation. The directness of expression and sensitiveness to the poets' moods should commend these works to those who are bold enough to tackle their difficulties.[8]

The Dark Night of the Soul

Rubbra's next choral work, Op. 41, no. 1, is a setting of *The Dark Night of the Soul* by St John of the Cross (1542–91). This Spanish mystic, who was one year younger than El Greco, was born Juan de Yepes y Alvarez, but changed his name to Juan de la Cruz when, in 1563, he entered the Carmelite Order, and promoted the Carmelite reforms of St Teresa of Avila. Running afoul of the anti-reformists, he was imprisoned in 1577 at Toledo until his escape nine months later. While he was jailed he wrote some of his greatest mystical poems including, possibly, the poem which is the subject of this work. He and El Greco, whom he may have met during his imprisonment, have much in common, for each man recorded mystical experiences in his respective medium.

Concerning the poem, Rubbra tells us that

in the collected edition of St. John of the Cross's writings, the Saint's commentary on his own poem occupies about one hundred pages: even then, only three of its eight stanzas are dealt with. The poem is a potent condensation of spiritual experiences, and its opening lines... point to the use of a symbolism that, although rooted in everyday experiences, can, by exposition be relevant to the most intense, spiritual longings. I hesitated for a long time before attempting to set a poem packed with such inner meaning. Also, I felt I had to wait until my musical language was sufficiently wide to reveal something of the poem's intensity and yet remain at a subjective level.[9]

In view of the frequency with which the words 'mystical' and 'mysticism' are applied to Rubbra in terms of his thought and his role as a composer, it seems appropriate to try to understand what is meant by them. Accordingly, we begin with a standard encyclopedia definition:

Mysticism in religion and philosophy means the doctrine that God cannot be rightly apprehended by any ordinary process of knowledge, but only by an immediate intuition that transcends knowledge – an ecstatic vision or communion in which man becomes one with the Divine Being.[10]

A second definition also employs the key word 'immediate' in reference to an experience, and goes on to say that 'it is a state of insight – not derived through the mind at all – but a state which is completely illuminating, convincing and satisfying to the feelings.'[11]

The intense mysticism of both St John of the Cross and St Teresa of Avila often spoke of divine love as a flame or arrow that pierces the heart or wounds the soul, and this concept is expressed physically and to perfection in Bernini's unforgettable sculpture, *The Ecstasy of St Teresa*, above the altar in the Cornaro Chapel of Rome's Santa Maria della Vittoria. In one of his most memorable poems, *The Living Flame of Love*, St John writes, 'O burn that searest never! / O wound of deep delight.'

The important question that now arises is how mysticism is expressed or translated into musical works. It may seem fatuous to attempt an answer to this question, for it is obvious that we are dealing with a very slippery and elusive subject. Nevertheless, it is appropriate to make the attempt when one is dealing with composers to whom the word 'mystical' is regularly applied. The late works of Franck, practically all of Bruckner's music, certain works of Vaughan Williams, much of Messiaen's music, and many Rubbra works fall into this category. As a basic premise on which to build, I quote Elsie Payne on the subject:

> The term 'mystical' is so often – and aptly – applied to Rubbra's music, that it perhaps needs some definition here. It is most probably true to say that what most people mean by a mystical experience is an experience of reality that is direct, an end in itself. One need not discuss here the nature of reality – how far the experience of reality is a natural one, how far a supernatural one, or again how it may be evoked. All that matters in this connection is that it is some sort of sudden illumination. It never comes as the result of deliberation, nor does it lead to explanations or to any kind of practical activity, but only to itself. It is, in all, an experience to be enjoyed, not necessarily to be understood or explained. So-called mystical music cannot be sharply separated from any other music. For all good music is, to some extent, the expression of reality, all equally, in a way, the denial of mysticism, since the very act of communication must destroy the complete self-sufficiency of a mystical experience. Nevertheless, that which is mystically inclined is in a sense differentiated from the rest in that it uses the data of music deliberately to symbolize the immediacy and completeness of a mystical experience and to suggest an atmosphere of other-worldliness.[12]

It would naturally appear that any specific techniques employed to accomplish this end vary from composer to composer, and from work to work. Thus any discussion of them must await the consideration of individual works in which they appear.

The Dark Night of the Soul, which occupied Rubbra intermittently from 1936 to 1942, is scored for SATB, a small orchestra consisting of strings, woodwinds, two horns, trumpet and timpani, plus a contralto soloist, who 'should be a member of the choir and should sing her solos without moving from her position in the choir. When possible, the choir should consist of about thirty voices.' The text is a scarcely-disguised love poem in which Lover and Beloved are united – an allegorical way of describing an ecstatic union of the soul with God. The translation exists in two versions – one rhymed, the other unrhymed, both by E. Allison Peers – and the composer has set the second of these. This is a fortunate choice, for the strophic divisions are not as obvious as those in the rhymed version, and the narrative is more spontaneous, giving rise to a freer musical structure than might otherwise have been the case. In fact, except for some very short, largely motivic passages, the chorus and solo parts are through-composed. This would seem to be a deliberate attempt to mirror the unpredictable nature of the mystical experience. Unity is achieved by the frequent use of

Ex. 208

an orchestral figure (Example 208) that often overlaps, but its differing pitches and numerous harmonic variants contribute to the impression that each passage is, again, a spontaneous response to the ecstatic events of the poem. Even the literal repetition of the material of the three opening measures (but in a quite different metrical context) just prior to the solo that concludes the piece cannot dispel that impression. The figure is employed only twice in the voice parts.

Certainly, one of the most obvious ways of suggesting a vague, mystical experience is through vague, chromatic harmonies that are not so dissonant as to call undue attention to themselves, and the greater part of the texture in this work is made up of such harmonies. There is no real sense of a key except during the first choral passage, which is undergirded by a sustained E pedal.

Rhythmically, the work is very flexible, like all of Rubbra's music. Frequent metrical changes; the simultaneous employment of 6/4 during one of the contralto solos and the immediately following choral passage, while 4/4 is the designated orchestral metre; and fluctuating tempi ('the tempi of this work are so fluid that the metronome markings are approximations only') work together to mirror the rhapsodic nature of the mystical experience.

In the vocal parts there are three canonic entries, each of which dissolves into free but related material. The first, in a semi-parlando style between sopranos and altos, follows the orchestral introduction, and is at the lower fifth to the words, 'On a dark night, kindled in love with yearnings – O, happy chance! I went forth without being observed, my house being now at rest.' The *pianissimo* Es in the orchestra – the pedal mentioned above – under the voices except for the unaccompanied conclusion of the passage, contribute to the suspense inherent in the words. The second canonic entry, above a restlessly heaving orchestral line, is paired: altos and sopranos, tenors and basses, with a tritone between each voice in the pair, and a semitone between pairs. The resulting ambiguity, bolstered by the dual metres, and the orchestra's independent material, amply matches the line, 'Without light or guide, save that which burned in my heart.' The third canon, separated from the second by an orchestral interlude, is also paired: sopranos and tenors, altos and basses, the distance between all parts being a fifth. Giving way to free imitation just before its high, climactic point, the passage is more tonally oriented, the purpose being to match the stability of 'This light guided me more surely than the light of noonday.' As a foil to these polyphonic passages, two unaccompanied chordal sections provide variety. With their rich and distinctive harmonies, the words to which they are set stand out in sharp relief. The second such passage, to the lines, 'With his gentle hand he wounded my neck/ And caused all my senses to be suspended', ends the choir's participation in the work. Upon its conclusion there is heard the 2/4 repetition of the first three measures of the orchestral introduction, referred to above. The dissonance which ends the latter (see Example 208) is here sustained through the remaining thirteen measures while the contralto soloist sings in a parlando style the final lines: 'I remained, lost in oblivion; / My face I reclined on the Beloved, / All ceased, and I abandoned myself, / Leaving my cares forgotten among the lilies.' The effect of the weaving solo line above this sharp but *pianissimo* discord is unforgettable.

Both of the reviews of *The Dark Night of the Soul* date from 1943. The first, by Eric Blom, was printed in January and is probably a report of the first performance, which, according to the composer 'took place twelve years or more after I wrote [the piece]'.[13] The time lapse can be explained if we recall that in the early 1940s Rubbra undertook the revision of the work (see p.19). However, his memory may be faulty here, for twelve years after 1936, the year in which the piece was begun, would be 1948, and reconciling this date with 1943 is an impossibility. It is not likely that either review would have been written unless the work had received a hearing, for both writers' notices read as if the music had been personally experienced in performance.

> The mystic words conjure up a sort of El Greco picture in words, and by some kind of divination that feeling is admirably caught by the music, which is sombre and strange, but never strident or angular. There may still be people who call any music ugly which introduces discordant clashes or false relations, but they must be firmly disregarded as being incapable of differentiating between the haphazard and the truly creative. This music may incidentally produce what we call ugly sounds: it is as a whole intensely and burningly beautiful. The vocal writing is elaborately contrapuntal, and the composer understands what true counterpoint means: not ingenious interlacing of material of any sort, but of music that has a high melodic value in every separate part to begin with. [14]

> A passionate, darkly coloured setting of words by St. John of the Cross.... The music admirably recaptures the fervent symbolism of the text. A small choir of thirty voices (including a solo contralto) is suggested. They should be expert enough to handle easily the subtle chromaticism of the choral writing. [15]

The composer regarded the work as a deeply personal creation, a conviction amply supported by his statement that 'its importance ... in the development of my music gives it a special hold on my affections, even if its significance is so subjective as not to communicate itself to others.' [16]

The Dark Night of the Soul is the first piece in what was planned as a triptych. Op. 41, no. 2, is *O Unwithered Eagle Void* which is unpublished. It is set to a text by Cecil Collins, a personal friend of the composer's, and a painter as well as a poet. According to Rubbra, Collins

> was also interested in the then unfashionable serial music of Schoenberg. The intensely subjective nature of the words – for Collins was, and is, a visionary, his paintings occupying a unique, almost Blake-like place in modern art – turned my thoughts to a serialist technique that remained, however, intuitive rather than calculated. The third work in the triptych was to have been a setting of a Latin poem by St. Thomas Aquinas, but this remains incomplete. [17]

Three Bird Songs

The next choral work, Three Bird Songs, Op. 46, was written for children's unison voices and piano. It is published as part of a series, *For the Nines to Twelves*, in which other composers are represented. Both the poems and Rubbra's settings are delightful. The first, 'Robin Redbreast', is slightly tinged with sadness as befits the poem, written by W.H. Davies, whose preference for simple things is well represented here. The setting is not as simple, however, as first meets the eye, for the voice part and the accompaniment go their separate ways. John Clare (1793–1864), the poet of 'Little Trotty Wagtail', second in the set, was, like Davies, poor, a jack-of-all-trades, and a poet of simple, rural conditions and pleasures. Each eventually achieved some fame for his poetry. The three stanzas of the Clare poem are treated strophically and the top line of the accompaniment follows strictly the vocal line. Warlock, incidentally, set the same text, also as a unison choral piece. 'Pigeon and Wren', the shortest of the three pieces, is set to an anonymous text, apparently from Gloucestershire. The wren's half of the piece is twice as fast as the pigeon's and is sure to delight the children who sing it. All three numbers are refreshing contributions to the literature for children's voices and I heartily recommend them to those who might be looking for fresh material.

Five Madrigals

Op. 51 is a set of five madrigals to words by Thomas Campion (1567–1620) who, besides his distinguished poetry, also composed four books of ayres, plus a fifth in which the ayres of Philip Rosseter also appeared, and the songs for five masques. Rubbra's madrigals are, of course, unaccompanied, and are scored for SATB; although the third one has an important solo soprano part, and short 'ay me' exclamations for solo tenor and bass.

It seems appropriate to introduce these pieces with Eric Blom's extended comments, and then to supplement his more general remarks concerning the individual numbers with detailed explanations:

> A modern composer who sets out to write madrigals to English words must, of course, be well versed in sixteenth-century counterpoint; but more than that is expected of him if he is not to turn out mere period imitations. He must be that rare phenomenon, a twentieth-century musician who expresses himself with natural ease through the medium of polyphony. Edmund Rubbra is such a musician. These madrigals are modern and personal, yet carry on throughout in a spontaneous flow of parts which shows that polyphonic thinking is the composer's gift, not a manner assumed for a certain purpose.
>
> The Elizabethan influence is, of course, evident, and very properly so in settings of Campion, who wrote these poems for songs to the lute, not madrigals, though one of them, 'When to her lute Corinna sings', was so set by Robert Jones (1607). Mr. Rubbra follows Jones so far as to divide the poem into two distinct halves and to introduce a new subject for polyphonic treatment where a new poetic idea arises; but while his texture can be as elaborate and at the same time as lucid as that of any Tudor madrigalist, his music has a new harmonic audacity and more spaciousness of phrasing, gained by avoidance of the old composers' much more frequent cadential points of repose.[18]

By 'harmonic audacity' Blom is referring to sevenths of various kinds, as well as other dissonances – all of which arise as the result of the continuous poly-phonic motion, some of which involves a crossing of parts. As for the new figures associated with new textual ideas, they are two in number, one at the beginning of each stanza. The first one returns in 3/4 metre instead of the original 4/4, and although its fourth note is different, the characteristic drop of a fourth and major second is enough to identify its origin. A thorough reading of the score will reveal a surprisingly large amount of imitative details not readily noticed after the principal figures have been introduced. Some of these details are overlooked because an imitative entry, having ceased its imitation of a prior part, will interpose a note or a short figure between the imitation and a segment which, heard earlier in another part, is now imitated. An example of this occurs directly after the beginning of the piece when the bass, at the distance of one measure and pitched an octave lower, imitates the tenor for two and a half measures. A long-held note intervenes, and the bass continues by imitating the altos' second phrase. The listener, realizing he has heard that phrase before, feels obliged to ascertain where. There are other examples of the same thing – proof that Rubbra's contrapuntal skills are not rigid or pedantic, but are there to serve his particular needs as these arise.

One point not mentioned in the review is the almost radical alterations in the tempi. From a beginning *con moto* ($\downarrow$ = 56) – not a metronome marking that many will associate with the stated tempo – that lasts through the first stanza, the first change comes in measure 18 where the second stanza begins; the metronome direction here is $\downarrow$ = 104, almost twice as fast. At measure 26, the tempo is increased to $\downarrow$ = 120. The reason for these changes is, of course, the text. Concurrently with the third tempo the sopranos and tenors reach their highest points: A sharp and B. However, when the mood shifts from joy to sorrow, a *rallentando* to the end matches the words. But as no new tempo is indicated, discretion must be used.

The second madrigal, *I Care Not for These Ladies*, has three stanzas in a strictly strophic form. The texture is chordal except at the end where there is a canonic segment between soprano and tenor. Cross-relations are also apparent here – measure 4, C sharp in the tenor, followed by C natural in the bass – plus three other equally prominent examples. Westrup calls this piece 'a ballet in the homophonic style on Morley's model – the outward shape and structure suggest the end of the sixteenth century but the treatment of the raw material is personal.'[19]

Ex. 209

Beauty Is But A Painted Hell, third in the series, is very expressive in a melancholy way. With its chromaticisms and 'ay me' interjections, it is reminiscent of the Italian rather than English madrigal. Note in Example 209 the simultaneous use of E and E flat, although admittedly the clash is extremely short-lived. Examples of non-simultaneous cross-relations are also present, as in measure 7. Note also the 'foreign' F minor chord (although it is not spelled as such) in the seventh measure between chords of D major and the A major dominant, which itself leads to a D minor chord. In terms of structure, the piece is a slightly modified strophic design.

No. 4, *It Fell On A Summer's Day*, is a sprightly piece that is so completely diatonic as to contain no tones outside of E flat major. It is also thoroughly contrapuntal to the degree that the alto part has separate stanzas set in long notes in the manner of a *cantus firmus*, while the other parts weave freely imitative countermelodies around it. The design is strophic, and there are eight stanzas in all – highly compressed – since the alto part has its four stanzas, and the remaining parts their four. But the listener is led to believe that four stanzas comprise the whole piece. The text is quite risqué, but with no words anywhere vertically aligned, the listener is not likely to follow this complete narrative in miniature. As though to underscore the hedonistic irresponsibility of the text, the madrigal is to be performed *Allegretto – senza espressione*.

Though You Are Young, the concluding piece in the set, is the most thoroughgoing in polyphonic terms. Each of its three stanzas is introduced by a point of imitation in the Renaissance motet – and, to a lesser extent in the madrigal, both Italian and English – tradition. However, unlike that tradition, the imitative passages continue well beyond the five or so notes that comprise the distinctive motive, for here the entire passage is imitated in the other parts, both strictly and freely. Like the Renaissance pieces, the motive that introduces the first line of each of the three stanzas here is sufficiently different for the listener to mark off the stanzas for himself. A particularly interesting detail concerns point-of-imitation no. 3 when, instead of following the initial three-note descent of the bass motive, the other three parts ascend.

Another interesting detail is Rubbra's employment of the symbol for *tempus perfectum*: O. Just why he did this instead of using 3/2 is unclear. The harmony throughout the madrigal is the result of the interaction of the polyphony and, naturally, there are abrupt changes in the harmonic direction that have nothing to do with Renaissance practice. Blom mentions the 'recondite' harmony, and then summarizes the set as a whole by calling it

ripe and beautiful in its effect, as well as a remarkable proof that modern harmonic resources are still compatible with polyphony without forcing it either into flagrant violations or into submission to rules only too likely to produce aridly academic writing.[20]

Two Madrigals

Two further madrigals to Campion texts make up Op. 52 and speaking generally, both are similar to those of Op. 51. The first, *Leave Prolonging Thy Dis-
tress*, is very expressive, particularly during the long chromatic line to which
'To her for mercy crying' is set. After hearing passages like this, as well as
others in the following madrigal, *So Sweet Is Thy Discourse*, it is with a certain
amount of astonishment that one reads this review:

> 'How gladly would one praise his compositions if only one could find in them one
> drop of blood!' Thus Brahms on the works of his adoring friend, Heinrich von
> Herzogenberg. To apply this criticism to Rubbra's work as a whole would be
> monstrously unfair, but there are occasions, as here, when his music seems more
> remarkable for exquisite craftsmanship than for any general emotional warmth.
> Admirably written from the technical standpoint, these madrigals somehow give the
> impression of having been conceived in a kind of mental refrigerator, resulting in
> music that, for all its virtues, remains
>   'Faultily faultless, splendidly null.'
> All the same, what lovely workmanship![21]

Another major review has this to say:

> The composer once more applies the Elizabethan technique to his own idiom, and
> with very happy results. These settings are not less ingenious than those of the first
> set, but they are on the whole more genial. The music flows along happily without
> any sense of effort, and though it calls for a good choir is beautifully singable.[22]

The author of the first review (probably Charles Wilfrid Orr, who achieved
some status as a song composer) should have been more discreet, for he may
not have been aware that the Italian and English madrigal belonged to a period
in music history when 'emotional warmth' was a by-product, not a goal; Gesualdo
was a notable exception to this. It therefore follows that if a composer like
Rubbra was basing his madrigals generally on Renaissance techniques (and
there appears to be no doubt that he was), he would have conformed to the
style, allowing, of course, for his own harmonic traits. Assuming that this
reviewer was the song-composer, one can understand his comments, for with
influences coming from Hugo Wolf and Delius, plus his settings of Housman
and Rossetti, he was thinking of 'emotional warmth' in terms of late Romanti-
cism.

A third reviewer proved to be the most discerning in his awareness of how
Rubbra applied techniques other than chromaticism to suggest textual meanings. These certainly fall under the heading of 'emotional warmth', but in a way
that is consistent with Renaissance models:

> 'Leave prolonging thy distress' is fittingly illustrated by successive entries in canon,
> and falling fifths mark each of the entries in 'So sweet is they discourse', as if the
> composer wished to colour the joyous mood of the poem with a suggestion of
> regret. All these procedures form a subtle technique of musical symbolism which
> the Elizabethans would have been the first to endorse.[23]

The Morning Watch

The Morning Watch, Op. 55, to Henry Vaughan's magnificent poem, is one of Rubbra's finest choral works. Its origins are described in Chapter 1. It opens with a lengthy orchestral introduction, marked 'Slow and spacious'. Over a steady, pulsating beat, the melodic intervals of a falling semitone and a rising minor third are joined to form a five-note figure, which is one of the dominant characteristics, not just in the introduction, but throughout the remainder of the orchestral accompaniment. This figure is not at all prominent in the voice parts, which tend to be completely independent of the orchestra. Imitation plays a large part wherever the figure is used. A second figure, first presented as an answer to the questioning nature of the first, is equally important throughout the piece. The rising third of the first figure acquires a life of its own when it is detached, and as such its eloquence is unequalled. All of these are seen in the first two lines of the introduction, reproduced as Example 210.

Ex. 210

Another and longer figure begins on the upbeat to the sixth beat of measure 14, and continues through 15. The accented sixteenths and the falling fifth with which the figure begins dominate the second phase of the introduction. Close imitations follow each entry. The sixteenths are important because they provide the rhythmic impetus for most of the rest of the introduction.

Instead of principal themes, what we have just seen is a kind of passing in review of different configurations that employ basic intervallic material (minor thirds, seconds, fifths). Their eloquence certainly needs no defence. Neither does the fact that there appears to be no principal theme. Anything more definite might inhibit the continuity of the mystical experience expressed in this poem. A theme is finite in terms of a beginning and an end; it repeats itself in much the same way as it is first stated and definite tonalities are integral parts of its make-up. A mystical experience unfolds from an uncertain beginning, and moves in an unpredictable manner towards an unknown ending; it can never be repeated.

The chords underlying these figures are in a continual state of transition. Perhaps most noteworthy, in the introduction many of them are non-resolving dominant sevenths – both roots and inversions – a fact that immediately recalls the opening of the Fourth Symphony, a work that was already in existence.

Vaughan's poem is clearly divided into two approximately equal parts. The first is full of exultation: 'O joys! Infinite sweetness! with what flowers / And shoots of glory, my soul breaks and buds!' Part 2 begins, 'Prayer is the world in tune, a spirit-voice, and vocal joys / Whose echo is heaven's bliss.' It continues to the end in a somewhat subdued and meditative style. The musical setting faithfully portrays these moods. In Part 1, the listener is swept along by gradual tempo increases ($\downarrow$ = 40 at the start through 72 and 96 to 112) and changes in volume to the final climax on the words, 'Thus all is hurled / In sacred hymns and order, the great chime / And symphony of nature.' The chorus parts are predominantly block-chordal and there are some *divisi* passages from time to time in all parts.

Adding greatly to the continually mounting excitement and sense of exultation are the orchestral triplets which, in scale patterns derived from the germinating melodic third of the beginning, underlie the chorus throughout all of Part 1. Cross-rhythms consisting of figures A and B are heard in a two-against-three pattern, but the dominant cross-rhythm cutting across the triplets is a heavily accented, four-note, bell-like figure composed of quarters. Beginning in the middle registers of the orchestra, it foreshadows 'the great chime' of the text. Marked *fortissimo* in the measure where the chorus begins its 'Thus all is hurled' passage, it dominates the orchestra throughout the following passage in the form of an ostinato in two parts in stretto. From 'thus' through 'order', the chorus parts are set in consecutive fifths in four-part organum style that reaches a B in the soprano and tenor. The *tessitura* remains high (sustained As occur twice) through 'nature'.

The transition to Part 2 of the text is an expressive orchestral interlude, which begins *molto rallentando* immediately upon cessation of the voices; by the next measure the tempo is $\downarrow$ = 88, and the dynamic level is *piano*. The interlude introduces two new features, one of which is rhythmic, the other melodic. The former, consisting of constantly repeating dotted quarters and eighths, completely pervades the orchestral fabric for the remainder of the motet in the newly adopted 3/2 metre. The melodic element is, again, motivic and is composed of five descending notes in a scale pattern that includes an overlap when the figures complete and restart their patterns. Beneath the final choral statements, the motive is altered to include repetitions of pattern *A. B* reappears briefly in the quiet orchestral postlude. As in the first half, there are tempo fluctuations: $\downarrow$ = 88, 96, 132, 96, *molto meno mosso* and, finally, *adagio*.

The chorus parts throughout Part 2 are still independent of the orchestra, but there is less block harmony in favour of more imitation, although the final lines are set to unison and octave passages.

There are two reviews of this work which, like others in this book, express opposing points of view. The first is by Ivor Keys:

> it is a pity that this work is at present published only in vocal score, because it invites comparison with Bax's setting of the same words, and without indications of the scoring seems far greyer than the Bax, and far greyer than the eager and ecstatic words.[24]

It would appear from these remarks that Keys did not hear the first performance of *The Morning Watch* on 22 November 1946 at the Albert Hall on the occasion of the first St Cecilia's Day Festival. Had he been there it is difficult to see how he could have thought the orchestration 'grey'. A more recent performance of the motet by the Scottish Philharmonic Singers and the BBC Scottish Symphony Orchestra, broadcast on Radio 3, indicates otherwise. The exuberance of the strings in high registers, the horn passages sounding through everything, plus the small details of instrumentation, all deny the greyness that Keys thought he observed in the vocal score.

In a 1981 review of the work in connection with the Radio 3 series that celebrated Rubbra's eightieth year, there are these words:

> Rubbra has seldom done anything better: the whole structure, growing inevitably and organically from the motivic seeds of a noble orchestral prelude, seems... to be conceived in a single breath, and set down in a single surge of creative inspiration. As ever with Rubbra, nothing is done for mere sensation's sake – but it is a powerful, gripping work that should be heard more often.[25]

Had the reviewer, Calum MacDonald, felt the same way about the instrumentation, it seems fair to assume that he would have said so.

The Revival

The Revival, Op. 58, also on a Henry Vaughan poem, was completed in August 1944, two years before the completion and first performance of *The Morning Watch* – proof that one cannot always rely on opus numbers to indicate the chronology of a work. Like *The Morning Watch* it is a motet, scored for SATB but having no *divisi* parts. It is also shorter, *a cappella*, and in proportion to its size, more polyphonic.

The poem to which the music is set has fourteen lines, but because of the division into two stanzas of six and eight lines respectively, the iambic tetrameter, and rhyme scheme, it is not a sonnet. Its title more properly derives from the second stanza where spring's awakening is described, but the first stanza, in which the relationship of God to men is the subject, gives meaning to the following stanza. Rubbra's setting follows this plan by making a distinction in terms of key, metre and tempo. Part 1, with a four-sharp key signature, fluctuates between C sharp minor and E major with a later gravitation to D major via shifting harmonies. Part 2, with no key signature until a reversion to four sharps near the end, is a combination of D minor-F major plus a strong feeling of A minor. However, the restoration of the four sharps fails to end the ambiguity completely until about two and a half measures before the end. The differences in metre and tempo between the two parts are simple: 4/4 and a slow tempo for Part 1, and 3/4 and a faster pace for the second.

With no accompaniment to aid in the delineation of mood or atmosphere, the work in its intimacy is reminiscent of the Five Motets. Like some of them, it is also a balanced mixture of polyphony and homophony. From the composer's setting two passages may be commented upon: the first, just prior to Part 2, is to the words, 'some drops and dews of future bliss'. Here, all the previous imitative entries and eighth-note motion change to block harmonies on longer values, *subito pianissimo* and *poco rallentando* – all obviously meant to emphasize the text. The other passage occurs in the second part to the words, 'The lofty groves in express Joyes / Reply unto the Turtle's voice.' What stands out here are the cross-relations resulting from the canon in the first line between the sopranos and tenors: G sharp as leading tone to A, followed by G natural in a descending pattern. The same idea is found in the second line where B is leading tone to C, and B flat appears in the descending figure. While some of Rubbra's other cross-relations are far more pungent, these draw attention to the gentle text.

The brief review of the work reads as follows:

> [It] has the appearance of a superbly written answer to a B.Mus. paper, with slight licence in regard to modulation and rhythmic variety.... It should be in the hands of all choirmasters who think either that motet writing is an art of the past, or that it cannot enshrine the choicest expression of a modern genius, or that its use need imply affectation or exhibitionism. Rubbra's motet has permanent worth.[26]

Missa Cantuariensis

The next work, *Missa Cantuariensis* or 'Canterbury Mass', Op. 59, represents the composer's first venture in setting a liturgical text. It is the earliest and largest of the Masses, and with the exception of the *Credo* is unaccompanied. In Rubbra's words,

> [It] was primarily designed for use on festival occasions. Commissioned by Canterbury Cathedral during the 1939–1945 War, I was specifically asked to set the words of the English rites of 1662 and 1928. The commission came when I was serving in the Army, and to complete it in time for the first performance by the Canterbury Cathedral choir in a concert of English church music on July 20, 1946, I had to start work on the Mass before I was demobilised towards the end of 1945. This difficulty, however, was not so great as it sounds, as I was in an Army Music Group that, although frequently shifting its location, did allow me a certain amount of quiet and

leisure. I remember working on the opening *Kyrie* while stationed at our Headquarters in Chelsea, and much of the *Sanctus*, *Benedictus* and *Gloria* was written in the music room of the Cathedral when I was stationed in Canterbury.[27]

In conformity with the English rites of 1662 and 1928, the text is, of course, in English. Music for the usual prayer responses is provided in the score, but not included in the recording by the St Margaret's Westminster, Singers despite its listing on both the record sleeve and record. The *Gloria in excelsis* concludes the work rather than appearing in its usual position between the *Kyrie* and *Credo* – one of the major differences between the Roman Catholic Mass and the Anglican Communion Service.

With respect to performance, there are these helpful hints from the composer: 'the work is scored for two separate choirs, which ideally should be spatially separate, so that the effect of the overlapping interplay of choral sounds achieves maximum clarity.'[28] And in order to ensure 'maximum clarity', these words appear in the score: 'the metronome markings are valid for the particular acoustics of Canterbury Cathedral, and should be modified, preferably on the slow side, when the Mass is sung in other buildings.' So far as key is concerned, 'the work has no overriding key, but all the movements start from the note G and then branch out independently from this. It can thus be said that the Mass is centrally based *on* G, but is not *in* G.'[29]

As a whole the Mass is well diversified and balanced with respect to polyphonic and chordal usage, not only as between the several sections but also within sections. This balance is at once apparent in the *Kyrie* where, after the opening chordal petition by both choruses, staggered entries carry the individual petitions of the various parts. The first *Kyrie*, that is, the collection of statements of 'Lord have mercy upon us', ends quietly in block harmony. Two points are important throughout this first *Kyrie*, and they are mentioned in order of how they are most likely to affect the listener: first, the generous use of that peculiarly English sound of harmonic cross-relations, and second, the upward and downward leap of a fifth that characterizes the individual parts. The second point needs no elaboration, but the first is of prime interest because of the distinctive sound wherever and whenever it is used.

Near the end of the 'Christ have mercy' section a short but very expressive passage occurs when, in Rubbra's words, 'the counterpoint gives way to massed harmonies which, in the process of overlapping and echoing achieves also a

Ex. 211

semitonal downward shift of key.'[30] This passage is shown in Example 211, where the parallel fifths between soprano and bass play an effective role in defining the harmonic limits of the passage. In a large cathedral like Canterbury, or even in the smaller church wherein the recording was made, this passage is enormously compelling.

Following the simple responses to the prayers, there comes a surprise in the form of the accompanied *Credo*. Since Rubbra never does anything without a cogent reason, the listener will be mystified until he reads the following explanation:

> At first sight it might seem inconsistent, possibly incongruous, to insert into an otherwise unaccompanied work a movement which has an important organ accompaniment. But I felt strongly that the *Credo* should somehow be isolated in its texture from the other movements, in order to underline the difference between a solitary *personal* statement of belief and the act of corporate worship and appeal. Also the music moves mostly at the unison or octave, with counterpoint making but two brief appearances.[31]

For these articles of faith the choirs are joined, as though to emphasize the strength of belief through communal affirmation; thus there are four instead of eight parts. The movement also features baritone and tenor solos alternating with the full men's parts. Although the movement as a whole is very expressive, the high point begins with 'and was crucified', continuing through the Ascension clause. At the first point the tempo changes from *Con moto* to *Adagio*, there is a hush, and all four parts sing the same notes – the sopranos and basses two octaves apart, the altos and tenors in unison. By this simple procedure the all-important words are thrown into relief and further intensified by the *pianissimo* dynamic and the high register – the sopranos and tenors reach a high A in the course of the slow-moving eighths. Following this passage there is a close (two beats) two-part canon at the fifth between the soloists on the words, 'He suffered and was buried'. This expands to a four-part canon for full chorus at the octave to a different note pattern on the words, 'And the third day'. The remainder of the Resurrection text is set to a simple but most effective chain of suspensions that employs two sets of parallel fifths and octaves. The accompaniment throughout the movement is, except for a very short passage, an entirely independent entity, underlining with authority the strong, virile statements of Christian belief, and quietly supporting the more subjective ones. One feels that Rubbra's decision to provide an accompaniment is absolutely right, ample proof, if any were needed, that he

> is intent only on writing music – *his* music; and what he needs for that music he will use.... Any musical device is right if it secures the result he intends to convey – and the only thing that matters *is* the result.[32]

The *Sanctus*, *Benedictus* and *Agnus Dei* are described by the composer in the following paragraph:

The *Sanctus* is based on a very simple three-note motif consisting of an upward and downward movement of a minor third, but the quiet echoing of this by the trebles and altos of the two choirs, and the later addition to this texture of a *pianissimo* scale-wise motif on overlapping tenors is designed to accentuate the intensely prayerful mood. This is broken into by the *forte* canonic harmonies of the middle section. The modally simple theme in octaves that opens the *Benedictus* is the lynchpin that holds the music together when, later, it is surrounded by contrapuntal complications. Such complications overspill into the following *Agnus Dei*, which consists entirely of quiet canonic movement involving all eight parts.[33]

Of course, this description does not and cannot convey the atmosphere engendered by these three sections, much less its translation into sound. In each instance, the simplest means produce sensitive results that are deeply satisfying aesthetically. For example, in the *Sanctus* where the more usual and loud exuberance associated with this text is replaced by the prayerfulness Rubbra sought, the overlapping entries of the first part give an almost vivid impression of individual beings quietly and reverently praising God. These individual expressions give way to corporate responses in the second half where a more massive canonic statement leads to block harmonies on 'Glory be to Thee'. At the end there is a return to the quiet entries.

In the *Benedictus* the same quiet joy pervades the music. The 'Hosannas' are dominated by a simple, five-note scale figure from G down to C and back again (there is some use of this figure in the first half). Its presentation in canon links the parts in such a manner as to suggest a ladder joining earth and heaven, an impression brought about by the simultaneous ascending and descending figures. The impression is strengthened when the Mass is performed in a resonantly alive church.

The *Agnus Dei* is entirely canonic. Two motives are present: the first sharply falling in keeping with the penitential nature of the text, the second gently rising and falling on the words, 'Have mercy'. A quiet urgency pervades the whole movement as one entry after another takes up the petition. The first motive is shown in Example 212 as it passes from part to part. This canon is

Ex. 212

much more effectively managed than the one in *Vain Wits and Eyes*, no. 2 of the Five Motets. There, the composer acknowledged that his technical achievement had made the individual parts 'indistinguishable'. In the same passage that contains this admission he describes the remedies that were applied to the 'similarly complex canon for two choirs' in the *Agnus Dei* of this Mass:

[it] was made much more accessible to the ear; first, by the initial leap of a sixth in each canonic entry, thus distinguishing all the entries, second, by raising the pitch of the last four entries to a fifth above, third, by the *pianissimo* of the dynamics.[34]

The *Gloria in Excelsis* is by far the most difficult of the Mass movements. Not only is the *tessitura* very high, the sopranos rather frequently having to sing Gs and As, while there are three B flats, but the fast tempo in keeping with the jubilation of the text renders the frequent staggered entries difficult. Such entries imply, of course, contrapuntal treatment of some sort, and examples are encountered immediately with the commencement of the strict, double canon between the choirs on the opening lines of the text. Less strict imitation and some block writing occur in due course until the start of the four fugal entries in Choir 1 on the words, 'O Lord God, only begotten Son, Jesu Christ'. Although the fugue does not continue, there are many imitative passages through to the end.

The first of the two reviews given below contains some reservations, but the critic's overall impression of the work is good:

> The Mass contains abundant examples of Rubbra's polyphonic mastery and sure musical architecture. If it can be sung in tune it cannot fail to be imposing and devotional. But that 'if' is a big one, as some London listeners and singers already know. Unfortunately, the difficulties in intonation are mostly concentrated in the opening Kyrie. When polyphony without abstruse modulation achieves such success later it appears that the dice is unnecessarily loaded against the choir here.... There is, however, some remarkable choral writing in three-octave unison at the phrase 'and was crucified', and the Resurrection clauses are given music which, although deliberately undramatic, is telling in its intensity.... Technical accomplishment could hardly go farther than in the Agnus Dei, where the first and third clauses are set to a canon 8 in 2 and the second clause to a canon 4 in 1. The constant *pianissimo* stream of prayer thus depicted is expressive and effective in the highest degree.[35]

The second review contains no reservations:

> The way in which he achieves spiritual kinship with the preclassical Mass by almost entirely modern means puts this among the most important church compositions of today.[36]

Magnificat and *Nunc Dimittis*

The *Magnificat* and *Nunc Dimittis* for SATB and organ, Op. 65, was written in the late 1940s, not long after the completion of the *Missa Cantuariensis*. However, several important works for other media intervened between the two. These included the Cello Sonata, Op. 60; the Festival Overture, Op. 62; and the Fifth Symphony, Op. 63. When Rubbra returned to choral writing, he was to provide another work for the Anglican liturgy – this time, Evensong. Both canticles have received short settings and the writing in each is relatively uncomplicated, but the entirely independent organ accompaniment offers no help whatsoever to the choir. There is a minimum of *divisi* sections in both canticles, and the *Nunc Dimittis* consists solely of unison block passages – a nice contrast to the *Magnificat*'s mixture of block harmonies and imitative entries. An unusual feature that links the two canticles is the identical *Gloria Patri*, whose organ accompaniments are noteworthy in that they are made up of a two-measure ostinato. Pedal dexterity and a steady rhythmic sense are essential if the pedal triplets and the running eighths in the manual are to be fitted together successfully.

Missa in Honorem Sancti Dominici

In 1948, Rubbra celebrated his conversion to Catholicism by composing the unaccompanied *Missa in Honorem Sancti Dominici*, Op. 66. The title has no significance other than the fact that Rubbra was received into the church on the Feast of St Dominic, 4 August. It is altogether different from its predecessor, as the composer makes clear in the following passages:

> this setting of the Mass was designed for normal liturgical use. The six movements are, therefore, as succinct as I could possibly make them, and in this respect the work differs greatly from the much more expansive *Missa Cantuariensis*. Also, unlike the latter, it did not owe its origin either to a commission or to a request for such a work, but purely to an inner compulsion to express my beliefs in music to be used within the framework of the liturgy.
>
> The first performance, however, was very much at odds with this prime intention, for, in celebrating its twentieth birthday, the Fleet Street Choir under T.B. Lawrence gave the Mass its premiere in a concert at the Royal Academy of Music on October 26, 1949, a concert that was graced by the presence of the Queen. Since then the Mass has generally assumed its legitimate function as an aid to worship, and a later English version widened its use. [This version, adapted by the composer, is entitled Holy Communion Service in A, and designated as Op. 66a].[37]

Further clarification is provided by Rubbra's remarks concerning, first, the choice of language, and second, the key scheme of the new Mass. As for the language difference, Rubbra considers the *Missa Cantuariensis* to be more national because it is in the English Cathedral tradition, while the Latin employed in the *Missa in Honorem Sancti Dominici* released him from 'any allegiance to national traditions. I am inside the words, warmly and emotionally identifying myself with their universal appeal'.[38] The key scheme, he says, 'is much more unified than that of the *Missa Cantuariensis*, gravitating mainly between A and C as points of departure and arrival, but the harmonies and key centres within these confines are much more fluid than this simple scheme would suggest'.[39]

Stressing that he wanted this Mass to be 'simple enough for the average choir', the composer has included some significant suggestions concerning performance:

> The attitude of the performer toward this work – and indeed to my work generally – should not be one of a withdrawn austerity, just because the look of the printed page is plain and unadorned. Everything, from a hushed *pianissimo* to a *fortissimo*, was

dramatically conceived, and every marked nuance should therefore be overstated rather than understated. As the exact degree of statement can never be indicated, this must of course be left to the individual intuition of the conductor. But I do want to stress that this is not austere music: it may seem emaciated in its printed appearance, but red blood runs in its veins! The textural reserve of my music comes from an inherent dislike of padding and an unmotivated busyness. Every voice in the texture – and this applies to a symphony as well as to the work under discussion – has its melodic part to play in moulding the architecture of the music.[40]

Although the composer's explanation of the basic architecture of this work requires a lengthy quotation, his insights and perceptive observations are too valuable to omit:

In the Anglican Communion Service the *Gloria* is placed last, thus giving an opportunity to the composer for an impressive climax to the whole work. But the ritual of the Roman Catholic church, in putting the *Gloria* second, makes the solving of the overall musical form peculiarly difficult. This difficulty is not present if the work is used exclusively for liturgical purposes, for the spacing of the various numbers so cuts up the music that, if each section is formally self-contained, there is no need for a more unifying thread than is given by, say, a basic key and its related centres, or, as in Byrd's Five Part Mass, a kind of leitmotiv that links the various sections together. If, however, the composer – as is most likely – envisages concert performances in which the relatedness of the various movements adds to the overall musical effect, then special attention must be given to the formal unity of the whole. In my Latin Mass, I have treated the *Kyrie*, *Gloria*, and *Credo* as together constituting three related sections, linking the *Sanctus*, *Benedictus*, and *Agnus Dei* in like manner. In effect, there are two movements, each of three sections. Moreover, the C sharp in the A major chord of the final 'pacem' of the *Agnus Dei* clarifies the ambiguity of the unfilled-in fifth with which the *Kyrie* begins and ends, thus completing the tonal circle of the music.
    In the first three sections (constituting the first 'movement') the linkages are by key, rhythm, and interval. The *Kyrie* is in A minor, but with an inner modal content which includes B flat and G natural instead of the usual B natural and G sharp: the *Gloria* is in C major, with B flat again prominent.... The rhythmic linkage between these two movements is found in the dotted rhythm of measure 1 of the *Gloria*, which is a diminished version of the rhythm of the ending of the *Kyrie*, ...
    In the *Credo*, the alto voice has the same interval (fourth) and notes in measure 1 as in the beginning of the *Gloria*, and the idea is extended canonically, the slight time-lapse serving to emphasize the fourth, and to break up rhythmically what would be two not very interesting consecutive fifths.
    The linking procedure is altered in the last three sections (constituting the second 'movement'). Here the note A is the basic starting point – and the interval of a third is predominant in melodic movement... (The same process was more extended in the *Missa Cantuariensis*, in which all six movements start from a G that has no fixed significance in any particular scale until a certain direction has been taken.)[41]

The *Kyrie* in its mere two pages achieves a massively Romanesque feeling, caused by the block harmonies, which contain empty fifths moving in an organum-like texture. Strengthening this medieval flavour are the occasional dissonances found between the buttressing fifths, and the rhythm which, although in metrical patterns of 4/2, 6/2 and 7/2, seems totally unmetred, for it is governed by the textual accents. The *Christe eleison* section is particularly moving as

> the rhythm and the harmonic centres become unsettled, and the quiet but intense music is dominated by an expressive phrase that achieves colouristic contrast by giving it alternately to altos and tenors, surrounding it with chromatically shifting fifths on trebles and basses [shown in Example 213].[42]

Ex. 213

Unlike the *Kyrie*, where the writing is generally for five and six parts, and occasionally seven, the *Gloria*, except for one brief passage shortly after the beginning, is in four parts. The composer remarks that its opening measures 'are unusual for a liturgical work in that I set the words *Gloria in excelsis Deo* instead of using the traditional plainsong motif. This is because I wanted to link this opening with the rhythm of the *Kyrie* ending.'[43] Following the next line of text there is an *Allegro* section, the beginning of which, 'Laudamus te, benedicimus te', is startlingly like Poulenc's setting of exactly the same words in his *Gloria*. But the resemblance is only fleeting and the skill shown in this closely-knit *Allegro* gives rise to passages whose joyful interpretation of the words remains in the memory long after the resemblance has been noted and forgotten. The skill involves counterpoint, but in this instance it is so subtly worked in as to be imperceptible to even the trained listener. Beginning with 'Laudamus te' and ending with 'Glorificamus te', there is paired imitation between the bass and alto, and between the soprano and tenor parts. The reason for the inability of the listener to hear this imitative activity is that the basses, although in their high register, are eclipsed by the sopranos who are in theirs; and second, the altos, also pitched high, sing shorter note values under a still dominating soprano part. Before the altos complete their imitation of the basses, the sopranos start their portion of the material on a high A, effectively cancelling the altos, who are singing the same rhythm in the same pattern a fifth lower. The tenor imitation of the soprano *can* be heard, but it tends to be buried in the general jubilation. This entire imitative passage is a perfect example of superb technical ability which is used as a means to an end rather than an end in itself. Certainly if these contrapuntal techniques were not present here, the whole passage would not be so effective. Much more obvious is the exact paired imitation from 'Domine Deus' – where the key changes from D flat major to C sharp minor – to 'omnipotens'. There, the voices enter in staggered fashion, beginning with the basses and finishing with the sopranos. In a reference to this *Allegro* section, Rubbra remarked that, 'except for brief sections, [it] is contrapuntal in the accepted sense, although the purist might find much to quarrel with!'[44]

The *Credo* begins with the usual priest's intonation and is composed primarily of block harmonies, although there are short contrapuntal sections. There is a wonderfully free rhythmic flow, suggested by the words and implemented by a liberal use of 5/2 metre interspersed with 4/2 and 3/2 in which the first named is divided by dotted lines into sub-measures of 3 + 2 and 2 + 3. This free flow reaches a high point in the 'Et in Spiritum Sanctum' clause which, as the composer remarks, 'in the speech-like freedom and similar motion of all seven parts, recalls early medieval organum'.[45] 'Medieval', although not in the organum sense, can also be applied to the previously sung 'Et incarnatus' and 'Crucifixus' sections, both of which are quietly and darkly intoned in a gently undulating manner. Each is infused with a soft luminosity that reminds one of a glowing fresco or the panels of an altarpiece.

The *Sanctus*, *Benedictus* and *Agnus Dei* are miniatures, each but two pages in length. Concerning the first of these, the composer explains that

> [it] is divided into two halves, one *pianissimo* and one *forte*. The tonal effect desired in the first section is that of the reverberations of a bell after the main note has been sounded. On paper, it looks as though the overlapping As in all four voices lead to an accumulation of tone, but that is not desirable, the individual entries merely adding a vibrational throb to the sustained note. Similarly, the notes with a stress and *tenuto* line over them should never be preceded by a crescendo. The *forte* second section uses the same melodic material, but a diminished fifth higher. Finally, this material is raised another tone, so that the ending is in a clear F major.[46]

The same bell-like effect is present in the *Sanctus* of the *Missa Cantuariensis*, except that there the motion is an upward third, stated once, instead of the downward third found in the present work and stated twice. The 5/2 metre, divided into alternating 2 + 3 and 3 + 2 patterns, combines with the slow tempo to create a sense of space in which all motion seems to be suspended. It is truly a magical moment.

In introducing the *Benedictus*, Rubbra mentions that

> this key, or rather this chord [see the concluding sentence in the above citation], is taken over by the *Benedictus*, which then proceeds to dovetail the basic melodic material of the *Sanctus* in such a way that five keys are stated in as many bars [Example 214]. Once C sharp minor has been established, this remains the key of the music from the 'qui venit' until the end.[47]

Ex. 214

The planning that obviously went into the 'qui venit' section is quite extraordinary, yet it is something that must be pointed out, for the resulting subtleties will escape everyone, including the professional musician. Rubbra reveals this plan in the following passage:

> The contrapuntal entries of the voices in the 'qui venit' are characterized by the progressive enlargement of the interval with which the phrase begins:
>
> | | | |
> |---|---|---|
> | D sharp-E | (second), | tenor. |
> | G sharp-B | (third), | bass. |
> | B-E | (fourth), | soprano. |
> | E-B | (fifth), | alto. |
> | A-F sharp | (sixth), | tenor. |
> | C sharp-B | (seventh), | bass. |
> | B-B | (octave), | soprano. |
>
> These enlargements must be made as clear as possible in performance.[48]

The *Agnus Dei*, marked *Adagio* like the two preceding movements, is characterized 'by the juxtaposition of unrelated triads and the minimum of counterpoint'.[49] Most of it is, indeed, fashioned from block harmonies, but a touch of counterpoint at each 'miserere nobis' as well as the concluding 'dona nobis pacem' provides a balance. The unrelated triads occur in a pattern that is the same for each of the 'Agnus Dei' petitions except that in the last the pattern is transposed to conform to the cadence in the preceding measure. That cadence, in turn, was decided by the choice of triads after the second 'Agnus Dei'. Rubbra, aware of the intonational problems here, tells us that 'the whole effect of the piece depends on retaining clarity of pitch when moving to unrelated triads. Its slowness does, though, give time for this accuracy of pitch to be prepared.'[50] As he said in a passage quoted above, 'the tonal circle of the music' is completed when the C sharp in the final chord of this movement 'clarifies the ambiguity of the unfilled-in fifth' with which the work began.

The impact of the Mass upon the listener is extraordinary, for its many deeply expressive passages remain for long in the memory. Space permits the mention of only a few: the organum sounds in the *Kyrie* and the poignant sounds of the 'Christe eleison' petitions; the dark hues of the 'et incarnatus' and 'crucifixus' sections of the *Credo*; the bell-like *Sanctus*; and the entire *Agnus Dei*.

The major review of the Mass contains highly complimentary statements:

> a work so impressive and so beautiful as to overshadow the usual round of Festival Hall concert-giving ... it speaks with restraint the direct and unmistakable language of personal conviction.... It seems to me that in his new Mass Rubbra has steered with perfect judgment between a tame pastiche-style and excessively chromatic 'word-painting'.... It is possible that these open fifths symbolize for the composer some sort of absolute: recalling medieval organum, they suggest simple faith, or the abstract notion of Divinity. Musically they come like a draught of clear water. They enable the composer to diverge into new and distant keys without the chromatic deliquescence of modulation. Some of its key-changes, often enharmonically achieved, are remote and very beautiful.[51]

In a letter of 8 April 1950, the composer Lennox Berkeley mentioned having

> much enjoyed your Mass at Westminster [Cathedral] this morning. It is beautifully done – dignified and simple. I admired, too, very much the way you managed to find a suitable style without falling into the pastiche of polyphonic music which so easily happens when people write for the actual service in church.

Festival Te Deum

Just as with the two Masses, the first in English, the second in Latin, so it is with the two *Te Deums*. Op. 71, the Festival *Te Deum*, was commissioned by the Arts Council of Great Britain for the Festival of Britain in 1951 and it is scored for soprano solo, SATB chorus in which there is a large amount of doubling, and orchestra. Although an organ reduction of the orchestral score has been provided (by Dr C.S. Lang), it is to be used only when an orchestra is unavailable. Thus it is suitable for an Anglican service of Morning Prayer, but it should be emphasized at the start that the rhythmic difficulties in both voice and organ, as well as the *divisi* parts, and the very high *tessitura* present problems serious enough to preclude service performance in any but large churches and cathedrals having well-trained choirs, large organs and very capable organists.

The rhythmic patterns are one of the work's main characteristics. Within the basic 6/4 metre the first pattern occurs shortly after the opening when four dotted quarters in the voice parts are superimposed on the accompaniment's normal six-beat pulse. Farther on, the vocal pattern changes to three half-notes over the accompaniment's basic 6/4, and this new pattern also appears, heavily accented, in the accompaniment itself. Just before the first and longer of the two soprano solos, set to 'When Thou tookest upon Thee to deliver man', and continuing through the solo and much of the rest of the work, triplet patterns appear in both voice and accompaniment. Some of these passages oppose a triplet containing half-notes in the solo and vocal lines to another comprised of quarters in the accompaniment, and both types occur together in accompanimental passages.

Most of the vocal writing in the *Te Deum* consists of block harmonies in parallel motion which, together with the many *divisi* passages expand the number of parts to six and sometimes eight. When to these characteristics are added the often high *tessiturae* of the soprano and tenor parts (As, B flats and Bs) plus the independent accompaniment, the effect is rather like that of a modern adaptation of a joyous and exciting medieval organum.

Nine Tenebrae Motets

The Nine Tenebrae Motets for unaccompanied mixed voices which comprise Op. 72 are intended for performance at Maundy Thursday Matins. The three sections of the work consist of three motets each, and are subtitled First, Second and Third Nocturn. A ten-year period separates the motets of the First Nocturn from those of the Second and Third (1951–61).

For those not familiar with the services of *Tenebrae*, these solemn and impressive rites are observed at Matins and Lauds (before daybreak and at sunrise respectively) on Maundy Thursday, Good Friday and Holy Saturday. Today these rites are observed on the evenings preceding the days for which the liturgical texts are prescribed and they are composed of alternating antiphons and psalms, lessons and responsories – a different set of each prescribed for each day. It should be understood that in strict usage all of these items are set to Gregorian chants, as can be seen in the *Liber Usualis* (pp.621ff). The word 'tenebrae' itself occurs in one of the Good Friday responsories ('Tenebrae factae sunt' or, freely translated, 'Darkness was over all'). It graphically describes the nature of the rites, as seen in the following rubrics:

> On this day and the following two days at Matins, after the silent recitation of the *Pater Noster*, *Ave Maria*, and *Credo*, the Office begins directly with the first Antiphon. At the end of each Psalm of Matins and of Lauds, one of the fifteen candles is extinguished on the triangular candlestick before the altar, the candle at the top being left lighted…. During the canticle *Benedictus* at Lauds, the six candles on the altar are likewise extinguished one by one, from each side alternately, at every second verse, so that by the last verse all are extinguished. All other lights and lamps in the church are also put out. During the repetition of the Antiphon *Traditor*, the lighted candle is taken from the top of the candlestick and hidden behind the altar at the Epistle side. [Following a concluding prayer], a noise is made by knocking on the stalls of choir until the lighted candle reappears from behind the altar. All then rise and retire in silence.[52]

The hiding and subsequent reappearance of the lighted candle symbolizes Christ, the Light of the World – a Light that is inextinguishable.

The portions of the *Tenebrae* service that particularly attract composers are the twenty-seven responsories – nine for each of the three Matins, each Matin being divided into three Nocturns with three responsories in each. The texts of all deal with the Passion, and are thus highly subjective, providing opportunities for expressive music which includes word-painting.

So far as Rubbra's settings are concerned, it is important to realize that despite the lapse in time between the first three motets and the six later ones, the decision to include all nine in one opus number indicates that the work was conceived as a unit. More to the point, the composer regarded it as a triptych: 'But a nearer approach to the subjective spirit of the triptych is made in the later unaccompanied choral works: the nine Tenebrae Motets'.[53]

Of course, the most obvious external characteristic of the triptych structure is the division of the Maundy Thursday motets into three Nocturns. However, each Nocturn itself is a small triptych, for the second motet of each possesses some singular characteristic that distinguishes it from its flanking motets. These characteristics are, of course, musical, but in each instance they arise from the more intensely subjective nature of the central text in each Nocturn. Thus we may assume that the original authors of the texts used these central ones as focal points for the worshipper. But we can go even further than this in suggesting that the three days over which the *Tenebrae* rites are spread represent a very large triptych with the Good Friday services forming the central panel – a plausible assumption considering that the events of Good Friday are central to the Passion. The texts bear this out, for *Tenebrae factae sunt* stands at the exact centre of the Good Friday portion, and thus of the entire three days. Even the altar candles form a *visual* triptych: the three tall candles on either side, the fifteen in the centre with the Light of the World as the focal point of all the candles.

Returning to Rubbra's Maundy Thursday settings, the middle text of each of the three Nocturns places in relief a particularly poignant moment in the Passion. In the First and Third Nocturns these texts deal with the human frailties of those surrounding Jesus in the Garden of Gethsemane, as they are revealed in His words. The central text of the Second Nocturn presents the stark reality of the Betrayal.[54] In like manner, Rubbra's settings of these focal points stand out from their surrounding texts.

The First Nocturn motets were 'written for the 75th birthday of Charles Kennedy Scott', a noted choral conductor, founder of performance organizations devoted to the advancement of English choral music, and author of important volumes on singing.

Scott responded to Rubbra's dedication in a letter of 18 October 1951:

> It's very good of you to celebrate my old age by composing that fine motet in my honour [perhaps at this point Scott had received only the first of the three motets]. I could not have expected such a welcome gesture on your part – it is somewhat of a consolation (for all your trouble) that others will be able to share the gift, as well as myself. Thank you *very much.*

I'm doing your Mass at Bideford and Exeter this weekend [*Missa in Honorem Sancti Dominici*], and the Tenebrae will be sung at the Oriana Easter Concert on March 23rd. It will fit in so well, then, with a very unusual motet of Morales which you may know, 'Emendemus in melius'.

The titles of the first and third motets are *In Monte Oliveti* and *Ecce Vidimus Eum*. The beginning of the scene on the Mount of Olives when Jesus prays, 'if it be possible, let this cup pass from me', is set to a modal melody centring around D, and harmonized by soft dissonances. The inevitable outcome of the drama is heightened by an austerely chordal style. On the words, 'the spirit is willing, but the flesh is weak', the unresolved dominant sevenths, seen in the Fourth Symphony and the orchestral introduction to *The Morning Watch*, add to the feeling of unrest, as does the faster tempo. The motet is scored for SATB with *divisi* tenor in the first five and a half measures. The versicles, 'Watch and pray, that ye may not enter into temptation', are taken by simultaneously sounding soloists: soprano, alto and bass.

In *Ecce Vidimus Eum*, 'Behold, we have seen him disfigured', and continuing with the familiar words, 'He hath borne our griefs and carried our sorrows', the overall style is declamatory. Within this framework the tragic intensity of the words is emphasized by the richer sonorities of the SSAATTBB setting, the relentless block harmonies, and the unusual and sometimes abrupt chromatic changes in which all of the parts participate. In both of these motets, Rubbra has followed the Gregorian practice of repeating the line (or lines) of text which immediately precedes the versicles. In *Ecce Vidimus Eum* a second ending is provided for this purpose.

The middle responsory is *Tristis Est Anima Mea*. Although it begins in a chordal style with short chordal passages later on, its dominant characteristic is a rhythmically free and flowing soprano melody. This melody engages the attention for several reasons: it is in sharp contrast to the prevailing chordal style of the Nocturn as a whole; it is placed above long-held chords in the three lower parts; and the angular nature of its first segment seems to suggest the pathos of the words, 'Ye shall run away', while the calm and conjunct second segment (which is separated from the first segment by a very small chordal passage) summarizes the resignation of 'and I will go to be sacrificed for you'. The first appearance of this melody in the chorus soprano line is in contrast to its second appearance for solo soprano. There the loneliness and resignation are more poignant. Again, the versicles divide the two statements of this melody.

The three motets comprising the Second Nocturn are set to texts that are entirely concerned with the Betrayal, the great drama of Maundy Thursday, and they are accordingly tension-filled to a greater degree than the motets of the First and Third Nocturns. Bearing the completion date of the Feast of Christ the King, 1961 (the last Sunday of October), they are dedicated to Alec Robertson, English musicologist and author of *The Interpretation of Plainchant* (1937); *Dvořák* in the Master Musician Series (1944); and other works.

Again, the second motet is the focal point of its triptych, but this time it also functions as the centrepiece of the entire work because of its text: *Judas Mercator Pessimus* which, in describing the very act of betrayal, is the most tragic. The composer has recognized this uniqueness by placing augmented fourths and diminished fifths – the most unstable and restless of intervals – in positions of great melodic prominence throughout the motet. These tritones with their root-lessness, used melodically and harmonically, suggest most powerfully the turmoil of the scene in the Garden of Gethsemane.

The theme of which these intervals are so important a constituent is a heavily marked, chant-like ostinato, although the latter word must not be interpreted too strictly for the following reasons: the theme's second statement is an inversion of the first and there is a two and a half measure solo quartet passage whose material represents a real departure from the theme in that the augmented and diminished intervals are entirely absent. But as this brief passage occurs at almost the midpoint of the motet, it is a division in the structure, for the second half of the motet is an exact repetition of the first half except for the final cadence and some insignificant details. Thus save for this quartet passage, the listener accepts the theme throughout as an ostinato, not just because of the frequent tritones which are, of course, the same size in the inverted version, but also because these intervals occur at the same points in each statement of the theme, and in the same metrical pattern.

The octave pairing of voices – alto and bass, soprano and tenor – concentrates and intensifies the theme as well as giving it depth. The opening *forte* statement (Example 215), is scored for the first pair, which then continues with closely related material – including the characteristic intervals – while the soprano and tenor present the inversion, *forte*. At its conclusion the altos and basses are again alone for two measures before being joined by sopranos singing in octaves, and tenors, both stating the original version. The solo quartet then takes over for its short passage, the second half commences with altos and basses – *divisi* and *pianissimo* – and everything is a restatement of the first half. The final and overwhelming impression which remains with the listener is the inexorable quality of the theme which, with its tritones, underlines the doom inherent in the text. It is interesting that when I pointed out the centrality of this motet in the entire work, Rubbra was not aware that this was so.

In sharp contrast to the harmonic ambiguity of *Judas Mercator Pessimus*, the two flanking motets, *Amicus Meus* and *Unus Ex Discipulis*, are strongly rooted in C minor, but with middle sections in less sharply defined tonalities. The same sense of impending doom is present, but in both motets it is less dramatic and more subtle – even chilling at times.

The opening and closing material of both motets consists of tightly controlled, small, repeating and largely conjunct intervals whose basic reference point is some form of the C minor triad. In *Amicus Meus* the central interval is the ascending and descending minor third, mostly filled in but also nicely balanced

Ex. 215

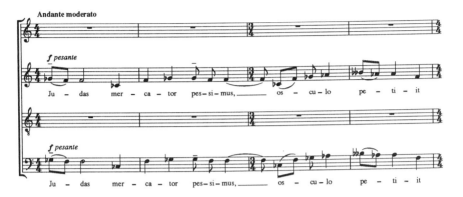

by occasional leaps of a third. The motet's first half is in strict canon at the octave and at the distance of one measure, and it is between soprano and tenor, alto and bass. This causes some of the C minor reference points to contain other tones – D, B flat, A flat – thus creating a feeling of restlessness appropriate to the words, 'My friend betrayed me with a kiss.'

In *Unus Ex Discipulis* the movement is at times very chromatic, and when the chromaticism is combined with the opening *pianissimo* in a slow tempo, and the restless consecutive fifths in the bass, the hopeless atmosphere is almost palpable. Adding to that atmosphere is the heaviness of the six parts. The opening phrase is shown in Example 216. When this phrase is repeated near the end of the motet, its first half has been redistributed with respect to parts. The altos and the lower line of the basses sing the sopranos' top line, while sustained notes have been given to the sopranos and tenors. The sound and the effect of these changes is to darken the texture and underline the tragedy of the scene. The second half of the phrase is set as before.

Whereas the Second Nocturn motets are at least 50 per cent polyphonic, those of the Third Nocturn are predominantly chordal. They were composed for

Ex. 216

the 1962 Cork Festival and bear the date, Advent 1961. The dedication is to Denys Darlow and the Tilford Bach Choir.

As with the central motets of the two preceding Nocturns, so the middle motet of this Nocturn has features not found in either of its neighbours. Its text, *Una Hora Non Potuistis*, is dramatic in terms of its unanswered questions, a quality brought out at once by a four-part unison passage whose rising and falling pitches, detached notes and carefully shaded dynamics pose the question, 'Could ye not watch one hour with me?' The following phrase in paired parts and two-part harmony completes the question with 'ye that were ready to die for me?' Although both phrases are immediately repeated for the next question, 'Or see ye not Judas, how he sleepeth not, but maketh haste to betray me to the Jews?', the setting is less dramatic, the unison writing having been replaced by part-writing. A dramatic and chordal middle section of slightly over five measures in six, seven and eight parts, again paired, intervenes with harmonies consisting of unrelated triads. The motet ends with a final statement of the opening phrases, harmonized for the most part as in its earlier statements.

The companion motets are more difficult and present problems for the singers. Arising from several sources, these may be briefly summarized: first, there is a larger percentage of *divisi* parts which call for five or six real parts rather than duplications of one kind or another; second, both the chromatic and, at times, very dissonant harmonies can cause serious intonational problems; and third, the tenors are required to sing a number of As and even a B flat in *Eram Quasi Agnus Innocens*, the first motet. In *Seniores Populi*, the third motet, there is a succession of consecutive, root-position triads, the majority of which are unrelated to one another. Inevitably, these are rather potent reminders of similar passages in the music of both Holst and Vaughan Williams. For all of these reasons, the motets of the Third Nocturn are less likely to be performed than those of the first two.

Owing to the ten-year gap between the First Nocturn and the two following, there is not, to my knowledge, a comprehensive review of the work as a whole. There are, however, two short reviews of the First Nocturn:

> Dr. Rubbra portrays the sombre message of his text by the simplest means. All these are mainly homophonic, probably because they are intended for their particular liturgical purpose and would become too extended with contrapuntal treatment. No. 3 is in eight parts throughout, the other two are in four parts; and all contain beautiful sounds.[55]

The equally enthusiastic second reviewer emphasizes different points:

> These three Tenebrae settings prove that within a comparatively simple harmonic structure, and without technical complexity, a composer of Rubbra's calibre can achieve both intensity of feeling and complete unity with the words. Such a satisfying fusion of the aural arts is rarely met in modern choral music.[56]

The two later Nocturns are included as part of a larger review in which a later choral work is considered:

> The parts are often in pairs at the outset of a point of imitation, and textures of great richness are achieved through dividing the voices. Of the two sets, those of the Third Nocturn place a great strain on the singers and require voices which are inexhaustible engines, but those of the second are not so fierce in their demands and are more expressive. Most effective is the way the last sentence of the response is reset after the versicle, being varied but recognizably similar music.[57]

Despite the difficulties in all three Nocturns, all nine motets are well worth the efforts needed to ensure outstanding performances, and they should not deter choral conductors from including them in their repertoires, either as concert pieces or as appropriate motets for Holy Week services. Insofar as the Catholic liturgy for which they were written is concerned, it is a great pity that today's modernized and popularized church seems to provide no place for motets of this high calibre.

Three Motets

Three *a cappella* motets comprise Op. 76. The dedicatory note informs us that they were 'written for and dedicated to The Friends' School, Saffron Walden on the occasion of its 250th anniversary, 1952'. Appropriately, one of the texts is by a Quaker, James Nayler, although the middle motet in which it appears is unusual in that his poem is combined with the *Beatitudes*. This feature, together with its greater length in comparison with its flanking neighbours, suggests another triptych.

The first motet, *Let Us Now Praise Famous Men* (Ecclesiasticus 44), is set straightforwardly in 5/4 metre with very brief changes to 7/4 and 3/4, and longer stretches of 4/4. The rhythmic flow is supple with a division of the 5/4 metre that conforms to the rhythm of the text at any particular time. Triplet patterns play an important part in all of the metres. The texture is block chordal and the effect of the entire motet is that of recitative. As in the *Tenebrae* motets, there is *divisi* writing, and some pairing of parts. One unusual feature is the organ pedal on G, held for the length of the motet. In a note at the bottom of the score, the composer says, 'should there be no organ available this pedal note can be played either as a timpani roll, or by means of octave tremolando on the piano. If the choir is large a combination of organ pedal and timpani would be effective.' Whichever is used, the pedal has the effect of strongly orienting the tonality to G (minor in this instance), although the final measure consists of a V of V above which an alto soloist suddenly appears with the words 'liveth for evermore' over the held chord. There is thus no formal cadence in the accepted sense, but assuming that the second motet is to be sung immediately, the transition from G, A, C sharp, E, A (reading upward) to a chord of E minor with an A instead of a G is not abrupt.

One of the interesting side issues that comes into play in any discussion of text-setting, whether it be choral music or songs, is the opportunity for brief comparisons when another composer has set the same words. In this instance the composer is Vaughan Williams, and his setting of *Let Us Now Praise Famous Men* is entirely different from the Rubbra motet. The basic difference – noticeable immediately – is that the former displays to perfection its composer's extroverted side, the vigour of which is apparent in the unison setting, and the march-like accompaniment. Its chord structure is very simple and the left-hand, quarter-note octaves, in many places resembling an ostinato, have a forward drive that brooks no interference. Its designation as an 'anthem' in contradistinction to Rubbra's 'motet' may not seem important, especially in view of the fact that a Latin text is not involved, but there is, none the less, a subtle difference that is felt rather than explained.

Rubbra's second motet takes its title from James Nayler's poem, *There Is A Spirit*. This Quaker theologian (1616–60) was born in Yorkshire, and later became a devoted follower of George Fox, the founder of Quakerism. He suffered severe penalties for his beliefs: the pillory, branding on his forehead with hot irons, and the spiking of his tongue. He wrote sermons, poems and various Quaker writings. The serenity of his spirit in the face of such treatment is evident from the opening of his poem: 'There is a spirit which I feel that delights to do no evil, nor to revenge any wrong, but delights to endure all things, in hope to enjoy its own in the end.' The decision to couple this text with the *Beatitudes* was a good one, for the gentleness and humility of the *Beatitudes* is in total harmony with Nayler's poem. Rubbra solves the complexities by assigning the *Beatitudes* to the SATB choir, and Nayler's poem to a solo soprano. The choir leads off, and at the fifth measure the poem begins. Careful attention to the proper balance between choir and soloist is evident from the directions given the choir at the very start: *sempre piano-pianissimo ma con espress*. Accordingly, only the solo part is provided with changes in dynamic levels, but when the solo part ends approximately two-thirds of the way through, such changes are transferred to the choir. While the choir and soloist are together the balance between the two is preserved in another way: the choir is given a narrow range, the notes of which with few exceptions lie well below those of the soloist. The choir's melodic material is chant-like, with many repeated notes. The soloist's material, on the other hand, is exuberant, more flexible and rhythmically independent of the choir. The soloist thus stands out from the choir but yet never dominates it.

When both texts finish simultaneously, another text – presumably by Nayler – is taken up by the choir alone, except for the four final measures where the soloist joins in. The choral style during this section is the same as that of the *Beatitudes*, but frequent metre changes accommodate the textual rhythms, and, as mentioned above, dynamic markings appear now that the soloist is resting. The number of parts increases from four to eight as the section progresses, and the motet ends exultantly for both choir and soloist.

The third motet, *Except the Lord Build The House*, takes its title from the first verse of Psalm 127, but the second half of this very short piece is a setting of verses 1 and 18 of Psalm 115: 'Not unto us, O Lord, but unto Thy name give glory', and so on. It is largely polyphonic, consisting of two very small and loosely defined sections, the first of which is dominated by a four-note motive. Beginning with the sopranos and descending in order, this motive appears in stretto at a two-beat interval with the altos and basses singing its inversion. This same plan is kept for the next statements, although the tenor's entry is altered and the bass inversion is pitched a minor third lower. Thereafter, there are five more entries, the last two of which are well into the second section. This section opens with verse 1 of Psalm 115, chanted at the fifth in organum style by the tenors and basses under a four-part chord held in the top voice parts. These latter parts retain their *divisi* status through to the end and do, in fact, sing a four-part version of the first section's motive before stating their own, new motive. The undivided tenors and basses have their own new motive in stretto, and the rest of the motet consists of alternating statements of these two. Verse 18 of the Psalm starts with the men's new motive. Harmonically, this motet is interesting because of the dissonances created by the contrapuntal movement.

While in all three motets there are some difficult places that involve intonational problems, a reasonably competent choir should be able to perform all three successfully. Any one of them can be sung in a general service situation if it were to prove impractical to perform the work as a whole.

Song of the Soul

For the text of his Op. 78 Rubbra returned to St John of the Cross in a translation by Roy Campbell, who, in a letter of 14 January 1953, enthusiastically gave his permission for its use:

I should be honoured and thrilled to have my translation set to music by you: and I shouldn't dream of charging anything. Funnily enough by a very rare coincidence, I had a letter by the same mail today from Graham Greene asking if he can quote several verses from the same translation in his forthcoming play, 'The Living Room'. As far as I can remember I have never even been asked for a quotation before from any of my work, let alone the far greater honour of having it set to music by a famous composer...

My friends Constant Lambert, Willie Walton, Cecil Gray and Philip Heseltine and Bernard van Dieren all said that my work could not be set to music. The last three tried and failed: and Gray wrote about the alleged impossibility of doing so in his autobiography 'Musical Chairs'.

Subtitled 'In intimate communication and union with the love of God', the *Song of the Soul* was 'especially written for the London Bach Society' in the early 1950s, and is scored for a chorus of SSATBB, strings, harp and timpani. The mysticism which is so much a part of the text of *The Dark Night of the Soul* is just as apparent here, but it is more ardent and intense than in the earlier poem. The imagery mentioned in connection with St John and St Teresa appears here: 'O flame of love, so living. / How tenderly you force / To my soul's inmost core your fiery probe!' And later: 'O cautery most tender! O gash that is my guerdon!'

Elsie Payne has some specific answers with regard to how Rubbra expressed the mysticism of this particular text:

Rubbra succeeded in the *Song of the Soul* in projecting into musical terms an experience which is not only humanly passionate but also rarefied or mystical. How? By melody which is forthright, positive and rhythmical, yet unmetrical and ambiguous in tonality and modality; by harmony which is lavish and varied but again insecure in tonality and frequently made up of bottomless 6/4 chords; by an instrumentation which, though colourful, is light and ephemeral, with much emphasis on harp timbre: and by an overall vivacity and sense of continuity in spite of a fluctuating momentum and a basically episodic formality. All his devices are unobtrusive. There is nothing, for instance, in Rubbra's mystical expression as arresting or ecstatic as in Tippett's *Vision of St. Augustine*, or in Messiaen's devastating *Et Expecto Resurrectionem Mortuorum*. Rubbra's music is indeed much more subtle in all respects.[58]

As is so often true in Rubbra's music, there is a germinal motive which gives rise to much, if not most, of what follows. It is seen in Example 217, where it is readily apparent that *b* is the inversion of *a*. The melodic fragment that rides atop the second-inversion chords of *a* and *b*, is pliable enough to generate new

Ex. 217

intervals such as those seen in measures 2–4 of the example. This basic material continues to expand and change as the work moves on.

The dissonances created by the interaction of these chords with the basic E flat major tonality are a distinctive feature of this work, yet they are neither strident nor disturbing. They are quite necessary, however, for the text generates a good deal of tension that must be expressed musically. Just because a text is said to be mystical and thus ambiguous and difficult to understand is no guarantee that the experience it describes is necessarily placid or trance-like. Many such experiences are quite the opposite, and produce agitation of one kind or another. Rubbra was aware of this and his setting of this text is more dissonant than that of the milder *The Dark Night of the Soul*.

The basic plan with regard to the choral forces concerns their division into two groups, sometimes equal, sometimes not, thereby creating an antiphonal effect when they are separated, and a massed double-choir sound when they are together. When the voice parts enter on the last beat of measure 4, the top three – SSA – come in first, followed on the final beat of measure 5 by the bottom three – TBB. After the initial entry, each entry of either group is accompanied by long, held notes in the other; and the second-inversion triads of the type seen in the example retain their individuality in both groups. On the last beat of measure 9 all six parts are joined in block harmony, but again the 6–4 chords remain independent. Another arrangement of the choral forces consists of first sopranos – *divisi* – and second sopranos with the *divisi* altos and the three lower parts beneath. The upper parts in this arrangement exchange their 6–4 chords in favour of root-position triads, which are also unrelated to one another. For the major part of the rest of the motet block-chord, double-choir sound prevails, and with but small exceptions the lower three parts are duplicates at the lower octave of the upper three. The closing measures quietly recall a portion of the opening section.

Immediately after the first massed choir section on the words, 'Since now you've no misgiving, end it', the cellos and basses in measure 17 quietly introduce a melodic line that seems at first sight to constitute a totally fresh idea that is unrelated to anything preceding it. However, close examination reveals that it is derived from the melodic contours of the chords in the third and fourth measures of Example 217. The A flat, G, D in the lower strings comes from the E flat, D, G, while E sharp, F sharp, B stems from B, C, G. Of course, the order in the new melodic line is the reverse of that in the chords, and the leap is a fourth instead of a fifth. This material, continuing beneath the vocal lines, quickly rises to the top of the orchestra where, in a typically Rubbran fashion, an ostinato appears and tension is built up until, at measure 36, the texture becomes chordal again, but the chords employed bear no resemblance to the initial second-inversion triads. The melody atop these new chords sometimes follows the vocal line, but more often it is independent.

One's subjective feeling at the conclusion of the *Song of the Soul* is that some sort of unusual experience has occurred. There is a sense of fulfilment that is deeply satisfying. For a more detailed personal reaction, both to the composer and the work, I quote remarks made to me in a letter of 14 July 1980, by Sister Jane Cicely, a member of an Anglican order. She writes:

> My contact with Rubbra was about thirty years ago when I was a professional musician. I was singing with Dr. Paul Steinitz's choir, the London Bach Society, and around the early 1950s we studied and sang a work by Edmund Rubbra, which if I remember aright was still in manuscript, perhaps photocopied.... Certainly he came to some of our rehearsals, and made a lasting impression on me as a quiet man of depth, somehow empowered by a rare humility.

After identifying the work as the *Song of the Soul*, she continues:

> The music spoke deeply to me and so lit up the words that hitherto unknown vistas of prayer were opened. The composer's presence with us added to what was an unforgettable experience.

Later, in a taped interview of 23 July, Sister Jane recalled more specific impressions of the work:

> I found that spiritually that setting of the *Song of the Soul* spoke to me beyond what I knew it was saying. The text I think in those days wouldn't have spoken to me. But the combination of the text and what the music said, which was *beyond* words (which is what prayer means to me), affected me to a degree that I have remembered all these years, without remembering any detail – no detail – of the music at all.

Sister Jane's memory of the poem as an uplifting experience in itself is in sharp, even ridiculous, contrast to the reaction expressed in the following passage:

> So sensuous is the imagery that I have had the unusual experience of having the *Song of the Soul* turned down for performance by the choir of a music school (which shall be nameless) because of the unsuitability of the words for young singers. St. John of the Cross would have been amused.[59]

In the same article and immediately preceding this extraordinary revelation, the composer has made available some information regarding the work:

> *Song of the Soul*, although written some fifteen years after *The Dark Night of the Soul*, is in many ways a companion work. True, the orchestral forces have been reduced to strings, the resulting greater homogeneity of sound being illuminated by a harp and made more dramatic by timpani, but the chromatic element remains as a sensuous part of the texture. The chromaticism, however, is less obviously there (a sign perhaps of the work's greater maturity); it is present in the opposition of harmonies – e.g. E flat major against G major or B major [see *a* and *b* in Example 217] – rather than in the thematic lines themselves. But the two works are, in a very real sense, complementary, as the words of *Song of the Soul*... are a description, using the imagery of earthly love, of the rapture of attainment when the soul has finally ceased its struggles through the dark night.[60]

Following a performance of the work at St Bartholomew's, Smithfield, on 17 June 1953, this review appeared:

> one of those supremely satisfying experiences – rare, for that matter – that leaves one spiritually exalted and musically stabilised. There was the feeling that for once one had recognized, by an instinct one could not but trust, a great work; and more,

that as the work passed by, with that treacherous speed music affects, it came close enough for one to imagine that it almost pleaded to be recognized for what it was. And of course one could not stay simply hearing but had to listen, a profoundly rewarding exercise.

Rubbra has chosen lines from a translation by Roy Campbell of the words of St. John of the Cross. It is a mystical vision, or rather the mystic's well-known, absolutely attested experience of spiritual union with God. Not unexpectedly its terms are those of physical ecstasy and one shudders to think what might have been the result of adding music to these unblushingly intimate expressions of spiritual sensuality had the musician been a sophisticated soul and an unsophisticated artist. With an unfaltering step Rubbra paces these ineffable distances. His gait is steady, his vision direct. The colour of his harmonies is warm, but he uses his polytonal counterpoint in such easy false relationships that one is not conscious of any excess of emotion. Looking at the score one discovers, in fact, not so much his as one's own emotion there. The quality of sound his texture produces is extraordinarily translucent.

As for the performance by the London Bach Society for whom the work was written, these thoughts about the music could hardly have been so vividly retained in the memory unless it had been good. As indeed it was; the best type of professionally trained amateur work, well directed by Paul Steinitz and altogether excellently presented.[61]

The night after the St Bartholomew's performance Paul Steinitz wrote the following letter to Rubbra from a ship:

Although you will not get it for some time, I must write and thank you for the great privilege of being able to conduct that wonderful work of yours last night. It is an experience I shall never forget, and it is living with me now to such an extent that I cannot settle down to a book this evening, but must write to you first.

If there is a broadcast of it, what do you think about doing it from St. Bartholomew's? The sound is so wonderful there, but there are snags from the broadcasting point of view; as soon as the number of strings is increased, the balance to us will be hopeless, unless we could keep the choir where it was and have the orchestra at the side of them (where the first block of seats is, as you come in, on the *left*).

May you write many more works of this calibre! Thank you again for so kindly writing it specially for us...

P.S. I suppose there is no chance of recording 'Song of the Soul'?

Miscellaneous small works

Between *Song of the Soul* and the next major choral work, there are five unaccompanied pieces – all short. In fact, choral composition assumed a decidedly subordinate place between this work and the Festival Gloria. This is because the Sixth and Seventh Symphonies, the Piano Concerto, Op. 85, and the Improvisation for Violin and Orchestra took precedence, and these five short pieces were fitted in here and there. *Star of the Mystic East*, Op. 81 for SATB is the first of these. It is set to a text by C.H.O. Daniel, Provost of Worcester College, Oxford, from 1903 to 1919, and it is dedicated to the Provost, Dean and Fellows of that College (where Rubbra taught for many years). It is a simple Christmas carol whose three stanzas are set to the same music – a seven-measure sentence with several metre changes, and a block chordal style consisting of basic triads and sevenths.

The most important of the five pieces is *Salutation*, Op. 82, also scored for SATB. A note inside the score reads

> This part-song is one of a collection commissioned by the Arts Council of Great Britain and composed to mark the occasion of the Coronation of Her Majesty Queen Elizabeth II. The collection was published by Messrs. Stainer and Bell Ltd. under the title, 'A Garland for the Queen'.

Ten poets and ten composers altogether were invited to contribute. The other composers were Bliss, Bax, Tippett, Vaughan Williams, Berkeley, Ireland, Howells, Finzi and Rawsthorne. The work as a whole can be considered as a modern equivalent to *The Triumphs of Oriana*, the collection of madrigals honouring the first Elizabeth. The set was first performed on 1 June 1953, the eve of Coronation Day, in the Royal Festival Hall. The poet for Rubbra's contribution was Christopher Hassall (1912–63). Besides his work as a poet, Hassall was the biographer of Rupert Brooke and Sir Edward Marsh, and the librettist for Walton's *Troilus and Cressida* and Bliss's *Tobias and the Angels*. He was also a talented composer. His *Salutation* makes no direct reference to the Queen, but is metaphoric. It first refers to the sad aftermath of the Second World War and as it progresses, suggests a prospect of better things to come.

Rubbra's sensitive setting follows the mood of this rather striking poem from the depression of 'We are still in the valley, the dark valley; / Scarred walls where the willow herb / Opens her healing flower' to the exultation of 'But thanks be to God, we go a hopeful journey, / For our land is a land of lingering winter, / Blessed with the Spring for Queen.' The music throughout the piece is illustrative to a greater degree than might be expected of Rubbra, yet this is natural, for in addition to its general moods the poem also projects definite images. Thus in the soprano and alto parts, 'the dark valley' is set to descending triplets that are dissonant with the remaining voices. When the willow herb 'opens her healing flower', the sopranos, again assigned triplets, soar quickly to an A flat and then descend more slowly to a C which, when it is joined to notes in the other parts, produces a pure C major chord. The rapid opening of the flower and its ability to heal the 'scarred walls', symbolized by the purity of the C major chord, are examples of musical imagery at its best. So also is the sombre passage that follows: 'And what scarred memories! O God of battles, / What terrible, proud thoughts has thou made our daily meat, / What burden of proud sorrow!' By the simple expedient of having all the parts except the altos and second basses retain their notes through 'scarred memories', Rubbra subtly darkens the harmony on these words to C minor as E flat is sounded by the altos. The second basses then descend to two A flats and a G. 'Memories' is set to a C major 6–4 chord on the first syllable, but the rest of the word becomes a neutral emptiness when the E natural is removed. The darkness continues musically through the remaining words of the passage.

The mood of both poem and music alters abruptly with 'With faffling banners, bells, all manner of music, / The old is made new, / Our thoughts are morning thoughts, / And our songs are a salutation.' The darkness of the valley returns momentarily in musical imagery heard previously and the piece ends triumphantly with the words cited earlier.

Salutation is a fine work that is suitable for performance at anytime; simply because it was composed for a special occasion, it should not be thought of as having fulfilled or outlived its purpose. In terms of its place in the larger work, *A Garland for the Queen*, it is judged to be 'the most interesting, and in quality the finest' along with the contributions of Bliss, Tippett and Howells, because of the 'polyphonic ideas.... Fifty years ago block-chords were our natural habitation; in 1953 we have returned, or advanced, to a contrapuntal frame of mind.'[62]

Two very contrasting arrangements of pre-existing melodies follow: *Dance to Your Daddie*, Op. 84 (SATB), a Scottish nursery song, and *Mary Mother*, Op. 90 (SSATB), a Portuguese folksong. The first is inscribed to Elizabeth Poston, composer, writer and pianist, who also collected folksongs. The piece, marked *Allegro*, has a dancing, sparkling rhythm and a merry quality. The melody is distributed among the parts and boisterous chains of open, consecutive fifths add to the fun.

Mary Mother is a tender Christmas carol containing four stanzas. The parts to which the melody and its attendant block harmonies are assigned – no matter which stanza is involved – are designated 6/8, 3/4. The remaining parts, whether above or below, are in 6/8 metre and their function is essentially one of furnishing a background, for they have been given running counterpoints on the syllable 'ah' (except for one texted passage). Ending each stanza is a refrain, identified by the melody in the first sopranos plus the change in all parts to 2/4 for one measure, followed by two measures of 3/4. Each of the refrain cadences is modal. As for the distribution of parts and harmonic structure, stanzas 1 and 4 are identical, but variety in the middle stanzas is obtained through reassignment of parts. This results, of course, in different harmonic combinations – one of the great charms of this little piece. Throughout the carol, the rhythmic play is very flexible, not only vertically between the double-metred parts and the 6/8 background, but also horizontally as the double-metred voices alternate from 6/8 to 3/4 and back again.

The fifth and final piece in this group of short works is *Entrez-y Tous En Sureté*, Op. 93, another charming Christmas carol, this time to an untranslated text by the seventeenth-century French poet, Christin Prost. A note in the score informs us that the tune was written in 1924 and arranged for SATB in 1956. The melody is long-breathed and in the Aeolian mode with a sprinkling of F and G sharps. The harmony is also predominantly modal with the addition of some sevenths. There are two stanzas; at the beginning of the second the tenors have the melody for six measures (it is marked 'soli'), before surrendering it to the sopranos, who take it to the end. The composer's directions at the start of the tenors' solo state that 'if there are not sufficient tenors to give weight to this line the music of the first verse should be repeated for six bars, then continue as on page 4, bar 3.' Concessions such as this show that the piece is practical for the average choir and both this and the Portuguese carol should find their way into the Christmas repertoire.

The brief review of these Christmas pieces opens with the statement that 'Edmund Rubbra has given us two gems... "Mary Mother" ... has a delicious flavour and, in spite of dissonances, the voice parts are not difficult to sing.' *Entrez-y Tous En Sureté* 'in the style of a chorale is very pleasing.'[63]

Festival Gloria

Op. 94, *Festival Gloria*, in Latin, was 'commissioned by and dedicated to St. Paul's Cathedral Choir', and is scored for unaccompanied double choir with soprano and baritone soli. Near the end of the work there are some *divisi* sections within both decani and cantoris choirs (Soprano I, II, III and Alto I, II, III), but because of doublings there are not sixteen independent parts.

The festive atmosphere of praise and adoration that marks, roughly, the first third of the *Gloria* text, is well reflected in the first seventy-four measures of the work. The tempo is *Allegro* and, except for several explicitly marked changes, it remains so throughout this section. The texture here is chordal, but each choir has different material – not *thematic* material, for thinking of it in that sense would be a mistake. Nevertheless, even though such material is lacking, there is a distinct and recognizable focus that, by concentrating on the movement of unrelated triads, produces a similarity in the overall sound, thus promoting unity.

With the ushering in of a second section by the soprano soloist, the quieter and more subjective portions of the text are before us. The tempo is initially *Andante*. During the twelve-measure solo, the choirs are separated into antiphonal bodies that sing alternating passages so designed that all moving parts occur during the soloist's held notes and vice versa. At the conclusion of the solo, the tempo changes to *Adagio* and what at first appears to be a fugue subject complete with stretto answer issues quietly from the tenors and altos in the *cantoris* choir on the words, 'qui tollis peccata mundi'. The intervallic structure of this 'subject' is so well balanced, and the totality of it so beautiful that one wishes Rubbra had decided to write at least a short fugue on it (Example 218). But following the incomplete alto and bass entries – the latter in the *decani* choir –

Ex. 218

the music charts a different but not wholly unrelated course. Spatially, this entire passage is striking in the way the sound crosses from one side of the chancel to the other. At the petition, 'suscipe deprecationem nostram', all eight parts join together in singing, *forte*, massive, unrelated first-inversion triads composed of eighths and sixteenths. The baritone then enters for his only solo of just over four measures on the 'qui tollis' petition, while at the same time longer value chords continue softly. As the soloist finishes, an extraordinary passage begins: a two-measure chant-like, melodic, rhythmic, and harmonic ostinato involving all four *decani* parts on the words, 'qui sedes ad dexteram Patris'. At the same time, on the *cantoris* side of the chancel entirely different figures are heard in paired parts – a different figure for each pair. The whole passage increases in volume and tension until, to different but similar figures in each choir, the climax is reached on 'altissimus Jesu Christe'.

The start of the ostinato figure is shown in Example 219. A lovely touch is then provided by the soprano's solo phrase, which overlaps the beginning of the

Ex. 219

final section: the *Allegro* setting of 'cum Sancto Spiritu'. Here, *divisi* writing creates three soprano and alto parts in each choir. These plus the two men's parts in each choir produce a massive sound. However, numerous doublings mean that there are not sixteen independent parts and at the start of this final section, both choirs are not always singing at the same time, for there are several imitative entries, the *decani* side leading off and the *cantoris* following.

As for reviews of this work, it is obvious from the following quote that the writer had not heard the music. His remarks appear at the end of an uncomplimentary review of the next choral work, and that notice will appear in due course. As for the *Festival Gloria*, it

> shows a flash of the old fire and originality. One would like to hear the passage of piled-up dissonances *pp allegro* on pp. 16–19 sung by a choir [the 'cum Sancto Spiritu' section described above]; it should sound fascinating. This looks like a fine work.'[64]

Another review reads as follows:

> Edmund Rubbra's *Festival Gloria*... received its first performance in the Festival Hall on 7 October 1957... the work ended the first part of a concert of both sacred

and secular music given by the Choir of St. Paul's Cathedral and the Kalmar Chamber Orchestra, under Dr. John Dykes Bower...

Rubbra's *Gloria* was none the less the revelatory item, for the demands it makes on the singers are formidable, and they were fearlessly and splendidly met. The texture throughout is fresh and clean, nicely calculated in its harmonic and contrapuntal aspects, and also in its dynamic range. There is about it more of the feeling of light and air than about Rubbra's earlier choral works, yet the *Gloria* touches the composer's most personal vein.[65]

Haec Est Domus Domini

Op. 95, *Haec Est Domus Domini* – subtitled Motet for the Dedication of a Church – might be thought of as appropriate only on those rare occasions when a church building is consecrated, yet in its later English version as *This Is Truly The House of God*, it is entirely suitable as an anthem for use in any Protestant denomination. Doubtlessly this is what prompted the translation. It is a very short piece – four pages – and it is scored for unaccompanied SATB choir with no *divisi* parts. Its text is derived from the Responsory for Matins of Mass, 'Terribilus est' and Psalm 83. Both texts appear in the *Liber Usualis* at the appropriate places. The structure is a perfectly balanced ternary form in which the words dealing with the house of God are set in the first and third sections, while in the *B* section the words from the Psalm are set to different music. The *A* sections are composed of simple triads entirely devoid of dissonances in a mostly chordal context of quarters and eighths, while the middle section has a flowing style characterized by triplets and some dissonances.

The unnecessarily acid tone of the aforementioned review, reproduced below, calls for an explanation:

> Someone once said of Stravinsky's ?th period that each new work was like another piece from a roll of wall-paper with a repeating pattern. Rubbra's 'Haec est Domus Domini' rather reminds me of this remark; it is short and simple, and could be inserted into any one of a number of similar things without occasioning surprise. Is it an immutable law that as soon as a great spiritual force decays the art associated with it decays also? Church music is in a trough; and Rubbra has seemingly ceased to develop; a grey mist hangs over his work. A pity[66]

One wonders if the reviewer has overlooked or is ignorant of the fact that this motet (and others like it by far inferior composers) was designed to supply a need in a church of modest size with an amateur choir of very modest abilities. The church in question is the one to which the piece is inscribed: St Augustine's in High Wycombe together with its choir. Certainly anyone conversant with the situation of Catholic choirs in England will realize that they are not the equals of Church of England choirs, even in fairly large towns. Therefore, simplicity is a virtue as is an uncomplicated texture.

The Givers

The Givers, Op. 96, for unaccompanied SATB choir, is another of Rubbra's very few secular choral pieces. 'Written especially in honour of the 85th birth-day of Ralph Vaughan Williams', it is set to a three-stanza poem by Louis MacNeice (1907–1963), author of numerous volumes of poetry, as well as a study of Yeats, and translator of Aeschylus's *Agamemnon* and Goethe's *Faust*. Rubbra's thoughtful choice of this poem clearly shows his great esteem for Vaughan Williams for, although there is no reference anywhere in it to any particular person, its title and the 'uniqueness' of which the poet writes both point to a rare type of personality – one not often encountered.

Again, four pages suffice. The form is strophic, carefully modified in ac-cordance with the slightly different poetic rhythms. Also, at the end of the second stanza there are some note differences in all parts, which, of course, mean harmonic differences. The final cadence is also new. Many passages include *divisi* writing such that the average number of parts increases to five, six and eight. The music is very expressive, both in the way its chromaticism gently highlights significant words, and in the use of second-inversion triads which serve to stress the music's quietly soothing character, but without the weakness that 6–4 chords sometimes impart.

In Honorem Mariae Matris Dei

In Honorem Mariae Matris Dei, Op. 97, is the first of Rubbra's three cantatas. It was composed for the Lourdes centenary, but it is eminently suitable for the Advent season. Its text which, despite the Latin title, is in English, consists of selected passages from the Old and New Testaments – *Ecclesiastes*, *Isaiah*, the *Song of Solomon* and Luke's Gospel – plus an appropriate Collect, and is so arranged as to form a continuous narrative of the Virgin Mary's visit to her cousin, Elizabeth, who, at an advanced age, is also expecting a child. The scriptural peak of the visit is Mary's recitation, in Luke, of what came to be called the *Magnificat*, although the first three verses only are used. While Mary is singing these, Elizabeth's exclamations as recorded in Luke are also heard, but they are set so that each one begins under a held note at the end of Mary's solo passages. Her part is sung by a soprano and Elizabeth's by a contralto. The narrative portions are entrusted to an SATB mixed choir and a children's choir (SSA). In addition, two short passages assigned to an angel – the first giving out the Isaiah prophecy ('Maid shall be with child and shall bear a son that shall be called Emmanuel') and the second directing Mary to 'see how it fares with thy cousin Elizabeth', and so on – are sung by the mixed choir. The accompani-ment is for organ or orchestra.

The music throughout the cantata has a relaxed, exultant and rhapsodic sound, echoing the same qualities in the words. Melodically, this is expressed in lines that are sometimes modal and which employ repeated notes. At other times, particularly in the two solo parts, there are figures showing a balance between high and low notes. Rhythmically, everything is moulded to the words, and a free-flowing, recitative-like style emerges, marked by triplets as textual needs dictate. Harmonically, in the choral parts, parallel motion involving complete triads is uppermost, although passages in parallel octaves are also heard. There are three *divisi* passages in the mixed choir, the first occurring at one of the text's high points: 'And Elizabeth was filled with the Holy Ghost so that she cried out', and so on.

The score contains the organ version of the accompaniment, and the fact that it is laid out in three staves with great care taken as to registration and manual changes may indicate that Rubbra preferred the organ over the orchestral version. Whichever version is used, the accompaniment remains independent of the voices except for short passages where it parallels the children's choir. However, despite the independence, there is often a subtle kinship with the voices so that the melodic elements are quietly exchanged or expanded upon.

It is significant that in the following extract, Rubbra, by placing this cantata in the company of others to which the term 'mystical' has been applied, further reveals his affinities as well as the natural bent of his mind: 'something of the inner nature of the St. John of the Cross and Hopkins works [*Inscape*, to be discussed later] is found in the Cantata.'[67] I must confess that I find it difficult to place this work in this category, for I think it is far inferior. First, I do not accept that any of its texts are mystical in the sense of the St John of the Cross and Gerard Manley Hopkins texts: second, the music is inferior to all of these other works. There is too much reliance on the virtually predictable movements of unrelated triads and in time this becomes tiresome and self-defeating. I cannot altogether rid myself of the impression that the cantata which, after all, was written to commemorate a particular occasion, observed by many thousands of people around the world, is encircled by an aura indicative of mass appeal – not that the composer intended it that way. My impression is certainly strengthened by the circumstances surrounding the cantata's first performances:

> Has it ever happened to a British composer before (or for that matter to any composer) to have a new work performed simultaneously in six different cities? The composer in question was Edmund Rubbra, the work was his cantata *In Honorem Mariae Matris Dei*, and the occasion was the Six Halls Festival to commemorate the first centenary of the shrine at Lourdes. The Festival was held on 10 February [1958], the eve of the centenary in London, Manchester, Liverpool, Newcastle, Bradford and Birmingham. At the Royal Albert Hall in London the cantata was sung by the Schola Polyphonica and five hundred school children, with Sylvia Fisher and Constance Shacklock as soloists, the Goldsbrough Orchestra, and John Pritchard conducting. A serene and radiant work, owing something perhaps to Holst... the cantata made a pleasing impression.[68]

My opinion of the cantata falls far short of the sentiments put forth by Pirie in his review:

Rubbra is a more serious case. For some time now I have felt a definite slackening off; his First Symphony was so full of promise. I cannot pretend that his later religious music appeals to me personally at all. The words of the present cantata have been arranged from the Old and New Testaments by Fr. Hanshell, S.J., and I must say that the order in which they are placed seems to me to detract from the original unsentimental purity of their meaning. The music, too, appears to me to carry sentiments that I cannot share. The treatment of the name of the least sentimental, most powerful and least respectable Artist [Jesus] who ever lived, at the bottom of p.13 of this score, is a case in point. I feel that the whole shows a mixture of barrenness and sentimentality rather distressingly typical of much late Rubbra. I do wish it were not so.[69]

A final comment: if the words of the cantata had been arranged in any other order the narrative aspect of the work would have been seriously impaired, if not destroyed.

Missa à 3

Rubbra's third Mass, *Missa à 3*, Op. 98, 'was commissioned by the Church Music Association of England to meet a demand for a liturgical work that asked for fewer voices and that would be more accessible for general use'.[70] Written for an *a cappella* choir of soprano, alto (or tenor) and bass, it is really a *Missa brevis* because of the omission of the *Credo*. However, throughout most of the work each of the three lines could function as an independent and acceptable melody. In fact, sections of the Mass could conceivably be sung by any two parts, a circumstance that suggests the medieval method of composing a three-part motet by writing the parts individually rather than simultaneously. In view of Rubbra's conception of polyphonic music as being the result of independent melodic lines that interact with one another, such a suggestion is not so far-fetched as it may seem. But the medieval atmosphere extends to more concrete instances in both the *Kyrie* and the *Gloria* where the voices are sometimes so close together that the total vertical range from top to bottom is less than an octave. Other medieval similarities include modal harmonies, empty fifths, an abundance of parallel fifths, and at one point in the *Kyrie* a double leading-tone cadence (measures 21–2).

Melodically, the generous use of D throughout the *Kyrie* and in the first half of the *Gloria* conveys the impression that this note is the final of the first mode rather than the tonic note of D minor. This impression is bolstered by the behaviour of the melody between the strong, empty cadences, for in both movements the A flats-G sharps used in conjunction with the D remind one of the medieval principle that any dissonances are acceptable in a passage provided that that passage is defined at its beginning and end by consonant intervals or chords on strong beats. While it must be conceded that these A flats-G sharps are members of independent triads, their position in the melodic line of the *Kyrie* produces a tritone relationship with the D which, because of the brevity of the phrases, is not erased so far as the ear is concerned. And a tritone relationship in medieval music was considered to be the ultimate dissonance – the 'diabolus in musica'. In the *Gloria* the G sharps are employed as leading tones to A, but the impression remains the same and for the same reason. Example 220 shows the first phrase of the *Kyrie* where most of these items appear.

Ex. 220

Perhaps the most widely known and publicized section of the Mass is the first half of the *Sanctus*, sometimes cited as a classic example of tritonality. In Example 221 it can be seen that Rubbra has written three key signatures, but it

Ex. 221

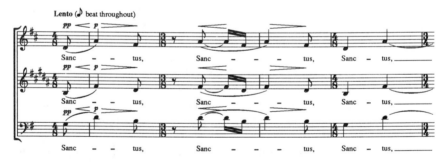

must be said that unless they are actually seen, a tritonal analysis will probably not occur to most theorists. It is, of course, true that if each of the three lines is sung separately, the same melody is set up in each of the three keys: D, B and G. However, when the lines are sung simultaneously, the *heard* as opposed to the *seen* is nothing but a juxtaposition of unrelated triads. In fact, because of the sopranos' A and the basses' D the overall tonality in the first seven measures is D major. Even the dominant of D is sounded on the last beat of measure 6, leading one to expect a cadence in that key in the next measure. Instead, the resolution is to B major, hardly a startling change.

The interesting question that now arises is why three key signatures were used if a tritonal analysis is invalid. My own view is that they were used in order to avoid accidentals, thus making each vocal line simpler and more understandable for the average singer to whom the Mass is addressed. The same question can be asked regarding certain of the three-part canons in Holst's Six Canons for Equal Voices where each voice is written in a different key, and here again the answer appears to be the same. However, in the final analysis the reasons for employing multiple key signatures are as unimportant as the presence of the signatures themselves and we return to the conviction, expressed a number of times in this book, that it is the ear, not the eye, that is the ultimate judge of what is occurring in any piece of music. This is a very elementary concept, yet it is astonishing how many analysts are misled by what they see on paper. Rubbra sums up the problem when, in discussing two of Holst's canons, he says:

> On paper there may be two or more conflicting keys, but the moment they are placed together in a complete texture distinction of key is obliterated, and in its place is a totality of new sounds, which must be accepted in their entirety. When yellow and blue are mixed to produce green the basic colours no longer exist visually. [Following his discussion of Holst's second canon and its three apparently different keys, he concludes that] the eye sees complications but the ear hears none.[71]

The publicity accompanying all such passages too often results in failure to regard them apart from the technical processes that brought them into being. In other words, their significance as artistic expressions is overlooked and not appreciated. Worse still, the total work of which the passage or movement in question is only a part tends to be neglected in favour of the notorious section. Examples of this abound in music history, one being the attention lavished on the canons and mathematical proportions in Ockeghem's Masses to the detriment of the music overall as an expressive force. The situation is the same here.

Small as it is, the first half of the *Sanctus* deserves attention not as an encyclopedic curiosity but as a deeply felt setting of the *Sanctus* text. This is Rubbra's third setting of these words, yet in spite of the three key signatures its similarity to the settings in the two previous Masses is so striking as to rule out coincidence as a factor. Indeed, the first sections of all three movements appear to be three aspects of an ideal which the composer envisioned as proper for the opening words of this text. All have slow settings in which triads, gently oscillating by thirds (and it makes no difference whether the intervallic movement is up or down), create delicate bell-like sounds, perhaps associated in Rubbra's mind with the Sanctus bell of the Catholic liturgy. A comparison between the second and third measures of the *Missa à 3 Sanctus* and measures 1 and 2 of the same movement in the *Missa in Honorem Sancti Dominici* shows that the two passages are almost identical. The only real exception is that the vertical alignment of notes in the *Missa à 3* precludes the reverberation effect present in both of the previous settings. In all three *Sanctus* movements the exultant mood is reserved for the later portions of the text.

The *Benedictus* is only thirteen measures long, but its structure is highly organized. This consists of a strict canon between sopranos and basses at a distance of one measure and at the octave. Adjustments are made in two places when the sopranos' C sharp is changed to C natural in the bass part. The melody from which the canon is formed is contained in one five-measure phrase and it is repeated once before the 'hosanna' section. During this section the basses, with one small change, complete their canonic participation, but continue to imitate in canon the first four notes of the 'hosanna' prior to the final cadence. Throughout the whole of the movement the middle voice has an independent melody which, with the exception of two G sharps and an E flat and a G flat, has a Gregorian sound.

Of the five movements, the *Agnus Dei* seems to embody the most personal expression; accordingly, it is the most poignant. Both of these qualities arise from the downward movement of the diminished fifth in the first measure, and the upward leap of the same interval from measure 1 to 2, as well as the chromaticism in the third and fourth measures. Strict imitation is a feature of this movement also, for at beat 2 of measure 5 the basses begin a complete statement of the sopranos' melody. However, even though there is an overlapping of the two parts, the imitation cannot in any way be called a canon because of the distance – four measures and one beat – between the originating voice and its duplicate. The start of this imitation appears in Example 222. Also shown in measure 6 is a cross-relation between the A natural of the middle

Ex. 222

voice and the A flat of the basses. This also contributes to the expressiveness. The beginning of a bracket under the last soprano note in the example signifies another passage, although a very short one of five notes, which is reproduced an octave lower and in stretto by the middle voice.

A wonderful instance on a miniature scale of the composer's subtlety in reintroducing previously heard material comes when the basses sing the two measures with which the sopranos opened the movement. Above this bass entry there is an open fifth (C-F) between the sopranos and the middle part, which is sustained until the basses complete the phrase. The suspended movement allows the bass entry to be clearly heard, and to be recognized as a new element in the reintroduction of this haunting phrase. After the basses have sounded the two A flats on 'Dei', the sopranos and, indeed, the other parts repeat the passage from 'qui' through 'mundi', as seen in the example. The 'dona nobis pacem' phrase is, again, very poignant. It consists of oscillating minor thirds in the three parts and the persistent cross-relations between the middle and bass parts (C flat-C natural) plus the final fall of a diminished fifth (C flat-F) in the soprano line have created in the short span of three measures a gentle pessimism – perhaps even melancholy is not too strong a word. It is as if one wants and needs to believe in peace, but facts cannot at present support that dream.

Autumn

For John Clare's poem, *Autumn*, Op. 99, for SSA with piano accompaniment, Rubbra has provided a setting that contains vigorous, attractive melodies in the vocal lines and a persistent, rising *arpeggio* figure in the accompaniment. With the exception of two 3/8 measures, the metre is 5/8 throughout with a pattern of 3 + 2 and two, widely separated 2 + 3 measures. The tempo is *Allegretto*.

Despite the poem's three-stanza structure, the musical form is obscure, owing to the very similar turns of phrase in the exuberant voice parts, which the listener is certain he has heard before when, in fact, he has not. While the situation in the accompaniment is different, owing to the unifying force of the *arpeggio* figure, the overall effect structurally is that the work is through-composed. This is not inappropriate in view of the changing imagery of the poem, which centres around a description of a dry and hot autumnal landscape.

The texture of *Autumn* is entirely chordal in the vocal parts and with very few exceptions the chords are root and first-inversion triads.

Lord, With What Care

Lord, With What Care, Op. 107, is an unaccompanied SATB motet that was composed for the Llandaff Cathedral Choir for the 1960 Llandaff Festival. The poem, a sonnet, is by George Herbert (1593–1633), one of the metaphysical poets. Born in Wales, educated at Trinity College, Cambridge, he assumed the vicarage of a small country parish in his last years. He was a friend of John Donne and is considered to have written some of the best religious poetry in English. The present poem describes how, after all the precautions taken by our parents, schoolmasters and church authorities, 'all these fences and their whole array / One cunning bosome sinne blows quite away'.

As might be expected, there are some *divisi* passages in this setting, but their number and difficulty cannot compare with those in many of Rubbra's other choral works. So far as structure is concerned, the sonnet form with its epigrammatic couplet at the end following a cumulative course suggests a through-composed setting, but such is not the case here. Yet, it is not possible to discover a specific plan with reference to any usual structure, for the music creates its own form. There are literal and almost literal repetitions of the eloquent music to which the first four lines are set, and they are easily identifiable as material that was previous heard. However, the treatment of some of these repeated segments is very subtle in terms of rhythmic changes, reshuffling of parts and the choice of a new key.

The material of the motet is divisible into three basic segments, marked *a*, *b*, and *c* in Example 223. The first segment is restricted in its repetitions to the

Ex. 223

final cadence and two internal ones. Each of these is fully harmonized in a very beautiful and satisfying way, yet in each instance the harmonies and distribution of the parts is different, with the greatest difference occurring in the final cadence. There, the bass line is assigned the ascending segment under a held chord in the remaining three parts. An added C flat between the two B flats at the top of the ascent is poignantly expressive. Even more expressive is the harmony that results when the moving lines in all parts except the soprano create dissonances. It all adds up to one of the most beautiful cadences in Rubbra's choral music (Example 224).

Segment *b* with its characteristic drop of an augmented second but minus its first beat is reproduced in measures 17–18. However, it is segment *c* that provides more extended passages through the repetitions of the rising thirds as well as phrase extensions. All subsequent statements of *c* include the distinctive sound of the cross-relations between A and A flat (and vice versa) as seen in the example where they are marked. In measures 29–32, measures 5–9 are repro-

Ex. 224

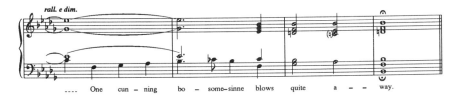

duced a half-step higher with all of the harmonies intact, but moved up so that the alto is now the second soprano, the tenor part is given to the altos, and so on. Thus the tone colour is changed through a subtlety in rescoring.

New music is introduced to match 'anguish of all sizes, / Fine nets and stratagems', and it is repeated a whole step higher for later words. In each case a short canon between sopranos and tenors is established.

To my ears the eight pages of this motet represent Rubbra's choral writing at its best. There is not an unnecessary note in it, yet nowhere is there any sense of abruptness or over-conciseness. The harmonies are beautifully thought out, and the dissonances create just enough tension before they are resolved. On a small scale, it is a perfectly realized work.

Up, O My Soul

Up, O My Soul, Op. 108, composed to a paraphrase by Henry Vaughan of Psalm 104, is entirely different from the rather inward-looking motet we have just considered. Again, it is an unaccompanied work for mixed voices – an anthem – and the dedication is to the Choir of Dean Close School, Cheltenham. It received its first performance at the 1960 Cheltenham Festival. It is a straight-forward setting of a text devoted to the praise of God, and as such it is full of vigour. Many of the traits in Rubbra's choral music are present here: *divisi* parts on a relatively large scale; frequent metrical changes designed to accommodate textual accents; and many unrelated triads.

Probably the most interesting part of the work centres around the short section, 'When thou doest hide thy face' and ending with 'And they to dust return'. These more introspective words are set to hitherto unused figures that consist of two and four sixteenths. Assigned to paired parts – alto and bass, soprano and tenor – they alternate so that when one pair has the figure, the other pair sings sustained notes, thus allowing each pair to dominate and so to highlight the entire passage. A further point worthy of comment is that, rather surprisingly, these more subjective words are not set to a reduced tempo, but are maintained at the *con spirito* level intended for the whole anthem.

The opening and closing portions of the anthem are dominated by passages containing chains of opposed perfect fifths – one chain in the top two parts, and the other in the bottom two – moving in contrary motion. In between these passages are others of a weightier nature in which the texture has expanded to five- and six-note chords in accordance with the *divisi* direction. In all such passages the contrary motion of the opening and closing sections has been largely preserved.

The Beatitudes

It is interesting to compare Rubbra's two settings of *The Beatitudes*. It will be recalled that the first setting was in conjunction with James Nayler's *There Is A Spirit* and that the style was simple and chant-like. The later setting, Op. 109, for unaccompanied SSA, is more difficult and complex despite the reduction in the number of parts. The individual melodic lines present no particular problems, although there are some awkward intervals, for example, a downward leap of a tenth in the first soprano part. However, when the three parts are joined, intonational problems arise as new tonalities momentarily assume prominence, and these are compounded when the parts cross, as they frequently do. Rhythmically, this setting of *The Beatitudes* is very flexible in comparison to the earlier setting. Here triplet figures, freely distributed among the parts, are to be found in twenty of the sixty measures. They keep the texture, much of which is chordal, moving forward in a way that is graceful and pliant, yet never hurried, and tempo also contributes to the flexibility.

One of the triplet figures, almost always preceded and followed by a quarter note, functions not in a thematic sense, as there is no theme, but as a reference point and unifying device. Although it is used frequently, it is incorrect to say that 'at each repetition of the word "Blessed" the same motive appears',[72] for three of the *Beatitudes* are not so introduced. The figure first appears at the very beginning in the alto part, to be followed a beat later by its inversion in the two soprano parts. The inverted figures are a fifth apart and with the original entry they form a major triad on C. At measure 42, the original figure appears in the first soprano voice, and its inversions are in the two lower parts, also a beat later. From time to time throughout the work, the triplet figure appears at different pitches. There are several instances of cross-relations, and the parallel fifths so often met in Rubbra's music are much in evidence.

The review from which the above quotation was extracted calls the piece 'rather difficult but well worth the effort involved... the interest is sustained throughout the piece. This should fill a gap in the SSA repertory.'[73]

Lauda Sion

Lauda Sion, Op. 110, completed on 2 December 1960, is one of the peaks in Rubbra's choral output. It is scored for an *a cappella* double mixed choir, and soprano and baritone soli. Critical reviews of it have been uniformly enthusiastic, the only negative remarks being confined to practical matters such as range. The first major review reads as follows:

> What more exciting sound is there in all music than a double choir in a resonant building? The combination of richness and flexibility, of grandeur and sensitivity, of power and subtlety can be overwhelming. Two pieces realize the possibility of this style: Schütz's 'Unser Herr Jesus Christus in der Nacht da er verraten ward' and Rubbra's 'Lauda Sion'.... Rubbra has captured the bolder, more fiery aspects of double-choir effects in his setting of words by St. Thomas Aquinas. He obviously delights in pitting one choir against the other, or upper against lower voices and any number of other variants of scoring familiar from Palestrina, Gabrieli and Schütz onwards. The words are clothed in natural, seemingly inevitable notes, underlay is precise and phrasing well thought out on the practical level. The music is not easy, however; it will take a skilled choir to finish up in tune, despite the fact that there are few intervals in any part to cause trouble.[74]

St Thomas Aquinas's text and the Gregorian chant to which it is set constitute one of the five sequences retained by the Catholic Church. The Festival of Corpus Christi for which this sequence is prescribed honours the Eucharist, and was instituted in 1264 by Pope Urban IV – ten years before the death of St Thomas. It was directed that it be celebrated on the Thursday after Trinity Sunday, although in some countries it is observed on the Sunday following Trinity. Antoine Brumel (*c*.1450–1520) set the odd-numbered stanzas in a motet and Palestrina wrote three motets and a Mass on this text, the Mass being of the parody type with one of the motets serving as the model.

A word needs to be said concerning the inadequacy of the textual translation, found on the facing page of the score. Not only is it a very free, rhymed and therefore inaccurate rendition in terms of detail, but its stanzaic divisions are confusing when compared to those of the original Latin. Where the latter consists of twenty-four stanzas of three and four lines, the translation presents us with thirteen stanzas of six, eight and five lines. A simple solution to the problem, adopted here, is to preface each of the Latin stanzas throughout

Ex. 225

Rubbra's score with the number corresponding to the stanzas in the *Liber Usualis*. In this way, the composer's treatment of the individual stanzas can be examined and compared.

We begin by quoting the basic opening material as it is stated in the soprano parts of both choirs (Example 225). The supporting material in the three lower voices of each choir is also identical until measure 7 when the first divergences occur. There is a distinctly Lydian flavour in the rising scale figure as well as in other places in the example. Also to be noted are the diminutions of the initial scale figure in measures 3 and 4, together with the short canon between the tenor and soprano voices. The basic material as shown is repeated exactly to the same words between stanzas 8 and 9 and again between 18 and 19, at which point there is an extension of the text to different music. The second repetition departs from the original statement and the first repetition in that, minus basses, it begins in Choir I, and when Choir II enters the disposition of parts is quite different from both previous statements, although the essentials are preserved.

In arithmetical terms and based on the total of 233 measures in the work, a structure emerges in which the full statement of the opening material begins in measures 1, 65 and 150; while the initial words with portions of its music commences in measure 33; and the same words with different music are repeated, starting with measures 89 and 181. These complete statements, together with the partial ones constitute structural members, and even the textual repetitions with different music are recognizable elements in the design. Such guideposts are important because the almost constant overlaps, which occur when stanzas end and succeeding ones start, preclude cadences and clearly delineated sections.

Rubbra has obviously thought of the stanzas as units because he has given most of them individual musical figures. This is, perhaps, risky when one reflects that the duration of each stanza is seldom more than a page and a half. Thus the figures must be terse, incisive and interesting enough to engage one's attention. This has not often been a problem for the composer in any of his music; he solves it here in his usual way by introducing imitation in a number of stanzas, with the result that figures are prolonged to a desired length. Motivic expansion and extension are other ways in which he achieves the same result. It goes without saying that he is also aware that there must be significant differences among the figures with respect to melodic content, contours, and so on. For example, a conjunct figure may be preceded or followed by a disjunct one, although this is not always the pattern, for conjunct figures are sometimes juxtaposed. But certainly the most interesting and memorable figures are those containing disjunct intervals. The first such instance occurs as early as stanza 3 where a five-note figure in three parts, arranged vertically in unrelated triads, is imitated in close stretto entries, producing in parallel motion a triadic pattern dominated by cross-relations. The figures to which stanzas 7 and 8 are set are other notable examples. Stanza 12 has material that consists of two disjunct patterns joined together, and first presented in a paired stretto entry by the sopranos and altos of Choir I at the distance of an augmented sixth. A second paired entry, employing different pitches but preserving the same distance, soon follows in the women's parts of Choir II. An independent tenor statement in Choir I, consisting of only the first disjunct pattern, completes the imitations. In Example 226, note how Rubbra varies the second disjunct figure by having the women of Choir II jump an octave before the figure is announced.

Ex. 226

In no way do any of the figures, conjunct or disjunct, appear as attempts to mirror the content of the words, a recognition that the text is concerned with Christian dogma and as such is too general for such treatment. There is a world of difference between the scholasticism of St Thomas Aquinas and the ecstatic mysticism of St John of the Cross, and this difference is abundantly reflected in Rubbra's treatment of each.

Rubbra's economical use of material is evident throughout this work. For example, the entire material of stanza 2 reappears in the ninth stanza where it is exchanged: Choir II sings what Choir I had sung and *vice versa*. The texture in stanza 9 is also lightened by the absence of any men's parts except for a two-measure passage. This was accomplished by the simple procedure of assigning the four parts of Choir I in stanza 2 to *divisi* women's parts in stanza 9. Other examples of economy can be found in stanza 8 where the preceding stanza's material is inverted, using different note values; in stanzas 10 and 11 where some of the same music is shared; and in 19 and 20 where basic materials are shared at different pitches. In all of these instances variety is achieved by reassigning material to different parts and/or choirs. An internal example of contrapuntal alteration is found in stanza 10 where the men of Choir II invert the material of the corresponding parts in Choir I.

The soprano and baritone soloists, who, according to the composer, 'should preferably belong to the choir', make their only appearance shortly before the end of the work. The reason for the delay appears to be that their role is to introduce music that is to become the dominant factor for the rest of the time. Although the sacramental Bread and Wine are the principal subjects of St Thomas's poem, they have up to this point been woven into the text in a tapestry-like fashion. Now, and for the rest of the work, the focus is primarily on the Bread, 'Ecce panis Angelorum', and it seems plausible to suggest that the soloists are intended to represent angels whose special function is to pro-claim this divine gift. This they do, accompanied by silence from the choirs except for an unobtrusive cadential chord, sustained in Choir II beneath the soprano's first five measures. Their music, melodically identical, is comfortable within the range of their respective voices. The baritone's solo, pitched a fourth below his counterpart, begins in an overlapping way under a sustained B at the end of the soprano's line, but his final four and a half measures are sung not by him but by the altos and basses of Choir II at the distance from each other of an octave. This is a subtle way of involving the choirs in what will be the climactic material of the work. A glance at Example 227 shows that this melody not only

Ex. 227

strikes a balance between conjunct and disjunct elements, but that it is longer and more complete than any of the earlier melodies. When it is understood that this melody is never absent from the start of the solo passages to the final cadence, the inescapable conclusion is that Rubbra intended both it and its text to be culminating points.

The soprano and baritone solos are settings, respectively, of stanzas 21 and 22. The music of these solos is transferred to the choirs where it is continued to the end of the work, but at the same time it is combined with the patterns to which stanzas 23 and 24 – the final stanzas – are set. These new patterns function as counterpoints to the principal melody, for they are almost entirely conjunct, with contours composed of gently rising and falling curves. Rhythmi-cally, owing to notes of various values as well as ties, they lack a forward drive.

The distribution of all three melodies has been carefully worked out. Those associated with stanzas 23 and 24 are restricted to Choir I, but the principal melody migrates from choir to choir. After the latter's second half has been heard in Choir II, there are three complete statements: the first in Choir I, the second in Choir II, and the third also in Choir II but reinforced by the basses of Choir I. Following a powerful climax for both choirs, the tempo broadens considerably, and the motet ends quietly.

The musically educated layman, the professional musician and the student will benefit from studying this score, for their observations will reveal a painstaking care expended on every facet of its composition. Details such as the independent and contrasted melodic figures in the stanzas have been mentioned, but space considerations preclude a discussion of the subtle intervallic changes that occur in many of them as they unfold. Similarly, there are numerous other instances concerning the thought given to how the materials were to be distributed to the choirs. Still another facet is dynamics. A study of the score will show how meticulously this element was planned. The many markings are precise and if they are obeyed literally, the overall design of the work as well as its details will emerge as the composer intended.

Finally, all of the careful planning connected with the composition of this or any work is in vain unless correct performance practices are observed. This means that *Lauda Sion* as a spatially conceived work must be performed with spatial separations thoroughly in mind. A wide chancel and, for a concert performance, a wide stage are absolutely essential, plus good reverberation time in each situation. We certainly owe this much to Gabrieli, Schütz, Rubbra and every other polychoric composer.

The second major review of this work is mostly descriptive, but there are points in it that deserve mention:

> Rubbra's liking for parallel chordal movement is much in evidence, but the technique is used with great impact, for instance on page 5 in the very striking passage 'Laudis thema specialis'. [These words begin stanza 3, and the passage has been cited above for its disjunct properties.] At the sequence beginning 'sit laus plena, sit jucunda', [stanza 5] however, which is another bold touch, the second tenors have to sustain a passage of several bars between top F and A flat (they later have bottom B to cope with) [near the end of stanza 15] while the first tenors are silent. This seems to militate against a satisfactory performance, and at the same time to be unnecessary.... The piece is well constructed and very effective, though open to criticism on the question of vocal compass.[75]

I find the criticism pertaining to compass misleading because of the terminology. The writer is referring to the tenors of Choir II and Choir I which, in his review are 'second' and 'first' tenors respectively. If both choirs are equally matched in capabilities, as they certainly should be, there ought not to be an inference that the 'first' tenors should be helping. Second, there are numerous places in both choirs where not just the tenors but also the sopranos are coping with a high compass. Third, *Lauda Sion* is not a work for the faint-hearted, and those choirs that do not have the resources to manage the high notes must not attempt it.

Cantata di Camera

In Alan Blyth's review of a retrospective concert of Rubbra's music in London's Purcell Room on 24 April 1969, there is an interesting comparison between *Lauda Sion* and *Cantata di Camera*, Op. 111, Rubbra's next choral work. He says, 'texture and polyphony are beautifully judged in this piece [*Lauda Sion*] to fit the contemplative text, which drew a much more inspired response from Rubbra than Patrick Carey's lachrymose lines did in the rather awkward *Cantata di Camera*.'[76]

The latter work, subtitled 'Crucifixus pro Nobis', was 'commissioned by and dedicated to The Riverside Choir, New York City, and its Director, Richard Weagly'. Scored for solo tenor, mixed choir of sixteen picked voices, flute, violin, cello, harp and organ, it contains four connected movements. The first three are settings of poems by the seventeenth-century poet, Patrick Carey, and the fourth movement 'is an arrangement of the last of the composer's Five Sonnets of Spenser for tenor and string orchestra, Op. 42'.

Little is known of Carey's life. He was the son of Sir Henry Carey, first Viscount Falkland. Sent to France at an early age to be reared a Catholic, he remained there for three years, after which he went to Italy for twelve years. In spite of reports that he took orders, he did not, although later he became a Benedictine monk in Douai, France. Leaving the order within a year because, physically, he could not stand the strict diet, he returned to England. His work, *Trivial Poems and Triolets*, was published in 1651. Reading the three Carey poems set here, 'Christ in the Cradle', 'Christ in the Garden' and 'Christ in His Passion', one is compelled to call them not only 'lachrymose' but also maudlin. However, Rubbra deserves praise for skilfully avoiding any traces of sentimentality in his settings.

'Most Glorious Lord of Life' – Sonnet 68 from Edmund Spenser's long sonnet sequence, *Amoretti* – is, of course, vastly superior to the Carey poems. Rubbra's decision to reuse this poem and the musical setting he provided for it in Op. 42 has resulted in a certain imbalance from the literary standpoint. However, it makes sense in terms of a connective link for its subject – the triumph of Easter and its effect on men – is a natural consequence of Carey's third poem, 'Christ in His Passion'. Rather than providing a new musical setting for Spenser's poem, modifications in the earlier setting seem logical in view of the fact that the tenor solo is an extension of the dominant role played by the soloist in the preceding movements.

However, notwithstanding the appropriateness of both poem and setting, a certain inconsistency characterizes the cantata, for the first three movements are perceived as one unit, poetically and musically, while the fourth seems to stand by itself. Perhaps this incongruity was what Blyth was referring to when he termed the cantata 'rather awkward'. The inconsistency is apparent in the cantata's melodic and rhythmic elements. The melodic contour of the solo part in the first three movements is varied and occasionally florid, while rhythmically there is flexibility that is expressed in a variety of note values, a generous use of rests and frequent tempo changes. The Spenser movement on the other hand has a solo line containing fewer notes and with abrupt contour changes being divided more evenly over a longer span. The rhythm is more regular, there is less variety in note values, a restricted use of rests and no tempo change until the concluding *Allargando*. In fact, it is not an exaggeration to speak here of a rhythmic drive.

It should not be assumed, however, that the first three movements of this cantata lack individuality merely because they share the characteristics noted above. Quite the contrary, for a steady progression from the fragility of 'Christ in the Cradle' through the intervening movements to the forcefulness of 'Most Glorious Lord of Life' is perceptible. While the tenor solos are the common bond which unites all of the movements, it is the accompaniments that really distinguish one movement from another. The choir is not a significant factor, for it is totally absent in the first two movements and its role in the remaining ones varies.

The fragile nature of 'Christ in the Cradle' stems from its text, which portrays a cold and shivering Jesus whom neither Joseph nor Mary can protect. This atmosphere is stressed in the solo line where words like 'shake', 'pale', 'pretty', 'lost' and 'frozen' are highlighted by particular figures. However, with the possible exception of the figure for 'shake' – C, D flat, C in a sixteenth-note pattern – all the figures are abstractions, designed to draw attention to the key words. The accompaniment also conveys the bleak atmosphere in a fragmented, mosaic-like structure in which one or two instruments briefly assume prominence, and then yield to one or more of their fellows. The figures assigned to them are quite distinctive and stand out in relief, particularly when some are doubled so that an octave or two separates the top and bottom voices. During the sounding of some of these figures sustained passages of several measures duration – most consisting of empty fifths in the double-stopped string parts as well as in the organ part – further emphasize the bareness of the scene.

It will be recalled from the discussions of the symphonies and other orchestral music that Rubbra strongly favours the harp and that it is included among the instruments in a majority of those works. When, as here, it is a member of a small ensemble accompanying a choral work, its role is necessarily more prominent because of the fewer instruments. This is true to a degree in the *Cantata di Camera*, although the harp's participation in the second and fourth movements is slight. In 'Christ in the Cradle' the harp stands out owing to a persistent rhythmic grouping of bare, consecutive fifths. The rhythmic pattern within the prevailing 6/8 metre is reproduced in Example 228, where it will be seen that the interplay of unrelated fifths creates dissonances intended to further the cheerless atmosphere. Contrary to what might seem to be the start of a long passage made from similar figures, the opposite is true: measures of rest and arpeggiated chords intervene between reappearances of the figure. Thus instead of overdoing the atmosphere, there is a subtle underplaying of it. At the

Ex. 228

end of the movement the harp accompaniment acquires depth through a series of syncopated and accented *arpeggio* chords, some of which contain dissonances.

The text of 'Christ in the Garden' offers a melodramatic contrast to that just seen, for instead of the coldness associated with the cradle, we are told, 'Look, how he glows for heat! / What flames come from his eyes!' The same sort of imagery follows later in 'His very heart burns in each part; / A fire his breast doth sear: / For all this flame; / To cool the same / He only breathes a sigh and weeps a tear.' One can only speculate on the composer's reasons for choosing so mediocre and unpromising a text, but by treating it generally he managed to provide an acceptable setting. The fragmentation of the cradle scene gives way to a texture in which the semi-declamatory and, at times, melismatic tenor solo blends with a contrapuntal and rhythmically fluid accompaniment, which is shared by the organ and strings. The flute pursues a relatively independent course, although at one point it doubles a portion of the solo two octaves higher. The harp's only prominent passage consists of a doubling for four measures of the organ's left-hand part.

'Christ in His Passion' is, understandably, the most intense of the four movements both textually and musically. Carey views Christ's sufferings through the eyes of a spectator who, in the musical setting, is the tenor soloist. The sixteen-voice choir, making its first appearance in the cantata, assumes three roles. In the first of these at the start of the movement, the choir is made up of sympathetic bystanders who intone the syllable 'ah' in hushed voices to six-part dissonant chords (the altos and basses are divided). This passage is more dramatic than a mention of it might indicate, for it is strongly supported in the cello and harp parts by a heavily accented, rhythmic figure. At the same time the harp's arpeggiated chords are doubling the choir's most important notes. The effect in the slow 6/8 metre is that of a funeral march. Most of this passage is a background for the soloist's exclamations, 'What bruises do I see! / What hideous stripes are those! / Could any cruel be / Enough to give such blows?' The choir drops out, and the soloist continues, accompanied by strings and organ, his text dealing with the indignities visited upon Christ. The choir's very short, second passage follows and its function is to narrate the final, tragic events: 'Through hands and feet sharp nails they beat: / And now the cross they rear.' The four parts sing the same music, the women and men each in unison and one octave apart.

The choir's third role as questioner and general observer of the scene is the most important, judged by the use of the word 'chorale'[77] and the choir's *a cappella* status. The passage is introduced by a short baritone solo. The first two lines of the choir's text are in the form of questions that contain obvious references to the first two movements: 'Why did he shake for cold? / Why did he glow for heat?' Musically, these questions are matched in the soprano part by two very subtle quotations from the first and second movements respectively. After a brief reference to the symbols of the Passion – the 'stripes', 'thorns', 'cross', and so on – the choir resumes its questioning with 'Why, O why suffered he?' This is repeated five times, and the answer is provided by the tenor during the repetitions: ''Twas for thy sake. Thou, thou didst make Him all those torments bear.' The contours of his melodic line and the number of notes in that line are in direct contrast with the simple nature of the chorale tune. Taken together, soloist and choir complement each other in what is a very expressive passage that, fortunately, has nothing of the bathos of Carey's poetic exaggerations.

The final movement is an arrangement of the last piece in Rubbra's Five Spenser Sonnets for solo tenor and string orchestra. The poem, although containing references to Easter as an event – 'Most glorious Lord of life, that on this day / Didst make thy triumph over death and sin' – also stresses the broad and enduring meaning of the Resurrection in the lines, 'So let us love, dear love, like as we ought, / Love is the lesson which the Lord us taught.'

The strength and assertiveness of the poem are carried over into Rubbra's setting through forceful, energetic figures whose sixteenth-note motion is constant throughout the movement. The tempo in an almost undeviating 2/4 metre is *Vivo aperto*, ♩ = 92 (in the original setting, the metronomic indication is 96). The solo line and chorus parts are composed principally of eighth notes with a scattering of sixteenths here and there. However, not to be overlooked are the accented quarters with which the solo begins, and which are a prominent feature in the choir during most of the latter's isolated passages. In the Spenser Sonnets these choral passages were assigned to the cellos, violins and, at the end, the tenor soloist. In the cantata they are much more conspicuous.

Although there is one sharp in the key signature, the real key is perceived not as G but as D, owing not just to the absence of C sharps but to the presence of a very large number of D pedal points. In fact, except for a small section where some F naturals and B flats are to be found, the entire movement/song impresses the listener as consisting of one long D major chord. A transposed Mixolydian mode is also suggested, an impression not cancelled by a scattering of C sharps, and the modal feeling is further buttressed by the tenor's opening line and some of the ensemble's sixteenth-note figures (Example 229).

Of particular interest is the adaptation of the string orchestra accompaniment in the Spenser Sonnets to the chamber ensemble in the cantata. Since absolutely nothing is omitted, the adaptation consists of the reassignment of material from one group to the other, plus the transfer to the choir of suitable passages that

Ex. 229

were originally instrumental; these latter have already been mentioned. The tenor solo in both versions is, of course, the same. In the matter of reassignments, the cello, understandably, retains most of its original music. The flute, as might be expected, borrows most of its part from the first violins, but one extended passage is a replica – two octaves higher – of the tenor solo. Surprisingly, the bulk of the violin's music in the cantata comes not from the first violins of the original setting, but from the seconds, but in this arrangement, the organ is the dominant instrument and its music is a summation of all of the principal parts in the earlier piece. The right hand at some points plays extended passages derived from the first violins, while at the same time the left hand is occupied with material from either the viola or the cello parts. At other places the distribution of the original material is different with respect to the hands. Of course, the very few pedal passages are transcriptions of the cello and bass lines. As for the harp, its function in the cantata movement is purely one of emphasis, and its arpeggiated chords on strong as well as weak beats contain some of the notes assigned to a number of the original instruments.

Opportunities to hear the Five Spenser Sonnets and the *Cantata di Camera* are at the moment almost nonexistent, so it is therefore impossible to render any kind of judgement as to which of the last-movement settings is more effective as music, quite apart from the use to which each piece is put. Indeed, such a judgement might not be possible anyway, since personal preferences come into play with respect to the quite different sounds produced by each piece. For what it may be worth, my present inclination is to choose the original setting because the strings create a homogeneous sound against which the soloist is placed in relief. In the more colourful but diffused cantata arrangement the soloist appears to have to work harder to make himself effective, and since his part is difficult at times in terms of intonation, problems are more likely.

The cantata as a whole has many fine moments and the writing of it proves that an inferior text – with the exception of the Spenser poem – can be overcome in the musical setting. This is certainly not always the case, either in Rubbra's or other composers' music.

Three Hymn Tunes

Of the simple, four-part *a cappella* settings comprising Three Hymn Tunes, Op. 114, the first two, 'Prayer to Jesus' and 'That Virgin's Child Most Meek' were published in *The Cambridge Hymnal* in 1967. The second of these also appears in the *New Catholic Hymnal* along with no. 3, 'Queen of Mercy'. The poem for no. 1, known as 'Richard de Castre's Prayer to Jesus', is contained on pages 28–30 of Lambeth Manuscript 853, *c*.1430, in the Archbishop of Canterbury's Lambeth Palace Library. There are fourteen stanzas in Middle English of which the composer has chosen six – nos 1, 6, 8, 11, 12, 14 – but in a modified version. Who Richard de Castre was is not known; it is unlikely that we shall ever learn anything about him.

The situation with regard to John Gwynneth (*c*.1495–*c*.1562), the poet of the second hymn, is very different. Born in Wales, he was both a Catholic priest and a composer, his achievements in the latter sphere attracting more attention than those in the former. Thomas Morley must have held him in high regard for, although he is not cited in the text, he is listed among English 'authorities' at the end of *A Plaine and Easie Introduction to Practicall Musicke* (1597). Unfortunately, all of Gwynneth's music has been lost except for the bass of a four-part song entitled 'My Love Mournyth', found in a book of 1530 entitled *XX Songes, IX of iiii Partes and XI of Thre Partes*, 'the only polyphonic music printed in England before the Reformation'.[78] His carol has four stanzas, the first two of which mention the purpose of the Incarnation. The last two are in the form of a personal prayer to Jesus, and thus resemble Richard de Castre's text.

The third text, 'Queen of Mercy' by Rev. Brian Foley, is a prayer to the Virgin Mary. Its modernity is apparent through the use of the contemporary pronouns 'you' and 'your' rather than the age-old 'thou' and 'thy'.

The hymn tunes were composed by Rubbra himself and their names – 'St. Colette', 'St. Non's' and 'Mater Misericordiae' – were chosen by him for personal reasons. Both the tunes and their harmonizations show a definite affinity for Tudor church music, but nowhere are there slavish imitations, merely a modern synthesis of earlier practices. In the tunes, conjunct and disjunct elements are well balanced and changes in melodic direction are entirely natural. As for the harmonizations, inner parts flow easily and independently with details momentarily standing out, but never detracting from the principal melodies.

Te Deum

In the *Te Deum*, Op. 115, Rubbra's second setting of this text, there is a reversion to large-scale *a cappella* writing in eight parts (SSAATTBB). The work is inscribed 'To the Lord Mayor and the City of London for Performance at the

Opening Service of the Festival of the City of London in St. Paul's Cathedral on July 9, 1962'.

Aside from the obvious dissimilarities in performance media, there is a world of difference between this *Te Deum* and the Op. 71 setting. The key to the differences, perhaps even their origin, may lie in the languages employed: English in the earlier setting, Latin here. Latin, being far removed from our everyday experience, but at the same time having associations derived from ecclesiastical usage over many centuries, suggests timelessness and permanence – qualities reinforced by the text. Musically, these qualities are embodied in what is, much of the time, a non-metrical structure (in spite of the very frequent metrical changes), and they are portrayed by massive and sometimes static harmonies moving slowly in parallel, triadic blocks.

Another quality, not found in the earlier *Te Deum* but which strongly colours this one, is a subjectivity that in places is mystical. The musical means for conveying this subjectivity are reserved for special sections, and Rubbra's intuitive sensitivity not just to words alone, but to the ideas behind them has determined where these sections should be. Perhaps strangely, they occur not at those textual passages that deal with Christ's relationship to humanity – from 'Thou art the King of Glory, O Christ' through 'We believe that thou shalt come to be our judge' – a known quantity, so to speak, but at unexpected points where the theological concepts are abstract and difficult for the mind to grasp. But even these are sometimes softened by the warmth and mystery of Divine Grace, as it is silently directed towards humanity: 'Also the Holy Ghost, the Comforter'.

The work falls into three clearly delineated sections which can be thought of as a triptych – an imaginative approach to the text, which I do not recall seeing in other settings of the Te Deum. The central panel features an impersonal Christ of the kind portrayed in glory in a Byzantine mosaic. The left panel contains the abstract theological statements, and the images of innumerable hosts praising God, while the right panel is filled with the various petitions. The slow first section ends with the double bar in measure 53, giving way to the vigorous and heavily accented *allegro* theme which characterizes the *B* section. This central panel concludes in measure 87, and the third section is, again, slow. Neither of the two *A* sections can be said to have a defined theme in the sense of a first-section statement and a third-section return of basic material. Instead, the two sections are alike in mood and tempo, although there is one abbreviated passage in the concluding *A* which duplicates a longer one in the first *A*, but this is not enough to negate what has just been said.

With respect to the harmonic structure, the signature of four flats, unchanged throughout the work, is no guarantee that A flat is to be understood as the central tonality for the bulk of the piece. Indeed, because of the strongly modal characteristics it would be more accurate to refer to A flat and all other keys as tonal centres, within which modality is operative. The replacement of one such centre by another is accomplished not by the usual modulatory processes, but by abrupt means, which are, however, ameloriated by an ingenious use of pedal points. One of these in each side panel provides a tone common to a number of centres. These pedals are both a stabilizing influence and an expressive force. Strictly speaking, some of them are not pedals at all, but tones sounded in both the melodic line and the other parts. In this capacity they are quitted and returned to so frequently (usually by means of upper and lower auxiliary tones) as to make them seem like legitimate pedals. In order to distinguish them from the latter, the term 'pseudo-pedal' will be used.

The relationship between tonal centres is a third, including thirds whose relationship is enharmonic; there is one instance in section 3 where it is a second. Thus in the opening section A flat is followed by C, both undergirded by a common C pedal; E and A flat complete the section, each having a pseudo-pedal as foundation. In the middle section the tonal centres are A flat, E, G, B, A flat and E, followed by three measures where the tonality is nebulous. The tonal centres in the third section are C, E minor, F for the first half, and again a C pedal serves as a common tone for centres on A flat, C and A flat in the second half.

Marked 'Spacious ($\rfloor$ = 60 circa)', the *Te Deum* begins *fortissimo* and in a most imposing fashion. This atmosphere continues for two pages before an important change occurs, and in them the raw material composing the work is set out: the melodic and harmonic interval of a third. Relationships involving both dimensions are simultaneously established, for while the first sopranos move majestically in half notes from C through D flat to E flat, the C pedal mentioned above is heard in the first altos and both bass parts. C as the mediant of the A flat triad functions as a lighter foundation than if A flat were used. As the basic material develops in the soprano parts, *divisi* passages appear, resulting in dissonances not just between the soprano parts but also in relation to the C pedal, and an austere splendour marks these pages. Example 230 shows the piano reduction

Ex. 230

of the first nine and a half measures. At the beginning a mirror image of the first sopranos' initial figure is seen simultaneously in the second alto part.

The entire mood of these two pages changes abruptly when, on the second half of 'veneratur' a *subito pianissimo* ushers in the first of the subjective portions which, like some of those to follow, suddenly becomes otherworldly and mystical, as though some invisible barrier had been crossed. The text responsible for this change reads 'To thee Cherubim and Seraphim continually do cry, Holy, Holy, Holy, Lord God of Sabaoth'. Everything becomes hushed and faraway; time seems nonexistent. The means for conveying these impressions are the dynamic level; the continuing C pedal now transformed into a tonic; the ethereal C major chord sustained in the women's parts for two and a half measures; the absence of any bass parts; the generally conjunct melodic lines whose soothing oscillations within a narrow compass interact to create a continuous and indefinite murmur that seems to negate rhythm in the metrical sense; and an explicit modality. The cumulative effect of all these elements has induced an atmosphere of quiet but intense adoration.

This mystical atmosphere deepens when the *Sanctus* is reached and we are at once made aware that here is yet another *Sanctus* in the general mould of those in the three Masses: gently rocking minor thirds and *pianissimos*. However, two new elements are introduced in this setting: a bracketed figure in the two alto parts, for which the composer supplies a 9/8 metre signature while retaining the barlines for the prevailing 3/4 metre; and mild dissonances that result in harmonic ambiguities. Both of these elements are responsible for promoting the mystical character of the passage, for the mildly indistinct sound, when combined with the soft dynamic level, gives the fleeting impression of a far-off multitude of supernatural beings forever praising God.

Beginning with the 'majestatis gloriae tuae' segment, the basses re-enter and remain virtually throughout the rest of the first and most of the second section. The subjective treatment continues through the passages dealing with the Apostles, Prophets, Martyrs, Holy Church and the first two Persons of the Trinity. But the Latin equivalent of 'Also the Holy Ghost, the Comforter' calls forth another mystical response which is perhaps more intense than the *Sanctus* passage. Like the latter it is introduced by an instantaneous shift in tonal centres, in this instance from E to A flat, and by a *pianissimo* prepared in a one-measure *diminuendo*. The mystery associated with the Holy Ghost is symbolized by a clouded texture, moving in an *adagio* tempo, and containing two unlike elements: alternating C and A flat chords arranged in a parallel configuration a major third apart and a horizontal line centred around A flat – one of the pseudo-pedals. The notes of the chords are assigned to divided first and second sopranos, divided first tenors, and unison second tenors. Thus each chord contains seven notes, and E and E flat are in a pattern of continuous cross-relations. The second element, the pseudo-pedal, appears in the two alto and bass parts, carefully marked *mezzo piano* so that it will stand out from the chords. Beginning one beat after the chords in the 5/8 metre, its various notes form dissonances with the chords, thus contributing further to the sense of mystery. The entire passage appears in Example 231.

Ex. 231

The mystical mood of the Holy Ghost segment is completely shattered by the rhythmic drive and vigour of the second section, and the contrast is dramatic. The soft *adagio* gives way to a heavily accented *allegro* whose dynamics are consistently *forte* and *fortissimo*, and the chordal texture, not only of the passage just quitted but also of the first section as a whole, is replaced by a contrapuntal texture. An inflexible, seven-note figure commands attention throughout the section. Its rigidity admirably matches the concept of a Byzantine Christ, which is central to this section. Its three initial appearances take the form of a close, three-part stretto, and are arranged so that the entries sound an A flat triad in the following order: A flat (altos and basses), E flat (sopranos), C (tenors). The continuation of each of the seven-note figures throughout the section is different in terms of both melody and rhythm and I shall refer to these as melodic suffixes. In Example 232 the three initial entries are marked and the

Ex. 232

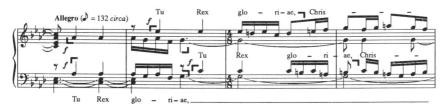

start of each melodic suffix is shown except for that connected to the A flat entry of the basses. Its beginning is delayed until the termination of the G pedal immediately after the illustration.

Because the intervallic conformations are always the same for each entry, accidentals having no relationship to the then current tonal centre lead away via the melodic suffixes to new centres. Looking now at the example more closely, the D, B and A naturals show very clearly that a transition is in progress, and the continuation of the passage beyond the illustration confirms this. G major appears to be the certain destination, but an abrupt shift to E major rules this out simultaneously with the appearance of the seven-note figure. This new round of statements is different from the last in two respects: a mirror version of the figure accompanies the tenor and the soprano entries, and a momentary bitonal conflict is implied because all of the women's parts are in G major. After the men's E major entry, they too veer towards G, but the overlap in entries is what causes the harmonic clash. Much the same processes continue from here to the end of the section as the music is propelled from tonal centre to tonal centre; the final centre, however, is formed not by the seven-note figure but by the materials emanating from it. A climactic *fortissimo* that features empty parallel fifths in five parts above a sustained triad on 'Judex crederis esse venturus' brings the section to an end.

Section 3 returns to the subjectivity and mysticism of the first section, but the intensity is greater because of the material itself and the higher registers in the soprano parts. The introduction of the mystical segments is accomplished, however, by the same means: an abruptly new triad, accompanied by soft dynamics (an exception to the softness occurs when the C tonal centre in measure 122 is announced *forte* in comparison with the *subito pianissimo* prescribed for the same change in measure 9). The first passage of the new section is centred on C, but the activity is concentrated in the men's parts under a chant-like octave G pedal in the altos. Their material is composed of a series of four-part, parallel, first-inversion chords reminiscent of English discant. This changes when activity shifts to the women's parts above the men's sustained A flat, first-inversion triad. Their parallel chords consist of empty fifths. A descending scale in the second soprano part, and a portion of the same scale in longer note values in the first tenors sets the stage for the most intensely mystical passage of the entire work: a sudden resolution to E minor in all of the parts, followed by six measures of minor, second-inversion triads (except for one diminished chord), arranged in a predominantly rising and falling parallel line. These chords are sung by three soprano soloists – *piano* – no mean feat in view of the high register (A naturals and one B flat for the topmost soprano).

Beneath the soloists is a chant-like E minor chord, scored for first altos, tenors and first basses, soon to be joined by the second bass part. The dynamic level is *pianissimo*. The text reads, 'Make them [thy servants] to be numbered with thy saints in glory everlasting'. The entire passage is one of the most expressive and beautiful in Rubbra's choral music. And the resolution of the passage is equally beautiful, for the combination of the F sharp minor chords in the solo parts and the E minor chords in the underlying voices softly melts into a serene and totally satisfying F major sonority. The imagery of the whole passage seems clear: the space between the three soloists and the lower parts represents the vast difference between heaven, where the saints dwell in glory, and the world of men below. In this respect it reminds one, in spirit only, of the passage in the 'Hostias' of Berlioz's *Requiem* where three flutes and three trombones symbolize the void between heaven and earth.

From the F major chord (measure 99) there flows an *adagio* and *pianissimo* figure shared by all of the first parts, while in each second part a derivative of it is simultaneously sounded. Since all of the entries are in stretto and are completed in slightly more than one page, a highly concentrated segment results, which seems very much in keeping with the text's intensity: 'Salvum fac populum tuam Domine' ('O Lord save thy people'). The figure appearing in all of the first parts comes from measures 37–8.

The segment beginning 'Per singulos dies benedicimus te' contains elements of the material with which the *Te Deum* opened, and a little over two pages later there is a literal repetition of most of the music of section 1 up to the 'Sanctus'. Two more pages, and the work ends *fortissimo* in triumphant splendour.

While space does not permit a detailed account of the modality with which the *Te Deum* is saturated, it would be a mistake to leave the work without recognizing the importance of its role. In this instance modality is considerably more than a flavouring. Rather, it is an organic element present in virtually all of the material. When it is not *explicitly* present in some of the principal melodic lines, its presence can be inferred because of the way in which these lines are interpreted with respect to the tonal centre prevailing at that moment. Thus on the very first page, reproduced in Example 230, the D flats in the soprano parts are heard not as the fourth degree of the A flat scale but as the lowered second degree of the C minor scale, and therefore the second degree of a transposed Phrygian scale. Such a conclusion is only possible if the Cs, so insistently sounded in the first alto and bass parts, are accepted as a tonic. They are, until A flats appear and establish the tonal centre as A flat and not C minor. But modal traits still persist, for in the second half of the passage the F flat, G flat, A flat succession of notes is transposed Aeolian. In the immediately following passage both Phrygian and Lydian characteristics are found in the context of C major: C, D flat, E flat; and C through F sharp. Many more modal examples are to be seen.

In Example 231 the mysticism associated with the Holy Ghost is represented not by modality or diatonicism but by the whole-tone scale: F sharp = G flat, G sharp = A flat, and so on.

A Spring Carol Sequence

Rubbra's next four opus numbers are filled with small pieces in other genres, but with *A Spring Carol Sequence*, Op. 120, choral composition was resumed. 'Commissioned by the "Farnham Herald" for the Farnham Festival, 1963', it is written in an idiom as far removed from that of the *Te Deum* as can be imagined – one best described as 'popular' in the finest sense of that word. It is scored for SSA (there is one *divisi* passage of sustained chords, consisting of three soprano and, soon after, two alto parts) and accompaniment of one flute, one oboe and two clarinets, or an ensemble of recorders. 'If recorders are used, it is suggested that, for the sake of balance, at least three should be used for each part.' The work is entirely suitable for any spring choral festival or concert in which something out of the ordinary is desired and its length of five to six minutes is a further inducement in the planning of a diversified programme.

Rubbra drew upon *The Oxford Book of Carols* for both words and music. The three carols that comprise the piece are 'Love Is Come Again', 'All In The Morning' and 'May Day Garland'. His colourful and interesting arrangements are spread over four continuous sections, the first of which contains stanzas 1 and 2 and the refrain of the first carol. Since each stanza and refrain is repeated, this section is the longest. The second and third sections are given over to the second and third carols respectively, and the fourth balances the structure when the last two stanzas and refrain of 'Love Is Come Again' are presented, this time with no repeats.

The text of the first carol is by Rev. J.M.C. Crum (1872–1958), Canon of Canterbury from 1928 to 1943. The Farnham commission takes on special meaning because of Rev. Crum's associations with the town: from 1913 to 1928 he was Rector of Farnham and he died there after becoming Canon Emeritus. The borrowed tune to which his Easter carol is set is the *c.*seventeenth-century French Dorian melody, *Noël Nouvelet*, best known as the source of Marcel Dupré's brilliant work for organ, Variations On A Noël.

The words and music of the other carols are traditional. 'All In The Morning' has nine stanzas altogether, arranged in two parts and covering in narrative form important events in Christ's life. The first part contains five stanzas and forms a unit from Christmas to Candlemas (2 February), and the remaining four stanzas in Part II encompass Holy Wednesday, Sheer Thursday (or Maundy Thursday; 'sheer' is derived from an Icelandic word meaning to cleanse, purify), Good Friday and Easter. Rubbra, of course, chose Part II for the present work. From *The Oxford Book of Carols* we learn that 'the text has been completed from *Old Castleton Christmas Carols*, edited by the late Rev. W.H. Shawcross. Melody and first verse of text from Mr. Hall, Castleton, Derbyshire'.[79] As for 'May Day Garland', more extensive notes from the same source tell us that

> This... might be sung in church at May-time when Evensong is over, by one or two girls carrying a branch of may.
> The words and tune were taken by Geoffrey and Martin Shaw from an English girl... in the Boro' Polytechnic, London, *c.*1917; she had brought them from Northamptonshire.[80]

The composer's arrangements of these tunes are at all times appropriate, and the countermelodies are uncomplicated and easily singable by amateurs. One of the work's interesting and unusual features is the persistence in the accompaniment throughout much of 'All In The Morning' of the spirited, five-note figure with which 'Love Is Come Again' begins. The figure jumps from one instrument to another, and is heard at various pitches. In two places it is extended to include all twelve notes in the first phrase of 'Love Is Come Again'. Besides helping to unify the work, these appearances provide a lively, eighth-note rhythm that is needed in the second carol whose tune and mood are sombre relative to 'Love Is Come Again'. With the same tempo indication, the second carol would be too heavy without the relief supplied by this figure.

From a harmonic standpoint, the work is more interesting than a cursory examination might indicate. All of the stanzas of 'Love Is Come Again' are solidly in G minor, the key in which the carol is harmonized by Martin Shaw in *The Oxford Book of Carols*. But whereas 'All In The Morning' is clearly in the Aeolian mode (except for three accidentals in the last line) in Vaughan Williams's harmonization, Rubbra puts the first stanza in G major keeping, however, the original pitches of the Aeolian setting. That there is no doubt of his intent is made clear by the accented G pedals in the low register of the clarinets, as well as the change to an F sharp in the signature. There are also other changes, for the second stanza is in D major, and the third and last are in C minor. 'May Day Garland' starts in E flat major – the key used by Shaw in his harmonization – and moves to G major for the third and fourth stanzas. The work returns to the G minor of the opening section as stanzas 3 and 4 of 'Love Is Come Again' conclude the piece.

Moving to a more localized level, the harmonizations of the borrowed melodies are relatively simple, ranging from unison and octave passages to those containing two- and three-part harmony. There are occasional mild dissonances in the voice parts, caused usually by contrapuntal movement, but several pungent dissonances occur between the vocal lines and the frequently independent accompaniment. Almost all of the dissonances of whichever kind are to be found in the Sheer Thursday and Good Friday portions of 'All In The Morning'. However, nowhere in this charming work are there harmonic problems (or, indeed, problems of any other sort) that a good amateur choir and woodwind ensemble cannot overcome.

Continuing his lifelong interest in carols, Rubbra next turned in Op. 121 to an arrangement of *Infant Holy*, a Polish tune of unknown origin. The translation of the two-stanza Polish text – author unknown – by Edith M.G. Reed first appeared in *Music and Youth* and *Panpipes* in December 1925. Both publications, the latter a music magazine for younger children, were edited by Miss Reed from 1923 to 1926.

In Rubbra's tasteful arrangement the simple, childlike tune has been altered from its usual 3/4 setting to one in 3/2 metre. This change removes the two-note upbeat, which precedes the first measure and recurs regularly on the third beat of succeeding measures. These notes are now the first beat of every measure, so that what in the hymnal versions is an accented beat becomes an unstressed second beat. This perhaps psychological change has a profound effect, for what is too often a monotonously singsong carol has been transformed to become smoothly flowing. That this was the composer's intent is apparent from the tempo – *Andante* ($\bullet = 88$) – and his statement that 'the dignity and beauty is lost if sung too quickly. Beat in crotchets (i.e. divided minims) but keep the flow and simplicity, with lightly-sung quavers.' The quavers are a reference to the conjunct eighth-note figures, which are distributed among the three lower parts, adding harmonic interest as they interact with the slower-moving voices. As the piece progresses the figures become more frequent. A steady *crescendo* in measures 9–12 leads to a two-measure *fortissimo* and the composer's wishes are again made known: 'Ensure that excitement of the TB *Nowells* is felt in the climax of bars 13 and 14.' In the final two measures the level is *pianissimo*, and the eighth-note movement ceases.

Inscape

> But as air, melody, is what strikes me most of all in music, and design in painting, so design, pattern or what I am in the habit of calling 'inscape' is what I above all aim at in poetry.[81]

So wrote Gerard Manley Hopkins in a letter of 15 February 1879 to his friend and contemporary, Robert Bridges, England's future poet laureate. Rubbra has chosen this word 'inscape' as an inclusive title for his important Op. 122 settings of four of Hopkin's finest poems plus a two-line fragment that concludes the work. Much of Hopkin's poetry is obscure and thus Rubbra's settings will take on more meaning if some explanations of it are included here, but these, in turn, require some knowledge of the poet's life and character.

Hopkins was born in 1844 of staunchly Anglican parents. Following a rather precocious childhood, he entered Balliol College, Oxford, in 1863 at a time when the University was experiencing deep religious divisions, a result of the intellectual conflicts between the Anglo-Catholics and the Low Church adherents. Soon, Hopkins found himself in total sympathy with the Anglo-Catholics. It was but a step to Roman Catholicism; while he was still an undergraduate Hopkins was received into the church by then Father John Henry Newman, himself a convert to Catholicism in 1845, and later Cardinal. From 1868 to 1877 Hopkins willingly submitted to the rigorous discipline of Jesuit training, and in the latter year he was ordained a priest. After serving in various posts he died in 1889 of typhoid fever.

'Hopkins's character was a meeting-place of opposed qualities: asceticism and the love of beauty; toughness and sensitivity; quickness of sensuous response and a taste for theoretical speculation.'[82] Dominating these opposites was a burning intensity, which showed itself in two areas: an intellectual curiosity about everything which entered his conscious life, and an acute need to excel in everything he undertook, whether poetic or religious (in many ways both these were fused into one). He had always been subject to periods of deep melancholy, and during the final five years of his life these were intensified into long cycles of acute mental pain and self-loathing which, according to his journals and letters, left him virtually paralysed.

Insofar as his poetry is concerned, Hopkins's 'choking aspirations to excellence'[83] were revealed in continuous experimentation involving metre, rhyme schemes, the use of 'compound adjectives, inversions of word-order, compression and elipsis'.[84] The two terms commonly associated with Hopkins's innovations are 'inscape' and 'sprung rhythm'. Although the first of these has already been defined in the poet's own words, a more restrictive meaning is pertinent here because of Hopkins's declaration that 'my verse is less to be read than heard'.[85] Thus there is an analogy to music. Where sprung rhythm is concerned the analogy is closer, for 'it consists of scanning by accents or stresses alone, without any account of the number of syllables, so that a foot may be one strong syllable, or it may be many light and one strong.'[86] In another passage Hopkins says, poetry 'must be spoken; *till it is spoken it is not performed*, it does not perform, it is not itself. Sprung rhythm gives back to poetry its true soul and self.'[87] As a way of implementing his ideas Hopkins developed a system of stress marks as an aid in performing his poetry. Towards the end of his life musical terms appear in his performance suggestions for particular poems or lines: '"Thou art indeed just, Lord" must be read *adagio molto* and with great stress.' One of his last sonnets, 'Spelt from Sibyl's Leaves', 'should be almost sung: it is most carefully timed in *tempo rubato*' and its 'long rests' should be observed.[88] However, before we push the analogy too far, Hopkins's 'love of music was more satisfied by actual music than by attempts to turn language into music; we know that in his final years he wanted to be a composer rather than a poet'.[89] (He did actually write some music which he submitted to Sir Robert Stewart, Professor of Music at Trinity College, Dublin, during his tenure at University College in that city.)

The four poems set by Rubbra in the present work are sonnets, although the first, 'Pied Beauty', is a curtal (or curtailed) sonnet, which Hopkins explained as having been 'constructed in proportions resembling those of the sonnet proper, namely, 6 + 4 instead of 8 + 6, with however a halfline tailpiece.'[90] All of the poems were written in 1877, the final year of Hopkins' three-year stay at St Beuno's, a Jesuit training centre situated in the hills of North Wales. These are by no means simple nature poems. Each has underlying theological meanings and one of them, 'God's Grandeur', is especially pertinent in the light of today's ecological concerns.

Inscape is described as a Suite for Mixed Voices, Strings and Harp (or Pianoforte). It owes its existence to a commission for a work to be performed at the 1965 Stroud Festival of Religious Drama and the Arts. Each poem is allotted a separate movement with its own key signature and tempo. There is no attempt to provide a linkage between the movements on the basis of key. Aside from the exact reproduction in the two-page 'Epilogue' of material from 'Pied Beauty', there are no direct thematic links between the movements. There are some *divisi* sections, and except in rare instances the vocal parts and the accompaniments are separate entities.

In addition to critical judgements, a description of the basic materials in the first and second movements appears below in the first of the two principal reviews:

> Design underpins each movement: an apt musical idea (e.g. in the first, *Pied Beauty*, a scale from dominant to dominant which within the 6/8 metre keeps shifting its accents; in the second a three-note tag and its inversion) developed, not forced, while the words are sung in springy, sensitive lines. I like the way Rubbra's mind moves, and his honest, sterling, carefully written music.[91]

In 'Pied Beauty' Hopkins 'gives glory to God for the rich colour-dappling of the world of nature. In lines 8–11 he praises the Father of all this ever-changing variety and contrast, whose own beauty is eternal, therefore "past change".'[92] Thus we read, 'Glory be to God for dappled things- / For skies of couple-colour as a brinded cow' and this image is followed by others of like nature.

The general well-being and contentment expressed in the poem are echoed in the tranquillity and easy grace of the music, one of the main characteristics of which is the rising and falling scale figure mentioned in the review. This figure is confined to the accompaniment except for the movement's final section, where it is duplicated in all of the vocal lines. In a number of instances the figure is a two- and three-octave affair, while at other times its one-octave span is immediately repeated in another instrumental part by means of a one-note overlap. In both cases the effect is somewhat like that heard in certain Bach organ preludes, where the extended and unbroken scale passages, constantly renewed, seem limitless. (A prime example is the Prelude in E minor which precedes the famous 'Wedge' fugue.)

Another accompanimental figure of equal importance consists of rocking octaves, but this is never shared with the voice parts. Its springy quality is particularly appropriate to the vigour and enthusiasm of the poem, while the scale figure suggests the continuity of those of God's creations of which Hopkins wrote. The alternation and interaction of these two figures provide the framework for several variants of the figures themselves.

The choral writing is a blend of block harmonies and moving parts, some of the latter being imitative, and there is a good balance of conjunct and disjunct patterns. Except for the sharing of the scale figure, voices and accompaniment are independent of one another. The vocal phrases are arranged so that a cadential *effect* rather than a cadence in the accepted sense coincides with the end of eight of the poem's eleven lines. Each of these has sustained notes – most in all four parts – and all except the final cadence are followed by measures containing rests. The accompaniment, however, forms a continuous running fabric.

All of these pseudo-cadences mark off distinct harmonic sections, the keys of which appear below: the sequence is shown by the arrows.

E major   →   G sharp minor   →   D sharp minor

| D major | → | ambiguous | → | D minor/major |
| B major | → | E major |

The instrumental interludes generate the modulations, and the extreme brevity of some of the former accounts for the abruptness in the latter. Yet nowhere is there any sense that the leisurely pace of the music has quickened. However, as we shall see, some of the keys shown above are not as clear-cut as they appear.

We begin our harmonic analysis of this movement by enlarging on the remark in Porter's review: 'a scale from dominant to dominant'. The key signature throughout the movement shows four sharps, but unless that signature is *seen* the listener will not accept E major as the tonic key, for the constantly repeating Bs in the leaping octave figure throughout the first four measures are interpreted as the tonic of B major/minor. Not until the ascending scale from B to B with its intervening notes, including A natural, is there certainty that preparations are under way for the establishment of E major as the tonic key. Hence Porter's 'dominant to dominant'. Rubbra takes his time – ten and a half measures – before E major is established by the entry of the women's parts. All of the choral passages are short, so that no key remains in effect for long. Thus not two measures after the conclusion of the men's entry, G sharp minor is established by reintroducing the dominant octaves and interpreting them as the third of G sharp minor when an open fifth in that key is sounded. At the end of the G sharp minor choral passage, D sharp – V in G sharp minor – becomes the tonic of D sharp minor. At the conclusion of the choral entries in the latter key, the first abrupt modulation takes the music to D major in an unusual passage of just three measures. The D sharp octaves move to what is basically a C sharp triad, but minus G sharp. Then C minor is introduced enharmonically when D sharp = E flat, E sharp = F and, for the implied G sharp, an A flat is substituted. In the third measure of the modulation naturals and sharps are introduced by

Ex. 233

contrary motion, and D major is reached in the measure that contains the vocal entries. The passage appears in Example 233.

In the above register of keys the word 'ambiguous' appears in place of a key for the following reason: after the establishment of D major and its confirmation in both voice parts and accompaniment, the D octaves with which the passage concludes are retained as a pedal in the strings while above them broken E flat minor triads are given to the harp. In performance, both parts are equally strong, thus making it impossible to choose one key over the other. The situation is further complicated when the women's parts enter one octave apart, for their music traverses a segment of the whole-tone scale that is focused on B flat. The next passage, although similarly clouded, is more easily explained: the leaping string octaves on D are continued but they have been moved to the top of the ensemble, second-inversion D major chords form a foundation, and a different pattern of broken E flat minor triads in the harp form a middle part. In the vocal lines above this a paired, canonic passage between the women's and the men's parts oscillates in contrary motion on a dissonant D minor chord. Later in the same passage a dissonant D major takes control.

There is, of course, a good reason for all of this cloudiness and ambiguity: the words. The passages just described encompass the most obscure portions of the poem: 'All things counter, original, spare, strange; / Whatever is fickle, freckled (who knows how?) / With swift, slow; sweet, sour; adazzle, dim.' In these lines, Rubbra has singled out 'spare', 'strange', 'sour', 'adazzle' and 'dim' for special treatment, and the accented dissonances on these words are most effective, and the always-moving accompaniment adds to the obscurity with its dissonant harmony.

For the final two lines of the poem the music very audibly disengages itself from ambiguities and in the longest orchestral passage of the movement the music is steered through a D minor/F major passage to a clear B major via a sequential pattern in which G flat and E flat are enharmonically altered to F sharp and D sharp. Modality also has a part to play in the passage. With the assertion of B major the voices enter *forte* with the confident, forceful words, 'He fathers-forth whose beauty is past change'. The rocking B octaves and the 'dominant to dominant' scales are reintroduced – the latter also scored for the voices – E major is established once more, and the movement ends jubilantly on a chorus of 'Praise him' repetitions.

No analysis of 'Pied Beauty' would be complete without mention of the rhythmic vitality which animates every measure. Basically, this vitality is the product of the combined rhythmic patterns of the vocal lines and the accompaniment, but within each of these elements there are conflicting patterns, more so in the accompaniment than in the voices. Except for the harmonically clouded section, which is in 3/4, the fundamental metre is 6/8, but triple patterns are almost continually cutting across it. Other more subordinate but none the less effective patterns contribute to the vitality, many of them in the form of

syncopations, and their interactions with the conflicting metres help to emphasize the buoyancy of the poem.

Hopkins's sonnet, 'The Lantern Out of Doors', was

> written in the year of his ordination [1877], [and] is one of [his] 'priestly' poems in
> the sense that it is one of a number that he produced expressing his vocational
> concerns. In this case the poem is one of faith; that where human, priestly care must
> fail or cease when 'death or distance' intervene, the overseeing Providence of Christ
> has an eternal care for all men, wherever they may be.[93]

The expressiveness in Rubbra's setting of this poem is to my mind one of the
peaks in his choral music. The 'three-note tag and its inversion', to quote Porter
again, open the movement. (Actually, it is a four-note tag.) Both forms of the
figure are shown in Example 234. It may seem strange, even arbitrary to show

Ex. 234

the inverted form in the exposed melodic line and the generating form in the
bass, but the more frequent appearances of the latter in all parts tend to support
my decision even though the inverted form is prominent at times in the melodic
line. In the final analysis the matter is unimportant. What is important is that
both forms of the figure are responsible for the unfolding of much of the
movement. A particularly effective, though short, phrase results from the linear
union of the original and inverted forms. Yet none of these various manifestations
of the motive – original, inverted, or any combination of the two – is omnipresent.
Their influence, however, is apparent in passages where they are absent, because
the fourths which are so prominent in both forms are detached and lead either a
separate existence or become parts of new configurations. An eloquent example
of the latter can be seen in the orchestral interlude between measures 24 and 30.
The new figure is reproduced at various pitches in the strings and accompanying
it throughout the passage are syncopated major seconds in the harp. Everything
grows from the line, 'With, all down darkness wide, his wading light?' The
intensity of those words as exemplified in their setting is continued in the
orchestral harmonies of the interlude. The entire passage appears as Example
235.

The new, bracketed figure in the example is the first in a series of short
ostinatos, and in the last measure of the illustration a new form of the first
ostinato can be seen, minus its first note. This five-note figure is then repro-

Ex. 235

duced one octave lower, its sixteenths creating a graceful flow that beautifully underscores the equally graceful contour of the tenor and bass lines, set one octave apart. The poetic line suggests this easy grace: 'Men go by me whom either beauty bright / In mould or mind or what not else makes rare.' There is a slight rhythmic modification in measures 34–5 when the two last sixteenths are replaced by eighths.

The longest and most prominent ostinato is composed of rising rather than falling fourths. There are eleven statements of the six-note pattern, scored for cellos and basses, and directed to be played *pizzicato* and with heavy accents. The composer has bracketed each statement so as to emphasize the triple framework, which cuts directly across the barlines of the 4/8 metre. Except for four rather widely separated harp chords, the ostinato patterns in this first half of what is the movement's final section are the sole accompaniment under the six vocal lines. Hence the obviousness of the ostinato, which is still conspicuous in the second half of the section where it is joined by the rest of the orchestra.

The choral writing in this movement as everywhere in *Inscape* is superior and one of the most memorable passages is also one of the most simple and economical. Set to the words, 'Christ minds; Christ's interest, what to avow or amend / There, eyes them, heart wants, care haunts', the passage is the six-voiced one just mentioned. Its six parts are really three, for the men double the women. We have met Rubbra's parallel, triadic writing before – notably in *Lauda Sion* and the *Te Deum*, Op. 115 – but here the effect is warmer owing to the non-theological text. Also, the passage, isolated by rests on either end, is self-contained, and not a part of an abstract continuum. In Example 236, note

Ex. 236

the beautifully moulded contour of the melody, and how 'haunts' is made to stand out by means of a simple, semitone movement. To conserve space, the men's parts have been omitted.

In sum, this short but highly expressive movement contains in microcosmic form two of the traits most associated with Rubbra: the evolution of an entire texture from a melodic germ cell, and the employment of ostinato techniques. Yet neither characteristic is ever carried to extremes, for, as musical maturity has come to the composer, so has a gradual relaxation of the former relentlessness associated with these and other techniques.

The sonnet to which the music of the third movement is set – 'Spring' – contains in its octave some of Hopkin's most joyous lines. However, as Robinson points out,

> spring is for Hopkins a condition rather than a season. He does not treat it as a passing from winter nor as a movement towards autumn, and it is hardly distinct from summer for him... Hopkin's nature poems are poems about the growing time of year and the strong and lively youthfulness of man. In winter, in age, he was scarcely interested.[94]

McChesney's briefer comment explains the more sober sestet by telling us that the origins of spring's loveliness go back 'to its original source – Paradise – the Garden of Eden and the innocence of mankind before the Fall'.[95]

Rubbra's setting of this poem follows the division made explicit by the shift in emphasis from the octave to the sestet. However, instead of employing new material for the sestet as many composers would probably have done, Rubbra has adapted some of his primary material to meet the new poetic content. Thus the unified approach that is such a striking feature of the two previous movements is again demonstrated. However, the economical use of material is by no means confined to the external divisions suggested by the poem's structure. It is also an internal feature to a quite astonishing degree, for beginning at once the first three and a half measures of the joyously animated orchestral material are simultaneously augmented in the harp part. Since the augmentation consumes six and a half measures, it follows that a certain amount of imitative or free material occupies the remaining measures of the generating statement. There are three restatements of these opening measures, and three similar augmentations which take the music to almost the midpoint of the movement. It must be admitted that only the first statement and its augmentation are entirely audible as the succeeding statements have the choir with which to contend. In order to compensate for the equally enthusiastic choral passages pitch adjustments have been made in each of the ensuing statements: under the first choral entry the passage is transposed a minor tenth higher; beneath the second entry the augmentation is in the topmost part, and the transposition is a major ninth higher than the generating figures (the original figures are in the middle); and under the third choral entry the passage is two octaves higher. The poem and its musical setting are best described as loud and exuberant – at least in the octave – and the general atmosphere encourages a certain confusion to which both orchestra and choir can legitimately contribute. This means that the loss of details in the hearing are to be expected.

The musical setting of the poem's octave, containing some new music as well as fragments of the original proceed in a headlong fashion to the sober and thoughtful sestet that begins, 'What is all this juice and all this joy? / A strain of the earth's sweet being in the beginning / In Eden garden.' Hopkins's restrained question and answer are matched by music of the utmost simplicity. Rubbra has set these lines for four-part women's voices in soft, slowly-moving block harmonies whose shifting triads are almost unbearably poignant, coming as they do after the buoyant rhythms and gentle dissonances of the octave. The only accompaniment consists of irregularly placed harp chords. The men's voices enter in unison, *pianissimo*, under the sustained chord that concludes the women's entry, and which the composer directs is to be held 'as long as possible'. The lines which the men sing read, 'Have, get, before it cloy, / Before it cloud, Christ, lord, and sour with sinning.' The accompaniment consists of an accented, ostinato figure in both top and bottom, separated by harp chords and moving in a measured tread of slow quarter notes. This figure is directly related to the generating figure at the start of the movement. The word 'sour' is given special emphasis by a dissonance in the orchestra. The re-entry of the women over a long-held E flat in the men's parts brings another reminder of the original material.

The final passage of the movement tends towards G major, but this tonality is not confirmed until B naturals are sounded just before the cadence, but even after the voices have become silent, an unexpected B flat major chord leaves the issue in doubt for an instant until G is finally decided upon.

The concluding sonnet, 'God's Grandeur', 'contrasts the devitalizing and smearing effect produced by man on the face of the earth, with the ever-springing freshness of the life of nature'.[96] Just as in 'Spring' this contrast is given expression in the sestet, but in the musical setting the distinction between the octave and the sestet is not as conspicuous as it was in the preceding movement.

The tempo indication, *Largo e grandioso*, matches the text, the first line of which reads, 'The world is charged with the grandeur of God.'[97] The two measures of striding octaves in the accompaniment – accented and *fortissimo* – which open the movement, set the stage for the mainly declamatory style of the choral forces and these octaves continue as the principal accompanimental feature. Again, as in 'The Lantern Out of Doors', ostinatos are an important factor. The first, a six-note descending octave figure in the uppermost parts, supports the lines beginning, 'And all is seared with trade', and ending with the unpleasant 'and shares man's smell'. The second ostinato is a three-note affair, also in octaves and in the upper reaches, but assuming slightly different rhythmic figures. It is under the second line of the sestet, 'There lives the dearest freshness deep down things.' The sense of exhilaration permeating the music for this and the next two lines is what sets the octave and the sestet apart rather than textural changes of the type seen in 'Spring'. The two final lines, 'Because the Holy Ghost over the bent / World broods with warm breast and with ah! bright wings', are set to soaring harmonies that beautifully portray their mystical fervour.

The two-page 'Epilogue' completes and rounds off the whole work. Except for minor details its accompaniment is the same as that found in the first and last two pages of 'Pied Beauty' and its choral parts are the same as those of the last two pages in the same movement. The text, entitled 'Summa', reads 'All glory be ascribed to / The Holy Three in One'.

The other major review of *Inscape* is also affirmative: the composer 'has captured the difficult rhythms of Hopkins's poems.... The whole work... is a model of skilful and economical writing.'[98]

The importance to Rubbra of *Inscape* is evident from the fact that he compared it with his two earlier settings of St John of the Cross, noting first that all three works are 'for mixed voices and small instrumental resources'. After pointing out that *Inscape* is 'not a continuous work' in contrast with its predecessors, he continues with a textual comparison:

the words, although mystical, are responses to natural beauty by one who believes that 'the world is charged with the grandeur of God'. There is sometimes a sultry and overpowering magnificence in St. John of the Cross's words: with Hopkins the language, although forged by the impact of natural things on one sensitive to them, never lets the reader be unaware of God's immanence. These differences affect the music of *Inscape*, which is much more varied in its idiomatic behaviour than its predecessors.[99]

Pentecostal Hymn

Rubbra's next three choral works are relatively short. The first of these, Pentecostal Hymn (*Nocte Surgentes*), Op. 123, is to a text perhaps by Alcuin of York (*c.*735–804), the Anglo-Saxon churchman and scholar who, after having met Charlemagne, became the principal teacher and leader in the Carolingian Renaissance. The three-stanza poem, translated into prose by Rubbra and printed in the front of the score, reads as follows:

> Rising before dawn, let us meditate on the Psalms and sing hymns to the Lord. Thus, in union with the saints, may we be found worthy to enter heaven and live there for ever. We pray that the blessed God, whose glory is sempiternal, may grant us this.

The piece was written 'for Denys Darlow and the Tilford Bach Festival Choir' and was completed on the Feast of St Thomas Aquinas, 7 March 1964.

The work received the following excellent review:

> Rubbra's vocal music is more a twentieth century equivalent of tenth-century organum than of sixteenth-century polyphony; and he achieves his striking harmonic effects largely by using triadic harmony in a novel manner. This fine work is for SAATBB. The lines are thoroughly vocal and there is much stepwise progression. It is a work for large and experienced choirs only; but well-performed, with Rubbra's meticulous dynamics carefully followed, it would sound superb.[100]

Stylistically, the piece is divided into two parts, the first of which contains the triads mentioned in the above review. These are arranged so that the three members of a triad in root position are assigned to the three bottom parts, while a different triad, also in root position, is distributed in like manner and simultaneously in the three top parts. The resulting six-note harmony is not so dissonant as might be thought. The harmonic combination that recurs most often in the course of the first two pages is composed of an F sharp, A, C sharp triad topped by one consisting of B, D, F sharp. This combination is the reference point to which other triadic combinations gravitate and all of the triads together support a Gregorian-type melody, formed by the movement of the topmost notes. As the upper triads move up and down, the foundation triads move in contrary motion. The total effect is that of an austere, massive, contrary-motion organum, but of course a more dissonant one.

Part II, comprising the last three pages of this five-page work, also has a Gregorian flavour, but the flowing eighth and sixteenth-note texture is contrapuntal. Imitative entries are prominent at the beginning of this part and when all of the voices are in a more generalized kind of imitation continues to add interest. Two unusual metre signatures appearing successively for one measure each are meant to indicate in unequivocal terms how the composer wishes the note groupings in each measure to be interpreted: $\frac{8+1}{8}$ and $\frac{3+3+2}{8}$ instead of the more usual 9/8 and 8/8, which would not have conveyed his intentions adequately because of the conventional patterns associated with these metres.

In the first of these two measures the sopranos are divided, remaining so for the rest of the piece, and the music reverts to the chordal writing of Part I, though not to the same degree. Imitation on a small scale is a factor and the piece ends on an inconclusive chord. The triadic writing in the work is reminiscent on a miniature scale of the similar writing in *Lauda Sion* and the *Te Deum*, Op. 115.

And When The Builders

The second of these three short choral works is the anthem for mixed voices (SATB) and organ, *And When the Builders*, Op. 125, composed in 1964. It bears a dedication to the 'Provost and Fellows of Worcester College, Oxford, on the occasion of the 250th Anniversary of the Incorporation of the College as Worcester College on 14 July 1714'. The text is from Ezra, Chapter 3, verses 10 to the end and Rubbra's setting has given us one of his most straightforward and uncomplicated works.

Except for a subdued section for sopranos only ('this can be sung by a solo voice if desired') which depicts the weeping of the priests, Levites and others who remembered the old temple, the piece is festive in a dignified way. The texture is overwhelmingly chordal and the dynamic level is mostly *forte* to *fortissimo*. The organ immediately establishes a tonal centre on D, and this is reinforced by lengthy pedals. In fact, Ds in the pedal occur in forty-two of the fifty-four measures, thus anchoring the tonality but also permitting harmonic excursions away from it in both the organ and vocal lines. One of the main strengths of this anthem is the consistent gravitation back to the D tonal centre after each excursion. The most lengthy deviation comes in the section for sopranos only. This is an anthem that is entirely suitable for festival services where volume and impressiveness are important; the current recording, made in St Paul's Cathedral, accomplishes both aims most admirably. The final reverberation is thrilling.

Bonny Mary O!

With *Bonny Mary O!*, Op. 126, a momentary return is made to the secular world. The poem, by John Clare, portrays a charming little genre scene: a fine morning with bird songs (robin and wren), swallows swooping, cowslips in bloom, and so on. The scene changes to evening and milking chores, at which time the poet hopes to meet Bonny Mary and make her his. The reader is aware of Bonny Mary before this, however, for her name appears from the beginning almost as a refrain.

Rubbra's setting, 'written specially for the Contemporary Arts Festival of Olympia, Washington 1964', is for SATB with piano accompaniment. Everywhere the music matches the extroverted enthusiasm of the text. It is cast in a clear, two-part form in which *B* is almost twice the length of *A*: thirty-two measures as opposed to eighteen. After *B* has run its course, both sections are repeated. Significant changes are found in the four, climactic closing measures of the piece. Otherwise, insofar as the repeats are concerned, there are only very slight alterations in the vocal lines, and these are intended to accommodate syllabic differences. However, the simplicity of the text does not extend to the music, for there are difficulties, particularly in the *B* sections where the combination of the vocal parts and the accompaniment present rhythmic complications. Also the very high notes (A and B flats) in both soprano and tenor lines are problems for inexperienced choirs.

In Die et Nocte Canticum

In Die et Nocte Canticum, Op. 129, for Choir (SATB) and Orchestra is the second choral work (after *Inscape*) which Rubbra called a 'suite'. Aside from the division of the work into separate movements the term, as in *Inscape*, has little significance, although purists might argue that it is at least partially justified by the presence in each work of dance-like movements: 'Pied Beauty' and 'Spring' in *Inscape*, and 'Hymn at Dawn' and 'Hymn to Spring' in the present work. Certainly neither of the other two movements in *Inscape* nor the remaining movement here, 'Hymn Before Sleep', qualify as dance movements.

The title of the work was supplied by the then Vice Provost (1965) of Worcester College, Oxford, A.N. Bryan-Brown, who also provided the English synopses of the Latin poems. The title is appropriate not only because of the references to dawn and sleep, but also because Rubbra provided two discrete orchestral movements, 'Aubade' at the beginning and 'Nocturne' at the end. Neither of these is included in the published score and the composer must have realized that many, if not most, of the performances of the suite would of necessity omit these short movements. Indeed, his note in the score remarks that 'if necessary the three choral movements can be sung as a separate suite, but they gain greatly if preceded and followed by the purely orchestral movements.' At least the premiere of the work at the University of Sussex in 1965 upon the occasion of the New Universities Festival, for which the suite was commissioned, included these movements, for a 'combined choir and orchestra from the six new Universities: East Anglia, Essex, Lancaster, Keele, Sussex and York' performed the piece.

The text to which 'Hymn at Dawn' was set is by St Ambrose (*c*.340–397), one of the Church Fathers. He was Bishop of Milan from 374 until his death, author of hymns known as Ambrosian, and the churchman responsible for introducing into the Milanese liturgy the chants later called Ambrosian. These were one of the precursors of Gregorian chant. His poem expresses the hope that the three Persons of the Trinity, each in his individual manner, will guide us on this new and promising day.

The forceful rhythms of the music in an *Allegro con spirito* tempo emphasize the vigorous, extroverted character of the voice parts and accompaniment. In both elements a Stravinskyian flavour, stemming from the orchestra's percussive, accented and syncopated chords, is distinctively noticeable. The first of several orchestral patterns in which this is true appears in Example 237. On

Ex. 237

the last half of the third beat in measure 4 the sopranos and tenors enter, separated by an octave, with a slightly different version of the initial pattern (bracketed in the example). Three measures later there is an overlap as the altos and basses – also an octave apart – enter with their version. Most of the rest of the movement in the vocal lines consists of subtle developments of this material plus repetitions of some of the versions. Much of the writing continues to be paired with each pair having the same music and even when all four parts are together this is still true. Thus instead of four independent vocal lines there are really only two most of the time and the consequence is that the music gains in clarity and vitality.

A second series of chords, marked *subito piano* and composed of mild dissonances, is equally Stravinskyian in its syncopations. It supports two softly expressive paired entries – altos and basses, sopranos and tenors – and also serves as a link between the patterns illustrated above and the repetition of those patterns. Its later restatement under the same softly expressive passage for altos and basses only connects two different versions of the basic material of the example.

A third orchestral pattern, really an ostinato, is more memorable for its series of descending octaves in quarter notes than for the sustained chords beneath. There are six statements, five of which are scored for high strings and the sixth for low strings. Each statement forms, in effect, a gapped scale after each beginning note: G flat, E flat, D, B, B flat, G, G flat, E flat. Shortly before the end of the movement the series is repeated a major second lower. One of the interesting things about both series is that the sustained chord beneath each statement of the eight notes is different, and thus the harmony is different.

The central movement in the suite, 'Hymn to Spring', is also extroverted but in an entirely different way from its predecessor. Put in an *Allegretto grazioso* tempo, the mood is light and vibrant as befits the text, a Goliardic poem from the Benediktbeuren Manuscript. The poem is a celebration of spring's arrival, and appropriate mention is made of flowers, new leaves, bird songs and the turning of youth to thoughts of love. Thus a secular poem has been sandwiched between two religious works.

The nine-measure orchestral introduction, the first portion of which appears as Example 238, provides the basic material for the entire movement in the

Ex. 238

orchestra certainly, but to a far less audible and visible extent in the vocal parts. There are two aspects to this introduction: first, the individual cell of four sixteenths plus its subsidiaries – a resolution and an upbeat to the next cell; second, the aggregate of all of these, together with the vocal parts, constitutes a large structural section. From the example, it can be seen that there is both repetition and variation with respect to the cellular units, and this mixture extends to the entire accompaniment.

As for the structural division, the first section, which includes the introduction, extends through measure 41 insofar as the vocal parts are concerned, but an exact repeat of the whole section starts one measure earlier in 40 with an abbreviated portion of the orchestral introduction, and this ends in measure 76. There ensues a rather interesting concluding section of twenty-eight measures with enough vocal and orchestral differences to justify considering it as a *B* in an *A*-repeat *B* binary form. This still holds true even when it is discovered that the material is in reality a new synthesis of most of the previously used material. Also, about two thirds of the text used in the first *A* section is reused here in the *B*. Such textual repetition is rare in Rubbra's choral music as well as in his songs, and it calls for comment, for one of this composer's strongest traits is his unfailing instinct for knowing when a work – however small – a movement in a larger work, and the larger work itself is complete. (It must be said that in some cases this characteristic has led to abrupt endings.) In 'Hymn to Spring' Rubbra's motive for repeating the first portion of the text appears to support the structural design. The *B* section is rhythmically, melodically and dynamically climactic: a series of *fortissimo*, rushing sixteenths set in the strings reacts asymmetrically with the voice parts, while a brief round of imitative entries is followed by massive octave and chordal passages for all four parts, the latter having a consistently high soprano line. To have used this material in the *B* section of a ternary structure, and repeated the *A* as its concluding section would have robbed the movement of its final climax. A similar mistake would have occurred if *B* had been substituted for the repeating *A*, for the movement in its *Allegretto* tempo would then have seemed too short. Finally, to have provided new music for the words of the repeating *A* would have resulted in a through-composed movement, something that Rubbra obviously did not want.

Some of the ways in which the introductory orchestral material has been transferred or adapted to new uses in the vocal parts may now be detailed, but as implied above only a very few examples are apparent. Except for a small rhythmic alteration the most obvious derivative is a literal, four-part transposition of the first introductory measure and its resolution in the next measure (measures 14–15, 49–50). Next, the three sixteenths and their resolution on C in measures 30–31 and 65–6 are transpositions of an easily overlooked ascending octave figure in the lower strings just after Example 238 (measures 6–7). In the *B* section the initial *divisi* passage for sopranos and altos (measures 77–80) is an extraction of the lower and upper neighbour figures of measure 4, and it retains the fourth between the upper parts and the third between the lower voices. The figure in the short imitative passage mentioned above is an exact replica of the figure in measures 11–12 and 46–7, but tracing the lineage of the original figure is impossible. Thus to conclude this brief survey of derivatives, the best that can be said is that while there are very few *literal* uses of the introductory material in the vocal parts, the drive and enthusiasm of the latter are reflections of the orchestral rhythms, and the harmonic structures of the introduction are also present in the vocal lines.

'Hymn Before Sleep', the last of the choral movements, is an appropriately quiet, *Lento* setting of a poem by Prudentius (or to give him his full name, Aurelius Prudentius Clemens), 348–405, the first major Christian Latin poet, who was born in Spain. He wrote such important works as *Peristephanon*, *Psychomachia* and *Cathemerinon*, the last consisting of a group of twelve hymns, the first six of which mark out particular hours that Christians should observe in their daily devotions. Among these are 'Morning Hymn', 'Hymn Before the Repast', 'Hymn for the Lighting of the Lamp' and so on. The poem that is the basis of this movement is no. 6 in the set and of its thirty-eight, four-line stanzas, Rubbra chose the third, fourth, fifth and last.

The importance of the outer, orchestral movements in the suite becomes plain only when 'Hymn Before Sleep' is reached. The centrepiece of the three choral movements is the same as that of the five-member structure: 'Hymn to Spring'. Admittedly, the resulting arch structure is not symmetrical, because the vigour of 'Hymn At Dawn' is not balanced by the soothing calm of 'Hymn Before Sleep'. However, without the orchestral movements the asymmetry is exaggerated; with them the quietness at the start of 'Aubade' and the stillness at

Ex. 239

the conclusion of 'Nocturne' provide a broader base, and the position of 'Hymn to Spring' as the apex of the structure now seems well-founded. Thus the omission of the orchestral movements in performance cancels the carefully thought-out design, a fact implied in the composer's statement that the choral movements 'gain greatly' if the orchestral movements are included.

The selected stanzas for 'Hymn Before Sleep' are descriptive of the benefits afforded by sleep including physical relaxation, relief from mental anguish and grief, and the forgetfulness of pain. However, even though sleep has taken charge, the heart remembers Christ.

The musical setting for these thoughts conveys in a most beautiful fashion the atmosphere surrounding sleep. The ostinato figure in the accompaniment is an important element, for its slow-moving, descending octaves acquire a hypnotic effect with repetition (Example 239). Variety is achieved by later alterations in the pitches of the series and monotony is avoided by dispensing with the ostinatos altogether in portions of the movement. The voice parts are languid not just in the example but throughout the movement, and their empty, consecutive fifths in measures 3–5 contribute to the empty, drained feeling that is so commonly experienced prior to sleep. That feeling is reinforced at numerous other points in the piece, even in the measures where Christ is remembered, for well before then and continuing until almost the end, softly moving octaves in the four vocal lines interact with shifting harmonies in the accompaniment, and the effect is poignant and enervating. It is also a poignant passage harmonically because of the dissonances between voices and accompaniment. Dissonances between the individual voice parts also occur in the movement and they serve to emphasize the indefiniteness associated with sleep.

In his short review of *In Die et Nocte Canticum*, Hugh Ottaway singled out 'Hymn to Spring' for special notice: 'This movement is Rubbra in his most unbuttoned vein – the Rubbra who admires Orff's *Carmina Burana* – and its companions, in their different ways, should prove equally telling.'[101]

Veni Creator Spiritus

Veni Creator Spiritus, Op. 130, is a setting for mixed choir and brass instruments, or organ, of the Latin hymn for Whit Sunday. The author is unknown, but the hymn is thought to date from the ninth century. Commissioned by the BBC, Rubbra completed the score on the Feast of the Epiphany 1966 and its first performance took place at the Promenade Concert of 5 August of the same year.

Although this work is relatively short – eleven pages – it is one of the composer's choral masterpieces. It is certainly not lacking in reviews and some of these are lavish, yet discriminating, in their praise. I begin with four brief newspaper notices:

Short choral works of this kind show Rubbra's quietly rapturous style at its purest and most impressive; the progression from gently clashing second at the outset to complex overlapping chords at the climax is calculated with a fine sense of sonority and balance.[102]

left a deep impression... inward-looking and devotional... Like all the late works of this composer, the short piece bears the stamp of ripe technical mastery, and beyond that generates a compelling sense of majesty and awe.[103]

in the manner of another and greater Opus 130 it found its argument on the key of B flat major.... Rubbra's use of polyphony provides a fair echo of late Beethoven.[104]

Rubbra's neglect is recent and unjust, although his monolithic *Veni Creator Spiritus*... may not convince the unbeliever.[105]

Allan Jefferis speaks of its 'sublime Holstian coda',[106] but it was left to Andrew Porter to write the most detailed review:

In any case the work has its basis in the alternation, or combination, of swelling brass sonorities with the chording and carefully spaced discording, of the chorus. The sound has sometimes a Brucknerian splendour, and sometimes the full, gentle surge of Bruckner's *piano* writing for similar forces... *Veni Creator* is a noble, thoughtful composition which will worthily fill our cathedrals whenever the right forces can be gathered together.[107]

Concerning a need for 'the right forces', there cannot be the slightest doubt: the work presents a formidable challenge in at least two areas, neither of which is apparent at the beginning of the piece in spite of the sopranos' B flat in the first phrase. This is a forerunner of things to come, for A flats, As, B flats and Bs are plentiful, and there is one C. The tenors' *tessitura* is also high, although the extreme notes are not so frequent. The 'complex overlapping chords at the climax' are certainly another area of difficulty for any but professional singers, and they will be considered in due course.

First, mention must be made of the accompaniment. The composer's first choice is a brass ensemble composed of four horns, two trumpets, two tenor trombones, bass trombone and tuba. Although the substitute organ accompaniment seems entirely adequate, it lacks the force and colour of the brass ensemble, and for this reason the latter should be supplied whenever and wherever possible.

The work's monolithic nature is revealed at the very beginning in a phrase that is memorable for its bold melodic contour as well as for the seconds and sevenths that constitute its harmonic structure. With some exceptions these characteristics dominate the remainder of the work in both the voice parts and the accompaniment. However, the sound of these intervals is not as forbidding as the mention of them might appear, for their effect is veiled rather than strident. This is the result of the contexts in which they are employed, and the soft dynamic level in many of the passages where they are most prominent; in both capacities the mystical character of the words is considerably enhanced. Example 240 shows the opening phrase. The characteristic melodic contour and the attendant harmonies as seen there are exactly reproduced only once, and

Ex. 240

then at the start of the final third of the work (measures 50–53), but the second half of just the contour appears in close stretto formation – first soprano, first tenor and accompaniment – immediately following the *fortissimo* climax (measures 64–5). Variants of the contour are frequent, the most notable instance occurring in measures 19–21 where the rising and falling fifths have been replaced by octaves, and the rising and falling fourths by minor thirds. Other variants are less obvious because their intervals are smaller than the fifths or fourths. Also, most of the less conspicuous variants are rhythmically different.

In the middle portion of the work the emphasis is less on the vertical structure and more on the horizontal movement of individual lines. Most of these lines have evolved in some way from the first phrase. Thus in a number of instances the rising and falling contour is clearly present, but the bold leaps are missing owing to interpolated connective notes on either side of the apex note. Rubbra's skill in the areas of improvisation and development has furnished several different examples of such treatment and, of course, phrase extensions are also found. The rocking alto part in measures 32–3 is clearly borrowed from the alto of the example, and so on.

The accompanimental figures are less easily traced to a source, but a careful inspection shows that the reverse contours seem to have been derived from the dips in the bass line of measure 3. Other figures simply grow out of the preceding material in a natural and inevitable way. Certainly the most important accompanimental feature in the work is the presence of the seconds and sevenths; there is no disputing the fact that their crisp bite is more effective when they are given to the brass ensemble rather than to the organ.

In a postcard note dated 31 August [1966] Charles Mackerras, the conductor for the 5 August premiere of the work wrote:

> Your kind letter has reached me out here on holiday in the Island of Elba.
> I am absolutely delighted that you found our performance of your 'Veni Creator Spiritus' so good. What a lovely piece it is; as you yourself say, it is a pleasant change from the usual 'hearty' approach to that beautiful text.
> I have enjoyed working on it very much.

Creature-Songs to Heaven

Creature-Songs to Heaven, Op. 134, is a four-movement work that was 'written for the centenary in 1969 of the Coloma Convent Grammar School, Croydon, Surrey'. It is scored for SSA, string quartet (or string orchestra) and piano, but there is no doubt regarding the composer's preference: 'this piano part incorporates both strings and solo piano part, and should be used only when a string quartet (or string orchestra) is not available.' The four charming poems to which the equally attractive music is set were written by Carmen Bernos de Gasztold, a French nun who lived and worked at the Benedictine Abbey of Saint Louis du Temple at Limon-par-Igny. She wrote two books of poetry: *Prayers From the Ark*, containing twenty-seven poems, and *The Beasts' Choir* with twenty-six, both published by the Abbey's private press. The poems selected by Rubbra were taken from the second book, with translations by Rumer Godden. In them, as with all of the poems from this book, plaintive petitions rise to God from each of the little creatures – the mother hen; the snail, who must carry his heavy house on his back; the ladybird; and the peacock, who wishes he had a more attractive voice.

In his review of the performance of the work at St John's, Smith Square, by Trinity School Boy's Choir of Croydon on 20 May 1970, Henry Raynor mentions the 'series of Job-like questions' addressed to God, as well as 'the dissonant polyphony of each movement resolving into a radiantly diatonic but always different Amen'.[108] The dissonances are, like those in *Veni Creator Spiritus*, formed from seconds and sevenths. The seconds particularly are effective in the accompaniments to 'The Mother Hen' where their *staccato* groupings suggest the clucking of barnyard hens, and 'The Ladybird' where the delicate whirr of tiny wings is depicted. They are less in evidence in 'The Snail', but are again prominent in 'The Peacock'. There are also numerous dissonances in the voice parts, particularly in 'The Mother Hen' and 'The Peacock'. When these react with those in the accompaniments the intonational difficulties for the voices can be formidable.

The prosaic nature of the translations means that the melodic style is largely declamatory in all four movements with a predominance of block harmonies. However, in some instances these block passages are deceptive, for when they are closely inspected they are seen to consist of lines in which there is close stretto imitation. One such passage fills the last page of 'The Ladybird'.

Rhythmically, the movements are straightforward and uncomplicated, and their tempi are governed by the subject matter of their texts. Thus 'The Mother Hen' is marked *Allegretto con spirito*, and 'The Snail', not surprisingly, is to be performed *Lento e pesante*. The same contrast prevails between the third and fourth movements: *Poco allegretto ed amabile* for 'The Ladybird' (my personal favourite among the four) and *Lento e con dignità* for 'The Peacock'.

The 'radiantly diatonic but always different Amen' which brings each movement to a close is, in each case, the culmination of a distinctive thought. In the first movement the thought is somewhat ambiguous as the mother hen says, 'Lord, my heart is so choked with loving care, how can I say amen?' Here, the amen is gentle and extended over four and a half measures. The snail is more abrupt, for all of his thoughts take the form of complaints, and he concludes with an almost demanding request for 'a paradise of lettuces... and the warmth of a thunder shower'. His amen is loud and appropriately blunt. The ladybird, on the other hand, recognizes her relationship to 'Our Lady', and is happy for 'each blade of Your grass', and so thankful that God made her 'so that no one is afraid of me; a little toy, a mite of comfort and laughter'. Her amens are joyful and long-lasting. Finally, the peacock asks the Lord to 'let a day come, a heavenly day, when my inner and outer selves will be reconciled in perfect harmony.' This is a reference to his 'discordant cry', which is 'humiliating', and to the splendour of his outward appearance. His amen is short.

Creature-Songs to Heaven is a thoroughly delightful work that deserves to be heard not once but many times. It reveals the lighter side of Rubbra's musical personality, a side not often displayed. It is by no means easy, and much rehearsal time is needed to ensure a good performance, for besides the technical difficulties there are subtleties of expression to be resolved. However, because of the string quartet or string orchestra requirement, it is highly unlikely that the work will receive many performances, but with the substitution of an excellent piano accompaniment prepared by the composer the chances are increased. Even here there are options, for one or more movements can be excerpted without doing violence should it prove impractical to perform the entire work. Such a solution is surely preferable to no performances at all.

The Holy Dawn

The Holy Dawn, Op. 135, is an unaccompanied Christmas carol for SATB set to a poem consisting of four rather mediocre stanzas. Strophic in form, its music is complete in eight measures except for two and one-third measures at the conclusion of the fourth stanza. The tonality is a modally inflected G minor with gentle dissonances that are created by the flow of the individual parts. The result is music of tenderness and quality.

Natum Maria Virgine

Natum Maria Virgine, Op. 136, more commonly known as the 'Advent Cantata', was 'written for the Tilford Bach Festival Choir and Orchestra, at the request of Denys Darlow, and was first performed by them on November 30, 1968, at the Queen Elizabeth Hall, London'. It is scored for baritone solo, mixed choir and small orchestra which includes harp and bells, but there is also an organ accompaniment for use when an orchestra is unavailable. There are four sections entitled respectively, Recitative, Aria (both for baritone), Acrostic Hymn and Chorale. Each of these is set to a text from a different source. Although double bars separate the sections, the music is continuous.

Anyone either hearing this cantata or studying its score will quickly realize that he is in the presence of one of Rubbra's major choral works. It may not seem so at first because the four texts suggest a disjointed patchwork, especially when it is discovered that three are in English and one is in Latin, but the texts flow easily from one to another, and the music traces a logical, well-planned progression from the dissonances of the first three sections – some of which are reminiscent of Messiaen – to the undisputed but far from simple A flat major tonality of the fourth section. In essence, it is a progression from a mystical outlook, symbolized by the indefiniteness of the dissonances, to an open and rational perspective embodied in the A flat setting.

The English words for the baritone recitative come from two sources: the Epistle of St Paul to the Hebrews, 10:37, and the much longer Responsory of the First Nocturn of Matins for the Third Sunday of Advent, a translation from the Latin. The text from Hebrews, 'He that shall come, will come, and will not tarry', is set to a very disjunct phrase seen in Example 241. It follows a ten-

Ex. 241

measure accompanimental introduction, whose clouded dissonances suggest and perhaps anticipate mystical experiences. Also present are the unrelated triads that are so much a part of other mystical works like the Op. 115 *Te Deum*. The beginning of this introduction appears in Example 242.

Ex. 242

The recitative continues with words from the Responsory: 'For He is our Saviour', scored for SAA as a kind of background commentary to the baritone, whose passages alternate with the women's. His first passage from the new source is set to, 'and there shall be no more fears in our borders'. The women then repeat their words to new music, and an orchestral interlude restates the first four measures of the introduction (see Example 242), but with harmonic and slight melodic changes. The soloist continues with 'He shall tread down all our iniquities, and cast all our sins into the depths of the sea.' The section concludes with more new music for 'He is our Saviour', scored now for SATB in a paired, close stretto.

Three distinctive features of this first section should be mentioned. First, the smooth connection between the one sentence from Hebrews and the sentences from the Third Responsory. The flow from one to the other is so natural that one could be pardoned for thinking that the entire text came from one source. The fact that these widely separated lines fit together so well is another proof of the composer's discriminating knowledge of literature. The second characteristic of this section is the balance struck between the highly disjunct solo line and the relatively conjunct choral phrases. This serves to highlight the solo and to establish the choir's role as one of merely emphasizing the point that 'He is our Saviour'. Third, and most important from the listener's standpoint, are the accumulated but not unpleasant dissonances that result from the interactions in the accompaniment of dissonant chords and tone clusters with a moving line. There are also many sustained chords, and these impart a sense of timelessness. Since the notes of both the solo and the choral parts are incorporated in one way or another into the accompaniment, there are few dissonances between the two elements.

The aria which follows is set to a poem by Digby Mackworth Dolben (1848–67), who received his basic education at Eton, where he developed a gift for writing poetry, most of which was religious and devotional in nature. Dolben's unmistakable tendencies towards Catholicism also came to the fore at this time. In 1864 at the age of sixteen he became an Anglican Benedictine monk, but in 1867 his career was tragically ended when he drowned in the River Welland during the time he was preparing to enter Oxford University. His poems were later edited with a memoir by his friend, Robert Bridges. This poem expresses the disillusionment of youth when, in the first line of each of the first three stanzas, something asked for – Peace, Truth, Love – is found to be wanting. In view of Dolben's tragic death there is bitter irony in the final stanza: 'I asked for Thee / And Thou didst come / To take me home / Within Thy Heart to be.'

The composer's designation of section 2 as an aria assumes that, in contrast with the freedoms in the recitative, some sort of formal structure will be adopted. In this instance the choice conforms to the poetic structure which, in terms of number and length of lines, is the same throughout the poem. More-over, as all four stanzas start with the same words – 'I asked for', followed by one of the words listed above – at least some of the musical structure is determined by this constant factor. Accordingly, an identical four-note pattern opens the first three stanzas (the fourth stanza is entirely independent of its predecessors because of the reference to God, which requires special treatment). The material following this pattern is different for all three stanzas, but rela-tionships between the later stanzas and the first are easily distinguished. The

Ex. 243

differences are created by intervallic changes, and more variety is provided through a different pitch level for each of the initial four-note patterns. All of the music for the opening stanza is seen in Example 243. An important point to be noted is the severely syllabic nature of the line. This is just as true in the following stanzas, and it limits the length of the aria.

The accompaniment to this stanza is, like the others, composed of two melodic elements: those that are completely independent and those that duplicate material contained in the solo line, but not necessarily the solo line of the moment. An example of the later use of solo material is found in the last two measures of the example where the bold figure in measures 1–2 is included in both the violin and viola parts. Another important segment of the solo line – the six-note figure of measure 3 and its concluding note in the fourth measure – is twice duplicated in the accompaniment to stanza 2.

It would be remiss to leave the aria without directing attention to its accompanimental harmonies, some of the most beautiful and satisfying in Rubbra's choral music. Noticeable immediately beneath stanza 1 (Example 243) are the harmonies made by the viola and bass lines, both of which are limited ostinatos, and their interactions with the sustained B. (Incidentally, this is a good place to plead for the orchestral version of the accompaniment, for the two-measure ostinato figure in the violas is an altered continuation of the same figure given out by the solo clarinet and before that by the solo horn.) The dissonances are, of course, the result of the moving parts, and they multiply and become richer with the appearance of still more parts. Both they and the restless ostinatos reinforce the disillusionment of the words, but two magical moments each dispel the accumulated dissonances, and both serve to introduce new stanzas. They share a common origin, for each is a simple chord that is formed by stationary notes and chromatic half-step movement. The first of these is a first-inversion E flat major chord, and it establishes a new tonal centre and reorients the soloist as he begins stanza 2: 'I asked for Truth', and so on. Again, dissonances accumulate, and a first-inversion D flat major chord performs the same function at the start of stanza 3. The music employed to introduce and accompany the last stanza, 'I asked for Thee', followed by the spiritual comfort of God's response, is reminiscent momentarily of a small segment of the orchestral introduction to *The Morning Watch*. There is the same throbbing bass, the four accented sixteenths and the gathering intensity.

That Rubbra thought of the recitative and aria as one unit appears to be confirmed by the virtually identical orchestral passage that encloses them, for the introduction whose beginning is shown in Example 242 is repeated at the end of the aria. The passage has been shortened from ten to eight measures, transposed up one whole tone, and is missing only several non-essential notes. In addition, the orchestration is identical. Accordingly, the usual statement that the cantata's structure consists of four parts seems in need of revision. Still another factor should be considered in the solving of this formal problem: the differences in style that set the sections apart. The recitative and aria form one common style and, as we shall soon see, each of the forthcoming sections has its own style. There are reasons for this seeming disparity, and they will be explored in due course. Finally, the proportions in terms of sectional lengths seem more reasonable if a three-section structure is proposed: 68 measures, 95 measures and 48 measures.

The next section of the cantata is much the longest. Its text is excerpted from a Latin acrostic hymn in which the letters at the beginnings of strophes are in alphabetical order. Each strophe contains four lines. The text's author, about whom little is known, is Caelius Sedulius, born *c*.450. He seems to have become a priest and to have lived in a religious community, judging from accounts in his writings of various people whom he met there. The authenticity of Sedulius's authorship has been questioned, but the Venerable Bede is firm in his attribution. The poem, which proceeds acrostically through the entire alphabet, is a summons to the faithful to praise Christ by means of a description of the principal events of his life. Two excerpts from the hymn are widely used in church services: the section from A through G at Lauds for Christmas Day, and sections H, I, L and N on the Feast of the Epiphany. The first of these excerpts is employed here.

From the deeply personal, really private, Dolben poem to the Sedulius hymn is a big step, and some sort of transition from one to the other is necessary. This function is fulfilled by the unrelated, parallel triads at the end of the aria through their close relationship to the unrelated triads that characterize much of the accompaniment to the Latin hymn. There are important differences between the triadic sets, for the triads at the beginning of the recitative and at the end of the aria have an almost passive air owing to the relatively slow movement of the upper chords against the long-held lower one. In the hymn, on the other hand, the combination of the *con moto* tempo and the metrical regularity, in which unrelated triads are sounded simultaneously, produces a far more discordant texture. One may with good reason question the appropriateness of such a texture in view of the positive nature of the Advent story. The answer I propose is that the text is theological and therefore formal, and the jubilation, although shared by all believers, is essentially impersonal. The clash of these unrelated triads is equally impersonal.

The accompaniment does contain elements other than unrelated triads. There are dissonant passages containing similarly constructed chords with common tones, and in quality and rhythmic vitality they are reminiscent of Stravinsky, for there is the same kind of rigid austerity. There is also one freely imitative passage whose notes for a short time are those of part of a paired imitative choral passage several measures back. This is one of the few instances in which the accompaniment has anything much to do with the material of the choral parts.

The choral parts are, in their own way, equally impersonal and austere, and the choice of a Latin text emphasizes these qualities (Stravinsky chose Latin for the same reasons in *Oedipus Rex*). In several places the voices proceed in octaves and unisons, particularly when there are clashes between unrelated triads in the accompaniment. At other places consecutive octaves filled in with thirds and fourths impart a distinctive organum sound. There are two passages containing paired, imitative writing and the baritone soloist has two short but widely separated passages, the first with choral accompaniment and the second with orchestra only. (Incidentally, the cantata's title, *Natum Maria Virgine*, is sung at the very end of the first strophe, just before the soloist's first passage.)

There is no doubt that Rubbra intended the hymn to be the focal point and climax of the whole cantata. Its effect on the listener, particularly when an orchestra is involved (as it should be, for I remain totally convinced that an organ cannot possibly substitute for the orchestral colours indicated in the score), must be overwhelming. There is majesty, jubilation of a kind one imagines in connection with the medieval church, and genuine excitement.

The final section of the cantata is entitled 'Chorale' with a subheading, 'Tune from Cantata No. 27, Bach'. It will undoubtedly surprise many that Bach's cantata has nothing to do with Advent, but was composed for the 16th Sunday after Trinity. Its title is 'Wer weiss, wie nahe mir ein Ende?' or 'Who Knows How Near Is My Last Hour?' Thus one is led to the conclusion that Rubbra was attracted to the chorale melody, and that it served his purpose in the present work. The text, however, is the fourth stanza of an Advent hymn, 'Lo! He Comes With Clouds Descending', by Charles Wesley, the brother of John Wesley, founder of Methodism. The words of this stanza, coupled with the strength of Bach's chorale melody provide a joyous ending to the work (Example 244).

Ex. 244

For the first and only time in his Advent Cantata Rubbra employs a key signature: A flat, as we see in the example. It is a whole step lower than Bach's B flat, the most likely reason for the change being that the preceding Latin hymn ends in C major over a C pedal. This pedal is extended beneath the A flat harmonies at the beginning of the chorale, thus becoming the mediant of the new key – a very common but pleasing transition. The vocal parts do not, however, enter at this point, for the entire chorale is first presented orchestrally. Both versions – orchestral and vocal – are harmonized the same.

The work received a very favourable, major review:

The whole is evolutionary writing, the solo meditation and questioning of the first half [an adherent of the two-part structure] admirably balanced by the choral statement of the latter part. One discerns a fresh vigour of harmonic freedom in the composer's style which, earlier on in the work, could keep one guessing. It is in the final beautifully-woven chorale setting that the more familiar Rubbra is unmistakable. The whole bears a highly-wrought and individual stamp, distinctive in idea and treatment. It will need competent handling.[109]

Missa Brevis

Rubbra's next choral work is the *Missa Brevis*, Op. 137, written in 1969 and scored for treble voices (T1, T2, A) and organ. It was composed for the Trinity School Boys' Choir, Croydon, which gave it its first London performance at St John's, Smith Square, on 20 May 1970 (at the same presentation as *Creature-Songs to Heaven*). The layout of the vocal lines is not as simple as the above scoring would seem to indicate, for in the *Kyrie* and the *Gloria* particularly, the number of parts often runs to four, and in the first of these sections to five. There are no doublings in the *Sanctus* and *Agnus Dei*, and only two unimportant and very small instances of doublings in the *Benedictus*.

Structurally, the *Kyrie* is a perfectly balanced, small ternary form, each of whose sections contains five measures. The key signature of three flats is only a very general guide to the tonality, which can best be described in the identical *A* sections as a modally modified C major because of the very frequent E and A naturals together with a sprinkling of F sharps. The close proximity in the *A* sections and, of course, in separate parts, of the few E flats and the E naturals produce cross-relations which impart a spicy flavour to the texture. More colourful flavour is provided by the frequent seconds – mostly minor – that result from the movement of parts. There are also three- and five-note tone clusters.

The harmonies of the *Kyrie* can be easily summarized: they are basically static despite the movement of parts. The only really significant movement is in the first treble part insofar as the *A* sections are concerned (Example 245), for the oscillating motion in the lower parts creates harmonic repetitions. While this is somewhat less true in the 'Christe eleison' portion, the increase in the

Ex. 245

melodic movement in the lower parts is not great enough to alter the above assessment.

The *Gloria* is not only the longest but also the most complex of the movements. All of its material is derived from and is an extension of the melodic contours of each of the three vocal lines as these are seen in a vertical arrangement in the second and third measures (the first measure is for organ alone). The basic material in these two measures is closely related in the sense that its melodic members are essentially different aspects of the same thing. The two treble lines in the second measure are identical: E flat, F, E flat – a simple upper neighbour relationship. Below them the alto part sings the inversion, a lower neighbour progression. In the third measure a descending scale figure of four notes in the first treble line is balanced in the second treble and alto parts by an ascending scale figure of four notes, these latter lines a perfect fourth apart. If one includes the notes on which the scale figures resolve, further upper and lower neighbour progressions are formed. Later in the movement the fourths assume prominence in an important passage involving all three parts.

Structurally, the *Gloria* is through-composed, but because of the heavy concentration of motivic figures derived from the second and third measures the movement is totally unified, and the absence of a formal plan in no way detracts from the music or the listener's perception of it.

The *Sanctus* has strong family resemblances to the same movement in the three preceding Masses: a slow starting tempo – *Adagio* in this instance; a *pianissimo*, bell-like sound during the first portion of the text; a rocking motion in which at some point in the setting of the word 'Sanctus' ('Holy' in the *Missa Cantuariensis*) at least the top part returns to its initial note; unrelated parallel triads somewhere in the movement; and a change of mood in the 'Pleni sunt coeli' section during which an imitative texture may have been introduced, as here. None of this is intended to imply any sort of submission to a formula, but rather to indicate that, in each case, we are witnessing a highly personal response to a text that obviously meant a great deal to the composer. Two new elements are introduced in this setting: an accompaniment, and the employment of the same music for the 'Hosanna in excelsis' texts which conclude both the *Sanctus* and its companion piece, the *Benedictus*. The accompaniments are also identical. Only the tonality is changed: D flat major to C major.

The words, 'Benedictus qui venit in nomine Domini' are set twice to the same music, but the settings are exactly a semitone apart. Because of the independent melodic and rhythmic nature of the three parts and the numerous accidentals contained in each, the tonalities are indefinite, but the first four-measure setting gravitates to C sharp minor and the second to C minor, although neither cadence has a third degree. The harmonic uncertainty has produced both rich and unexpected progressions, which are very beautiful.

Between the concluding *Agnus Dei* and the opening *Kyrie* an extraordinary unity has been achieved through the ingenious procedure of transferring the *Kyrie*'s entire vocal content to the *Agnus Dei*, where it forms the organ accompaniment. The latter's vocal lines are entirely new, composed of flowing triplets and eighths which contrast strongly with the accompaniment's eighths and quarters. The melody is very Gregorian in character and may even have been borrowed. The vocal writing is mostly unison, a wise decision in view of the dissonances between voice parts and accompaniment. Two independent lower parts throughout the movement would have created additional dissonances with the accompaniment, and the combined complex and thick textures would have obscured the beautifully flowing and graceful melody.

Not surprisingly, the *Agnus Dei* shares a ternary plan with the *Kyrie* and the vocal lines participate in this structure to the same degree as the borrowed accompaniment. Finally, as implied here in the *Agnus Dei*, there is little relationship between the voices and the accompaniment all through the Mass.

> It is an intense, meditative work, making no concessions to the youth of its performers, for Rubbra's long-phrased, pliantly linear style evolves very chromatic polyphony of extreme dissonance. It is concise and shapely, restrained enough for liturgical use.[110]

There followed in Op. 143, composed in the early 1970s, an isolated setting of the *Agnus Dei* text in English in which modern usage such as 'give us your peace' reflects the current changes not only in Catholicism but also in the Protestant denominations. Thus this work of just twenty-six measures, scored for unaccompanied SATB choir, is suitable anywhere. The tempo is *moderato* and there is no *divisi* writing. However, there is enough crossing of parts – mainly involving the alto and tenor lines – to cause untrained singers some anxious moments. Another problem could be accurate intonation, for there are many chromatic intervals, some followed by wide leaps, that indicate temporary shifts in tonality. Once these problems are solved the music readily falls into place and is perceived as one long continuous sentence with short gaps between notes occurring only in the three lower voices. Moving parts are more frequent in the middle and at the end of the piece, and they impart a sense of urgency to the textual petitions. Despite the moving parts, the piece is non-imitative. The tempo must not be too slow or the music's single arch-like sweep will be seriously compromised. Short, in this case, does not mean insignificant, for the work shows Rubbra at the height of his powers. It gives the impression of having been written during one composing session.

This Spiritual House Almighty God Shall Inhabit

The words for *This Spiritual House Almighty God Shall Inhabit*, Op. 146, a motet for *a cappella* SATB choir, were taken from Rahere's *Vision of St. Bartholomew*. Rahere (there does not appear to be another name associated with him) was born during the reign of William the Conqueror, followed a clerical career, and became Prebendary of St Paul's Cathedral in 1111. Legend has it that he was court jester to Henry I prior to his churchly life. He made a pilgrimage to Rome where, while recovering from a fever, he made a solemn vow to build a hospital and church in honour of St Bartholomew, whom he had seen in a vision. Upon his return to England Henry I granted land for this purpose, and in 1123 Rahere began the building of St Bartholomew's Hospital, Smithfield, and its adjoining Augustinian priory. Rahere died in 1143, and his tomb may be seen on the north side of the sanctuary of the priory church. In addition, a set of painted panels beneath the organ depicts the life of this visionary. The occasion for which this piece was composed in 1973 commemorated the 850th anniversary of the start of Rahere's building programme.

The motet can be considered a ternary structure, for there are identical *A* sections of five and a half and six measures respectively that enclose a comparatively large *B* section of nineteen measures. The general effect of the piece as a whole is one of great dignity and seriousness, but both qualities are nicely tempered by frequent and graceful triplets, some of which are a natural response to the rhythm of the words, but more often intended to lighten and balance these attributes. The music's principal interest resides in its harmonic makeup. Indeed, there is strong evidence for believing that two chords have given rise to the *A* sections, for their often-heard, pungent sounds colour and dominate the texture. Each of the chords is a seventh, and the characteristic sound throughout the sections derives, first, from the progressions of the first chord to the second – 'pseudo-resolutions', and second, the different arrangements of the notes in both chords.

For proper identification of both chords as sevenths (see measure 1 in Example 246) the spelling of certain of their notes must be enharmonically

Ex. 246

changed. The root of the first chord is C flat, so in order to get a seventh the basses' F sharp must be read as G flat. The chord is in its second inversion. The root is G in the second chord, and the tenors' C flat must be interpreted as B. The chord is in its third inversion. Looking at the remainder of the example, new arrangements of both chords may be seen, and these continue in the three measures beyond the example. Judging from the exact repetitions including text in the final *A* section, the composer wished this characteristic sound to remain with the listener.

The comparatively lengthy *B* section contains none of these harmonies, thus avoiding the tedium resulting from too much of the same sound. Its chord structure, founded on a more active bass line, has produced more varied harmonies, most of which are accidental in the sense of having been created through linear movement in all of the parts, and this process has produced more consonances than will be noted in the *A* sections. The *fortissimo* climax of the motet occurs just prior to the reintroduction of *A*, and *divisi* writing expands the parts to seven. The passage features one of Rubbra's most common characteristics: a sequence of unrelated chords moving in parallel motion.

A favourable review remarks that 'the composer's handling of words ... reflects his innate sympathy with religious texts. The music, beautifully moulded, should only be tackled by singers of ripe technique and musicianship.'[111]

Blessed Be He

Blessed Be He, Op. 147, was written in 1974 'for St. Peter's Church, Monkwearmouth on the occasion of the 1300th anniversary of the birth of St. Bede and of the foundation of the monastic house of Wearmouth'. All that remains of the church is at the west end, which includes a tower and a lower porch, the rest of the church having been covered by the sea. The tunnel vault at the entrance is the earliest vault in England.

The text for this unaccompanied SATB anthem is by Georgina Cook 'after a passage from the Venerable Bede's "History of the English Church and People", 2 Ch.13'. The words in the title occur only at the very end of the poem, and are a natural consequence of what has gone before. The poem's first half tells of the brevity and darkness of man's life, while the second half is an exhortation: 'O let us then / With gladness hear all men / That bring us word, / How Heaven's fair Lord / Here for love's sake did tread', and so on to 'Blessed be He'.

It seems proper to call the musical structure through-composed even though the melodic element in the opening soprano line does recur in the middle of the second half. However, the very different rhythms and reharmonizations of this brief passage have created a context dissimilar enough from the original statement to justify a through-composed designation. In the last analysis, it is the impression of the anthem's having been written in one spontaneous, creative burst that is the determining factor in the matter of structure and this is, of course, a response to the forward sweep of the words.

The piece opens majestically in chordal style to the words, 'O hear, O hark!' However, independently moving parts then become the norm throughout the work. From beginning to end the music is uninterrupted, for the very few rests are neutralized by movement in other parts and, of course, the composer's carefully placed breath checks are no hindrance to the flow. The music for each half is different in accord with the textual moods, the first half being sombre and subdued after the opening words, while the second half becomes increasingly exultant. The principal ways in which the two halves are differentiated is through the introduction in the second half of sixteenth-note figures, a *con moto* that is followed by gradually slowing tempi, and explicit dynamic markings that bring the anthem to a *fortissimo* and triumphant close. Another difference is the greater incidence in the second half of high soprano notes.

The common factor uniting the halves is dissonance, brought about by the movement of parts. Some of this movement consists of unrelated parallel triads and four-part chords pitted against thirds in another part – clear evidence that *divisi* writing has expanded the basic four parts to five and six. In fact, the greater part of the anthem consists of five and six parts. Other, less massive dissonances may be found, and they too result from individual part movement. Because of the constant rhythmic flow, none of the dissonances of whichever type endures long, and with no accompaniment to add weight they are never too heavy. Their expressive power manifests itself in two ways: in the first half the dissonances underline the cheerless atmosphere of such lines as 'Lo how the life of man / Is in our sight / No longer than / When a bird taketh flight / Out of the bitter night.' In the second half they accentuate the elation of the lines quoted at the start of our discussion by introducing the feeling of confused excitement that such elation is likely to foster.

The following review of the work will acquire more meaning if it is read with the foregoing discussion in mind. After saying that Rubbra's treatment of Georgina Cook's words shows 'rare sensitivity', the review continues: 'The music... is rich and spacious. Dr. Rubbra's poetic sensibilities are as deft as ever, and he uses the idiom with consummate skill.'[112]

Three Greek Folksongs

The Three Greek Folksongs, Op. 151, are for unaccompanied SATB, and are free arrangements of the respective tunes. The tunes were gathered and the texts were translated by M.D. Calvocoressi, perhaps best known for his study of the music of Musorgsky. Additions, presumably in both areas, were furnished by Rubbra. The work was 'commissioned by the Ruth Draddy Memorial Trust for the Cork International Choral and Folk Dance Festival 1977 and first performed by the Reading Phoenix Choir under their Conductor Norman Morris'. The work can be thought of as a balanced suite, whose first and third pieces reflect the general similarities in mood of their texts, while the slow and quiet middle piece offers an expressive contrast based on its words.

The first piece is called 'The Gifts', and in it the narrator asks the 'merry dancers' to 'let me through, please, quickly! for I love a dark-eyed beauty. At market I am due, please.' There, he will sell his cheese and butter so as to buy a golden bracelet, but that is not all. He will also sell his eggs and chickens, and buy a golden wedding ring. In addition to the given text there are also numerous instances of 'hey, nonnis' and 'la, la, las' scattered throughout the parts.

The tempo of the piece is *Allegretto con spirito* (♩ = *c*.60); and the key is D minor. The first eight measures are scored for *divisi* tenors and basses and the first statement of the tune begins in the baritone part in measure 2. However, in the next measure the tune moves to the first tenors who complete it in measure 8. The sopranos have the second statement, the tenors and basses the third. From there to the end this distribution is exactly repeated, making six statements in all. Between each statement there is connecting material in the form of extensions consisting of figures belong to the tune. Example 247 shows the

Ex. 247

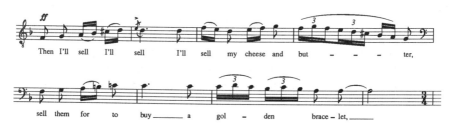

third statement, shared by the tenors and basses. It was chosen because of the text underlay, as both of the soprano statements are set to the words and syllables cited above.

Not all of the interest in this piece resides in the tune alone even though its statements stand out from the surrounding parts in various ways, one of which is the louder dynamic level. Nearly everything in those parts not containing the tune at any given time can be traced directly to the latter, the most obvious derivatives being the figures in the third and fourth measures of the example. In most cases the direction of the figures in the third measure has been reversed, and interesting variants of the triplet sixteenths in measure 4 are plentiful. In two instances the sopranos' augmentation of the tune's opening measure forms the start of what can be considered a subordinate theme whose continuation includes the features just mentioned.

Taking into account the tempo, the intonational problem posed by the augmented second in the tune's first and fourth measures, and the triplet sixteenths in the fourth measure, the tune is difficult for even the experienced singer. These same difficulties occur in the surrounding parts, but fortunately there are not too many dissonances – probably owing to the semi-popular nature of the piece – and they are quickly negotiated. The harmony remains firmly committed to D minor and, following a *poco allargando*, the piece ends on the dominant in which C sharp, although previously sounded, is absent from the final, held chord. There is an easy transition from this chord to the starting notes of the middle piece: unison F sharps in the men's parts.

In B minor, and with a metre signature of 7/8 and a tempo indication of *Lento* (♪= c.80) *e molto espressivo*, 'A Wreath of Basil' is the shortest and most unusual of the three folksong arrangements. The first of its three, gentle stanzas tells of weaving a basil wreath 'as soft as moonbeams to crown thee, resting on thy raven tresses'. In the second stanza the wreath is to be entrusted to the sea and in the third it will 'speak to thee of thine own home, of our village, of green fields and flow'ring meadows, and of thy patient lover, who awaits thee'.

As a result of the strophic form in which the piece is cast, the entire musical content consists of twelve measures plus a two-measure cadence at the conclusion of the third stanza. The tune is confined to the tenor part except for the first three measures during which the basses sing in unison with them. The chief characteristics of the tune itself are the leap of an augmented second (G-A sharp), and the filled-in intervals of an augmented fourth and a diminished fifth (E-A sharp; C sharp-G). Both the tune and the unobtrusive counterpoint that accompanies it in the women's parts, and later in the bass part, have the same *pianissimo* level which, together with the virtually non-pulsating 7/8 metre, contribute greatly to the expressiveness of the piece. A sense of ensemble has been created in which the folk-tune is but one element and, at times, not necessarily the most important one. However, the listener is made subtly aware of the tune because the words of the text are restricted to it except for the cadence, where an echo of the final words is heard in the women's parts.

The last piece is called 'The Suitors' and its text keeps the reader guessing as to who it is that is seen approaching. 'Lyoulia, who's coming? It's a suitor surely.' A footnote to the score tells us that '"lyoulia" is an exclamation equivalent to "good gracious!"' The young men named are Petro, Michael, Spiro, Manolaki, Costa, Andreas and Thano. But it is none of these! 'It is Yannis whom you love so dearly, and well he knows it.... Hark! the wedding bells are ringing.' This charming little scene fills four stanzas.

In Rubbra's setting the metre is a continuous 3/4, and the tempo is *Moderato* (♪= 132). The first fifteen measures of the sixteen-measure tune are scored for sopranos accompanied by an alto counterpoint; the final measure overlaps the beginning of the second stanza in which the tune is mostly given out by the tenors and then completed in the women's parts. The layout in the third stanza is identical to the second even to the accompanying counterpoints, but in the final strophe the distribution and even the tune's melodic properties are varied.

Although there is a B flat in the key signature, the majority of the Bs in the tune have been converted to naturals. In fact, during the course of the first four measures the tune appears to be solidly in G major, for not only is there an absence of F naturals but there is a strongly dominant feeling in the fourth measure as the tune rises from quarter-note A to quarter-note D. However, there is no such sense of G major in the alto accompaniment, for F natural is an important note, and D exerts a strong claim as a tonic. When the two parts are joined an entirely different sound is generated, as each part loses its identity. Yet, contrary to what might be supposed, the sum of the two parts does not suggest bitonality but rather a wayward G major. In the seventh measure the tonality of both tune and counterpoint has shifted to a modified C major, which persists until the start of the second stanza. But here, instead of the expected return to some sort of G major, there is a further strengthening of C major when three accented and rising quarters per measure are introduced into the counterpoints. Including their B naturals, these notes outline the C major scale from G to E, and from G to G with a drop to C. The same is true, of course, in the duplicate third stanza. Despite the changes in stanza 4, there is a return to modified tonalities: G followed by C.

Prayer for the Queen

This short *a cappella* piece, Op. 152, is Rubbra's contribution to the Queen's Silver Jubilee in 1977. Scored for SATB, it was 'commissioned by the Apollo Society and first performed at the Haymarket Theatre, London, on July 3rd 1977 by the Richard Hickox Singers'. The text is by Wordsworth, and is 'part of an untitled poem inscribed in a copy of his works that Wordsworth sent to Queen Victoria for the Royal Library at Windsor'. The words are typical of the fashionable hyperbole that greeted monarchs and other public figures in earlier periods and Rubbra has given them an enthusiastic setting.

The piece is through-composed in a *Lento e molto sostenuto* tempo. The composer's usual, flexible metre changes, designed to accommodate the words, are much in evidence, as is the use of triplets for the same purpose. There is a good balance between independently moving parts and block writing. In the second half of the piece the *divisi* writing increases the number of parts to six and seven. As for the musical material itself, it is obvious that Rubbra was fulfilling a commission for the observance of a great public occasion and the result is primarily a piece of public music. This is not to say that it is devoid of interest, but the stilted language certainly does not offer much opportunity for individual expression. This is particularly true in the opening portion of the piece where Wordsworth's exaggerated homage to the Queen suggests a great outpouring of sound, and this is exactly what happens. However, as one would expect from this composer, the outburst is carefully disciplined and the first way in which this control is revealed is in the matter of key: B flat major is prevented from clearly establishing itself until the end of what is really the first section. The frequency of the dominant and subdominant continually beguiles the listener into thinking that a final resolution is imminent, but there is more to it than this, for the constantly moving and interwoven parts create momentary dissonances that blur these and other chords belonging to the tonality. This oblique musical treatment matches the indefinite goal of the encomium: 'Queen, Wife and Mother! May all judging Heav'n / Show'r with a bounteous hand on thee and thine / Felicity that only can be given on earth to goodness blest by grace divine.' And just as the grandiloquence of the words must soon run its course, so the music near the end of these words becomes slower and quieter.

The poem's next four lines address the Queen in a more down-to-earth manner: 'Lady! devoutly honoured and beloved / Through every realm confided to thy sway: / May'st thou pursue thy course by God approved, / And He will teach thy people to obey.' Sensing the greater importance of these words, Rubbra has thrown each line into relief against sustained notes in some other part(s). Thus the first line is scored for altos and tenors under a sustained B flat and D in the *divisi* sopranos; the second line is scored for *divisi* sopranos above major seconds in the divided altos and tenors, and so on. During this second section, there is a shift in the tonality from the hard-won B flat to C major, and the latter key lasts until the midpoint of the poem's concluding four lines. These last lines promise that following a reign 'yet firm and staid', the 'earthly crown thy brows have worn [shall] Be changed for one whose glory cannot fade'. The music regains some of the impersonality of the beginning, and the piece ends in *fortissimo* triumph on a B flat chord.

While certainly not of major importance, and probably not performable at any occasion other than that for which it was composed, this piece proves that a public work, rather than being trite and loud, can be sensitively conceived. Choosing only the most obvious area – structure – the three quite discrete sections, each matched to its text in terms of mood, demonstrate that a through-composed piece does not necessarily lack shape.

How Shall My Tongue Express?

In the motet, *How Shall My Tongue Express...?*, Op. 155, for a *cappella* SATB, the composer who has consistently responded to the challenge imposed by an intense religious text is again evident. The poem is by Francis Quarles (1592–1644). Educated at Christ's College, Cambridge, and at Lincoln's Inn, Quarles wrote pamphlets defending Charles I. These led to the sequestration of his property and the destruction of his manuscripts. In 1635 there appeared a book of short poems entitled *Emblems*, of which the present poem is the eleventh. Each poem is based on a scriptural text, followed by quotations from the Church Fathers and an epigram; and each consists of various metres. Some of the poems are in dialogue form: 'Eve and the Serpent'; 'Jesus and the Soul'; and 'Flesh and the Spirit'. The motet 'was commissioned by the Aldwyn Consort for performance at the 1977 Malvern Festival'.

The two impressive opening lines of Quarles's poem have received a setting whose soaring power propels the listener to the close of the passage. Although

too long to be sung in one breath the passage was obviously conceived as a
unit, and its continuity should be carefully respected by the adoption of a
judicious breathing plan. The melody, shown in Example 248, is readily divisible

Ex. 248

into segments that are used and reused in various combinations throughout the
rest of the motet, and all of them are composed of melodic intervals that have
become associated with Rubbra throughout his career. They include the partially
filled-in diminished fifth, and the falling fourth and fifth. Connecting these
characteristic intervals are minor seconds and thirds. However, this motet is not
an example of the Rubbran technique of allowing a work to grow from intervals
or motives established at the beginning. Proof that it is not so constructed is
provided in measures 14–17 when the four opening measures are exactly reproduced a fourth lower in all four parts. Even prior to that, the first three
measures of the melody plus the falling fourth reappear in the tenor part in
measures 10–12 a minor third lower, but in a different rhythmic pattern.

Having at the beginning of the motet established a striking theme and then
reproduced the first part of it in two places, the composer is free to break it into
its several parts so as to form a new synthesis. Actually, this process has begun
before the transposition in measures 14–17, for in 12 and 13 the diminished
fifth is twice outlined by the tenors in a descending scale, the two scales being
connected by an ascending diminished triad. But such passages tend to be
'paper music', for while they are readily seen in the score, they are not so easily
heard, particularly here where the sopranos dominate.

In subsequent portions of the motet appearances of the diminished fifth are
infrequent, its place having been taken by the falling fifth. The dominant figure
in the second half of the piece is that of measures 5–7, consisting of the rising
thirds and falling fifths. Following an alto and tenor passage containing this
figure, set in octaves between sustained notes in the other parts, a new phase of
the motet begins in which there are imitative entries of the kind found in the
Renaissance motet. However, the figure that dominates this phase is not new in
the usual sense, for it is the one just mentioned, but with the third filled in on
either side of the falling fifth, it *seems* new. This altered figure does not initiate
the round of entries, that distinction having been awarded to the tenors in the

form of an inversion. The alto and bass entries as well as those that follow are all inverted. The resemblance to the Renaissance motet lies in the fact that the continuation of the short figure used in each of the entries is different in each case. Thus what, in effect, Rubbra has done here is to revive the Renaissance points-of-imitation technique, even though there is no further instance of it.

The treatment of dissonance in this motet calls for comment, for in all cases it is bold and effective even though the dissonances invariably result from the melodic movement of the individual parts of the chord structure beneath the quoted melody. The first dissonance involves the tied F in the second measure with an F sharp in the bass and a D in the tenor; the alto note is a tied C. The part-movement causing the dissonance has its origin in the 6-4 chord on the strong, first beat of the first measure, Rubbra having never had qualms about how or where he employs second inversion triads (probably to the great dismay of the theory pedants). Yet the tenors' F and the basses' A are merely the starting notes of inversions of the sopranos' D, F, E, D figure, but in order for the above-mentioned dissonances to occur under the tied-over F, the F and A in the lower parts must be lengthened to whole notes, which is just what happens. The 6/4 chord is, of course, sounded again on a strong beat when, in the third measure, all four parts return to their starting notes. The upward sweep to the A flat and the descent to D are harmonized on the second and fourth beats by B flat and G major respectively. The first beat of measure 4 is, again, a 6/4 chord but minus its third (F). The next important dissonance occurs in the middle of measure 4 when, under the first F, a held C sharp in the bass clashes with a C natural in the altos. Moving on to the fifth measure, the neutrality of another 6-4 chord under D in which F is missing gives way to two measures of concentrated dissonances, all caused by each of the three underlying parts nearing the end of what, in each case, is a totally acceptable and independent melody. The deeply satisfying A flat minor concord, reached in the second half of measure 7, lingers throughout measure 8 where it is emphasized by the syncopated soprano and alto lines – a calculated way of preparing the listener for the resolution of the entire passage. This seemingly occurs in the ninth measure on a first-inversion G major chord, but a master stroke postpones it until measure 10 when an intervening syncopated dissonance under the sopranos' B flat highlights the word 'ravished' in a most poignantly expressive manner. Much of the rest of the motet demonstrates equal skill in the handling of dissonance.

Mass in Honour of St Teresa of Avila

We pass now from one of Rubbra's finest, short choral works to his fifth and final Mass, Op. 157, written 'in honour of St Teresa of Avila (1515–1582)'. Completed on 18 January 1981, it was meant to commemorate the 400th anniversary of the saint's death. It was first performed by the BBC Singers, conducted by John Poole, on a 1981 Radio 3 broadcast. The work is scored for unaccompanied SATB choir and, like the two previous Masses, it lacks a *Credo*.

Although this Mass is but twelve pages long, it is Rubbra's last major choral work, for the three works that follow are small in comparison. Thus 'major' must be understood and interpreted in a relative sense. The Mass was written during a time of generally declining health and it is my considered opinion that, realizing that, Rubbra set out to compose a work that was intended to summarize some of the principal features of his style. I purposely did not use 'choral style', for by now it should be obvious that these features and techniques are not confined to any one compositional category. Naturally, it is only in the large categories – the symphonies, concertos, and certain chamber works, as well as in the larger choral pieces – that they can be brought to full fruition, but it is interesting to discover how satisfactorily some of these technical processes can be exploited in a relatively small work such as this Mass.

One of the attributes that energizes parts of the Mass is some particular interval in either its melodic or harmonic form. Other similarly constructed works are the Tenth and Eleventh Symphonies, where, respectively, the diminished fifth and the perfect fifth generated everything; and in the present chapter, *Judas Mercator Pessimus*, midpoint of the Nine Tenebrae Motets, is built wholly on the diminished fifth. In the St Teresa Mass, the *Sanctus* is composed almost entirely of ascending and descending, vertical (harmonic), conjunct fourths. On the first of its two pages, one set of fourths appears in the *divisi* soprano line while, simultaneously, a second set moves at exactly half the pace in the *divisi* alto line. Even if the lower set began with the same series as the upper there would be dissonances, although these would be mild. But the lower set is pitched a fifth lower, resulting in harsher dissonances which are somewhat mitigated by the *pianissimo* and *piano* dynamics. The arc in the upper set presents a contrast with the undeviating rise in the lower line, and this is also a factor in terms of the dissonances produced, but at the start of the third measure both sets alight on G-D. The second phrase is similarly scored, but with a different relationship in terms of curves. At the end of the third phrase during which fourths in the alto line have been exchanged for sevenths and ninths, the men's parts enter for the first time. The texture thickens as the layers of fourths increase, but only briefly, for the men are soon assigned octaves below the women's fourths. The movement ends with *fortissimo* dynamics.

Rubbra's final setting of the *Sanctus* text is very different from its four predecessors. There are no rocking figures and close imitations in other parts that, together, generate the bell-like reverberations that are so distinctive in the earlier settings. Here, the sound is austere and impersonal and, at times, strongly reminiscent of medieval organum. There is also a quasi-Gregorian flavour. And the way in which the fourths are used here refutes the notion that a particular interval in a Rubbra work or movement is *always* to be regarded as a nucleus from which everything grows. In this instance the fourths are not structural but atmospheric. Although they are in constant motion, they are static in the sense that they remain fourths.

The same static situation resulting from the non-growth of intervals prevails in the *Agnus Dei*, where there is a two-layered texture consisting of fifths and fourths in the women's parts, and thirds in the men's sections. Occasional directional changes and skips in each layer produce other intervals for a very short period before there is a return to the prevailing intervals. There is also the same wave-like motion as in the *Sanctus*, but the presence of the thirds is responsible for a warmer sound, and the inevitable dissonances created by the interaction of the upper intervals with the thirds are relatively mild. This warmth, which seems to be in response to the more personal nature of the words, is made more apparent by the *pianissimo* that dominates the majority of the movement. The structure of the movement is ternary with a cadential adjustment at the end.

The *Benedictus*, which at thirteen measures is the shortest of the Mass movements, is illustrative of another frequently encountered Rubbran procedure: lines whose contrary motions produce mirror images (derived from the 'topsy-turvydom' of the composer's childhood experience). A major difference in this movement is the fact that the mirror images are not omnipresent like the intervals in the *Sanctus* and *Agnus Dei*. Nevertheless, they are very prominent in the opening measures. They are not true mirror images because of differences in the intervallic content, but only a pedantic purist would dispute the mirror *effect*. Thus A, C, D, A in the first soprano line is inverted to A, G, F, A in the second altos, and the same discrepancy affects the first tenor and second bass lines. The inner lines in both the women's and men's parts proceed in parallel motion, but there is no mistaking the divergence of the outer lines even though the mirror images are imperfect. The same sort of inexact pattern is produced at the end of the movement in the undivided men's parts: under a sustained D-G in the sopranos and altos: $\begin{smallmatrix} D\ G\ F\text{ sharp}\ E\ D \\ G\ F\text{ sharp}\ G\ A\ B \end{smallmatrix}$ A drop to $\begin{smallmatrix} C \\ A \end{smallmatrix}$ leads to a $\begin{smallmatrix} D \\ G \end{smallmatrix}$ cadence. These final three measures plus the preceding three have a distinctively, joyous organum sound, generated by the open fifths in all four parts at the start and finish of the concluding passage, the contrary motion under the sustained fifths, and the clash of the ninth and seventh.

Owing to its greater length, the *Gloria* can support a larger number of typical Rubbra traits. These include short mirror images and imitative passages; parallel triadic chords; parallel fifths; and a pairing of parts (soprano, tenor; alto, bass). The movement is difficult from the intonational standpoint because of the chromatic semitones in individual parts and dissonant intervals of various kinds between the parts. The movement is full of the enthusiasm that one has come to expect when Rubbra sets a *Gloria* text, or, indeed, any text in which praise is a factor.

I have left the *Kyrie* until last because, in my estimation, it is not only the expressive peak of the Mass, but on a small scale it is one of Rubbra's finest choral achievements. My reasons for this assessment are several. First, the growth possibilities of the initial four-note figure are realized both melodically and rhythmically, as shown in the bracketed portions of Example 249. Note

Ex. 249

how in the soprano line the listener is at once drawn into the movement through the halved note values, and the shift to the second half of the first beat. And the upward leap is altered to a fourth in measures 5–6. The most involved passage in Example 249 is seen in measures 6–7 where the brackets show two overlapping statements of the figure. They in turn merge to create a larger unit, which is a perfectly realized instance of subtle melodic and rhythmic expansion. This expansion continues beyond the example when the D natural in the tenor line leaps up to G, and taking the descending soprano scale figure in measure 7 as its point of departure, initiates a series of complete and partial descending eighth-note scales; these are shared by all of the parts. The direct ascent in quarters from E to A (sopranos, measures 9–10) comes from the tenor line in measures 2–4. The gradually falling, wave-like motion in all parts (9–12) is strikingly beautiful, for the harmonies suddenly grow darker as they merge into

B flat minor. Appoggiaturas and a suspension augment the uncertain atmosphere.

A second reason for my enthusiastic assessment concerns the 'Christe eleison', or *B* section of this ternary form. Flowing directly from the B flat minor harmony of the concluding 'Kyrie' section, it occupies just six measures. It too can trace its ancestry to the tenor passage mentioned above, as well as to the rising third in the sopranos at measure 3. An element of tension is introduced into these petitions through the *subito pianissimos* and the accented first syllable of 'Christe', and it mounts during the two-measure long, third petition. Here, paired parts (soprano, tenor; alto, bass) ascend to a D major chord by whole steps; a major third separates the pairs, and the pairs are one beat apart. It is this 'out of phase' situation plus a *crescendo* and accented notes that are responsible for the increase in tension. The transition from the 'Christe eleisons' to the restatement of the 'Kyries' is flawlessly managed: the D major chord drops a semitone, and the altos' 'Kyrie' emerges from under the sustained D flat chord, a totally unexpected development.

A third but equally important reason is the utterly satisfying sound of the A flat, F sharp and A major chords, marked with asterisks in Example 249. These points of temporary stability are arrived at so naturally as to bring the word 'inevitable' to mind. Each chord serves to emphasize more sharply the restlessness of the intervening passages. The first two of these chords are repeated in the abbreviated last section of the movement, but the third is replaced by empty fifths on G, a sound that is sustained during the movement's final two and a half measures, and relieved only by the altos' chromatic line. The hollow fifths are confirmed at the end when the altos return to G.

Finally, I readily acknowledge that there are those who, seeing a diversity of styles in this Mass, will conclude that Rubbra was an eclectic composer with no individual style. The truth is, of course, that Rubbra *was* eclectic but in the best sense, for he took the ingredients that he needed from whatever source, and mingled them with his own traits to create a distinctive and unmistakably personal style. This Mass is thus no different in this regard from any of his other works.

St Teresa's Bookmark

Rubbra's next choral work also has connections with the 400th anniversary of St Teresa's death, but in a quite different way. Completed on 5 August 1981, Op. 159 is a setting of a text by the saint herself, entitled *St Teresa's Bookmark*: 'Let naught disturb thee, / Naught fright thee ever, / All things are passing; / God changeth never. // Patience e'er conquers; / With God for thine own / Thou nothing dost lack; / He suffices alone!' Not great poetry, surely, but none the less comforting in any age.

Rubbra's setting for SAB and organ bears a dedication to the choirmaster and choir of his own church in Gerrards Cross, Buckinghamshire – St Joseph's Priory Church. It seems certain that, in addition to the absence of a tenor part, some concessions were made to accommodate the limitations of what must be a choir of modest size and ability. These include a range in which G is the topmost soprano note (and not too many of them); several instances of unison and octave writing; and extended passages during which the organ accompaniment duplicates all of the voice parts. Yet almost a third of the anthem's thirty-five measures contains *divisi* writing, which increases the parts to four, and at the end, five. Also, there are passages of enough moderate difficulty to pose a challenge. The most notable of these comprises the *B* section of what is another modified ternary form; it is both rhythmically and melodically demanding, particularly in view of the fact that the accompaniment pursues an independent course, offering support in but one measure. However, the composer knew the capabilities of the choir for which he was writing and we can be sure that he neither depreciated nor overestimated its competence.

The material of the anthem consists of long, gently flowing, sinuous lines whose tranquillity is in keeping with that of the words. These lines are beautifully balanced, not only in terms of the rise and fall in the soprano part but also with regard to the two lower parts. Indeed, the melodic interest is not confined to the top line, for in most passages either one of the lower parts would be acceptable as a main melody. Part of the reason for this is because some of the melodic segments in the soprano line appear as inversions – mirror images – in one of the other lines. Another contributing factor is the presence of parallel triads similar to those in previous Rubbra choral works. It stands to reason that if an attractive top line is reproduced a third and fifth below, those lines will be just as appealing. In sum, all of these features will, one hopes, attract choirmasters, Catholic and Protestant, who seek a superior anthem.

Introit

In what proved to be his penultimate choral work, 'commissioned by the BBC for its 60th birthday celebration at St. Paul's Cathedral on July 12th, 1982', Rubbra turned to W.H. Auden for his text. Although Op. 162 is entitled *Introit*, this is not the title of Auden's poem, for the words were extracted from 'In Memory of W.B. Yeats'. They read, 'In the deserts of the heart / Let the healing fountain start, / In the prison of his days / Teach the free man how to praise.' Rubbra's setting is short – three pages – and is for *a cappella* SSATB choir. However, its brevity should in no way influence the listener to conclude that here is an unimportant work. On the contrary, two very impressive characteristics engage his immediate attention: first, the massive sound of the block harmonies; second, the long phrases. Both were much in evidence during the thrilling first performance at St Paul's. Another feature, but one less likely to be noticed, is the overall, vertical division of the work into two distinct layers: the two soprano lines and the three lower parts. The former are less consistent in terms of the intervals that separate them than the latter, where parallel sixths on the order of English medieval discant are the norm. It is the interaction between these layers that produces the dissonances that are heard from time to time throughout the work.

The material which forms the first long phrase bears a definite family relationship to the opening phrase of *Blessed Be He*, as seen in Example 250. The

Ex. 250

basic ingredients are the same, although, of course, the details are different. There is the same upward leap at the start of each phrase, but the B between the A and E in the *Introit* is one of the differences. The really close resemblance comes at the point where, in each phrase, E leaps to A, followed by G/G sharp, F, E, G. The descent to E is through F in *Blessed Be He*, but in the *Introit* it is devious, and consumes a measure before the E on 'start' is reached. Beyond these phrase likenesses, there are no further resemblances between the two pieces.

Many times throughout this book particular intervals and note patterns have been shown to be the fountainheads of numerous movements, as well as shorter pieces like these two choral works. In some cases, these intervals and patterns undoubtedly were the result of thoughtful deliberations, but not even the composer's analyses can always dispel the impression that they came first and *then* were found to be suitable for development. In my view, this is entirely as it should be. As for the similarities between these choral pieces, it is my view that they demonstrate the unconscious aspect of Rubbra's art. Yet, despite the same general melodic contour, how appropriately different are the results. The unadorned and severely plain contour in *Blessed Be He* fits the exhortation, 'O hear, O hark! This dirge we sing.' In the *Introit* the contour is altogether more sinuous, but at the same time relaxed, for the words, quoted above, are hopeful and positive. All of the remaining phrases are equally long and similar in their construction. The third phrase is the first phrase repeated. The *tessitura*, already high as seen in the second half of the first phrase, becomes higher on the third page when A flats, As, Bs and one C are found.

Psalm 122

Rubbra's last choral work, the penultimate work in his total output, is Psalm 122, Op. 164, for unaccompanied SATB choir. Only verses 1 and 9 were set and the anthem, completed on 4 April 1984, bears a dedication to the choir of St Andrew's Cathedral, Aberdeen. *Divisi* writing occurs at one time or another in all parts except the tenor, and in two places the number of parts reaches six.

The first and third sections, for, again, this is a modified ternary structure, begin with a stretto inversion in the alto part of the sopranos' initial four notes, but these are the anthem's only imitative passages. Again, in places the texture is stratified: parallel sixths in the soprano and *divisi* alto parts (and vice versa) as opposed to the more freely composed lower parts. In other short passages where six lines are present, two sets of parallel sixths move along together. In all cases, the lines are flowing, and the anthem does not impart the sense of massiveness that the sixths might suggest. Assisting the flow is the 6/8 metre, and the introduction of triplets when the metre is altered to 4/8, 2/4 and 3/4.

Conclusion

The reader may wonder at the lack of reviews and critical comments with respect to those choral works that come after *Blessed Be He*. Unfortunately, despite my search of all of the usual journals, and some less commonly known, I have been unable to find any. This lapse is not so serious in the case of the shorter pieces, but certainly one has the right to expect that the St Teresa Mass would have been reviewed. This failure to review not just the last choral works but also works in other genres during the same period demonstrates rather decisively the extent to which Rubbra has been curtly relegated to the past.

Even more deplorable than the lack of choral reviews in Rubbra's last years is the almost total absence from the programmes of performing organizations of *any* of his choral works. Can this be attributed to conductors who, seeing the considerable difficulties of works such as *Lauda Sion* and the Op. 115 *Te Deum*, to name but two, are reluctant to put forth the effort necessary for a first-rate performance? Is it unawareness of the existence of these and other works? And surely the best of Rubbra's anthems to Latin and English texts, as well as a Mass movement if not the whole Mass, could and should be included on the programmes of smaller choral groups. Such anthems and Mass movements should also be sung by cathedral choirs during Evensong. They would be a welcome relief from over-reliance on some of the standard cathedral fare of the late nineteenth and early twentieth centuries.

Finally, in this chapter we have dealt with an impressively large body of choral music, the quality of which is extremely high. Under such circumstances not everything can be or is a masterpiece, but there is a surprisingly large number of high peaks. Among these, and in the order of their opus numbers, I would unhesitatingly name Five Motets, *The Dark Night of the Soul*, *The Morning Watch*, *Missa Cantuariensis*, *Missa in Honorem Sancti Dominici*, *Song of the Soul*, *Missa à 3*, *Lauda Sion*, the *Te Deum* of Op. 115, *Inscape*, and *Veni Creator Spiritus*. There are, of course, lesser summits but peaks none the less. It is here that I place a number of the Nine Tenebrae Motets, *Lord, With What Care*, *Blessed Be He*, *How Shall My Tongue Express*?; and selected movements from larger works such as *Beauty Is But A Painted Hell*, and *Though You Are Young*, from Five Madrigals; and the *Kyrie* from the St Teresa Mass. There will undoubtedly be some professional musicians as well as laymen who will disagree with some of my choices, but that is as it should be. In most instances, my reasons are given in the course of the discussions.

Notes

1   Sleeve-note to the recording of *Dormi Jesu* on RCA LRLI 5119. Op. 3, no. 2 is an unaccompanied SSA version of the same text.
2   Elsie Payne, 'Non-Liturgical Choral Music', *Edmund Rubbra: Composer*, p.78.
3   'Edmund Rubbra Writes About The Development of His Choral Music', *The Listener*, 6 June 1968, p.748.
4   Tape of 26 July 1980.
5   Edmund Rubbra, *Counterpoint: A Survey*, pp.46–7.
6   Unidentified reviewer, *MT*, May 1936, p.455.
7   Eric Blom, *M&L* 19, no. 2, April 1938, p.233.
8   J.A. Westrup, *MMR*, December 1937, p.233.
9   'Edmund Rubbra Writes About The Development of His Choral Music', *The Listener*, 6 June 1968, p.748.
10   *The American Peoples Encyclopedia* (Chicago: Spencer Press, Inc., 1957), p.14, p.231.
11   Raynor C. Johnson, *The Imprisoned Splendour* (New York: Harper & Brothers, 1953), p.299.
12   Payne, *op. cit.*, p.80.
13   'Edmund Rubbra Writes About The Development of His Choral Music', *The Listener*, 6 June 1968, p.748.
14   Eric Blom, *M&L* 24, no. 1, January 1943, pp.63–4.
15   J.A. Westrup, *MMR*, September 1943, p.161.
16   'Edmund Rubbra Writes About The Development of His Choral Music', *The Listener*, 6 June 1968, p.748.
17   *ibid.*
18   Eric Blom, *M&L* 21, no. 2, April 1940, p.200.
19   J.A. Westrup, *MMR*, December 1939, p.312.
20   Blom, *op. cit.*, p.200.
21   C.W.O., *MR*, August 1943, pp.207–8.
22   J.A. Westrup, *MMR*, September 1943, p.161.
23   Edward Lockspeiser, *M&L* 24, no. 4, October 1943, p.253.
24   Ivor Keys, *M&L* 28, no. 3, July 1947, p.292.
25   Calum MacDonald, *The Listener*, 10 December 1981, p.731.
26   Arthur Hutchings, *MT*, January 1947, pp.27–8.
27   Sleeve-note to the recording of *Missa Cantuariensis* on RCA LRLI 5119.
28   *ibid.*

29 *ibid.*
30 *ibid.*
31 *ibid.*
32 Harold Truscott, 'Style and Orchestral Technique', *Edmund Rubbra: Composer*, p.19.
33 Sleeve-note to the recording of *Missa Cantuariensis* on RCA LRLI 5119.
34 Rubbra, *Counterpoint: A Survey*, p.47.
35 Ivor Keys, *M&L* 27, no. 4, October 1946, p.272.
36 Colin Mason, *Tempo*, no. 1, New Series, September 1946, p.27.
37 Sleeve-note to the recording of *Missa in Honorem Sancti Dominici* on RCA LRLI 5119.
38 Edmund Rubbra, 'Missa in Honorem Sancti Dominici', in *The Composer's Point of View*, Robert Stephan Hines (ed.) (Norman: University of Oklahoma Press, 1963), p.104.
39 Sleeve-note to the recording of *Missa in Honorem Sancti Dominici* on RCA LRLI 5119.
40 Rubbra, *op. cit.*, pp. 104, 110.
41 *ibid.*, pp.105–6.
42 Sleeve-note to the recording of *Missa in Honorem Sancti Dominici* on RCA LRLI 5119.
43 *ibid.*
44 *ibid.*
45 *ibid.*
46 Rubbra, *op. cit.*, p.109.
47 *ibid.*
48 *ibid.*, pp.109–10.
49 Sleeve-note to the recording of *Missa in Honorem Sancti Dominici* on RCA LRLI 5119.
50 Rubbra, *op. cit.*, p.110.
51 Desmond Shawe-Taylor, 'A St. Dominic Mass', *The New Statesman and Nation*, 25 October 1952.
52 *Liber Usualis* (Tournai: Desclée & Co., 1934), pp.621, 652–3.
53 'Edmund Rubbra Writes About The Development of His Choral Music', *The Listener*, 6 June 1968, p.749.
54 Free translations of the motet texts appear inside the front cover of each Nocturn, and it is these that are used in the following discussion.
55 Bernard Rose, *M&L* 36, no. 2, April 1955, p.196.
56 Basil Ramsey, *MT*, July 1955, p.370.
57 James Dalton, *M&L* 43, no. 4, October 1962, p.381.
58 Payne, *op. cit.*, pp.80–81. It is interesting that Rubbra reviewed *The Vision of St. Augustine* in *The Listener*, 13 January 1966, p.74.
59 'Edmund Rubbra Writes About The Development of His Choral Music', *The Listener*, 6 June 1968, p.749.
60 *ibid.*, pp.748–9.
61 Scott Goddard, *MT*, August 1953, p.373.
62 William Mann, *M&L* 35, no. 1, January 1954, p.70.
63 Douglas Hopkins, *MT*, November 1957, p.617.
64 Peter Pirie, *M&L* 38, no. 4, October 1957, p.410.
65 Ernest Bradbury, *MT*, December 1957, p.680.
66 Pirie, *op. cit.*, pp.409–10.
67 'Edmund Rubbra Writes About The Development of His Choral Music', *The Listener*, 6 June 1968, p.749.
68 Harold Rutland, *MT*, April 1958, p.208.

69   Peter Pirie, *M&L* 39, no. 3, July 1958, p.319.
70   Rubbra, 'Missa in Honorem Sancti Dominici', in *The Composer's Point of View*, p.110.
71   Rubbra, *Counterpoint: A Survey*, pp.42–3.
72   David Wulstan, *MT*, May 1962, p.337.
73   *ibid.*
74   David Lumsden, *M&L* 43, no. 2, April 1962, pp.181–2.
75   Wulstan, *op. cit.*, p.337.
76   Alan Blyth, *MT*, June 1969, p.652.
77   The word 'chorale' seems inappropriate as well as misleading here since no preexistent German Lutheran tune is used. On the other hand, as we shall see in the *Sinfonia Sacra* (Symphony No. 9), the word appears three times in connection with Lutheran tunes, identified together with their composers.
78   Frank Ll. Harrison, *Music In Medieval Britain* (London: Routledge & Kegan Paul, Ltd, 1958), pp.419–20. Further information on Gwynneth's music, including works he claimed to have written, appears in *NGD*, 7, p.861–2.
79   Percy Dearmer, R. Vaughan Williams, Martin Shaw, *The Oxford Book of Carols* (London: Oxford University Press, 1928), p.35.
80   *ibid.*
81   Printed at the front of the score of *Inscape*.
82   Bernard Bergonzi, *Gerard Manley Hopkins* (New York: Macmillan Publishing Co., Inc., 1977), p.26.
83   John Robinson, *In Extremity* (Cambridge: Cambridge University Press, 1978), p.10 of Preface.
84   Comments on and examples of these devices appear in Donald McChesney, *A Hopkins Commentary* (New York: New York University Press, 1968), pp.25–7.
85   Quoted in McChesney, *op. cit.*, p.33.
86   *ibid.*, p.16.
87   Quoted in Robinson, *op. cit.*, p.68.
88   *ibid.*, p.75.
89   Bergonzi, *op. cit.*, pp.188–9.
90   McChesney, *op. cit.*, p.71.
91   Andrew Porter, *MT*, December 1965, p.961.
92   McChesney, *op. cit.*, p.70.
93   *ibid.*, p.76.
94   Robinson, *op. cit.*, p.82.
95   McChesney, *op. cit.*, p.59.
96   *ibid.*, p.54. Hopkins experienced firsthand the desolation that industry can produce when he served a parish in Liverpool and journeyed to such places as St Helens.
97   Sir Arthur Bliss set the same poem as a choral work in 1969, using this line for his title.
98   David Wulstan, *M&L* 47, no. 2, April 1966, p.180.
99   'Edmund Rubbra Writes About The Development of His Choral Music', *The Listener*, 6 June 1968, p.749.
100 Arthur Milner, *MT*, May 1966, p.443.
101 Hugh Ottaway, *MT*, August 1966, p.707.
102 Desmond Shawe-Taylor, *The Sunday Times*.
103 Mosco Carner, *The Times*.
104 Edward Greenfield, *The Manchester Guardian*.
105 Stephen Walsh, *The Sunday Telegraph*
106 Allan Jefferis, *MT*, October 1967, p.924.
107 Andrew Porter, *MT*, September 1966, pp.787–8.

108   Henry Raynor, *MT*, July 1970, p.723.
109   Elizabeth Poston, *MT*, September 1970, p.921.
110   Raynor, *op. cit.*, p.723.
111   William Varcoe, *MT*, January 1975, p.75.
112   William Varcoe, *MT*, October 1975, p.911.

10   The songs

Of all the genres in which Rubbra worked the least known is his songs. Yet fifty-one have been published, ranging from Op. 2 (1921) to Op. 148 (1974). Of these, thirty-eight are grouped within opus numbers, but some of the earliest songs belonging to a particular opus have been published separately. Textually, as with the choral music, there is the same wide-ranging choice of poets, but perhaps the most interesting thing about this body of songs is the variety of accompaniments. Only twenty of the songs have accompaniments designated specifically for piano. The rest call for string quartet, string orchestra, harp, and so on; one early song has no accompaniment whatsoever. The piano is permitted as a substitute in some cases, and an accompaniment for it has been provided, but the impression is strong that it should be used only as a last resort. In all others where a piano accompaniment has been provided it is a reduction of the instrumental parts, and is intended 'for rehearsal only'. Such restrictive accompaniments have undoubtedly militated against frequent performances, but then the songs with piano accompaniments have fared no better. Since many of these songs qualify as chamber works, they could, and should, be included in programmes featuring string quartets and other appropriate combinations.

Rosa Mundi

Rubbra's first published song, *Rosa Mundi*, Op. 2, dates from 1921. Rachel Annand Taylor wrote the poem which, as its title implies, has a religious theme: 'The rose of the world hangs high on a thorny tree' is the first line. Both the vocal line and the two muted violins forming the accompaniment have a simple lyricism that is hauntingly expressive. It is difficult to say whether this or the alternative piano version is the more effective. The piano accompaniment includes all of the violins' notes, but it also duplicates the vocal line at a number of points – something the violins do not do. Its chordal structure is, of course, richer than the two violin lines, and at the same point in each of the three stanzas where there is a mirror image as voice and accompaniment move in contrary motion the piano is more assertive. (These examples of the composer's 'topsy-turvydom' are the earliest in his music.)

Harmonically, the song is also interesting. Although it has a key signature of two flats, neither B flat nor G minor is the true key, both ruled out by the preponderance of As and Ds in the vocal line. F major is strongly favoured because of the consistent harmonization of the As by Fs, but when the vocal line ascends to D, D minor seems the logical choice. However, neither of these keys is completely satisfactory because of the consistent presence of E flat, which imparts a strong modal flavour which is transposed Phrygian. Such ambiguities occurring in this early piece are clear indications of the subtleties to come in much of Rubbra's later music. One further subtlety is heard at the end when an unambiguous G minor accompanimental harmony is sounded on the unaccented fourth beat of the penultimate measure, but it is followed in the concluding measure by instrumental silence. The singer has been holding a D throughout the penultimate measure, and continues doing so in the last measure where there is also a *fermata*. Thus D modal/minor is confirmed by the singer, who must make this plain by holding the D long enough.

The reader will be surprised to learn of the importance attached to this little song by the composer. Most composers do not care to dwell on their first efforts, considering them to be juvenilia, but as late as 1971 Rubbra wrote that *Rosa Mundi*

> so excited Holst as to make me feel that I had discovered a lyrical direction for my music that I could happily follow in the knowledge that the root of it was in myself. I think it would be true to say that this little song was the point of departure for my future development.[1]

Op. 4

From 1922 comes Op. 4, which contains two short songs. The first of these is entitled *The Mystery*, to a poem by Ralph Hodgson. Its subject matter is related to *Rosa Mundi* in that a rose is again central to its religious thought. There are two four-line stanzas, and in his one-page setting the composer treats them strophically with only very slight note changes in the concluding stanza. This is the song which has no accompaniment. Its rhythmic freedom is expressed by the metre signatures 3/4, 2/4 and *Lento ma con rubato*. Melodically, its gentle curving line is pure, untransposed Aeolian, all contained within the span of a major seventh.

The second song in Op. 4 is *Jesukin*, with text by St Ita (480–570). The accompaniment is for harp or piano, but the arpeggiated chords throughout are a clear indication of the composer's preference. The song is strophic, based on three stanzas of four lines each. In each stanza subtle melodic and rhythmic changes are introduced in the vocal line, not in order to conform to changing textual accents but simply to introduce variety. A check of the vocal lines shows that at some of the points where changes are introduced the same melodic and rhythmic figures used previously could have easily been repeated. Variety is also introduced in the accompaniment. The harmony for each stanza remains substantially the same, but details in the chordal structure are different. There are, for example, two ostinatos, one in the second and the other in the third stanza. Harmonically, the song is less modal than either of the two thus far considered. Although the key signature shows four sharps, the tonal centre is a solid F sharp minor with a raised sixth and a lowered seventh, giving the song a Dorian flavour. A 5/4 metre with a division of 3 + 2 is the dominant rhythmic characteristic.

O My Deir Hert

I approached *O My Deir Hert*, Op. 5, with some misgivings. Having been familiar since my boy-chorister days with Peter Warlock's *Balulalow*, an exquisitely sensitive setting of the same text[2] for soprano solo and SATB, I was only cautiously optimistic. I am happy to report that Rubbra's setting is worthy in every respect. There are interesting points of similarity between them, but the question of influences is not involved, although some might maintain that the chronology of the settings suggests otherwise. Such a view would be superficial. Warlock's piece, composed in 1919 as a solo song with piano accompaniment, remained unpublished until 1923. Rubbra composed his in 1922, probably quite unaware of Warlock's setting, as there is no evidence that he and Warlock ever met. There is also no evidence that Rubbra's setting was published at the same time, for the only form in which the song is available is the composer's 1952 revision. This, together with *O Excellent Virgin Princess*, was published in 1953 under the title *Ave Maria Gratia Plena*, Two Medieval Songs for Voice and String Quartet.

The poem contains two stanzas of four lines each and for his setting Rubbra adopted a modified strophic plan. Despite the two-flat signature, the key is neither B flat nor G minor but D minor, a fact emphasized by the tonic pedal which, with two very unimportant exceptions, persists throughout the entire song. Other consistent features are the undeviating E flats in the voice part, which lend a Phrygian flavour to the song (however a very small number of E naturals do appear in the quartet accompaniment), and parallel triads, which are equally present throughout the song. All of these features appear in Example 251. Also seen is the melisma in measures 3–4, repeated note-for-note at the corresponding place in the second stanza, where the first syllable of 'evermoir' is sung. The climactic point of the song comes at the place in stanza 2 which corresponds with 'prepare thy creddil in my spreit' (Example 251). The vocal line reaches a high G and then drops to D. Following the melodic changes which this climax entails, there are others until the contour seen in measures 3 and 4 leads the way to the final cadence.

Ex. 251

One interesting metrical change involves a new melodic fragment immediately following the climax, and it comes at the point where the rhythm of the words departs very slightly from the prevailing iambic tetrameter: a measure of 5/4 in a 3 + 2 pattern is substituted for the 4/4 metre that is present everywhere else. Warlock in his setting makes a rhythmic adjustment at exactly the same place and if nothing else, these treatments demonstrate the responsiveness of both composers to textual nuances.

Although Rubbra does not specify a particular voice here (very many of the songs are unspecified in this regard), *O My Deir Hert* is effective for either soprano or tenor.

Op. 8

In the two published songs of Op. 8, written in 1923 (no. 3, *Who Is Sylvia?*, is in manuscript), Rubbra turned away from explicitly religious texts. The first, *Cradle Song*, on a poem by Padraic Colum, the Irish poet and playwright, contains two references to the Virgin Mary which are central to the poem's meaning, but the poem itself is not about her. Its two stanzas are addressed to 'men from the fields', who, in the first stanza, are asked to 'come gently within', for 'Mavourneen [Irish for 'my darling'] is going away from me and from you,/Where Mary will fold him/With mantle of blue!' In the second stanza the baby will be freed from 'reek of the smoke/And cold of the floor'. At the end 'Mary puts round him her mantle of blue.'

The composer has set this humble and moving scene as a lullaby in A minor, but with his usual flatted seventh. The vocal line and piano accompaniment each has its own melody, and this fact gives added interest to the song. The singer will likely experience an intonational problem at the same point in each stanza where there is an abrupt change of harmony. As seen in Example 252 the change throws into relief the pathos of the scene.

Ex. 252

In this song as in others already discussed, the final stanza contains subtle differences in both voice and accompaniment. Those in the vocal line of *Cradle Song* are fewer than in the earlier songs simply because a lullaby requires a primarily undeviating melody and accompaniment. So it is that the accompaniment contains note rearrangements without disturbing the harmony, but still enough to guarantee variety. As this chapter moves on we shall see greater adjustments in final stanzas that can be said to correspond to the final sections in symphony, concerto and chamber music movements where recapitulations are varied widely from expositions. Such procedures have been frequently met in Rubbra's works and it is not inaccurate to suggest that in his early songs he began to adopt the idea, albeit on a very small scale.

At the very beginning of Act 3 of Shakespeare's *Henry VIII*, a play now recognized by scholars as having been written in collaboration with, most probably, John Fletcher, Katherine of Aragon, Henry's Queen, in a melancholy mood directs one of her women to 'take thy lute, wench: my soul grows sad with troubles.' The song that comes forth from her servant's lips is *Orpheus With His Lute*, thought to be by Fletcher. Rubbra in his D minor setting of its two stanzas, Op. 8, no. 2, 'captures both the mood and the situation', to quote Stephen Banfield at the start of his short analysis. 'His "lute" chords, of which there are only three – two ninths, and a superposition of C and D triads – supply the poignancy and the lute-like function of punctuating the vocal line without getting in the way of it.'[3] These chords are, of course, rolled.

The rhythmic flow is determined by the double metre signature – 2/4, 3/4 – and this allows the phrase structure to expand and contract in accordance with the text. Some phrases are longer than others and in order not to violate the sense of the poetic lines careful breath control is required. For example, the first three lines as printed in Shakespeare are, 'Orpheus with his lute made trees,/And the mountain-tops that freeze,/Bow themselves, when he did sing.' This is one long arch of thought that, ideally, should be sung with one breath. Probably to encourage this the composer in his setting has omitted all of the punctuation seen above. 'Sing', set to a D, is the obvious goal of these lines (Example 253). The same melodic line is found in the next stanza, but there the

Ex. 253

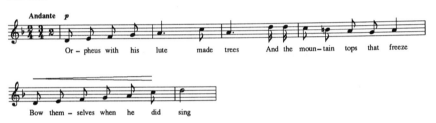

textual requirements mean different rhythmic emphases: 'Everything that heard him play,/Even the billows of the sea,/Hung their heads and then lay by.' 'Lute' in the first stanza was given a beat and a half because it is a key word, but 'heard' at the corresponding place in the second stanza is absorbed into the line as one eighth note among twelve. The whole phrase, couched in eighths and two sixteenths moves without interruption to 'by'. The song's climax on the words, 'killing care and grief of heart,/Fall asleep, or, hearing, die', is carefully thought out. 'Killing' has an *allargando* and a *crescendo* associated with it that lead to a *forte* and an accent on 'care'. 'Grief' is semi-isolated by being set to three accented notes, while a tiny break separates 'or hearing' and 'die'. These words are also accented. Of all the songs so far considered, this setting shows the greatest sensitivity to textual nuances.

Op. 13

A period of two years separates the songs of Op. 8 and the three that make up Op. 13 (1925). For the first of these new songs Rubbra chose the poem, *Out in the Dark*, by Edward Thomas (1878–1917). It can be inferred from the year of his death that Thomas was killed in the Great War; but while this is correct, it would be wrong to assume that he was a 'war poet' in the same sense that

Siegfried Sassoon, Wilfred Owen and others of their generation were. Of Thomas's 144 poems, all written between 3 December 1914 and 13 January 1917, very few deal with the War *per se*. Prior to the composition of his first poem all of his works were in prose, but a meeting and subsequent friendship with Robert Frost encouraged his shift to poetry. *Out in the Dark* is his penultimate poem, written on 24 December 1916 at High Beech, Essex, where he was stationed for a time after his enlistment in the army, and it reflects the natural beauty of his surroundings: 'Out in the dark over the snow/The fallow fawns invisible go/With the fallow doe;/And the winds blow/Fast as the stars are slow.' This first stanza is followed by three others whose gathering tensions are impressive. One can almost feel in the second stanza the approach of night: 'Stealthily the dark haunts round/And, when a lamp goes, without sound/At a swifter bound/Than the swiftest hound,/Arrives, and all else is drowned.' Fear enters the scene in the third stanza when 'I and star and wind and deer/Are in the dark together near', and so on.

The song's structure is an interesting adaptation of strophic form and there is no doubt that the composer has taken pains to make the necessary alterations so as to provide for correct accents and syllabification in succeeding stanzas. There are also minor note changes at these points. But the greatest modifications in the strophic plan occur near and at the ends of stanzas where the poet has introduced a thought that is unexpected or climactic. These changes occupy about half of the musical content of the stanza, and there is no doubt that they are effective. In my opinion Rubbra's setting overall is not entirely successful. Rhythmically, the song needs more variety, for the almost unvarying flow of eighths in the accompaniment becomes rather monotonous and the metre changes from 12/8 to 15/8, 9/8, 6/8, and so on, make no appreciable difference. Neither do the dotted quarter, arpeggiated chords – all of which are associated in some way with the eighth-note movement. Perhaps the intent was to portray the dark of night in soothing terms, but as a reading of the poem will show such an interpretation is not really appropriate. It is true that the poem is neither dramatic nor inclined to tell a story in the sense of cumulative events, but there is in it a nameless disquiet that is not adequately reflected in the music. The ending of the song is not entirely convincing, either. Thomas's last stanza reads, 'How weak and little is the light,/All the universe of sight,/Love and delight,/Before the might,/If you love it not, of night.' Instead of ending the vocal line where Thomas finishes the poem, the composer repeats 'If you love it not'. Doing so gets him back into the principal key of D major, following a lengthy excursion to B flat minor, but at the price of an unnecessary redundance, which weakens the effect of the poet's last line. This marks one of the very few times in Rubbra's choral or vocal music in which such a liberty is taken.

If *Out in the Dark* is unsatisfactory in some respects, the second song of Op. 13, *A Hymn to the Virgin*, is a little gem. The text is an anonymous Middle English poem containing five stanzas of which Rubbra selected the first and fourth. Like *Jesukin* with which it has been published, the accompaniment is for harp or piano, but the composer's preference is strongly indicated by his direction that 'if this accompaniment is played on the piano it should sound as harp-like as possible'.

The fifteenth-century text, whose manuscript source is Egerton 613, British Museum, is, like many others of the time, a mixture of Middle English and Latin in which there is a separate rhyme scheme for each. The poem is a general expression of praise and gratitude to the Virgin for having borne 'Jhesu, Hevene king', but it also contains a prayer to her: 'Ic crie to the, thou se to me [turn to me], Levedy, praye thi sone for me,/Tam pia, that ic mote come to the, Maria.' In Rubbra's setting of the fourth stanza (the second in the song) there surely is an error in the printed score. The poem goes 'Rosa sine spina' – 'Rose without thorn', but in the score *sine* is missing, an omission that makes the line unintelligible. Musically, *sine* can be easily inserted, for on the same notes in the first stanza *maris* is sung before *stella*.

Rubbra's setting is pure, original Aeolian in its A to A compass through the first half of each stanza. The second half introduces F and C sharps in a partially unaccompanied vocal line, marked *rubato*. Indeed, the differences between the two halves in each stanza are great enough to suggest an internal binary structure. Yet each half beautifully complements the other and unity is achieved through a quiet, shared elegance and dignity that perfectly suit the subject. The accompaniment is very simple and entirely chordal. A large part of it consists of alternating triads and sevenths in root position and the freely-flowing combination of voice and accompaniment is brought about by frequent

Ex. 254

changes of metre. Example 254 shows the vocal line in the concluding stanza's second half.

Taking into account that a medieval text is the song's *raison d'être*, it is rather startling to read that *A Hymn to the Virgin* 'is too deliberately medieval, and the retention of the old spelling and phraseology (some of which has to be explained in foot-notes) is surely "precious".'[4] One wonders how the setting of a medieval poem can be 'too deliberately medieval'. Of course the reviewer failed to mention that common triads and sevenths are not indigenous to medieval settings. Had he noted their presence he might have phrased his review differently. The miracle is that the composer has somehow convinced us that these chords *do* sound natural and authentic. As for the 'old spelling and phraseology', a translation into modern English and a rearrangement of portions of the text would have totally destroyed the medieval atmosphere. And why *not* educate the singer and the public by means of footnoted explanations? The large, modern collection in which this poem appears is similarly footnoted throughout, a feature for which every reader must be grateful.

The final song of Op. 13 is a setting of Shakespeare's *It Was A Lover and His Lass*, from Act 5, scene 3 of *As You Like It*; among composers contemporary with Rubbra who set the same text are Warlock and Finzi. Of Shakespeare's four stanzas Rubbra omitted the second.

The regularity of the undeviating 6/8 metre, with its two prominent accents per measure throughout much of the song, imparts an earthy exuberance to the *Allegretto* setting. However, the rhythmic impulse is varied for one measure in each of the refrains by the employment of two groups of duplets in both voice and piano.

There is no key signature, a circumstance that left Rubbra free to experiment with two modal axes: a basic one built on G in the piano, and a subordinate one revolving around D in the voice. There are no E flats or F sharps in the piano part and no C sharps in the vocal line, although in one measure of the refrain in each stanza there are C sharps in the accompaniment. Of the two elements it is the piano that stands on firmer ground, for in its rocking, eighth-note bass pattern G is present in all but one measure per stanza, and it is present in every measure of the right-hand part. On the other hand, D in the vocal line is ambiguous because at certain points it is a strongly accented first beat in the measure. Yet when this occurs it is always harmonized by a G minor or major triad, or a chord with no third. A, the dominant of D, is also prominent on third beats where it is harmonized by A or F major triads, but there are clashes between the G and D modal centres. However, in the last analysis this division into modal elements is 'eye' music as seen in the score. In performance, especially at the tripping, *Allegretto* tempo, it is unheard, and one is aware of the clashes between voice and piano in a hazy, subliminal kind of way because of the fast tempo.

It appears that Rubbra's experiment with modal mixing was in the reviewer's mind when he said, 'the result hardly justifies his daring. The words call for more light-heartedness than is here.'[5]

The Night

Another song from 1925 is *The Night*, Op. 14, set to Hilaire Belloc's beautiful poem; other settings are by Warlock, and Ivor Gurney. Belloc, French-born and Oxford-educated, became a British subject shortly after his graduation. Known chiefly for his many books and essays on historical subjects, he also wrote light, humorous verse as well as serious poetry, of which *The Night* is an example. To summarize briefly, the poet asks the night to give him repose: 'And let the far lament of them / That chaunt the dead day's requiem / Make in my ears, who wakeful lie, / Soft lullaby.' The fourth and final stanza is particularly beautiful: 'Fold your great wings about my face, / Hide dawning from my resting-place, / And cheat me with your false delight, / Most Holy Night.'

Rubbra's approach to the poem is that of a gentle, soothing lullaby, but without the rhythmic connotations that usually accompany that word. The metre is 4/8 rather than the innocent, 'rocking cradle' 6/8 with its stereotyped figure. Yet a distinctive rhythmic figure, used throughout the song in the piano's left hand, subtly suggests sleep. The right hand has a syncopated figure that forms about half of the top line of a mostly chordal texture, and some of the interior flow of notes in this hand creates a separate melodic line. The C sharp minor tonality is challenged repeatedly by recurring F sharps on strong beats in the left hand, as well as by other notes in the right hand, but the resulting dissonances are gentle enough to suggest the indefinite boundaries surrounding sleep. The vocal line shows a good balance between conjunct and disjunct elements.

Structurally, the song is of the modified strophic type with a very small change occurring near the end of stanza 2 – so small that only two measures are involved before a return is made to the patterns with which the first stanza closes. The principal modification involves a brief transition to an indefinite tonality, composed of elements of F minor, C minor and E flat major, and lasting for just half of stanza 3. In the second half, a return to the original material is easily managed, although the restoration of C sharp minor is not made 'official' until the stanza's penultimate measure.

The composer must have received encouragement from the following review:

> 'The Night' provides for some beautiful words by Belloc which have been crying out for a good musical setting and have now got it. The song has originality of outlook without the feebleness of control which often goes with that quality.... There is one bar, the eleventh, whose sliding ninth rather irritates as it passes, there and later on when it recurs. The colour seems foreign to the general design, and to the composer's palette. But this is a detail in a very good piece of work.[6]

While I agree that this is a fine song, it cannot, in my estimation compare with Warlock's magnificent setting.

Rune of Hospitality

Rubbra's next song, *Rune of Hospitality*, Op. 15, is a setting of an 'old Gaelic rune, recovered by Kenneth Macleod'. The song, composed in 1925 but revised in 1970, bears a dedication to Hugh Mackay, one of the key figures in The Arts League of Service Travelling Theatre, with which Rubbra was associated for a short period. The poem, at least in translation, is unrhymed, and tells how 'I saw a stranger yestreen;/I put food in the eating place,/Drink in the drinking place,/Music in the list'ning place;/And in the sacred name of the Triune,/He blessed myself and my house,/My cattle and my dear ones./And the lark said in her song,/Often goes the Christ in the stranger's guise.'

The music for this charming fable occupies just seventeen measures. Except for a recurring triplet figure and its resolution – G, F̃, A, G – used in both voice and piano as a unifying device, though not always simultaneously, the song is through-composed. The rhythm is totally moulded to the words, which are set in a chant-like, short-note style, the unit of value being the eighth. Consequently, frequent metre changes are to be seen. The accompaniment is primarily chordal, providing a nice balance for the moving eighths in the vocal line, and the harmonies are very simple, consisting of triads and sevenths. The key is G minor with Rubbra's usual lowered seventh and there are no modulations. The raised third in the piano part in the middle and at the end of the song provides just the right touch. Ottaway refers to the song as 'a nicely shaped miniature'.[7] It is an excellent choice for singers who are looking for 'something different', for its unusual text and sensitive setting should have a wide audience appeal.

Op. 17

For the two songs of Op. 17, composed in 1926, Rubbra turned to Ben Jonson (*A Prayer*) and James Thomson (*Invocation to Spring*). The music for the first of these is charmingly noncommittal, seemingly an attempt to match what appears to be a not altogether serious petition. Everything points in that direction, for as the song progresses it is the music that emphasizes the growing doubts about taking the poem too literally. It does this in several ways: first, the too serene E flat major tonality imparts a blandness inconsistent with a genuinely penitential prayer, which is what this prayer purports to be. Second, the rather busy eighth-note activity in both vocal line and accompaniment through most of the song does little to stress a particular word or group of words. Two instances of this are 'A broken heart/Is my best part' and 'For sin's so sweet,/As minds ill-bent/Rarely repent,/Until they meet/Their punishment.' Third, the climax of the vocal line on the word 'stern' in 'If Thou hadst not/Been stern to me', is not dwelt on at all, but moves on at once to the next thought. Finally, the accompaniment plays its part in promoting the irony. It is a continuously moving line of mostly four-note chords – two notes per hand – that consists, like the vocal line, of gently rising and falling scale figures. Most of the time the piano does not follow the voice and this independence places some strain on the singer. Also, occasionally, there is contrary motion, including some between piano and voice. The cumulative effect of all this motion is to weaken the resolve and the concentration that penitential prayer demands, and thus to strengthen the gentle irony of the poem. The result is a delightful song, yet one whose subtlety can easily be missed by those who interpret the poem too literally. For them, the composer's setting will seem wide of the mark in terms of its failure properly to address the poem as they see it.

Invocation to Spring is a setting of the opening four lines of 'Spring' in James Thomson's enormous four-part work, *The Seasons*, which in the final 1746 edition runs to 5,541 lines. The descriptive style and blank verse in which the work is written do not, of course, lend themselves to strophic treatment even if Rubbra had chosen more than four lines for his setting. Thus this miniature of just ten measures is through-composed insofar as the vocal line is concerned. Unity is ensured by a tightly-knit accompaniment consisting almost entirely of a repeating two-measure phrase along the tops of the right-hand chords. The full, two-handed accompaniment seems overloaded at times, considering the delicacy of the poem, and when the *con moto* tempo is taken into account some of the chords are unnecessarily awkward for the pianist. Also, in a song whose light vocal line is composed of flowing eighths, it is puzzling to find such a large percentage of the eighth-note chords with stress marks above them. They tend to cancel the easy flow that the composer wrote into the voice part. Yet, despite these faults the song can be effectively performed, given sensitive musicians aware of the pitfalls.

A Duan of Barra

For his next song, *A Duan of Barra*, Op. 20, Rubbra chose a beautiful three-stanza poem by Murdoch Maclean. A note in the score tells us that 'duan' is a little song. The locale is, of course, the outer Hebridean Isle of Barra. The subject of the poem is similar to that of *Rune of Hospitality*, but it is more som-bre: 'The Son of God shall pass tonight,/Shall pass at midnight dreary,/The Son of Mary, weary.' After a second-stanza admonition to 'leave the stranger's door ajar', the third stanza commands us to 'Sweep the hearth and pile the peat,/And set the board with bread and meat;/The Son of God may take it,/The Son of Mary brake it.'

Rubbra's setting has all the outward appearances of being strophic, but there are too many differences in both the voice and accompaniment for the term to be entirely valid, therefore we shall refer to the structure as modified strophic. The metre is a gentle, rocking 6/8, marked 'Always quiet, but with motion'. There is no key signature, but the tonality is an unequivocal E minor with a lowered seventh. The gentle rise and fall of the vocal line is exquisitely

balanced, as is the melody atop the piano chords. One of the delightful surprises in this song is the discovery of a significant number of canonic and near-
canonic imitations between the vocal melody and the piano melody; and the use
of the word 'discovery' is evidence of their unobtrusiveness. The passages in
which they are contained flow so naturally out of and back into the surrounding
texture as to attract little or no attention. Yet their absence would certainly
reduce the song's effectiveness.

The harmonies of which the accompaniment is composed are basically static,
but their relative immobility is a consequence not so much of the almost
omnipresent pedals – one at the bottom (C-G), the other in the middle (E) – as
the chords themselves. These are of the added-note and tone cluster types. The
pedals provide a firm foundation above which the chords, for all their fullness,
never convey an impression of heaviness. Example 255 shows the first stanza.

Ex. 255

Op. 22

Op. 21, *Soontree*, a lullaby to words by Nora Hopper, dates from 1928 but remains in manuscript. Op. 22 from the same year contains two songs, *Take, O Take Those Lips Away* to Shakespeare's well-known text from Act 4, scene 1 of *Measure for Measure* and *Why So Pale and Wan?* by Sir John Suckling. The first of these texts has also received settings by a number of composers contemporaneous with Rubbra, among them Bernard van Dieren, Peter Warlock's friend and mentor, and Warlock himself, who wrote three settings, the third of which was lost or destroyed. Rubbra's setting bears a dedication to Maurice Jacobson, a close friend from the RCM days, and his very sensitive response to Shakespeare's love-struck text is a little gem. Just twenty-one measures long, it contrasts two different elements in such a way as to create a wholly unified texture without detracting from the independence of either.

It appears as though the composer has taken special pains with his vocal line, for its flow is more carefully moulded to the implications of the words than in some of his preceding songs. A careful reading of Example 256 will

Ex. 256

show that the goal of the first phrase is 'lips away', certain to attract attention because of its devious contour and high position. Attention is still concentrated on 'lips' by means of the repeating C sharps. The hesitation on 'sweetly' seems just right. In the next phrase the unexpected change to A flat, announced by a rolled A flat chord, prepares the listener for the sharp rise to 'break of day'. However, note that the scale figure ascends, not conventionally through D flat to E flat, but through D natural to E natural. 'Break of day' is set to the same contour as 'lips away' except that it is higher. 'Lights', before the drop to C sharp, is placed on the highest note of the song and the three rapidly descending sixteenths, the only such values in the song except for those following the dotted eighths, focus our attention on 'that do mislead'. 'Morn' is then pitched higher but not as high as 'Lights', for had it received a higher note the latter word would have been robbed of its preeminence.

Except for unimportant and tiny details the rest of the vocal line repeats what is shown in the example. However, it should not be assumed that the song can be automatically classified as strophic even though elements of strophic form are certainly present. Modified strophic form is a more plausible choice, but even its treatment is unconventional, for music from the first part of the song is reintroduced in an order different from that of its original presentation. Thus the music for 'But my kisses bring again', the line following the end of the illustration, is set to the same notes as 'That so sweetly were forsworn', allowing for two F sharps instead of the earlier C sharps. Shakespeare's repetition of 'bring again' is a three-note phrase extension but set to notes not previously heard. Then comes the song's final line, 'Seals of love, but seal'd in vain,/Seal'd in vain', set to the music of the first four measures.

The accompaniment is basically chordal but flowing lines associated with the chords serve as connectives and give variety. Most of the chords themselves are harmonically unrelated, parallel constructions with similar intervallic distances between notes. They also traverse a segment of the whole tone scale as they fall and rise. Of course, by this time in the century such writing had become firmly established, making it difficult to determine whose influence this might suggest. Thus the use of the term, 'Holstian' in mentioning these 'shifting triads' seems ill-advised.[8] It is true that Rubbra himself listed chords of this nature in an article describing some of Holst's characteristics,[9] but that does not necessarily imply that he got them from his teacher.

The important element in this song is the happy relationship between the vocal line and the chord stream. As the latter falls and the former rises, dissonances are produced at just the right points with respect to the text. One further item worth mentioning is that the piano continues for five measures after the voice ceases, making this the longest postlude to date in Rubbra's songs.

Why So Pale and Wan?, the second song of Op. 22, is a setting of a poem that is typical of the carefree wit of its author, Sir John Suckling (1609–42), who incidentally is given credit for inventing the game of cribbage. Rubbra's song reflects that wit in both voice and piano by means of a melody couched in an eighth-note patter style, and an accompaniment composed of quarter-note, dissonant chords directed to be played *staccato*, although in the second half of the song some of these are marked *legato*. Despite Suckling's three rhymed stanzas, Rubbra adopted a free form design in which only the vocal line repeats anything, and then just one-measure scale figures. The accompaniment has no repetitions of any kind.

In order of opus numbers two songs come between *Why So Pale and Wan?* and *A Widow Bird Sate Mourning*, but neither was published. The first, *The Song of the Laverock* (the Scottish word for 'lark'), Op. 23, for voice, strings and harp to words by F.C. Boden (1928), was discarded by the composer. The second, *Ballad of Tristram* to a text translated from the Icelandic, and designated for tenor and small orchestra as Op. 26, was composed in 1930, but it remains in manuscript.

A Widow Bird Sate Mourning

A Widow Bird Sate Mourning, Op. 28, is a setting of the little song sung by Archy, the court fool, in Shelley's unfinished historical drama, *Charles the First*. The words stand at the beginning of scene 5, and are the last in the fragment. The song, written in 1930, bears a dedication to Hubert Foss, music editor of Oxford University Press from 1924 to 1941. He published this song as well as several we have already considered (the total number being somewhat larger than the figure mentioned by the composer in Chapter 1). All were reissued by Lengnick at later dates.

The structure of this two-stanza poem is modified strophic, but with some unusual features: at the start of stanza 2 the melody for the first line of text is different from the corresponding place in stanza 1, yet the piano part is the same. As the stanza moves into its second line an entire measure in the accompaniment is omitted, and the vocal line at that point is altered. This produces a situation in which the faithfully repeating accompaniment and the 'wayward' vocal line are out of phase for about a measure and a half with respect to the corresponding place in the first stanza. The vocal line's final measure is very different from its first-stanza counterpart, and the piano's concluding solo measures contain material borrowed from earlier segments. All of this is more important than it might at first appear, for it offers proof of the increasingly relaxed sense of structure that is becoming more and more apparent in Rubbra's songs.

The metre is 12/8 and the tempo is marked *Lento espressivo*. Much of the time in both voice and piano the rhythm is two against three. The tonality is E minor, reinforced in the accompaniment by the equivalent of a dominant pedal: B, C, B, C, B, C, and so on, filling up the 12/8 measure. This pattern moves easily from one hand to the other and from one octave to another and it is discontinued for no more than one or two beats in four of the song's nineteen measures. Most of the time the pedal is in one of the middle parts, and dissonances have been created through the interaction of chords and moving parts with it. The mainly static harmony and the undulating pedal have combined to produce a quiet, almost colourless texture which is ideally suited to the portrayal of the numbing cold and deadness of winter: 'A widow bird sate mourning for her love/Upon a wintry bough;/The frozen wind crept on above,/The freezing stream below.' In the vocal line the melody rises and falls as it wills and no attempt is made to delineate any particular word. This impersonal atmosphere is enhanced by the three-measure piano prelude, the four-measure interlude and the two-measure postlude, the most extended solo piano passages in Rubbra's songs thus far.

Four Medieval Latin Lyrics

In 1932 Rubbra composed what eventually became his first large-scale work for solo voice and accompaniment: Four Medieval Latin Lyrics, Op. 32, for baritone and string orchestra. (It will be recalled that in his autobiographical account Rubbra said that these were originally written for *a cappella* choir, but finding them too difficult for this medium, he reworked them after the Second World War and in their new form they were published in 1949.) The English translations were made by the composer and the work was dedicated to the baritone, Robert Irwin.

The source for the first three poems is a thirteenth-century manuscript found at the Monastery of Benediktbeuren, south of Munich. It contains some two hundred sacred and secular songs, most of them without music, and is best known today for the title bestowed on it in 1847 by its discoverer: *Carmina Burana*. The title has a special meaning for the thousands of listeners familiar with Carl Orff's work of the same name, composed in 1935–6. The poems, dealing with the pleasures of love and drinking, spring, fate in the form of Fortune's wheel, and so on, were written by the Goliards – wandering students as well as young clerics in minor ecclesiastical orders. Some of the latter appear to have been defrocked for their disreputable activities. They flourished from the last half of the tenth century to the early part of the thirteenth.

Each of the four pieces in Rubbra's set bears a title that refers to either a musical or literary form of the Middle Ages, and this is followed by the first line of the Latin text (except for no. 4 where no Latin *incipit* is given). Thus no. 1 is entitled 'Rondel', a generic word which, in the Middle Ages, referred to a type of composition containing a repeating element such as a recurring refrain. That exactly describes the present piece and Rubbra has adapted the principle to his own use. The Latin title is 'Tempus est iocundum', and those familiar with Orff's *Carmina Burana* will recognize it as constituting the twenty-second

Ex. 257

item in that work. Some stanzas appearing in Rubbra's setting are not present in the Orff and vice versa.

Rubbra's setting of this text, which describes the springtime desire of a youth for 'one sweet maiden', is marked *Allegro vivace e sempre leggiero* ($\downarrow$ = 160). All of the essential material of the entire ninety measures is contained in Example 257, where stanza and refrain are identified by S and R respectively. In line with the composer's tendency to alter materials that are repeated, some succeeding stanzas and refrains are varied both rhythmically and melodically. More liberties can be taken with the refrains than with the stanzas because the textual repetition in the former is a constant identifying factor. Simple key changes – D minor to E minor and back several times as well as excursions to G minor and A minor – add interest and variety.

The orchestral accompaniment becomes increasingly exciting through the introduction of canonic passages, and as they multiply it is evident that the composer is thoroughly enjoying himself. However, realizing that the orchestra can grow too enthusiastic, the following caution is printed at the bottom of the first page: 'the dynamics of the accompaniment in this setting should always be on a lower level than those of the voice.' Here, as in the three remaining pieces the strings are divided much of the time.

The second piece of the set is entitled *Plaint*, a literary word without any reference to a specific musical form. The poem, 'Dum estas inchoatur', is a youthful lament for a love that is not returned: 'O that my heart, sore-wounded/ With unrequited love/Might in desolate longing...', and so on. This setting, the shortest of the work, employs a standard figure for the portrayal of grief: a repeating chromatic bass in the manner of a ground that, somewhat surprisingly, ascends rather than descends. It is not consistent in its repetitions, for some are different with regard to notes and the lengths of the segments. Above this line the upper strings combine to produce chords which emphasize the mournful character of the piece. The vocal line consists mostly of eighth notes and it is wholly independent of the orchestra.

The third number is called *Pastoral*. The text, 'Ecce, chorus virginum', is a call to 'Happy maidens, come and play,/Come and play together,/While the sun his morning ray/Gilds the springtime weather', and so on. Rubbra's tempo indication is *Giocoso* ($\downarrow$. = 144) in a 12/8 metre, one of the standard metres for a pastoral. Both soloist and orchestra are faithful to the joyous mood in lilting melodies that gracefully rise and fall. The principal focus of interest is in the orchestra, where dissonances, some gentle and others biting, produce a joyous sense of confusion that is appropriate to the 'merry laughter' as the maidens 'dance and pipe together'. At the point where 'the blackbird sings his lay' the violins and cellos imitate with trills. The overall effect of the accompaniment is that of a thirteenth-century piece in the first rhythmic mode ($\downarrow$ $\flat$$\downarrow$ $\flat$$\downarrow$ $\flat$$\downarrow$ $\flat$) and the harmonic clashes that result from the moving parts, although in a contemporary idiom, are also consistent with the medieval style.

The last piece, *Planctus* or *Lament*, again presupposes no particular musical form. The poem by Peter Abélard (1079–1142), the extraordinary French scholastic philosopher, theologian and teacher, is his celebrated lament of David for Jonathan: 'Could I share thy grave with thee,/Happy then my death would be.'

The tempo indication is *Lento* (♪= 66) and the strings are muted throughout the piece. Insofar as the orchestra is concerned the style is decidedly chromatic, but the vocal line is considerably less so. It does not seem too far-fetched to suggest a carefully calculated purpose behind such a discrepancy: the muted chromaticism of the accompaniment depicts in *general* terms the desolation that goes hand in hand with grief, while the stark and colourless vocal line represents the difficulty of expressing the stunning force of a *personal* grief. The passage beginning in measure 4, immediately following the lines quoted above, is typical of the entire song and is shown in Example 258. In structural terms

Ex. 258

Planctus is a clear example of ternary form. Except for changes in note values that allow for the words, the second *A* is a duplicate of the first.

All things considered, this entire work is effective and should be heard. It is, of course, impossible to know what the work was like as an unaccompanied choral piece, but if certain works in that genre as discussed in Chapter 9 are any criteria, the difficulties must have been considerable. It seems reasonable to suppose that many of the present string parts were vocal lines in the choral work. If that supposition is true the clashing dissonances in the medieval-sounding third piece certainly caused problems, particularly when sung up to tempo. Whether the baritone's part throughout the present work was the original soprano line is impossible to say for sure; it would seem that much of it is the same.

In Dark Weather

Mary Webb's *In Dark Weather* was the vehicle for Rubbra's next song, Op. 33, composed in 1932, and his setting of it prompted the following favourable review:

> 'In Dark Weather' is a setting of a beautiful little quiet pastoral poem by Mary Webb. It describes a scene in late winter when, though no sign of spring yet shows, there is already a feeling of coming change....
>
> The composer has admirably realized this sentiment in his quiet but truly distinguished song. If one describes it as of the New English or Vaughan Williams School, this must be taken as a rough generalization, and not as suggesting any weak derivativeness. The opening is bare and chill, with an E tolling deep in the bass. Gradually the music is enriched, but not over-enriched. The composer is a modern but sensitive harmonist, and has avoided the welter of mere experimentation. The voice part is perfectly singable, though a wide compass is required – two octaves, in fact, if the last phrase is sung as the composer would have it, with the high B. But optional notes are allowed here, reducing the compass to an octave and a minor sixth.[10]

A more detailed examination of the score reveals several points of interest, the first of which is that each of the poem's three stanzas is set to a different vocal line and not even the reappearance in the second stanza of a two-measure segment from the first alters that fact. Indeed, one receives the impression that the reappearance was unplanned. Thus while it is safe to say that the vocal line is through-composed, the term cannot strictly apply to the song as a whole for reasons to be pursued presently. The second point concerns three sharply rising segments in the vocal line, each marked with a *crescendo*. The first of these, in the second stanza, is intensive rather than descriptive insofar as suggesting images conveyed by the words: 'No lambs across the fields have cried.' The unexpected 'not yet' following these words is appropriately isolated. The other rising segments, both in stanza 3, are descriptive: 'But whorl by whorl the green fronds climb', a reference to the bracken in stanza 2, and 'The warm buds swell beneath the rime.'

Even more interesting is the accompaniment, whose repeating segments are responsible for the rejection of the through-composed idea. These are composed of two very dissimilar figures, the first of which, occupying one measure, fills the first twelve. In sound, it is frankly impressionistic, embracing three very soft and delicate grace notes that precede the prime note of each measure, which in every case is a dotted half in the 3/4 metre. The 'E tolling deep in the bass' is a half note on the second beats. Three factors have combined to produce the impressionistic quality: the incomplete dominant ninths – the missing root being B flat – formed from D, F, A flat, C, though not in that order; the veiled, muted sound made by *una corda*; and the blurring effect of a held pedal. The tolling Es are outside the harmonic framework until changes in the grace notes at the bottom of the page, but they too add to the delicate, blurring sound that is so much a part of impressionistic music.

The second of the two figures mentioned at the start of the last paragraph completely dominates the remainder of the song, although it is introduced most of the time by the grace notes just discussed. It is a right-handed figure, made up of expanding chromatic intervals, although there are two instances of contracting intervals. At the end of the song a third melodic line is added, and the

Ex. 259

figure ascends triumphantly in octaves, symbolizing the advent of spring. A passage from the second stanza showing both accompanimental figures as well as the voice part appears as Example 259. It should be noted that the grace note figure has lost its impressionistic trait.

A significant interval in the song is the upward leap of a fifth. When it first appears in the voice part on the first page, and during the second stanza in our illustration, it seems relatively unimportant. But the emphasis it acquires on the words 'not yet', and in the stressed echoing notes of the accompaniment immediately following imparts a sense of expectancy. This feeling continues as the interval and its echo are heard during the ten-measure interlude between stanzas 2 and 3. In general terms this interlude is a transition between the winter of the first stanzas and the first stirrings of spring in the third. The change is symbolized by four measures of new material, urged on by a *crescendo* and a small *accelerando*. When the peak is reached the remaining six measures return to the music of the kind seen in the example. It is almost as though one should not raise one's hopes too high, for spring has its own mysterious schedule. But when the voice proclaims that 'whorl by whorl the green fronds climb', and so on, the accompaniment, still keeping the rising figures in the right hand, adds accented octaves, marked *piano ma pesante*, in the left hand. The rising fifth from E to high B in the vocal line on the last word of the song in the line 'For life does not forget' is immensely effective, for there is no doubt now that the expectations aroused by the earlier fifths are fully realized. The *crescendo* ending the vocal line continues through the piano's five-measure postlude. For me, this is one of Rubbra's finest songs.

Five Spenser Sonnets

The next ten songs, divided into two sets of five songs each, occupy two opus numbers – 42 and 43 – and date from 1935. The words for both sets come from Edmund Spenser's enormous sonnet-sequence, *Amoretti* (eighty-nine poems), written for Elizabeth Boyle, who in 1594 became his second wife. The first set, entitled Five Spenser Sonnets is scored for tenor and string orchestra and bears a dedication to its first performers – the tenor, William Herbert and the Kathleen Riddick String Orchestra.

For the opening song of this set Rubbra chose the second sonnet, whose subject is the 'unquiet thought, whom at the first I bred,/Of the inward bale of my love pined heart;/And sithens [since] have with sighs and sorrows fed.' The poet commands this thought to 'break forth at length out of the inner part' so that it may 'seek some succour both to ease my smart/And also to sustain thyself with food.' However, if the thought should chance to meet 'that fairest proud', it should 'fall lowly at her feet:/And with meek humbleness and afflicted mood,/Pardon for thee, and grace for me entreat.' If she grants this all is well; if not, both the thought and the poet will die.

These sombre musings are matched by a solidly chordal foundation, above which an undulating chromatic melody pursues its course in the violins. Because of the *divisi* writing that has given all parts except the basses their separate staff the sonorities are rich, although unison and octave doublings have restricted the harmonies to four parts. As is usual in Rubbra's songs the vocal line has its own melody, some parts of which are also chromatic. Following a moderate alternation of metres the song settles down to its principal metre – 6/4. The tempo is marked *Lento* (♩ = 84). The change of thought contained in the concluding rhymed couplet of the Spenserian sonnet is reflected in a drum-beat-like E flat pedal.

The next song, a contrapuntal setting of Sonnet 4, is more interesting. The poem celebrates the New Year, and looks forward to 'new delight', 'fresh love', 'lusty spring'. The tempo is appropriately *Allegro* (♩ = 96). The ceaseless contrapuntal movement in which all the instruments except the basses are involved is also shared by the vocal line, whose participation is every bit as vigorous. Accordingly, there is little doubling of parts, and this has resulted in a thinner texture. The dynamic range is mostly *mezzo forte* and *forte*; *staccato* markings and accents abound.

The thematic material is made up of several motives which are combined and recombined so as to form continuous and ever changing, interlocking lines. The first such motives and the line formed from them is seen in Example 260 as

Ex. 260

they appear in the piano reduction, five measures prior to the soloist's entry. But another line containing variants of some of the original motives plus two new ones – three *staccato* eighths and a sequence of falling fifths – soon dominates the texture from measures 23 through 68, by far the largest portion of the song. The singer also takes an active role in presentations of this line, which, as seen in a violin statement (Example 261), would appear to make an excellent fugue subject, and, in fact, this statement initiates a fairly strict fugato with tonic-dominant relationships and close stretto entries. The qualifying adjective,

Ex. 261

'fairly', is a reference to the absence of the falling fifths in the vocal line and first violins. Some, but not all of the statements that precede and follow the fugato section are less stringent in that they are shorter and have different endings. As such, they are merely inexact imitative entries.

The song concludes with a soft seven-measure, *molto meno mosso* section, which matches the mood of the sonnet's final couplet: 'Then you fair flower, in whom fresh youth doth reign,/Prepare yourself new love to entertain.' A series of quiet, quarter-note chords below and then above a sustained B flat pedal underlies a subdued, but flowing vocal line. However, the song is not permitted to end in this serious vein for, beneath the tenor's final, sustained B flat, the orchestra repeats its opening passage up to and including the chord in the middle of the third measure of Example 260. The original tempo and dynamic level are also reproduced.

The third song is a setting of Sonnet 6, a poem that addresses the subject of a long-lasting love versus one 'of baser kind'. Such a love 'is harder won' and the poet compares it to the 'dureful oak, whose sap is not yet dried', and which needs a long time 'ere it conceive the kindling fire:/But when it once doth burn, it doth divide/Great heat, and makes his flames to heav'n aspire.' The concluding couplet provides the customary change of thought: 'Then think not long in taking little pain,/To knit the knot, that ever shall remain.'

Sonnet 6 is marked *Lento ma non troppo* ($\downarrow$ = 88), or just a shade faster than the tempo of Sonnet 2, the opening song, and like it there is a fluctuation between 3/2 and 4/2 metres. Other similarities include the chordal texture, composed of non-imitative moving parts, and the partial dichotomy of diatonicism and chromaticism. Here, as in Sonnet 2 it is the accompaniment that is generally chromatic, and the vocal line that is mainly diatonic. However, there is an important difference between the chromaticism of these two settings, that of the earlier song being harmonic by virtue of its function as the agent of change in a lengthy transitional passage. In Sonnet 6 the chromaticism is both harmonic and melodic, its harmonic role being the same as in Sonnet 2. The melodic chromaticism is entirely linear and seems to be directed towards underscoring the love-sick atmosphere of the poem. The song's opening passage reveals an unhurried, semitonal ascent and descent through F sharp minor, while the vocal line above is solidly diatonic. The by now familiar mirror image, formed by the contrary motion in the *divisi* first violin parts, is also present in the passage.

Sonnet 43 is another *Lento ma non troppo* setting, but the tempo is slower ($\downarrow$ = 76). The poem is the most expressive of the five, and Rubbra's setting is eminently worthy of it. The poet is in a quandary as to whether he should speak his love or be silent, for 'if I speak, her wrath renew I shall:/And if I silent be, my heart will break,/Or choked be with overflowing gall.' He decides that silence is to be his course, and that she, 'with her deep wit' will be able to read the love that is in his eyes.

The elements we have observed in the two preceding *Lento* settings are also present here: fluctuating metres, the dichotomy of diatonicism and chromaticism, and the meticulous attention paid to dynamic shadings. The separation of diatonic and chromatic elements is complete except for a very short and accented chromatic descent in the voice part. Moving from B to F sharp, it is obviously intended to stress the words, 'to plead'.

The vocal line begins with a figure that, quite surprisingly, never reappears in the voice, although at several points later in the song its three ascending notes lead one to expect the whole figure. However, it is by no means wasted, for in the orchestra it completely dominates the proceedings in two places: measures 9–15 and 27–9. There seems to be no particular reason for the figure's absence from the vocal line after its early appearance and it would be idle to speculate. However, there may be a plausible connection between its early appearance in the voice and its later orchestral statements, for when it is assigned to the voice the words are 'Shall I then silent be...?' and when the orchestra takes it up the poet is complaining about the 'tyranny' he is undergoing, for his heart is in 'thrall' and his tongue is restrained so that 'neither I may speak nor think at all,/But like a stupid stock in silence die.' Certainly the drooping figure underscores the disconsolate atmosphere.

However, a far more potent contributor to the overall atmosphere, and one that is active from the very start is the melodic chromaticism of the descending chords – a series that occupies four measures and is then immediately repeated for another four. Beneath the eight measures a G pedal in the lower strings provides a foundation, but it is an insecure and uneasy foundation in two respects: first, it is the mediant and not the tonic of E minor, the overall key of the song, which the soloist has established in the first measure as he sets forth the figure referred to above; and, second, it is a note with which all of the chords except two are dissonant. This last would not be true if the chords were concordant within themselves, but D naturals against D sharps, E flats against E naturals, and so on, are the rule. Three chords only are consonant – the opening E major, the closing E minor and a C sharp minor chord. Of these the G sharps in the first and third are at odds with the G pedal. All this may seem quite harsh, but the *pianissimo* level and the *con sordino* timbre (the latter to be observed throughout the song) create a veiled, indistinct sound of great beauty.

Another phase of the accompaniment is common to many slow movements and pieces in nearly all of the genres in which Rubbra worked: a series of repeated notes, usually arranged in a melodic pattern, in which some form of syncopation is often present. A similarly constructed passage appeared in Sonnet 6. Neither passage is long and each soon gives way to other Rubbra hallmarks: repeated notes in a chromatically descending pattern, and repeated notes on the same pitch. All such patterns, whether in small pieces or in symphonic movements, underline the gravity of a text or an instrumental mood.

It is no accident that, with the exception of the *Allegro* setting of Sonnet 4, the vocal lines of these poems have received scant attention. The reason for this is soon apparent: the unity achieved in Sonnet 4 is complete and entirely satisfactory, for the vocal line and accompaniment seem to have sprung from one creative impulse. This unity is lacking in the first two *Lento* settings, but in Sonnet 43 the vocal line is more direct and better focused than in the two earlier *Lentos*. This more disciplined vocal line with its fewer abrupt directional changes may have resulted from a conscious effort on the composer's part to craft a voice part that differed substantially from the preceding *Lentos*. Perhaps the basic problem is that three slow settings out of five songs is both limiting and unbalanced. Had the composer chosen poems with more diverse subject matter the result would undoubtedly have been songs with greater contrasts. It would appear that he recognized these limitations, and in his struggle to overcome them, he met with only partial success.

The vigorous and lusty fifth song, a setting of Sonnet 68, 'Most Glorious Lord of Life', was treated in the previous chapter where Rubbra's choral arrangement formed the fourth movement of the *Cantata di Camera*.

Amoretti

In Chapter 1 Rubbra told how Joseph Williams (now Stainer and Bell) had approached him for 'a couple of works... as they were building up their new catalogue of music'. One of these works was the second group of five Spenser settings, bearing the title of the poet's sonnet-sequence, *Amoretti*. Besides the identifying title there are significant differences with respect to the first series and one can assume that these were the fruits of the revisions which Rubbra made before he submitted the work. Undoubtedly realizing that a string orchestra severely limited performance possibilities, he substituted a string quartet and even authorized a piano in lieu of that. The really important changes, however, concern the greater simplicity and directness of the music. (A nice touch in the Joseph Williams score of 1942 is the prefacing of each song with its sonnet in Elizabethan English.)

The first song is a setting of Sonnet 78, 'Lackyng my love, I go from place to place,/Lyke a young fawne, that late hath lost the hynd;/And seeke each where, where last I sawe her face,/Whose ymage yet I carry fresh in mynd.' The only tempo indication is ♩ = 60; and like the remaining songs in this series there is no key signature.

Noticeable right from the start is a closer partnership between voice and accompaniment, each of which demonstrates the changes mentioned above. And the choice of this particular sonnet was a happy one, for the imagery evoked by the poet as he goes 'from place to place' seeking his love is amusingly depicted in the seemingly aimless rise and fall of the vocal line, and the unexpected and unrelated chords of the accompaniment that suggest one place after another. The act of searching is given expression in the opening measure as voice and accompaniment immediately head in different directions (Example

Ex. 262

La - ckyng - my   love,   I   go   from place to   place,   Lyke a   young

262). This musical portrayal is both sly and subtle, and an Elizabethan would have appreciated these qualities and enjoyed the gentle humour of the passage. However, during the next four lines the poet becomes increasingly distressed and anxious: 'I seeke the fields with her late footing synd;/I seeke her bowre with her late presence deckt./Yet nor in field nor bowre I can her fynd;/Yet field and bowre are full of her aspect.' Musically these feelings are expressed by pungent, ascending dissonances between the cello and viola – B sharp versus A sharp; C sharp versus B sharp; D against C sharp, and so on – while in the vocal line only the shortest of breaths may be taken between 'synd' and 'I', as the poet presses forward with his unhappy tale. Gradually the dissonances cease as the poet becomes more and more resigned to not finding his love. By the time the couplet arrives he is at peace: 'Ceasse then, myne eyes, to seeke her selfe to see;/And let my thoughts behold her selfe in mee.' These lines are simply and expressively set, accompanied by a rising, *pianissimo* line arranged as a sequence. The interrelationship of the vocal line with this sequential passage produces shifting harmonies within the context of the A flat minor (G sharp minor) that, with the exception of the unstable passages in the middle, dominates the song. A chordal descent in the last two measures ends the song in A flat major.

The frame of mind that has pervaded the first song is completely swept away when 'Fresh Spring, the herald of loves mighty king' bursts upon the scene in a setting of Sonnet 70. Marked *Allegro festivo e bucolico* ($\downarrow$ = 138), the song has an infectious enthusiasm that is expressed in a never wavering swirl of sound. The freely-flowing vocal line is through-composed. Two dissimilar but complementary elements appearing simultaneously form the bulk of the accompaniment. One is a line of detached, heavily accented and disjunct quarter notes that produce a robust and hearty melody well suited to the words. The other is a very common figure made from three sixteenths preceded by a sixteenth rest. At times these groups are so arranged as to form a melody. A structure of sorts is created when the first ten measures of accompaniment are repeated, but the interesting point is how well the through-composed vocal line spans both statements.

The sonnet's seventh and eighth lines – 'Tell her [my love] the joyous time will not be staid,/Unlesse she doe him [spring] by the forelock take' – bring a change of mood in the music, which includes a four-measure *forte*, *allargando* and a complete change in the accompanimental patterns. The vocal line *seems* different owing to the tempo change, the two beats on a high G on 'tell', and the generally high *tessitura*, but it is not substantially different from what has gone before and the characteristics that identify the line as through-composed remain. The original accompanimental patterns – but to different notes – return, but they are soon replaced by triplets. A five-measure return of the original pattern and a chordal ascending scale bring this setting to its conclusion.

In the final analysis it is best to view this song as a compromise between the impulsive and unstructured enthusiasm of the vocal line and the structured accompaniment, which, however, is not so organized as to inhibit the former in any way. The song is very quickly over, the duration being one and a half minutes according to the note in the score.

The third song, a setting of Sonnet 89, the concluding poem in Spenser's sequence, is a full two minutes longer in performance. The poet likens his mourning for his absent mate to that of a dove, who 'in her songs, sends many a wishfull vow/For his returne that seemes to linger late.' Nothing will comfort him 'but her owne joyous sight', and until that time comes, 'Dark is my day, whyles her fayre light I mis,/And dead my life that wants such lively blis.'

Rubbra's setting carries no tempo marking other than ♩ = 52; and unlike the two previous songs in this series where there are changing metres, the 4/2 is constant throughout. The poem's gloomy mood has been caught and admirably expressed by the composer, but a word of caution is in order with regard to performance, for of all these Series 2 settings this has the most pitfalls for both the singer and the instrumentalists. The slow tempo and the regularity of the beat must not be exaggerated. Should they be, the result will inevitably produce a plodding and over-accented interpretation. The string players must be especially careful not to overdo their accents. These potential problems are eased in the song's middle section where the tempo is *più mosso*, ♩ = 72, but the accents on the first and third beats are still a danger if not properly handled. The return of tempo 1 for the couplet (quoted above) gives us a new idea in which the accompaniment's two accents per measure are replaced by four, evenly stressed chords. These occupy the first measure only of an expressive, two-measure segment that is heard three times.

The entire vocal line is through-composed, but the accompaniment has sufficient repeated elements to give it a kind of structure even though none of them returns in exactly the same way or to the same harmonies. The principal accompanimental element for the song's first half is a descending scale from E: major to begin with and chromatic later on. Suspensions are another important factor. Altogether, this is an expressive and beautiful setting, but it should be performed by only sensitive and experienced musicians.

Sonnet 37 is the text for the fourth setting and it is not an exaggeration to say that the subject matter of the poem is responsible for the main musical idea, first announced by the singer in the manner of a recitative over a *pianissimo* and almost stationary cello line. Its first half is skilfully introduced at the point where the full quartet enters for the first time, and it is here that the link between words and music becomes apparent. The second quatrain reads, 'Is it that mens frayle eyes, which gaze too bold,/She may entangle in that golden snare;/And, being caught, may craftily enfold/Theyr weaker harts, which are not wel aware?' The connection is between 'that golden snare' – a reference to her 'golden tresses' in the first line (Example 263) and the three stretto entries

Ex. 263

of the bracketed segment in the example, which overlap so closely as to suggest a mesh or web. This analogy is appropriate not only aurally by virtue of the close texture and inflexibility of the material, but also visually because of the three accented quarters that, in their dense stretto arrangement of nine successive Es, present a barrier-like appearance. In succeeding statements the material is condensed by the joining of the three stressed notes to the chromatic figure at the start of measure 2 (the latter is pitched a half-step lower than the repeated notes). Three such statements occur in tandem, and five stretto statements are found near the end. In all of these rather stern figures there is no escaping the sense of entrapment. (Although the allusions and material are entirely different, one is reminded of the similarly impersonal figure used by Bach in his larger chorale-prelude setting of 'These Are The Holy Ten Commandments'.)

Between these statements of the stretto figure there are other, more relaxed segments, one of which is a one-measure series of descending chords containing notes moving in contrary directions. Following the first appearance of these chords there are two sequential repetitions at the distance of a descending major second. A similar situation is found at the end of the song, but the third sequential member continues its descent. The words during this passage are 'Fondnesse it were for any, being free,/To covet fetters, though they golden bee.' Beneath the last word a soft statement of the stern figure concludes the song.

It seems odd that following its opening, recitative-like statement of the song's principal material, the vocal line's references to it are few and far between. Yet the word-painting that is such an important part of this material is not left entirely to the accompaniment, for a fine example of it occurs in the vocal line when 'she may entangle' is sung to a melisma of fifteen notes, grouped into triplets and set to an appropriately undulating line. This is one of the few melismas to be found in Rubbra's songs and its purpose here is unmistakeable.

The fifth and final song of *Amoretti* is a relaxed setting of Sonnet 40's cheerful and pleasant text: 'Mark when she smiles with amiable cheare,/And tell me whereto can ye lyken it.' The relaxation extends to all components of the song – the tempo, *Moderato grazioso* ($\downarrow$ = 112); the vocal line, which possesses a simple elegance; and particularly the accompaniment, whose gracefully rising and falling chains of eighths provide a ribbon of continuous movement right to the final chord. Associated with and embedded in the strands of eighth notes are short, accented segments, of which some are indirectly related to segments in the vocal line. Still others bear a closer relationship. One belonging to the latter category is shared by the first violin and cello in a stretto arrangement. But the closest link between voice and accompaniment comes when, during three measures of rest for the voice, the latter's opening music is given to the first violin.

The different accompanimental forces used in these ten settings of Spenser make it impossible to regard the two series as forming a song-cycle, but it might be interesting to consider how they could be thought of as such. Of course, liberties would have to be taken by reducing the string orchestra of the first series to the quartet of the second, or upgrading the 'reduction for rehearsal' piano accompaniments of the first series to the piano alternatives in the second. Of these options, the second is the more practical and the least likely to offend the purist, but the first would be preferable in terms of accompanimental richness. Both options would enable all ten songs to be performed as a unit, but such a cycle would be loose in the sense that the poems are all by the same poet and on the same general subject: love. A serious obstacle might be the absence of a tonal link between any song and its successor. While such links are not essential to the success of a song-cycle, they do promote a sense of continuity and unity.

Of the two principal reviews of *Amoretti* reproduced below, the first by Arthur Hutchings is certainly the more probing and the more perceptive. In my opinion, it is not only an accurate assessment, but it is even more valuable because it comes from the pen of a genuine Rubbra admirer:

> Britten writes brilliantly for small and occasional resources. Not so Rubbra, whose limitation – the inability to unbend easily – is at least shared with Beethoven. He needs room in which to work. The same modulation which makes a tremendous

swerve when time has established tonal contacts becomes incidental, maybe congesting, in the line of a song. The sonnets are not congested, but they are too serious; Rubbra's sincerity maintains an intensity throughout, which, with his particular turn of genius, should grow in the due course of a long movement. One could remember one of his biggest symphonic movements in fewer hearings than one of these sonnets demands. And if one of Rubbra's champions says: 'Ah... but the motet and madrigal were full of recalcitrant parts...' I must reply: 'Yes. With plenty of blanks. Besides, the motet repeated each phrase, if only contrapuntally, and so *moved* to its intense moments.' Rubbra writes a whole sonnet with the intensity found only in part of a motet... see, for instance, No. 3, 'Lyke As The Culver.'[11]

Westrup in his more inclusive review summarizes several of the work's strongest points:

> The problems of the sonnet are solved here with apparent ease [we are not told what those problems are]. The vocal line flows smoothly and is at the same time an integral part of the texture. One has the impression not that the voice is supported by the quartet but that five parts are associated on equal terms. The cadences of all five songs are beautifully handled. The music is both personal and faithful to the mood of the words. These are distinguished settings which call for the utmost artistry in performance.[12]

Six years and ten opus numbers intervened before Rubbra's next song. The gap was filled with the first four symphonies, the Five Madrigals, the Farnaby Improvisations, and works of lesser importance. Such gaps became increasingly frequent as larger works occupied the composer, but the growing artistic maturity that led to them also extended into the realm of the smaller works – a fact not always appreciated.

Nocturne

Nocturne, Op. 54, was composed in 1941 to a poem by the Greek lyric poet, Alcman, who was born in Sardis, Lydia, in 630 BC. He lived first as a slave, and later as a freedman in Sparta. He wrote *Parthenia*, which were songs for choruses of virgins; bridal hymns; and poems in praise of love and wine. In *Nocturne*, translated by H.T. Wade-Gery, we are told of all the things that sleep: 'the far peaks, the great ravines, the foothills, and the streams. Asleep are trees, and hivèd bees', and so on.

Perhaps the simple, direct imagery of Alcman's poem as opposed to the elaborate and artificial imagery of Spenser is what makes this song so immediately attractive. The poetry has a more universal appeal, for certainly today's reader can more easily identify with the vivid scene painted by Alcman – including 'the glooming seas, the monsters in their deeps' – than he can with the bewildered, love-sick youth in some of the *Amoretti* sonnets. Not surprisingly, Rubbra's setting reflects this difference and as one listens, the wish that the composer had set more poems depicting emotions and situations experienced by the *average* person recurs again and again. Had he done so his body of songs might have matched those of Warlock and Finzi, for it seems evident that he was most successful as a song composer when he chose simpler texts such as *The Night, In Dark Weather* and *Nocturne*.

Rubbra's setting of the latter is for medium voice and piano in a 3/4 metre, marked *Andante piacevole*. In a three-measure introduction the piano established just the right framework for suggesting not only the peace associated with night, but also the depth of a profound sleep. Peace is communicated by way of a major key (G flat), very little motion and a *pianissimo* dynamic. Deep sleep is suggested by wide, vertical spacing in the chordal fabric and recurring rhythmic figures. A sense of mystery is also introduced by means of rich sonorities and some gentle dissonances whose exact components are veiled by the lower chord members. A very subtle touch is the distinct Lydian flavour of some of the progressions – an obvious connection with the poet's place of birth. All of these features appear in Example 264 and once begun, they continue throughout the song.

Ex. 264

At the midpoint another component is introduced for a total of five and a half measures, but then allowed to disappear. Its presence illustrates one of the remarkable things about Rubbra's music: the ease and, particularly, the unobtrusiveness with which small bits of contrapuntal writing are suddenly injected into a prevailing homophonic context. In this instance a series of high chords is duplicated two octaves lower in a close stretto arrangement. Of course the texture has thereby become more dense, but not to the extent of obscuring the vocal line.

As for the vocal line *per se*, its soothing languor and gentle movement are perfect vehicles for the words. A particularly beautiful touch comes during the final line, 'And every bird, its wide wings folded, sleeps.' The setting of the last two words is one of the most sensitive moments in all of Rubbra's songs, and it is so simply managed. The downward octave leap on 'folded' seems physically to suggest the verb, while the descending chords –again with a Lydian flavour – delicately carry out the action more gradually. Then the emphasis on 'sleeps', denoted not only by the accent but also an intervening rest. A second chord series – this time containing cross-relations between the C sharp in the first chord and C natural in the third – continues to suggest the descent into sleep.

From a practical standpoint the singer needs the rest preceding the F flat on 'sleeps' because the latter must be held for eight and a half beats. The song concludes with substantially the same chordal harmonies as those which opened it.

Three Psalms

Three Psalms for Low Voice and Piano, Op. 61, dates from 1946, following a hiatus in song composition of five years. Some important works composed during the interval were *The Morning Watch*, *Soliloquy*, *Missa Cantuariensis* and the Cello Sonata. Rubbra selected Psalms 6, 23 and 150, each of which bears a dedication to Kathleen Ferrier.

> In the first, 'O Lord, rebuke me not in thine anger', the soul's passionate cry is strikingly set to as expressive a declamatory line as the composer has ever given us, with a no less effective accompaniment, mainly ostinato with the left hand duplicating the right two octaves lower. Some of the resonances of the piano part in the slow tempo Largo seem to be audible more to the composer's ear than to an ordinary listener's, but the occasional lacuna may well be accepted as in keeping with the style of the piece.[13]

To put some detail on these remarks: the declamatory line, indicated to be sung *parlando*, is entirely through-composed – not at all surprising in view of the increasingly large number of Rubbra songs where this is the case. Such treatment is primarily a response to the text being set and in Psalm 6 there is a distinct progression from the petitions with which it begins, through the complaining stage, to the confidence of the concluding lines. The dramatic nature of the vocal line is confirmed and emphasized by its compass: one note under two octaves – F sharp to E – the greatest spread of the three Psalms; the separation of each petition or declamatory statement from its neighbour by rests; and, of course, the petitions and statements themselves. Some of the latter contain examples of word-painting, the most interesting of which is the tortuous, chromatic figure to which 'groaning' is set.

The ostinato that makes up the accompaniment is sounded eight times. However, between statements 6 and 7 there is a short variant, while between the seventh and eighth a kind of parenthesis, consisting of different figures that

Ex. 265

fill four measures, intervenes between *a* and the two *b* statements into which the ostinato is divided (Example 265). With one exception the two-octave duplication of the *b* statements is preserved, but some variety is introduced into the *a* statements by means of notes interposed between its main beats. As these notes change in successive entries, so do the harmonies. (If in reading or listening to this ostinato the reader is reminded of two previously cited passages, he is quite correct: the *Grave* theme that begins the last movement of the Fourth Symphony, and the passacaglia theme from the Seventh Symphony, which was, of course, composed years later. Although these are family rather than literal resemblances, the passacaglia theme is more closely akin.)

Considered now as a whole the vocal line and accompaniment are fused into a most sensitive partnership, capable of rapid adjustments to the changing moods of the text. It is remarkable that the seemingly inflexible ostinato can be made to sound stern or gentle as required and by the simplest means: harmonic changes of an elementary nature and dynamic changes. The vocal line's sensitivity to the words is, of course, more obvious, being a matter of linear inflection. In the final analysis the compatibility of two such diverse elements is the central achievement of this song.

Ivor Keys points out in his review of the next song that 'it is with surprise that one finds much the same technique applied to "The Lord Is My Shepherd"'.[14] On the surface this appears to be an accurate observation, but a more searching inquiry shows it to be superficial and ultimately incorrect. His remark may be a reference to the little figure and its inversion, both of which are shared by voice and accompaniment (unlike the situation in Psalm 6), or, more likely, it may be to the larger unit of which these figures are a part. If it is to the latter, then one must be prepared to accept that 'the same technique' has produced an ostinato whose length is approximately eight measures. In view of the fact that these measures are filled with a smoothly flowing, lyrical line with none of the terseness so often associated with an ostinato, this theory must be called into question even though there are two repetitions of the eight measures. But here, another objection arises: the repetitions depart radically from the prototype, each in a different way and for a different reason – matters that will be dealt with shortly.

The two figures that appear so often and so prominently in Psalm 23 may be compared with the figures in Psalm 6. The latter, particularly b^1 and b^2, are austere and inflexible even when their dynamic level is soft; those in Psalm 23 are mild and rounded. It is even possible to think of them as written out ornaments (Example 266). And so, for all of the above reasons the theory that any part of this accompaniment contains an ostinato in the sense in which the word is usually understood is fallacious.

The remainder of Keys's review also calls for clarification:

> the piano writing becomes on occasion even barer [than that of Psalm 6], and singers may well feel that the composer might have given them more help in achieving the tenderness that the familiar words inevitably invoke. The hearing of a

Ex. 266

devoted performance only strengthens the impression of this conflict of manner and sentiment.[15]

An examination of the score reveals that there are, indeed, 'barer' patches in the piano part – places where the texture has been reduced to two lines. Of course, the two *b* patterns in Psalm 6 are always in two parts, but the affective consequences in each case are entirely different, as are the means used to achieve them. In Psalm 6 the impersonality of the two-octave separation of parts is clearly apparent – almost physically experienced. In Psalm 23, measure 5, two lines begin to move away from one another, and when each reaches its destination in measure 6, they are over three octaves apart. Yet the emotive effect is one of warmth, for the upper line soars to its climactic point, and there is a liquid flow in the scalic movement of both hands. In measures 7–8 the writing becomes even more spare as right-hand sixteenths and left-hand quarters descend in scalic motion into the depths. At the start of the passage the distance is three octaves, but the quicker motion of the sixteenths reduces this to two octaves at the end. The reason behind the passage is the text: 'He leadeth me beside the still waters.' 'Still' also implies depth. Another two-part descending passage appropriately accompanies 'the valley of the shadow of death'.

The tenderness thought by the reviewer to be in short supply seems quite adequate. One can sense it in the gently curving lines of both voice and piano and it is particularly apparent in two carefully marked places: the *tenuto* and accents above 'my shepherd' and the *rallentando* and *pianissimo* of 'beside the still waters'. At other points, such as the beautifully sculpted line, 'for Thou are with me; Thy rod and staff, they comfort me', discreet and expressive emphases are the performer's prerogative, as they always are.

To return now to the subject of deviations from the original eight-measure phrase, measure 13, which equals measure 6, provides an excellent example of the ease with which Rubbra moves from one tonality to another by simply inflecting the notes of the repeated material before introducing something new.

The topmost accompanimental line in measure 6 – cited above in connection with bare patches – is a restatement of x^1 (Example 266). In 13 it is moved down a half step: from B minor/D major to D flat minor/E flat minor. This change is followed in 14 by a new descending line – also cited above – which accompanies 'the valley of the shadow of death'. From the end of 15 and into 16, x^1 appears in both hands in G flat, but under a held-out B flat, F sharp (= G flat) appears, and x^1 resumes its original tonality. The third eight-measure statement then begins, only to be altered halfway through measure 22 with the introduction of more new material intended to match the exuberance of 'Thou anointest my head with oil; my cup runneth over.'

The *forte* statement of x^1 accompanying 'over' in the line just quoted leads one to expect a fourth eight-measure phrase that, if not wholly faithful to the original, will introduce changes on the order of those just reported. But as we have seen many times before, Rubbra seldom does the obvious or expected. In this instance the final page of the song marks a total departure from any of the phrases, and well it should, for the text confidently proclaims that 'Surely goodness and mercy shall follow me', and so on to the end. The words 'mercy', 'dwell' and 'Lord' are given extra emphasis by being partially set to thirty-seconds. The tonality throughout this final page is an undeviating D major and its effect in both voice and piano is that of a triumphant, cadential chord. The accompaniment considerably furthers this impression with two series of accented, eighth-note patterns that dominate the surrounding sixteenth-note movement. A certain pianistic dexterity is required because of the hand crossing and the arrangement of the first pattern in octaves. Although no *crescendo* is indicated throughout the last page, it is difficult to hold back in view of the enthusiasm written into both voice and piano parts – an enthusiasm that brings the song to a *fortissimo* conclusion.

For the final song of this set Rubbra selected the familiar text of Psalm 150, 'Praise ye the Lord', followed in due course by the naming of the various instruments – trumpet, psaltery, harp, organ, and so on – with which He is to be praised. As Keys remarks, 'the voice part is difficult in both time and intonation, but does not demand an excessive compass.'[16] The metre is 6/8 with no changes, and the tempo is *Allegro risoluto*.

The rhythmic difficulties for the singer begin almost at once, but it is not the three quarters cutting across the 6/8 on the first syllable of 'sanctuary' that pose the problem. It is the two sixteenths in the next measure – 6 – that must be precisely fitted in between a quarter, tied over from the previous measure, and a dotted quarter. The difficulty is compounded by the rather tongue-twisting nature of the two short syllables – 'tu-a' sung to the sixteenths. An even more awkward spot comes three measures later when 'firmament' is set to two sixteenths, a quarter tied to the first of two succeeding sixteenths, and another quarter. In both instances the piano is very assertive in its 6/8 patterns and this multiplies the difficulties. Thereafter, except for the need to be a bit cautious, the singer's rhythmic problems are over.

The intonational difficulties are far more serious. They begin about a third of the way through the song when the F major tonic is quitted in favour of some indefinite harmonies on the way to a clear D major. They are really the fault of the accompaniment which, by the way, offers no help of any consequence to the singer. They are made worse in the transitional passages because of dissonances between voice and piano. When, presently, there is an abrupt return to F major from D major the listener has not had time to adjust to the sudden change. This is another example of the problem mentioned by Hutchings in connection with the *Amoretti* sonnets: a modulation or transition that has little room in which to manoeuvre, and which fails to convince the listener of the composer's intent. I suspect the passage will never sound right. Simply put, these intonational problems are not the singer's fault.

There is no end to the energy put forth in the accompaniment and this has its good and bad points. On the plus side is the 'joyful noise' made unto the Lord. The main negative aspect is that the process employed in the making of that noise is sometimes ruthless, for imitative figures assigned to each hand proceed to their logical goals regardless of the clashes en route or at the phrase endings. When, as occasionally happens, the vocal line comes into conflict with these imitative voices the sense of key is weakened, and the listener is puzzled and confused – all the more in view of the strong tonal context in which the song as a whole has been conceived. To ensure as accurate a performance as possible in these ambiguous areas, it is strongly recommended that singers with a wide vibrato do not attempt this song.

O Excellent Virgin Princess

In his Op. 77 of 1952 Rubbra returned to the string quartet as the accompanimental medium for *O Excellent Virgin Princess*. As mentioned earlier, this song and *O My Deir Hert* were published together in 1953. The poem, simple and touching, is the concluding section of a longer poem by François Villon (1431–80), called *His Mother's Service to Our Lady*, probably composed in 1450. The English translation is by Dante Gabriel Rossetti.

The metre signature is 6/4, 7/4 and the entire song up to the penultimate twelfth measure is composed of measures that alternate between these. In each of the 7/4 measures a dotted line divides the material into beats of 3 + 4. The tempo is marked, 'Slow'.

The vocal line pursues a leisurely, beautifully flowing and unstructured course above an equally leisurely accompaniment. The latter, however, is very carefully structured, for it is built on just two measures of music whose metrical design follows the alternating pattern mentioned above. Following the two initial measures there are five repetitions of the pattern. Everything, including the disposition of the four parts, is repeated exactly, with two small exceptions: the viola and cello parts of the opening measure are exchanged in succeeding repetitions, and in the penultimate measure normal adjustments are made in preparation for the cadence.

What is revealed in this accompaniment is a clever, modern adaptation of the isorhythmic and isomelic techniques found in the medieval French motet. The rhythmic segment, known as the *talea,* and the melodic segment or *color,* are here exactly equal in length: two measures (in the French prototype this is unusual).[17] The freedom of the vocal line is particularly satisfying, for it perfectly complements and balances the accompaniment's predictable regularity. It totally ignores the patterns beneath it as it arches across barlines. The expression markings throughout the song in both voice and quartet are numerous and if carefully observed they are quite sufficient to overcome any sense of rigidity in the organized patterns. The dynamic level ranges from *piano* to *forte.*

Singers and instrumentalists would do well to perform both this song and its companion, *O My Deir Hert,* as a unit on the same programme. The wide span of the opus numbers – 5 and 77 – means nothing, for it will be recalled that *O My Deir Hert* was revised in 1952, the same year in which *O Excellent Virgin Princess* was composed. The medieval poems, their treatment and the quartet accompaniments link them together. The key relationship also promotes a smooth transition: *O My Deir Hert* ends on a D major chord following a D minor/ Phrygian context and *O Excellent Virgin Princess* is in F major. This easy access with respect to key suggests that the composer intended the songs to be performed as a unit.

Ode to the Queen

This three-movement work for medium voice and orchestra, Op. 83,

> was commissioned by the BBC for the 1953 Coronation Week, and was first performed by Anne Wood and the BBC Symphony Orchestra under Sir Malcolm Sargent on June 6 of that year.
>
> The first poem is taken from Crashaw's 'Upon the King's Coronation', the second from Davenant's 'To the Queen: Entertained at Night by the Countess of Anglesey', and the third from Campion's 'A relationship of the Late Royal Entertainment given by the Right Honourable the Lord Knowles at Cawsome House near Reading to our most gracious Queene, Queene Anne, 1613'.[18]

The queen referred to is Anne of Denmark, the wife of James I.

These songs are, owing to their texts, public music for a very special occasion and once performed in the fulfilment of that purpose they stand only a very small chance of ever being heard again. This is even more true where a large orchestra is involved. Piano reductions (one is provided here) are certainly not satisfactory substitutes, particularly as in this work, where brilliant fanfares, trills, string tremolos and other orchestral effects are necessary adjuncts.

The first song, 'Sound Forth Celestial Organs', is by far the longest of the three. The starting metre signature is 3/4, but as the piece moves on there is a variety of other metres with frequent changes from one to the other. The dominant one proves to be 6/8. *Moderato quasi una fantasia* is the designated tempo with a subheading of ♩ = 144 *ma molto flessibile*.

The song opens with a thirty-one measure orchestral introduction that contains all of the above-mentioned effects. Just prior to the singer's *forte* entrance the tempo has been slowed substantially so that the words of the title and those that follow may ring out in all their majesty. The style is decidedly declamatory, and much of the rest of the song proceeds in like manner. Tempo I returns in measure 122 when the opening orchestral flourishes are repeated note for note. The same *Allargando molto* precedes the singer's entrance, and her first four measures are exactly as before. But the exultation of 'Shine forth, ye flaming sparks of Deity' and the lines that immediately follow gradually wanes. The orchestral support is reduced to tremolo strings, and the mood takes on the nature of a petition: 'Fix'd in your spheres of glory, shed from thence/The treasures of our lives, your influence.' A tranquil, hushed *Adagio* brings the song to its conclusion with the words, 'For if you set, who may not justly fear/The world will be one ocean, one great tear?'

The direction 'quasi una fantasia', has more meaning here than is often the case, for instead of suggesting, as it so often does, some vague, generalized atmosphere, it points back to a particular period in music history that exhibits prototypes of some figures seen and heard in this song. The period is that of John Bull (*c*.1562–1628) and Giles Farnaby (*c*.1563–1640), two of the most eminent composers for the virginal, and the figures in the present song that bring them to mind are the flourishes and runs in sixteenths and thirty-seconds. They are important features in the improvisatory-type pieces of these composers. However, their presence here is no more a slavish imitation of the originals than are the isorhythmic and isomelic techniques in Op. 77. Once again the breadth of Rubbra's knowledge and understanding of earlier periods has been demonstrated, but even more significant is the imagination he displayed in seeing a chronological link between the poet of his first song and composers of the same period. It was a happy discovery, for in finding new uses for older idioms and applying them to this song a far more interesting accompaniment was created. It is refreshing to find that an elaborate, metaphorical text, selected for a great occasion, does not have to be cluttered with the customary, predictable fanfares that have grown stale with overuse. The figures seen in Example 267 are typical and come from the orchestral interlude.

An important aspect of the *fantasia*, both as a type (form is the wrong word) and as a later style derived from it, is its rhythmic freedom and flexibility. Rubbra's direction, *ma molto flessibile*, is an acknowledgement of this. But it should be understood that the means whereby flexibility is achieved are unwritten, for except in over-edited editions of Renaissance and Baroque music the pages indicate nothing. Since the composer and performer of all such pieces were one and the same no directions were needed. This fact does not, of course, help the modern performer, who must rely on his knowledge of the basic style

Ex. 267

as well as his innate sense of taste. The conductor and singer of 'Sound Forth Celestial Organs' must do the same, for Rubbra likewise has rightly included no directions to indicate where *accelerandos* and *ritardandos* should be applied.

The setting of Sir William Davenant's 'Fair As Unshaded Light', the second of these songs, is exceptionally beautiful, the delicacy of the poem having been superbly and sensitively matched. The key is G minor (although the song finishes on the dominant), and the metre signature is 8/8 with an explicit division of beats indicated: $\frac{3+2+3}{8}$. The tempo and expressive indication are *Poco adagio e tranquillo* ($\flat$= 50).

The rhythmic pattern is more subtle than the above figures indicate, for with very few exceptions syncopations dominate the orchestra. Gentle, soft dissonances are also plentiful. Against this interesting combination the vocal line pursues an independent course both rhythmically and melodically, as seen in Example 268 where the opening lines appear. Note the momentary dissonances between voice and accompaniment in measures 2 and 3 which, however, are mitigated by the soft dynamic levels in each element. Four measures later the rather haunting vocal line in measures 2–5 is duplicated in its entirety in the orchestra to the same syncopated chords of the example. Still later, the figure in measure 2 has been detached and given mainly to the orchestra. However, four of its statements have been rhythmically altered to even sixteenths and placed in an imitative texture, the only passage in the song given over to counterpoint. Almost immediately, the detached figure in its original note values and pitches is heard twice more in the orchestra. Earlier, some suspensions, created very simply by the syncopated movement of parts, provide a lovely accompaniment below the gentle vocal line. Altogether, this is a very memorable piece, entirely devoid of the pomp and pageantry usually associated with coronation music,

Ex. 268

but not at all out of place here. The music faithfully carries out the gentle beauty of the poem, which is, unfortunately, too long to be reproduced here.

The final piece to Campion's 'Yet Once Again, Let Us Our Measures Move', marks a return to the exultant mood of the first song, but in place of the orchestral flourishes and runs that play such an important part in the latter, the style here is unadorned, even plain. It demonstrates the composer's awareness that he is dealing with a poem whose unpretentious, simple enthusiasm is poles apart from the elaborate and artificial imagery of the first text. In conformity with this mood, everything is simpler: the metre is an unswerving ¢; the tempo is *Allegretto*, ♩ = 84; and the key is an unambiguous B flat. Indeed, of the sixty-eight measures, sixty-one stress the tonic. The majority of this total contains a combination of a repeating, accented B flat pedal accompanied by material in both voice and orchestra that is strongly centred on the tonic. Yet this is not tiresome, for enough is occurring to sustain interest at a high level. The orchestral movement is almost entirely in eighth-note figures during which imitation is an important feature at times. The figures have a Baroque-like cast and one in particular – the fanfare in fifths, heard in the middle and end of the song – is an almost direct quotation from the third movement of Bach's Brandenburg Concerto No. 2.

The vocal line has a simple, almost Handelian majesty befitting the occasion. It is brought about by a good balance of scalic and disjunct motion, the latter involving leaps of a fifth and an octave. The soloist's first eighteen measures are exactly reproduced in the song's last third to the same words except for 'Welcome, O welcome, ever-honoured Queen'. The rearrangement of some of the accompanimental elements under the second appearance of the soloist's material gives variety.

It is shameful that no notices of Ode to the Queen, either pro or con, can be found in any of the major musical journals around or after the time of its first performance. Yet the coronation efforts of other composers were duly reported. In fact, it is ironic that Rubbra himself reviewed some of them in his regularly allotted space in *The Monthly Musical Record*.

Two Sonnets

Three years elapsed between the Ode and Rubbra's next songs. In the interim the Piano Concerto, Op. 85, and the Machaut Fantasia were composed. The Sonnets were first performed at the Wigmore Hall on 9 June 1955 as part of the Arts Council's series of concerts devoted to English song.

> The new work – settings of two sonnets by William Alabaster (1567–1640) comprising an interlocked diptych for baritone, viola and piano – was performed by Bruce Boyce, Watson Forbes and the composer. The two slow songs, 'Upon the Crucifix' and 'On the Reed of Our Lord's Passion', were grave, darkly-coloured, deeply-felt meditations in a vein which Mr. Rubbra has made very much his own. The first song, whose texture was first rate, seemed to unfold rather more naturally than the second which did not altogether escape a certain lack of contrast, both within itself and with the first 'tableau'. The intimate commentary and occasional solo excursions of the viola were throughout beautifully managed.[19]

The diptych, No. 87 in the opus list, was completed appropriately enough during Holy Week of 1955, and bears the dedication 'For Antoinette, April 21, 1955'.

Alabaster had an interesting religious life. Following his graduation from Trinity College, Cambridge, he was appointed Chaplain to Robert Devereux, Earl of Essex, in 1596, but in the very next year he was converted to Catholicism. In their intensity his sonnets can be said to reflect this experience. He was soon arrested and stripped of his Anglican orders. He eventually deserted the Catholic Church, and by 1613–14 was again an Anglican. He later took a Doctor of Divinity at Cambridge and served James I as his Chaplain.

The first sonnet, *Upon the Crucifix*, sets forth two quite distinct emotional states and the musical setting closely parallels each of them. The first communicates a sense of deep satisfaction and inner peace: 'Now I have found thee I will evermore/Embrace this standard where thou sitts above', and so on. The music for these opening lines is a perfect expression of this sense; every element of voice and accompaniment has its part in this perfection. In Example 269, where the viola part has been omitted, note the feeling of permanence conveyed by the middle and low ranges of the repeating D major chords. 'Found' engages our attention at once because of its higher and longer note as well as the gentle dissonance to which it is set.

Ex. 269

The immediately following poetic lines and their musical setting become increasingly tense in response to the growing fervour: 'Feede greedie eyes, and from hence never rove;/Sucke hungrie Soule of this eternall store;/Issue my hart from thie two leaved dore,/And lett my lippes from kissinge not remove.' The first of these lines is still solidly rooted in D major, but then the tonality becomes fluid and transient, going first to A flat major (a tritone relationship), and thence via an indefinite A major to an equally ill-defined F minor. An instantly recognizable and distinctive harmony is introduced for 'eternall store' through the interaction of voice and accompaniment. Although this harmony is nothing more complicated than that produced by false relations, it stands out from its surroundings. This same, characteristic sound is heard several more times during the course of the song.

A four-measure instrumental interlude ushers in the second of the two emotional states mentioned above: one of intense longing as the poet cries, 'O thatt I weare transformed into love,/And as a plant might springe upon this flower.' The music of the interlude is freely imitative, leading one to expect a continuation of this change when the vocal line resumes, but this does not happen, probably because an overly busy accompaniment would tend to detract from the intensity of the words. In fact, the accompaniment, in returning to the chordal texture of the song's first part, assumes an almost Spartan simplicity. Both piano and viola have just three chords per measure during the new triple metre: rolled chords for the former, triply and quadruply-stopped, *pizzicato* chords for the latter. In both parts these chords oscillate between C and B major with a later alternation between D minor and C major. Rocking pedals on B and E underscore the restless longing as they interact dissonantly with the C major and D minor chords respectively. Above all this the vocal line consists mainly of sixteenths with a few quarters and eighths reserved for the most important words. Its compass is narrow and it is centred around B – features that in a quiet and moving way emphasize the longing.

The characteristic sound produced by the false relations is again prominent as the song nears its end. Subtle differences in the sequential repetitions prevent the harmonies from becoming too easily predictable. These false relations are contained within a six-measure section where the metre has been altered to 2/4. The accompaniment has also been changed in the piano to rolled, syncopated chords whose rather throbbing effect emphasizes the intensity of the religious longing: 'And kisse his feete with my ambitious boughes,/And clyme along uppon his sacred brest,/And make a garland for his wounded browes.'

With the three-measure conclusion, marked *Adagio calmato*, the deep inner peace of the song's first third is restored as the soloist sings, 'Lord soe I am, if heare my thoughts may rest.' The final D chord, containing no third and held over into the first measure of the second song seems, very gently, to symbolize the emptiness of the soul following its extraordinary confession.

That emptiness persists through the first three measures of *On the Reed of Our Lord's Passion*, for the piano is silent while the viola appears to search for some sort of permanence and stability, a quest symbolized by a recitative-like line, marked *liberamente* and *intenso*. It is characterized by short segments, frequent use of the tritone and disjunct intervals. When the voice enters just after the viola line concludes, its opening material is substantially what we have just heard, although it is pitched higher. This material, composed of the falling tritone, rising fourth and falling second, is a perfect vehicle for the lack of fulfilment in the words, 'Long tyme hath Christ (long tyme I must confesse)/ Held me a hollowe Reede within his hande.' Near the end of the next two measures the music assumes a more purposeful shape as the goal is made clear: 'Had not his grace supplied mine emptines.'

The piano accompaniment following its low, single-line entry beneath the viola's last measure is chordal when the voice begins in the fifth measure. Marked *pulsato* and *pianissimo*, the chords are arranged in groups of three identical chords – three groups per measure. Each group differs from that which precedes and follows. The harmonies are chromatic in both directions, and some are mildly dissonant. Thus the unsettled, searching atmosphere of the vocal line is gently underscored but, at the same time, rhythmically controlled, for whereas the viola's preceding solo is to be played *liberamente*, the vocal line is held in check by the piano's regularity.

Neither the vocal line nor the accompaniment of the middle section in what is, essentially, a ternary structure quite matches the impressiveness of the first section. This small lapse is confined to just four measures, for the section's remaining four are devoted to an exact restatement (at a lower and, consequently, darker pitch) of the viola's solo line. The fault is traceable to a temporary reliance on such commonplace devices as suspensions in the piano and scalic figures in the vocal line.

In the song's final section the chordal groups return, although many of the chords and their progressions from one group to another are different. The vocal line again clothes the poetry with a worthy expressiveness, and some of the new chords produce richer harmonies than those heard in the first section. The growing intensity of the religious experience clearly shows in the words: 'Still let mee growe upon that livinge lande,/Within that wounde which iron did impresse,/And made a springe of bloud flowe from thie hande.' The music mirrors the same growing excitement, made all the more intense because it is discreetly held in check. Two climactic points are found in the quoted lines: 'wounde', on a B and harmonized by a chord which can be interpreted as either G sharp minor or E major (without the E), but with a low, repeated C pedal. A small *crescendo* leads to a *mezzo forte* and an accent above the note, and when all things are considered the 'wounde' can almost be felt. The second point, the climax of the song, occurs on 'springe'. Set to a sixteenth, two thirty-seconds and a dotted eighth, it attracts attention by its intricate figure, its high position, the *forte* dynamic, and the chord which underlies it (B flat minor with a C pedal). The word is approached and left in such a way as to ensure its importance.

The following lines end the poem: 'Then will I gather sapp, and rise, and stand/That all that see this wonder maye expresse/Upon this grounde how well growes barrennes.' 'Wonder' is the obvious high point, and in both arriving at and leaving it great care has been taken with the vocal line. The balance struck between the gentle descents and ascents in the rise to the accented and *forte* E on the first syllable of 'wonder' is beautifully calculated. Two measures are needed for the rise, but the fall from this climactic point is swift and sharp, occupying only one measure during which the intervals are much wider.

A final touch that demonstrates how far the composer has come in his mastery of the art of song composition occurs at the end when he forges a totally convincing transition to the same music – vocal and instrumental – that he wrote for the conclusion of *Upon the Crucifix*.

Following concentrated study and many hearings of this diptych, which overall I regard as one of Rubbra's finest achievements in the genre, one is somewhat puzzled by the statement in Mitchell's review concerning the 'lack of contrast' between the two songs, and within the second song itself. Granted that this criticism may be valid, the question arises as to whether the composer intended either or both contrasts. Although there is no certain answer, I tend to think that he did not want them, his probable reason being that they would upset, perhaps even destroy, the concentrated religious ecstasy of these meditations.

I conclude my consideration of this work with the other important review:

The two Rubbra sonnets have a positively Counter-Reformation air. Rubbra is a more complex musical personality than some might think; the progress from the iron polyphony of yelling[!] voices in his First Symphony to the vague textures, heavy with thought, on which diatonic fragments ride, in his latest orchestral works, is a striking one; no less striking is the contrast between the formal expanse of his Protestant Mass [*Missa Cantuariensis*] and the luminous concentration of his Catholic one [*Missa in Honorem Sancti Dominici*]. These settings of William Alabaster are almost embarrassingly explicit. From the onset of the first sonnet with its poignant semitonal clash against throbbing chords to the *molto espress.* at the end of the second sonnet we are in a world of exacerbated religious emotion. Alabaster's sonnets, to a later age, are full of obvious sexual imagery; and Rubbra's music matches them with weaving voices and yearning harmonies. Musically, in a detached and purely technical sense, they are masterly: assured, mature writing that says just what it wants to say. The rest is decidedly a matter of taste, although it is possible that as we get used to these songs we may accept them as we accept the equally emotional religious Lieder in Hugo Wolf's 'Spanisches Liederbuch'.[20]

No Swan So Fine

Two of Rubbra's finest works, the Seventh Symphony and Improvisation for Violin and Orchestra, separate the diptych from *No Swan So Fine*, Op. 91. The poem is by Marianne Moore, the only American poet he ever set. Born in St Louis in 1887, and educated at Bryn Mawr College, she became a librarian in New York and from 1925–9 was Editor of *The Dial*, a well-known literary magazine, founded in 1880. (It is not to be confused with the magazine of the same name, which was the organ of the American Transcendental Movement during the time of Emerson and Thoreau.) Moore's poems, contained in several volumes, are intellectual and tightly controlled with frequent touches of irony. Her unrhymed lines read like matter-of-fact prose, and do not at all suggest themselves as candidates for musical settings. Nevertheless, Rubbra took on the challenge.

The song was in response to a request from Sophie Wyss, a Swiss-born singer (1897) who, in 1925, settled in England. She gave concerts throughout the British Isles, Europe and Australia, but she was also known as an opera singer. She is particularly remembered for her efforts on behalf of contemporary British composers. In her recitals and chamber concerts for the BBC from 1927–64, she gave the first performance of Britten's *Les Illuminations*, as well as songs by Lennox Berkeley, Alan Rawsthorne, Peter Racine Fricker and Elizabeth Maconchy, to name but a few. Many of these songs were commissioned by her and written especially for her voice. *No Swan So Fine* was one of these and, appropriately, is inscribed to her.

The particular circumstances surrounding its composition are these: it was part of a song-cycle on the general subject of birds, to which a number of composers contributed. It seems natural to suppose that the mention of Rubbra's contribution in a short interview given by Miss Wyss might have elicited a reaction or a judgement from her, but unfortunately these were not forthcoming.[21]

The swan of Moore's poem is not live but a

chintz china one with fawn-brown eyes and toothed gold collar on to show whose bird it was. Lodged in the Louis Fifteenth candelabrum tree of cockscomb-tinted buttons, dahlias, sea urchins, and everlastings, it perches on the branching foam of polished sculptured flowers, at ease and tall.

The specific location of this swan seems undisputed for the poem's first line reads, 'No water so still as the dead fountains of Versailles.' The swan's 'gondoliering legs' obviously suggested the *quasi-barcarolle* with which Rubbra qualified his *Lento* direction. The choice of style not only shows his subtle sense of humour, but also the painstaking care with which he studied every detail of his texts.

This is a most attractive and unpretentious song, set in B flat major but with numerous D and A flats. Its vocal line flows naturally in response to the syllabification of the poem's prosaic style, but this very style precludes – and rightly so – a structured, memorable vocal melody. Nevertheless, the first line is set to two distinctive figures, but only the first of these reappears later in the voice part. Both figures are repeated in the piano accompaniment in what appears to be a casual, unplanned fashion. When they appear in the latter they ride very briefly along the tops of a continuous series of thirds, whose unabashed chromaticism rocks back and forth in a semi-popular vein that lends considerable weight to the gondolier-*barcarolle* theory. Perhaps the china swan was Venetian in origin.

A closer look at the vocal line shows that the principal rhythmic currency is composed of sixteenths. These urge the rhythm along in an almost conversational way. Yet there is ample rhythmic variety in the frequent syncopations. Melodically, the conversational effect – so right for the prose-like poetic style – is enhanced by quite a narrow range within individual phrases. The greatest spread in any phrase – an octave – is reserved for the poetic climax that begins with the line already quoted: 'it perches... at ease and tall.'

The accompaniment's most prominent feature is the trill in the right-hand part, present in sixteen of the song's twenty-five measures and of those no fewer than eleven contain two trills. They must all be executed within the space of one beat and since all but three are double trills involving thirds with no possibility of help from the left hand, the song is off limits to all but able pianists. The left hand is, of course, occupied with maintaining the gentle 6/8 *barcarolle* rhythm, the regularity of which is offset by the right hand's frequent dotted rhythms and occasional syncopations.

A probably unanswerable question is whether death is the underlying subject of Moore's poem as evidenced by such lines as, 'the dead fountains of Versailles,' and her last line, 'the king is dead.' And, of course, the swan is inanimate.

The following review says nothing of this, but the remark with respect to the accompaniment is enigmatic enough to suggest that the *barcarolle* connection may have occurred to the writer:

> Although at first sight Rubbra's vocal line does little more than follow the inflections of a short ornate poem, it sings well, and the song is greatly helped by the cunning yet quiet piano part, full of unexpected things.[22]

Cantata Pastorale

Rubbra's next work for solo voice consists of three short movements to be performed without interruption, for the final measures of nos 1 and 2 flow into nos 2 and 3 respectively. I quote from one of the two reviews:

> A new Cantata Pastorale (Op. 92) by Edmund Rubbra lent special interest to the recorder recital given by Carl Dolmetsch at Wigmore Hall on 1 February [1957]; the words (translations of Plato and medieval Latin lyrics) are set for soprano voice with accompaniment of recorder [treble], cello and harpsichord.... The pure tone and clear words of Joan Alexander were a great asset in this striking and beautiful work, and Mr. Dolmetsch to whom the composer dedicated the piece also had excellent collaboration in Joseph Saxby, harpsichord, and Arnold Ashby, cello.[23]

The 'Pastorale' of the title is a reference to the subject matter of each of the three poems.

The first movement is set to words by Plato, translated by Walter Leaf. The poem is divided into two stanzas of four lines each. The first calls for the Dryads, 'rocky fountains' and 'bleating sheep' to become still because 'Pan is playing'. The second stanza tells of the fountain and tree nymphs 'round him, dancing, dancing'. Rubbra's setting has corresponding divisions, but they are very unequal in length, the 6/16 dancing section containing forty-three measures to the sixteen of the first part.

The first section, in 4/8 metre and marked *Lento*, opens with a four-measure instrumental passage during which a five-note scale segment is firmly established in both the recorder and harpsichord parts (Example 270). That this

Ex. 270

segment and others like it in the remaining movements seem exotic to Western ears is evident, particularly in view of their constant repetitions. Suggestions as to their origins appear in both reviews. In hers, Joan Chissell remarks that 'the composer admits to having been influenced by a five-note Indian scale.'[24] For his part Arthur Hutchings referred to the notes as 'intervals of Near-Eastern and

Greek scales'.[25] In view of the Platonic text the temptation to theorize about the 'Greek scales', ancient or modern, is strong, but Rubbra's admission cannot be disputed. Writing his review seven years later, it is possible that Hutchings was unaware of this admission. However, Rubbra reiterated it in the early 1960s, just prior to Hutchings's review, when Murray Schafer observed, 'you are very much interested in oriental music though outwardly there is little trace of this in your own music.' In his reply the composer observed that

> one can be influenced by the exteriors of music and by the interiors. It is the interior view of oriental music that has influenced me the most – the controlled improvisation on limited material that eventually builds up, in the hands of a fine oriental musician, into a big satisfying structure. I have tried to express myself in a similar way in the first movement of my piano concerto and this is why that work is dedicated to Ali Akbar Khan. The exterior exoticisms of mode and rhythm, fascinating as they are, are, for me, not as important. I can only think of one isolated work in which this aspect of oriental music has influenced me. In a little piece for voice, recorder, harpsichord and cello I have used a melodic motif that I heard played by an Indian musician as the basic theme of the work.[26]

The ensemble as a totality in the first part projects a deliciously sensuous effect. To mention the components briefly, the recorder, following its basic presentation of the given tones in Example 270, has several varied figures – both ascending and descending – in which the basic tones are arranged differently. The harpsichord's principal role is confined to the presentation of the segment in the form of *glissandi*, arranged in groups of nine and eighteen notes. The cello's *con sordino* part is purely harmonic and supportive with one small exception. The vocal line introduces tones outside the basic five-note segment, and these plus the segment form a balanced, ornamented melody that extends from D sharp up to G. The entire section is rather typical of the sort of music generally associated with Pan and his syrinx.

There is a slight overlap as the final phrase of the languorous first section ends in the dancing boisterousness of the second section. Although the *Lento* is retained, the leaping figures in the voice and recorder parts, some of which are syncopated while others are examples of hemiola, seem faster than they really are. The harpsichord now has a chordal texture in which the outline of the descending tetrachord is clearly heard in the right hand. Later, other and more conventional figures are given priority, and the cello assumes a very active role in contrast with its previously supportive duties. What is surprising is the presence of a purely instrumental postlude, occupying twenty-four measures after the voice has completed its presentation. (This compares with the previous nineteen measures during which the voice was the dominant entity.) What is the purpose of such a disproportionately long postlude? If its aim is to prolong the excitement of the dance then it is a miscalculation, for the most interesting and alive rhythmic figures have ceased. What remains is much calmer, and without the voice to give it focus it is too long and drawn out. Ultimately, it becomes slower and softer in preparation for the second movement into which it quietly flows, coming to rest on a sustained C major chord.

The text of the new movement is taken from the Manuscript of St Augustine at Canterbury, translated by Helen Waddell. Spring in all its beauty and phases has arrived. 'I see it with my eyes,/I hear it with my ears,/But in my heart are sighs/And I am full of tears.' It is the age-old story of beauty depicted by so many poets as causing pain, either in itself or owing to circumstances usually connected with love. And so, 'Do thou, O spring most fair,/Squander thy care/On flower and leaf and grain./Leave me alone with pain!' The tempo is *Adagio* and the vocal line which begins at once on the second beat of the 3/4 metre is to be sung *pianissimo* and 'subdued'.

The same intervals as those used in the first movement are present here, but in different arrangements. The filled-in tetrachord is no longer in evidence in either the voice or instrumental ensemble, thus giving the movement a much less 'exotic' flavour. C major is the central tonality, and deviations from it are very short, ranging from one or two chords at a time to no more than two measures. The tonality is controlled largely by a C pedal in the cello together with Cs at the bottom of the harpsichord's rolled, C major chords. The recorder is silent for the first eleven and the concluding ten measures, as well as five in the middle. Its most active participation comes during what can be considered a small *B* section in a ternary structure, and its function in this section is to accompany the voice – the only instrument to do so. Its music at this point consists mostly of groups of sixteenths. The movement as a whole is effective, and it contrasts well in its melancholy expressiveness with the joyousness of the final movement into which it flows effortlessly.

As in three of the Four Medieval Latin Lyrics of Op. 32 the text for the last movement is drawn from the same Goliardic source: the manuscript from the Benediktbeuern Monastery. The translation is not, however, by the composer as in the earlier work, but by Helen Waddell. The subject matter is virtually the same as that of the middle movement – the arrival of spring – but without the personal sorrow introduced there. In its place is the impersonal, 'O lads be gay of mood/For love himself now leads you to the lasses.'

The first two measures of the new movement, which is in an undeviating 6/8, are marked *poco accelerando*, and these lead to the prevailing *Allegretto moderato*. Whether it would have been more effective to have introduced the new tempo in the new metre in the very first measure, thus taking the listener by surprise, is a matter of preference. Arguments can be advanced for both approaches, but the composer undoubtedly wished the bitter-sweet atmosphere only gradually to be dispelled.

The music consists of recurring segments of the basic material, this time far more obvious than in the second movement because the original order of tones has been restored. However, these notes are confined to the accompaniment where, in the harpsichord part, they take the form of three ostinato patterns, one of which is composed entirely of *staccato* sixteenths arranged in two parallel lines one octave apart. The recorder part is varied between its own ostinato figure, short versions of the original descending tetrachord and other related material. The cello part is filled with leaping figures of various kinds that provide the necessary harmonic foundation. The vocal line adequately expresses the innocent joyousness of the scene.

In the last line of his review, Hutchings calls this work a 'cantata' (which, in reality, is correct, although 'solo cantata' would have been more accurate) and goes on to say that it is 'worthy of its dedication to Carl Dolmetsch [and] should make a distinguished recital item'. But he then remarks that 'it is not the unique Rubbra of his polyphonic music.'[27] Of course the work is not to be compared with the polyphony of the symphonies and other music. A more appropriate observation would have recognized the unity of the work, achieved by the use in all three movements of the generating tetrachord.

The Jade Mountain

The Jade Mountain, Op. 116, completed in December 1962, is a very unusual work. It is a setting for harp and high voice of five poems of the T'ang Dynasty (618–906 AD), translated from the Chinese by the American poet, playwright and translator Witter Bynner (1881–1968). Bynner's early poetic style was lyrical, resulting in two volumes of poetry (1917 and 1920). In 1951 he wrote a biography of D.H. Lawrence, entitled *Journey With Genius*. His translation of the 300 poems comprising *The Jade Mountain* was undertaken in 1929 with the help of a Chinese doctor.

Rubbra's cycle is dedicated to Ann Griffiths, the harpist for whom he had composed other works and to the soprano, Elizabeth Robinson. Stephen Banfield has caught the spirit and substance of these songs in his brief summary, although with reference to two of his statements I have reservations.

> In the exquisite, contemplative Chinese poetry, the emotion is articulated by a form of objective correlative, in which colourful pictures and situations are depicted, but in neutral terms. The music acts likewise. It does not comment on or colour the poetry, but sets up a detached neutral correlative of its own, which mirrors the equilibrium, not the underlying emotion.... Both the voice parts and the harmony, owing little to classical Western procedures, tend to float on a limited number of pitches, derived from non-Western modes.[28]

Before the songs are explored individually two further general points regarding the cycle as a whole deserve mention. The first has to do with the overall structure, which is in the form of an arch. This is, of course, the natural result of the position of these poems in the cycle and of the musical fabric with which the poems are clothed. Thus poems 1 and 5 have serious subject matter, nos 2 and 4 are light in content, while the third poem falls somewhere between these opposites. Musically, there is a similar balance, reflected in tempi and lengths: songs 1 and 5 are marked *Lento* (thirty-six measures) and *Largo* (thirty-one measures) respectively; nos 2 and 4 are designated *Vivace* (twenty-seven measures) and *Con moto* (twenty-six measures), but no. 3 is marked *Andante* and is the shortest of the set with but five measures of 10/4 metre, divided into 6 + 4, and a concluding 2/4 measure.

The remaining point concerns the texture of the five songs: each consists of repeating accompanimental segments, above which are freely evolving vocal lines. Thus there is a carefully imposed unity, both with regard to the cycle as a whole and the internal structure of the individual songs.

The first poem, 'A Night Thought On Terrace Tower', is by Wêi Chuang: 'Far through the night a harp is sighing/With a sadness of wind and rain in the strings.' After a short, further description of the scene the poem concludes with 'While I still have been hoping that my old friend would come./There are no more messengers I can send him,/Now that the wild geese have turned south.'

Ex. 271

The principal feature of the harp accompaniment is the parallel movement in both hands of unrelated triads, some of which are in the second inversion while others are in root position. In some cases different triads appear together, one in each hand, and these naturally cause dissonances. However, as seen in Example 271, dissonances arising from two other sources are an important characteristic from the start. The first source is the generally static and segmented melody that rides in both hands along the tops of the chords and the second is the added notes attached to many of the chords. Halfway through the song these patterns change in favour of still unrelated but dissonance-free chords that, at first, rise and fall, and then occur in alternating low and high registers. An entirely new idea dominates the closing portion when an ostinato figure in triplets is introduced. This has a distinctly dissonant flavour and as such a wonderfully mysterious, indefinite atmosphere is created, which is enhanced by the harmonics indicated for all of the left-hand notes.

The very free and expressive vocal line, whose beginning is shown in Example 271, encompasses the widest range of the five songs: E above middle C to B above the staff. A particular portion of this line as well as a section of the accompaniment are responsible for my first reservation regarding a part of Banfield's summary. He claims that 'the music... does not comment on or colour the poetry' and that the 'underlying emotion' is not mirrored in it. Yet it seems more than probable that the rests separating 'while', 'still' and 'I' in the line, 'While still I have been hoping' are intended to suggest the uncertainties associated with hope. 'I have been hoping that my old friend would come' is set to faster note values following the separations, as though the poet were trying to reassure himself. 'Come', on the high B, and held for a whole measure, is the poetic and musical climax of the song. The immediately ensuing ostinato, described above, seems to express the grey cheerlessness of 'there are no more messengers I can send him,/Now that the wild geese have turned south.' Most of the words in these last two lines are set to the lowest pitches in the song, and they also express the subdued atmosphere.

The second poem, 'On Hearing Her Play The Harp', by Li Tüan, paints a very charming picture of a woman whose 'hands of white jade by a window of snow/Are glimmering on a golden fretted harp.' This miniature concludes in a delightfully mischievous vein: 'And to draw the quick eye of Chou Yü,/She touches a wrong note now and then.'

The musical setting begins with a six-measure harp introduction whose material carries on through the song in one way or another. It is composed of two contrasting elements divided between the hands. The right-hand element is a falling and rising, arpeggiated B major chord, arranged in three groups of six notes each. Its 8*va* placement and *pianissimo* level have combined to give it a delicate, whirring sound. The left-hand element is composed of two lines of melody whose intervals are in consistent contrary motion, thus producing a mirror image as they contract and expand. In the fourth and fifth measures these intervals are inverted – a minor sixth becomes a major third, a fourth turns into a fifth, and so on. The interaction of the right- and left-hand elements has produced an interesting mixture of a tonal foundation (right hand) and a strongly modal melody in the left hand. However, this mixture is more evident in the score than in the hearing, for the *vivace* tempo and the mostly *pianissimo* level have combined to create an effect of indistinctness which is very pleasing. That effect is modified when the vocal line enters in the seventh measure, for its modality reinforces that of the accompaniment.

A very abrupt harmonic shift occurs in the middle of the song when the left-hand intervals, the top and bottom lines of which have provided the modal flavour, are replaced by C major arpeggios with the same shape and grouping as their B major counterparts. Placed in the harp's mid-range and marked *forte*, they are more clearly heard than the B major *arpeggios*. Above these, however, in the right hand, intervals associated with B major are alternated with one another. Thus we are presented with a clear case of bitonality which is, indeed, strengthened when the right hand resumes its original B major arpeggio against the left hand's continuing C major version. The song ends with an exact repetition of its accompanimental beginnings.

In addition to its modal characteristics the vocal line also contains two notes – D sharp and C sharp – that fit into the context of B major. They do not, however, appear until close to the end of the soloist's part. The C sharp is the more interesting of the two, for it is present only when the harpist, in an effort to win Chou Yü's attention, 'touches a wrong note now and then'. I suggest that the C sharps can be interpreted as a sly and subtle example of word-painting, for the accompaniment at this point is sounding the C naturals which it has had throughout most of the song. This time, they are even accented to draw attention to them. Therefore the clash with the C sharp is intended. But the fact that it is the singer and not the harpist who has the 'wrong note' should not put us off the track, for if the C sharp were assigned to the harp the listener would not notice it. To think that the composer would, or even should, ignore an obvious chance to match text and music is to adopt a stiffly purist approach that does not seem to stand scrutiny.

The centrepiece of the set is the very short third song, 'An Autumn Night Message', by Wêi Ying-Wu: 'As I walk in the cool of the autumn night,/ Thinking of you, singing my poem,/I hear a mountain pine cone fall./You also seem to be awake.' My second reservation regarding Banfield's summary is that the entire chord structure of this piece, as well as the vocal line derived from it, can be explained within the framework of Western harmonic practice; no non-Western scale is involved. The harp accompaniment consists entirely of five statements of the following ten-beat measure, divided into 6 + 4, and a concluding measure in which the opening two beats are repeated (Example 272). Carefully observe the harp chords. The A sharps should be interpreted as the enharmonic equivalents of B flat; the chord then becomes a second-inversion structure (with D flat at the bottom). Turning momentarily to the setting of the concluding line of the song, 'You also seem to be awake', the key of B flat

Ex. 272

minor is firmly established through the sounding of A natural – the leading tone
of the key – on each side of a B flat. This is then followed by the tracing of the
minor third – B flat up to D flat and back again. Having accepted that the
tonality of the song is B flat minor, the harp chords fall into place as second
inversions of VI: D flat, G flat, B flat. The Cs in the moving part atop the
chords are appoggiaturas to the B flats and D flats. The E and F flats are, like
the Cs, tones foreign to the basic chord. The whole-note C in the four-beat
section of the measure is merely a long appoggiatura that does not resolve until
the quarter-note C in the repeated chord set falls to B flat.

The vocal line is just as easily analysed: all of its notes except a high A flat
and the A naturals just mentioned are contained in the harp chord, and are
freely arranged to form a melody. The fact that this melody, when measured
against the chordal structure, is highly unstable should not modify the validity
of the foregoing analysis. A simple test involving the holding out of the VI $^6_4$
chord minus the moving line on top will show the static nature of the whole
song, and the silent resolution which the listener is supplying: to I in B flat
minor. However, even after the A naturals and the rest of the final line establish
the tonality, the song is left unresolved, for in the 2/4 measure the opening two
beats are repeated.

Song no. 4, 'A Song Of The Southern River', to a poem by Li Yi, tells in a
light-hearted way of a woman's disillusionment: 'Since I married the merchant
of Ch'üt'ang/He has failed each day to keep his word./Had I thought how
regular the tide is,/I might rather have chosen a river boy.' These words are
given a very relaxed setting that leaves no doubt as to a central tonality: A
major. However, all of the Fs are left unsharped in the accompaniment, but in
the vocal line they are sharped. There is no clash between the inflected and
uninflected Fs, because, with two small exceptions F natural is not sounded
when the voice is active.

The relaxed, amiable atmosphere is immediately evident in the running
sixteenths of the six-measure harp introduction. The dominance of A major is
not undermined by the presence in the harpist's left hand of chords which are
dissonant with the sixteenths. With the entry of the voice in measure 7 a one-
measure, repeating pattern is established, which encompasses all parts of the
accompaniment. Its most noticeable feature is an abrupt, downward-moving
figure in octaves in the right hand. Upon the completion of five measures of

these repetitions, the accompaniment of the song's second half is a reproduction of the first half. The music of the vocal line – equally relaxed – is different
for each stanza.

The fifth and final song in the cycle is called, 'Farewell To A Japanese
Buddhist Priest Bound Homeward' and the poet is Ch'ien Ch'i. The poem is
perhaps the most strikingly beautiful of the three serious songs: 'You were
foreordained to find the source./Now, tracing your way in a dream/There where
the sea floats up the sky,/You wane from the world in your fragile boat./The
water and the moon are as calm as your faith,/Fishes and dragons follow your
chanting,/And the eye still watches beyond the horizon/The holy light of your
single lantern.'

The musical setting begins with a five-measure introduction whose repetitions beneath the vocal line have the effect of a ground bass even though there
is a two-measure interruption, and a shortened statement. The vocal line, seen
in Example 273, through 'sky' is repeated from 'You wane' on through 'faith',

Ex. 273

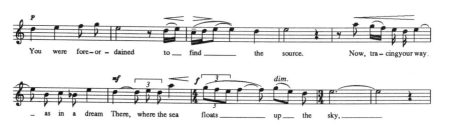

adjustments in syllabification accounting for minor rhythmic differences. Seven
measures from the end of the song a rising and falling intervallic figure in
sixteenths is introduced in the right hand of the accompaniment.

It all sounds so simple, and it is, but one should not allow oneself to be
lulled into thinking that this song is in any way inferior to either the first or
third. On the contrary, it is the culmination of the cycle, both poetically and
musically. To quote Banfield again, 'the sense of peace is complete, even unto
Nirvana.'[29] From the viewpoint of Rubbra's interest in and knowledge of Eastern philosophies and religions, this text in particular would have represented a
summation for him of the basic tenet of renunciation of self, thereby making
possible a final freedom and union with God. Because such a goal is best
described in simple, physical terms that involve an easily imagined scene ('Der
Abschied' from Mahler's *Das Lied von der Erde* is probably the best-known
example), the music must also be stripped of all non-essentials. Rubbra's setting fits that description and so, in its different way, does Mahler's.

Salve, Regina

For his penultimate song, published three years later in 1966, Rubbra turned to a specifically Catholic text in his setting of the Marian antiphon, *Salve, Regina*. Written for 'Low Voice (Contralto, Baritone or Counter-tenor) and Piano (or Harpsichord)', its opus number designation is 119.

Following the greatly simplified and scaled-down style of *The Jade Mountain* the music for *Salve, Regina* seems complex – some might even say overloaded. The melody is convincingly Gregorian, but it is of Rubbra's own composition. Even though there is an accompaniment, this remains relatively simple through the first ten measures of the song. A certain restlessness, in keeping with the text as a whole, pervades the accompaniment from the beginning, well before the words assume the intensity of the later petitions. This restlessness is manifested in a basic idea that is composed of repeating right-hand octave Es, plus the same note at the bottom of the left hand. In the 4/8 metre these notes occur on the first and third beats. Within this framework are running triplets and eighths.

The very first statement of this idea is at odds with the vocal line in terms of tonality, but 'tonality' must be understood here in its widest and most general sense, for the two running lines of the accompaniment are modal, as is the vocal line. Interpreting the latter first, the overall tonality of the line is E major/minor, but the words 'Salve, Regina' are set to a transposed Mixolydian, while

Ex. 274

'Mater misericordiae' is untransposed Phrygian. The balance of the line is a mixture of an indeterminate mode and a clear E major. The modal lines of the accompaniment are untransposed Phrygian for the triplets and an untransposed Aeolian (or natural A minor) for the eighths. The two accompanimental modes – consonant with each other – create harmonic uncertainties when the vocal line is placed above them. Although the dissonances are not great, they are enough to contribute to the restless feeling mentioned above, and the rhythmic mixture in the piano also adds to it. Example 274 shows the opening seven measures.

Following the conclusion of Rubbra's composed chant, a measure of accompaniment marked *drammatico* leads to a restatement of the first half of the chant. New material then ensues. Tonally, the entire passage eventually gravitates to G sharp minor, but within this context the modal characteristics are retained. The texture becomes more dissonant and agitated as the petitions to the Virgin increase in intensity.

The drama that has accumulated in the second section is maintained and intensified in the final section, which is also the longest. Except for very small segments, nothing of the chant remains. The principal figures of the accompaniment return several times in altered form, but the biggest change concerns the full, rolled chords, divided between the hands. From a rhythmic viewpoint, the most interesting of these are the groups of three per measure which, in 4/8 metre, indicate slow-moving triplets. These and the two groups of triplets in the voice combine to produce the rhythm so often heard in Rubbra's music: three beats cutting across a measure of six. The stress marks over all of the chords, the dynamic marks and the *appassionato* and *intenso* directions are visible indications of the increasingly insistent petitions. The song ends calmly and quietly with 'O clemens, O pia, O dulcis virgo Maria.'

Fly, Envious Time

Rubbra's last song, Op. 148, is a setting of Milton's poem of 1645, *Fly, Envious Time*. It was composed in 1974 for the Milton Tercentenary Festival, and bears the inscription, 'In Memoriam Gerald Finzi'. Its assertive, triumphant character is in keeping with Milton's poem, but for that character to be convincing some precautions are necessary. First, the tempo must not become slower than is indicated – *con moto ma liberamente*, ♩ = 44 circa – except where *ritardandos* are directed. Second, some of the vocal phrases are long, and the proper tempo must be maintained or the momentum will be lost. Another reason for moving the tempo along is to prevent the rather elaborate piano accompaniment from sounding stodgy. Yet the majesty of Milton's lines is never in jeopardy so long as the stated metronome marking is not exceeded.

Like a number of the preceding songs, the vocal line of *Fly, Envious Time* is through-composed, while the accompaniment contains elements that are repeated.

In this instance these elements are more insistently present than in some of the composer's other songs. Perhaps Banfield's assertion that 'the heavy counterpoint which sometimes, under the necessity for thematic argument, bogs down [the song]'[30] is a reference to this frequency. Yet, as shown in Example 275, the

Ex. 275

repeating segment – seen here in its initial appearance – is not heavy. On the contrary, the detached notes in the continuous eighth-note movement act as a kind of springboard to the repetitions as well as to the subordinate segments. And the well-considered tempo and the eighth-note movement in all but nine measures of the accompaniment preclude any bogging down. The repeating segment is not employed excessively, or in a relentless fashion in order to accommodate a 'thematic argument'. In fact, in the song's second half, its appearances are restricted to just two. Its main function, in sum, appears to be that of providing a reference point in the interest of unity – something that is essential when a vocal line is through-composed.

It will be noted in Example 275 that there is a rhythmic interplay between voice and piano. This continues in one form or another until close to the end of the song. At that point sixteenth notes appear in both parts as the tempo – *Lento e calmo* – broadens in preparation for the end. The dynamic level has been steadily increasing in keeping with the exultant words, 'Then, all this earthy grossness quit,/Attired with stars we shall forever sit,/Triumphing over Death, and Chance, and Thee, O Time!' Although harmonically there is nothing new in this song, there are abrupt shifts of tonality, and some dissonant clashes, early examples of which can be seen in the illustration. *Fly, Envious Time* is neither an easy song, nor is it as immediately attractive as some of the composer's other songs, but it is well written, and in time it grows on one.

Conclusion

In attempting a fair assessment of Rubbra's songs, several factors must be taken into account. First, Rubbra was neither a Warlock nor a Finzi, both of whom attained the front rank with their songs. Indeed, song composition appeared to be second nature for them to the degree that nearly every song gives the impression (correct or otherwise) of having been created in one spontaneous surge.

Second, it is very apparent that both Warlock and Finzi possessed a basic and unswerving instinct for the subtleties associated with song composition, and demonstrated it in practically every song. One does not sense this instinct in Rubbra except in connection with particular songs that are scattered throughout his career. In other words, this natural instinct is not consistently present and a fair number of songs appear to have represented a struggle for the composer. However, even certain songs wherein a struggle seems to have taken place are above average and there are some songs which are, in my opinion, masterpieces.

Third, in the light of Rubbra's considerable achievements in the fields of the symphony and concerto, it is very easy to overlook or underrate his song output. This is as true of the critics and commentators as it is of the average listener, but the latter can be more easily excused than those who make a profession of acquainting themselves with new music as it is written and published.

The songs whose titles appear below are, in my judgement, fully equal to some of the best that Warlock and Finzi wrote. The particular qualities that distinguish them have already been covered in the text and my judgements are based on the observations contained there. Among the separate songs (and these are in no particular order) are *A Duan of Barra*; *Take, O Take Those Lips*

Away; *In Dark Weather*; *Nocturne*; and *O My Deir Hert*. Of the cycles, the finest by far is *The Jade Mountain*, each of whose five songs is perfectly matched to its text. Second among the sets is Four Medieval Latin Lyrics; again the mood of each poem is sensitively reproduced in entirely appropriate music. As for the remaining sets, certain songs stand out from their fellows: *Upon the Crucifix* from Two Sonnets by William Alabaster; and Psalms 6 and 23 from Three Psalms. The Five Spenser Sonnets and *Amoretti* display the greatest inequalities among the individual songs, but this fact does not, of course, rule out the probability that all ten songs are entirely acceptable to both performers and audiences. As in the other cycles, certain songs stand out in the memory: Sonnet 4 from the first set and Sonnets 78, 37 and 40 from *Amoretti*. Of these, Sonnets 4 and 37 are particularly striking because their contrapuntal complexities are, in each instance, a spontaneous and wholly natural expression of the words and the subtleties behind them.

In conclusion, although Rubbra's contribution to the literature of the song may seem slight in comparison with that of other song composers, enterprising singers will find much to interest and challenge them in his work.

Notes

1 'Edmund Rubbra, Now 70, Looks At His Eight Symphonies', *The Listener*, 27 May 1971, p.690.
2 On pp.5–7 of Newsletter 37 of the Peter Warlock Society for August 1986, there appears an interesting article, primarily by Patrick Mills, concerning the source of *Balulalow* as a text. He points out on p.6 that Warlock supposed the text to have originated in the sixteenth or seventeenth century, and that Herbert Howells, who set the text in 1922, thought it was by an anonymous author. Rubbra, whose setting also dates from 1922, held the same view as Howells. Actually, the poem's two stanzas are part of Luther's *Vom Himmel Hoch* and the free translation of these was the work of the Scottish Wedderburn brothers – James, John and Robert.
3 Stephen Banfield, 'Rubbra's Songs', *Edmund Rubbra: Composer*, pp.89–90.
4 B.V., *MT*, December 1925, p.1103.
5 *ibid.*
6 T.A., *MT*, March 1927, p.233.
7 Hugh Ottaway, *MT*, February 1972, p.187.
8 Banfield, *op. cit.*, p.89.
9 Edmund Rubbra, 'Some Technical Characteristics', in Stephen Lloyd and Edmund Rubbra (eds) *Gustav Holst: Collected Essays* (London: Triad Press, 1974), p.30.
10 Richard Capell, *MMR*, March–April 1933, p.61.
11 Arthur Hutchings, *MT*, April 1944, p.116.
12 J.A. Westrup, *MMR*, September 1943, p.160.
13 Ivor Keys, *M&L* 29, no. 1, January 1948, p.112.
14 *ibid.*
15 *ibid.* I also heard a recent 'devoted performance' of this song, but I detected no such conflict, nor have I in my study of it.
16 *ibid.*
17 Readers wishing to learn more about the isorhythmic motet and its technical

characteristics can find a concise explanation in Donald Jay Grout's previously cited *A History of Western Music*, pp.119–22.

18   Printed in the front of the score. In Chapter 1, p.22, Rubbra tells how he imagined Kathleen Ferrier's voice for the work. Unfortunately, Ferrier's final illness prevented her from singing it.

19   Donald Mitchell, *MT*, August 1955, p.434.

20   Peter Pirie, *M&L* 37, no. 4, October 1956, p.422.

21   'Sophie Wyss In Conversation With John Skiba', *Composer*, no. 59, Winter 1976–77, p.35.

22   Ivor Keys, *M&L* 40, no. 1, January 1959, p.94.

23   Joan Chissell, *MT*, March 1957, p.157.

24   *ibid.*

25   Arthur Hutchings, *M&L* 45, no. 2, April 1964, p.202.

26   Quoted in Murray Schafer, 'Edmund Rubbra', *British Composers in Interview* (London: Faber and Faber, 1963), p.68.

27   Hutchings, *op. cit.*, p.202.

28   Banfield, *op. cit.*, p.93.

29   *ibid.*, p.94.

30   *ibid.*, p.93.

11 Miscellaneous Works

Music for the theatre

The number of Rubbra's works that do not fit any of the categories already considered is small, but several of them are important because they reveal the composer's interest in music for the theatre, an interest of which most Rubbra supporters are probably unaware. How many of them know, for example, that in 1933 he wrote a one-act opera called *The Shadow*, formerly entitled *Bee-bee-bei*? In Chapter 1 Rubbra referred to this opera as having been fostered by his interest in Eastern philosophy and religion. That he tried to bring it to the attention of at least one influential person is substantiated by the following letter of 3 October 1933, to Francis Clive Carey, a well-known baritone. It was in his capacity as a London opera producer that Rubbra wrote to him:

> I am enclosing an introduction from Mr. Holst. I have a one-act opera which I should very much like you to hear if you are interested and can spare the time. I could easily come and play it to you if you would kindly let me know a convenient time.

The opera, which as Op. 36 falls between the original version of the First String Quartet and the Five Motets, remains in manuscript. However, the lengthy account of the plot in an undated and unnamed newspaper would appear to indicate that the opera was performed at least once. This work marked both the beginning and the end of Rubbra's operatic venture, thus, and also because of the unusual story line, it seems appropriate to quote the plot in full.

> To a poetic yet far from sombre text by Mr. Sturge Moore, Mr. Edmund Rubbra has recently composed an opera in one act, the scene of which is Kashmir in the 16th century.
> The action takes place in the shop at Srinagar of Yekbal, a carpet merchant. He is the father of the beauteous Beebeebei. The plot deals with the rivalry between two of this young person's admirers, the one Prince Fureed, the other Teimoor, a soldier of the guard.
> The girl holds kind hearts to rank above coronets, and the end of the piece shows the boastful prince discomfited and the soldier with his true love in his arms. But there are various vicissitudes before this point is reached.

The carpet merchant, while minding his shop, keeps an eye on his daughter by means of a large mirror, which makes her room visible to anyone in the shop. The young soldier is caught by his princely master in the act of kissing the girl's reflection in this mirror. Furious, the prince orders him to be bastinadoed, but the prince's father, a gentle soul, pleads for mercy, saying that since the young man kissed not the girl but her shadow, justice demands that not his feet but only the shadow of his feet should be bastinadoed. This formal punishment is forthwith performed with Oriental punctilio, to the accompaniment of wild music.

The soldier is then banished, and the field is clear for the prince to plead his cause with Beebeebei. He fails, however, to capture her fancy with his description of the house he has designed for her. She calls the promised house a cage. Meanwhile Teimoor has noiselessly crawled back into the shop. At an opportune moment he nets the overbearing prince's head in a sash, and at once throws him into a boat which is drifting in the stream which we see at the back of the shop.

That is, so far as the opera goes, the end of Prince Fureed, and the rest of the piece is concerned with the declarations of the two lovers. The whole has a strong flavour of Arabian Nights fantasy [in fact, the Lengnick catalogue says that the libretto has its origins in an Arabian Nights story].[1]

As we know from Chapter 1, Rubbra composed incidental music for a number of plays. Most of these scores were written during his association with The Arts League of Service Travelling Theatre, and included music for Velona Pilcher's anti-war play, *The Searcher*; Ezra Pound's translation of *Hagoromo*, a Japanese Noh play; Hardy's *The Dynasts*; and *Mahomed and The Spider* (author unknown). The highly entertaining details relating to some of the problems encountered in connection with the first two titles appear in Chapter 1.

Rubbra's largest and most ambitious undertaking in the area of incidental music was his score for *Macbeth*. Never published, the score is in the Shakespeare Memorial Library at Stratford-upon-Avon; and Plate 2 shows the title page in Rubbra's handwriting. It lists all the scenes for which music was written, together with the timings for some of them. The play was produced at the Library on 21 June 1946, under Michael MacOwan's direction with the music recorded by the Boyd Neel Orchestra. Rubbra recalled that his music was not an unqualified success, owing to the musical inadequacies of some of the actors, who were required to speak some of their lines to musical rhythms. The most logical lines for such treatment are those of the three witches and in the score these appear at the proper places accompanied by staffless notes in the rhythms and accents of the words. The music, having been recorded, was too low in volume to be heard, and Rubbra's carefully planned rhythms were badly distorted.

Another play for which Rubbra composed incidental music was Ben Jonson's savage comedy, *Volpone*. The Westminster Theatre's production (no date given) received an extremely enthusiastic notice in yet another unidentified newspaper, and its drama critic had this to say about Rubbra's contribution:

Even the music is exceptional; Mr. Edmund Rubbra, writing for the queer combination of clarinet, oboe and bassoon alone, has composed harshly ingenious bleatings which suggest the grotesque capers of the three deformed freaks who are Volpone's servants.[2]

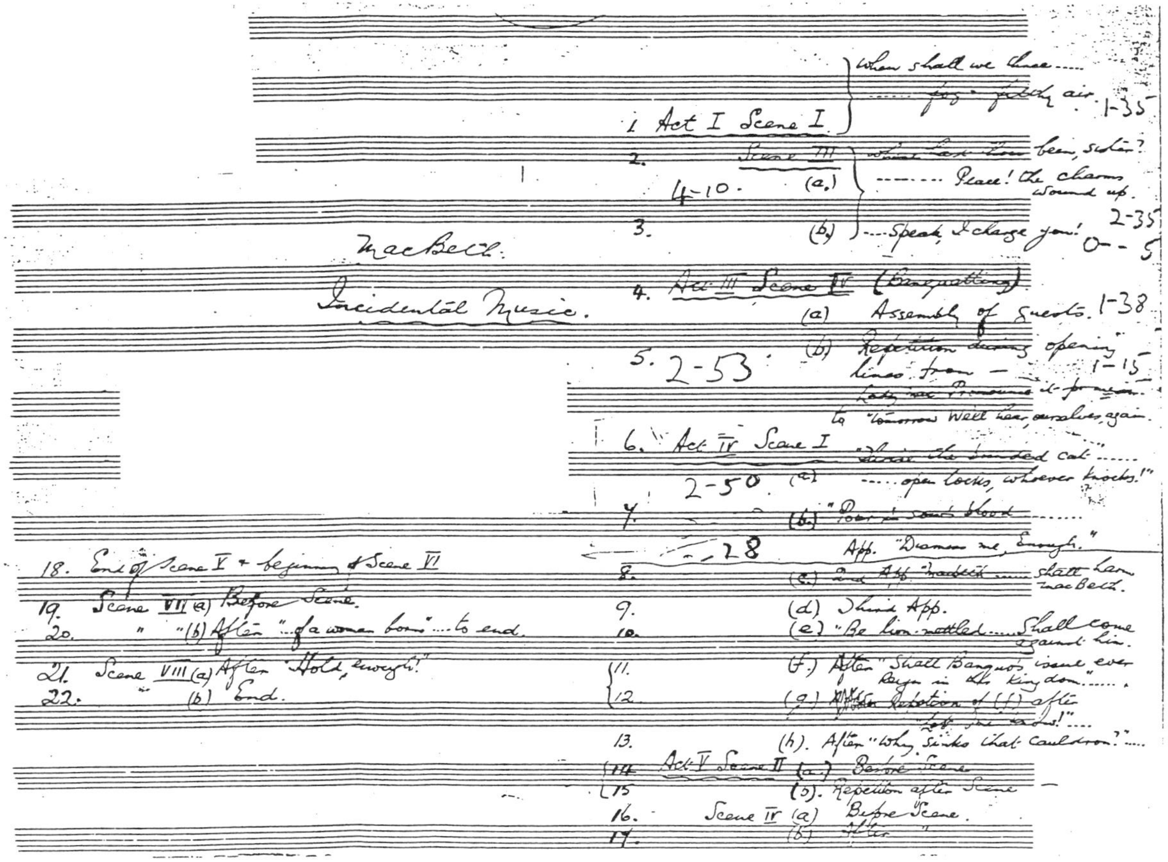

Macbeth.

Incidental Music.

1. Act I Scene I — "When shall we three..." "...fog & filthy air." 1–35

2. Scene II (a.) — "Peace! the charm..." "Drum up." 2–35
   (b) — "...Speak & charge you..." 0–5
   4–10.

4. Act III Scene II (Banqueting) (a) Assembly of Guests. 1–38
   (b) Musician plays Fanfare 1–15
   5. 2–53.

6. Act IV Scene I — "...Drum within..." 2–50
   7. (b) "Double, double..." 1–28

8. App. "Damn'd be..."
9. (c) 2nd App. "Macbeth! Macbeth! Macbeth!"
10. (d) 3rd App. "Be lion mettled..."
11. (e) "Be lion mettled... Shall live..." ...
12. (f) After "Shall Banquo's issue ever..." Reign in this kingdom...
13. (g) After "Rebellious head..."
14. Act V Scene I (h) After "...oh, so that Cauldron...?"
15. (i) Scene after
16. Scene IV (a) Repetition after Scene
17. (b) Before Scene

18. End of Scene I & beginning of Scene VI
19. Scene VII (a) Before Scene
20. (b) After — "...a woman born..." to end.
21. Scene VIII (a) After "Hold, enough!"
22. (b) End.

Plate 2

A paragraph on the music for the Dartington Dance-Mime Group, composed in 1935–6, appeared towards the end of Chapter 1. This completes the survey of Rubbra's music associated with the theatre.

Works for brass

A second and smaller category of music that has found no place in the preceding chapters consists of three works for brass. Taking them in order of opus number and year of composition, Variations on *The Shining River* for Brass Band, Op. 101, is the first. In the following programme note, Rubbra explains the genesis of the work, and introduces us to the music itself:

> This work was written as a test piece for the Brass Band Championship of Great Britain held at the Albert Hall, London, in 1958. I was at first diffident about accepting such a commission, as I did not have the specialised knowledge demanded by the peculiarities of brass band scoring, where everything except the bass trombone and drums is written in the treble clef! But the late Frank Wright, who was a recognised authority in the world of brass band music, assured me that if I would go ahead with the piece and then meet him to discuss the sounds I had in mind, he would translate what I wanted into brass band terms. This was done.
>
> The six variations have their origin not, as might be supposed in the tune of a folksong or something of a similar nature, but in a complete piano piece I wrote a few years earlier as part of a collection of teaching pieces [Op. 74, No. 9]. I felt that the slow legato quality of the music, its subdued tone-colour and the rhythmic opposition of twos and threes would serve as an excellent preliminary test in brass band playing. In Variation I ('First Dance') there is a lively opposition of legato and staccato, while Variation II ('Cradle Song') relies for its effectiveness on a subtle balancing of quiet harmonic ingredients. Variation III ('Pageant') raises the dynamics to *forte* and demands alert dotted rhythms. 'Ostinato' (IV) has mainly five beats to the bar, and its material overlaps into the 'Second Dance' (V). The last Variation, 'Lament', is in many ways the most difficult, as its rhythmic freedom demands perfect coordination of instruments. The Coda returns briefly to the opening theme.[3]

The theme is a transcription of the entire thirty-four measures of the original piano piece; the triplet movement against the eighths of the theme in the original is also preserved, but in very different note patterns. The key has been changed from the G major of the piano piece to F major. The first six measures of the theme, reproduced in Example 276, are enough to show the tranquil mood and the flowing lines, and both of these continue throughout the entire thematic presentation. Also, the structure of the presentation is that of the piano piece – a symmetrical ternary form (see p.267).

Ex. 276

As a set of variations, this is certainly among the most elusive of all Rubbra's works in this genre from the standpoint of theme recognition. The only variation in which any thematic segment is readily identifiable is the Fourth. An example of the difficulty is furnished as early as Variation I where, in accordance with the character of the music, the metre has been altered to 3/4, and the tempo to *Allegretto*. The figure in measure 6 of Example 276, plus G, A, B flat in the measure just beyond the example, serves as the nucleus of a new melody whose gracefulness is consistent with the dance rhythm. However, the listener will not identify this melody with any part of the theme, and it is difficult even for the analyst to discover its origins exactly. The metre change, and especially the accentual changes, have totally disguised the figure.

The rocking fifths and fourths in the continuing 3/4 of 'Cradle Song' are obviously intended to simulate the rocking of a cradle, but since they comprise a standard way of portraying this, it seems pointless to say that they are derived from the very occasional fourths and fifths contained in the theme. If they were so derived, it was surely the result of an unconscious process. These intervals, together with others, form a distinctive melody whose only relationship to the theme resides in its harmonic organization: the minor mode of 'Cradle Song' corresponds to that of the *B* section of the theme. The expressive quality is also the same, for in each instance there is a gentle and rather wistful melancholy. In 'Cradle Song' that feeling is intensified through the careful use of muted dissonances.

'Pageant' derives the rocking fifths and fourths of its melodic line from those of 'Cradle Song', but almost everything else in the piece is scalic or otherwise conjunct. There are no figures in the theme to which these are linked. The mood is stately and ceremonial.

The ostinatos of Variation IV, set in 5/4 metrical patterns whose divisions are 3 + 2, consist of seven-note figures. These are arranged so that an eighth rest and three eighths and a quarter fill the first part of the measure; following the dotted line, two eighths and a quarter complete the ostinato pattern. Each of these parts ends with the upward leap of a fourth, and the complete figures are variously marked with accents or *staccato* dots. They dominate the entire Variation to the extent that certain passages that do refer unambiguously to the theme are almost inaudible. These latter passages are in long notes, but are, at first, not entirely literal replicas of the opening two measures of the theme because their starting notes are not the mediant of the key, as is the case in the theme's first statement (Example 276). Closer to the end of the Variation the first six measures of the theme are faithfully reproduced but, as I have indicated above, the ostinatos all but overwhelm them.

The 'Second Dance' of Variation V is very short – really just a transition from the ostinato variation to the final 'Lament'. Like its predecessor in Variation II, it is in 3/4 metre and its descending three-note figure seems to be related to similar figures in 'First Dance'.

Variation VI, 'Lament', is beautifully conceived and sensitively scored. Only the vaguest of references to the theme are contained in the delicate roulades, composed of sixteenths and thirty-seconds, that are the outstanding and pervasive feature of this piece. The scalic, undulating rise and fall of the passages containing these figures require, as Rubbra said above, 'perfect coordination of instruments', a problem made more difficult by the groups of five, six and nine notes that distinguish many of these passages. Trills precede and follow each of the roulades and the tempo – *Molto meno mosso* – is to be interpreted 'freely'. In fact, any rigidity of tempo would ruin the Variation in the same way as a Chopin nocturne would be spoiled. The roulades are scored for the cornets, solo E flat horn and the euphonium. Those instruments not participating in the roulades have been assigned notes of longer duration, as well as long, sustained notes. The dynamic level throughout the Variation varies from *piano* to *mezzo piano* only. The sound, therefore, is wonderfully mellow.

The coda repeats not the whole theme, but just that portion from the beginning of section *B* in the ternary plan to the end, plus a five-measure cadential passage containing a *crescendo* to a final *fortissimo* chord for all instruments.

Although in these variations the melodic theme has been all but ignored, a situation bound to be confusing to the layman who expects to hear clear references to it from time to time, there are general similarities to the basic harmonic plan of the theme. It is these that the listener must be prepared to accept *in lieu* of the much more easily recognized melodic line or its fragments. A set of variations so constructed is every bit as legitimate as one that refers constantly to a theme or to fragments thereof. One thing, however, that is puzzling: in his programme notes, Rubbra never mentions thematic relationships of any kind, emphasizing instead the special technical problems that must be met and overcome in the competitive situation for which the work was written. One wonders why both aspects were not included in his notes.

Rubbra's second work for brass is his *Fanfare for Europe*, Op. 142, commissioned by the Guildhall School and dedicated to the Lord Mayor of London. It bears a completion date of December 1972 and its obvious purpose was to celebrate the entry of Britain into the European Economic Community, an event that occurred on 1 January 1973. It would seem that the six trumpets in C for which the Fanfare is scored were meant to represent the six original members of the Community: Belgium, France, Italy, Luxembourg, The Netherlands and West Germany. There is no doubt, however, about the three notes on which the piece is based, and which are named on the title page and at the head of the score: E-E-C. However, there is enough variety in Rubbra's employment of these notes to forestall monotony, and the brevity of the piece – thirty-four full measures – and the *Allegretto con spirito* tempo also serve this end.

The asymmetrical ternary form of the piece ensures still more variety by way of a tiny *B* section that contains just four measures of B major/D major harmony, plus a fifth measure that modulates back to C. The second measure of this miniature section repeats in B major the three statements of the notes that inspired the *Fanfare*. These notes are, quite naturally, first heard in the opening measure of the work where they are given out by the six trumpets in unison and octaves; the dynamic level is *forte* (see Example 277). The sense of excitement

Ex. 277

and elation has been noticeably increased by the progressively faster rhythmic patterns in which the notes have been cast. These are also employed in later measures: the B major passage, the first measure of the returning *A*, and in one more place, but in each instance the unison and octaves have been replaced by chords and moving parts in certain of the other trumpets. Elsewhere, the three notes appear in other contexts and in other values, but there are also materials during which the notes are entirely absent. The work ends triumphantly on a sustained, *fortissimo* chord.

The third work in the brass category is the Canzona for St. Cecilia, Op. 158. The occasion for which it was commissioned was the Royal Concert in the Festival Hall on 18 November 1981. This is an annual affair held on or close to 22 November, the feast day of St Cecilia. Its purpose is to augment the Musicians Benevolent Fund as well as the funds of similar organizations. The Queen and Prince Philip, patrons of the event, were in attendance that evening.

In a short explanation of his Canzona in the costly and beautifully produced concert brochure, Rubbra has demonstrated a refreshingly new approach to pieces honouring this patron saint of music:

> As St. Cecilia is often pictured as seated at an organ, I thought it appropriate that instead of the usual fanfare I should write a three-minute solemn-sounding piece that would approximate to organ sounds, beginning as quietly as possible with muted brass and growing to a resounding climax, *fortissimo*.[4]

Commenting on this explanation the day after the concert, the reviewer for the *Guardian* observed that 'it was a welcome reminder that some composers still keep their words-to-music ratio in realistic proportion.'[5]

Another review on the following day tells how

> players from the Royal Military School of Music, conducted by Lt-Col George Evans, who are regular guests at the celebration, did sound remarkably organ-like in this 'three-minute solemn-sounding piece' as Rubbra calls it: firm and sure of step, its strong, terse progress towards a fortissimo climax moves through lines of individuated sound, drawing out and dissolving back into the texture with all the skill of sensitively selected organ registration.[6]

Finally, we read that

> The traditional patron saint of our art and, thus, of the occasion, was paid homage to somewhat unconventionally by Edmund Rubbra's 'Canzona for St. Cecilia' (a name

sadly enough claimed by latest research to have resulted from a misreading of the Latin caecitas, meaning blindness). Given that the saint is often pictured seated at an organ, Dr. Rubbra decided that throughout his three-minute piece the trumpeters and brass of the Royal Military School of Music, conducted by Lt-Col G. E. Evans, should simulate the tone colours of that celestial instrument.[7]

In the totality of Rubbra's achievement the Canzona is very much a minor work, but its first performance was part of an important occasion that the BBC broadcast live on Radio 3. Hopefully, it will be included not only on future Royal Concert programmes but also on other occasions that require a brass ensemble work of this calibre. Like so many of Rubbra's works, both large and small, it deserves more than the one performance it received.

The melody with which it opens ('theme' seems inappropriate because of the brevity of the piece and the fact that it is through-composed) has been placed in relief in the high range of the solo trumpet, where its softly undulating, conjunct line suggests the timeless tranquility of the cloister. Supporting this melody are slow-moving chords in the middle brass, which gradually rise higher until they become subordinated to the melodic lines of other instruments. A fascinating interplay of granitic harmony with individual, contrapuntal lines ensues, eventually reaching the loud climax mentioned in Rubbra's programme notes. However, in addition to the organ-like sounds thereby achieved, there is the unmistakable sound of an actual organ on the final, *fortissimo* chord in the BBC's broadcast performance. With no mention of the organ's use in Rubbra's summary or in the reviews, the full sound of the Festival Hall's organ is totally unexpected. Although this is a very small detail, one wonders why it was overlooked.

The condition of Rubbra's health prevented his attendance at the Royal Concert, just as it had the preceding year when his Eleventh Symphony received its first performance. This circumstance explains the opening sentence in a letter of 20 November 1981, from John Denison, Chairman of The Royal Concert that annually honours St Cecilia:

> I hope that the radio transmission of Wednesday evening's Royal Concert came over well, and that you were satisfied with the performance. As you know, I had sent Colonel Evans some very precise suggestions following on our various telephone conversations, and so far as I can gather he had followed them implicitly. To my ears at least, it sounded truly impressive, and I cannot say better than that you gave us exactly what we asked for in the most glorious form.
>
> For your reference, I enclose copies of such press notices as we have found.
>
> I think Colonel Evans hopes that there may be other occasions when he can use this piece, but, in any case, may I send you my personal thanks and those of the Committee for responding so magnificently.

Sinfonietta for large string orchestra

The last work that Rubbra was to write, and which is by far the most important and impressive in the miscellaneous category is the Sinfonietta for Large String

Orchestra, Op. 163. It was commissioned by the Albany (New York) Symphony Orchestra for performance in 1986 as part of the tricentennial celebration of the founding of New York's capital city. This orchestra, like the Louisville Symphony earlier, for which Rubbra had composed his Improvisation for Violin and Orchestra, is one of the leading American organizations in the matter of commissioning new music. George Lloyd's Eleventh Symphony, conducted by the composer, was yet another new work by an Englishman to receive its world premiere during the same season that heard the Rubbra premiere. The latter took place on 5 December 1986, in the nearby city of Troy simply because the orchestra's policy is to present its Friday concerts in that city and its Saturday performances in Albany. I was a guest of the orchestra for that performance, conducted by Julius Hegyi, the orchestra's permanent conductor. This is a work that ranks alongside such other string orchestra masterpieces as Barber's Adagio for Strings and Vaughan Williams's Tallis Fantasia.

The extraordinary vigour and strength of this music have combined to produce one of Rubbra's most dynamic and optimistic works. The fact that its entire second half is a note-for-note transcription (except for a short passage at the very end) of the Fantasy Fugue for Piano, Op. 161, does not imply weakness or a decrease in inventive powers. According to Michael Hill, for whom the piano piece was written, Rubbra had 'encountered a block which he simply could not break through until it occurred to him that the intervallic structure of the Fantasy Fugue was related to that of the string piece'.[8] Most composers experience such blocks from time to time, but in this instance Rubbra was enough worried about his solution to ask Hill whether he objected to the wholesale transcription of his piece, and upon being assured that his friend and former pupil did not, said, 'Well, I'm glad that's off my chest; I've been concerned about it.'[9]

While I fully accept Rubbra's reason for the incorporation of the Fantasy Fugue into the second half of the Sinfoniettta, I feel that his solution may also have been motivated by another but unspoken reason: the realization that he might not live to complete the commission unless he resorted to some kind of drastic action. Support for this idea can, it seems to me, be read into the words 'Deo gratias', written at the end of the score over the date of composition: 1984–85.

The Sinfonietta is through-composed and entirely improvisatory in feeling, something that seems very right and appropriate for this composer's final undertaking, for his inclinations and talents have always lain in this direction no matter what the formal structures of his works may have dictated. The first section is essentially a fantasia and the great majority of its melodic movement is conjunct in spite of the skips seen in the four opening measures (Example 278) but the scale-wise motion in measures 5–7 is the norm for Part I. There are, of course, other disjunct intervals throughout this first half, but they are mainly leaps of an octave or more. A number of these appear in the example where their function is seen as one of changing the melodic direction in several

Ex. 278

parts. There is more to it than this, for as the work progresses a certain amount
of excitement is built up when scalic passages ascend to the higher reaches of
the violins. Besides the melodic factor, harmonic and dynamic elements also
contribute to this excitement, which is then released when the melodic line
changes direction by dropping an octave or further.

At first, the solid wall of sound in this first half of the Sinfonietta appears to
militate against the probability of finding some segment that is responsible for
the melodic fabric. But Rubbra's musical sensibilities have almost always found
some motive, segment or interval that can serve as a generating force; becoming aware of this predilection is half the problem, and the other half is the

identification of those first causes. In this instance the generating force involves nothing more than the final application of what came to be the composer's favourite interval: the fourth. It is employed here melodically, and sounded twice in the *pizzicato* eighths of the cello part in the opening measure of Example 278. A glance at the rest of the example will show other instances of the melodic fourth in both its ascending and descending forms. Most obvious are the stressed *pizzicato* fourths in the second violin and viola parts of measures 6–7, and Rubbra's intention to highlight them is proved by the syncopated rhythms in which they are set. They are heard again in the *fortissimo* closing passage of Part I (measures 74–5), but on different notes and with the syncopations absent.

Part II (*Lento* $\downarrow$ = *c*.72) is the same length as Part I and the halves are connected by the remains of a *sforzando*, triple-stopped, A flat chord in the basses. Thus the key is the same as that of the opening chord in the first measure of Example 278. The idea of transcribing the Fantasy Fugue was brilliant for two reasons: first, in its new setting for strings the transcription is enormously effective – more so, to my mind, than the original piano version; and second, because it fits perfectly in this particular place for the reason that the level of emotional intensity beyond the climax in measures 74–8 (the end of Part I) cannot be sustained. The broad and quiet fugue subject (Example 152, p.278) with which the transcription opens provides the necessary relief. Yet it is not long before the transcription itself builds to climaxes more powerful than those in the original piano piece (it is instructive to compare the two scores in this regard, for the later version contains doublings, string tremolos and other small changes), but the emphasis is, of course, on counterpoint. And so, with a first part more like a prelude or fantasia and a fugal second part, a balance has been struck.

Most of the harmonies in the Sinfonietta are the result of the melodic interactions of the instrumental parts – a common Rubbra characteristic – and these are often rich. Another harmonic trait is also present in this work: progressions which, in a very short space, direct the music to a temporary yet quite unexpected tonality that is unrelated to what the ear has begun to accept as the defined tonality. The first three measures of Example 278 afford a perfect instance of this kind of writing: a modified A flat major is the accepted tonality in the first one and a half measures, but then a dissonant C major chord and a D flat chord take us unexpectedly to B major. Thereafter, the harmony is transitional until an unstable D flat major is reached in the middle of measure 6. This is also arrived at abruptly, this time by half-step movement: modulation by chromaticism, another favourite Rubbra technique. Yet it all sounds so completely natural and unforced, and the ear accepts the sudden changes without question. The final chord of the Sinfonietta which is, of course, the final chord of the Fantasy Fugue for Piano, illustrates the Rubbran practice of substituting an entirely different cadential chord for the one the listener is expecting to hear. In this case, a D major chord seems inevitable, but instead the work comes to an end on an F major chord – a very logical choice in view of the harmonies up to that point, but still unexpected.

Critical comment in the press was unanimously enthusiastic:

> As the composer of eleven symphonies and a considerable body of chamber music and choral works, Rubbra has been acknowledged a master among 20th-century British composers.
>
> That he has not achieved the popularity of, say, Britten has to do with a certain introverted quality to his music. He was a composer who shied away from the openly dramatic, although the processes of his music could engender considerable tension.
>
> The 'Sinfonietta' is a distillation of Rubbra's esthetic, a ruminative but impassioned piece that belies the lighthearted connotations of its title. 'Fantasia and Fugue' might be a more apt title, actually, though the fugue quickly dissolves in freer writing.
>
> Strands of melody are intertwined in sometimes heated harmonic tension; textures are thickened by dividing the strings, setting into high relief a passage for four soloists (a tribute, perhaps, to Vaughan Williams)....
>
> Though only thirteen minutes long, it's easily worth the price of the concert.[10]

The above notice appeared the day of the concert, in effect advertising the night's performance. An excellent and forward-looking policy, showing that the reviewer had had a rehearsal experience with a new work; also good for the listener, who can gain some idea as to what the new work is all about. Would that this policy were more widespread.

Two days later, and following the dual performances, Cantrell wrote again:

> The prize, to my ears, was Edmund Rubbra's 'Sinfonietta for Large String Orchestra,' composed last year on an ASO commission. (It proved to be the late English composer's last work.)
>
> The title, with its lighthearted connotations is misleading: 'Fantasia and Fugue' might be better, especially in relating the piece to a rich English heritage of string music going back to the 16th century. Here, as in the Tudor viol fantasias, the bittersweet modal inflections seem almost otherworldly; the friction of intertwining voices (with textures thickened by dividing the strings) yields emotional incandescence. In little space – some thirteen minutes – much is compressed.[11]

Finally, in the leading newspaper of another city close to Albany, we read that the Sinfonietta 'sits very comfortably within a British tradition of string suites: gorgeously crafted, harmonically rich. There's nothing obtuse or threatening about it, and brief enough to make its statement without cloying.'[12]

The composer fittingly dedicated this final work to his sons, Adrian and Julian.

Notes

1   Printed on the inside front cover of *Edmund Rubbra: Composer*.
2   *ibid.*
3   Edmund Rubbra, programme notes for Variations on *The Shining River*.

4   Edmund Rubbra, programme notes for the *Canzona for Saint Cecilia*.
5   Andrew Keener, *Guardian*, 19 November 1981.
6   Hilary Finch, *The Times*, 19 November 1981.
7   Peter Stadlen, *The Daily Telegraph*, 20 November 1981.
8   Michael Hill, 'Edmund Rubbra: A Personal Memoir', *Worcester College Record*, 1987, p.23.
9   *ibid.*
10 Scott Cantrell, *The Albany Times Union*, 5 December 1986.
11 *ibid.*, 7 December 1986.
12 B.A. Nilsson, *The Schenectady Gazette*, 8 December 1986.

12   Conclusions and summaries

Summarizing the style of any composer in a meaningful way is never a simple task, but in the case of one who, like Rubbra, pursued a singularly independent course that ignored the styles of most of his contemporaries, it becomes even more difficult. One might think it would be easier owing to the absence in Rubbra's music of any of the complexities associated with dodecaphony, to say nothing of more recent trends. However, in his quiet and unassuming way Rubbra was something of a pioneer in his application of polyphony to the symphony as well as to other genres where, in each instance, it is a generating force rather than a decorative adjunct. Add to this his admission that he had no idea where the music was going next, and the difficulties are then compounded by the problems of structure which arise. The improvisatory element is yet another complicating factor.

No composer is immune to influences, but Rubbra was more fortunate than some owing to his late start, plus the fact that in Holst and R.O. Morris he encountered no overbearing musical personalities but, rather, guides who, by suggestions and encouragement, allowed him to develop in his own way. This is not to deny that a Holstian influence is present for one element in particular – the ostinato – recurs again and again throughout Rubbra's works. However, whereas with Holst it is more often a succession of repeated, descending notes in the bass (in essence, a decorative device), in Rubbra's music it forms an organic part of the structure: the often complex ostinato figures grow out of previously stated thematic material. Being no longer confined to the bass as in Holst, they are distributed throughout all parts, thereby generating a considerable amount of gathering tension as in the first movement of the Second Symphony. Here, Rubbra incorporated and transformed the ostinato, making it serve his purpose in a new and individual way. A second Holstian characteristic – the frequent use of 5/4 and 7/4 metres – is also present throughout Rubbra's music, but the prevalence of these in much twentieth-century music rules out Holst as the sole source.

Among others, Sibelius is sometimes mentioned as having exerted an influence on Rubbra and it is certainly true that there are reminders: mainly orchestral combinations and colours, and the way in which melodic fragments eventually coalesce into a theme. Yet neither the fragments nor the theme are Sibelian in character and to call such reminders 'influences' is both destructive and misleading: destructive because the untutored reader/listener has no alternative but to believe the judgements of those 'authorities'. The 'destruction' of Rubbra's Second Symphony in a few paragraphs under the heading 'Sibelius' Eighth At Last!' is a case in point (see pp.64–65); still other reminders are the Ravelian and Bartókian passages in the First Quartet (p.303). There are also a few measures in the passacaglia movement of the Seventh Symphony where there is a strong hint of Shostakovich. However, to call any of these reminders 'influences' is wrong.

The most frequently mentioned influence is said to emanate from Elizabethan music, and Rubbra himself was largely to blame for the wide circulation of the idea when he told A.L. Lloyd in 1949 that he was 'trying to bring the contrapuntal texture of the Elizabethans into the wider instrumental forms'.[1] He undoubtedly regretted having said this, for some writers and reviewers have drawn totally unwarranted conclusions as a result. One of the more extreme examples concerns the symphonies, which are described by one writer as being 'by nature expanded madrigals, descendants of the Elizabethan fantasia'.[2] Once said, variants of such stereotypes inevitably find their way into other assessments and this has, of course, happened. In a 1971 radio talk, Hugh Ottaway sought to mitigate the damage, and rightly observed that it is the *spirit* of Elizabethan music rather than literal resemblances which inform certain Rubbra movements. I disagree, however, with Ottaway's choice of the Scherzo Polimetrico from the Second Quartet as an illustration of that spirit, for the rhythmic complexity of twentieth-century music is much closer to hand than that of the sixteenth-century madrigal tradition which Ottaway felt was the rhythmic source. At the close of his remarks Ottaway admits that 'any thoughts of the madrigal or the fantasy are pushed well into the background where they properly belong'. If the connection with the *sound* of Elizabethan music is this tenuous, what criteria were used in the selection of this movement? To my ears even the spirit of Elizabethan music is missing in it.

In an apparent effort to rebut the critics Rubbra observed that

> writers have said I've been influenced by the Elizabethans. Whenever they say this I'm surprised for it has never occurred to me that analogies might be drawn.[3]

Had Rubbra in his remark to Lloyd used the expression 'contrapuntal texture' without alluding to any historical period, the controversy could have been avoided. Such a revised statement would have accurately described many of his symphonic movements and much else in the other genres, including some song accompaniments. Of course, in the choral area there is no doubting an Elizabethan flavour in the madrigals, but since these were set to Elizabethan texts such a flavour is expected.

The final word on supposed influences in Rubbra's music came from the composer himself, and is contained in the same interview as his comments above. Following Rubbra's remark that 'all composers throughout history have had the same problem of selecting from what was bequeathed in order to satisfy what it was necessary to express', Schafer asked, 'What have you found worth selecting?' The composer's answer is illuminating:

> This I couldn't tell you. I've never been conscious of selecting anything from the past in order to make use of it in my own work... I simply take what is relevant without knowing the sources.... When I study the music of the past, the antennae of my imagination automatically dwell on certain interesting features of the music I am studying, and later, unconsciously, some of these may find expression in my own music. I never take over an idea or a musical formula from an earlier epoch and use it as though it were a fixed and unalterable fact in its own right. Material of the past should be regarded as fertilizer for the imagination and if one assimilates it unconsciously, one avoids the danger of disrupting one's work through a conflict of styles.[4]

Two elements from the past that have helped to fertilize Rubbra's style are medieval organum, including later medieval procedures, and modality, the latter in more generous amounts than the former. In commenting on the three liturgical Masses (*Missa in Honorem Sancti Dominici*, *Missa à 3*, and Mass in Honour of St Teresa of Avila), *Lauda Sion* and the two *Te Deums*, Erik Routley correctly caught the essential flavour of these works, and in doing so dismissed the Elizabethan apologists:

> The influence of neo-medievalism is nowhere more evident than here. Sometimes there is a strangely angular and astringent effect – often produced by the combination of tonalities or by simple 'false relations', but it is the angularity of very early polyphonic music. You hear Byrd and Tallis less often than Dunstable when Rubbra is writing for the church.[5]

The granitic, austere sounds, some of them very much like medieval organum, of these and such other choral works as *And When The Builders* and *Up, O My Soul* are far removed from the contrapuntal textures with which Rubbra has always been associated, but their emphasis on harmony and its attendant verticality is no less an authentic facet of his style. It is true that much of Rubbra's harmonic structure is the by-product of the horizontal movement of individual contrapuntal lines and is, therefore, as unpredictable as the movement of the parts that produced it. The result is frequently quite dissonant, leading to some interesting harmonic situations, some of which have prompted a number of writers, Elsie Payne and Harold Truscott among them, to conclude that bitonality is present. When I asked the composer if he agreed with their analyses, he replied,

> if I do, it's quite incidental to the music. *They* might find bitonality there, but I did not put it in as such. I don't particularly like it as an idiom, although music I've studied, such as Eugene Goossens's *Kaleidoscope*, has a piece in two different keys which I used to play. But I don't consider bitonality as willed at all. It may happen, but it's not willed. I think in terms of counterpoint – lines – and if they happen to be bitonal at one point, it's only because the two lines coalesce and produce that effect.[6]

Thus the question of bitonality is really an academic one.

Similarly, it is not possible to point to a harmonic structure as having been planned, given Rubbra's singular method of composing: 'I never know where a piece is going to go next... I work each bar as I go along', and so on. Such a preconceived harmonic structure would have seriously restricted his imagination. It then follows that there is no guarantee that a movement will end in the key in which it began; most of the time it does not. Further harmonic freedom is ensured when important themes are restated in keys different from the original ones, and often the context surrounding themes is also different. Key signatures are frequently very imprecise indicators of the music's real tonal structure and the question inevitably arises as to why key signatures were used in the first place.

Nothing said thus far is meant to imply that harmony is an unimportant ingredient in Rubbra's music, merely that it cannot normally be thought of as a form-building agent. In the context of the composer's measure-to-measure procedure it is immensely expressive in two ways. First, there is the element that I shall call 'harmonic surprise'. There was in Rubbra's musical constitution the ability to sense in an almost uncanny way the point at which a melody should change its direction. That point is sometimes not the one that even a knowledgeable listener might have chosen, especially if the context suggests a continuation in the same vein. But after a few hearings the change sounds not only reasonable but inevitable. One realizes at such moments that one is part of a process of discovery and the exciting thing about it is that, in view of Rubbra's compositional procedures, discovery is the keyword for him too. It naturally follows that the harmony associated with the change in melodic direction is also full of surprises, no matter whether it has been produced accidentally through the movement of contrapuntal parts or has evolved beneath a homophonic melody. In either case, the harmony commands attention.

The second way in which Rubbra's harmony is expressive is eloquently demonstrated in the areas of modulation and transition (see Julius Harrison's remarks quoted on p.44). There are many instances of modulatory magic scattered throughout Rubbra's works, some of which have been treated in detail in this book.

Closely allied to modulatory and transitional passages but not necessarily employing either are the shifts – both gradual and sudden – from a contrapuntal to a homophonic texture, and, of course, the reverse is true. As usual with Rubbra there is always a good reason for such shifts, but the ease with which he makes them is extraordinary. In the case of those accomplished gradually, the listener is scarcely aware that any change is in progress, while the abrupt shifts are sometimes dramatic. Naturally, the harmonic structure shifts emphasis in accordance with the textural changes, but the determining factor in most instances is the melodic element. This is true even in those cases where the melody rides along the tops of chords which have, in effect, created the melody.

As for Rubbra's homophonic gifts (all too often forgotten), one need think only of the slow movement from the Fifth Symphony, the 'Canto' of the Sixth, and innumerable slower sections of *allegro* and *allegretto* movements. The same is true in the string quartets and concertos. In all such instances there is a wonderful singing quality in the melody and the supporting harmonies are full and rich.

Rubbra's orchestration has since the first two symphonies been subjected to a barrage of criticism. One of the more balanced pronouncements is from Julius Harrison:

> That gift for polyphonic writing, unapproached by any other British composer since the time of the Tudor madrigalists and Purcell, of necessity imposed some restrictions on the colourful orchestral presentation of his symphonic music. In pursuit of his high ideals colour was indeed too often made subservient to line. And so in the two earliest – the Second belongs to 1937 – there is in the general scoring a plodding sameness that has certainly dulled appreciation of the music's great worth. But when we reach the Third Symphony (1939), with its beautiful and rather Sibelian first movement and a mystical third that rises to a superb climax, the claims of counterpoint, harmony and orchestral colours are met in more equal proportions.[7]

The composer has, of course, his defenders in this area. Harold Truscott is one who maintains, quite rightly in my opinion, that the texture of the first two symphonies demanded and received the scoring required, and had the music of either symphony been different, the orchestration would necessarily have been different. This view received expression in the remarks made by Robert Layton, one of Rubbra's former pupils, in a radio interview conducted some months after the composer's death:

> I think his scoring was very germane to his thinking; and that attempts to thin it out or clean it up would, in fact, damage the whole concept that he had. I don't think that his ideal of colour corresponded to that of contemporary fashions at all.... His music does have an individual sonority. Take the opening of the Seventh for example. It's quite unlike anybody else when you get to know it, and his music does speak with a distinctive voice that summons you.

Had Rubbra heard Layton's remark about 'contemporary fashions' in orchestral colour, he would have concurred heartily, for he had expressed his views on this very point when he confessed to Murray Schafer that

> there is one characteristic of much contemporary music that bothers me. I feel the emphasis on colour and timbre to be an unfortunate thing because that is the most ephemeral part of music really. If a colour is implicit in stronger lines underneath, then very well; but so often today it is treated as too important a thing in itself. I don't deny that colour has fascination, but for me, it's no substitute for the real substance of art. You can't abstract the green from a leaf and still pretend the leaf exists.[8]

Schafer then asked Rubbra whether he was 'concerned with colour at all? You have been accused of "unimaginative" orchestration'. Rubbra replied,

Those who thus accuse me obviously have a different viewpoint from myself. There are many others who maintain my orchestration is completely appropriate. Colour is not something I can put on; it either is or is not in the ideas themselves. All my orchestral ideas are conceived in a certain orchestral colour, and this is part of the fundamental conception of them. For instance, the second subject of the first movement of my sixth symphony came to me clothed in woodwind colour. I could not have conceived it any other way. To go further in decking my themes out would, for me, introduce an element of distraction. Some critics may call the texture of my music dense or heavy – grey. Perhaps I like grey. People sometimes look at Rembrandt paintings and exclaim: 'Yes, but how dark it is!' What they don't realize is that this very darkness was part of Rembrandt's vision. You couldn't brighten them up without distorting the idea behind them.[9]

Beginning with his Third Symphony there is a noticeable lightening in Rubbra's scoring, but the changes emanated solely from the subject matter in accord with the composer's principles as stated above.

When the totality of Rubbra's *oeuvre* is considered, unity is one of its most important characteristics. This operates on two levels: the purely musical, and the religious and philosophical. The former aspect has been noted a number of times in this book, chiefly when a melodic fragment or phrase, cast in a particular rhythmic form and given a distinctive instrumentation, is employed as a focal point at both the beginning and end of a movement. The first movement of the Fifth Symphony with its poignant oboe phrase sounding the augmented fourth is a perfect example (see Example 36, p.106). Other instances of unity involve a very small unit such as a generating interval, which is carried over from movement to movement or section to section, the diminished fifth in the Tenth Symphony being an example.

Still another Rubbra trait which contributes not a little to the sense of unity, although in an indirect way, is his intuitive awareness of the place at which a movement or an entire work should end. Once a point has been made it is not endlessly hammered home (as in Nielsen's truly 'Inextinguishable' Symphony). In fact, sometimes one wishes that an especially beautiful phrase at or near the end of a movement or work could be heard just once more, but no; when Rubbra is through, he is through.

The unity that manifests itself religiously and philosophically is not so easily perceived or apprehended. It is religious in the universal rather than in the sectarian sense despite Rubbra's personal Catholicism and the Latin titles of many of his works. Which religious experience or combination of experiences induced it is immaterial, although I personally believe it was a blend of the most mystical and spiritual elements of Buddhism and Catholicism arrived at intuitively in response to the basic nature of Rubbra's personality. A perusal of the religious and philosophical section of the composer's library tends to support this view, for the emphasis is on such writings as those of St Teresa of Avila, St John of the Cross, Teilhard de Chardin and various works dealing with the contemplative aspects of Buddhism. Books that approach religion from a doctrinal and dogmatic viewpoint are conspicuously absent. The blend becomes richer and more humanized with the discovery of books that deal philosophically with the verse of the English metaphysical poets and that of such poets as Gerard Manley Hopkins. And, of course, there are the anthologies of their poetry.

The blending of these elements, if that is indeed the source, produced music which overflows with a basic optimism and sense of well-being; but both qualities are strong enough to impress the listener as having been fought for and won in some remote past. In that sense – and that sense only – Rubbra is like Bruckner: 'their symphonic canvases are both drawn from cooperative, rather than antagonistic musical material, toward climaxes which are expressions of ecstasy rather than confrontation.'[10] But a buildup of tension on the way to those climaxes is by no means ruled out. In Rubbra's case the lyricism endemic in all of his music, and which generates everything that happens both polyphonically and homophonically, can and does employ variants of itself in the creation of tensions. Yet such passages are softened and ennobled by the lyricism without diluting the very real drama with which many of them are imbued. Thus not only is musical unity enhanced, but the basic optimism and serenity (both words used in a spiritual sense) of the music are preserved, and it is possible to think of musical unity as having been extended to represent the unity ideally existing between man and man, and between man and God. This is what I think Rubbra intended and it is what I believe is meant by the unavoidably vague term, 'religious and philosophical unity'.

Over the years Rubbra received tributes in the form of letters from close friends, many of whom were fellow composers and performers. Some were in connection with first performances, while others celebrated special birthdays such as his seventieth and seventy-fifth. However, common to both types are warm statements of appreciation for Rubbra's overall career and the high standards he always maintained. It is appropriate now to reproduce several of these. The first is dated 17 February 1960, and is from someone whose signature is, unfortunately, undecipherable:

> I have just heard the performance of your Violin Concerto and am so impressed by its beauty I must find an outlet for my enthusiasm by this letter.
>
> Beauty is a word I find I can seldom apply to the compositions of today's composers and painters, but the irresistible beauty of the second movement of your Concerto... overwhelmed me: it is otherworldly, as I believe music should be – not the contrived expression of an egocentric composer.

On 21 May 1971, two days before Rubbra's seventieth birthday, the critic, Henry Raynor, wrote,

> I should not forgive myself if I didn't add my voice to the very many who are saying *ad multos annos* on Sunday morning. May I say that in an age of hit and miss, slipshod composition, when serious workmanship seems to count for little, and when music which thinks and feels deeply is very likely to be pushed on one side, it is an inspiration to many of us that you have continued to be yourself, without surrender or even compromise, and that we are always eager for more....

My wishes for very many happy returns of the day come with my thanks for what you have already given me.

The same sentiments are found in a letter of 24 May 1976, written by the composer's close friend, Bernard Stevens:

> In congratulating you on your 75th birthday and wishing you many more years of creative activity, I can't let the occasion pass without thanking you for all that knowing you and your work has meant for me all these years. Your great work has been not only a source of endless satisfaction in itself, but has been at the same time a constant source of encouragement to myself in its steadfastness and integrity, its refusal to be deflected from its path.

In addition to tributes contained in letters, there are testimonials to Rubbra's compositional skills and experience, for his advice was actively sought not only, as might be supposed, from former pupils now launched on their own composing careers, but also from a composer with the standing of Vaughan Williams. The latter was in the habit of asking close friends to attend a piano 'play-through' of a new composition, followed several weeks later by one at which 'musicians whose opinions he valued' were present. Among the composers were Bliss, Finzi, Howells and Rubbra. 'All were asked to be frankly critical and he would listen to all they had to say.'[11] In a letter of 22 April 1955, to Michael Kennedy in connection with his Eighth Symphony, Vaughan Williams remarked that he

> had a jury (A. Bliss, Gerald Finzi, Rubbra...) to sit on my new tune... and decide whether I had better go on with it. They decided to put it on the 'short list' with the proviso that it wanted a lot more revision (with that I entirely agreed).[12]

Finally, at the end of Ernest Bradbury's short notice of a 'distinguished and poetic account of one of the masterpieces of our day: Rubbra's Sixth Symphony' (admired also by Vaughan Williams along with the Third), as performed by the City of Birmingham Symphony Orchestra under Douglas Guest at the 1957 Three Choirs Festival in Worcester, there are these words: 'Here again, one thought, the future lies in safe and sensible hands.'[13] For me, this sentence epitomizes the essence of Rubbra's contribution to music. However, a cautionary word is in order here, for 'safe' should never be interpreted as suggesting a mind closed to innovation (one can be sure that Bradbury did not mean it in that sense). On the contrary, in his lyrical and polyphonic approach to composition Rubbra introduced a new way of viewing the symphony, the concerto and chamber music, but in an optimistic and spiritual manner that is entirely incompatible with the materialism of our turbulent and tragic century. It is this manner that kept him from enjoying the prominence that should have been his. He must have known the risks involved in pursuing a style comprised of such currently unpopular elements, but to doggedly maintain it in the face of misunderstanding, indifference and even animosity was an act of great courage for which he paid dearly. Of course, integrity always exacts its price, but in Rubbra's case that price has seemed inexcusably high.

Hopefully, the principal goal of this book has now been achieved: the objective study of a considerable body of music, the high quality of which should by now be obvious (I make no apologies whatsoever for my enthusiasm). However, the attainment of the book's second goal is dependent upon the future: a measurable increase in the number of performances of Rubbra's music from near zero at the moment to something approaching respectability. Every member of the musical community must share the blame for this deplorable neglect: programme planner, conductor, solo performer, chamber group, critic and commentator. During the years I have been occupied with the writing of this book, one question has been asked again and again whenever I have played records and tapes of principal Rubbra works: 'why is this composer's music unknown and unperformed?' My reply has been and still is, 'why, indeed?'

Notes

1   A.L. Lloyd, 'Rubbra: Heir of A Golden Age', *Picture Post*, 10 December 1949.
2   Frank Howes, *The English Musical Renaissance* (London: Secker & Warburg, 1966), p.258.
3   Quoted in Murray Schafer, 'Edmund Rubbra', *British Composers in Interview*, p.68.
4   *ibid.*, pp.67–8.
5   Erik Routley, *Twentieth Century Church Music* (New York: Oxford University Press, 1964), p.65.
6   Tape of 28 June 1980.
7   Julius Harrison, *The New Musical Companion*, p.275.
8   Quoted in Schafer, *op. cit.*, pp.69–70.
9   *ibid.*, p.70.
10   Louis Blois, 'The Symphonies of Edmund Rubbra: A Perspective', *American Record Guide*, p.4.
11   Michael Kennedy, *The Works of Ralph Vaughan Williams* (London: Oxford University Press, 1971), p.287.
12   *ibid.*, p.384.
13   Ernest Bradbury, *MT*, November 1957, p.628.

Appendix A: *British Composers in Interview*

The working methods and preferences of any artist in whatever field are always a matter of interest to the serious reader. Printed below are the questions asked by Murray Schafer of each of the composers in *British Composers in Interview* (Introduction, pp.18–22), and Rubbra's answers.

S. Do you compose at the piano?
R. I like to have one at hand.

S. Do you usually through-compose or sketch out sections independently?
R. Through-compose.

S. Do you revise extensively?
R. Very little. I work slowly and get things right before going on.

S. How many hours a day do you generally compose?
R. Six.

S. Can you estimate roughly how much work gets written at an average sitting?
R. Two bars to twenty bars.

S. How old were you when you wrote your first work of value, and what was this?
R. About thirty. Violin and piano sonata [No. 2].

S. Do you have a favourite composition among your own works?
R. Any of my later symphonies.

S.   Do you have any favourite composers?
R.   Monteverdi, Bach, Stravinsky and Shostakovich at their best.

Appendix B: Catalogue of the works of Edmund Rubbra

Opus	No.	Title	
1		*The Secret Hymnody.* Mixed Voices and Orchestra	MS
2		*Rosa Mundi.* Song	
3	No. 1	*The Virgin's Cradle Hymn.* Mixed Voices	
	No. 2	*The Virgin's Cradle Hymn.* Female Voices	
4	No. 1	*The Mystery.* Song. Unaccompanied Solo Voice	
	No. 2	*Jesukin.* Song	
5		*O My Deir Hert.* Solo Voice and String Quartet	
6		*Afton Water.* Mixed Voices	
7		*Dear Liza.* Two-Part Song	
8	No. 1	*Cradle Song.* Song	
	No. 2	*Orpheus.* Song	
	No. 3	*Who Is Sylvia?* Song	MS
9		Double Fugue. Orchestra	MS
10		*My Tocher's the Jewel.* Mixed Voices	
11		Violin Sonata No. 1	MS
12		*La Belle Dame Sans Merci.* Mixed Voices and Orchestra	MS
13	No. 1	*Out in the Dark.* Song	
	No. 2	*Hymn to the Virgin.* Song	
	No. 3	*It Was A Lover.* Song	
14		*The Night.* Song	
15		*Rune of Hospitality.* Song	
16		Phantasy. Two Violins and Piano	
17	No. 1	*A Prayer.* Song	
	No. 2	*Invocation to Spring.* Song	
18		Rhapsody. Soprano and 13 Instruments	MS

Opus	No.	Title	
	No. 2	*O Unwithered Eagle Void*. Mixed Voices and Orchestra	MS
42		Five Spenser Sonnets. Tenor and String Orchestra Sonnets 2, 4, 6, 43 and 68	
43		*Amoretti*: Five Spenser Sonnets. Tenor and String Quartet. Sonnets 78, 70, 89, 37 and 40	
44		Symphony No. 1	
45		Symphony No. 2	
46		Three Bird Songs. Children's Unison Voices and Piano	
	No. 1	*Robin Redbreast*	
	No. 2	*Little Trotty Wagtail*	
	No. 3	*Pigeon and Wren*	
47		Orchestration of the Handel Variations by Brahms	
48		*Prism*. Ballet Music	MS
49		Symphony No. 3	
50		Improvisations on Virginal Pieces by Giles Farnaby for Orchestra	
		Farnaby's Conceit	
		His Dreame	
		His Humour	
		Loth to Depart	
		Tell Me, Daphne (Variations)	
51		Five Madrigals. Mixed Voices	
		When to Her Lute Corinna Sings	
		I Care Not for These Ladies	
		Beauty Is But A Painted Hell	
		It Fell On A Summer's Day	
		Though You Are Young	
52		Two Madrigals. Mixed Voices	
		Leave Prolonging Thy Distress	
		So Sweet Is Thy Discourse	
53		Symphony No. 4	
54		*Nocturne*. Song	
55		*The Morning Watch*. Mixed Voices and Orchestra	
56		*A Tribute*. Orchestra	
57		*Soliloquy* for Solo Cello and Orchestra	
58		*The Revival*. Mixed Voices	
59		*Missa Cantuariensis*. Mixed Voices	
60		Cello Sonata	
61		Three Psalms for Low Voice and Piano Psalms 6, 23, 150	

Opus	No.	Title
78		*Song of the Soul*. Mixed Voices and Orchestra
79		*Meditation*. Organ
80		Symphony No. 6
81		*Star of the Mystic East*. Mixed Voices
82		*Salutation*. Mixed Voices
83		Ode to the Queen. Contralto and Orchestra
84		*Dance To Your Daddie*. Mixed Voices
85		Concerto in G for Piano and Orchestra
86		Fantasia on a Theme of Machaut. Recorder, String Quartet and Harpsichord
87		Two Sonnets for Medium Voice, Viola and Piano
	No. 1	*Upon the Crucifix*
	No. 2	*On the Reed of Our Lord's Passion*
88		Symphony No. 7
89		Improvisation for Violin and Orchestra
90		*Mary Mother*. Mixed Voices
91		*No Swan So Fine*. Song
92		*Cantata Pastorale*. High Voice, Recorder, Harpsichord and Cello
93		*Entrez-y Tous En Sureté*. Mixed Voices
94		*Festival Gloria*. Mixed Voices
95		*Haec Est Domus Domini*. Mixed Voices
96		*The Givers*. Mixed Voices
97		*In Honorem Mariae Matris Dei*. Soprano and Contralto Soli, Children's Choir, Mixed Voices and Orchestra
98		*Missa à 3*. Mixed Voices
99		*Autumn*. Women's Voices and Piano
100		Sonata for Oboe and Piano
101		Variations On *'The Shining River'* Brass Band
102		*Pezzo Ostinato*. Solo Harp
103		Concerto for Violin and Orchestra
104		Introduction, Aria and Fugue. Harpsichord
105		Variations on a Phrygian Theme. Solo Violin
106		*Notturno*. Recorder Quartet.
107		*Lord, With What Care*. Mixed Voices
108		*Up, O My Soul*. Mixed Voices
109		*The Beatitudes*. Women's Voices
110		*Lauda Sion*. Soprano, Baritone Soli and Mixed Voices
111		*Cantata di Camera*. Solo Tenor, Mixed Voices and Instrumental Ensemble

Opus	No.	Title
130		*Veni Creator Spiritus*. Mixed Voices and Brass
131		Eight Preludes for Piano
132		Symphony No. 8
133		Violin Sonata No. 3
134		*Creature-Songs to Heaven*. Treble Voices, String Quartet and Piano
	No. 1	'The Mother Hen'
	No. 2	'The Snail'
	No. 3	'The Ladybird'
	No. 4	'The Peacock'
135		*The Holy Dawn*. Mixed Voices
136		Advent Cantata. Baritone Solo, Mixed Voices and Small Orchestra
137		*Missa Brevis*. Treble Voices and Organ
138		Piano Trio No. 2
139		Graded Pieces for Piano
	No. 1	Study in Sixths
	No. 2	Study in Tonality
	No. 3	Study in Thirds
	No. 4	Study in Cantabile Chord Playing
140		Symphony No. 9 (*Sinfonia Sacra*)
141		*Transformations*. Solo Harp
142		*Fanfare for Europe*. Six Trumpets
143		*Agnus Dei*. Mixed Voices
144		Graded Pieces for Violin and Piano
	No. 1	*Swinging*
	No. 2	*Strolling*
	No. 3	*Riding*
	No. 4	*Gliding*
	No. 5	*Striding*
145		Symphony No. 10 (*Sinfonia da Camera*)
146		*This Spiritual House Almighty God Shall Inhabit*. Mixed Voices
147		*Blessed Be He*. Mixed Voices
148		*Fly, Envious Time*. Song
149		*Resurgam*. Overture for Orchestra
150		String Quartet No. 4
151		Three Greek Folksongs. Mixed Voices
	No. 1	*The Gift*
	No. 2	*A Wreath of Basil*
	No. 3	*The Suitors*
152		*Prayer for the Queen*. Mixed Voices

Opus No.	Title
153	Symphony No. 11
154	Fantasia on a Chord. Recorder and Harpsichord
155	*How Shall My Tongue Express?* Mixed Voices
156	Duo for Cor Anglais and Piano
157	Mass In Honour of St Teresa of Avila. Mixed Voices
158	Canzona for Brass
159	*St Teresa's Bookmark*. Mixed Voices and Organ
160	Invention on the Name of Haydn. Piano
161	Fantasy Fugue. Piano
162	*Introit*. Mixed Voices
163	Sinfonietta for Large String Orchestra
164	Psalm 122. Mixed Voices

Selected bibliography

During the course of Edmund Rubbra's long career a number of articles marking his progress at various stages have appeared in leading musical journals. Most of these consist of no more than two pages, and the material which they contain is so general as to be of little interest or value to the reader. However, other articles that also fall into the category of 'progress reports' are more specific in content, and these are included in the bibliography.

A second category of articles consists of items that deal with the symphonies in general, while others concentrate on particular symphonies. In both instances the most valuable contributions are by Hugh Ottaway who, before his untimely death, was engaged in writing a book on these works. Other significant articles and reviews in this area also appear in the bibliography.

Finally, there are Rubbra's articles on the various genres of his music, all containing valuable information and insights into his working methods. Excerpts from these have been incorporated at appropriate places in the book.

Banfield, Stephen (1977) 'Rubbra's Songs', in Lewis Foreman (ed.) *Edmund Rubbra: Composer*, Rickmansworth: Triad Press, pp.89–95.

Bergonzi, Bernard (1977) *Gerard Manley Hopkins*, New York: Macmillan Publishing Co., Inc.

Blois, Louis (1984) 'The Symphonies of Edmund Rubbra: A Perspective', *American Record Guide*, May, pp.3–8.

Cruft, Adrian (1971) 'Edmund Rubbra: A Broadcast Tribute', *Royal College of Music Magazine*, Spring, pp.63–4.

———— (1986) 'Edmund Rubbra CBE (1901–1986): A Personal Memoir', *Royal College of Music Magazine*, Summer, pp.43–5.

Elder, Eleanor (1939) *Travelling Players: The Story of The Arts League of Service*, London: Frederick Muller Ltd.

Evans, Edwin (1945) 'Edmund Rubbra', *The Musical Times*, February–March, pp.41–5; 75–8.

Foreman, Lewis (1977) 'Recorder Music', in Lewis Foreman (ed.) *Edmund Rubbra: Composer*, Rickmansworth: Triad Press, pp.71–5.

Goddard, Scott (1954) 'Rubbra's New Symphony', *The Listener*, 11 November, p.829.

Hill, Michael (1987) 'Edmund Rubbra: A Personal Memoir', *Worcester College Record*, pp.17–23.

Hutchings, Arthur (1946) 'Edmund Rubbra', in A.L. Bacharach (ed.) *British Music of Our Time*, Harmondsworth: Pelican Books, pp.200–8.

——— (1939) 'Edmund Rubbra's Second Symphony', *Music and Letters* 20, October, pp.374–80.

——— (1940) 'Rubbra's Third Symphony', *The Musical Times*, September, pp.361–4.

——— (1941) 'Rubbra's Third Symphony: A Study of Its Texture', *The Music Review*, February, pp.14–28.

Jacobson, Maurice (1935) 'The Music of Edmund Rubbra', *The Monthly Musical Record*, February, pp.32–3.

McChesney, Donald (1968) *A Hopkins Commentary*, New York: New York University Press.

Mellers, Wilfrid (1939) 'Edmund Rubbra and Symphonic Form', *Scrutiny*, June, pp.56–72.

——— (1943) 'Rubbra and the Dominant Seventh: Notes On An English Symphony', *The Music Review*, August, pp.145–56. Reprinted in Mellers (1947) *Studies in Contemporary Music*, London: Dennis Dobson, Ltd.

——— (1940) 'Rubbra's No. 3', *Scrutiny*, September, pp.120–30.

Milligan, Stuart (1966) 'An Analysis of the Later Symphonic Style of Edmund Rubbra', unpublished MA thesis, Eastman School of Music, University of Rochester.

Ottaway, Hugh (1952) 'A Note On Edmund Rubbra', *Musical Opinion*, April, pp.401–3.

——— (1956) 'A Note On Rubbra's Sixth Symphony', *Musical Opinion*, August, pp.653–5.

——— (1950) 'Edmund Rubbra and His Fifth Symphony', *Hallé*, April, pp.1–5.

——— (1950) 'Introducing Edmund Rubbra', *Hallé*, January, pp.12–15.

——— (1955) 'Edmund Rubbra's Sixth Symphony', *Hallé*, March, pp.1–5.

——— (1955) 'Rubbra's Sixth Symphony', *The Musical Times*, October, pp.527–9.

——— (1966) 'Edmund Rubbra and His Recent Works', *The Musical Times*, September, pp.765–8.

——— (1977) 'The Symphonies', in Lewis Foreman (ed.) *Edmund Rubbra: Composer*, Rickmansworth: Triad Press, pp.30–42.

Payne, Elsie (1955) 'Edmund Rubbra', *Music and Letters* 36, October, pp.341–56.

——— (1955) 'Rubbra's Sixth Symphony', *The Monthly Musical Record*, October, pp.201–7.

————— (1955) 'Some Aspects of Rubbra's Style', *The Music Review*, August, pp.198–217.

————— (1977) 'Non-Liturgical Choral Music', in Lewis Foreman (ed.) *Edmund Rubbra: Composer*, Rickmansworth: Triad Press, pp.77–85.

Robinson, John (1978) *In Extremity: A Study of Gerard Manley Hopkins*, Cambridge: Cambridge University Press.

Rooper, Jasper (1967) 'The Symphonies of Edmund Rubbra: An Appreciation', *Royal College of Music Magazine*, Spring, pp.7–11.

Rubbra, Edmund (1931) 'R.O. Morris As Teacher', *The Monthly Musical Record*, September, pp.264–5.

————— (1939) 'Edmund Rubbra's Second Symphony: A Note By the Composer', *Tempo*, January, p.8.

————— (1949) 'Symphony No. 5 in B flat, Op. 63', *The Music Review*, February, pp.27–35.

————— (1949) 'R.O. Morris: An Appreciation', *Music and Letters* 30, April, pp.107–8.

————— (1960) *Counterpoint: A Survey*, London: Hutchinson University Library.

————— (1963) '*Missa in Honorem Sancti Dominici*', in Robert Stephan Hines (ed.) *The Composer's Point of View*, Norman: University of Oklahoma Press, pp. 103–10.

————— (1964) 'String Quartet No. 3, Op. 112', *Musical Events*, July, pp.8–9.

————— (1968) 'Edmund Rubbra Writes About The Development of His Choral Music', *The Listener*, 6 June, pp.748–9.

————— (1970) 'Edmund Rubbra Writes About His Eighth Symphony', *The Listener*, 31 December, p.925.

————— (1971) 'Edmund Rubbra, Now 70, Looks At His Eight Symphonies', *The Listener*, 27 May, p.690.

————— (1973) 'Edmund Rubbra Writes About His *Sinfonia Sacra*', *The Listener*, 15 February, p.220.

————— (1975) 'Towards Symphony No. 7', in Peter Dickinson (ed.) *Twenty British Composers: The Feeney Trust Commissions*, Chester Music.

Rubbra, Edmund and Stephen Lloyd (eds) (1974) *Gustav Holst: Collected Essays*, Rickmansworth: Triad Press.

Schafer, Murray (1963) 'Edmund Rubbra', in *British Composers in Interview*, London: Faber & Faber.

Simmons, Walter (1979–82) Reviews of Symphonies 2, 5, 6, 8, *Fanfare*, July–August 1979; July–August 1981; September–October 1982.

Stevens, Bernard (1971) 'Rubbra At Seventy', *Royal College of Music Magazine*, Autumn, pp.99–100.

Stevenson, Ronald (1977) 'Concerted Works', in Lewis Foreman (ed.) *Edmund Rubbra: Composer*, Rickmansworth: Triad Press, pp.43–9.

Tiedman, Richard (1979) 'Rubbra: Neglected Symphonist', *American Record Journal*, September, pp.37–9.

Truscott, Harold (1977) 'Chamber Music', in Lewis Foreman (ed.) *Edmund Rubbra: Composer*, Rickmansworth: Triad Press, pp.53–69.

———— (1977) 'Style and Orchestral Technique', in Lewis Foreman (ed.) *Edmund Rubbra: Composer*, Rickmansworth: Triad Press, pp.18–29.

Westrup, J.A. (1942) 'Edmund Rubbra's Fourth Symphony', *The Musical Times*, July, p.204.

General Index

Index of Rubbra's Works